THE DECLINE AND FALL

OF THE

ROMAN EMPIRE.

BY

EDWARD GIBBON, ESQ.

WITH NOTES,

BY THE REV. H. H. MILMAN.

A New Edition,

TO WHICH IS ADDED

A COMPLETE INDEX OF THE WHOLE WORK.

IN FIVE VOLUMES.

VOL. III.

NEW YORK:
AMERICAN BOOK EXCHANGE,
TRIBUNE BUILDING.
1880.

THE JOHN A. GRAY PRESS
AND STEAM TYPE-SETTING OFFICE,
18 JACOB STREET,
NEW YORK.

THE DECLINE AND FALL

OF THE

ROMAN EMPIRE.

CHAPTER XXXIX.

ZENO AND ANASTASIUS, EMPERORS OF THE EAST.—BIRTH, EDUCA-
TION, AND FIRST EXPLOITS OF THEODORIC THE OSTROGOTH.—
HIS INVASION AND CONQUEST OF ITALY.—THE GOTHIC KINGDOM
OF ITALY.—STATE OF THE WEST.—MILITARY AND CIVIL GOV-
ERNMENT.—THE SENATOR BOETHIUS.—LAST ACTS AND DEATH
OF THEODORIC.

AFTER the fall of the Roman Empire in the West, an interval
of fifty years, till the memorable reign of Justinian, is faintly
marked by the obscure names and imperfect annals of Zeno, Anastasius, and Justin, who successively ascended to the throne of
Constantinople. During the same period, Italy revived and flourished under the government of a Gothic king, who might have
deserved a statue among the best and bravest of the ancient Romans.

Theodoric the Ostrogoth, the fourteenth in lineal descent of the
royal line of the Amali,[1] was born in the neighborhood of Vienna [2]
two years after the death of Attila.* A recent victory had restored the independence of the Ostrogoths ; and the three brothers, Walamir, Theodemir, and Widimir, who ruled that warlike
nation with united counsels, had separately pitched their habitations in the fertile though desolate province of Pannonia. The
Huns still threatened their revolted subjects, but their hasty attack was repelled by the single forces of Walamir, and the news

---

* The date of Theodoric's birth is not accurately determined. We can hardly err,
observes Manso, in placing it between the years 453 and 456. Manso, Geschichte des
Ost-Gothischen Reiches, p. 14.—M.

of his victory reached the distant camp of his brother in the same auspicious moment that the favorite concubine of Theodemir was delivered of a son and heir. In the eighth year of his age, Theodoric was reluctantly yielded by his father to the public interest, as the pledge of an alliance which Leo, emperor of the East, had consented to purchase by an annual subsidy of three hundred pounds of gold. The royal hostage was educated at Constantinople with care and tenderness. His body was formed to all the exercises of war, his mind was expanded by the habits of liberal conversation ; he frequented the schools of the most skilful masters ; but he disdained or neglected the arts of Greece ; and so ignorant did he always remain of the first elements of science, that a rude mark was contrived to represent the signature of the illiterate king of Italy.[3] As soon as he had attained the age of eighteen, he was restored to the wishes of the Ostrogoths, whom the emperor aspired to gain by liberality and confidence. Walamir had fallen in battle ; the youngest of the brothers, Widimir, had led away into Italy and Gaul an army of barbarians, and the whole nation acknowledged for their king the father of Theodoric. His ferocious subjects admired the strength and stature of their young prince ;[4] and he soon convinced them that he had not degenerated from the valor of his ancestors. At the head of six thousand volunteers, he secretly left the camp in quest of adventures, descended the Danube as far as Singidunum, or Belgrade, and soon returned to his father with the spoils of a Sarmatian king whom he had vanquished and slain. Such triumphs, however, were productive only of fame, and the invincible Ostrogoths were reduced to extreme distress by the want of clothing and food. They unanimously resolved to desert their Pannonian encampments, and boldly to advance into the warm and wealthy neighborhood of the Byzantine court, which already maintained in pride and luxury so many bands of confederate Goths. After proving, by some acts of hostility, that they could be dangerous, or at least troublesome, enemies, the Ostrogoths sold at a high price their reconciliation and fidelity, accepted a donative of lands and money, and were intrusted with the defence of the Lower Danube, under the command of Theodoric, who succeeded, after his father's death, to the hereditary throne of the Amali.[5]

A hero, descended from a race of kings, must have despised the base Isaurian who was invested with the Roman purple, without any endowments of mind or body, without any advantages of royal birth, or superior qualifications. After the failure of the Theodosian line, the choice of Pulcheria and of the senate might be justified in some measure by the characters of Marcian and Leo, but the latter of these princes confirmed and dishonored his reign by the perfidious murder of Aspar and his sons, who too rigorously exacted the debt of gratitude and obedience. The inheritance of Leo and of the East was peaceably devolved on his infant grandson, the son of his daughter Ariadne ; and her Isaurian husband, the fortunate Trascalisseus, exchanged that barbarous sound for the Grecian appellation of Zeno. After the decease of the elder Leo, he approached with unnatural respect the throne of his son, humbly received, as a gift, the second rank in the empire, and soon excited the public suspicion on the sudden and premature death of his young colleague, whose life could no longer promote the success of his ambition. But the palace of Constantinople was ruled by female influence, and agitated by female passions : and Verina, the widow of Leo, claiming his empire as her own, pronounced a sentence of deposition against the worthless and ungrateful servant on whom she alone had bestowed the sceptre of the East.[6] As soon as she sounded a revolt in the ears of Zeno, he fled with precipitation into the mountains of Isauria, and her brother Basiliscus, already infamous by his African expedition,[7] was unanimously proclaimed by the servile senate. But the reign of the usurper was short and turbulent. Basiliscus presumed to assassinate the lover of his sister ; he dared to offend the lover of his wife, the vain and insolent Harmatius, who, in the midst of Asiatic luxury, affected the dress, the demeanor, and the surname of Achilles.[8] By the conspiracy of the malcontents, Zeno was recalled from exile ; the armies, the capital, the person, of Basiliscus, were betrayed ; and his whole family was condemned to the long agony of cold and hunger by the inhuman conqueror, who wanted courage to encounter or to forgive his enemies.* The haughty spirit of Verina was still incapable of submission or repose. She provoked the enmity of a favorite general, embraced his cause as soon as he was disgraced, created a new emperor in Syria and Egypt,† raised an army of seventy thousand men, and persisted to the last moment of her life in a fruitless rebellion, which, according to the fashion of the age, had been predicted by Christian hermits and Pagan magicians. While the East was afflicted by the passions of Verina, her daughter Ariadne was distinguished by the female virtues of mildness and fidelity ; she followed her husband in his exile, and after his res-

---

* Joannes Lydus accuses Zeno of timidity, or, rather, of cowardice ; he purchased an ignominious peace from the enemies of the empire, whom he dared not meet in battle ; and employed his whole time at home in confiscations and executions. Lydus, de Magist. iii. 45, p. 230.—M.

† Named Illus.—M.

toration, she implored his clemency in favor of her mother. On the decease of Zeno, Ariadne, the daughter, the mother, and the widow of an emperor, gave her hand and the Imperial title to Anastasius, an aged domestic of the palace, who survived his elevation above twenty-seven years, and whose character is attested by the acclamation of the people, "Reign as you have lived!"[9] *

Whatever fear or affection could bestow, was profusely lavished by Zeno on the king of the Ostrogoths ; the rank of patrician and consul, the command of the Palatine troops, an equestrian statue, a treasure in gold and silver of many thousand pounds, the name of son, and the promise of a rich and honorable wife. As long as Theodoric condescended to serve, he supported with courage and fidelity the cause of his benefactor : his rapid march contributed to the restoration of Zeno ; and in the second revolt, the *Walamirs*, as they were called, pursued and pressed the Asiatic rebels, till they left an easy victory to the Imperial troops.[10] But the faithful servant was suddenly converted into a formidable enemy, who spread the flames of war from Constantinople to the Adriatic ; many flourishing cities were reduced to ashes, and the agriculture of Thrace was almost extirpated by the wanton cruelty of the Goths, who deprived their captive peasants of the right hand that guided the plough.[11] On such occasions, Theodoric sustained the loud and specious reproach of disloyalty, of ingratitude, and of insatiate avarice, which could be only excused by the hard necessity of his situation. He reigned, not as the monarch, but as the minister of a ferocious people, whose spirit was unbroken by slavery, and impatient of real or imaginary insults. Their poverty was incurable ; since the most liberal donatives were soon dissipated in wasteful luxury, and the most fertile estates became barren in their hands ; they despised, but they envied, the laborious provincials ; and when their subsistence had failed, the Ostrogoths embraced the familiar resources of war and rapine. It had been the wish of Theodoric (such at least was his declaration) to lead a peaceful, obscure, obedient life on the confines of Scythia, till the Byzantine court, by splendid and fallacious promises, seduced him to attack a confederate tribe of Goths, who had been engaged in the party of Basiliscus. He marched from his station in Mœsia, on the solemn assurance that before he reached Adriano-

---

* The Panegyric of Procopius of Gaza (edited by Villoison in his Anecdota Græca, and reprinted in the new edition of the Byzantine historians by Niebuhr, in the same vol. with Dexippus and Eunapius, viii. p. 483, 516), was unknown to Gibbon. It is vague and pedantic, and contains few facts. The same criticism will apply to the poetical panegyric of Priscian, edited from the MS. of Bobbio by Ang. Mai. Priscian, the grammarian, Niebuhr argues from this work, must have been born in the African, not in either of the Asiatic Cæsareas. Pref. p. xi.—M.

ple, he should meet a plentiful convoy of provisions, and a re-enforcement of eight thousand horse and thirty thousand foot, while the legions of Asia were encamped at Heraclea to second his operations. These measures were disappointed by mutual jealousy. As he advanced into Thrace, the son of Theodemir found an inhospitable solitude, and his Gothic followers, with a heavy train of horses, of mules, and of wagons, were betrayed by their guides among the rocks and precipices of Mount Sondis, where he was assaulted by the arms and invectives of Theodoric the son of Triarius. From a neighboring height, his artful rival harangued the camp of the *Walamirs*, and branded their leader with the opprobrious names of child, of madman, of perjured traitor, the enemy of his blood and nation. " Are you ignorant," exclaimed the son of Triarius, " that it is the constant policy of the Romans to destroy the Goths by each other's swords ? Are you insensible that the victor in this unnatural contest will be exposed, and justly exposed, to their implacable revenge ? Where are those warriors, my kinsmen and thy own, whose widows now lament that their lives were sacrificed to thy rash ambition ? Where is the wealth which thy soldiers possessed when they were first allured from their native homes to enlist under thy standard ? Each of them was then master of three or four horses ; they now follow thee on foot, like slaves, through the deserts of Thrace ; those men who were tempted by the hope of measuring gold with a bushel, those brave men who are as free and as noble as thyself." A language so well suited to the temper of the Goths excited clamor and discontent ; and the son of Theodemir, apprehensive of being left alone, was compelled to embrace his brethren, and to imitate the example of Roman perfidy.[12] *

In every state of his fortune, the prudence and firmness of Theodoric were equally conspicuous ; whether he threatened Constantinople at the head of the confederate Goths, or retreated with a faithful band to the mountains and sea-coast of Epirus. At length the accidental death of the son of Triarius[13] destroyed the balance which the Romans had been so anxious to preserve, the whole nation acknowledged the supremacy of the Amali, and the Byzantine court subscribed an ignominious and oppressive treaty.[14] The senate had already declared, that it was necessary to choose a party among the Goths, since the public was unequal to the sup-

---

* Gibbon has omitted much of the complicated intrigues of the Byzantine court with the two Theodorics. The weak emperor attempted to play them one against the other, and was himself in turn insulted, and the empire ravaged, by both. The details of successive alliance and revolt, of hostility and of union, between the two Gothic chieftains, to dictate terms to the emperor, may be found in Malchus.—M.

port of their united forces ; a subsidy of two thousand pounds of gold, with the ample pay of thirteen thousand men, were required for the least considerable of their armies ; [15] and the Isaurians, who guarded not the empire but the emperor, enjoyed, besides the privilege of rapine, an annual pension of five thousand pounds. The sagacious mind of Theodoric soon perceived that he was odious to the Romans, and suspected by the barbarians : he understood the popular murmur, that his subjects were exposed in their frozen huts to intolerable hardships, while their king was dissolved in the luxury of Greece, and he prevented the painful alternative of encountering the Goths, as the champion, or of leading them to the field, as the enemy, of Zeno. Embracing an enterprise worthy of his courage and ambition, Theodoric addressed the emperor in the following words : "Although your servant is maintained in affluence by your liberality, graciously listen to the wishes of my heart ! Italy, the inheritance of your predecessors, and Rome itself, the head and mistress of the world, now fluctuate under the violence and oppression of Odoacer the mercenary. Direct me, with my national troops, to march against the tyrant. If I fall, you will be relieved from an expensive and troublesome friend : if, with the divine permission, I succeed, I shall govern in your name, and to your glory, the Roman senate, and the part of the republic delivered from slavery by my victorious arms." The proposal of Theodoric was accepted, and perhaps had been suggested, by the Byzantine court. But the forms of the commission, or grant, appear to have been expressed with a prudent ambiguity, which might be explained by the event ; and it was left doubtful, whether the conqueror of Italy should reign as the lieutenant, the vassal, or the ally, of the emperor of the East. [16]

The reputation both of the leader and of the war diffused a universal ardor ; the *Walamirs* were multiplied by the Gothic swarms already engaged in the service, or seated in the provinces, of the empire ; and each bold barbarian, who had heard of the wealth and beauty of Italy, was impatient to seek, through the most perilous adventures, the possession of such enchanting objects. The march of Theodoric must be considered as the emigration of an entire people ; the wives and children of the Goths, their aged parents, and most precious effects, were carefully transported ; and some idea may be formed of the heavy baggage that now followed the camp, by the loss of two thousand wagons, which had been sustained in a single action in the war of Epirus. For their subsistence, the Goths depended on the magazines of corn which was ground in portable mills by the hands of their women ; on the milk and flesh of their flocks and herds ; on the casual produce of the chase, and upon the contributions which they might impose on all who should presume to dispute the passage, or to refuse their friendly assistance. Notwithstanding these precautions, they were exposed to the danger, and almost to the distress, of famine, in a march of seven hundred miles, which had been undertaken in the depth of a rigorous winter. Since the fall of the Roman power, Dacia and Pannonia no longer exhibited the rich prospect of populous cities, well-cultivated fields, and convenient highways : the reign of barbarism and desolation was restored, and the tribes of Bulgarians, Gepidæ, and Sarmatians, who had occupied the vacant province, were prompted by their native fierceness, or the solicitations of Odoacer, to resist the progress of his enemy. In many obscure though bloody battles, Theodoric fought and vanquished ; till at length, surmounting every obstacle by skilful conduct and persevering courage, he descended from the Julian Alps, and displayed his invincible banners on the confines of Italy.[17]

Odoacer, a rival not unworthy of his arms, had already occupied the advantageous and well-known post of the River Sontius, near the ruins of Aquileia, at the head of a powerful host, whose independent *kings* [18] or leaders disdained the duties of subordination and the prudence of delays. No sooner had Theodoric gained a short repose and refreshment to his wearied cavalry, than he boldly attacked the fortifications of the enemy ; the Ostrogoths showed more ardor to acquire, than the mercenaries to defend, the lands of Italy ; and the reward of the first victory was the possession of the Venetian province as far as the walls of Verona. In the neighborhood of that city, on the steep banks of the rapid Adige, he was opposed by a new army, re-enforced in its numbers, and not impaired in its courage : the contest was more obstinate, but the event was still more decisive ; Odoacer fled to Ravenna, Theodoric advanced to Milan, and the vanquished troops saluted their conqueror with loud acclamations of respect and fidelity. But their want either of constancy or of faith soon exposed him to the most imminent danger ; his vanguard, with several Gothic counts, which had been rashly intrusted to a deserter, was betrayed and destroyed near Faenza by his double treachery ; Odoacer again appeared master of the field, and the invader, strongly intrenched in his camp of Pavia, was reduced to solicit the aid of a kindred nation, the Visigoths of Gaul. In the course of this History, the most voracious appetite for war will be abundantly satiated ; nor can I much lament that our dark and imperfect materials do not afford a more ample narrative of the distress of Italy, and of the fierce conflict, which was finally decided by the abilities, experience, and valor of the Gothic king. Immediately before the battle of Verona, he visited the tent of his mother [19] and sister, and requested, that on a day, the most illustrious festival of his life, they would adorn him with the rich garments which they had worked with their own hands. "Our glory," said he, "is mutual and inseparable. You are known to the world as the mother of Theodoric; and it becomes me to prove, that I am the genuine offspring of those heroes from whom I claim my descent." The wife or concubine of Theodemir was inspired with the spirit of the German matrons, who esteemed their sons' honor far above their safety; and it is reported, that in a desperate action, when Theodoric himself was hurried along by the torrent of a flying crowd, she boldly met them at the entrance of the camp, and, by her generous reproaches, drove them back on the swords of the enemy. [20]

From the Alps to the extremity of Calabria, Theodoric reigned by the right of conquest; the Vandal ambassadors surrendered the Island of Sicily, as a lawful appendage of his kingdom; and he was accepted as the deliverer of Rome by the senate and people, who had shut their gates against the flying usurper. [21] Ravenna alone, secure in the fortifications of art and nature, still sustained a siege of almost three years; and the daring sallies of Odoacer carried slaughter and dismay into the Gothic camp. At length, destitute of provisions and hopeless of relief, that unfortunate monarch yielded to the groans of his subjects and the clamors of his soldiers. A treaty of peace was negotiated by the bishop of Ravenna; the Ostrogoths were admitted into the city, and the hostile kings consented, under the sanction of an oath, to rule with equal and undivided authority the provinces of Italy. The event of such an agreement may be easily foreseen. After some days had been devoted to the semblance of joy and friendship, Odoacer, in the midst of a solemn banquet, was stabbed by the hand, or at least by the command, of his rival. Secret and effectual orders had been previously despatched; the faithless and rapacious mercenaries, at the same moment, and without resistance, were universally massacred; and the royalty of Theodoric was proclaimed by the Goths, with the tardy, reluctant, ambiguous consent of the emperor of the East. The design of a conspiracy was imputed, according to the usual forms, to the prostrate tyrant; but his innocence, and the guilt of his conqueror, [22] are sufficiently proved by the advantageous treaty which *force* would not sincerely have granted, nor *weakness* have rashly infringed. The jealousy of power, and the mischiefs of discord, may suggest a more decent apology, and a sentence less rigorous may be pronounced against a crime which was necessary to introduce into Italy a generation of public felicity. The living author of this felicity was audaciously praised in his own presence by sacred and profane orators ; [23] but history (in his time she was mute and inglorious) has not left any just representation of the events which displayed, or of the defects which clouded, the virtues of Theodoric. [24] One record of his fame, the volume of public epistles composed by Cassiodorus in the royal name, is still extant, and has obtained more implicit credit than it seems to deserve. [25] They exhibit the forms, rather than the substance, of his government ; and we should vainly search for the pure and spontaneous sentiments of the barbarian amidst the declamation and learning of a sophist, the wishes of a Roman senator, the precedents of office, and the vague professions, which, in every court and on every occasion, compose the language of discreet ministers. The reputation of Theodoric may repose with more confidence on the visible peace and prosperity of a reign of thirty-three years ; the unanimous esteem of his own times, and the memory of his wisdom and courage, his justice and humanity, which was deeply impressed on the minds of the Goths and Italians.

The partition of the lands of Italy, of which Theodoric assigned the third part to his soldiers, is *honorably* arraigned as the sole injustice of his life.* And even this act may be fairly justified by the example of Odoacer, the rights of conquest, the true interest of the Italians, and the sacred duty of subsisting a whole people, who, on the faith of his promises, had transported themselves into a distant land. [26] Under the reign of Theodoric, and in the happy climate of Italy, the Goths soon multiplied to a formidable host of two hundred thousand men, [27] and the whole amount of their families may be computed by the ordinary addition of women and children. Their invasion of property, a part of which must have been already vacant, was disguised by the generous but improper name of *hospitality ;* these unwelcome guests were irregularly dispersed over the face of Italy, and the lot of each barbarian was adequate to his birth and office, the number of his followers, and the rustic wealth which he possessed in slaves and cattle. The distinctions of noble and plebe-

* Compare Gibbon, ch. xxxvi. vol. ii. p. 512, etc.—Manso observes that this division was conducted, not in a violent and irregular, but in a legal and orderly manner. The barbarian, who could not show a title of grant from the officers of Theodoric appointed for that purpose, or a prescriptive right of thirty years, in case he had obtained the property before the Ostro-Gothic conquest, was ejected from the estate. He conceives that estates too small to bear division paid a third of their produce.—Geschichte des Ost-Gothischen Reiches, p. 82.—M.

ian were acknowledged ; [28] but the lands of every freeman were exempt from taxes,* and he enjoyed the inestimable privilege of being subject only to the laws of his country.[29] Fashion, and even convenience, soon persuaded the conquerors to assume the more elegant dress of the natives, but they still persisted in the use of their mother-tongue ; and their contempt for the Latin schools was applauded by Theodoric himself, who gratified their prejudices, or his own, by declaring, that the child who had trembled at a rod, would never dare to look upon a sword.[30] Distress might sometimes provoke the indigent Roman to assume the ferocious manners which were insensibly relinquished by the rich and luxurious barbarian ; [31] but these mutual conversions were not encouraged by the policy of a monarch who perpetuated the separation of the Italians and Goths ; reserving the former for the arts of peace, and the latter for the service of war. To accomplish this design, he studied to protect his industrious subjects, and to moderate the violence, without enervating the valor, of his soldiers, who were maintained for the public defence. They held their lands and benefices as a military stipend : at the sound of the trumpet they were prepared to march under the conduct of their provincial officers ; and the whole extent of Italy was distributed into the several quarters of a well-regulated camp. The service of the palace and of the frontiers was performed by choice or by rotation ; and each extraordinary fatigue was recompensed by an increase of pay and occasional donatives. Theodoric had convinced his brave companions, that empire must be acquired and defended by the same arts. After his example, they strove to excel in the use, not only of the lance and sword, the instruments of their victories, but of the missile weapons, which they were too much inclined to neglect ; and the lively image of war was displayed in the daily exercise and annual reviews of the Gothic cavalry. A firm though gentle discipline imposed the habits of modesty, obedience, and temperance ; and the Goths were instructed to spare the people, to reverence the laws, to understand the duties of civil society, and to disclaim the barbarous license of judicial combat and private revenge.[32]

Among the barbarians of the West, the victory of Theodoric had spread a general alarm. But as soon as it appeared that he was satisfied with conquest and desirous of peace, terror was changed into respect, and they submitted to a powerful mediation, which was uniformly employed for the best purposes of reconcil-

---

* Manso (p. 100) quotes two passages from Cassiodorus to show that the Goths were not exempt from the fiscal claims.—Cassiodor. i. 19, iv. 14.—M.

ing their quarrels and civilizing their manners.[33] The ambassadors who resorted to Ravenna from the most distant countries of Europe, admired his wisdom, magnificence,[34] and courtesy; and if he sometimes accepted either slaves or arms, white horses or strange animals, the gift of a sun-dial, a water-clock, or a musician, admonished even the princes of Gaul of the superior art and industry of his Italian subjects. His domestic alliances,[35] a wife, two daughters, a sister, and a niece, united the family of Theodoric with the kings of the Franks, the Burgundians, the Visigoths, the Vandals, and the Thuringians, and contributed to maintain the harmony, or at least the balance, of the great republic of the West.[36] It is difficult in the dark forests of Germany and Poland to pursue the emigrations of the Heruli, a fierce people who disdained the use of armor, and who condemned their widows and aged parents not to survive the loss of their husbands, or the decay of their strength.[37] The king of these savage warriors solicited the friendship of Theodoric, and was elevated to the rank of his son, according to the barbaric rites of a military adoption.[38] From the shores of the Baltic, the Æstians or Livonians laid their offerings of native amber[39] at the feet of a prince, whose fame had excited them to undertake an unknown and dangerous journey of fifteen hundred miles. With the country[40] from whence the Gothic nation derived their origin, he maintained a frequent and friendly correspondence: the Italians were clothed in the rich sables[41] of Sweden; and one of its sovereigns, after a voluntary or reluctant abdication, found a hospitable retreat in the palace of Ravenna. He had reigned over one of the thirteen populous tribes who cultivated a small portion of the great island or peninsula of Scandinavia, to which the vague appellation of Thule has been sometimes applied. That northern region was peopled, or had been explored, as high as the sixty-eighth degree of latitude, where the natives of the polar circle enjoy and lose the presence of the sun at each summer and winter solstice during an equal period of forty days.[42] The long night of his absence or death was the mournful season of distress and anxiety, till the messengers, who had been sent to the mountain tops, descried the first rays of returning light, and proclaimed to the plain below the festival of his resurrection.[43]

The life of Theodoric represents the rare and meritorious example of a barbarian, who sheathed his sword in the pride of victory and the vigor of his age. A reign of three-and-thirty years was consecrated to the duties of civil government, and the hostilities, in which he was sometimes involved, were speedily terminated by the conduct of his lieutenants, the discipline of his troops, the

arms of his allies, and even by the terror of his name. He reduced, under a strong and regular government, the unprofitable
countries of Rhætia, Noricum, Dalmatia, and Pannonia, from the
source of the Danube and the territory of the Bavarians,[44] to the
petty kingdom erected by the Gepidæ on the ruins of Sirmium.
His prudence could not safely intrust the bulwark of Italy to such
feeble and turbulent neighbors ; and his justice might claim the
lands which they oppressed, either as a part of his kingdom, or
as the inheritance of his father. The greatness of a servant, who
was named perfidious because he was successful, awakened the
jealousy of the emperor Anastasius ; and a war was kindled on
the Dacian frontier, by the protection which the Gothic king, in
the vicissitude of human affairs, had granted to one of the descendants of Attila. Sabinian, a general illustrious by his own
and father's merit, advanced at the head of ten thousand Romans ; and the provisions and arms, which filled a long train of
wagons, were distributed to the fiercest of the Bulgarian tribes.
But in the fields of Margus, the Eastern powers were defeated by
the inferior forces of the Goths and Huns ; the flower and even
the hope of the Roman armies was irretrievably destroyed ; and
such was the temperance with which Theodoric had inspired his
victorious troops, that, as their leader had not given the signal of
pillage, the rich spoils of the enemy lay untouched at their feet.[45]
Exasperated by this disgrace, the Byzantine court despatched two
hundred ships and eight thousand men to plunder the sea-coast of
Calabria and Apulia : they assaulted the ancient city of Tarentum, interrupted the trade and agriculture of a happy country,
and sailed back to the Hellespont, proud of their piratical victory
over a people whom they still presumed to consider as their *Roman* brethren.[46] Their retreat was possibly hastened by the activity of Theodoric ; Italy was covered by a fleet of a thousand
light vessels,[47] which he constructed with incredible despatch ;
and his firm moderation was soon rewarded by a solid and honorable peace. He maintained, with a powerful hand, the balance of
the West, till it was at length overthrown by the ambition of
Clovis ; and although unable to assist his rash and unfortunate
kinsman, the king of the Visigoths, he saved the remains of his
family and people, and checked the Franks in the midst of their
victorious career. I am not desirous to prolong or repeat [48] this
narrative of military events, the least interesting of the reign of
Theodoric ; and shall be content to add, that the Alemanni were
protected,[49] that an inroad of the Burgundians was severely chastised, and that the conquest of Arles and Marseilles opened a free
communication with the Visigoths, who revered him as their na-

tional protector, and as the guardian of his grandchild, the infant son of Alaric. Under this respectable character, the king of Italy restored the Prætorian præfecture of the Gauls, reformed some abuses in the civil government of Spain, and accepted the annual tribute and apparent submission of its military governor, who wisely refused to trust his person in the palace of Ravenna.[50] The Gothic sovereignty was established from Sicily to the Danube, from Sirmium or Belgrade to the Atlantic Ocean ; and the Greeks themselves have acknowledged that Theodoric reigned over the fairest portion of the Western empire.[51]

The union of the Goths and Romans might have fixed for ages the transient happiness of Italy ; and the first of nations, a new people of free subjects and enlightened soldiers, might have gradually arisen from the mutual emulation of their respective virtues. But the sublime merit of guiding or seconding such a revolution was not reserved for the reign of Theodoric : he wanted either the genius or the opportunities of a legislator ; [52] and while he indulged the Goths in the enjoyment of rude liberty, he servilely copied the institutions, and even the abuses, of the political system which had been framed by Constantine and his successors. From a tender regard to the expiring prejudices of Rome, the barbarian declined the name, the purple, and the diadem, of the emperors ; but he assumed, under the hereditary title of king, the whole substance and plenitude of Imperial prerogative.[53] His addresses to the Eastern throne were respectful and ambiguous : he celebrated, in pompous style, the harmony of the two republics, applauded his own government as the perfect similitude of a sole and undivided empire, and claimed above the kings of the earth the same pre-eminence which he modestly allowed to the person or rank of Anastasius. The alliance of the East and West was annually declared by the unanimous choice of two consuls ; but it should seem that the Italian candidate who was named by Theodoric accepted a formal confirmation from the sovereign of Constantinople.[54] The Gothic palace of Ravenna reflected the image of the court of Theodosius or Valentinian. The Prætorian præfect, the præfect of Rome, the quæstor, the master of the offices, with the public and patrimonial treasurers,* whose functions are painted in gaudy colors by the rhetoric of Cassiodorus, still continued to act as the ministers of state. And the subordinate care

---

* All causes between Roman and Roman were judged by the old Roman courts. The comes Gothorum judged between Goth and Goth ; between Goths and Romans (without considering which was the plaintiff), the comes Gothorum, with a Roman jurist as his assessor, making a kind of mixed jurisdiction, but with a natural predominance to the side of the Goth. Savigny, vol. i. p. 290.—M.

of justice and the revenue was delegated to seven consulars, three correctors, and five presidents, who governed the fifteen *regions* of Italy according to the principles, and even the forms, of Roman jurisprudence.[55] The violence of the conquerors was abated or eluded by the slow artifice of judicial proceedings ; the civil administration, with its honors and emoluments, was confined to the Italians ; and the people still preserved their dress and language, their laws and customs, their personal freedom, and two thirds of their landed property.* It had been the object of Augustus to conceal the introduction of monarchy ; it was the policy of Theodoric to disguise the reign of a barbarian.[56] If his subjects were sometimes awakened from this pleasing vision of a Roman government, they derived more substantial comfort from the character of a Gothic prince, who had penetration to discern, and firmness to pursue, his own and the public interest. Theodoric loved the virtues which he possessed, and the talents of which he was destitute. Liberius was promoted to the office of Prætorian præfect for his unshaken fidelity to the unfortunate cause of Odoacer. The ministers of Theodoric, Cassiodorus,[57] and Boethius, have reflected on his reign the lustre of their genius and learning. More prudent or more fortunate than his colleague, Cassiodorus preserved his own esteem without forfeiting the royal favor ; and after passing thirty years in the honors of the world, he was blessed with an equal .term of repose in the devout and studious solitude of Squillace.†

As the patron of the republic, it was the interest and duty of

---

* Manso enumerates and develops at some length the following sources of the royal revenue of Theodoric : 1. A domain, either by succession to that of Odoacer, or a part of the third of the lands was reserved for the royal patrimony. 2. Regalia, including mines, unclaimed estates, treasure-trove, and confiscations. 3. Land-tax. 4. Aurarium, like the Chrysargyrum, a tax on certain branches of trade. 5. Grant of monopolies. 6. Siliquaticum, a small tax on the sale of all kinds of commodities. 7. Portoria, customs. Manso, 96, 111. Savigny (i. 285) supposes that in many cases the property remained in the original owner, who paid his tertia or third of the produce, to the crown, vol. i. p. 285.—M.

— † Cassiodorus was of an ancient and honorable family ; his grandfather had distinguished himself in the defence of Sicily against the ravages of Genseric ; his father held a high rank at the court of Valentinian III., enjoyed the friendship of Ætius, and was one of the ambassadors sent to arrest the progress of Attila. Cassiodorus himself was first the treasurer of the private expenditure to Odoacer, afterwards " count of the sacred largesses." Yielding with the rest of the Romans to the dominion of Theodoric, he was instrumental in the peaceable submission of Sicily ; was successively governor of his native provinces of Bruttium and Lucania, quæstor, magister, palatii, Prætorian præfect, patrician, consul, private secretary, and, in fact, first minister of the king. He was five times Prætorian præfect under different sovereigns, the last time in the reign of Vitiges. This is the theory of Manso, which is not unencumbered with difficulties. M. Buat had supposed that it was the father of Cassiodorus who held the office first named. Compare Manso, p. 85, etc., and Beylage, vii. It certainly appears improbable that Cassiodorus should have been count of the sacred largesses at twenty years old.—M.

the Gothic king to cultivate the affections of the senate [58] and people. The nobles of Rome were flattered by sonorous epithets and formal professions of respect, which had been more justly applied to the merit and authority of their ancestors. The people enjoyed, without fear or danger, the three blessings of a capital, order, plenty, and public amusements. A visible diminution of their numbers may be found even in the measure of liberality ; [59] yet Apulia, Calabria, and Sicily, poured their tribute of corn into the granaries of Rome ; an allowance of bread and meat was distributed to the indigent citizens ; and every office was deemed honorable which was consecrated to the care of their health and happiness. The public games, such as the Greek ambassador might politely applaud, exhibited a faint and feeble copy of the magnificence of the Cæsars : yet the musical, the gymnastic, and the pantomime arts, had not totally sunk in oblivion ; the wild beasts of Africa still exercised in the amphitheatre the courage and dexterity of the hunters ; and the indulgent Goth either patiently tolerated or gently restrained the blue and green factions, whose contests so often filled the circus with clamor and even with blood. [60] In the seventh year of his peaceful reign, Theodoric visited the old capital of the world ; the senate and people advanced in solemn procession to salute a second Trajan, a new Valentinian ; and he nobly supported that character by the assurance of a just and legal government, [61] in a discourse which he was not afraid to pronounce in public, and to inscribe on a tablet of brass. Rome, in this august ceremony, shot a last ray of declining glory ; and a saint, the spectator of this pompous scene, could only hope, in his pious fancy, that it was excelled by the celestial splendor of the New Jerusalem. [62] During a residence of six months, the fame, the person, and the courteous demeanor of the Gothic king, excited the admiration of the Romans, and he contemplated, with equal curiosity and surprise, the monuments that remained of their ancient greatness. He imprinted the footsteps of a conqueror on the Capitoline hill, and frankly confessed that each day he viewed with fresh wonder the forum of Trajan and his lofty column. The theatre of Pompey appeared, even in its decay, as a huge mountain artificially hollowed and polished, and adorned by human industry ; and he vaguely computed, that a river of gold must have been drained to erect the colossal amphitheatre of Titus. [63] From the mouths of fourteen aqueducts, a pure and copious stream was diffused into every part of the city ; among these the Claudian water, which arose at the distance of thirty-eight miles in the Sabine mountains, was conveyed along a gentle though constant declivity of solid arches, till it descended on the summit of the Aventine hill. The long and spacious vaults which had been constructed for the purpose of common sewers, subsisted, after twelve centuries, in their pristine strength ; and these subterraneous channels have been preferred to all the visible wonders of Rome.[64] The Gothic kings, so injuriously accused of the ruin of antiquity, were anxious to preserve the monuments of the nation whom they had subdued.[65] The royal edicts were framed to prevent the abuses, the neglect, or the depredations of the citizens themselves ; and a professed architect, the annual sum of two hundred pounds of gold, twenty-five thousand tiles, and the receipt of customs from the Lucrine port, were assigned for the ordinary repairs of the walls and public edifices. A similar care was extended to the statues of metal or marble of men or animals. The spirit of the horses, which have given a modern name to the Quirinal, was applauded by the barbarians ; [66] the brazen elephants of the *Via sacra* were diligently restored ; [67] the famous heifer of Myron deceived the cattle, as they were driven through the forum of peace ; [68] and an officer was created to protect those works of art, which Theodoric considered as the noblest ornament of his kingdom.

After the example of the last emperors, Theodoric preferred the residence of Ravenna, where he cultivated an orchard with his own hands.[69] As often as the peace of his kingdom was threatened (for it was never invaded) by the barbarians, he removed his court to Verona[70] on the northern frontier, and the image of his palace, still extant on a coin, represents the oldest and most authentic model of Gothic architecture. These two capitals, as well as Pavia, Spoleto, Naples, and the rest of the Italian cities, acquired under his reign the useful or splendid decorations of churches, aqueducts, baths, porticos, and palaces.[71] But the happiness of the subject was more truly conspicuous in the busy scene of labor and luxury, in the rapid increase and bold enjoyment of national wealth. From the shades of Tibur and Praeneste, the Roman senators still retired in the winter season to the warm sun, and salubrious springs, of Baiae ; and their villas, which advanced on solid moles into the Bay of Naples, commanded the various prospect of the sky, the earth, and the water. On the eastern side of the Adriatic, a new Campania was formed in the fair and fruitful province of Istria, which communicated with the palace of Ravenna by an easy navigation of one hundred miles. The rich productions of Lucania and the adjacent provinces were exchanged at the Marcilian fountain, in a populous fair, annually dedicated to trade, intemperance, and superstition. In the solitude of Comum, which had once been animated by the mild

genius of Pliny, a transparent basin above sixty miles in length
still reflected the rural seats which encompassed the margin
of the Larian lake ; and the gradual descent of the hills was
covered by a triple plantation of olives, of vines, and of chest-
nut trees.[72] Agriculture revived under the shadow of peace,
and the number of husbandmen was multiplied by the redemption of captives.[73] The iron mines of Dalmatia, a gold
mine in Bruttium, were carefully explored, and the Pomptine
marshes, as well as those of Spoleto, were drained and cultivated
by private undertakers, whose distant reward must depend on the
continuance of the public prosperity.[74] Whenever the seasons
were less propitious, the doubtful precautions of forming magazines of corn, fixing the price, and prohibiting the exportation,
attested at least the benevolence of the state ; but such was the
extraordinary plenty which an industrious people produced from a
grateful soil, that a gallon of wine was sometimes sold in Italy for
less than three farthings, and a quarter of wheat at about five
shillings and sixpence.[75] A country possessed of so many valuable
objects of exchange soon attracted the merchants of the world,
whose beneficial traffic was encouraged and protected by the
liberal spirit of Theodoric. The free intercourse of the provinces
by land and water was restored and extended ; the city gates
were never shut, either by day or by night ; and the common saying, that a purse of gold might be safely left in the fields, was
expressive of the conscious security of the inhabitants.

A difference of religion is always pernicious, and often fatal, to
the harmony of the prince and people : the Gothic conqueror had
been educated in the profession of Arianism, and Italy was devoutly attached to the Nicene faith. But the persuasion of Theodoric was not infected by zeal ; and he piously adhered to the
heresy of his fathers, without condescending to balance the subtile arguments of theological metaphysics. Satisfied with the
private toleration of his Arian sectaries, he justly conceived himself to be the guardian of the public worship, and his external
reverence for a superstition which he despised, may have nourished
in his mind the salutary indifference of a statesman or philosopher.
The Catholics of his dominions acknowledged, perhaps with reluctance, the peace of the church ; their clergy, according to the
degrees of rank or merit, were honorably entertained in the palace
of Theodoric ; he esteemed the living sanctity of Cæsarius[76] and
Epiphanius,[77] the orthodox bishops of Arles and Pavia ; and
presented a decent offering on the tomb of St. Peter, without any
scrupulous inquiry into the creed of the apostle.[78] His favorite
Goths, and even his mother, were permitted to retain or embrace

the Athanasian faith, and his long reign could not afford the example of an Italian Catholic, who, either from choice or compulsion, had deviated into the religion of the conqueror.[79] The people, and the barbarians themselves, were edified by the pomp and order of religious worship ; the magistrates were instructed to defend the just immunities of ecclesiastical persons and possessions ; the bishops held their synods, the metropolitans exercised their jurisdiction, and the privileges of sanctuary were maintained or moderated according to the spirit of the Roman jurisprudence.[80] With the protection, Theodoric assumed the legal supremacy, of the church ; and his firm administration restored or extended some useful prerogatives which had been neglected by the feeble emperors of the West. He was not ignorant of the dignity and importance of the Roman pontiff, to whom the venerable name of POPE was now appropriated. The peace or the revolt of Italy might depend on the character of a wealthy and popular bishop, who claimed such ample dominion both in heaven and earth ; who had been declared in a numerous synod to be pure from all sin, and exempt from all judgment.[81] When the chair of St. Peter was disputed by Symmachus and Laurence, they appeared at his summons before the tribunal of an Arian monarch, and he confirmed the election of the most worthy or the most obsequious candidate. At the end of his life, in a moment of jealousy and resentment, he prevented the choice of the Romans, by nominating a pope in the palace of Ravenna. The danger and furious contests of a schism were mildly restrained, and the last decree of the senate was enacted to extinguish, if it were possible, the scandalous venality of the papal elections.[82]

I have descanted with pleasure on the fortunate condition of Italy ; but our fancy must not hastily conceive that the golden age of the poets, a race of men without vice or misery, was realized under the Gothic conquest. The fair prospect was sometimes overcast with clouds ; the wisdom of Theodoric might be deceived, his power might be resisted, and the declining age of the monarch was sullied with popular hatred and patrician blood. In the first insolence of victory, he had been tempted to deprive the whole party of Odoacer of the civil and even the natural rights of society ;[83] a tax unseasonably imposed after the calamities of war, would have crushed the rising agriculture of Liguria ; a rigid pre-emption of corn, which was intended for the public relief, must have aggravated the distress of Campania. These dangerous projects were defeated by the virtue and eloquence of Epiphanius and Boethius, who, in the presence of Theodoric himself, successfully pleaded the cause of the people ;[84] but if the royal ear was open to the voice of truth, a saint and a philosopher are not always to be found at the ear of kings. The privileges of rank, or office, or favor, were too frequently abused by Italian fraud and Gothic violence, and the avarice of the king's nephew was publicly exposed, at first by the usurpation, and afterwards by the restitution of the estates which he had unjustly extorted from his Tuscan neighbors. Two hundred thousand barbarians, formidable even to their master, were seated in the heart of Italy ; they indignantly supported the restraints of peace and discipline ; the disorders of their march were always felt and sometimes compensated ; and where it was dangerous to punish, it might be prudent to dissemble, the sallies of their native fierceness. When the indulgence of Theodoric had remitted two thirds of the Ligurian tribute, he condescended to explain the difficulties of his situation, and to lament the heavy though inevitable burdens which he imposed on his subjects for their own defence.[85] These ungrateful subjects could never be cordially reconciled to the origin, the religion, or even the virtues, of the Gothic conqueror ; past calamities were forgotten, and the sense or suspicion of injuries was rendered still more exquisite by the present felicity of the times.

Even the religious toleration which Theodoric had the glory of introducing into the Christian world, was painful and offensive to the orthodox zeal of the Italians. They respected the armed heresy of the Goths ; but their pious rage was safely pointed against the rich and defenceless Jews, who had formed their establishments at Naples, Rome, Ravenna, Milan, and Genoa, for the benefit of trade, and under the sanction of the laws.[86] Their persons were insulted, their effects were pillaged, and their synagogues were burnt by the mad populace of Ravenna and Rome, inflamed, as it should seem, by the most frivolous or extravagant pretences. The government which could neglect, would have deserved such an outrage. A legal inquiry was instantly directed ; and as the authors of the tumult had escaped in the crowd, the whole community was condemned to repair the damage ; and the obstinate bigots, who refused their contributions, were whipped through the streets by the hand of the executioner.* This simple act of justice exasperated the discontent of the Catholics, who applauded the merit and patience of these holy confessors. Three hundred pulpits deplored the persecution of the church ; and if the chapel of St. Stephen at Verona was demolished by the command of Theodoric, it is probable that some miracle hostile to his name and dignity had been performed

---

* See History of the Jews, vol. iii. p. 217.—M.

on that sacred theatre. At the close of a glorious life, the king of
Italy discovered that he had excited the hatred of a people whose
happiness he had so assiduously labored to promote ; and his mind
was soured by indignation, jealousy, and the bitterness of
unrequited love. The Gothic conqueror condescended to disarm
the unwarlike natives of Italy, interdicting all weapons of offence,
and excepting only a small knife for domestic use. The deliverer
of Rome was accused of conspiring with the vilest informers
against the lives of senators whom he suspected of a secret and
treasonable correspondence with the Byzantine court.[87] After the
death of Anastasius, the diadem had been placed on the head of a
feeble old man ; but the powers of government were assumed by
his nephew Justinian, who already meditated the extirpation of
heresy, and the conquest of Italy and Africa. A rigorous law,
which was published at Constantinople, to reduce the Arians by
the dread of punishment within the pale of the church, awakened
the just resentment of Theodoric, who claimed for his distressed
brethren of the East the same indulgence which he had so long
granted to the Catholics of his dominions.* At his stern command, the Roman pontiff, with four *illustrious* senators, embarked
on an embassy, of which he must have alike dreaded the failure or
the success. The singular veneration shown to the first pope who
had visited Constantinople was punished as a crime by his jealous
monarch ; the artful or peremptory refusal of the Byzantine court
might excuse an equal, and would provoke a larger, measure of
retaliation ; and a mandate was prepared in Italy, to prohibit,
after a stated day, the exercise of the Catholic worship. By the
bigotry of his subjects and enemies, the most tolerant of princes
was driven to the brink of persecution ; and the life of Theodoric
was too long, since he lived to condemn the virtue of Boethius
and Symmachus.[88]

The senator Boethius [89] is the last of the Romans whom Cato or
Tully could have acknowledged for their countryman. As a
wealthy orphan, he inherited the patrimony and honors of the
Anician family, a name ambitiously assumed by the kings and
emperors of the age ; and the appellation of Manlius asserted his
genuine or fabulous descent from a race of consuls and dictators,

---

* Gibbon should not have omitted the golden words of Theodoric in a letter which
he addressed to Justin : That to pretend to a dominion over the conscience is to
usurp the prerogative of God ; that by the nature of things the power of sovereigns
is confined to external government ; that they have no right of punishment but
over those who disturb the public peace, of which they are the guardians ; that the
most dangerous heresy is that of a sovereign who separates from himself a part of
his subjects, because they believe not according to his belief. Compare Le Beau,
vol. viii. p. 63.—M.

who had repulsed the Gauls from the Capitol, and sacrificed their sons to the discipline of the republic. In the youth of Boethius the studies of Rome were not totally abandoned ; a Virgil [90] is now extant, corrected by the hand of a consul ; and the professors of grammar, rhetoric, and jurisprudence, were maintained in their privileges and pensions by the liberality of the Goths. But the erudition of the Latin language was insufficient to satiate his ardent curiosity ; and Boethius is said to have employed eighteen laborious years in the schools of Athens, [91] which were supported by the zeal, the learning, and the diligence of Proclus and his disciples. The reason and piety of their Roman pupil were fortunately saved from the contagion of mystery and magic, which polluted the groves of the academy ; but he imbibed the spirit, and imitated the method, of his dead and living masters, who attempted to reconcile the strong and subtile sense of Aristotle with the devout contemplation and sublime fancy of Plato. After his return to Rome, and his marriage with the daughter of his friend, the patrician Symmachus, Boethius still continued, in a palace of ivory and marble, to prosecute the same studies. [92] The church was edified by his profound defence of the orthodox creed against the Arian, the Eutychian, and the Nestorian heresies ; and the Catholic unity was explained or exposed in a formal treatise by the *indifference* of three distinct though consubstantial persons. For the benefit of his Latin readers, his genius submitted to teach the first elements of the arts and sciences of Greece. The geometry of Euclid, the music of Pythagoras, the arithmetic of Nicomachus, the mechanics of Archimedes, the astronomy of Ptolemy, the theology of Plato, and the logic of Aristotle, with the commentary of Porphyry, were translated and illustrated by the indefatigable pen of the Roman senator. And he alone was esteemed capable of describing the wonders of art, a sun-dial, a water-clock, or a sphere which represented the motions of the planets. From these abstruse speculations, Boethius stooped, or, to speak more truly, he rose to the social duties of public and private life : the indigent were relieved by his liberality ; and his eloquence, which flattery might compare to the voice of Demosthenes or Cicero, was uniformly exerted in the cause of innocence and humanity. Such conspicuous merit was felt and rewarded by a discerning prince : the dignity of Boethius was adorned with the titles of consul and patrician, and his talents were usefully employed in the important station of master of the offices. Notwithstanding the equal claims of the East and West, his two sons were created, in their tender youth, the consuls of the same year. [93] On the memorable day of their inauguration, they proceeded in solemn pomp from their pal-

ace to the forum amidst the applause of the senate and people ; and
their joyful father, the true consul of Rome, after pronouncing an
oration in the praise of his royal benefactor, distributed a triumphal
largess in the games of the circus. Prosperous in his fame and
fortunes, in his public honors and private alliances, in the cultivation of science and the consciousness of virtue, Boethius might
have been styled happy, if that precarious epithet could be safely
applied before the last term of the life of man.

A philosopher, liberal of his wealth and parsimonious of his
time, might be insensible to the common allurements of ambition,
the thirst of gold and employment. And some credit may be due
to the asseveration of Boethius, that he had reluctantly obeyed
the divine Plato, who enjoins every virtuous citizen to rescue the
state from the usurpation of vice and ignorance. For the integrity
of his public conduct he appeals to the memory of his country.
His authority had restrained the pride and oppression of the royal
officers, and his eloquence had delivered Paulianus from the dogs
of the palace. He had always pitied, and often relieved, the distress of the provincials, whose fortunes were exhausted by public
and private rapine ; and Boethius alone had courage to oppose
the tyranny of the barbarians, elated by conquest, excited by
avarice, and, as he complains, encouraged by impunity. In these
honorable contests his spirit soared above the consideration of
danger, and perhaps of prudence ; and we may learn from the
example of Cato, that a character of pure and inflexible virtue is
the most apt to be misled by prejudice, to be heated by enthusiasm,
and to confound private enmities with public justice. The disciple
of Plato might exaggerate the infirmities of nature, and the
imperfections of society ; and the mildest form of a Gothic kingdom, even the weight of allegiance and gratitude, must be insup-
portable to the free spirit of a Roman patriot. But the favor and
fidelity of Boethius declined in just proportion with the public
happiness ; and an unworthy colleague was imposed, to divide and
control the power of the master of the offices. In the last gloomy
season of Theodoric, he indignantly felt that he was a slave ; but
as his master had only power over his life, he stood without arms
and without fear against the face of an angry barbarian, who had
been provoked to believe that the safety of the senate was incompatible with his own. The senator Albinus was accused and
already convicted on the presumption of *hoping*, as it was said, the
liberty of Rome. " If Albinus be criminal," exclaimed the orator,
" the senate and myself are all guilty of the same crime. If we
are innocent, Albinus is equally entitled to the protection of the
laws." These laws might not have punished the simple and

barren wish of an unattainable blessing ; but they would have shown less indulgence to the rash confession of Boethius, that, had he known of a conspiracy, the tyrant never should.[94] The advocate of Albinus was soon involved in the danger and perhaps the guilt of his client ; their signature (which they denied as a forgery) was affixed to the original address, inviting the emperor to deliver Italy from the Goths ; and three witnesses of honorable rank, perhaps of infamous reputation, attested the treasonable designs of the Roman patrician.[95] Yet his innocence must be presumed, since he was deprived by Theodoric of the means of justification, and rigorously confined in the tower of Pavia, while the senate, at the distance of five hundred miles, pronounced a sentence of confiscation and death against the most illustrious of its members. At the command of the barbarians, the occult science of a philosopher was stigmatized with the names of sacrilege and magic.[96] A devout and dutiful attachment to the senate was condemned as criminal by the trembling voices of the senators themselves ; and their ingratitude deserved the wish or prediction of Boethius, that, after him, none should be found guilty of the same offence.[97]

While Boethius, oppressed with fetters, expected each moment the sentence or the stroke of death, he composed, in the tower of Pavia, the *Consolation of Philosophy ;* a golden volume not unworthy of the leisure of Plato or Tully, but which claims incomparable merit from the barbarism of the times and the situation of the author. The celestial guide, whom he had so long invoked at Rome and Athens, now condescended to illumine his dungeon, to revive his courage, and to pour into his wounds her salutary balm. She taught him to compare his long prosperity and his recent distress, and to conceive new hopes from the inconstancy of fortune. Reason had informed him of the precarious condition of her gifts ; experience had satisfied him of their real value ; he had enjoyed them without guilt ; he might resign them without a sigh, and calmly disdain the impotent malice of his enemies, who had left him happiness, since they had left him virtue. From the earth, Boethius ascended to heaven in search of the SUPREME GOOD ; explored the metaphysical labyrinth of chance and destiny, of prescience and free will ; of time and eternity ; and generously attempted to reconcile the perfect attributes of the Diety with the apparent disorders of his moral and physical government. Such topics of consolation, so obvious, so vague, or so abtruse, are ineffectual to subdue the feelings of human nature. Yet the sense of misfortune may be diverted by the labor of thought ; and the sage who could artfully combine in the same work the various

riches of philosophy, poetry, and eloquence, must already have
possessed the intrepid calmness which he affected to seek.   Suspense, the worst of evils, was at length determined by the ministers
of death, who executed, and perhaps exceeded, the inhuman
mandate of Theodoric.   A strong cord was fastened round the
head of Boethius, and forcibly tightened, till his eyes almost
started from their sockets ; and some mercy may be discovered
in the milder torture of beating him with clubs till he expired.[98]
But his genius survived to diffuse a ray of knowledge over the
darkest ages of the Latin world ; the writings of the philosopher
were translated by the most glorious of the English kings,[99] and
the third emperor of the name of Otho removed to a more honorable
tomb the bones of a Catholic saint, who, from his Arian persecutors, had acquired the honors of martyrdom, and the fame of
miracles.[100]   In the last hours of Boethius, he derived some comfort from the safety of his two sons, of his wife, and of his father-
in-law, the venerable Symmachus.   But the grief of Symmachus
was indiscreet, and perhaps disrespectful : he had presumed to
lament, he might dare to revenge, the death of an injured friend.
He was dragged in chains from Rome to the palace of Ravenna ;
and the suspicions of Theodoric could only be appeased by the
blood of an innocent and aged senator.[101]

Humanity will be disposed to encourage any report which
testifies the jurisdiction of conscience and the remorse of kings ;
and philosophy is not ignorant that the most horrid spectres are
sometimes created by the powers of a disordered fancy, and the
weakness of a distempered body.   After a life of virtue and glory,
Theodoric was now descending with shame and guilt into the
grave ; his mind was humbled by the contrast of the past, and
justly alarmed by the invisible terrors of futurity.   One evening,
as it is related, when the head of a large fish was served on the
royal table,[102] he suddenly exclaimed that he beheld the angry
countenance of Symmachus, his eyes glaring fury and revenge,
and his mouth armed with long sharp teeth, which threatened to
devour him.   The monarch instantly retired to his chamber, and,
as he lay, trembling with anguish cold, under a weight of bed-
clothes, he expressed, in broken murmurs to his physician
Elpidius, his deep repentance for the murders of Boethius and
Symmachus.[103]   His malady increased, and after a dysentery,
which continued three days, he expired in the palace of Ravenna,
in the thirty-third, or, if we compute from the invasion of Italy,
in the thirty-seventh year of his reign.   Conscious of his approaching end, he divided his treasures and provinces between his two
grandsons, and fixed the Rhone as their common boundary.[104]

Amalaric was restored to the throne of Spain. Italy, with all the conquests of the Ostrogoths, was bequeathed to Athalaric ; whose age did not exceed ten years, but who was cherished as the last male offspring of the line of Amali, by the short-lived marriage of his mother Amalasontha with a royal fugitive of the same blood.[105] In the presence of the dying monarch, the Gothic chiefs and Italian magistrates mutually engaged their faith and loyalty to the young prince, and to his guardian mother ; and received, in the same awful moment, his last salutary advice, to maintain the laws, to love the senate and people of Rome, and to cultivate with decent reverence the friendship of the emperor.[106] The monument of Theodoric was erected by his daughter Amalasontha, in a conspicuous situation, which commanded the city of Ravenna, the harbor, and the adjacent coast. A chapel of a circular form, thirty feet in diameter, is crowned by a dome of one entire piece of granite : from the centre of the dome four columns arose, which supported, in a vase of porphyry, the remains of the Gothic king, surrounded by the brazen statues of the twelve apostles.[107] His spirit, after some previous expiation, might have been permitted to mingle with the benefactors of mankind, if an Italian hermit had not been witness, in a vision, to the damnation of Theodoric,[108] whose soul was plunged, by the ministers of divine vengeance, into the volcano of Lipari, one of the flaming mouths of the infernal world.[109]

CHAPTER XL.

THE emperor Justinian was born[1] near the ruins of Sardica (the modern Sophia), of an obscure race[2] of barbarians,[3] the inhabitants of a wild and desolate country, to which the names of Dardania, of Dacia, and of Bulgaria, have been successively applied. His elevation was prepared by the adventurous spirit of his uncle Justin, who, with two other peasants of the same village, deserted, for the profession of arms, the more useful em-

ployment of husbandmen or shepherds.[4] On foot, with a scanty
provision of biscuit in their knapsacks, the three youths followed
the high road of Constantinople, and were soon enrolled, for their
strength and stature, among the guards of the emperor Leo.
Under the two succeeding reigns, the fortunate peasant emerged
to wealth and honors ; and his escape from some dangers which
threatened his life was afterwards ascribed to the guardian angel
who watches over the fate of kings. His long and laudable service in the Isaurian and Persian wars would not have preserved
from oblivion the name of Justin ; yet they might warrant the
military promotion, which in the course of fifty years he gradually obtained ; the rank of tribune, of count, and of general ;
the dignity of senator, and the command of the guards, who
obeyed him as their chief, at the important crisis when the emperor Anastasius was removed from the world. The powerful
kinsmen whom he had raised and enriched were excluded from
the throne ; and the eunuch Amantius, who reigned in the palace, had secretly resolved to fix the diadem on the head of the
most obsequious of his creatures. A liberal donative, to conciliate the suffrage of the guards, was intrusted for that purpose in
the hands of their commander. But these weighty arguments
were treacherously employed by Justin in his own favor ; and as
no competitor presumed to appear, the Dacian peasant was invested with the purple by the unanimous consent of the soldiers,
who knew him to be brave and gentle, of the clergy and people,
who believed him to be orthodox, and of the provincials, who
yielded a blind and implicit submission to the will of the capital.
The elder Justin, as he is distinguished from another emperor of
the same family and name, ascended the Byzantine throne at the age
of sixty-eight years ; and, had he been left to his own guidance,
every moment of a nine years' reign must have exposed to his subjects the impropriety of their choice. His ignorance was similar
to that of Theodoric ; and it is remarkable that, in an age not destitute of learning, two contemporary monarchs had never been
instructed in the knowledge of the alphabet.* But the genius of
Justin was far inferior to that of the Gothic king : the experience
of a soldier had not qualified him for the government of an empire ; and though personally brave, the consciousness of his own
weakness was naturally attended with doubt, distrust, and political apprehension. But the official business of the state was diligently and faithfully transacted by the quæstor Proclus ;[5] and

---

* St. Martin questions the fact in both cases. The ignorance of Justin rests on
the secret history of Procopius, vol. viii. p. 8. St. Martin's notes on Le Beau.—M.

the aged emperor adopted the talents and ambition of his nephew Justinian, an aspiring youth, whom his uncle had drawn from the rustic solitude of Dacia, and educated at Constantinople, as the heir of his private fortune, and at length of the Eastern empire.

Since the eunuch Amantius had been defrauded of his money, it became necessary to deprive him of his life. The task was easily accomplished by the charge of a real or fictitious conspiracy ; and the judges were informed, as an accumulation of guilt, that he was secretly addicted to the Manichæan heresy.[6] Amantius lost his head ; three of his companions, the first domestics of the palace, were punished either with death or exile ; and their unfortunate candidate for the purple was cast into a deep dungeon, overwhelmed with stones, and ignominiously thrown, without burial, into the sea. The ruin of Vitalian was a work of more difficulty and danger. That Gothic chief had rendered himself popular by the civil war which he boldly waged against Anastasius for the defence of the orthodox faith, and after the conclusion of an advantageous treaty, he still remained in the neighborhood of Constantinople at the head of a formidable and victorious army of barbarians. By the frail security of oaths, he was tempted to relinquish this advantageous situation, and to trust his person within the walls of a city, whose inhabitants, particularly the *blue* faction, were artfully incensed against him by the remembrance even of his pious hostilities. The emperor and his nephew embraced him as the faithful and worthy champion of the church and state ; and gratefully adorned their favorite with the titles of consul and general ; but in the seventh month of his consulship, Vitalian was stabbed with seventeen wounds at the royal banquet ;[7] and Justinian, who inherited the spoil, was accused as the assassin of a spiritual brother, to whom he had recently pledged his faith in the participation of the Christian mysteries.[8] After the fall of his rival, he was promoted, without any claim of military service, to the office of master-general of the Eastern armies, whom it was his duty to lead into the field against the public enemy. But, in the pursuit of fame, Justinian might have lost his present dominion over the age and weakness of his uncle ; and instead of acquiring by Scythian or Persian trophies the applause of his countrymen,[9] the prudent warrior solicited their favor in the churches, the circus, and the senate, of Constantinople. The Catholics were attached to the nephew of Justin, who, between the Nestorian and Eutychian heresies, trod the narrow path of inflexible and intolerant orthodoxy.[10] In the first days of the new reign he prompted and gratified the popular enthusiasm against the memory of the deceased emperor. After a schism of thirty-four years, he reconciled the proud and angry spirit of the Roman pontiff, and spread among the Latins a favorable report of his pious respect for the apostolic see. The thrones of the East were filled with Catholic bishops devoted to his interest, the clergy and the monks were gained by his liberality, and the people were taught to pray for their future sovereign, the hope and pillar of the true religion. The magnificence of Justinian was displayed in the superior pomp of his public spectacles, an object not less sacred and important in the eyes of the multitude than the creed of Nice or Chalcedon : the expense of his consulship was esteemed at two hundred and twenty-eight thousand pieces of gold ; twenty lions and thirty leopards were produced at the same time in the amphitheatre, and a numerous train of horses, with their rich trappings, was bestowed as an extraordinary gift on the victorious charioteers of the circus. While he indulged the people of Constantinople, and received the addresses of foreign kings, the nephew of Justin assiduously cultivated the friendship of the senate. That venerable name seemed to qualify its members to declare the sense of the nation, and to regulate the succession of the Imperial throne : the feeble Anastasius had permitted the vigor of government to degenerate into the form or substance of an aristocracy ; and the military officers who had obtained the senatorial rank were followed by their domestic guards, a band of veterans, whose arms or acclamations might fix in a tumultuous moment the diadem of the East. The treasures of the state were lavished to procure the voices of the senators, and their unanimous wish, that he would be pleased to adopt Justinian for his colleague, was communicated to the emperor. But this request, which too clearly admonished him of his approaching end, was unwelcome to the jealous temper of an aged monarch, desirous to retain the power which he was incapable of exercising ; and Justin, holding his purple with both his hands, advised him to prefer, since an election was so profitable, some older candidate. Notwithstanding this reproach, the senate proceeded to decorate Justinian with the royal epithet of *nobilissimus ;* and their decree was ratified by the affection or the fears of his uncle. After some time, the languor of mind and body, to which he was reduced by an incurable wound in his thigh, indispensably required the aid of a guardian. He summoned the patriarch and senators ; and in their presence solemnly placed the diadem on the head of his nephew, who was conducted from the palace to the circus, and saluted by the loud and joyful applause of the people. The life of Justin was prolonged about four months ; but from the instant of this ceremony he was considered as dead to the empire, which acknowledged Justinian, in the forty-fifth year of his age, for the lawful sovereign of the East.[11]

From his elevation to his death, Justinian governed the Roman empire thirty-eight years, seven months, and thirteen days. The events of his reign, which excite our curious attention by their number, variety, and importance, are diligently related by the secretary of Belisarius, a rhetorician, whom eloquence had promoted to the rank of senator and præfect of Constantinople. According to the vicissitudes of courage or servitude, of favor or disgrace, Procopius[12] successively composed the *history*, the *panegyric*, and the *satire* of his own times. The eight books of the Persian, Vandalic, and Gothic wars,[13] which are continued in the five books of Agathias, deserve our esteem as a laborious and successful imitation of the Attic, or at least of the Asiatic, writers of ancient Greece. His facts are collected from the personal experience and free conversation of a soldier, a statesman, and a traveller ; his style continually aspires, and often attains, to the merit of strength and elegance ; his reflections, more especially in the speeches, which he too frequently inserts, contain a rich fund of political knowledge ; and the historian, excited by the generous ambition of pleasing and instructing posterity, appears to disdain the prejudices of the people, and the flattery of courts. The writings of Procopius[14] were read and applauded by his contemporaries :[15] but, although he respectfully laid them at the foot of the throne, the pride of Justinian must have been wounded by the praise of a hero, who perpetually eclipses the glory of his inactive sovereign. The conscious dignity of independence was subdued by the hopes and fears of a slave ; and the secretary of Belisarius labored for pardon and reward in the six books of the Imperial *edifices*. He had dexterously chosen a subject of apparent splendor, in which he could loudly celebrate his genius, the magnificence, and the piety of a prince, who, both as a conqueror and legislator, had surpassed the puerile virtues of Themistocles and Cyrus.[16] Disappointment might urge the flatterer to secret revenge ; and the first glance of favor might again tempt him to suspend and suppress a libel,[17] in which the Roman Cyrus is degraded into an odious and contemptible tyrant, in which both the emperor and his consort Theodora are seriously represented as two dæmons, who had assumed a human form for the destruction of mankind.[18] Such base inconsistency must doubtless sully the reputation, and detract from the credit, of Procopius : yet, after the venom of his malignity has been suffered to exhale, the residue of the *anecdotes*, even the most disgraceful facts, some of which had been tenderly hinted in his public history, are established by their internal evidence, or the authentic monuments of the times.[19] * From these various materials, I shall now proceed to describe the reign of Justinian, which will deserve and occupy an ample space. The present chapter will explain the elevation and character of Theodora, the factions of the circus, and the peaceful administration of the sovereign of the East. In the three succeeding chapters I shall relate the wars of Justinian, which achieved the conquest of Africa and Italy ; and I shall follow the victories of Belisarius and Narses, without disguising the vanity of their triumphs, or the hostile virtue of the Persian and Gothic heroes. The series of this and the following volume will embrace the jurisprudence and theology of the emperor ; the controversies and sects which still divide the Oriental church ; the reformation of the Roman law, which is obeyed or respected by the nations of modern Europe.

I. In the exercise of supreme power, the first act of Justinian was to divide it with the woman whom he loved, the famous Theodora,[20] whose strange elevation cannot be applauded as the triumph of female virtue. Under the reign of Anastasius, the care of the wild beasts maintained by the green faction at Constantinople was intrusted to Acacius, a native of the Isle of Cyprus, who, from his employment, was surnamed the master of the bears. This honorable office was given after his death to another candidate, notwithstanding the diligence of his widow, who had already provided a husband and a successor. Acacius had left three daughters, Comito,[21] THEODORA, and Anastasia, the eldest of whom did not then exceed the age of seven years. On a solemn festival, these helpless orphans were sent by their distressed and indignant mother, in the garb of suppliants, into the midst of the theatre : the green faction received them with contempt, the blues with compassion ; and this difference, which sunk deep into the mind of Theodora, was felt long afterwards in the administration of the empire. As they improved in age and beauty, the three sisters were successively devoted to the public and private pleasures of the Byzantine people ; and Theodora, after following Comito on the stage, in the dress of a slave, with a stool

---

* The Anecdota of Procopius, compared with the former works of the same author, appear to me the basest and most disgraceful work in literature. The wars, which he has described in the former volumes as glorious or necessary, are become unprofitable and wanton massacres ; the buildings which he celebrated, as raised to the immortal honor of the great emperor, and his admirable queen, either as magnificent embellishments of the city, or useful fortifications for the defence of the frontier, are become works of vain prodigality and useless ostentation. I doubt whether Gibbon has made sufficient allowance for the "malignity" of the Anecdota ; at all events, the extreme and disgusting profligacy of Theodora's early life rests entirely on this virulent libel.—M.

on her head, was at length permitted to exercise her independent talents. She neither danced, nor sung, nor played on the flute ; her skill was confined to the pantomime arts ; she excelled in buffoon characters, and as often as the comedian swelled her cheeks, and complained with a ridiculous tone and gesture of the blows that were inflicted, the whole theatre of Constantinople resounded with laughter and applause. The beauty of Theodora [22] was the subject of more flattering praise, and the source of more exquisite delight. Her features were delicate and regular ; her complexion, though somewhat pale, was tinged with a natural color ; every sensation was instantly expressed by the vivacity of her eyes ; her easy motions displayed the graces of a small but elegant figure ; and either love or adulation might proclaim, that painting and poetry were incapable of delineating the matchless excellence of her form. But this form was degraded by the facility with which it was exposed to the public eye, and prostituted to licentious desire. Her venal charms were abandoned to a promiscuous crowd of citizens and strangers, of every rank, and of every profession : the fortunate lover who had been promised a night of enjoyment, was often driven from her bed by a stronger or more wealthy favorite ; and when she passed through the streets, her presence was avoided by all who wished to escape either the scandal or the temptation. The satirical historian has not blushed [23] to describe the naked scenes which Theodora was not ashamed to exhibit in the theatre. [24] After exhausting the arts of sensual pleasure, [25] she most ungratefully murmured against the parsimony of Nature ; [26] but her murmurs, her pleasures, and her arts, must be veiled in the obscurity of a learned language. After reigning for some time, the delight and contempt of the capital, she condescended to accompany Ecebolus, a native of Tyre, who had obtained the government of the African Pentapolis. But this union was frail and transient ; Ecebolus soon rejected an expensive or faithless concubine ; she was reduced at Alexandria to extreme distress ; and in her laborious return to Constantinople, every city of the East admired and enjoyed the fair Cyprian, whose merit appeared to justify her descent from the peculiar island of Venus. The vague commerce of Theodora, and the most detestable precautions, preserved her from the danger which she feared ; yet once, and once only, she became a mother. The infant was saved and educated in Arabia, by his father, who imparted to him, on his death-bed, that he was the son of an empress. Filled with ambitious hopes, the unsuspecting youth immediately hastened to the palace of Constantinople, and was admitted to the presence of his mother. As he was never more seen, even after the decease of Theodora, she deserves the foul imputation of extinguishing with his life a secret so offensive to her Imperial virtue.

In the most abject state of her fortune and reputation, some vision, either of sleep or of fancy, had whispered to Theodora the pleasing assurance that she was destined to become the spouse of a potent monarch. Conscious of her approaching greatness, she returned from Paphlagonia to Constantinople ; assumed, like a skilful actress, a more decent character ; relieved her poverty by the laudable industry of spinning wool ; and affected a life of chastity and solitude in a small house, which she afterwards changed into a magnificent temple.[27] Her beauty, assisted by art or accident, soon attracted, captivated, and fixed the patrician Justinian, who already reigned with absolute sway under the name of his uncle. Perhaps she contrived to enhance the value of a gift which she had so often lavished on the meanest of mankind ; perhaps she inflamed, at first by modest delays, and at last, by sensual allurements, the desires of a lover, who, from nature or devotion, was addicted to long vigils and abstemious diet. When his first transports had subsided, she still maintained the same ascendant over his mind, by the more solid merit of temper and understanding. Justinian delighted to ennoble and enrich the object of his affection ; the treasures of the East were poured at her feet, and the nephew of Justin was determined, perhaps by religious scruples, to bestow on his concubine the sacred and legal character of a wife. But the laws of Rome expressly prohibited the marriage of a senator with any female who had been dishonored by a servile origin or theatrical profession : the empress Lupicina, or Euphemia, a barbarian of rustic manners, but of irreproachable virtue, refused to accept a prostitute for her niece ; and even Vigilantia, the superstitious mother of Justinian, though she acknowledged the wit and beauty of Theodora, was seriously apprehensive, lest the levity and arrogance of that artful paramour might corrupt the piety and happiness of her son. These obstacles were removed by the inflexible constancy of Justinian. He patiently expected the death of the empress ; he despised the tears of his mother, who soon sunk under the weight of her affliction ; and a law was promulgated in the name of the emperor Justin, which abolished the rigid jurisprudence of antiquity. A glorious repentance (the words of the edict) was left open for the unhappy females who had prostituted their persons on the theatre, and they were permitted to contract a legal union with the most illustrious of the Romans.[28] This indulgence was speedily followed by the solemn nuptials of Justinian and Theodora ; her

dignity was gradually exalted with that of her lover ; and, as
soon as Justin had invested his nephew with the purple, the patriarch of Constantinople placed the diadem on the heads of the
emperor and empress of the East. But the usual honors, which
the severity of Roman manners had allowed to the wives of
princes, could not satisfy either the ambition of Theodora or the
fondness of Justinian. He seated her on the throne as an equal
and independent colleague in the sovereignty of the empire, and
an oath of allegiance was imposed on the governors of the provinces in the joint names of Justinian and Theodora.[29] The Eastern world fell prostrate before the genius and fortune of the
daughter of Acacius. The prostitute, who, in the presence of
innumerable spectators, had polluted the theatre of Constantinople, was adored as a queen in the same city, by grave magistrates,
orthodox bishops, victorious generals, and captive monarchs.[30]

Those who believe that the female mind is totally depraved by
the loss of chastity, will eagerly listen to all the invectives of private envy, or popular resentment, which have dissembled the virtues of Theodora, exaggerated her vices, and condemned with
rigor the venal or voluntary sins of the youthful harlot. From
a motive of shame or contempt, she often declined the servile
homage of the multitude, escaped from the odious light of the
capital, and passed the greatest part of the year in the palaces
and gardens which were pleasantly seated on the sea-coast of the
Propontis and the Bosphorus. Her private hours were devoted to
the prudent as well as grateful care of her beauty, the luxury of
the bath and table, and the long slumber of the evening and the
morning. Her secret apartments were occupied by the favorite
women and eunuchs, whose interests and passions she indulged at
the expense of justice ; the most illustrious personages of the
state were crowded into a dark and sultry ante-chamber, and
when at last, after a tedious attendance, they were admitted to
kiss the feet of Theodora, they experienced, as her humor might
suggest, the silent arrogance of an empress, or the capricious levity of a comedian. Her rapacious avarice to accumulate an immense treasure may be excused by the apprehension of her husband's death, which could leave no alternative between ruin and
the throne ; and fear as well as ambition might exasperate Theodora against two generals, who, during the malady of the emperor, had rashly declared that they were not disposed to acquiesce in the choice of the capital. But the reproach of cruelty,
so repugnant even to her softer vices, has left an indelible stain on
the memory of Theodora. Her numerous spies observed, and zealously reported, every action, or word, or look, injurious to their

royal mistress. Whomsoever they accused were cast into her peculiar prisons,[31] inaccessible to the inquiries of justice ; and it
was rumored, that the torture of the rack or scourge had been inflicted in the presence of the female tyrant, insensible to the voice
of prayer or of pity.[32] Some of these unhappy victims perished in
deep, unwholesome dungeons, while others were permitted, after
the loss of their limbs, their reason, or their fortunes, to appear
in the world, the living monuments of her vengeance, which was
commonly extended to the children of those whom she had suspected or injured. The senator or bishop, whose death or exile
Theodora had pronounced, was delivered to a trusty messenger,
and his diligence was quickened by a menace from her own
mouth. " If you fail in the execution of my commands, I swear
by Him who liveth forever, that your skin shall be flayed from
your body." [33]

If the creed of Theodora had not been tainted with heresy, her
exemplary devotion might have atoned, in the opinion of her contemporaries, for pride, avarice, and cruelty. But if she employed
her influence to assuage the intolerant fury of the emperor, the
present age will allow some merit to her religion, and much indulgence to her speculative errors.[34] The name of Theodora was introduced, with equal honor, in all the pious and charitable foundations of Justinian ; and the most benevolent institution of his
reign may be ascribed to the sympathy of the empress for her less
fortunate sisters, who had been seduced, or compelled to embrace
the trade of prostitution. A palace, on the Asiatic side of the
Bosphorus, was converted into a stately and spacious monastery,
and a liberal maintenance was assigned to five hundred women,
who had been collected from the streets and brothels of Constantinople. In this safe and holy retreat they were devoted to perpetual confinement ; and the despair of some, who threw themselves headlong into the sea, was lost in the gratitude of the penitents, who had been delivered from sin and misery by their generous benefactress.[35] The prudence of Theodora is celebrated by
Justinian himself ; and his laws are attributed to the sage counsels of his most reverend wife, whom he had received as the gift of
the Deity.[36] Her courage was displayed amidst the tumult of the
people and the terrors of the court. Her chastity, from the moment of her union with Justinian, is founded on the silence of her
implacable enemies ; and although the daughter of Acacius
might be satiated with love, yet some applause is due to the firmness of a mind which could sacrifice pleasure and habit to the
stronger sense either of duty or interest. The wishes and prayers
of Theodora could never obtain the blessing of a lawful son, and

she buried an infant daughter, the sole offspring of her marriage.[37] Notwithstanding this disappointment, her dominion was permanent and absolute ; she preserved, by art or merit, the affections of Justinian ; and their seeming dissensions were always fatal to the courtiers who believed them to be sincere. Perhaps her health had been impaired by the licentiousness of her youth ; but it was always delicate, and she was directed by her physicians to use the Pythian warm baths. In this journey the empress was followed by the Prætorian præfect, the great treasurer, several counts and patricians, and a splendid train of four thousand attendants : the highways were repaired at her approach ; a palace was erected for her reception ; and as she passed through Bithynia, she distributed liberal alms to the churches, the monasteries, and the hospitals, that they might implore Heaven for the restoration of her health.[38] At length, in the twenty-fourth year of her marriage, and the twenty-second of her reign, she was consumed by a cancer ;[39] and the irreparable loss was deplored by her husband, who, in the room of a theatrical prostitute, might have selected the purest and most noble virgin of the East.[40]

II. A material difference may be observed in the games of antiquity : the most eminent of the Greeks were actors, the Romans were merely spectators. The Olympic stadium was open to wealth, merit, and ambition ; and if the candidates could depend on their personal skill and activity, they might pursue the footsteps of Diomede and Menelaus, and conduct their own horses in the rapid career.[41] Ten, twenty, forty chariots were allowed to start at the same instant ; a crown of leaves was the reward of the victor ; and his fame, with that of his family and country, was chanted in lyric strains more durable than monuments of brass and marble. But a senator, or even a citizen, conscious of his dignity, would have blushed to expose his person or his horses in the circus of Rome. The games were exhibited at the expense of the republic, the magistrates, or the emperors : but the reins were abandoned to servile hands ; and if the profits of a favorite charioteer sometimes exceeded those of an advocate, they must be considered as the effects of popular extravagance, and the high wages of a disgraceful profession. The race, in its first institution, was a simple contest of two chariots, whose drivers were distinguished by *white* and *red* liveries : two additional colors, a light *green*, and a cærulean *blue*, were afterwards introduced ; and as the races were repeated twenty-five times, one hundred chariots contributed in the same day to the pomp of the circus. The four *factions* soon acquired a legal establishment, and a mysterious origin, and their fanciful colors were derived from the various appearances of nature in the four seasons of the year ; the red dog-star of summer, the snows of winter, the deep shades of autumn, and the cheerful verdure of the spring.[42] Another interpretation preferred the elements to the seasons, and the struggle of the green and blue was supposed to represent the conflict of the earth and sea. Their respective victories announced either a plentiful harvest or a prosperous navigation, and the hostility of the husbandmen and mariners was somewhat less absurd than the blind ardor of the Roman people, who devoted their lives and fortunes to the color which they had espoused. Such folly was disdained and indulged by the wisest princes ; but the names of Caligula, Nero, Vitellius, Verus, Commodus, Caracalla, and Elagabalus, were enrolled in the blue or green factions of the circus : they frequented their stables, applauded their favorites, chastised their antagonists, and deserved the esteem of the populace by the natural or affected imitation of their manners. The bloody and tumultuous contest continued to disturb the public festivity, till the last age of the spectacles of Rome ; and Theodoric, from a motive of justice or affection, interposed his authority to protect the greens against the violence of a consul and a patrician, who were passionately addicted to the blue faction of the circus.[43]

Constantinople adopted the follies, though not the virtues, of ancient Rome ; and the same factions which had agitated the circus, raged with redoubled fury in the hippodrome. Under the reign of Anastasius, this popular frenzy was inflamed by religious zeal ; and the greens, who had treacherously concealed stones and daggers under baskets of fruit, massacred, at a solemn festival, three thousand of their blue adversaries.[44] From the capital this pestilence was diffused into the provinces and cities of the East, and the sportive distinction of two colors produced two strong and irreconcilable factions, which shook the foundations of a feeble government.[45] The popular dissensions, founded on the most serious interest, or holy pretence, have scarcely equalled the obstinacy of this wanton discord, which invaded the peace of families, divided friends and brothers, and tempted the female sex, though seldom seen in the circus, to espouse the inclinations of their lovers, or to contradict the wishes of their husbands. Every law, either human or divine, was trampled under foot, and as long as the party was successful, its deluded followers appeared careless of private distress or public calamity. The license, without the freedom, of democracy, was revived at Antioch and Constantinople, and the support of a faction became necessary to every candidate for civil or ecclesiastical honors. A secret attachment to the family or sect of Anastasius was imputed to the greens ; the blues were zealously devoted to the cause of orthodoxy and Justinian,[46] and their grateful patron protected, above five years, the disorders of a faction, whose seasonable tumults overawed the palace, the senate, and the capitals of the East. Insolent with royal favor, the blues affected to strike terror by a peculiar and barbaric dress, the long hair of the Huns, their close sleeves and ample garments, a lofty step, and a sonorous voice. In the day they concealed their two-edged poniards, but in the night they boldly assembled in arms, and in numerous bands, prepared for every act of violence and rapine. Their adversaries of the green faction, or even inoffensive citizens, were stripped and often murdered by these nocturnal robbers, and it became dangerous to wear any gold buttons or girdles, or to appear at a late hour in the streets of a peaceful capital. A daring spirit, rising with impunity, proceeded to violate the safeguard of private houses ; and fire was employed to facilitate the attack, or to conceal the crimes of these factious rioters. No place was safe or sacred from their depredations ; to gratify either avarice or revenge, they profusely spilt the blood of the innocent ; churches and altars were polluted by atrocious murders ; and it was the boast of the assassins, that their dexterity could always inflict a mortal wound with a single stroke of their dagger. The dissolute youth of Constantinople adopted the blue livery of disorder ; the laws were silent, and the bonds of society were relaxed : creditors were compelled to resign their obligations ; judges to reverse their sentence ; masters to enfranchise their slaves ; and fathers to supply the extravagance of their children ; noble matrons were prostituted to the lust of their servants ; beautiful boys were torn from the arms of their parents ; and wives, unless they preferred a voluntary death, were ravished in the presence of their husbands.[47] The despair of the greens, who were persecuted by their enemies, and deserted by the magistrates, assumed the privilege of defence, perhaps of retaliation ; but those who survived the combat were dragged to execution, and the unhappy fugitives, escaping to woods and caverns, preyed without mercy on the society from whence they were expelled. Those ministers of justice who had courage to punish the crimes, and to brave the resentment, of the blues, became the victims of their indiscreet zeal ; a præfect of Constantinople fled for refuge to the holy sepulchre, a count of the East was ignominiously whipped, and a governor of Cilicia was hanged, by the order of Theodora, on the tomb of two assassins whom he had condemned for the murder of his groom, and a daring attack upon his own life.[48] An aspiring candidate may be tempted to build his greatness on the public confusion, but it is the interest as well as duty of a sovereign to maintain the authority of the laws. The first edict of Justinian, which was often repeated and sometimes executed, announced his firm resolution to support the innocent, and to chastise the guilty, of every denomination and *color*. Yet the balance of justice was still inclined in favor of the blue faction, by the secret affection, the habits, and the fears of the emperor ; his equity, after an apparent struggle, submitted, without reluctance, to the implacable passions of Theodora, and the empress never forgot, or forgave, the injuries of the comedian. At the accession of the younger Justin, the proclamation of equal and rigorous justice indirectly condemned the partiality of the former reign. " Ye blues, Justinian is no more ! ye greens, he is still alive !" [43]

A sedition, which almost laid Constantinople in ashes, was excited by the mutual hatred and momentary reconciliation of the two factions. In the fifth year of his reign, Justinian celebrated the festival of the ides of January : the games were incessantly disturbed by the clamorous discontent of the greens : till the twenty-second race, the emperor maintained his silent gravity ; at length, yielding to his impatience, he condescended to hold, in abrupt sentences, and by the voice of a crier, the most singular dialogue [59] that ever passed between a prince and his subjects. Their first complaints were respectful and modest ; they accused the subordinate ministers of oppression, and proclaimed their wishes for the long life and victory of the emperor. " Be patient and attentive, ye insolent railers !" exclaimed Justinian ; " be mute, ye Jews, Samaritans, and Manichæans !" The greens still attempted to awaken his compassion. " We are poor, we are innocent, we are injured, we dare not pass through the streets : a general persecution is exercised against our name and color. Let us die, O emperor ! but let us die by your command, and for your service !" But the repetition of partial and passionate invectives degraded, in their eyes, the majesty of the purple : they renounced allegiance to the prince who refused justice to his people ; lamented that the father of Justinian had been born ; and branded his son with the opprobrious names of a homicide, an ass, and a perjured tyrant. " Do you despise your lives ?" cried the indignant monarch : the blues rose with fury from their seats ; their hostile clamors thundered in the hippodrome ; and their adversaries, deserting the unequal contest, spread terror and despair through the streets of Constantinople. At this dangerous moment, seven notorious assassins of both factions, who had been condemned by the præfect, were carried round the city, and afterwards transported to the place of execution in the suburb of Pera.

Four were immediately beheaded ; a fifth was hanged : but when the same punishment was inflicted on the remaining two, the rope broke, they fell alive to the ground, the populace applauded their escape, and the monks of St. Conon, issuing from the neighboring convent, conveyed them in a boat to the sanctuary of the church.[51] As one of these criminals was of the blue, and the other of the green livery, the two factions were equally provoked by the cruelty of their oppressor, or the ingratitude of their patron ; and a short truce was concluded till they had delivered their prisoners, and satisfied their revenge. The palace of the præfect, who withstood the seditious torrent, was instantly burnt, his officers and guards were massacred, the prisons were forced open, and freedom was restored to those who could only use it for the public destruction. A military force, which had been despatched to the aid of the civil magistrate, was fiercely encountered by an armed multitude, whose numbers and boldness continually increased ; and the Heruli, the wildest barbarians in the service of the empire, overturned the priests and their relics, which, from a pious motive, had been rashly interposed to separate the bloody conflict. The tumult was exasperated by this sacrilege, the people fought with enthusiasm in the cause of God ; the women, from the roofs and windows, showered stones on the heads of the soldiers, who darted firebrands against the houses ; and the various flames, which had been kindled by the hands of citizens and strangers, spread without control over the face of the city. The conflagration involved the cathedral of St. Sophia, the baths of Zeuxippus, a part of the palace, from the first entrance to the altar of Mars, and the long portico from the palace to the forum of Constantine : a large hospital with the sick patients was consumed ; many churches and stately edifices were destroyed, and an immense treasure of gold and silver was either melted or lost. From such scenes of horror and distress, the wise and wealthy citizens escaped over the Bosphorus to the Asiatic side ; and during five days Constantinople was abandoned to the factions, whose watchword, NIKA, *vanquish !* has given a name to this memorable sedition.[52]

As long as the factions were divided, the triumphant blues, and desponding greens, appeared to behold with the same indifference the disorders of the state. They agreed to censure the corrupt management of justice and the finance ; and the two responsible ministers, the artful Tribonian, and the rapacious John of Cappadocia, were loudly arraigned as the authors of the public misery. The peaceful murmurs of the people would have been disregarded : they were heard with respect when the city was in flames ; the quæstor and the præfect were instantly removed, and their offices

were filled by two senators of blameless integrity. After this popular concession, Justinian proceeded to the hippodrome to confess
his own errors, and to accept the repentance of his grateful subjects ; but they distrusted his assurances, though solemnly pronounced in the presence of the holy Gospels ; and the emperor,
alarmed by their distrust, retreated with precipitation to the
strong fortress of the palace. The obstinacy of the tumult was
now imputed to a secret and ambitious conspiracy, and a suspicion
was entertained that the insurgents, more especially the green faction, had been supplied with arms and money by Hypatius and
Pompey, two patricians, who could neither forget with honor, nor
remember with safety, that they were the nephews of the emperor
Anastasius.   Capriciously trusted, disgraced, and pardoned by the
jealous levity of the monarch, they had appeared as loyal servants
before the throne ; and, during five days of the tumult, they were
detained as important hostages ; till at length, the fears of Justinian prevailing over his prudence, he viewed the two brothers
in the light of spies, perhaps of assassins, and sternly commanded them to depart from the palace. After a fruitless representation, that obedience might lead to involuntary treason, they
retired to their houses, and in the morning of the sixth day, Hypatius was surrounded and seized by the people, who, regardless
of his virtuous resistance, and the tears of his wife, transported
their favorite to the forum of Constantine, and instead of a diadem
placed a rich collar on his head. If the usurper, who afterwards
pleaded the merit of his delay, had complied with the advice of
his senate, and urged the fury of the multitude, their first irresistible effort might have oppressed or expelled his trembling competitor. The Byzantine palace enjoyed a free communication with
the sea ; vessels lay ready at the garden stairs ; and a secret resolution was already formed, to convey the emperor with his family
and treasures to a safe retreat at some distance from the capital.

Justinian was lost, if the prostitute whom he raised from the
theatre had not renounced the timidity, as well as the virtues, of
her sex. In the midst of a council, where Balisarius was present,
Theodora alone displayed the spirit of a hero ; and she alone,
without apprehending his future hatred, could save the emperor
from the imminent danger, and his unworthy fears. " If flight,"
said the consort of Justinian, " were the only means of safety, yet
I should disdain to fly. Death is the condition of our birth ; but
they who have reigned should never survive the loss of dignity
and dominion. I implore Heaven that I may never be seen, not a
day, without my diadem and purple ; that I may no longer behold
the light when I cease to be saluted with the name of queen. If

you resolve, O Cæsar ! to fly, you have treasures ; behold the sea, you have ships ; but tremble lest the desire of life should expose you to wretched exile and ignominious death. For my own part, I adhere to the maxim of antiquity, that the throne is a glorious sepulchre.'' The firmness of a woman restored the courage to deliberate and act, and courage soon discovers the resources of the most desperate situation. It was an easy and a decisive measure to revive the animosity of the factions ; the blues were astonished at their own guilt and folly, that a trifling injury should provoke them to conspire with their implacable enemies against a gracious and liberal benefactor ; they again proclaimed the majesty of Justinian ; and the greens, with their upstart emperor, were left alone in the hipprodrome. The fidelity of the gods was doubtful ; but the military force of Justinian consisted in three thousand veterans, who had been trained to valor and discipline in the Persian and Illyrian wars. Under the command of Belisarius and Mundus, they silently marched in two divisions from the palace, forced their obscure way through narrow passages, expiring flames, and falling edifices, and burst open at the same moment the two opposite gates of the hipprodrome. In this narrow space, the disorderly and affrighted crowd was incapable of resisting on either side a firm and regular attack ; the blues signalized the fury of their repentance ; and it is computed, that above thirty thousand persons were slain in the merciless and promiscuous carnage of the day. Hypatius was dragged from his throne, and conducted, with his brother Pompey, to the feet of the emperor : they implored his clemency ; but their crime was manifest, their innocence uncertain, and Justinian had been too much terrified to forgive. The next morning the two nephews of Anastasius, with eighteen *illustrious* accomplices, of patrician or consular rank, were privately executed by the soldiers ; their bodies were thrown into the sea, their palaces razed, and their fortunes confiscated. The hippodrome itself was condemned, during several years, to a mournful silence : with the restoration of the games, the same disorders revived ; and the blue and green factions continued to afflict the reign of Justinian, and to disturb the tranquillity of the Eastern empire.[53]

III. That empire, after Rome was barbarous, still embraced the nations whom she had conquered beyond the Adriatic, and as far as the frontiers of Æthiopia and Persia. Justinian reigned over sixty-four provinces, and nine hundred and thirty-five cities ;[54] his dominions were blessed by nature with the advantages of soil, situation, and climate : and the improvements of human art had been perpetually diffused along the coast of the Mediterranean and the banks of the Nile from ancient Troy to the Egyptian Thebes. Abraham [55] had been relieved by the well-known plenty of Egypt ; the same country, a small and populous tract, was still capable of exporting each year, two hundred and sixty thousand quarters of wheat for the use of Constantinople ; [56] and the capital of Justinian was supplied with the manufactures of Sidon, fifteen centuries after they had been ·celebrated in the poems of Homer. [57] The annual powers of vegetation, instead of being exhausted by two thousand harvests, were renewed and invigorated by skilful husbandry, rich manure, and seasonable repose. The breed of domestic animals was infinitely multiplied. Plantations, buildings, and the instruments of labor and luxury, which are more durable than the term of human life, were accumulated by the care of successive generations. Tradition preserved, and experience simplified, the humble practice of the arts : society was enriched by the division of labor and the facility of exchange ; and every Roman was lodged, clothed, and subsisted, by the industry of a thousand hands. The invention of the loom and distaff has been piously ascribed to the gods. In every age, a variety of animal and vegetable productions, hair, skins, wool, flax, cotton, and at length *silk*, have been skilfully manufactured to hide or adorn the human body ; they were stained with an infusion of permanent colors ; and the pencil was successfully employed to improve the labors of the loom. In the choice of those colors [58] which imitate the beauties of nature, the freedom of taste and fashion was indulged ; but the deep purple [59] which the Phœnicians extracted from a shell-fish, was restrained to the sacred person and palace of the emperor ; and the penalties of treason were denounced against the ambitious subjects who dared to usurp the prerogative of the throne. [60]

I need not explain that *silk* [61] is originally spun from the bowels of a caterpillar, and that it composes the golden tomb, from whence a worm emerges in the form of a butterfly. Till the reign of Justinian, the silk-worms who feed on the leaves of the white mulberry-tree were confined to China ; those of the pine, the oak, and the ash, were common in the forests, both of Asia and Europe ; but as their education is more difficult, and their produce more uncertain, they were generally neglected, except in the little island of Ceos, near the coast of Attica. A thin gauze was procured from their webs, and this Cean manufacture, the invention of a woman, for female use, was long admired both in the East and at Rome. Whatever suspicions may be raised by the garments of the Medes and Assyrians, Virgil is the most ancient writer who expressly mentions the soft wool which was combed from the trees of the Seres or Chinese ; [62] and this natural error, less marvellous than the truth, was slowly corrected by the knowledge of a valuable insect, the first artificer of the luxury of nations. That rare and elegant luxury was censured in the reign of Tiberius, by the gravest of the Romans ; and Pliny, in affected though forcible language, has condemned the thirst of gain, which explores the last confines of the earth, for the pernicious purpose of exposing to the public eye naked draperies and transparent matrons. [63] * A dress which showed the turn of the limbs, and color of the skin, might gratify vanity, or provoke desire ; the silks which had been closely woven in China were sometimes unravelled by the Phœnician women, and the precious materials were multiplied by a looser texture, and the intermixture of linen threads. [64] Two hundred years after the age of Pliny, the use of pure, or even of mixed silks, was confined to the female sex, till the opulent citizens of Rome and the provinces were insensibly familiarized with the example of Elagabalus, the first who, by this effeminate habit, had sullied the dignity of an emperor and a man. Aurelian complained, that a pound of silk was sold at Rome for twelve ounces of gold ; but the supply increased with the demand, and the price diminished with the supply. If accident or monopoly sometimes raised the value even above the standard of Aurelian, the manufacturers of Tyre and Berytus were sometimes compelled, by the operation of the same causes, to content themselves with a ninth part of that extravagant rate. [65] A law was thought necessary to discriminate the dress of comedians from that of senators ; and of the silk exported from its native country the far greater part was consumed by the subjects of Justinian. They were still more intimately acquainted with a shell-fish of the Mediterranean, surnamed the silk-worm of the sea : the fine wool or hair by which the mother-of-pearl affixes itself to the rock, is now manufactured for curiosity rather than use : and a robe obtained from the same singular materials was the gift of the Roman emperor to the satraps of Armenia. [66]

A valuable merchandise of small bulk is capable of defraying the expense of land-carriage ; and the caravans traversed the whole latitude of Asia in two hundred and forty-three days from the Chinese Ocean to the sea-coast of Syria. Silk was immediately delivered to the Romans by the Persian merchants, [67] who frequented the fairs of Armenia and Nisibis ; but this trade, which in the intervals of truce was oppressed by avarice and jeal-

---

* Gibbon must have written *transparent* draperies and *naked* matrons. Though sometimes affected, he is never inaccurate.—M.

ousy, was totally interrupted by the long wars of the rival monarchies. The great king might proudly number Sogdiana, and even *Serica*, among the provinces of his empire ; but his real dominion was bounded by the Oxus ; and his useful intercourse with the Sogdoites, beyond the river, depended on the pleasure of their conquerors, the white Huns, and the Turks, who successively reigned over that industrious people. Yet the most savage dominion has not extirpated the seeds of agriculture and commerce, in a region which is celebrated as one of the four gardens of Asia ; the cities of Samarcand and Bochara are advantageously seated for the exchange of its various productions ; and their merchants purchased from the Chinese,[68] the raw or manufactured silk which they transported into Persia for the use of the Roman empire. In the vain capital of China, the Sogdian caravans were entertained as the suppliant embassies of tributary kingdoms, and if they returned in safety, the bold adventure was rewarded with exorbitant gain. But the difficult and perilous march from Samarcand to the first town of Shensi, could not be performed in less than sixty, eighty, or one hundred days : as soon as they had passed the Jaxartes they entered the desert ; and the wandering hordes, unless they are restrained by armies and garrisons, have always considered the citizen and the traveller as the objects of lawful rapine. To escape the Tartar robbers, and the tyrants of Persia, the silk caravans explored a more southern road ; they traversed the mountains of Thibet, descended the streams of the Ganges or the Indus, and patiently expected, in the ports of Guzerat and Malabar, the annual fleets of the West.[69] But the dangers of the desert were found less intolerable than toil, hunger, and the loss of time ; the attempt was seldom renewed, and the only European who has passed that unfrequented way, applauds his own diligence, that, in nine months after his departure from Pekin, he reached the mouth of the Indus. The ocean, however, was open to the free communication of mankind. From the great river to the Tropic of Cancer, the provinces of China were subdued and civilized by the emperors of the North ; they were filled about the time of the Christian æra with cities and men, mulberry-trees, and their precious inhabitants ; and if the Chinese, with the knowledge of the compass, had possessed the genius of the Greeks or Phœnicians, they might have spread their discoveries over the southern hemisphere. I am not qualified to examine, and I am not disposed to believe, their distant voyages to the Persian Gulf, or the Cape of Good Hope ; but their ancestors might equal the labors and success of the present race, and the sphere of their navigation might extend from the

Isles of Japan to the Straits of Malacca, the pillars, if we may apply that name, of an Oriental Hercules.[70] Without losing sight of land, they might sail along the coast to the extreme promontory of Achin, which is annually visited by ten or twelve ships laden with the productions, the manufactures, and even the artificers of China ; the Island of Sumatra and the opposite peninsula are faintly delineated[71] as the regions of gold and silver ; and the trading cities named in the geography of Ptolemy may indicate that this wealth was not solely derived from the mines. The direct interval between Sumatra and Ceylon is about three hundred leagues : the Chinese and Indian navigators were conducted by the flight of birds and periodical winds ; and the ocean might be securely traversed in square-built ships, which, instead of iron, were sewed together with the strong thread of the cocoanut. Ceylon, Serendib, or Taprobana, was divided between two hostile princes ; one of whom possessed the mountains, the elephants, and the luminous carbuncle, and the other enjoyed the more solid riches of domestic industry, foreign trade, and the capacious harbor of Trinquemale, which received and dismissed the fleets of the East and West. In this hospitable isle, at an equal distance (as it was computed) from their respective countries, the silk merchants of China, who had collected, in their voyages, aloes, cloves, nutmeg, and sandal wood, maintained a free and beneficial commerce with the inhabitants of the Persian Gulf. The subjects of the great king exalted, without a rival, his power and magnificence : and the Roman, who confounded their vanity by comparing his paltry coin with a gold medal of the emperor Anastasius, had sailed to Ceylon, in an Æthiopian ship, as a simple passenger.[72]

As silk became of indispensable use, the emperor Justinian saw with concern that the Persians had occupied by land and sea the monopoly of this important supply, and that the wealth of his subjects was continually drained by a nation of enemies and idolaters. An active government would have restored the trade of Egypt and the navigation of the Red Sea, which had decayed with the prosperity of the empire ; and the Roman vessels might have sailed, for the purchase of silk, to the ports of Ceylon, of Malacca, or even of China. Justinian embraced a more humble expedient, and solicited the aid of his Christian allies, the Æthiopians of Abyssinia, who had recently acquired the arts of navigation, the spirit of trade, and the seaport of Adulis,[73] * still deco-

---

* Mr. Salt obtained information of considerable ruins of an a cient town near Zulla, called Azoole, which answers to the position of Adulis. Mr. Salt was prevented by illness, Mr. Stuart, whom he sent, by the jealousy of the natives, from

rated with the trophies of a Grecian conqueror. Along the
African coast, they penetrated to the equator in search of gold,
emeralds, and aromatics ; but they wisely declined an unequal
competition, in which they must be always prevented by the
vicinity of the Persians to the markets of India ; and the emperor
submitted to the disappointment, till his wishes were gratified by
an unexpected event.   The gospel had been preached to the Indians : a bishop already governed the Christians of St. Thomas on
the pepper-coast of Malabar ; a church was planted in Ceylon,
and the missionaries pursued the footsteps of commerce to the extremities of Asia.[74]   Two Persian monks had long resided in
China, perhaps in the royal city of Nankin, the seat of a monarch
addicted to foreign superstitions, and who actually received an
embassy from the Isle of Ceylon.   Amidst their pious occupations,
they viewed with a curious eye the common dress of the Chinese,
the manufactures of silk, and the myriads of silk-worms, whose
education (either on trees or in houses) had once been considered
as the labor of queens.[75]   They soon discovered that it was impracticable to transport the short-lived insect, but that in the eggs
a numerous progeny might be preserved and multiplied in a distant climate.   Religion or interest had more power over the Persian monks than the love of their country : after a long journey,
they arrived at Constantinople, imparted their project to the emperor, and were liberally encouraged by the gifts and promises of
Justinian.   To the historians of that prince, a campaign at the
foot of Mount Caucasus has seemed more deserving of a minute
relation than the labors of these missionaries of commerce, who
again entered China, deceived a jealous people by concealing the
eggs of the silk-worm in a hollow cane, and returned in triumph
with the spoils of the East.   Under their direction, the eggs were
hatched at the proper season by the artificial heat of dung ; the
worms were fed with mulberry leaves ; they lived and labored in a
foreign climate ; a sufficient number of butterflies was saved to
propagate the race, and trees were planted to supply the nourishment of the rising generations.   Experience and reflection corrected the errors of a new attempt, and the Sogdoite ambassadors
acknowledged, in the succeeding reign, that the Romans were not
inferior to the natives of China in the education of the insects, and
the manufactures of silk,[76] in which both China and Constantinople have been surpassed by the industry of modern Europe.   I am
not insensible of the benefits of elegant luxury ; yet I reflect with

---

investigating these ruins : of their existence there seems no doubt.   Salt's 2d Journey, p. 452.—M.

some pain, that if the importers of silk had introduced the art of printing, already practised by the Chinese, the comedies of Menander and the entire decades of Livy would have been perpetuated in the editions of the sixth century. A larger view of the globe might at least have promoted the improvement of speculative science, but the Christian geography was forcibly extracted from texts of Scripture, and the study of nature was the surest symptom of an unbelieving mind. The orthodox faith confined the habitable world to *one* temperate zone, and represented the earth as an oblong surface, four hundred days' journey in length, two hundred in breadth, encompassed by the ocean, and covered by the solid crystal of the firmament.[77]

IV. The subjects of Justinian were dissatisfied with the times, and with the government. Europe was overrun by the barbarians, and Asia by the monks: the poverty of the West discouraged the trade and manufactures of the East: the produce of labor was consumed by the unprofitable servants of the church, the state, and the army; and a rapid decrease was felt in the fixed and circulating capitals which constitute the national wealth. The public distress had been alleviated by the economy of Anastasius, and that prudent emperor accumulated an immense treasure, while he delivered his people from the most odious or oppressive taxes.* Their gratitude universally applauded the aboli-

---

* See the character of Anastasius in Joannes Lydus de Magistratibus, l. iii. c. 45, 46, p. 230-232. His economy is there said to have degenerated into parsimony. He is accused of having taken away the levying of taxes and payment of the troops from the municipal authorities (the decurionate) in the Eastern cities, and intrusted it to an extortionate officer named Manus. But he admits that the imperial revenue was enormously increased by this measure. A statue of iron had been erected to Anastasius in the Hippodrome, on which appeared one morning this pasquinade:

Εἰκόνα σοὶ, βασιλεῦ κοσμοφθόρε, τήνδε σιδήρου

Στήσαμεν, ὡς χαλκῆς (οὔσαν), ἀτιμοτέραν (πολλόν, Anth.),

Ἀντὶ φόνου, πενίης τ' ὀλοῆς, λιμοῦ τε καὶ ὀργῆς

Ἡ (οἶς, Anth.) πάντα φθείρει σὴ φιλοχρημοσύνη.

Γείτονα δὴ Σκύλλης ὀλοὴν ἀνέθεντο Χάρυβδιν,

Ἄγριον ὠμηστὴν τοῦτον Ἀναστάσιον.

Δείδιθι καὶ σὺ, Σκύλλα, τεαῖς φρεσὶ, μή σε καὶ αὐτὴν

Βρώξῃ, χαλκείην δαίμονα κερματίσας.

This epigram is also found in the Anthology. Jacobs, vol. iv. p. 104, with some better readings.

This iron statue meetly do we place
To thee, world-wasting king, than brass more base;
For all the death, the penury, famine, woe,
That from thy wide-destroying avarice flow.
This fell Charybdis, Scylla, near to thee,
This fierce devouring Anastasius, see;

tion of the *gold of affliction*, a personal tribute on the industry of the poor,[78] but more intolerable, as it should seem, in the form than in the substance, since the flourishing city of Edessa paid only one hundred and forty pounds of gold, which was collected in four years from ten thousand artificers.[79] Yet such was the parsimony which supported this liberal disposition, that, in a reign of twenty-seven years, Anastasius saved, from his annual revenue, the enormous sum of thirteen millions sterling, or three hundred and twenty thousand pounds of gold.[80] His example was neglected, and his treasure was abused, by the nephew of Justin. The riches of Justinian were speedily exhausted by alms and buildings, by ambitious wars, and ignominious treaties. His revenues were found inadequate to his expenses. Every art was tried to extort from the people the gold and silver which he scattered with a lavish hand from Persia to France:[81] his reign was marked by the vicissitudes, or rather by the combat, of rapaciousness and avarice, of splendor and poverty; he lived with the reputation of hidden treasures,[82] and bequeathed to his successor the payment of his debts.[83] Such a character has been justly accused by the voice of the people and of posterity: but public discontent is credulous; private malice is bold; and a lover of truth will peruse with a suspicious eye the instructive anecdotes of Procopius. The secret historian represents only the vices of Justinian, and those vices are darkened by his malevolent pencil. Ambiguous actions are imputed to the worst motives; error is confounded with guilt, accident with design, and laws with abuses; the partial injustice of a moment is dexterously applied as the general maxim of a reign of thirty-two years; the emperor alone is made responsible for the faults of his officers, the disorders of the times, and the corruption of his subjects; and even the calamities of nature, plagues, earthquakes, and inundations, are imputed to the prince of the dæmons, who had mischievously assumed the form of Justinian.[84]

After this precaution, I shall briefly relate the anecdotes of avarice and rapine under the following heads: I. Justinian was so profuse that he could not be liberal. The civil and military officers, when they were admitted into the service of the palace, obtained an humble rank and a moderate stipend; they ascended

---

And tremble, Scylla! on thee, too, his greed,
Coining thy brazen deity, may feed.

But Lydus, with no uncommon inconsistency in such writers, proceeds to paint the character of Anastasius as endowed with almost every virtue, not excepting the utmost liberality. He was only prevented by death from relieving his subjects altogether from the capitation tax, which he greatly diminished.—M.

by seniority to a station of affluence and repose ; the annual pensions, of which the most honorable class was abolished by Justinian, amounted to four hundred thousand pounds ; and this domestic economy was deplored by the venal or indigent courtiers as the last outrage on the majesty of the empire. The posts, the salaries of physicians, and the nocturnal illuminations, were objects of more general concern ; and the cities might justly complain, that he usurped the municipal revenues which had been appropriated to these useful institutions. Even the soldiers were injured ; and such was the decay of military spirit, that they were injured with impunity. The emperor refused, at the return of each fifth year, the customary donative of five pieces of gold, reduced his veterans to beg their bread, and suffered unpaid armies to melt away in the wars of Italy and Persia. II. The humanity of his predecessors had always remitted, in some auspicious circumstance of their reign, the arrears of the public tribute, and they dexterously assumed the merit of resigning those claims which it was impracticable to enforce. " Justinian, in the space of thirty-two years, has never granted a similar indulgence ; and many of his subjects have renounced the possession of those lands whose value is insufficient to satisfy the demands of the treasury. To the cities which had suffered by hostile inroads, Anastasius promised a general exemption of seven years : the provinces of Justinian have been ravaged by the Persians and Arabs, the Huns and Sclavonians ; but his vain and ridiculous dispensation of a single year has been confined to those places which were actually taken by the enemy." Such is the language of the secret historian, who expressly denies that *any* indulgence was granted to Palestine after the revolt of the Samaritans ; a false and odious charge, confuted by the authentic record, which attests a relief of thirteen centenaries of gold (fifty-two thousand pounds) obtained for that desolate province by the intercession of St. Sabas.[65] III. Procopius has not condescended to explain the system of taxation, which fell like a hail-storm upon the land, like a devouring pestilence on its inhabitants : but we should become the accomplices of his malignity, if we imputed to Justinian alone the ancient though rigorous principle, that a whole district should be condemned to sustain the partial loss of the persons or property of individuals. The *Annona*, or supply of corn for the use of the army and capital, was a grievous and arbitrary exaction, which exceeded, perhaps in a tenfold proportion, the ability of the farmer ; and his distress was aggravated by the partial injustice of weights and measures, and the expense and labor of distant carriage. In a time of scarcity, an extraordinary requisition was

made to the adjacent provinces of Thrace, Bithynia, and Phyrgia :
but the proprietors, after a wearisome journey and a perilous navigation, received so inadequate a compensation, that they would
have chosen the alternative of delivering both the corn and price
at the doors of their granaries.   These precautions might indicate
a tender solicitude for the welfare of the capital ; yet Constantinople did not escape the rapacious despotism of Justinian.   Till
his reign, the Straits of the Bosphorus and Hellespont were open
to the freedom of trade, and nothing was prohibited except the
exportation of arms for the service of the barbarians.   At each of
these gates of the city, a prætor was stationed, the minister of Imperial avarice ; heavy customs were imposed on the vessels and
their merchandise ; the oppression was retaliated on the helpless
consumer ; the poor were afflicted by the artificial scarcity, and
exorbitant price of the market ; and a people, accustomed to depend on the liberality of their prince, might sometimes complain
of the deficiency of water and bread.[86]   The *aerial* tribute, without a name, a law, or a definite object, was an annual gift of one
hundred and twenty thousand pounds, which the emperor accepted from his Prætorian præfect ; and the means of payment
were abandoned to the discretion of that powerful magistrate.
IV. Even such a tax was less intolerable than the privilege of
monopolies,* which checked the fair competition of industry,
and, for the sake of a small and dishonest gain, imposed an arbitrary burden on the wants and luxury of the subject. . "As soon"
(I transcribe the anecdotes) "as the exclusive sale of silk was
usurped by the Imperial treasurer, a whole people, the manufacturers of Tyre and Berytus, was reduced to extreme misery, and
either perished with hunger, or fled to the hostile dominions of
Persia."   A province might suffer by the decay of its manufactures, but in this example of silk, Procopius has partially overlooked the inestimable and lasting benefit which the empire received from the curiosity of Justinian.   His addition of one seventh to the ordinary price of copper money may be interpreted
with the same candor ; and the alteration, which might be wise, appears to have been innocent : since he neither alloyed the purity,
nor enhanced the value, of the gold coin,[87] the legal measure of
public and private payments.   V. The ample jurisdiction required
by the farmers of the revenue to accomplish their engagements
might be placed in an odious light, as if they had purchased from

---

* Hullman (Geschichte des Byzantinischen Handels, p. 15) shows that the despotism of the government was aggravated by the unchecked rapacity of the officers.
This state monopoly, even of corn, wine, and oil, was in force at the time of the
first crusade.—M.

the emperor the lives and fortunes of their fellow-citizens. And a more direct sale of honors and offices was transacted in the palace, with the permission, or at least with the connivance, of Justinian and Theodora. The claims of merit, even those of favor, were disregarded, and it was almost reasonable to expect, that the bold adventurer, who had undertaken the trade of a magistrate, should find a rich compensation for infamy, labor, danger, the debts which he had contracted, and the heavy interest which he paid. A sense of the disgrace and mischief of this venal practice, at length awakened the slumbering virtue of Justinian ; and he attempted, by the sanction of oaths [83] and penalties, to guard the integrity of his government : but at the end of a year of perjury, his rigorous edict was suspended, and corruption licentiously abused her triumph over the impotence of the laws. VI. The testament of Eulalius, count of the domestics, declared the emperor his sole heir, on condition, however, that he should discharge his debts and legacies, allow to his three daughters a decent maintenance, and bestow each of them in marriage, with a portion of ten pounds of gold. But the splendid fortune of Eulalius had been consumed by fire, and the inventory of his goods did not exceed the trifling sum of five hundred and sixty-four pieces of gold. A similar instance, in Grecian history, admonished the emperor of the honorable part prescribed for his imitation. He checked the selfish murmurs of the treasury, applauded the confidence of his friend, discharged the legacies and debts, educated the three virgins under the eye of the empress Theodora, and doubled the marriage portion which had satisfied the tenderness of their father. [89] The humanity of a prince (for princes cannot be generous) is entitled to some praise ; yet even in this act of virtue we may discover the inveterate custom of supplanting the legal or natural heirs, which Procopius imputes to the reign of Justinian. His charge is supported by eminent names and scandalous examples ; neither widows nor orphans were spared ; and the art of soliciting, or extorting, or supposing testaments, was beneficially practised by the agents of the palace. This base and mischievous tyranny invades the security of private life ; and the monarch who has indulged an appetite for gain, will soon be tempted to anticipate the moment of succession, to interpret wealth as an evidence of guilt, and to proceed, from the claim of inheritance, to the power of confiscation. VII. Among the forms of rapine, a philosopher may be permitted to name the conversion of Pagan or heretical riches to the use of the faithful ; but in the time of Justinian this holy plunder was condemned by the sectaries alone, who became the victims of his orthodox avarice.[90]

Dishonor might be ultimately reflected on the character of Justinian ; but much of the guilt, and still more of the profit, was intercepted by the ministers, who were seldom promoted for their virtues, and not always selected for their talents.[91] The merits of Tribonian the quæstor will hereafter be weighed in the reformation of the Roman law ; but the economy of the East was subordinate to the Prætorian præfect, and Procopius has justified his anecdotes by the portrait which he exposes in his public history, of the notorious vices of John of Cappadocia.[92] * His knowledge was not borrowed from the schools,[93] and his style was scarcely legible ; but he excelled in the powers of native genius, to suggest the wisest counsels, and to find expedients in the most desperate situations. The corruption of his heart was equal to the vigor of his understanding. Although he was suspected of magic and Pagan superstition, he appeared insensible to the fear of God or the reproaches of man ; and his aspiring fortune was raised on the death of thousands, the poverty of millions, the ruins of cities, and the desolation of provinces. From the dawn of light to the moment of dinner, he assiduously labored to enrich his master and himself at the expense of the Roman world ; the remainder of the day was spent in sensual and obscene pleasures,† and the silent hours of the night were interrupted by the perpetual dread of the justice of an assassin. His abilities, perhaps his vices, recommended him to the lasting friendship of Justinian : the emperor yielded with reluctance to the fury of the people ; his victory was displayed by the immediate restoration of their enemy ; and they felt above ten years, under his oppressive administration, that he was stimulated by revenge, rather than instructed by misfortune. Their murmurs served only to fortify the resolution of Justinian ; but the præfect, in the insolence of favor, provoked the resentment of Theodora, disdained a power before which every knee was bent, and attempted to sow the seeds of discord between the emperor and his beloved consort. Even Theodora herself was constrained to dissemble, to wait a favorable moment, and, by an

---

* This view, particularly of the cruelty of John of Cappadocia, is confirmed by the testimony of Joannes Lydus, who was in the office of the præfect, and eye-witness of the tortures inflicted by his command on the miserable debtors, or supposed debtors, of the state. He mentions one horrible instance of a respectable old man, with whom he was personally acquainted, who, being suspected of possessing money, was hung up by the hands till he was dead. Lydus de Magist. lib. iii. c. 57, p. 254.—M.

† Joannes Lydus is diffuse on this subject, lib. iii c. 65. p. 268. But the indignant virtue of Lydus seems greatly stimulated by the loss of his official fees, which he ascribes to the innovations of the minister.—M.

artful conspiracy, to render John of Cappadocia the accomplice of his own destruction.* At a time when Belisarius, unless he had been a hero, must have shown himself a rebel, his wife Antonina, who enjoyed the secret confidence of the empress, communicated his feigned discontent to Euphemia, the daughter of the præfect ; the credulous virgin imparted to her father the dangerous project, and John, who might have known the value of oaths and promises, was tempted to accept a nocturnal, and almost treasonable, interview with the wife of Belisarius. An ambuscade of guards and eunuchs had been posted by the command of Theodora ; they rushed with drawn swords to seize or to punish the guilty minister : he was saved by the fidelity of his attendants ; but instead of appealing to a gracious sovereign, who had privately warned him of his danger, he pusillanimously fled to the sanctuary of the church. The favorite of Justinian was sacrificed to conjugal tenderness or domestic tranquillity ; the conversion of a præfect into a priest extinguished his ambitious hopes : but the friendship of the emperor alleviated his disgrace, and he retained, in the mild exile of Cyzicus, an ample portion of his riches. Such imperfect revenge could not satisfy the unrelenting hatred of Theodora ; the murder of his old enemy, the bishop of Cyzicus, afforded a decent pretence ; and John of Cappadocia, whose actions had deserved a thousand deaths, was at last condemned for a crime of which he was innocent. A great minister, who had been invested with the honors of consul and patrician, was ignominiously scourged like the vilest of malefactors ; a tattered cloak was the sole remnant of his fortunes ; he was transported in a bark to the place of his banishment at Antinopolis in Upper Egypt, and the præfect of the East begged his bread through the cities which had trembled at his name. During an exile of seven years, his life was protracted and threatened by the ingenious cruelty of Theodora ; and when her death permitted the emperor to recall a servant whom he had abandoned with regret, the ambition of John of Cappadocia was reduced to the humble duties of the sacerdotal profession. His successors convinced the subjects of Justinian, that the arts of oppression might still be improved by experience and industry ; the frauds of a Syrian banker were introduced into the administration of the finances ; and the example of

---

* According to Lydus, Theodora disclosed the crimes and unpopularity of the minister to Justinian, but the emperor had not the courage to remove, and was unable to replace, a servant, under whom his finances seemed to prosper. He attributes the sedition and conflagration called the *vika* (see p. 41) to the popular resentment against the tyranny of John, lib. iii. c. 70, p. 278. Unfortunately there is a large gap in his work just at this period.—M.

the præfect was diligently copied by the quæstor, the public and private treasurer, the governors of provinces, and the principal magistrates of the Eastern empire.[94]

V. The *edifices* of Justinian were cemented with the blood and treasure of his people ; but those stately structures appeared to announce the prosperity of the empire, and actually displayed the skill of their architects.   Both the theory and practice of the arts, which depend on mathematical science and mechanical power, were cultivated under the patronage of the emperors ; the fame of Archimedes was rivalled by Proclus and Anthemius ; and if their *miracles* had been related by intelligent spectators, they might now enlarge the speculations instead of exciting the distrust of philosophers.   A tradition has prevailed, that the Roman fleet was reduced to ashes in the port of Syracuse by the burning-glasses of Archimedes ;[95] and it is asserted that a similar expedient was employed by Proclus to destroy the Gothic vessels in the harbor of Constantinople, and to protect his benefactor Anastasius against the bold enterprise of Vitalian.[96]   A machine was fixed on the walls of the city, consisting of a hexagon mirror of polished brass, with many smaller and movable polygons to receive and reflect the rays of the meridian sun ; and a consuming flame was darted, to the distance, perhaps, of two hundred feet.[97]   The truth of these two extraordinary facts is invalidated by the silence of the most authentic historians ; and the use of burning-glasses was never adopted in the attack or defence of places.[98]   Yet the admirable experiments of a French philosopher[99] have demonstrated the possibility of such a mirror ; and, since it is possible, I am more disposed to attribute the art to the greatest mathematicians of antiquity, than to give the merit of the fiction to the idle fancy of a monk or a sophist.   According to another story, Proclus applied sulphur to the destruction of the Gothic fleet ;[100] in a modern imagination, the name of sulphur is instantly connected with the suspicion of gunpowder, and that suspicion is propagated by the secret arts of his disciple Anthemius.[101]   A citizen of Tralles in Asia had five sons, who were all distinguished in their respective professions by merit and success.   Olympius excelled in the knowledge and practice of the Roman jurisprudence.   Dioscorus and Alexander became learned physicians ; but the skill of the former was exercised for the benefit of his fellow-citizens, while his more ambitious brother acquired wealth and reputation at Rome.   The fame of Metrodorus the grammarian, and of Anthemius the mathematician and architect, reached the ears of the emperor Justinian, who invited them to Constantinople ; and while the one instructed the rising generation in the schools of eloquence, the other filled the capital and provinces with more lasting monuments of his art. In a trifling dispute relative to the walls or windows of their contiguous houses, he had been vanquished by the eloquence of his neighbor Zeno ; but the orator was defeated in his turn by the master of mechanics, whose malicious, though harmless, stratagems are darkly represented by the ignorance of Agathias. In a lower room, Anthemius arranged several vessels or caldrons of water, each of them covered by the wide bottom of a leathern tube, which rose to a narrow top, and was artificially conveyed among the joists and rafters of the adjacent building. A fire was kindled beneath the caldron ; the steam of the boiling water ascended through the tubes ; the house was shaken by the efforts of imprisoned air, and its trembling inhabitants might wonder that the city was unconscious of the earthquake which they had felt. At another time, the friends of Zeno, as they sat at table, were dazzled by the intolerable light which flashed in their eyes from the reflecting mirrors of Anthemius ; they were astonished by the noise which he produced from the collision of certain minute and sonorous particles ; and the orator declared, in tragic style to the senate, that a mere mortal must yield to the power of an antagonist, who shook the earth with the trident of Neptune, and imitated the thunder and lightning of Jove himself. The genius of Anthemius, and his colleague, Isidore the Milesian, was excited and employed by a prince, whose taste for architecture had degenerated into a mischievous and costly passion. His favorite architects submitted their designs and difficulties to Justinian, and discreetly confessed how much their laborious meditations were surpassed by the intuitive knowledge or celestial inspiration of an emperor, whose views were always directed to the benefit of his people, the glory of his reign, and the salvation of his soul.[102]

The principal church, which was dedicated by the founder of Constantinople to St. Sophia, or the eternal wisdom, had been twice destroyed by fire ; after the exile of John Chrysostom, and during the *Nika* of the blue and green factions. No sooner did the tumult subside, than the Christian populace deplored their sacrilegious rashness ; but they might have rejoiced in the calamity, had they foreseen the glory of the new temple, which at the end of forty days was strenuously undertaken by the piety of Justinian.[103] The ruins were cleared away, a more spacious plan was described, and as it required the consent of some proprietors of ground, they obtained the most exorbitant terms, from the eager desires and timorous conscience of the monarch. Anthemius formed the design, and his genius directed the hands of ten thousand workmen, whose payment in pieces of fine silver was never delayed beyond the evening. The emperor himself, clad in a linen tunic, surveyed each day their rapid progress, and encouraged their diligence by his familiarity, his zeal, and his rewards. The new Cathedral of St. Sophia was consecrated by the patriarch, five years, eleven months, and ten days from the first foundation ; and in the midst of the solemn festival Justinian exclaimed with devout vanity, " Glory be to God, who hath thought me worthy to accomplish so great a work ; I have vanquished thee, O Solomon !" [104] But the pride of the Roman Solomon, before twenty years had elapsed, was humbled by an earthquake, which overthrew the eastern part of the dome. Its splendor was again restored by the perseverance of the same prince ; and in the thirty-sixth year of his reign, Justinian celebrated the second dedication of a temple, which remains, after twelve centuries, a stately monument of his fame. The architecture of St. Sophia, which is now converted into the principal mosch, has been imitated by the Turkish sultans, and that venerable pile continues to excite the fond admiration of the Greeks, and the more rational curiosity of European travellers. The eye of the spectator is disappointed by an irregular prospect of half-domes and shelving roofs : the western front, the principal approach, is destitute of simplicity and magnificence ; and the scale of dimensions has been much surpassed by several of the Latin cathedrals. But the architect who first erected an *aerial* cupola, is entitled to the praise of bold design and skilful execution. The dome of St. Sophia, illuminated by four-and-twenty windows, is formed with so small a curve, that the depth is equal only to one sixth of its diameter ; the measure of that diameter is one hundred and fifteen feet, and the lofty centre, where a crescent has supplanted the cross, rises to the perpendicular height of one hundred and eighty feet above the pavement. The circle which encompasses the dome, lightly reposes on four strong arches, and their weight is firmly supported by four massy piles, whose strength is assisted, on the northern and southern sides, by four columns of Egyptian granite. A Greek cross, inscribed in a quadrangle, represents the form of the edifice ; the exact breadth is two hundred and forty-three feet, and two hundred and sixty-nine may be assigned for the extreme length from the sanctuary in the east, to the nine western doors, which open into the vestibule, and from thence into the *narthex* or exterior portico. That portico was the humble station of the penitents. The nave or body of the church was filled by the congregation of the faithful ; but the two sexes were prudently distinguished, and the upper and lower galleries were allotted for the more private devotion of the women. Beyond the northern and southern piles, a balustrade, terminated on either side by the thrones of the emperor and the patriarch, divided the nave from the choir ; and the space, as far as the steps of the altar, was occupied by the clergy and singers. The altar itself, a name which insensibly became familiar to Christian ears, was placed in the eastern recess, artificially built in the form of a demi-cylinder, and this sanctuary communicated by several doors with the sacristy, the vestry, the baptistery, and the contiguous buildings, subservient either to the pomp of worship, or the private use of the ecclesiastical ministers. The memory of past calamities inspired Justinian with a wise resolution, that no wood, except for the doors, should be admitted into the new edifice ; and the choice of the materials was applied to the strength, the lightness, or the splendor of the respective parts. The solid piles which contained the cupola were composed of huge blocks of freestone, hewn into squares and triangles, fortified by circles or iron, and firmly cemented by the infusion of lead and quicklime : but the weight of the cupola was diminished by the levity of its substance, which consists either of pumice-stone that floats in the water, or of bricks from the Isle of Rhodes, five times less ponderous than the ordinary sort. The whole frame of the edifice was constructed of brick ; but those base materials were concealed by a crust of marble ; and the inside of St. Sophia, the cupola, the two larger, and the six smaller, semi-domes, the walls, the hundred columns, and the pavement, delight even the eyes of barbarians, with a rich and variegated picture. A poet,[105] who beheld the primitive lustre of St. Sophia, enumerates the colors, the shades, and the spots of ten or twelve marbles, jaspers, and porphyries, which nature had profusely diversified, and which were blended and contrasted as it were by a skilful painter. The triumph of Christ was adorned with the last spoils of Paganism, but the greater part of these costly stones was extracted from the quarries of Asia Minor, the isles and continent of Greece, Egypt, Africa, and Gaul. Eight columns of porphry, which Aurelian had placed in the temple of the sun, were offered by the piety of a Roman matron ; eight others of green marble were presented by the ambitious zeal of the magistrates of Ephesus : both are admirable by their size and beauty, but every order of architecture disclaims their fantastic capitals. A variety of ornaments and figures was curiously expressed in mosaic ; and the images of Christ, of the Virgin, of saints, and of angels, which had been defaced by Turkish fanaticism, were dangerously exposed to the superstition of the Greeks. According to the sanctity of each object, the precious metals were distributed in thin leaves or in solid masses. The balustrade of the choir, the capitals of the pillars, the ornaments of the doors and galleries, were of gilt bronze ; the spectator was dazzled by the glittering aspect of the cupola ; the sanctuary contained forty thousand pounds weight of silver ; and the holy vases and vestments of the altar were of the purest gold, enriched with inestimable gems.   Before the structure of the church had arisen two cubits above the ground, forty-five thousand two hundred pounds were already consumed ; and the whole expense amounted to three hundred and twenty thousand : each reader, according to the measure of his belief, may estimate their value either in gold or silver ; but the sum of one million sterling is the result of the lowest computation.   A magnificent temple is a laudable monument of national taste and religion ; and the enthusiast who entered the dome of St. Sophia might be tempted to suppose that it was the residence, or even the workmanship, of the Deity. Yet how dull is the artifice, how insignificant is the labor, if it be compared with the formation of the vilest insect that crawls upon the surface of the temple !

So minute a description of an edifice which time has respected, may attest the truth, and excuse the relation, of the innumerable works, both in the capital and provinces, which Justinian constructed on a smaller scale and less durable foundations.[106]   In Constantinople alone, and the adjacent suburbs, he dedicated twenty-five churches to the honor of Christ, the Virgin, and the saints : most of these churches were decorated with marble and gold ; and their various situation was skilfully chosen in a populous square, or a pleasant grove ; on the margin of the sea-shore, or on some lofty eminence which overlooked the continents of Europe and Asia.   The church of the Holy Apostles at Constantinople, and that of St. John at Ephesus, appear to have been framed on the same model : their domes aspired to imitate the cupolas of St. Sophia ; but the altar was more judiciously placed under the centre of the dome, at the junction of four stately porticos, which more accurately expressed the figure of the Greek cross.   The Virgin of Jerusalem might exult in the temple erected by her Imperial votary on a most ungrateful spot, which afforded neither ground nor materials to the architect.   A level was formed by raising part of a deep valley to the height of the mountain. The stones of a neighboring quarry were hewn into regular forms ; each block was fixed on a peculiar carriage, drawn by forty of the strongest oxen, and the roads were widened for the passage of such enormous weights.   Lebanon furnished her loftiest cedars for the timbers of the church ; and the seasonable discovery of a vein of red marble supplied its beautiful columns, two of which, the supporters of the exterior portico, were esteemed the largest in the world. The pious munificence of the emperor was diffused over the Holy Land ; and if reason should condemn the monasteries of both sexes, which were built or restored by Justinian, yet charity must applaud the wells which he sunk, and the hospitals which he founded, for the relief of the weary pilgrims. The schismatical temper of Egypt was ill entitled to the royal bounty ; but in Syria and Africa, some remedies were applied to the disasters of wars and earthquakes, and both Carthage and Antioch, emerging from their ruins, might revere the name of their gracious benefactor.[107] Almost every saint in the calendar acquired the honors of a temple ; almost every city of the empire obtained the solid advantages of bridges, hospitals, and aqueducts ; but the severe liberality of the monarch disdained to indulge his subjects in the popular luxury of baths and theatres. While Justinian labored for the public service, he was not unmindful of his own dignity and ease. The Byzantine palace, which had been damaged by the conflagration, was restored with new magnificence ; and some notion may be conceived of the whole edifice, by the vestibule or hall, which, from the doors perhaps, or the roof, was surnamed *chalce*, or the brazen. The dome of a spacious quadrangle was supported by massy pillars ; the pavement and walls were incrusted with many-colored marbles—the emerald green of Laconia, the fiery red, and the white Phrygian stone, intersected with veins of a sea-green hue : the mosaic paintings of the dome and sides represented the glories of the African and Italian triumphs. On the Asiatic shore of the Propontis, at a small distance to the east of Chalcedon, the costly palace and gardens of Heræum [108] were prepared for the summer residence of Justinian, and more especially of Theodora. The poets of the age have celebrated the rare alliance of nature and art, the harmony of the nymphs of the groves, the fountains, and the waves : yet the crowd of attendants who followed the court complained of their inconvenient lodgings,[109] and the nymphs were too often alarmed by the famous Porphyrio, a whale of ten cubits in breadth, and thirty in length, who was stranded at the mouth of the River Sangaris, after he had infested more than half a century the seas of Constantinople.[110]

The fortifications of Europe and Asia were multiplied by Justinian : but the repetition of those timid and fruitless precautions exposes, to a philosophic eye, the debility of the empire.[111] From Belgrade to the Euxine, from the conflux of the Save to the mouth of the Danube, a chain of above fourscore fortified places was extended along the banks of the great river. Single watch-towers were changed into spacious citadels ; vacant walls, which the engineers contracted or enlarged according to the nature of the ground, were filled with colonies or garrisons ; a strong fortress defended the ruins of Trajan's bridge,[112] and several military stations affected to spread beyond the Danube the pride of the Roman name. But that name was divested of its terrors ; the barbarians, in their annual inroads, passed, and contemptuously repassed, before these useless bulwarks ; and the inhabitants of the frontier, instead of reposing under the shadow of the general defence, were compelled to guard, with incessant vigilance, their separate habitations. The solitude of ancient cities was replenished ; the new foundations of Justinian acquired, perhaps too hastily, the epithets of impregnable and populous ; and the auspicious place of his own nativity attracted the grateful reverence of the vainest of princes. Under the name of *Justiniana prima*, the obscure village of Tauresium became the seat of an archbishop and a præfect, whose jurisdiction extended over seven warlike provinces of Illyricum ; [113] and the corrupt appellation of *Giustendil* still indicates, about twenty miles to the south of Sophia, the residence of a Turkish sanjak.[114] For the use of the emperor's countrymen, a cathedral, a palace, and an aqueduct, were speedily constructed ; the public and private edifices were adapted to the greatness of a royal city ; and the strength of the walls resisted, during the lifetime of Justinian, the unskilful assaults of the Huns and Sclavonians. Their progress was sometimes retarded, and their hopes of rapine were disappointed, by the innumerable castles which, in the provinces of Dacia, Epirus, Thessaly, Macedonia, and Thrace, appeared to cover the whole face of the country. Six hundred of these forts were built or repaired by the emperor ; but it seems reasonable to believe, that the far greater part consisted only of a stone or brick tower, in the midst of a square or circular area, which was surrounded by a wall and ditch, and afforded in a moment of danger some protection to the peasants and cattle of the neighboring villages.[115] Yet these military works, which exhausted the public treasure, could not remove the just apprehensions of Justinian and his European subjects. The warm baths of Anchialus in Thrace were rendered as safe as they were salutary ; but the rich pastures of Thessalonica were foraged by the Scythian cavalry ; the delicious vale of Tempe, three hundred miles from the Danube, was continually alarmed by the sound of war ; [116] and no unfortified spot, however distant or solitary, could securely enjoy the blessings of peace. The Straits of Thermopylæ, which seemed to protect, but which had so often betrayed, the safety of Greece, were diligently strengthened by the labors of Justinian. From the edge of the sea-shore, through the forests and valleys, and as far as the summit of the Thessalian mountains, a strong wall was continued, which occupied every practicable entrance. Instead of a hasty crowd of peasants, a garrison of two thousand soldiers was stationed along the rampart; granaries of corn and reservoirs of water were provided for their use; and by a precaution that inspired the cowardice which it foresaw, convenient fortresses were erected for their retreat. The walls of Corinth, overthrown by an earthquake, and the mouldering bulwarks of Athens and Platæa, were carefully restored; the barbarians were discouraged by the prospect of successive and painful sieges: and the naked cities of Peloponnesus were covered by the fortifications of the Isthmus of Corinth. At the extremity of Europe, another peninsula, the Thracian Chersonesus, runs three days' journey into the sea, to form, with the adjacent shores of Asia, the Straits of the Hellespont. The intervals between eleven populous towns were filled by lofty woods, fair pastures, and arable lands; and the isthmus, of thirty-seven stadia or furlongs, had been fortified by a Spartan general nine hundred years before the reign of Justinian.[117] In an age of freedom and valor, the slightest rampart may prevent a surprise; and Procopius appears insensible of the superiority of ancient times, while he praises the solid construction and double parapet of a wall, whose long arms stretched on either side into the sea; but whose strength was deemed insufficient to guard the Chersonesus, if each city, and particularly Gallipoli and Sestus, had not been secured by their peculiar fortifications. The *long* wall, as it was emphatically styled, was a work as disgraceful in the object, as it was respectable in the execution. The riches of a capital diffuse themselves over the neighboring country, and the territory of Constantinople, a paradise of nature, was adorned with the luxurious gardens and villas of the senators and opulent citizens. But their wealth served only to attract the bold and rapacious barbarians; the noblest of the Romans, in the bosom of peaceful indolence, were led away into Scythian captivity, and their sovereign might view from his palace the hostile flames which were insolently spread to the gates of the Imperial city. At the distance only of forty miles, Anastasius was constrained to establish a last frontier; his long wall, of sixty miles from the Propontis to the Euxine, proclaimed the impotence of his arms; and as the danger became more imminent, new fortifications were added by the indefatigable prudence of Justinian.[118]

Asia Minor, after the submission of the Isaurians,[119] remained without enemies and without fortifications. Those bold savages, who had disdained to be the subjects of Gallienus, persisted two hundred and thirty years in a life of independence and rapine. The most successful princes respected the strength of the mountains and the despair of the natives; their fierce spirit was sometimes soothed with gifts, and sometimes restrained by terror; and a military count, with three legions, fixed his permanent and ignominious station in the heart of the Roman provinces.[120] But no sooner was the vigilance of power relaxed or diverted, than the light-armed squadrons descended from the hills, and invaded the peaceful plenty of Asia. Although the Isaurians were not remarkable for stature or bravery, want rendered them bold, and experience made them skilful in the exercise of predatory war. They advanced with secrecy and speed to the attack of villages and defenceless towns; their flying parties have sometimes touched the Hellespont, the Euxine, and the gates of Tarsus, Antioch, or Damascus;[121] and the spoil was lodged in their inaccessible mountains, before the Roman troops had received their orders, or the distant province had computed its loss. The guilt of rebellion and robbery excluded them from the rights of national enemies; and the magistrates were instructed, by an edict, that the trial or punishment of an Isaurian, even on the festival of Easter, was a meritorious act of justice and piety.[122] If the captives were condemned to domestic slavery, they maintained, with their sword or dagger, the private quarrel of their masters; and it was found expedient for the public tranquillity to prohibit the service of such dangerous retainers. When their countryman Tarcalissæus or Zeno ascended the throne, he invited a faithful and formidable band of Isaurians, who insulted the court and city, and were rewarded by an annual tribute of five thousand pounds of gold. But the hopes of fortune depopulated the mountains, luxury enervated the hardiness of their minds and bodies, and in proportion as they mixed with mankind, they became less qualified for the enjoyment of poor and solitary freedom. After the death of Zeno, his successor Anastasius suppressed their pensions, exposed their persons to the revenge of the people, banished them from Constantinople, and prepared to sustain a war, which left only the alternative of victory or servitude. A brother of the last emperor usurped the title of Augustus; his cause was powerfully supported by the arms, the treasures, and the magazines, collected by Zeno; and the native Isaurians must have formed the smallest portion of the hundred and fifty thousand barbarians under his standard, which was sanctified, for the first time, by the presence of a fighting bishop. Their disorderly numbers were vanquished in the plains of Phrygia by the valor and discipline of the Goths ; but a war of six years almost exhausted the courage of the emperor.[123] The Isaurians retired to their mountains ; their fortresses were successively besieged and ruined ; their communication with the sea was intercepted ; the bravest of their leaders died in arms ; the surviving chiefs, before their execution, were dragged in chains through the hippodrome ; a colony of their youth was transplanted into Thrace, and the remnant of the people submitted to the Roman government. Yet some generations elapsed before their minds were reduced to the level of slavery. The populous villages of Mount Taurus were filled with horsemen and archers : they resisted the imposition of tributes, but they recruited the armies of Justinian ; and his civil magrstrates, the proconsul of Cappadocia, the count of Isauria, and the prætors of Lycaonia and Pisidia, were invested with military power to restrain the licentious practice of rapes and assassinations.[124]

If we extend our view from the tropic to the mouth of the Tanais, we may observe, on one hand, the precautions of Justinian to curb the savages of Æthiopia,[125] and on the other, the long walls which he constructed in Crimæa for the protection of his friendly Goths, a colony of three thousand shepherds and warriors.[126] From that peninsula to Trebizond, the eastern curve of the Euxine was secured by forts, by alliance, or by religion ; and the possession of *Lazica*, the Colchos of ancient, the Mingrelia of modern, geography, soon became the object of an important war. Trebizond, in after-times the seat of a romantic empire, was indebted to the liberality of Justinian for a church, an aqueduct, and a castle, whose ditches are hewn in the solid rock. From that maritime city, a frontier line of five hundred miles may be drawn to the fortress of Circesium, the last Roman station on the Euphrates.[127] Above Trebizond immediately, and five days' journey to the south, the country rises into dark forests and craggy mountains, as savage though not so lofty as the Alps and the Pyrenees. In this rigorous climate,[128] where the snows seldom melt, the fruits are tardy and tasteless, even honey is poisonous : the most industrious tillage would be confined to some pleasant valleys ; and the pastoral tribes obtained a scanty sustenance from the flesh and milk of their cattle. The *Chalybians*[129] derived their name and temper from the iron quality of the soil ; and, since the days of Cyrus, they might produce, under the various appellations of Chaldæans and Zanians, an uninterrupted prescription of war and rapine. Under the reign of Justinian, they acknowledged the god and the emperor of the Romans, and seven fortresses were built in the most accessible passes, to exclude the ambition of the Persian monarch.[130] The principal source of the Euphrates descends from the Chalybian mountains, and seems to flow towards the west and the Euxine : bending to the south-west, the river passes under the walls of Satala and Melitene (which were restored by Justinian as the bulwarks of the Lesser Armenia), and gradually approaches the Mediterranean Sea ; till at length, repelled by Mount Taurus,[131] the Euphrates inclines his long and flexible course to the south-east and the Gulf of Persia. Among the Roman cities beyond the Euphrates, we distinguish two recent foundations, which were named from Theodosius, and the relics of the martyrs ; and two capitals Amida and Edessa, which are celebrated in the history of every age. Their strength was proportioned by Justinian to the danger of their situation. A ditch and palisade might be sufficient to resist the artless force of the cavalry of Scythia ; but more elaborate works were required to sustain a regular siege against the arms and treasures of the great king. His skilful engineers understood the methods of conducting deep mines, and of raising platforms to the level of the rampart : he shook the strongest battlements with his military engines, and sometimes advanced to the assault with a line of movable turrets on the backs of elephants. In the great cities of the East, the disadvantage of space, perhaps of position, was compensated by the zeal of the people, who seconded the garrison in the defence of their country and religion ; and the fabulous promise of the Son of God, that Edessa should never be taken, filled the citizens with valiant confidence, and chilled the besiegers with doubt and dismay.[132] The subordinate towns of Armenia and Mesopotamia were diligently strengthened, and the posts which appeared to have any command of ground or water were occupied by numerous forts, substantially built of stone, or more hastily erected with the obvious materials of earth and brick. The eye of Justinian investigated every spot ; and his cruel precautions might attract the war into some lonely vale, whose peaceful natives, connected by trade and marriage, were ignorant of national discord and the quarrels of princes. Westward of the Euphrates, a sandy desert extends above six hundred miles to the Red Sea. Nature had interposed a vacant solitude between the ambition of two rival empires ; the Arabians, till Mahomet arose, were formidable only as robbers ; and in the proud security of peace, the fortifications of Syria were neglected on the most vulnerable side.

But the national enmity, at least the effects of that enmity, had been suspended by a truce, which continued above fourscore years. An ambassador from the emperor Zeno accompanied the rash and unfortunte Perozes,* in his expedition against the Nepthalites,† or white Huns, whose conquests had been stretched from the Caspian to the heart of India, whose throne was enriched with emeralds,[133] and whose cavalry was supported by a line of two thousand elephants.[134] The Persians ‡ were twice circumvented, in a situation which made valor useless and flight impossible ; and the double victory of the Huns was achieved by military stratagem. They dismissed their royal captive after he had submitted to adore the majesty of a barbarian ; and the humiliation was poorly evaded by the casuistical subtlety of the Magi, who instructed Perozes to direct his attention to the rising sun.§ The indignant successor of Cyrus forgot his danger and his gratitude ; he renewed the attack with headstrong fury, and lost both his army and his life.[135] The death of Perozes abandoned Persia to her foreign and domestic enemies ; ‖ and twelve years of confusion elapsed before his son Cabades, or Kobad, could embrace any designs of ambition or revenge. The unkind parsimony of Anastasius was the motive or pretence of a Roman war ; [136] the Huns and Arabs marched under the Persian standard, and the fortifications of Armenia and Mesopotamia were, at that time, in a ruinous or imperfect condition. The emperor returned his thanks to the governor and people of Martyropolis for the prompt surrender of a city which could not be successfully defended, and the conflagration of Theodosiopolis might justify the conduct of their prudent neighbors. Amida sustained a long and destructive siege : at the end of three months the loss of fifty thousand of the soldiers of Cabades was not balanced by any prospect of success, and it was in vain that the Magi deduced a flattering prediction from the indecency of the women ¶ on the ramparts, who had revealed their most secret charms to the eyes of the assailants. At length, in a silent night, they ascended the most accessible tower, which was guarded only by some monks oppressed, after the duties of a festival, with sleep and wine. Scaling-ladders were applied at the dawn of day ; the presence of Cabades, his stern command, and his drawn sword, compelled the Persians to vanquish ; and

---

* Firouz the Conqueror—unfortunately so named. See St. Martin, vol. vi. p. 439.—M.

† Rather Hepthalites.—M.

‡ According to the Persian historians, he was misled by guides who used the old stratagem of Zopyrus. Malcolm, vol. i. p. 101.—M.

§ In the MS. Chronicle of Tabary, it is said that the Moubedan Mobed, or Grand Pontiff, opposed with all his influence the violation of the treaty. St. Martin, vol. vii. p. 254.—M.

‖ When Firoze advanced, Khoosh-Nuaz (the king of the Huns) presented on the point of a lance the treaty to which he had sworn, and exhorted him yet to desist before he destroyed his fame forever. Malcolm, vol. i. p. 103.--M.

¶ Gibbon should have written " some prostitutes." Proc. Pers. vol. i. p. 7.—M.

before it was sheathed, fourscore thousand of the inhabitants had expiated the blood of their companions. After the siege of Amida, the war continued three years, and the unhappy frontier tasted the full measure of its calamities. The gold of Anastasius was offered too late, the number of his troops was defeated by the number of their generals ; the country was stripped of its inhabitants, and both the living and the dead were abandoned to the wild beasts of the desert. The resistance of Edessa, and the deficiency of spoil, inclined the mind of Cabades to peace : he sold his conquests for an exorbitant price ; and the same line, though marked with slaughter and devastation, still separated the two empires. To avert the repetition of the same evils, Anastasius resolved to found a new colony, so strong, that it should defy the power of the Persian, so far advanced towards Assyria, that its stationary troops might defend the province by the menace or operation of offensive war. For this purpose, the town of Dara,[137] fourteen miles from Nisibis, and four days' journey from the Tigris, was peopled and adorned ; the hasty works of Anastasius were improved by the perseverance of Justinian ; and, without insisting on places less important, the fortifications of Dara may represent the military architecture of the age. The city was surrounded with two walls, and the interval between them, of fifty paces, afforded a retreat to the cattle of the besieged. The inner wall was a monument of strength and beauty : it measured sixty feet from the ground, and the height of the towers was one hundred feet ; the loop-holes, from whence an enemy might be annoyed with missile weapons, were small, but numerous ; the soldiers were planted along the rampart, under the shelter of double galleries, and a third platform, spacious and secure, was raised on the summit of the towers. The exterior wall appears to have been less lofty, but more solid ; and each tower was protected by a quadrangular bulwark. A hard, rocky soil resisted the tools of the miners, and on the south-east, where the ground was more tractable, their approach was retarded by a new work, which advanced in the shape of a half-moon. The double and treble ditches were filled with a stream of water ; and in the management of the river, the most skilful labor was employed to supply the inhabitants, to distress the besiegers, and to prevent the mischiefs of a natural or artificial inundation. Dara continued more than sixty years to fulfil the wishes of its founders, and to provoke the jealousy of the Persians, who incessantly complained, that this impregnable fortress had been constructed in manifest violation of the treaty of peace between the two empires.*

---

* The situation (of Dara) does not appear to give it strength, as it must have

Between the Euxine and the Caspian, the countries of Colchos, Iberia, and Albania, are intersected in every direction by the branches of Mount Caucasus; and the two principal *gates* or passes, from north to south, have been frequently confounded in the geography both of the ancients and moderns. The name of *Caspian* or *Albanian* gates is properly applied to Derbend,[138] which occupies a short declivity between the mountains and the sea: the city, if we give credit to local tradition, had been founded by the Greeks; and this dangerous entrance was fortified by the kings of Persia with a mole, double walls, and doors of iron. The Iberian gates [139] * are formed by a narrow passage of six miles in Mount Caucasus, which opens from the northern side of Iberia, or Georgia, into the plain that reaches to the Tanais and the Volga. A fortress, designed by Alexander perhaps, or one of his successors, to command that important pass, had descended by right of conquest or inheritance to a prince of the Huns, who offered it for a moderate price to the emperor: but while Anastasius paused, while he timorously computed the cost and the distance, a more vigilant rival interposed, and Cabades forcibly occupied the Straits of Caucasus. The Albanian and Iberian gates excluded the horsemen of Scythia from the shortest and most practicable roads, and the whole front of the mountains was covered by the rampart of Gog and Magog, the long wall which has excited the curiosity of an Arabian caliph [140] and a Russian conqueror.[141] According to a recent description, huge stones, seven feet thick,

---

been commanded on three sides by the mountains, but opening on the south towards the plains of Mesopotamia. The foundation of the walls and towers, built of large hewn stone, may be traced across the valley, and over a number of low rocky hills which branch out from the foot of Mount Masius. The circumference I conceive to be nearly two miles and a half; and a small stream, which flows through the middle of the place, has induced several Koordish and Armenian families to fix their residence within the ruins. Besides the walls and towers, the remains of many other buildings attest the former grandeur of Dara; a considerable part of the space within the walls is arched and vaulted underneath, and in one place we perceived a large cavern, supported by four ponderous columns somewhat resembling the great cistern of Constantinople. In the centre of the village are the ruins of a palace (probably that mentioned by Procopius) or church, one hundred paces in length, and sixty in breadth. The foundations, which are quite entire, consist of a prodigious number of subterraneous vaulted chambers, entered by a narrow passage forty paces in length. The gate is still standing; a considerable part of the wall has bid defiance to time, etc. M'Donald Kinneir's Journey, p. 438.—M.

* Malte-Brun, tom. viii. p. 12, makes three passes: 1. The central, which leads from Mosdok to Teflis, πύλαι καυκάσιαι. 2. The Albanian, more inland than the Derbend Pass. 3. The Derbend—the Caspian Gates. But the narrative of Colonel Monteith, in the Journal of the Geographical Society of London, vol. iii. p. i. 39, clearly shows that there are but two passes between the Black Sea and the Caspian; the central, the Caucasian, or, as Colonel Monteith calls it, the Caspian Gates, and the pass of Derbend, though it is practicable to turn this position (of Derbend) by a road a few miles distant through the mountains, p. 40.—M.

twenty-one feet in length or height, are artificially joined without iron or cement, to compose a wall, which runs above three hundred miles from the shores of Derbend, over the hills, and through the valleys of Daghestan and Georgia. Without a vision, such a work might be undertaken by the policy of Cabades ; without a miracle, it might be accomplished by his son, so formidable to the Romans, under the name of Chosroes ; so dear to the Orientals, under the appellation of Nushirwan. The Persian monarch held in his hand the keys both of peace and war ; but he stipulated in every treaty, that Justinian should contribute to the expense of a common barrier, which equally protected the two empires from the inroads of the Scythians.[142]

VII. Justinian suppressed the schools of Athens and the consulship of Rome, which had given so many sages and heroes to mankind. Both these institutions had long since degenerated from their primitive glory ; yet some reproach may be justly inflicted on the avarice and jealousy of a prince, by whose hand such venerable ruins were destroyed.

Athens, after her Persian triumphs, adopted the philosophy of Ionia and the rhetoric of Sicily ; and these studies became the patrimony of a city, whose inhabitants, about thirty thousand males, condensed, within the period of a single life, the genius of ages and millions. Our sense of the dignity of human nature is exalted by the simple recollection, that Isocrates[143] was the companion of Plato and Xenophon ; that he assisted, perhaps with the historian Thucydides, at the first representations of the Œdipus of Sophocles and the Iphigenia of Euripides ; and that his pupils Æschines and Demosthenes contended for the crown of patriotism in the presence of Aristotle, the master of Theophrastus, who taught at Athens with the founders of the Stoic and Epicurean sects.[144] The ingenuous youth of Attica enjoyed the benefits of their domestic education, which was communicated without envy to the rival cities. Two thousand disciples heard the lessons of Theophrastus ;[145] the schools of rhetoric must have been still more populous than those of philosophy ; and a rapid succession of students diffused the fame of their teachers as far as the utmost limits of the Grecian language and name. Those limits were enlarged by the victories of Alexander ; the arts of Athens survived her freedom and dominion ; and the Greek colonies, which the Macedonians planted in Egypt, and scattered over Asia, undertook long and frequent pilgrimages to worship the Muses in their favorite temple on the banks of the Ilissus. The Latin conquerors respectfully listened to the instructions of their subjects and captives ; the names of Cicero and

Horace were enrolled in the schools of Athens ; and after the perfect settlement of the Roman empire, the natives of Italy, of Africa, and of Britain, conversed in the groves of the academy with their fellow-students of the East. The studies of philosophy and eloquence are congenial to a popular state, which encourages the freedom of inquiry, and submits only to the force of persuasion. In the republics of Greece and Rome, the art of speaking was the powerful engine of patriotism or ambition ; and the schools of rhetoric poured forth a colony of statesmen and legislators. When the liberty of public debate was suppressed, the orator, in the honorable profession of an advocate, might plead the cause of innocence and justice ; he might abuse his talents in the more profitable trade of panegyric ; and the same precepts continued to dictate the fanciful declamations of the sophist, and the chaster beauties of historical composition. The systems which professed to unfold the nature of God, of man, and of the universe, entertained the curiosity of the philosophic student ; and according to the temper of his mind, he might doubt with the Sceptics, or decide with the Stoics, sublimely speculate with Plato, or severely argue with Aristotle. The pride of the adverse sects had fixed an unattainable term of moral happiness and perfection ; but the race was glorious and salutary ; the disciples of Zeno, and even those of Epicurus, were taught both to act and to suffer ; and the death of Petronius was not less effectual than that of Seneca, to humble a tyrant by the discovery of his impotence. The light of science could not indeed be confined within the walls of Athens. Her incomparable writers address themselves to the human race ; the living masters emigrated to Italy and Asia ; Berytus, in later times, was devoted to the study of the law ; astronomy and physic were cultivated in the musæum of Alexandria ; but the Attic schools of rhetoric and philosophy maintained their superior reputation from the Peloponnesian war to the reign of Justinian. Athens, though situate in a barren soil, possessed a pure air, a free navigation, and the monuments of ancient art. That sacred retirement was seldom disturbed by the business of trade or government ; and the last of the Athenians were distinguished by their lively wit, the purity of their taste and language, their social manners, and some traces, at least in discourse, of the magnanimity of their fathers. In the suburbs of the city, the *academy* of the Platonists, the *lycæum* of the Peripatetics, the *portico* of the Stoics, and the *garden* of the Epicureans, were planted with trees and decorated with statues ; and the philosophers, instead of being immured in a cloister, delivered their instructions in spacious and pleasant walks, which, at different hours, were consecrated to the exercises of the mind and body. The genius of the founders still lived in those venerable seats ; the ambition of succeeding to the masters of human reason excited a generous emulation ; and the merit of the candidates was determined, on each vacancy, by the free voices of an enlightened people. The Athenian professors were paid by their disciples : according to their mutual wants and abilities, the price appears to have varied from a mina to a talent ; and Isocrates himself, who derides the avarice of the sophists, required, in his school of rhetoric, about thirty pounds from each of his hundred pupils. The wages of industry are just and honorable, yet the same Isocrates shed tears at the first receipt of a stipend : the Stoic might blush when he was hired to preach the contempt of money ; and I should be sorry to discover that Aristotle or Plato so far degenerated from the example of Socrates, as to exchange knowledge for gold. But some property of lands and houses was settled by the permission of the laws, and the legacies of deceased friends, on the philosophic chairs of Athens. Epicurus bequeathed to his disciples the gardens which he had purchased for eighty minæ or two hundred and fifty pounds, with a fund sufficient for their frugal subsistence and monthly festivals,[146] and the patrimony of Plato afforded an annual rent, which, in eight centuries, was gradually increased from three to one thousand pieces of gold.[147] The schools of Athens were protected by the wisest and most virtuous of the Roman princes. The library, which Hadrian founded, was placed in a portico adorned with pictures, statues, and a roof of alabaster, and supported by one hundred columns of Phrygian marble. The public salaries were assigned by the generous spirit of the Antonines ; and each professor of politics, of rhetoric, of the Platonic, the Peripatetic, the Stoic, and the Epicurean philosophy, received an annual stipend of ten thousand drachmæ, or more than three hundred pounds sterling.[148] After the death of Marcus, these liberal donations, and the privileges attached to the *thrones* of science, were abolished and revived, diminished and enlarged ; but some vestige of royal bounty may be found under the successors of Constantine ; and their arbitrary choice of an unworthy candidate might tempt the philosophers of Athens to regret the days of independence and poverty.[149] It is remarkable, that the impartial favor of the Antonines was bestowed on the four adverse sects of philosophy, which they considered as equally useful, or at least, as equally innocent. Socrates had formerly been the glory and the reproach of his country ; and the first lessons of Epicurus so strangely scandalized the pious ears of the Athenians, that by his exile, and that of his antagonists, they silenced all vain disputes concerning the nature of the gods. But in the ensuing year they recalled the hasty decree, restored the liberty of the schools, and were convinced, by the experience of ages, that the moral character of philosophers is not affected by the diversity of their theological speculations.[150]

The Gothic arms were less fatal to the schools of Athens than the establishment of a new religion, whose ministers superseded the exercise of reason, resolved every question by an article of faith, and condemned the infidel or sceptic to eternal flames. In many a volume of laborious controversy, they exposed the weakness of the understanding and the corruption of the heart, insulted human nature in the sages of antiquity, and proscribed the spirit of philosophical inquiry, so repugnant to the doctrine, or at least to the temper, of an humble believer. The surviving sects of the Platonists, whom Plato would have blushed to acknowledge, extravagantly mingled a sublime theory with the practice of superstition and magic ; and as they remained alone in the midst of a Christian world, they indulged a secret rancor against the government of the church and state, whose severity was still suspended over their heads. About a century after the reign of Julian,[151] Proclus[152] was permitted to teach in the philosophic chair of the academy ; and such was his industry, that he frequently, in the same day, pronounced five lessons, and composed seven hundred lines. His sagacious mind explored the deepest questions of morals and metaphysics, and he ventured to urge eighteen arguments against the Christian doctrine of the creation of the world. But in the intervals of study, he *personally* conversed with Pan, Æsculapius, and Minerva, in whose mysteries he was secretly initiated, and whose prostrate statues he adored ; in the devout persuasion that the philosopher, who is a citizen of the universe, should be the priest of its various deities. An eclipse of the sun announced his approaching end ; and his life, with that of his scholar Isidore,[153] compiled by two of their most learned disciples, exhibits a deplorable picture of the second childhood of human reason. Yet the golden chain, as it was fondly styled, of the Platonic succession, continued forty-four years, from the death of Proclus to the edict of Justinian,[154] which imposed a perpetual silence on the schools of Athens, and excited the grief and indignation of the few remaining votaries of Grecian science and superstition. Seven friends and philosophers, Diogenes and Hermias, Eulalius and Priscian, Damascius, Isidore, and Simplicius, who dissented from the religion of their sovereign, embraced the resolution of seeking in a foreign land the freedom which was denied in their native country. They had heard, and they credulously believed, that the republic of Plato was realized in the despotic government of Persia, and that a patriot king reigned over the happiest and most virtuous of nations. They were soon astonished by the natural discovery, that Persia resembled the other countries of the globe ; that Chosroes, who affected the name of a philosopher, was vain, cruel, and ambitious ; that bigotry, and a spirit of intolerance, prevailed among the Magi ; that the nobles were haughty, the courtiers servile, and the magistrates unjust ; that the guilty sometimes escaped, and that the innocent were often oppressed. The disappointment of the philosophers provoked them to overlook the real virtues of the Persians ; and they were scandalized, more deeply perhaps than became their profession, with the plurality of wives and concubines, the incestuous marriages, and the custom of exposing dead bodies to the dogs and vultures, instead of hiding them in the earth, or consuming them with fire. Their repentance was expressed by a precipitate return, and they loudly declared that they had rather die on the borders of the empire, than enjoy the wealth and favor of the barbarian. From this journey, however, they derived a benefit which reflects the purest lustre on the character of Chosroes. He required, that the seven sages who had visited the court of Persia should be exempted from the penal laws which Justinian enacted against his Pagan subjects ; and this privilege, expressly stipulated in a treaty of peace, was guarded by the vigilance of a powerful mediator.[155] Simplicius and his companions ended their lives in peace and obscurity ; and as they left no disciples, they terminate the long list of Grecian philosophers, who may be justly praised, notwithstanding their defects, as the wisest and most virtuous of their contemporaries. The writings of Simplicius are now extant. His physical and metaphysical commentaries on Aristotle have passed away with the fashion of the times ; but his moral interpretation of Epictetus is preserved in the library of nations, as a classic book, most excellently adapted to direct the will, to purify the heart, and to confirm the understanding, by a just confidence in the nature both of God and man.

About the same time that Pythagoras first invented the appellation of philosopher, liberty and the consulship were founded at Rome by the elder Brutus. The revolutions of the consular office, which may be viewed in the successive lights of a substance, a shadow, and a name, have been occasionally mentioned in the present History. The first magistrates of the republic had been chosen by the people, to exercise, in the senate and in the camp, the powers of peace and war, which were afterwards translated to the emperors. But the tradition of ancient dignity was long revered by the Romans and barbarians. A Gothic historian applauds the consulship of Theodoric as the height of all temporal glory and greatness ;[156] the king of Italy himself congratulated those annual favorites of fortune who, without the cares, enjoyed the splendor of the throne ; and at the end of a thousand years, two consuls were created by the sovereigns of Rome and Constantinople, for the sole purpose of giving a date to the year, and a festival to the people. But the expenses of this festival, in which the wealthy and the vain aspired to surpass their predecessors, insensibly arose to the enormous sum of fourscore thousand pounds ; the wisest senators declined a useless honor, which involved the certain ruin of their families, and to this reluctance I should impute the frequent chasms in the last age of the consular *Fasti*. The predecessors of Justinian had assisted from the public treasures the dignity of the less opulent candidates ; the avarice of that prince preferred the cheaper and more convenient method of advice and regulation.[157] Seven *processions* or spectacles were the number to which his edict confined the horse and chariot races, the athletic sports, the music, and pantomines of the theatre, and the hunting of wild beasts ; and small pieces of silver were discreetly substituted to the gold medals, which had always excited tumult and drunkenness, when they were scattered with a profuse hand among the populace. Notwithstanding these precautions, and his own example, the succession of consuls finally ceased in the thirteenth year of Justinian, whose despotic temper might be gratified by the silent extinction of a title which admonished the Romans of their ancient freedom.[158] Yet the annual consulship still lived in the minds of the people ; they fondly expected its speedy restoration ; they applauded the gracious condescension of successive princes, by whom it was assumed in the first year of their reign ; and three centuries elapsed, after the death of Justinian, before that obsolete dignity, which had been suppressed by custom, could be abolished by law.[159] The imperfect mode of distinguishing each year by the name of a magistrate, was usefully supplied by the date of a permanent æra : the creation of the world, according to the Septuagint version, was adopted by the Greeks ;[160] and the Latins, since the age of Charlemagne, have computed their time from the birth of Christ.[161]

CHAPTER XLI.

CONQUESTS OF JUSTINIAN IN THE WEST.—CHARACTER AND FIRST
CAMPAIGNS OF BELISARIUS.—HE INVADES AND SUBDUES THE
VANDAL KINGDOM OF AFRICA.—HIS TRIUMPH.—THE GOTHIC
WAR.—HE RECOVERS SICILY, NAPLES, AND ROME.—SIEGE OF
ROME BY THE GOTHS.—THEIR RETREAT AND LOSSES.—SURREN-
DER OF RAVENNA.—GLORY OF BELISARIUS.—HIS DOMESTIC
SHAME AND MISFORTUNE.

WHEN Justinian ascended the throne, about fifty years after the
fall of the Western empire, the kingdoms of the Goths and Vandals had obtained a solid, and, as it might seem, a legal establishment both in Europe and Africa. The titles, which Roman victory had inscribed, were erased with equal justice by the sword of
the barbarians ; and their successful rapine derived a more venerable sanction from time, from treaties, and from the oaths of
fidelity, already repeated by a second or third generation of obedient subjects. Experience and Christianity had refuted the superstitious hope, that Rome was founded by the gods to reign forever over the nations of the earth. But the proud claim of perpetual and indefeasible dominion, which her soldiers could no
longer maintain, was firmly asserted by her statesmen and lawyers, whose opinions have been sometimes revived and propagated
in the modern schools of jurisprudence. After Rome herself had
been stripped of the Imperial purple, the princes of Constantinople assumed the sole and sacred sceptre of the monarchy ; demanded, as their rightful inheritance, the provinces which had
been subdued by the consuls, or possessed by the Cæsars ; and
feebly aspired to deliver their faithful subjects of the West from
the usurpation of heretics and barbarians. The execution of this
splendid design was in some degree reserved for Justinian. During the five first years of his reign, he reluctantly waged a costly
and unprofitable war against the Persians ; till his pride submitted to his ambition, and he purchased, at the price of four hundred and forty thousand pounds sterling, the benefit of a precarious truce, which, in the language of both nations, was dignified
with the appellation of the *endless* peace. The safety of the East
enabled the emperor to employ his forces against the Vandals ;
and the internal state of Africa afforded an honorable motive, and
promised a powerful support, to the Roman arms.[1]

According to the testament of the founder, the African kingdom had lineally descended to Hilderic, the eldest of the Vandal princes. A mild disposition inclined the son of a tyrant, the grandson of a conqueror, to prefer the counsels of clemency and peace ; and his accession was marked by the salutary edict, which restored two hundred bishops to their churches, and allowed the free profession of the Athanasian creed.[2] But the Catholics accepted, with cold and transient gratitude, a favor so inadequate to their pretensions, and the virtues of Hilderic offended the prejudices of his countrymen. The Arian clergy presumed to insinuate that he had renounced the faith, and the soldiers more loudly complained that he had degenerated from the courage, of his ancestors. His ambassadors were suspected of a secret and disgraceful negotiation in the Byzantine court ; and his general, the Achilles,[3] as he was named, of the Vandals, lost a battle against the naked and disorderly Moors. The public discontent was exasperated by Gelimer, whose age, descent, and military fame, gave him an apparent title to the succession : he assumed, with the consent of the nation, the reins of government ; and his unfortunate sovereign sunk without a struggle from the throne to a dungeon, where he was strictly guarded with a faithful counsellor, and his unpopular nephew the Achilles of the Vandals. But the indulgence which Hilderic had shown to his Catholic subjects had powerfully recommended him to the favor of Justinian, who, for the benefit of his own sect, could acknowledge the use and justice of religious toleration : their alliance, while the nephew of Justin remained in a private station, was cemented by the mutual exchange of gifts and letters ; and the emperor Justinian asserted the cause of royalty and friendship. In two successive embassies, he admonished the usurper to repent of his treason, or to abstain, at least, from any further violence which might provoke the displeasure of God and of the Romans ; to reverence the laws of kindred and succession, and to suffer an infirm old man peaceably to end his days, either on the throne of Carthage or in the palace of Constantinople. The passions, or even the prudence, of Gelimer compelled him to reject these requests, which were urged in the haughty tone of menace and command ; and he justified his ambition in a language rarely spoken in the Byzantine court, by alleging the right of a free people to remove or punish their chief magistrate, who had failed in the execution of the kingly office. After this fruitless expostulation, the captive monarch was more rigorously treated, his nephew was deprived of his eyes, and the cruel Vandal, confident in his strength and distance, derided the vain threats and slow preparations of the emperor of the East. Justinian resolved to deliver or revenge his friend, Gelimer to maintain his usurpation ; and the war was preceded, according to the practice of civilized nations, by the most solemn protestations, that each party was sincerely desirous of peace.

The report of an African war was grateful only to the vain and idle populace of Constantinople, whose poverty exempted them from tribute, and whose cowardice was seldom exposed to military service. But the wiser citizens, who judged of the future by the past, revolved in their memory the immense loss, both of men and money, which the empire had sustained in the expedition of Basiliscus. The troops, which, after five laborious campaigns, had been recalled from the Persian frontier, dreaded the sea, the climate, and the arms of an unknown enemy. The ministers of the finances computed, as far as they might compute, the demands of an African war ; the taxes which must be found and levied to supply those insatiate demands ; and the danger, lest their own lives, or at least their lucrative employments, should be made responsible for the deficiency of the supply. Inspired by such selfish motives (for we may not suspect him of any zeal for the public good), John of Cappadocia ventured to oppose in full council the inclinations of his master. He confessed, that a victory of such importance could not be too dearly purchased ; but he represented in a grave discourse the certain difficulties and the uncertain event. "You undertake," said the præfect, "to besiege Carthage : by land, the distance is not less than one hundred and forty days' journey ; on the sea, a whole year [4] must elapse before you can receive any intelligence from your fleet. If Africa should be reduced, it cannot be preserved without the additional conquest of Sicily and Italy. Success will impose the obligation of new labors ; a single misfortune will attract the barbarians into the heart of your exhausted empire." Justinian felt the weight of this salutary advice ; he was confounded by the unwonted freedom of an obsequious servant ; and the design of the war would perhaps have been relinquished, if his courage had not been revived by a voice which silenced the doubts of profane reason. "I have seen a vision," cried an artful or fanatic bishop of the East. "It is the will of Heaven, O emperor ! that you should not abandon your holy enterprise for the deliverance of the African church. The God of battles will march before your standard, and disperse your enemies, who are the enemies of his Son." The emperor might be tempted, and his counsellors were constrained, to give credit to this seasonable revelation : but they derived more rational hope from the revolt, which the adherents of Hilderic or Athanasius had already excited on the borders of the Vandal monarchy. Pudentius, an African subject, had privately signified his loyal intentions, and a small military aid restored the province of Tripoli to the obedience of the Romans. The government of Sardinia had been intrusted to Godas, a valiant barbarian : he suspended the payment of tribute, disclaimed his allegiance to the usurper, and gave audience to the emissaries of Justinian, who found him master of that fruitful island, at the head of his guards, and proudly invested with the ensigns of royalty. The forces of the Vandals were diminished by discord and suspicion ; the Roman armies were animated by the spirit of Belisarius ; one of those heroic names which are familiar to every age and to every nation.

The Africanus of new Rome was born, and perhaps educated, among the Thracian peasants,[5] without any of those advantages which had formed the virtues of the elder and younger Scipio ; a noble origin, liberal studies, and the emulation of a free state. The silence of a loquacious secretary may be admitted, to prove that the youth of Belisarius could not afford any subject of praise : he served, most assuredly with valor and reputation, among the private guards of Justinian ; and when his patron became emperor, the domestic was promoted to military command. After a bold inroad into Persarmenia, in which his glory was shared by a colleague, and his progress was checked by an enemy, Belisarius repaired to the important station of Dara, where he first accepted the service of Procopius, the faithful companion, and diligent historian, of his exploits.[6] The Mirranes of Persia advanced, with forty thousand of her best troops, to raze the fortifications of Dara ; and signified the day and the hour on which the citizens should prepare a bath for his refreshment, after the toils of victory. He encountered an adversary equal to himself, by the new title of General of the East ; his superior in the science of war, but much inferior in the number and quality of his troops, which amounted only to twenty-five thousand Romans and strangers, relaxed in their discipline, and humbled by recent disasters. As the level plain of Dara refused all shelter to stratagem and ambush, Belisarius protected his front with a deep trench, which was prolonged at first in perpendicular, and afterwards in parallel, lines, to cover the wings of cavalry advantageously posted to command the flanks and rear of the enemy. When the Roman centre was shaken, their well-timed and rapid charge decided the conflict : the standard of Persia fell ; the *immortals* fled ; the infantry threw away their bucklers, and eight thousand of the vanquished were left on the field of battle. In the next campaign, Syria was invaded on the side of the desert ; and Belisarius, with twenty thousand men, hastened from Dara to the relief of the province. During the whole summer, the designs of the enemy were baffled by his skilful dispositions : he pressed their retreat, occupied each night their camp of the preceding day, and would have secured a bloodless victory, if he could have resisted the impatience of his own troops.   Their valiant promise was faintly supported in the hour of battle ; the right wing was exposed by the treacherous or cowardly desertion of the Christian Arabs ; the Huns, a veteran band of eight hundred warriors, were oppressed by superior numbers ; the flight of the Isaurians was intercepted ; but the Roman infantry stood firm on the left ; for Belisarius himself, dismounting from his horse, showed them that intrepid despair was their only safety.*   They turned their backs to the Euphrates, and their faces to the enemy : innumerable arrows glanced without effect from the compact and shelving order of their bucklers ; an impenetrable line of pikes was opposed to the repeated assaults of the Persian cavalry ; and after a resistance of many hours, the remaining troops were skilfully embarked under the shadow of the night.   The Persian commander retired with disorder and disgrace, to answer a strict account of the lives of so many soldiers, which he had consumed in a barren victory.   But the fame of Belisarius was not sullied by a defeat, in which he alone had saved his army from the consequences of their own rashness : the approach of peace relieved him from the guard of the eastern frontier, and his conduct in the sedition of Constantinople amply discharged his obligations to the emperor.   When the African war became the topic of popular discourse and secret deliberation, each of the Roman generals was apprehensive, rather than ambitious, of the dangerous honor ; but as soon as Justinian had declared his preference of superior merit, their envy was rekindled by the unanimous applause which was given to the choice of Belisarius.   The temper of the Byzantine court may encourage a suspicion, that the hero was darkly assisted by the intrigues of his wife, the fair and subtle Antonina, who alternately enjoyed the confidence, and incurred the hatred, of the empress Theodora. The birth of Antonina was ignoble ; she descended from a family of charioteers ; and her chastity has been stained with the foulest reproach.   Yet she reigned with long and absolute power over the mind of his illustrious husband ; and if Antonina disdained the merit of conjugal fidelity, she expressed a manly friendship to Belisarius, whom she accompanied with undaunted resolution in all the hardships and dangers of a military life.[7]

---

* The battle was fought on Easter Sunday, April 19, not at the end of the summer.   The date is supplied from John Malala by Lord Mahon, p. 47.—M.

The preparations for the African war were not unworthy of the last contest between Rome and Carthage. The pride and flower of the army consisted of the guards of Belisarius, who, according to the pernicious indulgence of the times, devoted themselves, by a particular oath of fidelity, to the service of their patrons. Their strength and stature, for which they had been curiously selected, the goodness of their horses and armor, and the assiduous practice of all the exercises of war, enabled them to act whatever their courage might prompt ; and their courage was exalted by the social honor of their rank, and the personal ambition of favor and fortune. Four hundred of the bravest of the Heruli marched under the banner of the faithful and active Pharas ; their untractable valor was more highly prized than the tame submission of the Greeks and Syrians ; and of such importance was it deemed to procure a re-enforcement of six hundred Massagetæ, or Huns, that they were allured by fraud and deceit to engage in a naval expedition. Five thousand horse and ten thousand foot were embarked at Constantinople for the conquest of Africa ; but the infantry, for the most part levied in Thrace and Isauria, yielded to the more prevailing use and reputation of the cavalry ; and the Scythian bow was the weapon on which the armies of Rome were now reduced to place their principal dependence. From a laudable desire to assert the dignity of his theme, Procopius defends the soldiers of his own time against the morose critics, who confined that respectable name to the heavy-armed warriors of antiquity, and maliciously observed, that the word *archer* is introduced by Homer [8] as a term of contempt. "Such contempt might perhaps be due to the naked youths who appeared on foot in the fields of Troy, and lurking behind a tombstone, or the shield of a friend, drew the bow-string to their breast, [9] and dismissed a feeble and lifeless arrow. But our archers (pursues the historian) are mounted on horses, which they manage with admirable skill ; their head and shoulders are protected by a casque or buckler ; they wear greaves of iron on their legs, and their bodies are guarded by a coat of mail. On their right side hangs a quiver, a sword on their left, and their hand is accustomed to wield a lance or javelin in closer combat. Their bows are strong and weighty ; they shoot in every possible direction, advancing, retreating, to the front, to the rear, or to either flank ; and as they are taught to draw the bow-string not to the breast, but to the right ear, firm indeed must be the armor that can resist the rapid violence of their shaft." Five hundred transports, navigated by twenty thousand mariners of Egypt, Cilicia, and Ionia, were collected in the harbor of Constantinople. The smallest of these vessels may be computed at thirty, the largest at five hundred, tons ; and the fair average will supply an allowance, liberal, but not profuse, of about one hundred thousand tons,[10] for the reception of thirty-five thousand soldiers and sailors, of five thousand horses, of arms, engines, and military stores, and of a sufficient stock of water and provisions for a voyage, perhaps, of three months. The proud galleys, which in former ages swept the Mediterranean with so many hundred oars, had long since disappeared ; and the fleet of Justinian was escorted only by ninety-two light brigantines covered from the missile weapons of the enemy and rowed by two thousand of the brave and robust youth of Constantinople. Twenty-two generals are named, most of whom were afterwards distinguished in the wars of Africa and Italy : but the supreme command, both by land and sea, was delegated to Belisarius alone, with a boundless power of acting according to his discretion, as if the emperor himself were present. The separation of the naval and military professions is at once the effect and the cause of the modern improvements in the science of navigation and maritime war.

In the seventh year of the reign of Justinian, and about the time of the summer solstice, the whole fleet of six hundred ships was ranged in martial pomp before the gardens of the palace. The patriarch pronounced his benediction, the emperor signified his last commands, the general's trumpet gave the signal of departure, and every heart, according to its fears or wishes, explored, with anxious curiosity, the omens of misfortune and success. The first halt was made at Perinthus or Heraclea, where Belisarius waited five days to receive some Thracian horses, a military gift of his sovereign. From thence the fleet pursued their course through the midst of the Propontis ; but as they struggled to pass the Straits of the Hellespont, an unfavorable wind detained them four days at Abydus, where the general exhibited a memorable lesson of firmness and severity. Two of the Huns, who in a drunken quarrel had slain one of their fellow-soldiers, were instantly shown to the army suspended on a lofty gibbet. The national dignity was resented by their countrymen, who disclaimed the servile laws of the empire, and asserted the free privilege of Scythia, where a small fine was allowed to expiate the hasty sallies of intemperance and anger. Their complaints were specious, their clamors were loud, and the Romans were not averse to the example of disorder and impunity. But the rising sedition was appeased by the authority and eloquence of the general : and he represented to the assembled troops the obligation of justice, the importance of discipline, the rewards of piety and virtue, and the unpardonable guilt of murder, which, in his apprehension, was aggravated rather than excused by the vice of intoxication.[11] In the navigation from the Hellespont to Peloponnesus, which the Greeks, after the siege of Troy, had performed in four days,[12] the fleet of Belisarius was guided in their course by his master-galley, conspicuous in the day by the redness of the sails, and in the night by the torches blazing from the mast head. It was the duty of the pilots, as they steered between the islands, and turned the Capes of Malea and Tænarium, to preserve the just order and regular intervals of such a multitude of ships : as the wind was fair and moderate, their labors were not unsuccessful, and the troops were safely disembarked at Methone on the Messenian coast, to repose themselves for a while after the fatigues of the sea. In this place they experienced how avarice, invested with authority, may sport with the lives of thousands which are bravely exposed for the public service. According to military practice, the bread or biscuit of the Romans was twice prepared in the oven, and the diminution of one fourth was cheerfully allowed for the loss of weight. To gain this miserable profit, and to save the expense of wood, the præfect John of Cappadocia had given orders, that the flour should be slightly baked by the same fire which warmed the baths of Constantinople ; and when the sacks were opened, a soft and mouldy paste was distributed to the army. Such unwholesome food, assisted by the heat of the climate and season, soon produced an epidemical disease, which swept away five hundred soldiers. Their health was restored by the diligence of Belisarius, who provided fresh bread at Methone, and boldly expressed his just and humane indignation : the emperor heard his complaint ; the general was praised, but the minister was not punished. From the port of Methone, the pilots steered along the western coast of Peloponnesus, as far as the Isle of Zacynthus, or Zante, before they undertook the voyage (in their eyes a most arduous voyage) of one hundred leagues over the Ionian Sea. As the fleet was surprised by a calm, sixteen days were consumed in the slow navigation ; and even the general would have suffered the intolerable hardship of thirst, if the ingenuity of Antonina had not preserved the water in glass bottles, which she buried deep in the sand in a part of the ship impervious to the rays of the sun. At length the harbor of Caucana,[13] on the southern side of Sicily, afforded a secure and hospitable shelter. The Gothic officers who governed the island in the name of the daughter and grandson of Theodoric, obeyed their imprudent orders, to receive the troops of Justinian like friends and allies : provisions were liberally supplied, the cavalry was remounted,[14] and Procopius soon returned from Syracuse with correct information of the state and designs of the Vandals.   His intelligence determined Belisarius to hasten his operations, and his wise impatience was seconded by the winds.   The fleet lost sight of Sicily, passed before the Isle of Malta, discovered the capes of Africa, ran along the coast with a strong gale from the north-east, and finally cast anchor at the promontory of Caput Vada, about five days' journey to the south of Carthage.[15]

If Gelimer had been informed of the approach of the enemy, he must have delayed the conquest of Sardinia for the immediate defence of his person and kingdom.   A detachment of five thousand soldiers, and one hundred and twenty galleys, would have joined the remaining forces of the Vandals ; and the descendant of Generic might have surprised and oppressed a fleet of deep laden transports, incapable of action, and of light brigantines that seemed only qualified for flight.   Belisarius had secretly trembled when he overheard his soldiers, in the passage, emboldening each other to confess their apprehensions : if they were once on shore, they hoped to maintain the honor of their arms ; but if they should be attacked at sea, they did not blush to acknowledge that they wanted courage to contend at the same time with the winds, the waves, and the barbarians.[16]   The knowledge of their sentiments decided Belisarius to seize the first opportunity of landing them on the coast of Africa ; and he prudently rejected, in a council of war, the proposal of sailing with the fleet and army into the port of Carthage.*   Three months after their departure from Constantinople, the men and horses, the arms and military stores, were safely disembarked, and five soldiers were left as a guard on board each of the ships, which were disposed in the form of a semicircle.   The remainder of the troops occupied a camp on the sea-shore, which they fortified, according to ancient discipline, with a ditch and rampart ; and the discovery of a source of fresh water, while it allayed the thirst, excited the superstitious confidence, of the Romans.   The next morning, ome of the neighboring gardens were pillaged ; and Belisarius, 'er chastising the offenders, embraced the slight occasion, but the decisive moment, of inculcating the maxims of justice, moderation, and genuine policy.   " When I first accepted the commission of subduing Africa, I depended much less," said the general, " on the numbers, or even the bravery of my troops, than on the friendly disposition of the natives, and their immortal hatred of the Vandals.   You alone can deprive me of this hope ; if you con-

---

* Rather into the present Lake of Tunis. Lord Mahon, p. 92.—M.

tinue to extort by rapine what might be purchased for a little money, such acts of violence will reconcile these implacable enemies, and unite them in a just and holy league against the invaders of their country." These exhortations were enforced by a rigid discipline, of which the soldiers themselves soon felt and praised the salutary effects. The inhabitants, instead of deserting their houses, or hiding their corn, supplied the Romans with a fair and liberal market ; the civil officers of the province continued to exercise their functions in the name of Justinian ; and the clergy, from motives of conscience and interest, assiduously labored to promote the cause of a Catholic emperor. The small town of Sullecte,[17] one day's journey from the camp, had the honor of being foremost to open her gates, and to resume her ancient allegiance : the larger cities of Leptis and Adrumetum imitated the example of loyalty as soon as Belisarius appeared ; and he advanced without opposition as far as Grasse, a palace of the Vandal kings, at the distance of fifty miles from Carthage. The weary Romans indulged themselves in the refreshment of shady groves, cool fountains, and delicious fruits ; and the preference which Procopius allows to these gardens over any that he had seen, either in the East or West, may be ascribed either to the taste, or the fatigue, of the historian. In three generations, prosperity and a warm climate had dissolved the hardy virtue of the Vandals, who insensibly became the most luxurious of mankind. In their villas and gardens, which might deserve the Persian name of *Paradise*,[18] they enjoyed a cool and elegant repose ; and, after the daily use of the bath, the barbarians were seated at a table profusely spread with the delicacies of the land and sea. Their silken robes loosely flowing, after the fashion of the Medes, were embroidered with gold ; love and hunting were the labors of their life, and their vacant hours were amused by pantomimes, chariotraces, and the music and dances of the theatre.

In a march of ten or twelve days, the vigilance of Belisarius was constantly awake and active against his unseen enemies, by whom, in every place, and at every hour, he might be suddenly attacked. An officer of confidence and merit, John the Armenian, led the vanguard of three hundred horse ; six hundred Massagetæ covered at a certain distance the left flank ; and the whole fleet, steering along the coast, seldom lost sight of the army, which moved each day about twelve miles, and lodged in the evening in strong camps, or in friendly towns. The near approach of the Romans to Carthage filled the mind of Gelimer with anxiety and terror. He prudently wished to protract the war till his brother, with his veteran troops, should return from the conquest of Sardinia ; and he now lamented the rash policy of his ancestors, who, by destroying the fortifications of Africa, had left him only the dangerous resource of risking a battle in the neighborhood of his capital. The Vandal conquerors, from their original number of fifty thousand, were multiplied, without including their women and children, to one hundred and sixty thousand fighting men : * and such forces, animated with valor and union, might have crushed, at their first landing, the feeble and exhausted bands of the Roman general. But the friends of the captive king were more inclined to accept the invitations, than to resist the progress, of Belisarius ; and many a proud barbarian disguised his aversion to war under the more specious name of his hatred to the usurper. Yet the authority and promises of Gelimer collected a formidable army, and his plans were concerted with some degree of military skill. An order was despatched to his brother Ammatas, to collect all the forces of Carthage, and to encounter the van of the Roman army at the distance of ten miles from the city : his nephew Gibamund, with two thousand horse, was destined to attack their left, when the monarch himself, who silently followed, should charge their rear, in a situation which excluded them from the aid or even the view of their fleet. But the rashness of Ammatas was fatal to himself and his country. He anticipated the hour of the attack, outstripped his tardy followers, and was pierced with a mortal wound, after he had slain with his own hand twelve of his boldest antagonists. His Vandals fled to Carthage ; the highway, almost ten miles, was strewed with dead bodies ; and it seemed incredible that such multitudes could be slaughtered by the swords of three hundred Romans. The nephew of Gelimer was defeated, after a slight combat, by the six hundred Massagetæ : they did not equal the third part of his numbers ; but each Scythian was fired by the example of his chief, who gloriously exercised the privilege of his family, by riding, foremost and alone, to shoot the first arrow against the enemy. In the meanwhile, Gelimer himself, ignorant of the event, and misguided by the windings of the hills, inadvertently passed the Roman army, and reached the scene of action where Ammatas had fallen. He wept the fate of his brother and of Carthage, charged with irresistible fury the advancing squadrons, and might have pursued, and perhaps decided, the victory, if he had not wasted those inestimable moments in the discharge of a vain, though pious, duty to the dead. While his spirit was bro-

---

* 80,000—μυρίαδες ὀκτώ. Hist. Arc. c. 18. Gibbon has been misled by the translation. See Lord Mahon, p. 99.—M.

ken by this mournful office, he heard the trumpet of Belisarius, who, leaving Antonina and his infantry in the camp, pressed forwards with his guards and the remainder of the cavalry to rally his flying troops, and to restore the fortune of the day. Much room could not be found, in this disorderly battle, for the talents of a general ; but the king fled before the hero ; and the Vandals, accustomed only to a Moorish enemy, were incapable of withstanding the arms and discipline of the Romans. Gelimer retired with hasty steps towards the desert of Numidia : but he had soon the consolation of learning that his private orders for the execution of Hilderic and his captive friends had been faithfully obeyed. The tyrant's revenge was useful only to his enemies. The death of a lawful prince excited the compassion of his people ; his life might have perplexed the victorious Romans ; and the lieutenant of Justinian, by a crime of which he was innocent, was relieved from the painful alternative of forfeiting his honor or relinquishing his conquests.

As soon as the tumult had subsided, the several parts of the army informed each other of the accidents of the day ; and Belisarius pitched his camp on the field of victory, to which the tenth mile-stone from Carthage had applied the Latin appellation of *Decimus*. From a wise suspicion of the stratagems and resources of the Vandals, he marched the next day in order of battle, halted in the evening before the gates of Carthage, and allowed a night of repose, that he might not, in darkness and disorder, expose the city to the license of the soldiers, or the soldiers themselves to the secret ambush of the city. But as the fears of Belsiarius were the result of calm and intrepid reason, he was soon satisfied that he might confide, without danger, in the peaceful and friendly aspect of the capital. Carthage blazed with innumerable torches, the signals of the public joy ; the chain was removed that guarded the entrance of the port ; the gates were thrown open, and the people, with acclamations of gratitude, hailed and invited their Roman deliverers. The defeat of the Vandals, and the freedom of Africa, were announced to the city on the eve of St. Cyprian, when the churches were already adorned and illuminated for the festival of the martyr, whom three centuries of superstition had almost raised to a local deity. The Arians, conscious that their reign had expired, resigned the temple to the Catholics, who rescued their saint from profane hands, performed the holy rites, and loudly proclaimed the creed of Athanasius and Justinian. One awful hour reversed the fortunes of the contending parties. The suppliant Vandals, who had so lately indulged the vices of conquerors, sought an humble refuge in the sanctuary of the church ; while the merchants of the East were delivered from the deepest dungeon of the palace by their affrighted keeper, who implored the protection of his captives, and showed them, through an aperture in the wall, the sails of the Roman fleet. After their separation from the army, the naval commanders had proceeded with slow caution along the coast till they reached the Hermæan promontory, and obtained the first intelligence of the victory of Belisarius. Faithful to his instructions, they would have cast anchor about twenty miles from Carthage, if the more skilful seamen had not represented the perils of the shore, and the signs of an impending tempest. Still ignorant of the revolution, they declined, however, the rash attempt of forcing the chain of the port ; and the adjacent harbor and suburb of Mandracium were insulted only by the rapine of a private officer, who disobeyed and deserted his leaders. But the Imperial fleet, advancing with a fair wind, steered through the narrow entrance of the Goletta, and occupied, in the deep and capacious lake of Tunis, a secure station about five miles from the capital.[19] No sooner was Belisarius informed of their arrival, than he despatched orders that the greatest part of the mariners should be immediately landed to join the triumph, and to swell the apparent numbers, of the Romans. Before he allowed them to enter the gates of Carthage, he exhorted them, in a discourse worthy of himself and the occasion, not to disgrace the glory of their arms ; and to remember that the Vandals had been the tyrants, but that *they* were the deliverers, of the Africans, who must now be respected as the voluntary and affectionate subjects of their common sovereign. The Romans marched through the streets in close ranks, prepared for battle if an enemy had appeared : the strict order maintained by the general imprinted on their minds the duty of obedience ; and in an age in which custom and impunity almost sanctified the abuse of conquest, the genius of one man repressed the passions of a victorious army. The voice of menace and complaint was silent ; the trade of Carthage was not interrupted ; while Africa changed her master and her government, the shops continued open and busy ; and the soldiers, after sufficient guards had been posted, modestly departed to the houses which were allotted for their reception. Belisarius fixed his residence in the palace ; seated himself on the throne of Genseric ; accepted and distributed the barbaric spoil ; granted their lives to the suppliant Vandals ; and labored to repair the damage which the suburb of Mandracium had sustained in the preceding night. At supper he entertained his principal officers with the form and magnificence of a royal banquet.[20] The victor was respectfully served by the captive officers of the house-

hold ; and in the moments of festivity, when the impartial spectators applauded the fortune and merit of Belisarius, his envious
flatterers, secretly shed their venom on every word and gesture
which might alarm the suspicions of a jealous monarch. One day
was given to these pompous scenes, which may not be despised as
useless, if they attracted the popular veneration ; but the active
mind of Belisarius, which in the pride of victory could suppose a
defeat, had already resolved, that the Roman empire in Africa
should not depend on the chance of arms, or the favor of the people. The fortifications of Carthage * had alone been exempted
from the general proscription ; but in the reign of ninety-five
years they were suffered to decay by the thoughtless and indolent
Vandals. A wiser conqueror restored, with incredible despatch,
the walls and ditches of the city. His liberality encouraged the
workmen ; the soldiers, the mariners, and the citizens, vied with
each other in the salutary labor ; and Gelimer, who had feared to
trust his person in an open town, beheld, with astonishment and
despair, the rising strength of an impregnable fortress.

That unfortunate monarch, after the loss of his capital, applied
himself to collect the remains of an army scattered, rather than
destroyed, by the preceding battle ; and the hopes of pillage attracted some Moorish bands to the standard of Gelimer. He encamped in the fields of Bulla, four days' journey from Carthage ;
insulted the capital, which he deprived of the use of an aqueduct ;
proposed a high reward for the head of every Roman ; affected to
spare the persons and property of his African subjects, and
secretly negotiated with the Arian sectaries and the confederate
Huns. Under these circumstances, the conquest of Sardinia
served only to aggravate his distress : he reflected, with the deepest anguish, that he had wasted, in that useless enterprise, five
thousand of his bravest troops ; and he read, with grief and shame,
the victorious letters of his brother Zano,† who expressed a sanguine confidence that the king, after the example of their ancestors, had already chastised the rashness of the Roman invader.
"Alas ! my brother," replied Gelimer, "Heaven has declared
against our unhappy nation. While you have subdued Sardinia,
we have lost Africa. No sooner did Belisarius appear with a
handful of soldiers, than courage and prosperity deserted the
cause of the Vandals. Your nephew Gibamund, your brother

---

* And a few others (ὀλίγα ἄττα), Procopius states in his work De Edificiis, l.
vi. vol. i. p. 5.—M.
† Gibbon had forgotten that the bearer of the "victorious letters of his brother'
had sailed into the port of Carthage ; and that the letters had fallen into the hands
of the Romans. Proc. Vandal. l. i. c. 23.—M.

Ammatas, have been betrayed to death by the cowardice of their followers. Our horses, our ships, Carthage itself, and all Africa, are in the power of the enemy. Yet the Vandals still prefer an ignominious repose, at the expense of their wives and children, their wealth and liberty. Nothing now remains except the field of Bulla, and the hope of your valor. Abandon Sardinia ; fly to our relief ; restore our empire, or perish by our side.'' On the receipt of this epistle, Zano imparted his grief to the principal Vandals ; but the intelligence was prudently concealed from the natives of the island. The troops embarked in one hundred and twenty galleys at the port of Cagliari, cast anchor the third day on the confines of Mauritania, and hastily pursued their march to join the royal standard in the camp of Bulla. Mournful was the interview : the two brothers embraced ; they wept in silence ; no questions were asked of the Sardinian victory ; no inquiries were made of the African misfortunes : they saw before their eyes the whole extent of their calamities ; and the absence of their wives and children afforded a melancholy proof that either death or captivity had been their lot. The languid spirit of the Vandals was at length awakened and united by the entreaties of their king, the example of Zano, and the instant danger which threatened their monarchy and religion. The military strength of the nation advanced to battle ; and such was the rapid increase, that before their army reached Tricameron, about twenty miles from Carthage, they might boast, perhaps with some exaggeration, that they surpassed, in a tenfold proportion, the diminutive powers of the Romans. But these powers were under the command of Belisarius ; and, as he was conscious of their superior merit, he permitted the barbarians to surprise him at an unseasonable hour. The Romans were instantly under arms ; a rivulet covered their front ; the cavalry formed the first line, which Belisarius supported in the centre, at the head of five hundred guards ; the infantry, at some distance, was posted in the second line ; and the vigilance of the general watched the separate station and ambiguous faith of the Massagetæ, who secretly reserved their aid for the conquerors. The historian has inserted, and the reader may easily supply, the speeches [21] of the commanders, who, by arguments the most apposite to their situation, inculcated the importance of victory, and the contempt of life. Zano, with the troops which had followed him to the conquest of Sardinia, was placed in the centre ; and the throne of Genseric might have stood, if the multitude of Vandals had imitated their intrepid resolution. Casting away their lances and missile weapons, they drew their swords, and expected the charge : the Roman cavalry thrice passed the rivulet ; they were thrice repulsed ; and the conflict was firmly maintained, till Zano fell, and the standard of Belisarius was displayed. Gelimer retreated to his camp ; the Huns joined the pursuit ; and the victors despoiled the bodies of the slain. Yet no more than fifty Romans, and eight hundred Vandals, were found on the field of battle ; so inconsiderable was the carnage of a day, which extinguished a nation, and transferred the empire of Africa. In the evening Belisarius led his infantry to the attack of the camp ; and the pusillanimous flight of Gelimer exposed the vanity of his recent declarations, that to the vanquished, death was a relief, life a burden, and infamy the only object of terror. His departure was secret ; but as soon as the Vandals discovered that their king had deserted them, they hastily dispersed, anxious only for their personal safety, and careless of every object that is dear or valuable to mankind. The Romans entered the camp without resistance ; and the wildest scenes of disorder were veiled in the darkness and confusion of the night. Every barbarian who met their swords was inhumanly massacred ; their widows and daughters, as rich heirs, or beautiful concubines, were embraced by the licentious soldiers ; and avarice itself was almost satiated with the treasures of gold and silver, the accumulated fruits of conquest or economy in a long period of prosperity and peace. In this frantic search, the troops, even of Belisarius, forgot their caution and respect. Intoxicated with lust and rapine, they explored, in small parties, or alone, the adjacent fields, the woods, the rocks, and the caverns, that might possibly conceal any desirable prize : laden with booty, they deserted their ranks, and wandered without a guide, on the high road to Carthage ; and if the flying enemies had dared to return, very few of the conquerors would have escaped. Deeply sensible of the disgrace and danger, Belisarius passed an apprehensive night on the field of victory : at the dawn of day, he planted his standard on a hill, recalled his guards and veterans, and gradually restored the modesty and obedience of the camp. It was equally the concern of the Roman general to subdue the hostile, and to save the prostrate, barbarian ; and the suppliant Vandals, who could be found only in churches, were protected by his authority ; disarmed, and separately confined, that they might neither disturb the public peace, nor become the victims of popular revenge. After despatching a light detachment to tread the footsteps of Gelimer, he advanced, with his whole army, about ten days' march, as far as Hippo Regius which no longer possessed the relics of St. Augustin.[22] The season, and the certain intelligence that the Vandal had fled to an inaccessible country of the Moors, determined Belisarius to relinquish the vain pursuit, and to fix his winter quarters at Carthage. From thence he despatched his principal lieutenant, to inform the emperor, that in the space of three months he had achieved the conquest of Africa.

Belisarius spoke the language of truth. The surviving Vandals yielded, without resistance, their arms and their freedom : the neighborhood of Carthage submitted to his presence ; and the more distant provinces were successively subdued by the report of his victory. Tripoli was confirmed in her voluntary allegiance ; Sardinia and Corsica surrendered to an officer, who carried, instead of a sword, the head of the Valiant Zano ; and the Isles of Majorca, Minorca, and Yvica, consented to remain an humble appendage of the African kingdom. Cæsarea, a royal city, which in looser geography may be confounded with the modern Algiers, was situate thirty days' march to the westward of Carthage : by land, the road was infested by the Moors ; but the sea was open, and the Romans were now masters of the sea. An active and discreet tribune sailed as far as the Straits, where he occupied Septem or Ceuta,[23] which rises opposite to Gibraltar on the African coast : that remote place was afterwards adorned and fortified by Justinian ; and he seems to have indulged the vain ambition of extending his empire to the columns of Hercules. He received the messengers of victory at the time when he was preparing to publish the Pandects of the Roman law ; and the devout or jealous emperor celebrated the divine goodness, and confessed, in silence, the merit of his successful general.[24] Impatient to abolish the temporal and spiritual tyranny of the Vandals, he proceeded, without delay, to the full establishment of the Catholic church. Her jurisdiction, wealth, and immunities, perhaps the most essential part of episcopal religion, were restored and amplified with a liberal hand ; the Arian worship was suppressed ; the Donatist meetings were proscribed ;[25] and the synod of Carthage, by the voice of two hundred and seventeen bishops,[26] applauded the just measure of pious retaliation. On such an occasion, it may not be presumed, that many orthodox prelates were absent ; but the comparative smallness of their number, which in ancient councils had been twice or even thrice multiplied, most clearly indicates the decay both of the church and state. While Justinian approved himself the defender of the faith, he entertained an ambitious hope, that his victorious lieutenant would speedily enlarge the narrow limits of his dominion to the space which they occupied before the invasion of the Moors and Vandals ; and Belisarius was instructed to establish five dukes or commanders in the convenient stations of Tripoli, Leptis, Cirta, Cæsarea, and Sardinia, and to compute the military force of *palatines* or *borderers* that might be sufficient for the defence of Africa. The kingdom of the Vandals was not unworthy of the presence of a Prætorian præfect ; and four consulars, three presidents, were appointed to administer the seven provinces under his civil jurisdiction. The number of their subordinate officers, clerks, messengers, or assistants, was minutely expressed ; three hundred and ninety-six for the præfect himself, fifty for each of his vicegerents ; and the rigid definition of their fees and salaries, was more effectual to confirm the right, than to prevent the abuse. These magistrates might be oppressive, but they were not idle ; and the subtile questions of justice and revenue were infinitely propagated under the new government, which professed to revive the freedom and equity of the Roman republic. The conqueror was solicitous to extract a prompt and plentiful supply from his African subjects ; and he allowed them to claim, even in the third degree, and from the collateral line, the houses and lands of which their families had been unjustly despoiled by the Vandals. After the departure of Belisarius, who acted by a high and special commission, no ordinary provision were made for a master-general of the forces : but the office of Prætorian præfect was intrusted to a soldier ; the civil and military powers was united, according to the practice of Justinian, in the chief governor ; and the representative of the emperor in Africa, as well as in Italy, was soon distinguished by the appellation of Exarch.[27]

Yet the conquest of Africa was imperfect till her former sovereign was delivered, either alive or dead, into the hands of the Romans. Doubtful of the event, Gelimer had given secret orders that a part of his treasure should be transported to Spain, where he hoped to find a secure refuge at the court of the king of the Visigoths. But these intentions were disappointed by accident, treachery, and the indefatigable pursuit of his enemies, who intercepted his flight from the sea-shore, and chased the unfortunate monarch, with some faithful followers, to the inaccessible mountain of Papua,[28] in the inland country of Numidia. He was immediately besieged by Pharas, an officer whose truth and sobriety were the more applauded, as such qualities could seldom be found among the Heruli, the most corrupt of the barbarian tribes. To his vigilance Belisarius had intrusted this important charge ; and, after a bold attempt to scale the mountain, in which he lost a hundred and ten soldiers, Pharas expected, during a winter siege, the operation of distress and famine on the mind of the Vandal king. From the softest habits of pleasure, from the unbounded command of industry and wealth, he was reduced to share the poverty of the Moors,[29] supportable only to themselves by their ignorance of a happier condition. In their rude hovels, of mud and hurdles, which confined the smoke and excluded the light, they promiscuously slept on the ground, perhaps on a sheep-skin, with their wives, their children, and their cattle. Sordid and scanty were their garments; the use of bread and wine was unknown; and their oaten or barley cakes, imperfectly baked in the ashes, were devoured, almost in a crude state, by the hungry savages. The health of Gelimer must have sunk under these strange and unwonted hardships, from whatsoever cause they had been endured; but his actual misery was imbittered by the recollection of past greatness, the daily insolence of his protectors, and the just apprehension, that the light and venal Moors might be tempted to betray the rights of hospitality. The knowledge of his situation dictated the humane and friendly epistle of Pharas. "Like yourself," said the chief of the Heruli, "I am an illiterate barbarian, but I speak the language of plain sense and an honest heart. Why will you persist in hopeless obstinacy? Why will you ruin yourself, your family, and nation? The love of freedom and abhorrence of slavery? Alas! my dearest Gelimer, are you not already the worst of slaves, the slave of the vile nation of the Moors? Would it not be preferable to sustain at Constantinople a life of poverty and servitude, rather than to reign the undoubted monarch of the mountain of Papua? Do you think it a disgrace to be the subject of Justinian? Belisarius is his subject; and we ourselves, whose birth is not inferior to your own, are not ashamed of our obedience to the Roman emperor. That generous prince will grant you a rich inheritance of lands, a place in the senate, and the dignity of patrician: such are his gracious intentions, and you may depend with full assurance on the word of Belisarius. So long as Heaven has condemned us to suffer, patience is a virtue; but if we reject the proffered deliverance, it degenerates into blind and stupid despair." "I am not insensible," replied the king of the Vandals, "how kind and rational is your advice. But I cannot persuade myself to become the slave of an unjust enemy, who has deserved my implacable hatred. _Him_ I had never injured either by word or deed: yet he has sent against me, I know not from whence, a certain Belisarius, who has cast me headlong from the throne into this abyss of misery. Justinian is a man; he is a prince; does he not dread for himself a similar reverse of fortune? I can write no more: my grief oppresses me. Send me, I beseech you, my dear Pharas, send me, a lyre,[30] a sponge, and a loaf of bread." From the Vandal messenger, Pharas was informed of the motives of this singular request. It was long since the king of Africa had tasted bread ; a defluxion had fallen on his eyes, the effect of fatigue or incessant weeping ; and he wished to solace the melancholy hours by singing to the lyre the sad story of his own misfortunes. The humanity of Pharas was moved ; he sent the three extraordinary gifts ; but even his humanity prompted him to redouble the vigilance of his guard, that he might sooner compel his prisoner to embrace a resolution advantageous to the Romans, but salutary to himself. The obstinacy of Gelimer at length yielded to reason and necessity ; the solemn assurances of safety and honorable treatment were ratified in the emperor's name, by the ambassador of Belisarius ; and the king of the Vandals descended from the mountain. The first public interview was in one of the suburbs of Carthage ; and when the royal captive accosted his conqueror, he burst into a fit of laughter. The crowd might naturally believe, that extreme grief had deprived Gelimer of his senses ; but in this mournful state unseasonable mirth insinuated to more intelligent observers, that the vain and transitory scenes of human greatness are unworthy of a serious thought.[31]

Their contempt was soon justified by a new example of a vulgar truth ; that flattery adheres to power, and envy to superior merit. The chiefs of the Roman army presumed to think themselves the rivals of a hero. Their private despatches maliciously affirmed, that the conqueror of Africa, strong in his reputation and the public love, conspired to seat himself on the throne of the Vandals. Justinian listened with too patient an ear ; and his silence was the result of jealousy rather than of confidence. An honorable alternative, of remaining in the province, or of returning to the capital, was indeed submitted to the discretion of Belisarius ; but he wisely concluded from intercepted letters and the knowledge of his sovereign's temper, that he must either resign his head, erect his standard, or confound his enemies by his presence and submission. Innocence and courage decided his choice ; his guards, captives, and treasures, were diligently embarked ; and so prosperous was the navigation, that his arrival at Constantinople preceded any certain account of his departure from the port of Carthage. Such unsuspecting loyalty removed the apprehensions of Justinian ; envy was silenced and inflamed by the public gratitude ; and the third Africanus obtained the honors of a triumph, a ceremony which the city of Constantine had never seen, and which ancient Rome, since the reign of Tiberius, had reserved for the *auspicious* arms of the Cæsars.[32] From the palace of Belisarius, the procession was conducted through the principal streets to the hippodrome ; and this memorable day seemed to avenge the injuries of Genseric, and to expiate the shame of the Romans. The wealth of nations was displayed, the trophies of martial or effeminate luxury ; rich armor, golden thrones, and the chariots of state which had been used by the Vandal queen ; the massy furniture of the royal banquet, the splendor of precious stones, the elegant forms of statues and vases, the more substantial treasure of gold, and the holy vessels of the Jewish temple, which after their long peregrination were respectfully deposited in the Christian church of Jerusalem. A long train of the noblest Vandals reluctantly exposed their lofty stature and manly countenance. Gelimer slowly advanced : he was clad in a purple robe, and still maintained the majesty of a king. Not a tear escaped from his eyes, not a sigh was heard ; but his pride or piety derived some secret consolation from the words of Solomon,[33] which he repeatedly pronounced, VANITY ! VANITY ! ALL IS VANITY ! Instead of ascending a triumphal car drawn by four horses or elephants, the modest conqueror marched on foot at the head of his brave companions ; his prudence might decline an honor too conspicuous for a subject ; and his magnanimity might justly disdain what had been so often sullied by the vilest of tyrants. The glorious procession entered the gate of the hippodrome ; was saluted by the acclamations of the senate and people ; and halted before the throne where Justinian and Theodora were seated to receive the homage of the captive monarch and the victorious hero. They both performed the customary adoration ; and falling prostrate on the ground, respectfully touched the footstool of a prince who had not unsheathed his sword, and of a prostitute who had danced on the theatre : some gentle violence was used to bend the stubborn spirit of the grandson of Genseric ; and however trained to servitude, the genius of Belisarius must have secretly rebelled. He was immediately declared consul for the ensuing year, and the day of his inauguration resembled the pomp of a second triumph : his curule chair was borne aloft on the shoulders of captive Vandals ; and the spoils of war, gold cups, and rich girdles, were profusely scattered among the populace.

But the purest reward of Belisarius was in the faithful execution of a treaty for which his honor had been pledged to the king of the Vandals. The religious scruples of Gelimer, who adhered to the Arian heresy, were incompatible with the dignity of senator or patrician : but he received from the emperor an ample estate in the province of Galatia, where the abdicated monarch retired, with his family and friends, to a life of peace, of affluence, and perhaps of content.[34] The daughters of Hilderic were entertained with the respectful tenderness due to their age and misfortune ; and Justinian and Theodora accepted the honor of educating and enriching the female descendants of the great Theodosius. The bravest of the Vandal youth were distributed into five squadrons of cavalry, which adopted the name of their benefactor, and supported in the Persian wars the glory of their ancestors. But these rare exceptions, the reward of birth or valor, are insufficient to explain the fate of a nation, whose numbers, before a short and bloodless war, amounted to more than six hundred thousand persons. After the exile of their king and nobles, the servile crowd might purchase their safety by abjuring their character, religion, and language ; and their degenerate posterity would be insensibly mingled with the common herd of African subjects. Yet even in the present age, and in the heart of the Moorish tribes, a curious traveller has discovered the white complexion and long flaxen hair of a northern race ; [35] and it was formerly believed, that the boldest of the Vandals fled beyond the power, or even the knowledge, of the Romans, to enjoy their solitary freedom on the shores of the Atlantic Ocean. [36] Africa had been their empire, it became their prison ; nor could they entertain a hope, or even a wish, of returning to the banks of the Elbe, where their brethren, of a spirit less adventurous, still wandered in their native forests. It was impossible for cowards to surmount the barriers of unknown seas and hostile barbarians ; it was impossible for brave men to expose their nakedness and defeat before the eyes of their countrymen, to describe the kingdoms which they had lost, and to claim a share of the humble inheritance, which, in a happier hour, they had almost unanimously renounced. [37] In the country between the Elbe and the Oder, several populous villages of Lusatia are inhabited by the Vandals : they still preserve their language, their customs, and the purity of their blood ; support, with some impatience, the Saxon or Prussian yoke ; and serve, with secret and voluntary allegiance, the descendant of their ancient kings, who in his garb and present fortune is confounded with the meanest of his vassals. [38] The name and situation of this unhappy people might indicate their descent from one common stock with the conquerors of Africa. But the use of a Sclavonian dialect more clearly represents them as the last remnant of the new colonies, who succeeded to the genuine Vandals, already scattered or destroyed in the age of Procopius. [39]

If Belisarius had been tempted to hesitate in his allegiance, he might have urged, even against the emperor himself, the indispensable duty of saving Africa from an enemy more barbarous than the Vandals. The origin of the Moors is involved in darkness : they were ignorant of the use of letters. [40] Their limits can-

not be precisely defined ; a boundless continent was open to the
Libyan shepherds ; the change of seasons and pastures regulated
their motions ; and their rude huts and slender furniture were
transported with the same ease as their arms, their families, and
their cattle, which consisted of sheep, oxen, and camels.[41] During the vigor of the Roman power, they observed a respectful distance from Carthage and the sea-shore : under the feeble reign of
the Vandals, they invaded the cities of Numidia, occupied the
sea-coast from Tangier to Cæsarea, and pitched their camps, with
impunity, in the fertile province of Byzacium. The formidable
strength and artful conduct of Belisarius secured the neutrality of
the Moorish princes, whose vanity aspired to receive, in the emperor's name, the ensigns of their regal dignity.[42] They were astonished by the rapid event, and trembled in the presence of their
conqueror. But his approaching departure soon relieved the apprehensions of a savage and superstitious people ; the number of
their wives allowed them to disregard the safety of their infant
hostages ; and when the Roman general hoisted sail in the port of
Carthage, he heard the cries, and almost beheld the flames, of the
desolated province. Yet he persisted in his resolution ; and
leaving only a part of his guards to re-enforce the feeble garrisons,
he intrusted the command of Africa to the eunuch Solomon,[43]
who proved himself not unworthy to be the successor of Belisarius. In the first invasion, some detachments, with two officers
of merit, were surprised and intercepted ; but Solomon speedily
assembled his troops, marched from Carthage into the heart of
the country, and in two great battles destroyed sixty thousand of
the barbarians. The Moors depended on their multitude, their
swiftness, and their inaccessible mountains ; and the aspect and
smell of their camels are said to have produced some confusion in
the Roman cavalry.[44] But as soon as they were commanded to
dismount, they derided this contemptible obstacle : as soon as the
columns ascended the hills, the naked and disorderly crowd was
dazzled by glittering arms and regular evolutions ; and the menace of their female prophets was repeatedly fulfilled, that the
Moors should be discomfited by a *beardless* antagonist. The victorious eunuch advanced thirteen days' journey from Carthage, to
besiege Mount Aurasius,[45] the citadel, and at the same time the
garden, of Numidia. That range of hills, a branch of the great
Atlas, contains, within a circumference of one hundred and
twenty miles, a rare variety of soil and climate ; the intermediate
valleys and elevated plains abound with rich pastures, perpetual
streams, and fruits of a delicious taste and uncommon magnitude.
This fair solitude is decorated with the ruins of Lambesa, a Ro-

man city, once the seat of a legion, and the residence of forty thousand inhabitants. The Ionic temple of Æsculapius is encompassed with Moorish huts ; and the cattle now graze in the midst of an amphitheatre, under the shade of Corinthian columns. A sharp perpendicular rock rises above the level of the mountain, where the African princes deposited their wives and treasures ; and a proverb is familiar to the Arabs, that the man may eat fire who dares to attack the craggy cliffs and inhospitable natives of Mount Aurasius. This hardy enterprise was twice attempted by the eunuch Solomon : from the first, he retreated with some disgrace ; and in the second, his patience and provisions were almost exhausted ; and he must again have retired, if he had not yielded to the impetuous courage of his troops, who audaciously scaled, to the astonishment of the Moors, the mountain, the hostile camp, and the summit of the Geminian rock. A citadel was erected to secure this important conquest, and to remind the barbarians of their defeat ; and as Solomon pursued his march to the west, the long-lost province of Mauritanian Sitifi was again annexed to the Roman empire. The Moorish war continued several years after the departure of Belisarius ; but the laurels which he resigned to a faithful lieutenant may be justly ascribed to his own triumph.

The experience of past faults, which may sometimes correct the mature age of an individual, is seldom profitable to the successive generations of mankind. The nations of antiquity, careless of each other's safety, were separately vanquished and enslaved by the Romans. This awful lesson might have instructed the barbarians of the West to oppose with timely counsels and confederate arms, the unbounded ambition of Justinian. Yet the same error was repeated, the same consequences were felt, and the Goths, both of Italy and Spain, insensible of their approaching danger, beheld with indifference, and even with joy, the rapid downfall of the Vandals. After the failure of the royal line, Theudes, a valiant and powerful chief, ascended the throne of Spain, which he had formerly administered in the name of Theodoric and his infant grandson. Under his command, the Visigoths besieged the fortress of Ceuta on the African coast : but while they spent the Sabbath day in peace and devotion, the pious security of their camp was invaded by a sally from the town ; and the king himself, with some difficulty and danger, escaped from the hands of a sacrilegious enemy.[46] It was not long before his pride and resentment were gratified by a suppliant embassy from the unfortunate Gelimer, who implored, in his distress, the aid of the Spanish monarch. But instead of sacrificing these unworthy passions to the dictates of generosity and prudence, Theudes amused the ambassadors till he was secretly informed of the loss of Carthage, and then dismissed them with obscure and contemptuous advice, to seek in their native country a true know edge of the state of the Vandals.[47] The long continuance of the Italian war delayed the punishment of the Visigoths ; and the eyes of Theudes were closed before they tasted the fruits of his mistaken policy. After his death, the sceptre of Spain was disputed by a civil war. The weaker candidate solicited the protection of Justinian, and ambitiously subscribed a treaty of alliance, which deeply wounded the independence and happiness of his country. Several cities, both on the ocean and the Mediterranean, were ceded to the Roman troops, who afterwards refused to evacuate those pledges, as it should seem, either of safety or payment ; and as they were fortified by perpetual supplies from Africa, they maintained their impregnable stations, for the mischievous purpose of inflaming the civil and religious factions of the barbarians. Seventy years elapsed before this painful thorn could be extirpated from the bosom of the monarchy ; and as long as the emperors retained any share of these remote and useless possessions, their vanity might number Spain in the list of their provinces, and the successors of Alaric in the rank of their vassals.[48]

The error of the Goths who reigned in Italy was less excusable than that of their Spanish brethren, and their punishment was still more immediate and terrible. From a motive of private revenge, they enabled their most dangerous enemy to destroy their most valuable ally. A sister of the great Theodoric had been given in marriage to Thrasimond, the African king : [49] on this occasion, the fortress of Lilybæum [50] in Sicily was resigned to the Vandals ; and the princess Amalafrida was attended by a martial train of one thousand nobles and five thousand Gothic soldiers, who signalized their valor in the Moorish wars. Their merit was overrated by themselves, and perhaps neglected by the Vandals ; they viewed the country with envy, and the conquerors with disdain ; but their real or fictitious conspiracy was prevented by a massacre ; the Goths were oppressed, and the captivity of Amalafrida was soon followed by her secret and suspicious death. The eloquent pen of Cassiodorus was employed to reproach the Vandal court with the cruel violation of every social and public duty ; but the vengeance which he threatened in the name of his sovereign might be derided with impunity, as long as Africa was protected by the sea, and the Goths were destitute of a navy. In the blind impotence of grief and indignation, they joyfully saluted the approach of the Romans, entertained the fleet of Belisarius in the ports of Sicily, and were speedily delighted or alarmed by the surprising intelligence, that their revenge was executed beyond the measure of their hopes, or perhaps of their wishes. To their friendship the emperor was indebted for the kingdom of Africa, and the Goths might reasonably think, that they were entitled to resume the possession of a barren rock, so recently separated, as a nuptial gift from the Island of Sicily. They were soon undeceived by the haughty mandate of Belisarius, which excited their tardy and unavailing repentance. "The city and promontory of Lilybæum," said the Roman general, "belonged to the Vandals, and I claim them by the right of conquest. Your submission may deserve the favor of the emperor; your obstinacy will provoke his displeasure, and must kindle a war, that can terminate only in your utter ruin. If you compel us to take up arms, we shall contend, not to regain the possession of a single city, but to deprive you of all the provinces which you unjustly withhold from their lawful sovereign." A nation of two hundred thousand soldiers might have smiled at the vain menace of Justinian and his lieutenant : but a spirit of discord and disaffection prevailed in Italy, and the Goths supported, with reluctance, the indignity of a female reign.[61]

The birth of Amalasontha, the regent and queen of Italy,[52] united the two most illustrious families of the barbarians. Her mother, the sister of Clovis, was descended from the long-haired kings of the *Merovingian* race ;[53] and the regal succession of the *Amali* was illustrated in the eleventh generation, by her father, the great Theodoric, whose merit might have ennobled a plebeian origin. The sex of his daughter excluded her from the Gothic throne ; but his vigilant tenderness for his family and his people discovered the last heir of the royal line, whose ancestors had taken refuge in Spain ; and the fortunate Eutharic was suddenly exalted to the rank of a consul and a prince. He enjoyed only a short time the charms of Amalasontha, and the hopes of the succession ; and his widow, after the death of her husband and father, was left the guardian of her son Athalaric, and the kingdom of Italy. At the age of about twenty-eight years, the endowments of her mind and person had attained their perfect maturity. Her beauty, which, in the apprehension of Theodora herself, might have disputed the conquest of an emperor, was animated by manly sense, activity, and resolution. Education and experience had cultivated her talents ; her philosophic studies were exempt from vanity ; and, though she expressed herself with equal elegance and ease in the Greek, the Latin, and the Gothic tongue, the daughter of Theodoric maintained in her counsels a discreet and impenetrable silence. By a faithful imitation of the virtues, she revived the prosperity, of his reign ; while she strove, with pious care, to expiate the faults, and to obliterate the darker memory of his declining age. The children of Boethius and Symmachus were restored to their paternal inheritance ; her extreme lenity never consented to inflict any corporal or pecuniary penalties on her Roman subjects ; and she generously despised the clamors of the Goths, who, at the end of forty years, still considered the people of Italy as their slaves or their enemies. Her salutary measures were directed by the wisdom, and celebrated by the eloquence, of Cassiodorus ; she solicited and deserved the friendship of the emperor ; and the kingdoms of Europe respected, both in peace and war, the majesty of the Gothic throne. But the future happiness of the queen and of Italy depended on the education of her son ; who was destined, by his birth, to support the different and almost incompatible characters of the chief of a barbarian camp, and the first magistrate of a civilized nation. From the age of ten years,[54] Athalaric was diligently instructed in the arts and sciences, either useful or ornamental for a Roman prince ; and three venerable Goths were chosen to instil the principles of honor and virtue into the mind of their young king. But the pupil who is insensible of the benefits, must abhor the restraints, of education ; and the solicitude of the queen, which affection rendered anxious and severe, offended the untractable nature of her son and his subjects. On a solemn festival, when the Goths were assembled in the palace of Ravenna, the royal youth escaped from his mother's apartment, and, with tears of pride and anger, complained of a blow which his stubborn disobedience had provoked her to inflict. The barbarians resented the indignity which had been offered to their king ; accused the regent of conspiring against his life and crown ; and imperiously demanded, that the grandson of Theodoric should be rescued from the dastardly discipline of women and pedants, and educated, like a valiant Goth, in the society of his equals, and the glorious ignorance of his ancestors. To this rude clamor, importunately urged as the voice of the nation, Amalasontha was compelled to yield her reason, and the dearest wishes of her heart. The king of Italy was abandoned to wine, to women, and to rustic sports ; and the indiscreet contempt of the ungrateful youth betrayed the mischievous designs of his favorites and her enemies. Encompassed with domestic foes, she entered into a secret negotiation with the emperor Justinian ; obtained the assurance of a friendly reception, and had actually deposited at Dyrrachium, in Epirus, a treasure of forty thousand pounds of gold. Happy would it have been for her fame and safety, if she had calmly retired from barbarous faction to the peace and splendor of Constantinople. But the mind of Amalasontha was inflamed by ambition and revenge ; and while her ships lay at anchor in the port, she waited for the success of a crime, which her passions excused or applauded as an act of justice. Three of the most dangerous malcontents had been separately removed, under the pretence of trust and command, to the frontiers of Italy ; they were assassinated by her private emissaries ; and the blood of these noble Goths rendered the queen-mother absolute in the court of Ravenna, and justly odious to a free people. But if she had lamented the disorders of her son, she soon wept his irreparable loss ; and the death of Athalaric, who, at the age of sixteen, was consumed by premature intemperance, left her destitute of any firm support or legal authority. Instead of submitting to the laws of her country, which held as a fundamental maxim, that the succession could never pass from the lance to the distaff, the daughter of Theodoric conceived the impracticable design of sharing with one of her cousins, the regal title, and of reserving in her own hands the substance of supreme power. He received the proposal with profound respect and affected gratitude ; and the eloquent Cassiodorus announced to the senate and the emperor, that Amalasontha and Theodatus had ascended the throne of Italy. His birth (for his mother was the sister of Theodoric) might be considered as an imperfect title ; and the choice of Amalasontha was more strongly directed by her contempt of his avarice and pusillanimity, which had deprived him of the love of the Italians, and the esteem of the barbarians. But Theodatus was exasperated by the contempt which he deserved : her justice had repressed and reproached the oppression which he exercised against his Tuscan neighbors ; and the principal Goths, united by common guilt and resentment, conspired to instigate his slow and timid disposition. The letters of congratulation were scarcely dispatched before the queen of Italy was imprisoned in a small island of the Lake of Bolsena,[55] where, after a short confinement, she was strangled in the bath, by the order, or with the connivance, of the new king, who instructed his turbulent subjects to shed the blood of their sovereigns.

Justinian beheld with joy the dissensions of the Goths ; and the mediation of an ally concealed and promoted the ambitious views of the conqueror. His ambassadors in their public audience, demanded the fortress of Lilybæum, ten barbarian fugitives, and a just compensation for the pillage of a small town on the Illyrian borders ; but they secretly negotiated with Theodatus to betray the province of Tuscany, and tempted Amalasontha to extricate herself from danger and perplexity, by a free surrender of the kingdom of Italy. A false and servile epistle was subscribed, by the reluctant hand of the captive queen : but the confession of the Roman senators, who were sent to Constantinople, revealed the truth of her deplorable situation ; and Justinian, by the voice of a new ambassador, most powerfully interceded for her life and liberty.* Yet the secret instructions of the same minister were adapted to serve the cruel jealousy of Theodora, who dreaded the presence and superior charms of a rival : he prompted, with artful and ambiguous hints, the execution of a crime so useful to the Romans ; [56] received the intelligence of her death with grief and indignation, and denounced, in his master's name, immortal war against the perfidious assassin. In Italy, as well as in Africa, the guilt of a usurper appeared to justify the arms of Justinian ; but the forces which he prepared, were insufficient for the subversion of a mighty kingdom, if their feeble numbers had not been multiplied by the name, the spirit, and the conduct, of a hero. A chosen troop of guards, who served on horseback, and were armed with lances and bucklers, attended the person of Belisarius ; his cavalry was composed of two hundred Huns, three hundred Moors, and four thousand *confederates*, and the infantry consisted only of three thousand Isaurians. Steering the same course as in his former expedition, the Roman consul cast anchor before Catana in Sicily, to survey the strength of the island, and to decide whether he should attempt the conquest, or peaceably pursue his voyage for the African coast. He found a fruitful land and a friendly people. Notwithstanding the decay of agriculture, Sicily still supplied the granaries of Rome : the farmers were graciously exempted from the oppression of military quarters ; and the Goths, who trusted the defence of the island to the inhabitants, had some reason to complain, that their confidence was ungratefully betrayed. Instead of soliciting and expecting the aid of the king of Italy, they yielded to the first summons a cheerful obedience ; and this province, the first fruits of the Punic wars, was again, after a long separation, united to the Roman empire.[57] The Gothic garrison of Palermo, which alone attempted to resist, was reduced, after

---

* Amalasontha was not alive when this new ambassador, Peter of Thessalonica, arrived in Italy : he could not then secretly contribute to her death. "But (says M. de Sainte Croix) it is not beyond probability that Theodora had entered into some criminal intrigue with Gundelina ; for that wife of Theodatus wrote to implore her protection, reminding her of the confidence which she and her husband had always placed in her former promises." See on Amalasontha and the authors of her death, an excellent dissertation of M. de Sainte Croix in the Archives Littéraires, published by M. Vandenbourg, No. 50, t. xvii. p. 216.—G

a short siege, by a singular stratagem. Belisarius introduced his ships into the deepest recess of the harbor; their boats were laboriously hoisted with ropes and pulleys to the top-mast head, and he filled them with archers, who, from that superior station, commanded the ramparts of the city. After this easy, though successful, campaign, the conqueror entered Syracuse in triumph, at the head of his victorious bands, distributing gold medals to the people, on the day which so gloriously terminated the year of the consulship. He passed the winter season in the palace of ancient kings, amidst the ruins of a Grecian colony, which once extended to a circumference of two-and-twenty miles : [58] but in the spring, about the festival of Easter, the prosecution of his designs was interrupted by a dangerous revolt of the African forces. Carthage was saved by the presence of Belisarius, who suddenly landed with a thousand guards.* Two thousand soldiers of doubtful faith returned to the standard of their old commander : and he marched, without hesitation, above fifty miles, to seek an enemy whom he affected to pity and despise. Eight thousand rebels trembled at his approach ; they were routed at the first onset by the dexterity of their master : and this ignoble victory would have restored the peace of Africa, if the conqueror had not been hastily recalled to Sicily, to appease a sedition which was kindled during his absence in his own camp. [59] Disorder and disobedience were the common malady of the times ; the genius to command, and the virtue to obey, resided only in the mind of Belisarius.

Although Theodatus descended from a race of heroes, he was ignorant of the art, and averse to the dangers, of war. Although he had studied the writings of Plato and Tully, philosophy was incapable of purifying his mind from the basest passions, avarice and fear. He had purchased a sceptre by ingratitude and murder : at the first menace of an enemy he degraded his own majesty and that of a nation, which already disdained their unworthy sovereign. Astonished by the recent example of Gelimer, he saw himself dragged in chains through the streets of Constantinople : the terrors which Belisarius inspired were heightened by the eloquence of Peter, the Byzantine ambassador ; and that bold and subtle advocate persuaded him to sign a treaty, too ignominious to become the foundation of a lasting peace. It was stipulated, that in the acclamations of the Roman people, the name of the emperor should be always proclaimed before that of the Gothic king ;

---

* A hundred (there was no room on board for more). Gibbon has again been misled by Cousin's translation. Lord Mahon, p. 157.—M.

and that as often as the statue of Theodatus was erected in brass
or marble, the divine image of Justinian should be placed on its
right hand. Instead of conferring, the king of Italy was reduced
to solicit, the honors of the senate ; and the consent of the emperor was made indispensable before he could execute, against a
priest or senator, the sentence either of death or confiscation.
The feeble monarch resigned the possession of Sicily ; offered as
the annual mark of his dependence, a crown of gold of the weight
of three hundred pounds, and promised to supply, at the requisition of his sovereign, three thousand Gothic auxiliaries, for the
service of the empire. Satisfied with these extraordinary concessions, the successful agent of Justinian hastened his journey to
Constantinople ; but no sooner had he reached the Alban villa,[60]
than he was recalled by the anxiety of Theodatus ; and the dialogue which passed between the king and the ambassador deserves to be represented in its original simplicity. " Are you of
opinion that the emperor will ratify this treaty ? *Perhaps.* If he
refuses, what consequence will ensue ? *War.* Will such a war
be just or reasonable ? *Most assuredly : every one should act according to his character.* What is your meaning ? *You are a philosopher—Justinian is emperor of the Romans : it would ill become the
disciple of Plato to shed the blood of thousands in his private quarrel :
the successor of Augustus should vindicate his rights, and recover by
arms the ancient provinces of his empire.*" This reasoning might
not convince, but it was sufficient to alarm and subdue the weakness of Theodatus ; and he soon descended to his last offer, that
for the poor equivalent of a pension of forty-eight thousand
pounds sterling, he would resign the kingdom of the Goths and
Italians, and spend the remainder of his days in the innocent pleasures of philosophy and agriculture. Both treaties were intrusted
to the hands of the ambassador, on the frail security of an oath not
to produce the second till the first had been positively rejected.
The event may be easily foreseen : Justinian required and accepted the abdication of the Gothic king. His indefatigable
agent returned from Constantinople to Ravenna, with ample instructions ; and a fair epistle, which praised the wisdom and
generosity of the royal philosopher, granted his pension, with the
assurance of such honors as a subject and a Catholic might enjoy ;
and wisely referred the final execution of the treaty to the presence
and authority of Belisarius. But in the interval of suspense, two
Roman generals, who had entered the province of Dalmatia, were
defeated and slain by the Gothic troops. From blind and abject
despair Theodatus capriciously rose to groundless and fatal presumption,[61] and dared to receive, with menace and contempt, the

ambassador of Justinian ; who claimed his promise, solicited the allegiance of his subjects, and boldly asserted the inviolable privilege of his own character. The march of Belisarius dispelled this visionary pride ; and as the first campaign [62] was employed in the reduction of Sicily, the invasion of Italy is applied by Procopius to the second year of the GOTHIC WAR. [63]

After Belisarius had left sufficient garrisons in Palermo and Syracuse, he embarked his troops at Messina, and landed them, without resistance, on the opposite shores of Rhegium. A Gothic prince, who had married the daughter of Theodatus, was stationed with an army to guard the entrance of Italy ; but he imitated, without scruple, the example of a sovereign faithless to his public and private duties. The perfidious Ebermor deserted with his followers to the Roman camp, and was dismissed to enjoy the servile honors of the Byzantine court. [64] From Rhegium to Naples, the fleet and army of Belisarius, almost always in view of each other, advanced near three hundred miles along the sea-coast. The people of Bruttium, Lucania, and Campania, who abhorred the name and religion of the Goths, embraced the specious excuse that their ruined walls were incapable of defence : the soldiers paid a just equivalent for a plentiful market ; and curiosity alone interrupted the peaceful occupations of the husbandman or artificer. Naples, which has swelled to a great and populous capital, long cherished the language and manners of a Grecian colony ; [65] and the choice of Virgil had ennobled this elegant retreat, which attracted the lovers of repose and study, from the noise, the smoke, and the laborious opulence of Rome. [66] As soon as the place was invested by sea and land, Belisarius gave audience to the deputies of the people, who exhorted him to disregard a conquest unworthy of his arms, to seek the Gothic king in a field of battle, and after his victory, to claim, as the sovereign of Rome, the allegiance of the dependent cities. "When I treat with my enemies," replied the Roman chief with a haughty smile, "I am more accustomed to give than to receive counsel ; but I hold in one hand inevitable ruin, and in the other peace and freedom, such as Sicily now enjoys." The impatience of delay urged him to grant the most liberal terms ; his honor secured their performance : but Naples was divided into two factions ; and the Greek democracy was inflamed by their orators, who, with much spirit and some truth, represented to the multitude that the Goths would punish their defection, and that Belisarius himself must esteem their loyalty and valor. Their deliberations, however, were not perfectly free : the city was commanded by eight hundred barbarians, whose wives and children were detained at Ravenna as the pledge of their fidelity ; and even the Jews, who were rich and numerous, resisted, with desperate enthusiasm, the intolerant laws of Justinian. In a much later period, the circumference of Naples [67] measured only two thousand three hundred and sixty-three paces : [68] the fortifications were defended by precipices or the sea ; when the aqueducts were intercepted, a supply of water might be drawn from wells and fountains ; and the stock of provisions was sufficient to consume the patience of the besiegers. At the end of twenty days, that of Belisarius was almost exhausted, and he had reconciled himself to the disgrace of abandoning the siege, that he might march, before the winter season, against Rome and the Gothic king. But his anxiety was relieved by the bold curiosity of an Isaurian, who explored the dry channel of an aqueduct and secretly reported that a passage might be perforated to introduce a file of armed soldiers into the heart of the city. When the work had been silently executed, the humane general risked the discovery of his secret by a last and fruitless admonition of the impending danger. In the darkness of the night, four hundred Romans entered the aqueduct, raised themselves by a rope, which they fastened to an olive-tree, in the house or garden of a solitary matron, sounded their trumpets, surprised the sentinels, and gave admittance to their companions, who on all sides scaled the walls and burst open the gates of the city. Every crime which is punished by social justice was practised as the rights of war ; the Huns were distinguished by cruelty and sacrilege, and Belisarius alone appeared in the streets and churches of Naples to moderate the calamities which he predicted. " The gold and silver," he repeatedly claimed, " are the just rewards of your valor. But spare the inhabitants ; they are Christians, they are suppliants, they are now your fellow-subjects. Restore the children to their parents, the wives to their husbands ; and show them by your generosity of what friends they have obstinately deprived themselves." The city was saved by the virtue and authority of its conqueror ; [69] and when the Neapolitans returned to their houses, they found some consolation in the secret enjoyment of their hidden treasures. The barbarian garrison enlisted in the service of the emperor ; Apulia and Calabria, delivered from the odious presence of the Goths, acknowledged his dominion ; and the tusks of the Calydonian boar, which were still shown at Beneventum, are curiously described by the historian of Belisarius. [70]

The faithful soldiers and citizens of Naples had expected their deliverance from a prince, who remained the inactive and almost indifferent spectator of their ruin. Theodatus secured his person within the walls of Rome, while his cavalry advanced forty miles on the Appian way, and encamped in the Pomptine marshes ; which, by a canal of nineteen miles in length, had been recently drained and converted into excellent pastures.[71] But the principal forces of the Goths were dispersed in Dalmatia, Venetia, and Gaul ; and the feeble mind of their king was confounded by the unsuccessful event of a divination, which seemed to presage the downfall of his empire.[72] The most abject slaves have arraigned the guilt or weakness of an unfortunate master. The character of Theodatus was rigorously scrutinized by a free and idle camp of barbarians, conscious of their privilege and power : he was declared unworthy of his race, his nation, and his throne ; and their general Vitiges, whose valor had been signalized in the Illyrian war, was raised with unanimous applause on the bucklers of his companions. On the first rumor of the abdicated monarch fled from the justice of his country ; but he was pursued by private revenge. A Goth, whom he had injured in his love, overtook Theodatus on the Flaminian way, and, regardless of his unmanly cries, slaughtered him, as he lay prostrate on the ground, like a victim (says the historian) at the foot of the altar. The choice of the people is the best and purest title to reign over them ; yet such is the prejudice of every age, that Vitiges impatiently wished to return to Ravenna, where he might seize, with the reluctant hand of the daughter of Amalasontha, some faint shadow of hereditary right. A national council was immediately held, and the new monarch reconciled the impatient spirit of the barbarians to a measure of disgrace, which the misconduct of his predecessor rendered wise and indispensable. The Goths consented to retreat in the presence of a victorious enemy ; to delay till the next spring the operations of offensive war ; to summon their scattered forces ; to relinquish their distant possessions, and to trust even Rome itself to the faith of its inhabitants. Leuderis, an aged warrior, was left in the capital, with four thousand soldiers ; a feeble garrison, which might have seconded the zeal, though it was incapable of opposing the wishes, of the Romans. But a momentary enthusiasm of religion and patriotism was kindled in their minds. They furiously exclaimed, that the apostolic throne should no longer be profaned by the triumph or toleration of Arianism ; that the tombs of the Cæsars should no longer be trampled by the savages of the North ; and, without reflecting, that Italy must sink into a province of Constantinople, they fondly hailed the restoration of a Roman emperor as a new æra of freedom and prosperity. The deputies of the pope and clergy, of the senate and people, invited the lieutenant of Jus-

tinian to accept their voluntary allegiance, and to enter the city,
whose gates would be thrown open for his reception. As soon as
Belisarius had fortified his new conquests, Naples and Cumæ, he
advanced about twenty miles to the banks of the Vulturnus, contemplated the decayed grandeur of Capua, and halted at the separation of the Latin and Appian ways. The work of the censor,
after the incessant use of nine centuries, still preserved its pri-
mæval beauty, and not a flaw could be discovered in the large
polished stones, of which that solid, though narrow road, was so
firmly compacted.[73] Belisarius, however, preferred the Latin
way, which, at a distance from the sea and the marshes, skirted
in a space of one hundred and twenty miles along the foot of the
mountains. His enemies had disappeared : when he made his
entrance through the Asinarian gate, the garrison departed without molestation along the Flaminian way ; and the city, after
sixty years' servitude, was delivered from the yoke of the barbarians. Leuderis alone, from a motive of pride or discontent,
refused to accompany the fugitives ; and the Gothic chief himself, a trophy of the victory, was sent with the keys of Rome to
the throne of the emperor Justinian.[74]

The first days which coincided with the old Saturnalia, were
devoted to mutual congratulation and the public joy ; and the
Catholics prepared to celebrate, without a rival, the approaching
festival of the nativity of Christ. In the familiar conversation
of a hero, the Romans acquired some notion of the virtues which
history ascribed to their ancestors ; they were edified by the apparent respect of Belisarius for the successor of St. Peter, and his
rigid discipline secured in the midst of war the blessings of tranquillity and justice. They applauded the rapid success of his
arms, which overran the adjacent country, as far as Narni, Perusia, and Spoleto ; but they trembled, the senate, the clergy,
and the unwarlike people, as soon as they understood that he had
resolved, and would speedily be reduced, to sustain a siege
against the powers of the Gothic monarchy. The designs of Vitiges were executed, during the winter season, with diligence and
effect. From their rustic habitations, from their distant garrisons, the Goths assembled at Ravenna for the defence of their
country ; and such were their numbers, that, after an army had
been detached for the relief of Dalmatia, one hundred and fifty
thousand fighting men marched under the royal standard. According to the degrees of rank or merit, the Gothic king distributed arms and horses, rich gifts, and liberal promises ; he moved
along the Flaminian way, declined the useless sieges of Perusia
and Spoleto, respected the impregnable rock of Narni, and ar-

rived within two miles of Rome at the foot of the Milvian bridge. The narrow passage was fortified with a tower, and Belisarius had computed the value of the twenty days which must be lost in the construction of another bridge. But the consternation of the soldiers of the tower, who either fled or deserted, disappointed his hopes, and betrayed his person into the most imminent danger. At the head of one thousand horse, the Roman general sallied from the Flaminian gate to mark the ground of an advantageous position, and to survey the camp of the barbarians; but while he still believed them on the other side of the Tyber, he was suddenly encompassed and assaulted by their numerous squadrons. The fate of Italy depended on his life; and the deserters pointed to the conspicuous horse, a bay,[75] with a white face, which he rode on that memorable day. " Aim at the bay horse," was the universal cry. Every bow was bent, every javelin was directed, against that fatal object, and the command was repeated and obeyed by thousands who were ignorant of its real motive. The bolder barbarians advanced to the more honorable combat of swords and spears; and the praise of an enemy has graced the fall of Visandus, the standard-bearer,[76] who maintained his foremost station till he was pierced with thirteen wounds, perhaps by the hand of Belisarius himself. The Roman general was strong, active, and dexterous; on every side he discharged his weighty and mortal strokes: his faithful guards imitated his valor, and defended his person; and the Goths, after the loss of a thousand men, fled before the arms of a hero. They were rashly pursued to their camp; and the Romans, oppressed by multitudes, made a gradual, and at length a precipitate retreat to the gates of the city: the gates were shut against the fugitives; and the public terror was increased, by the report that Belisarius was slain. His countenance was indeed disfigured by sweat, dust, and blood; his voice was hoarse, his strength was almost exhausted; but his unconquerable spirit still remained; he imparted that spirit to his desponding companions; and their last desperate charge was felt by the flying barbarians, as if a new army, vigorous and entire, had been poured from the city. The Flaminian gate was thrown open to a *real* triumph; but it was not before Belisarius had visited every post, and provided for the public safety, that he could be persuaded, by his wife and friends, to taste the needful refreshments of food and sleep. In the more improved state of the art of war, a general is seldom required, or even permitted, to display the personal prowess of a soldier; and the example of Belisarius may be added to the rare examples of Henry IV., of Pyrrhus, and of Alexander.

After this first and unsuccessful trial of their enemies, the whole army of the Goths passed the Tyber, and formed the siege of the city, which continued above a year, till their final departure. Whatever fancy may conceive, the severe compass of the geographer defines the circumference of Rome within a line of twelve miles and three hundred and forty-five paces; and that circumference, except in the Vatican, has invariably been the same from the triumph of Aurelian to the peaceful but obscure reign of the modern popes.[77] But in the day of her greatness, the space within her walls was crowded with habitations and inhabitants; and the populous suburbs, that stretched along the public roads, were darted like so many rays from one common centre. Adversity swept away these extraneous ornaments, and left naked and desolate a considerable part even of the seven hills. Yet Rome in its present state, could send into the field about thirty thousand males of a military age;[78] and, notwithstanding the want of discipline and exercise, the far greater part, inured to the hardships of poverty, might be capable of bearing arms for the defence of their country and religion. The prudence of Belisarius did not neglect this important resource. His soldiers were relieved by the zeal and diligence of the people, who watched while *they* slept, and labored while *they* reposed: he accepted the voluntary service of the bravest and most indigent of the Roman youth; and the companies of townsmen sometimes represented, in a vacant post, the presence of the troops which had been drawn away to more essential duties. But his just confidence was placed in the veterans who had fought under his banner in the Persian and African wars; and although that gallant band was reduced to five thousand men, he undertook, with such contemptible numbers, to defend a circle of twelve miles, against an army of one hundred and fifty thousand barbarians. In the walls of Rome, which Belisarius constructed or restored, the materials of ancient architecture may be discerned;[79] and the whole fortification was completed, except in a chasm still extant between the Pincian and Flaminian gates, which the prejudices of the Goths and Romans left under the effectual guard of St. Peter the apostle.[80]

The battlements or bastions were shaped in sharp angles; a ditch, broad and deep, protected the foot of the rampart, and the archers on the rampart were assisted by military engines; the *balista*, a powerful cross-bow, which darted short but massy arrows; the *onagri*, or wild asses, which, on the principle of a sling, threw stones and bullets of an enormous size.[81] A chain was drawn across the Tyber; the arches of the aqueducts were made impervious, and the mole or sepulchre of Hadrian[82] was converted, for the first time, to the uses of a citadel. That venerable structure, which contained the ashes of the Antonines, was a circular turret rising from a quadrangular basis : it was covered with the white marble of Paros, and decorated by the statues of gods and heroes ; and the lover of the arts must read with a sigh that the works of Praxiteles or Lysippus were torn from their lofty pedestals, and hurled into the ditch on the heads of the besiegers.[63] To each of his lieutenants Belisarius assigned the defence of a gate, with the wise and peremptory instruction, that, whatever might be the alarm, they should steadily adhere to their respective posts, and trust their general for the safety of Rome. The formidable host of the Goths was insufficient to embrace the ample measure of the city ; of the fourteen gates, seven only were invested from the Praenestine to the Flaminian way ; and Vitiges divided his troops into six camps, each of which was fortified with a ditch and rampart. On the Tuscan side of the river, a seventh encampment was formed in the field or circus of the Vatican, for the important purpose of commanding the Milvian bridge and the course of the Tyber ; but they approached with devotion the adjacent church of St. Peter ; and the threshold of the holy apostles was respected during the siege by a Christian enemy. In the ages of victory, as often as the senate decreed some distant conquest, the consul denounced hostilities, by unbarring, in solemn pomp, the gates of the temple of Janus.[64] Domestic war now rendered the admonition superfluous, and the ceremony was superseded by the establishment of a new religion. But the brazen temple of Janus was left standing in the forum ; of a size sufficient only to contain the statue of the god, five cubits in height, of a human form, but with two faces, directed to the east and west. The double gates were likewise of brass ; and a fruitless effort to turn them on their rusty hinges revealed the scandalous secret, that some Romans were still attached to the superstition of their ancestors.

Eighteen days were employed by the besiegers to provide all the instruments of attack which antiquity had invented. Fascines were prepared to fill the ditches, scaling ladders to ascend the walls. The largest trees of the forest supplied the timbers of four battering-rams : their heads were armed with iron ; they were suspended by ropes, and each of them was worked by the labor of fifty men. The lofty wooden turrets moved on wheels or rollers, and formed a spacious platform of the level of the rampart. On the morning of the nineteenth day a general attack was made from the Praenestine gate to the Vatican : seven Gothic columns, with their military engines, advanced to the assault ; and.

the Romans, who lined the ramparts, listened with doubt and anxiety to the cheerful assurances of their commander. As soon as the enemy approached the ditch, Belisarius himself drew the first arrow ; and such was his strength and dexterity, that he transfixed the foremost of the barbarian leaders.

A shout of applause and victory was re-echoed along the wall. He drew a second arrow, and the stroke was followed with the same success and the same acclamation. The Roman general then gave the word, that the archers should aim at the teams of oxen ; they were instantly covered with mortal wounds ; the towers which they drew remained useless and immovable, and a single moment disconcerted the laborious projects of the king of the Goths. After this disappointment, Vitiges still continued, or feigned to continue, the assault of the Salarian gate, that he might divert the attention of his adversary, while his principal forces more strenuously attacked the Prænestine gate and the sepulchre of Hadrian, at the distance of three miles from each other. Near the former, the double walls of the Vivarium [85] were low or broken ; the fortifications of the latter were feebly guarded : the vigor of the Goths was excited by the hope of victory and spoil ; and if a single post had given way, the Romans, and Rome itself, were irrecoverably lost. This perilous day was the most glorious in the life of Belisarius. Amidst tumult and dismay, the whole plan of the attack and defence was distinctly present to his mind ; he observed the changes of each instant, weighed every possible advantage, transported his person to the scenes of danger, and communicated his spirit in calm and decisive orders. The contest was fiercely maintained from the morning to the evening ; the Goths were repulsed on all sides ; and each Roman might boast that he had vanquished thirty barbarians, if the strange disproportion of numbers were not counterbalanced by the merit of one man. Thirty thousand Goths, according to the confession of their own chiefs, perished in this bloody action ; and the multitude of the wounded was equal to that of the slain. When they advanced to the assault, their close disorder suffered not a javelin to fall without effect ; and as they retired, the populace of the city joined the pursuit, and slaughtered, with impunity, the backs of their flying enemies. Belisarius instantly sallied from the gates ; and while the soldiers chanted his name and victory, the hostile engines of war were reduced to ashes. Such was the loss and consternation of the Goths, that, from this day, the siege of Rome degenerated into a tedious and indolent blockade ; and they were incessantly harassed by the Roman general, who, in frequent skirmishes, destroyed above five thousand of their bravest troops. Their cavalry was unpractised in the use of the bow; their archers served on foot; and this divided force was incapable of contending with their adversaries, whose lances and arrows, at a distance or at hand, were alike formidable. The consummate skill of Belisarius embraced the favorable opportunities; and as he chose the ground and the moment, as he pressed the charge, or sounded the retreat,[56] the squadrons which he detached were seldom unsuccessful. These partial advantages diffused an impatient ardor among the soldiers and people, who began to feel the hardships of a siege, and to disregard the dangers of a general engagement. Each plebeian conceived himself to be a hero, and the infantry, who, since the decay of discipline, were rejected from the line of battle, aspired to the ancient honors of the Roman legion. Belisarius praised the spirit of his troops, condemned their presumption, yielded to their clamors, and prepared the remedies of a defeat, the possibility of which he alone had courage to suspect. In the quarter of the Vatican, the Romans prevailed; and if the irreparable moments had not been wasted in the pillage of the camp, they might have occupied the Milvian bridge, and charged in the rear of the Gothic host. On the other side of the Tyber, Belisarius advanced from the Pincian and Salarian gates. But his army, four thousand soldiers, perhaps, was lost in a spacious plain; they were encompassed and oppressed by fresh multitudes, who continually relieved the broken ranks of the barbarians. The valiant leaders of the infantry were unskilled to conquer; they died: the retreat (a hasty retreat) was covered by the prudence of the general, and the victors started back with affright from the formidable aspect of an armed rampart. The reputation of Belisarius was unsullied by a defeat; and the vain confidence of the Goths was not less serviceable to his designs than the repentance and modesty of the Roman troops.

From the moment that Belisarius had determined to sustain a siege, his assiduous care provided Rome against the danger of famine, more dreadful than the Gothic arms. An extraordinary supply of corn was imported from Sicily: the harvests of Campania and Tuscany were forcibly swept for the use of the city; and the rights of private property were infringed by the strong plea of the public safety. It might easily be foreseen that the enemy would intercept the aqueducts; and the cessation of the water-mills was the first inconvenience, which was speedily removed by mooring large vessels, and fixing mill-stones in the current of the river. The stream was soon embarrassed by the trunks of trees, and polluted with dead bodies; yet so effectual were the precautions of the Roman general, that the waters of the Tyber still continued to give motion to the mills and drink to the inhabitants : the more distant quarters were supplied from domestic wells ; and a besieged city might support, without impatience, the privation of her public baths. A large portion of Rome, from the Prænestine gate to the church of St. Paul, was never invested by the Goths ; their excursions were restrained by the activity of the Moorish troops : the navigation of the Tyber, and the Latin, Appian, and Ostian ways, were left free and unmolested for the introduction of corn and cattle, or the retreat of the inhabitants, who sought a refuge in Campania or Sicily. Anxious to relieve himself from a useless and devouring multitude, Belisarius issued his peremptory orders for the instant departure of the women, the children, and slaves ; required his soldiers to dismiss their male and female attendants, and regulated their allowance, that one moiety should be given in provisions, and the other in money. His foresight was justified by the increase of the public distress, as soon as the Goths had occupied two important posts in the neighborhood of Rome. By the loss of the port, or, as it is now called the city of Porto, he was deprived of the country on the right of the Tyber, and the best communication with the sea ; and he reflected, with grief and anger, that three hundred men, could he have spared such a feeble band, might have defended its impregnable works. Seven miles from the capital, between the Appian and the Latin ways, two principal aqueducts crossing, and again crossing each other, enclosed within their solid and lofty arches a fortified space,[87] where Vitiges established a camp of seven thousand Goths to intercept the convoy of Sicily and Campania. The granaries of Rome were insensibly exhausted, the adjacent country had been wasted with fire and sword ; such scanty supplies as might yet be obtained by hasty excursions, were the reward of valor and the purchase of wealth : the forage of the horses, and the bread of the soldiers, never failed : but in the last months of the siege, the people were exposed to the miseries of scarcity, unwholesome food,[88] and contagious disorders. Belisarius saw and pitied their sufferings ; but he had foreseen, and he watched the decay of their loyalty, and the progress of their discontent. Adversity had awakened the Romans from the dreams of grandeur and freedom, and taught them the humiliating lesson, that it was of small moment to their real happiness, whether the name of their master was derived from the Gothic or the Latin language. The lieutenant of Justinian listened to their just complaints, but he rejected with disdain the idea of flight or capitulation ; repressed their clamorous impatience for battle ; amused them with the prospect of sure and speedy relief ; and secured himself and the city from the effects of their despair or treachery. Twice in each month he changed the station of the officers to whom the custody of the gates was committed ; the various precautions of patrols, watch-words, lights, and music, were repeatedly employed to discover whatever passed on the ramparts ; out-guards were posted beyond the ditch, and the trusty vigilance of dogs supplied the more doubtful fidelity of mankind. A letter was intercepted, which assured the king of the Goths that the Asinarian gate, adjoining to the Lateran church, should be secretly opened to his troops. On the proof or suspicion of treason, several senators were banished, and the pope Sylverius was summoned to attend the representative of his sovereign, at his head-quarters in the Pincian palace.[89] The ecclesiastics, who followed their bishop, were detained in the first or second apartment,[90] and he alone was admitted to the presence of Belisarius. The conqueror of Rome and Carthage was modestly seated at the feet of Antonina, who reclined on a stately couch : the general was silent, but the voice of reproach and menace issued from the mouth of his imperious wife. Accused by credible witnesses, and the evidence of his own subscription, the successor of St. Peter was despoiled of his pontifical ornaments, clad in the mean habit of a monk, and embarked, without delay, for a distant exile in the East.* At the emperor's command, the clergy of Rome proceeded to the choice of a new bishop ; and after a solemn invocation of the Holy Ghost, elected the deacon Vigilius, who had purchased the papal throne by a bribe of two hundred pounds of gold. The profit, and consequently the guilt, of this simony, was imputed to Belisarius : but the hero obeyed the orders of his wife ; Antonina served the passions of the empress ; and Theodora lavished her treasures in the vain hope of obtaining a pontiff hostile or indifferent to the council of Chalcedon.[91]

The epistle of Belisarius to the emperor announced his victory, his danger, and his resolution. "According to your commands, we have entered the dominions of the Goths, and reduced to your obedience Sicily, Campania, and the city of Rome ; but the loss of these conquests will be more disgraceful than their acquisition was glorious. Hitherto we have successfully fought against the multitudes of the barbarians, but their multitudes may finally prevail. Victory is the gift of Providence, but the reputation of kings and generals depends on the success or the failure of their designs. Permit me to speak with freedom : if you wish that we should

---

* Le Beau, as a good Catholic, makes the Pope the victim of a dark intrigue. Lord Mahon (p. 225), with whom I concur, sums up against him.—M.

live, send us subsistence ; if you desire that we should conquer, send us arms, horses, and men. The Romans have received us as friends and deliverers : but in our present distress, *they* will be either betrayed by their confidence, or we shall be oppressed by *their* treachery and hatred. For myself, my life is consecrated to your service : it is yours to reflect whether my death in this situation will contribute to the glory and prosperity of your reign." Perhaps that reign would have been equally prosperous if the peaceful master of the East had abstained from the conquest of Africa and Italy : but as Justinian was ambitious of fame, he made some efforts (they were feeble and languid) to support and rescue his victorious general.   A re-enforcement of sixteen hundred Sclavonians and Huns was led by Martin and Valerian ; and as they reposed during the winter season in the harbors of Greece, the strength of the men and horses was not impaired by the fatigues of a sea-voyage ; and they distinguished their valor in the first sally against the besiegers. About the time of the summer solstice, Euthalius landed at Terracina with large sums of money for the payment of the troops : he cautiously proceeded along the Appian way, and this convoy entered Rome through the gate Capena,[92] while Belisarius, on the other side, diverted the attention of the Goths by a vigorous and successful skirmish.   These seasonable aids, the use and reputation of which were dexterously managed by the Roman general, revived the courage, or at least the hopes, of the soldiers and people. The historian Procopius was despatched with an important commission to collect the troops and provisions which Campania could furnish, or Constantinople had sent ; and the secretary of Belisarius was soon followed by Antonina herself,[93] who boldly traversed the posts of the enemy, and returned with the Oriental succors to the relief of her husband and the besieged city. A fleet of three thousand Isaurians cast anchor in the Bay of Naples, and afterwards at Ostia. About two thousand horse, of whom a part were Thracians, landed at Tarentum, and after the junction of five hundred soldiers of Campania, and a train of wagons laden with wine and flour, they directed their march on the Appian way, from Capua to the neighborhood of Rome. The forces that arrived by land and sea were united at the mouth of the Tyber. Antonina convened a council of war : it was resolved to surmount, with sails and oars, the adverse stream of the river ; and the Goths were apprehensive of disturbing, by any rash hostilities, the negotiation to which Belisarius had craftily listened. They credulously believed that they saw no more than the vanguard of a fleet and army, which already covered the Ionian Sea and the plains of Campania ; and the illusion was supported by the haughty language of the Roman general, when he gave audience to the ambassadors of Vitiges. After a specious discourse to vindicate the justice of his cause, they declared, that for the sake of peace, they were disposed to renounce the possession of Sicily. "The emperor is not less generous," replied his lieutenant, with a disdainful smile, "in return for a gift which you no longer possess : he presents you with an ancient province of the empire : he resigns to the Goths the sovereignty of the British Island." Belisarius rejected with equal firmness and contempt the offer of a tribute ; but he allowed the Gothic ambassadors to seek their fate from the mouth of Justinian himself ; and consented, with seeming reluctance, to a truce of three months, from the winter solstice to the equinox of spring. Prudence might not safely trust either the oaths or hostages of the barbarians, but the conscious superiority of the Roman chief was expressed in the distribution of his troops. As soon as fear or hunger compelled the Goths to evacuate Alba, Porto, and Centumcellæ, their place was instantly supplied ; the garrisons of Narni, Spoleto, and Perusia, were re-enforced, and the seven camps of the besiegers were gradually encompassed with the calamities of a siege. The prayers and pilgrimage of Datius, bishop of Milan, were not without effect ; and he obtained one thousand Thracians and Isaurians, to assist the revolt of Liguria against her Arian tyrant. At the same time, John the Sanguinary,[94] the nephew of Vitalian, was detached with two thousand chosen horse, first to Alba, on the Fucine Lake, and afterwards to the frontiers of Picenum, on the Hadriatic Sea. "In that province," said Belisarius, "the Goths have deposited their families and treasures, without a guard or the suspicion of danger. Doubtless they will violate the truce : let them feel your presence, before they hear of your motions. Spare the Italians ; suffer not any fortified places to remain hostile in your rear ; and faithfully reserve the spoil for an equal and common partition. It would not be reasonable," he added with a laugh, "that whilst we are toiling to the destruction of the drones, our more fortunate brethren should rifle and enjoy the honey."

The whole nation of the Ostrogoths had been assembled for the attack, and was almost entirely consumed in the siege of Rome. If any credit be due to an intelligent spectator, one third at least of their enormous host was destroyed, in frequent and bloody combats under the walls of the city. The bad fame and pernicious qualities of the summer air might already be imputed to the decay of agriculture and population ; and the evils of famine and pestilence were aggravated by their own licentiousness, and the unfriendly disposition of the country. While Vitiges struggled with his fortune, while he hesitated between shame and ruin, his retreat was hastened by domestic alarms. The king of the Goths was informed by trembling messengers, that John the Sanguinary spread the devastations of war from the Apennine to the Hadriatic ; that the rich spoils and innumerable captives of Picenum were lodged in the fortifications of Rimini ; and that this formidable chief had defeated his uncle, insulted his capital, and seduced, by secret correspondence, the fidelity of his wife, the imperious daughter of Amalasontha. Yet, before he retired, Vitiges made a last effort, either to storm or to surprise the city. A secret passage was discovered in one of the aqueducts ; two citizens of the Vatican were tempted by bribes to intoxicate the guards of the Aurelian gate ; an attack was meditated on the walls beyond the Tyber, in a place which was not fortified with towers ; and the barbarians advanced, with torches and scaling-ladders, to the assault of the Pincian gate. But every attempt was defeated by the intrepid vigilance of Belisarius and his band of veterans, who, in the most perilous moments, did not regret the absence of their companions ; and the Goths, alike destitute of hope and subsistence, clamorously urged their departure before the truce should expire, and the Roman cavalry should again be united. One year and nine days after the commencement of the siege, an army, so lately strong and triumphant, burnt their tents, and tumultuously repassed the Milvian bridge. They repassed not with impunity : their thronging multitudes, oppressed in a narrow passage, were driven headlong into the Tyber, by their own fears and the pursuit of the enemy ; and the Roman general, sallying from the Pincian gate, inflicted a severe and disgraceful wound on their retreat. The slow length of a sickly and desponding host was heavily dragged along the Flaminian way ; from whence the barbarians were sometimes compelled to deviate, lest they should encounter the hostile garrisons that guarded the high road to Rimini and Ravenna. Yet so powerful was this flying army, that Vitiges spared ten thousand men for the defence of the cities which he was most solicitous to preserve, and detached his nephew Uraias, with an adequate force, for the chastisement of rebellious Milan. At the head of his principal army, he besieged Rimini, only thirty-three miles distant from the Gothic capital. A feeble rampart, and a shallow ditch, were maintained by the skill and valor of John the Sanguinary, who shared the danger and fatigue of the meanest soldier, and emulated, on a theatre less illustrious, the military virtues of his great commander. The towers and battering-engines of the barbarians were rendered useless ; their attacks were repulsed ; and the tedious blockade, which reduced the garrison to the last extremity of hunger, afforded time for the union and march of the Roman forces. A fleet, which had surprised Ancona, sailed along the coast of the Hadriatic, to the relief of the besieged city. The eunuch Narses landed in Picenum with two thousand Heruli and five thousand of the bravest troops of the East. The rock of the Apennine was forced ; ten thousand veterans moved round the foot of the mountains, under the command of Belisarius himself ; and a new army, whose encampment blazed with innumerable lights, *appeared* to advance along the Flaminian way. Overwhelmed with astonishment and despair, the Goths abandoned the siege of Rimini, their tents, their standards, and their leaders, and Vitiges, who gave or followed the example of flight, never halted till he found a shelter within the walls and morasses of Ravenna.

To these walls, and to some fortresses destitute of any mutual support, the Gothic monarchy was now reduced. The provinces of Italy had embraced the party of the emperor ; and his army, gradually recruited to the number of twenty thousand men, must have achieved an easy and rapid conquest, if their invincible powers had not been weakened by the discord of the Roman chiefs. Before the end of the siege, an act of blood, ambiguous, and indiscreet, sullied the fair fame of Belisarius. Presidius, a loyal Italian, as he fled from Ravenna to Rome, was rudely stopped by Constantine, the military governor of Spoleto, and despoiled, even in a church, of two daggers richly inlaid with gold and precious stones. As soon as the public danger had subsided, Presidius complained of the loss and injury : his complaint was heard, but the order of restitution was disobeyed by the pride and avarice of the offender. Exasperated by the delay, Presidius boldly arrested the general's horse as he passed through the forum ; and, with the spirit of a citizen, demanded the common benefit of the Roman laws. The honor of Belisarius was engaged ; he summoned a council ; claimed the obedience of his subordinate officer ; and was provoked, by an insolent reply, to call hastily for the presence of his guards. Constantine, viewing their entrance as the signal of death, drew his sword, and rushed on the general, who nimbly eluded the stroke, and was protected by his friends ; while the desperate assassin was disarmed, dragged into a neighboring chamber, and executed, or rather murdered, by the guards, at the arbitrary command of Belisarius.[95] In this hasty act of violence, the guilt of Constantine was no longer remembered ; the despair and death of that valiant officer were secretly imputed to the revenge of Antonina ; and each of his colleagues, conscious of the same rapine, was apprehensive of the same fate. The fear of a common enemy suspended the effects of their envy and discontent ; but in the confidence of approaching victory, they instigated a powerful rival to oppose the conqueror of Rome and Africa. From the domestic service of the palace, and the administration of the private revenue, Narses the eunuch was suddenly exalted to the head of an army ; and the spirit of a hero, who afterwards equalled the merit and glory of Belisarius, served only to perplex the operations of the Gothic war. To his prudent counsels, the relief of Rimini was ascribed by the leaders of the discontented faction, who exhorted Narses to assume an independent and separate command. The epistle of Justinian had indeed enjoined his obedience to the general ; but the dangerous exception, " as far as may be advantageous to the public service," reserved some freedom of judgment to the discreet favorite, who had so lately departed from the *sacred* and familiar conversation of his sovereign. In the exercise of this doubtful right, the eunuch perpetually dissented from the opinions of Belisarius ; and, after yielding with reluctance to the siege of Urbino, he deserted his colleague in the night, and marched away to the conquest of the Æmilian province. The fierce and formidable bands of the Heruli were attached to the person of Narses ; [96] ten thousand Romans and confederates were persuaded to march under his banners ; every malcontent embraced the fair opportunity of revenging his private or imaginary wrongs ; and the remaining troops of Belisarius were divided and dispersed from the garrisons of Sicily to the shores of the Hadriatic. His skill and perseverance overcame every obstacle : Urbino was taken, the sieges of Fæsulæ, Orvieto, and Auximum, were undertaken and vigorously prosecuted ; and the eunuch Narses was at length recalled to the domestic cares of the palace. All dissensions were healed, and all opposition was subdued, by the temperate authority of the Roman general, to whom his enemies could not refuse their esteem ; and Belisarius inculcated the salutary lesson, that the forces of the state should compose one body, and be animated by one soul. But in the interval of discord, the Goths were permitted to breathe ; an important season was lost, Milan was destroyed, and the northern provinces of Italy were afflicted by an inundation of the Franks.

When Justinian first meditated the conquest of Italy, he sent ambassadors to the kings of the Franks, and adjured them, by the common ties of alliance and religion, to join in the holy enterprise against the Arians. The Goths, as their wants were more urgent, employed a more effectual mode of persuasion, and vainly strove, by the gift of lands and money, to purchase the friendship, or at least the neutrality, of a light and perfidious nation. [97] But the arms of Belisarius, and the revolt of the Italians, had no sooner shaken the Gothic monarchy, than Theodebert of Austrasia, the most powerful and warlike of the Merovingian kings, was persuaded to succor their distress by an indirect and seasonable aid. Without expecting the consent of their sovereign, ten thousand Burgundians, his recent subjects, descended from the Alps, and joined the troops which Vitiges had sent to chastise the revolt of Milan. After an obstinate siege, the capital of Liguria was reduced by famine ; but no capitulation could be obtained, except for the safe retreat of the Roman garrison. Datius, the orthodox bishop, who had seduced his countrymen to rebellion [98] and ruin, escaped to the luxury and honors of the Byzantine court ; [99] but the clergy, perhaps the Arian clergy, were slaughtered at the foot of their own altars by the defenders of the Catholic faith. Three hundred thousand males were *reported* to be slain ; [100] the female sex, and the more precious spoil, was resigned to the Burgundians ; and the houses, or at least the walls, of Milan, were levelled with the ground. The Goths, in their last moments, were revenged by the destruction of a city, second only to Rome in size and opulence, in the splendor of its buildings, or the number of its inhabitants ; and Belisarius sympathized alone in the fate of his deserted and devoted friends. Encouraged by this successful inroad, Theodebert himself, in the ensuing spring, invaded the plains of Italy with an army of one hundred thousand barbarians. [101] The king, and some chosen followers, were mounted on horseback, and armed with lances ; the infantry, without bows or spears, were satisfied with a shield, a sword, and a double-edged battle-axe, which, in their hands, became a deadly and unerring weapon. Italy trembled at the march of the Franks ; and both the Gothic prince and the Roman general, alike ignorant of their designs, solicited, with hope and terror, the friendship of these dangerous allies. Till he had secured the passage of the Po on the bridge of Pavia, the grandson of Clovis dissembled his intentions, which he at length declared, by assaulting, almost at the same instant, the hostile camps of the Romans and Goths. Instead of uniting their arms, they fled with equal precipitation ; and the fertile, though desolate provinces of Liguria and Æmilia, were abandoned to a licentious host of barbarians, whose rage was not mitigated by any thoughts of settlement or conquest. Among the cities which they ruined, Genoa, not yet constructed of marble, is particularly enumerated ; and the deaths of thousands, according to the regular practice of war, appear to have excited less horror than some idolatrous sacrifices of women and children, which were performed with impunity in the camp of the most Christian king. If it were not a melancholy truth, that the first and most cruel sufferings must be the lot of the innocent and helpless, history might exult in the misery of the conquerors, who, in the midst of riches, were left destitute of bread or wine, reduced to drink the waters of the Po, and to feed on the flesh of distempered cattle. The dysentery swept away one third of their army; and the clamors of his subjects, who were impatient to pass the, Alps disposed Theodebert to listen with respect to the mild exhortations of Belisarius. The memory of this inglorious and destructive warfare was perpetuated on the medals of Gaul, and Justinian, without unsheathing his sword, assumed the title of conqueror of the Franks. The Merovingian prince was offended by the vanity of the emperor; he affected to pity the fallen fortunes of the Goths; and his insidious offer of a fœderal union was fortified by the promise or menace of descending from the Alps at the head of five hundred thousand men. His plans of conquest were boundless, and perhaps chimerical. The king of Austrasia threatened to chastise Justinian; and to march to the gates of Constantinople : [102] he was overthrown and slain [103] by a wild bull, [104] as he hunted in the Belgic or German forests.

As soon as Belisarius was delivered from his foreign and domestic enemies, he seriously applied his forces to the final reduction of Italy. In the siege of Osimo, the general was nearly transpierced with an arrow, if the mortal stroke had not been intercepted by one of his guards, who lost, in that pious office, the use of his hand. The Goths of Osimo,* four thousand warriors, with those of Fæsulæ and the Cottian Alps, were among the last who maintained their independence; and their gallant resistance, which almost tired the patience, deserved the esteem of the conqueror. His prudence refused to subscribe the safe conduct which they asked, to join their brethren of Ravenna; but they saved, by an honorable capitulation, one moiety at least of their wealth, with the free alternative of retiring peaceably to their estates, or enlisting to serve the emperor in his Persian wars. The multitudes which yet adhered to the standard of Vitiges far surpassed the number of the Roman troops; but neither prayers, nor defiance, nor the extreme danger of his most faithful subjects, could tempt the Gothic king beyond the fortifications of Ravenna. These fortifications were, indeed, impregnable to the assaults of art or violence; and when Belisarius invested the capital he was soon convinced that famine only could tame the stubborn spirit of the barbarians. The sea, the land, and the channels of the Po, were

---

* Auximum, p. 122.—M.

guarded by the vigilance of the Roman general ; and his morality extended the rights of war to the practice of poisoning the waters,[105] and secretly firing the granaries[106] of a besieged city.[107] While he pressed the blockade of Ravenna, he was surprised by the arrival of two ambassadors from Constantinople, with a treaty of peace, which Justinian had imprudently signed, without deigning to consult the author of his victory. By this disgraceful and precarious agreement, Italy and the Gothic treasure were divided, and the provinces beyond the Po were left with the regal title to the successor of Theodoric. The ambassadors were eager to accomplish their salutary commission ; the captive Vitiges accepted, with transport, the unexpected offer of a crown ; honor was less prevalent among the Goths, than the want and appetite of food ; and the Roman chiefs, who murmured at the continuance of the war, professed implicit submission to the commands of the emperor. If Belisarius had possessed only the courage of a soldier, the laurel would have been snatched from his hand by timid and envious counsels ; but in this decisive moment, he resolved, with the magnanimity of a statesman, to sustain alone the danger and merit of generous disobedience. Each of his officers gave a written opinion, that the siege of Ravenna was impracticable and hopeless : the general then rejected the treaty of partition, and declared his own resolution of leading Vitiges in chains to the feet of Justinian. The Goths retired with doubt and dismay : this peremptory refusal deprived them of the only signature which they could trust, and filled their minds with a just apprehension, that a sagacious enemy had discovered the full extent of their deplorable state. They compared the fame and fortune of Belisarius with the weakness of their ill-fated king ; and the comparison suggested an extraordinary project, to which Vitiges, with apparent resignation, was compelled to acquiesce. Partition would ruin the strength, exile would disgrace the honor, of the nation ; but they offered their arms, their treasures, and the fortifications of Ravenna, if Belisarius would disclaim the authority of a master, accept the choice of the Goths, and assume, as he had deserved, the kingdom of Italy. If the false lustre of a diadem could have tempted the loyalty of a faithful subject, his prudence must have foreseen the inconstancy of the barbarians, and his rational ambition would prefer the safe and honorable station of a Roman general. Even the patience and seeming satisfaction with which he entertained a proposal of treason, might be susceptible of a malignant interpretation. But the lieutenant of Justinian was conscious of his own rectitude ; he entered into a dark and crooked path, as it might lead to the voluntary submission of the Goths ; and his dexterous policy persuaded them that he was disposed to comply with their wishes, without engaging an oath or a promise for the performance of a treaty which he secretly abhorred. The day of the surrender of Ravenna was stipulated by the Gothic ambassadors : a fleet, laden with provisions, sailed as a welcome guest into the deepest recess of the harbor : the gates were opened to the fancied king of Italy ; and Belisarius, without meeting an enemy, triumphantly marched through the streets of an impregnable city.[108] The Romans were astonished by their success ; the multitudes of tall and robust barbarians were confounded by the image of their own patience ; and the masculine females, spitting in the faces of their sons and husbands, most bitterly reproached them for betraying their dominion and freedom to these pygmies of the south, contemptible in their numbers, diminutive in their stature. Before the Goths could recover from the first surprise, and claim the accomplishment of their doubtful hopes, the victor established his power in Ravenna, beyond the danger of repentance and revolt.

Vitiges, who perhaps had attempted to escape, was honorably guarded in his palace ;[109] the flower of the Gothic youth was selected for the service of the emperor ; the remainder of the people was dismissed to their peaceful habitations in the southern provinces ; and a colony of Italians was invited to replenish the depopulated city. The submission of the capital was imitated in the towns and villages of Italy, which had not been subdued, or even visited, by the Romans ; and the independent Goths, who remained in arms at Pavia and Verona, were ambitious only to become the subjects of Belisarius. But his inflexible loyalty rejected, except as the substitute of Justinian, their oaths of allegiance ; and he was not offended by the reproach of their deputies that he rather chose to be a slave than a king.

After the second victory of Belisarius, envy again whispered, Justinian listened, and the hero was recalled. "The remnant of the Gothic war was no longer worthy of his presence : a gracious sovereign was impatient to reward his services, and to consult his wisdom ; and he alone was capable of defending the East against the innumerable armies of Persia." Belisarius understood the suspicion, accepted the excuse, embarked at Ravenna his spoils and trophies ; and proved, by his ready obedience, that such an abrupt removal from the government of Italy was not less unjust than it might have been indiscreet. The emperor received with honorable courtesy both Vitiges and his more noble consort ; and as the king of the Goths conformed to the Athanasian faith, he obtained, with a rich inheritance of land in Asia, the rank of senator and patrician.[110] Every spectator admired, without peril, the strength and stature of the young barbarians : they adored the majesty of the throne, and promised to shed their blood in the service of their benefactor. Justinian deposited in the Byzantine palace the treasures of the Gothic monarchy. A flattering senate was sometimes admitted to gaze on the magnificent spectacle ; but it was enviously secluded from the public view : and the conqueror of Italy renounced, without a murmur, perhaps without a sigh, the well-earned honors of a second triumph. His glory was indeed exalted above all external pomp ; and the faint and hollow praises of the court were supplied, even in a servile age, by the respect and admiration of his country. Whenever he appeared in the streets and public places of Constantinople, Belisarius attracted and satisfied the eyes of the people. His lofty stature and majestic countenance fulfilled their expectations of a hero ; the meanest of his fellow-citizens were emboldened by his gentle and gracious demeanor ; and the martial train which attended his footsteps left his person more accessible than in a day of battle. Seven thousand horsemen, matchless for beauty and valor, were maintained in the service, and at the private expense, of the general.[111] Their prowess was always conspicuous in single combats, or in the foremost ranks ; and both parties confessed, that in the siege of Rome, the guards of Belisarius had alone vanquished the barbarian host. Their numbers were continually augmented by the bravest and most faithful of the enemy ; and his fortunate captives, the Vandals, the Moors, and the Goths, emulated the attachment of his domestic followers. By the union of liberality and justice, he acquired the love of the soldiers, without alienating the affections of the people. The sick and wounded were relieved with medicines and money ; and still more efficaciously, by the healing visits and smiles of their commander. The loss of a weapon or a horse was instantly repaired, and each deed of valor was rewarded by the rich and honorable gifts of a bracelet or a collar, which were rendered more precious by the judgment of Belisarius. He was endeared to the husbandmen by the peace and plenty which they enjoyed under the shadow of his standard. Instead of being injured, the country was enriched by the march of the Roman armies ; and such was the rigid discipline of their camp, that not an apple was gathered from the tree, not a path could be traced in the fields of corn. Belisarius was chaste and sober. In the license of a military life, none could boast that they had seen him intoxicated with wine : the most beautiful captives of Gothic or Vandal race were offered to his embraces ; but he turned aside from their charms, and the husband of Antonina was never suspected of violating the laws of conjugal fidelity. The spectator and historian of his exploits has observed, that amidst the perils of war, he was daring without rashness, prudent without fear, slow or rapid according to the exigencies of the moment ; that in the deepest distress he was animated by real or apparent hope, but that he was modest and humble in the most prosperous fortune. By these virtues, he equalled or excelled the ancient masters of the military art. Victory, by sea and land, attended his arms. He subdued Africa, Italy, and the adjacent islands ; led away captives the successors of Genseric and Theodoric ; filled Constantinople with the spoils of their palaces ; and in the space of six years recovered half the provinces of the Western empire. In his fame and merit, in wealth and power, he remained without a rival, the first of the Roman subjects ; the voice of envy could only magnify his dangerous importance ; and the emperor might applaud his own discerning spirit, which had discovered and raised the genius of Belisarius.

It was the custom of the Roman triumphs, that a slave should be placed behind the chariot to remind the conqueror of the instability of fortune, and the infirmities of human nature. Procopius, in his Anecdotes, has assumed that servile and ungrateful office. The generous reader may cast away the libel, but the evidence of facts will adhere to his memory ; and he will reluctantly confess, that the fame, and even the virtue, of Belisarius, were polluted by the lust and cruelty of his wife ; and that the hero deserved an appellation which may not drop from the pen of the decent historian. The mother of Antonina [112] was a theatrical prostitute, and both her father and grandfather exercised, at Thessalonica and Constantinople, the vile, though lucrative, profession of charioteers. In the various situations of their fortune she became the companion, the enemy, the servant, and the favorite of the empress Theodora : these loose and ambitious females had been connected by similar pleasures ; they were separated by the jealousy of vice, and at length reconciled by the partnership of guilt. Before her marriage with Belisarius, Antonina had one husband and many lovers : Photius, the son of her former nuptials, was of an age to distinguish himself at the siege of Naples ; and it was not till the autumn of her age and beauty [113] that she indulged a scandalous attachment to a Thracian youth. Theodosius had been educated in the Eunomian heresy ; the African voyage was consecrated by the baptism and auspicious name of the first soldier who embarked ; and the proselyte was adopted into the family of his spiritual parents, [114] Belisarius and Antonina. Before they touched the shores of Africa, this holy kindred degenerated into sensual love : and as Antonina soon overleaped the bounds of modesty and caution, the Roman general was alone ignorant of his own dishonor. During their residence at Carthage, he surprised the two lovers in a subterraneous chamber, solitary, warm, and almost naked. Anger flashed from his eyes. "With the help of this young man," said the unblushing Antonina, "I was secreting our most precious effects from the knowledge of Justinian." The youth resumed his garments, and the pious husband consented to disbelieve the evidence of his own senses. From this pleasing and perhaps voluntary delusion, Belisarius was awakened at Syracuse, by the officious information of Macedonia ; and that female attendant, after requiring an oath for her security, produced two chamberlains, who, like herself, had often beheld the adulteries of Antonina. A hasty flight into Asia saved Theodosius from the justice of an injured husband, who had signified to one of his guards the order of his death ; but the tears of Antonina, and her artful seductions, assured the credulous hero of her innocence : and he stooped, against his faith and judgment, to abandon those imprudent friends, who had presumed to accuse or doubt the chastity of his wife. The revenge of a guilty woman is implacable and bloody : the unfortunate Macedonia, with the two witnesses, were secretly arrested by the minister of her cruelty ; their tongues were cut out, their bodies were hacked into small pieces, and their remains were cast into the Sea of Syracuse. A rash though judicious saying of Constantine, "I would sooner have punished the adulteress than the boy," was deeply remembered by Antonina ; and two years afterwards, when despair had armed that officer against his general, her sanguinary advice decided and hastened his execution. Even the indignation of Photius was not forgiven by his mother ; the exile of her son prepared the recall of her lover ; and Theodosius condescended to accept the pressing and humble invitation of the conqueror of Italy. In the absolute direction of his household, and in the important commissions of peace and war,[115] the favorite youth most rapidly acquired a fortune of four hundred thousand pounds sterling ; and after their return to Constantinople, the passion of Antonina, at least, continued ardent and unabated. But fear, devotion, and lassitude perhaps, inspired Theodosius with more serious thoughts. He dreaded the busy scandal of the capital, and the indiscreet fondness of the wife of Belisarius ; escaped from her embraces, and retiring to Ephesus, shaved his head, and took refuge in the sanctuary of a monastic life. The despair of the new Ariadne could scarcely have been excused by the death of her husband. She wept, she tore her hair, she filled the palace with her cries ; "she had lost the dearest of friends, a tender, a faithful, a laborious friend !'' But her warm entreaties, fortified by the prayers of Belisarius, were insufficient to draw the holy monk from the solitude of Ephesus. It was not till the general moved forward for the Persian war, that Theodosius could be tempted to return to Constantinople ; and the short interval before the departure of Antonina herself was boldly devoted to love and pleasure.

A philosopher may pity and forgive the infirmities of female nature, from which he receives no real injury : but contemptible is the husband who feels, and yet endures, his own infamy in that of his wife. Antonina pursued her son with implacable hatred ; and the gallant Photius [116] was exposed to her secret persecutions in the camp beyond the Tigris. Enraged by his own wrongs, and by the dishonor of his blood, he cast away in his turn the sentiments of nature, and revealed to Belisarius the turpitude of a woman who had violated all the duties of a mother and a wife. From the surprise and indignation of the Roman general, his former credulity appears to have been sincere : he embraced the knees of the son of Antonina, adjured him to remember his obligations rather than his birth, and confirmed at the altar their holy vows of revenge and mutual defence. The dominion of Antonina was impaired by absence ; and when she met her husband, on his return from the Persian confines, Belisarius, in his first and transient emotions, confined her person, and threatened her life. Photius was more resolved to punish, and less prompt to pardon ; he flew to Ephesus ; extorted from a trusty eunuch of his mother the full confession of her guilt ; arrested Theodosius and his treasures in the church of St. John the Apostle, and concealed his captives, whose execution was only delayed, in a secure and sequestered fortress of Cilicia. Such a daring outrage against public justice could not pass with impunity ; and the cause of Antonina was espoused by the empress, whose favor she had de served by the recent services of the disgrace of a præfect, and the exile and murder of a pope. At the end of the campaign, Belisarius was recalled ; he complied, as usual, with the Imperial mandate. His mind was not prepared for rebellion : his obedience, however adverse to the dictates of honor, was consonant to the wishes of his heart ; and when he embraced his wife, at the command, and perhaps in the presence, of the empress, the tender husband was disposed to forgive or to be forgiven. The bounty of Theodora reserved for her companion a more precious favor. `` I have found,'' she said, `` my dearest patrician, a pearl of inestimable value ; it has not yet been viewed by any mortal eye ; but the sight and the possession of this jewel are destined for my friend." * As soon as the curiosity and impatience of Antonina were kindled, the door of a bed-chamber was thrown open, and she beheld her lover, whom the diligence of the eunuchs had discovered in his secret prison. ' Her silent wonder burst into passionate exclamations of gratitude and joy, and she named Theodora her queen, her benefactress, and her savior. The monk of Ephesus was nourished in the palace with luxury and ambition ; but instead of assuming, as he was promised, the command of the Roman armies, Theodosius expired in the first fatigues of an amorous interview.† The grief of Antonina could only be assuaged by the sufferings of her son. A youth of consular rank, and a sickly constitution, was punished, without a trial, like a malefactor and a slave : yet such was the constancy of his mind, that Photius sustained the tortures of the scourge and the rack,‡ without violating the faith which he had sworn to Belisarius. After this fruitless cruelty, the son of Antonina, while his mother feasted with the empress, was buried in her subterraneous prisons, which admitted not the distinction of night and day. He twice escaped to the most venerable sanctuaries of Constantinople, the churches of St. Sophia and of the Virgin : but his tyrants were insensible of religion as of pity ; and the helpless youth, amidst the clamors of the clergy and people, was twice dragged from the altar to the dungeon. His third attempt was more successful. At the end of three years, the prophet Zachariah, or some mortal friend, indicated the means of an escape : he eluded the spies and guards of the empress, reached the holy sepulchre of Jerusalem, embraced the profession of a monk ; and the abbot Photius was employed, after the death of Justinian, to reconcile and regulate the churches of Egypt. The son of Antonina suffered all that an enemy can inflict : her patient husband imposed on himself the more exquisite misery of violating his promise and deserting his friend.

In the succeeding campaign, Belisarius was again sent against

---

* This, and much of the private scandal in the "Anecdota," is liable to serious doubt. Who reported all these private conversations, and how did they reach the ears of Procopius ?—M.

† This is a strange misrepresentation—he died of a dysentery ; nor does it appear that it was *immediately* after this scene. Antonina proposed to raise him to the generalship of the army—ἀλλά τις προτερήσασα δίκη νόσῳ ἁλόντα δυσεντερίας ἐξ ἀνθρώ–ων αὐτὸν ἀφανίζει. Procop. Anecd. p. 14. The sudden change from the abstemious diet of a monk to the luxury of the court is a much more probable cause of his death.—M.

‡ The expression of Procopius does not appear to me to mean this kind of torture : Φώτιον δὲ αἰκισμοῖς τε ἄλλοις ἀνδραποδώδεσι περιβαλοῦσα, καὶ ξάνασα κατά τε τῶν νόμων (leg. ὤμων) καὶ τοῦ νώτου πολλάς. Ibid.—M.

the Persians : he saved the East, but he offended Theodora, and perhaps the emperor himself. The malady of Justinian had countenanced the rumor of his death ; and the Roman general, on the supposition of that probable event, spoke the free language of a citizen and a soldier. His colleague Buzes, who concurred in the same sentiments, lost his rank, his liberty, and his health, by the persecution of the empress : but the disgrace of Belisarius was alleviated by the dignity of his own character, and the influence of his wife, who might wish to humble, but could not desire to ruin, the partner of her fortunes. Even his removal was colored by the assurance, that the sinking state of Italy would be retrieved by the single presence of its conqueror. But no sooner had he returned, alone and defenceless, than a hostile commission was sent to the East, to seize his treasures and criminate his actions ; the guards and veterans, who followed his private banner, were distributed among the chiefs of the army, and even the eunuchs presumed to cast lots for the partition of his martial domestics. When he passed, with a small and sordid retinue through the streets of Constantinople, his forlorn appearance excited the amazement and compassion of the people. Justinian and Theodora received him with cold ingratitude ; the servile crowd, with insolence and contempt ; and in the evening he retired with trembling steps to his deserted palace. An indisposition, feigned or real, had confined Antonina to her apartment ; and she walked disdainfully silent in the adjacent portico, while Belisarius threw himself on his bed, and expected, in an agony of grief and terror, the death which he had so often braved under the walls of Rome. Long after sunset a messenger was announced from the empress : he opened, with anxious curiosity, the letter which contained the sentence of his fate. " You cannot be ignorant how much you have deserved my displeasure. I am not insensible of the services of Antonina. To her merits and intercession I have granted your life, and permit you to retain a part of your treasures, which might be justly forfeited to the state. Let your gratitude, where it is due, be displayed, not in words, but in your future behavior." I know not how to believe or to relate the transports with which the hero is said to have received this ignominious pardon. He fell prostrate before his wife, he kissed the feet of his savior, and he devoutly promised to live the grateful and submissive slave of Antonina. A fine of one hundred and twenty thousand pounds sterling was levied on the fortunes of Belisarius ; and with the office of count, or master of the royal stables, he accepted the conduct of the Italian war. At his departure from Constantinople, his friends, and even the public, were persuaded, that as soon as he regained his freedom, he would renounce his dissimulation, and that his wife, Theodora, and perhaps the emperor himself, would be sacrificed to the just revenge of a virtuous rebel. Their hopes were deceived ; and the unconquerable patience and loyalty of Belisarius appear either *below* or *above* the character of a MAN.[117]

CHAPTER XLII.

STATE OF THE BARBARIC WORLD.—ESTABLISHMENT OF THE LOMBARDS ON THE DANUBE.—TRIBES AND INROADS OF THE SLAVONIANS.—ORIGIN, EMPIRE, AND EMBASSIES OF THE TURKS.—THE FLIGHT OF THE AVARS.—CHOSROES I. OR NUSHIRVAN, KING OF PERSIA.—HIS PROSPEROUS REIGN AND WARS WITH THE ROMANS.—THE COLCHIAN OR LAZIC WAR.—THE ÆTHIOPIANS.

OUR estimate of personal merit is relative to the common faculties of mankind. The aspiring efforts of genius, or virtue, either in active or speculative life, are measured, not so much by their real elevation, as by the height to which they ascend above the level of their age or country ; and the same stature, which in a people of giants would pass unnoticed, must appear conspicuous in a race of pygmies. Leonidas, and his three hundred companions, devoted their lives at Thermopylæ ; but the education of the infant, the boy, and the man, had prepared, and almost insured, this memorable sacrifice ; and each Spartan would approve, rather than admire, an act of duty, of which himself and eight thousand of his fellow-citizens were equally capable.[1] The great Pompey might inscribe on his trophies, that he had defeated in battle two millions of enemies, and reduced fifteen hundred cities from the Lake Mæotis to the Red Sea :[2] but the fortune of Rome flew before his eagles ; the nations were oppressed by their own fears, and the invincible legions which he commanded, had been formed by the habits of conquest and the discipline of ages. In this view, the character of Belisarius may be deservedly placed above the heroes of the ancient republics. His imperfections flowed from the contagion of the times ; his virtues were his own, the free gift of nature or reflection ; he raised himself without a master or a rival ; and so inadequate were the arms committed to his hand, that his sole advantage was derived from the pride and presumption of his adversaries. Under his command, the sub-

jects of Justinian often deserved to be called Romans : but the
unwarlike appellation of Greeks was imposed as a term of reproach by the haughty Goths ; who affected to blush, that they
must dispute the kingdom of Italy with a nation of tragedians,
pantomimes, and pirates.[3] The climate of Asia has indeed been
found less congenial than that of Europe to military spirit : those
populous countries were enervated by luxury, despotism, and superstition ; and the monks were more expensive and more numerous than the soldiers of the East. The regular force of the empire had once amounted to six hundred and forty-five thousand
men : it was reduced, in the time of Justinian, to one hundred
and fifty thousand ; and this number, large as it may seem, was
thinly scattered over the sea and land ; in Spain and Italy, in
Africa and Egypt, on the banks of the Danube, the coast of the
Euxine, and the frontiers of Persia. The citizen was exhausted,
yet the soldier was unpaid ; his poverty was mischievously
soothed by the privilege of rapine and indolence ; and the tardy
payments were detained and intercepted by the fraud of those
agents who usurp, without courage or danger, the emoluments of
war. Public and private distress recruited the armies of the
state ; but in the field, and still more in the presence of the enemy,
their numbers were always defective. The want of national spirit
was supplied by the precarious faith and disorderly service of barbarian mercenaries. Even military honor, which has often survived the loss of virtue and freedom, was almost totally extinct.
The generals, who were multiplied beyond the example of former
times, labored only to prevent the success, or to sully the reputation of their colleagues ; and they had been taught by experience,
that if merit sometimes provoked the jealousy, error, or even
guilt, would obtain the indulgence, of a gracious emperor. In
such an age, the triumphs of Belisarius, and afterwards of Narses,
shine with incomparable lustre ; but they are encompassed with
the darkest shades of disgrace and calamity. While the lieutenant of Justinian subdued the kingdoms of the Goths and Vandals,
the emperor,[5] timid, though ambitious, balanced the forces of the
barbarians, fomented their divisions by flattery and falsehood, and
invited by his patience and liberality the repetition of injuries.[6]
The keys of Carthage, Rome, and Ravenna, were presented to
their conqueror, while Antioch was destroyed by the Persians,
and Justinian trembled for the safety of Constantinople.

Even the Gothic victories of Belisarius were prejudicial to the
state, since they abolished the important barrier of the Upper
Danube, which had been so faithfully guarded by Theodoric
and his daughter. For the defence of Italy, the Goths evacu-

ated Pannonia and Noricum, which they left in a peaceful and flourishing condition : the sovereignty was claimed by the emperor of the Romans ; the actual possession was abandoned to the boldness of the first invader. On the opposite banks of the Danube, the plains of Upper Hungary and the Transylvanian hills were possessed, since the death of Attila, by the tribes of the Gepidæ, who respected the Gothic arms, and despised, not indeed the gold of the Romans, but the secret motive of their annual subsidies. The vacant fortifications of the river were instantly occupied by these barbarians ; their standards were planted on the walls of Sirmium and Belgrade ; and the ironical tone of their apology aggravated this insult on the majesty of the empire. " So extensive, O Cæsar, are your dominions, so numerous are your cities, that you are continually seeking for nations to whom, either in peace or war, you may relinquish these useless possessions. The Gepidæ are your brave and faithful allies ; and if they have anticipated your gifts, they have shown a just confidence in your bounty." Their presumption was excused by the mode of revenge which Justinian embraced. Instead of asserting the rights of a sovereign for the protection of his subjects, the emperor invited a strange people to invade and possess the Roman provinces between the Danube and the Alps ; and the ambition of the Gepidæ was checked by the rising power and fame of the LOMBARDS.[7] This corrupt appellation has been diffused in the thirteenth century by the merchants and bankers, the Italian posterity of these savage warriors : but the original name of *Langobards* is expressive only of the peculiar length and fashion of their beards. I am not disposed either to question or to justify their Scandinavian origin ;[8] nor to pursue the migrations of the Lombards through unknown regions and marvellous adventures. About the time of Augustus and Trajan, a ray of historic light breaks on the darkness of their antiquities, and they are discovered, for the first time, between the Elbe and the Oder. Fierce, beyond the example of the Germans, they delighted to propagate the tremendous belief, that their heads were formed like the heads of dogs, and that they drank the blood of their enemies, whom they vanquished in battle. The smallness of their numbers was recruited by the adoption of their bravest slaves ; and alone, amidst their powerful neighbors, they defended by arms their high-spirited independence. In the tempests of the north, which overwhelmed so many names and nations, this little bark of the Lombards still floated on the surface : they gradually descended towards the south and the Danube ; and, at the end of four hundred years, they again appear with their ancient valor and renown. Their manners were not less ferocious. The assassination of a royal guest was executed in the presence, and by the command, of the king's daughter, who had been provoked by some words of insult, and disappointed by his diminutive stature ; and a tribute, the price of blood, was imposed on the Lombards, by his brother the king of the Heruli. Adversity revived a sense of moderation and justice, and the insolence of conquest was chastised by the signal defeat and irreparable dispersion of the Heruli, who were seated in the southern provinces of Poland.[9] The victories of the Lombards recommended them to the friendship of the emperors ; and at the solicitations of Justinian, they passed the Danube, to reduce, according to their treaty, the cities of Noricum and the fortresses of Pannonia. But the spirit of rapine soon tempted them beyond these ample limits ; they wandered along the coast of the Hadriatic as far as Dyrrachium, and presumed, with familiar rudeness, to enter the towns and houses of their Roman allies, and to seize the captives who had escaped from their audacious hands. These acts of hostility, the sallies, as it might be pretended, of some loose adventurers, were disowned by the nation, and excused by the emperor ; but the arms of the Lombards were more seriously engaged by a contest of thirty years, which was terminated only by the extirpation of the Gepidæ. The hostile nations often pleaded their cause before the throne of Constantinople ; and the crafty Justinian, to whom the barbarians were almost equally odious, pronounced a partial and ambiguous sentence, and dexterously protracted the war by slow and ineffectual succors. Their strength was formidable, since the Lombards, who sent into the field several *myriads* of soldiers, still claimed, as the weaker side, the protection of the Romans. Their spirit was intrepid ; yet such is the uncertainty of courage, that the two armies were suddenly struck with a panic ; they fled from each other, and the rival kings remained with their guards in the midst of an empty plain. A short truce was obtained ; but their mutual resentment again kindled ; and the remembrance of their shame rendered the next encounter more desperate and bloody. Forty thousand of the barbarians perished in the decisive battle, which broke the power of the Gepidæ, transferred the fears and wishes of Justinian, and first displayed the character of Alboin, the youthful prince of the Lombards, and the future conqueror of Italy.[10]

The wild people who dwelt or wandered in the plains of Russia, Lithuania, and Poland, might be reduced, in the age of Justinian, under the two great families of the BULGARIANS [11] and the SCLAVONIANS. According to the Greek writers, the former, who touched the Euxine and the Lake Mæotis, derived from the Huns their name or descent; and it is needless to renew the simple and well-known picture of Tartar manners. They were bold and dexterous archers, who drank the milk, and feasted on the flesh, of their fleet and indefatigable horses; whose flocks and herds followed, or rather guided, the motions of their roving camps; to whose inroads no country was remote or impervious, and who were practised in flight, though incapable of fear. The nation was divided into two powerful and hostile tribes, who pursued each other with fraternal hatred. They eagerly disputed the friendship, or rather the gifts, of the emperor; and the distinction which nature had fixed between the faithful dog and the rapacious wolf was applied by an ambassador who received only verbal instructions from the mouth of his illiterate prince.[12] The Bulgarians, of whatsoever species, were equally attracted by Roman wealth: they assumed a vague dominion over the Sclavonian name, and their rapid marches could only be stopped by the Baltic Sea, or the extreme cold and poverty of the north. But the same race of Sclavonians appears to have maintained, in every age, the possession of the same countries. Their numerous tribes, however distant or adverse, used one common language (it was harsh and irregular), and were known by the resemblance of their form, which deviated from the swarthy Tartar, and approached without attaining the lofty stature and fair complexion of the German. Four thousand six hundred villages [13] were scattered over the provinces of Russia and Poland, and their huts were hastily built of rough timber, in a country deficient both in stone and iron. Erected, or rather concealed, in the depth of forests, on the banks of rivers, or the edge of morasses, we may not, perhaps, without flattery, compare them to the architecture of the beaver; which they resembled in a double issue, to the land and water; for the escape of the savage inhabitant, an animal less cleanly, less diligent, and less social, than that marvellous quadruped. The fertility of the soil, rather than the labor of the natives, supplied the rustic plenty of the Sclavonians. Their sheep and horned cattle were large and numerous, and the fields which they sowed with millet or panic [14] afforded, in the place of bread, a coarse and less nutritive food. The incessant rapine of their neighbors compelled them to bury this treasure in the earth; but on the appearance of a stranger, it was freely imparted by a people, whose unfavorable character is qualified by the epithets of chaste, patient, and hospitable. As their supreme god, they adored an invisible master of the thunder. The rivers and the nymphs obtained their subordinate honors, and the popular worship was expressed in vows and sacrifice. The Sclavonians disdained to obey a despot, a prince, or even a magistrate ; but their experience was too narrow, their passions too headstrong, to compose a system of equal law or general defence. Some voluntary respect was yielded to age and valor ; but each tribe or village existed as a separate republic, and all must be persuaded where none could be compelled. They fought on foot, almost naked, and, except an unwieldy shield, without any defensive armor : their weapons of offence were a bow, a quiver of small poisoned arrows, and a long rope, which they dexterously threw from a distance, and entangled their enemy in a running noose. In the field, the Sclavonian infantry was dangerous by their speed, agility, and hardiness ; they swam, they dived, they remained under water, drawing their breath through a hollow cane ; and a river or lake was often the scene of their unsuspected ambuscade. But these were the achievements of spies or stragglers ; the military art was unknown to the Sclavonians ; their name was obscure, and their conquests were inglorious.[15]

I have marked the faint and general outline of the Sclavonians and Bulgarians, without attempting to define their intermediate boundaries, which were not accurately known or respected by the barbarians themselves. Their importance was measured by their vicinity to the empire ; and the level country of Moldavia and Walachia was occupied by the Antes,[16] a Sclavonian tribe, which swelled the titles of Justinian with an epithet of conquest.[17] Against the Antes he erected the fortifications of the Lower Danube ; and labored to secure the alliance of a people seated in the direct channel of northern inundation, an interval of two hundred miles between the mountains of Transylvania and the Euxine Sea. But the Antes wanted power and inclination to stem the fury of the torrent ; and the light-armed Sclavonians, from a hundred tribes, pursued with almost equal speed the footsteps of the Bulgarian horse. The payment of one piece of gold for each soldier procured a safe and easy retreat through the country of the Gepidæ, who commanded the passage of the Upper Danube.[18] The hopes or fears of the barbarians ; their intestine union or discord ; the accident of a frozen or shallow stream ; the prospect of harvest or vintage ; the prosperity or distress of the Romans ; were the causes which produced the uniform repetition of annual visits,[19] tedious in the narrative, and destructive in the event. The same year, and possibly the same month, in which Ravenna surrendered, was marked by an invasion of the Huns or Bulgarians, so dreadful, that it almost effaced the memory of their past inroads. They spread from the suburbs of Constantinople to the

Ionian Gulf, destroyed thirty-two cities or castles, erased Potidæa, which Athens had built, and Philip had besieged, and repassed the Danube, dragging at their horses' heels one hundred and twenty thousand of the subjects of Justinian. In a subsequent inroad they pierced the wall of the Thracian Chersonesus, extirpated the habitations and the inhabitants, boldly traversed the Hellespont, and returned to their companions, laden with the spoils of Asia. Another party, which seemed a multitude in the eyes of the Romans, penetrated, without opposition, from the Straits of Thermopylæ to the Isthmus of Corinth ; and the last ruin of Greece has appeared an object too minute for the attention of history. The works which the emperor raised for the protection, but at the expense of his subjects, served only to disclose the weakness of some neglected part ; and the walls, which by flattery had been deemed impregnable, were either deserted by the garrison, or scaled by the barbarians. Three thousand Sclavonians, who insolently divided themselves into two bands, discovered the weakness and misery of a triumphant reign. They passed the Danube and the Hebrus, vanquished the Roman generals who dared to oppose their progress, and plundered, with impunity, the cities of Illyricum and Thrace, each of which had arms and numbers to overwhelm their contemptible assailants. Whatever praise the boldness of the Sclavonians may deserve, it is sullied by the wanton and deliberate cruelty which they are accused of exercising on their prisoners. Without distinction of rank, or age, or sex, the captives were impaled or flayed alive, or suspended between four posts, and beaten with clubs till they expired, or enclosed in some spacious building, and left to perish in the flames with the spoil and cattle which might impede the march of these savage victors.[20] Perhaps a more impartial narrative would reduce the number, and qualify the nature, of these horrid acts ; and they might sometimes be excused by the cruel laws of retaliation. In the siege of Topirus,[21] whose obstinate defence had enraged the Sclavonians, they massacred fifteen thousand males ; but they spared the women and children ; the most valuable captives were always reserved for labor or ransom ; the servitude was not rigorous, and the terms of their deliverance were speedy and moderate. But the subject, or the historian of Justinian, exhaled his just indignation in the language of complaint and reproach ; and Procopius has confidently affirmed, that in a reign of thirty-two years, each *annual* inroad of the barbarians consumed two hundred thousand of the inhabitants of the Roman empire. The entire population of Turkish Europe, which nearly corresponds with the provinces of Justinian, would perhaps be incapable of supplying six millions of persons, the result of this incredible estimate.[22]

In the midst of these obscure calamities, Europe felt the shock of a revolution, which first revealed to the world the name and nation of the TURKS.* Like Romulus, the founder † of that martial people was suckled by a she-wolf, who afterwards made him the father of a numerous progeny; and the representation of that animal in the banners of the Turks preserved the memory, or rather suggested the idea, of a fable, which was invented, without any mutual intercourse, by the shepherds of Latium and those of Scythia. At the equal distance of two thousand miles from the Caspian, the Icy, the Chinese, and the Bengal Seas, a ridge of mountains is conspicuous, the centre, and perhaps the summit, of Asia; which, in the language of different nations, has been styled Imaus, and Caf,[23] and Altai, and the Golden Mountains,‡ and the Girdle of the Earth. The sides of the hills were productive of minerals; and the iron forges,[24] for the purpose of war, were exercised by the Turks, the most despised portion of the slaves of the great khan of the Geougen. But their servitude could only last till a leader, bold and eloquent, should arise to persuade his countrymen, that the same arms which they forged for their masters, might become, in their own hands, the instruments of freedom and victory. They sallied from the mountain;[25] a sceptre was the reward of his advice; and the annual ceremony, in which a piece of iron was heated in the fire, and a smith's hammer § was successively handled by the prince and his nobles, recorded for ages the humble profession and rational pride of the Turkish nation. Bertezena,‖ their first leader, signalized their valor and his own in successful combats against the neighboring tribes; but when he presumed to ask in marriage the daughter of the great

---

* It must be remembered that the name of Turks is extended to a whole family of the Asiatic races, and not confined to the Assena, or Turks of the Altai.—M.

† Assena (the wolf) was the name of this chief. Klaproth, Tabl. Hist. de l'Asie, p. 114.—M.

‡ Altai, *i.e.*, Altun Tagh, the Golden Mountain. Von Hammer. Osman Geschichte, vol. i. p. 2.—M.

§ The Mongol Temugin is also, though erroneously, explained by Rubruquis, a smith. Schmidt, p. 376.—M.

‖ There appears the same confusion here. Bertezena (Bertè-Scheno) is claimed as the founder of the Mongol race. The name means the gray (blauliche) wolf. In fact, the same tradition of the origin from a wolf seems common to the Mongols and the Turks. The Mongol Bertè-Scheno, of the very curious Mongol History, published and translated by M. Schmidt, of Petersburg, is brought from Thibet. M. Schmidt considers this tradition of the Thibetane descent of the royal race of the Mongols to be much earlier than their conversion to Lamaism, yet it seems very suspicious. See Klaproth, Tabl. de l'Asie, p. 159. The Turkish Bertezena is called Thou-men by Klaproth, p. 115. In 552, Thou-men took the title of Kha-Khan, and was called Il Khan.—M.

khan, the insolent demand of a slave and a mechanic was contemptuously rejected. The disgrace was expiated by a more noble alliance with a princess of China ; and the decisive battle, which almost extirpated the nation of the Geougen, established in Tartary the new and more powerful empire of the Turks.* They reigned over the north : but they confessed the vanity of conquest, by their faithful attachment to the mountain of their fathers. The royal encampment seldom lost sight of Mount Altai, from whence the River Irtish descends to water the rich pastures of the Calmucks,²⁶ which nourish the largest sheep and oxen in the world. The soil is fruitful, and the climate mild and temperate : the happy region was ignorant of earthquake and pestilence ; the emperor's throne was turned towards the East, and a golden wolf on the top of a spear seemed to guard the entrance of his tent. One of the successors of Bertezena was tempted by the luxury and superstition of China ; but his design of building cities and temples was defeated by the simple wisdom of a barbarian counsellor. " The Turks," he said, " are not equal in number to one hundredth part of the inhabitants of China. If we balance their power, and elude their armies, it is because we wander without any fixed habitations, in the exercise of war and hunting. Are we strong ? we advance and conquer : are we feeble ? we retire and are concealed. Should the Turks confine themselves within the walls of cities, the loss of a battle would be the destruction of their empire. The bonzes preach only patience, humility, and the renunciation of the world. Such, O king ! is not the religion of heroes." They entertained, with less reluctance, the doctrines of Zoroaster ; but the greatest part of the nation acquiesced, without inquiry, in the opinions, or rather in the practice, of their ancestors. The honors of sacrifice were reserved for the supreme deity ; they acknowledged, in rude hymns, their obligations to the air, the fire, the water, and the earth ; and their priests derived some profit from the art of divination. Their unwritten laws were rigorous and impartial : theft was punished by a tenfold restitution ; adultery, treason, and murder, with death ; and no chastisement could be inflicted too severe for the rare and inexpiable guilt of cowardice. As the subject nations marched under the standard of the Turks, their cavalry, both men and horses, were proudly computed by millions ; one of their effective armies consisted of four hundred thousand soldiers, and in less than fifty years they were connected in peace and war with the

---

* Great Bucharia is called Turkistan ; see Hammer, 2. It includes all the vast steppes at the foot of the Altaï. The name is the same with that of the Turan of Persian poetic legend.—M.

Romans, the Persians, and the Chinese. In their northern limits, some vestige may be discovered of the form and situation of Kamptchatka, of a people of hunters and fishermen, whose sledges were drawn by dogs, and whose habitations were buried in the earth. The Turks were ignorant of astronomy ; but the observation taken by some learned Chinese, with a gnomon of eight feet, fixes the royal camp in the latitude of forty-nine degrees, and marks their extreme progress within three, or at least ten degrees of the polar circle.[27] Among their southern conquests the most splendid was that of the Nepthalites, or white Huns, a polite and warlike people, who possessed the commercial cities of Bochara and Samarcand, who had vanquished the Persian monarch, and carried their victorious arms along the banks, and perhaps to the mouth of the Indus. On the side of the West, the Turkish cavalry advanced to the Lake Mæotis. They passed that lake on the ice. The khan who dwelt at the foot of Mount Altai issued his commands for the siege of Bosphorus,[28] a city the voluntary subject of Rome, and whose princes had formerly been the friends of Athens.[29] To the east, the Turks invaded China, as often as the vigor of the government was relaxed : and I am taught to read in the history of the times, that they mowed down their patient enemies like hemp or grass ; and that the mandarins applauded the wisdom of an emperor who repulsed these barbarians with golden lances. This extent of savage empire compelled the Turkish monarch to establish three subordinate princes of his own blood, who soon forgot their gratitude and allegiance. The conquerors were enervated by luxury, which is always fatal except to an industrious people ; the policy of China solicited the vanquished nations to resume their independence ; and the power of the Turks was limited to a period of two hundred years. The revival of their name and dominion in the southern countries of Asia are the events of a later age ; and the dynasties, which succeeded to their native realms, may sleep in oblivion ; since *their* history bears no relation to the decline and fall of the Roman empire.[30]

In the rapid career of conquest, the Turks attacked and subdued the nation of the Ogors or Varchonites * on the banks of the

---

* The Ogors or Varchonites, from Var, a river (obviously connected with the name Avar), must not be confounded with the Uigours, the eastern Turks (v. Hammer, Osmanische Geschichte, vol. i. p. 3), who speak a language the parent of the more modern Turkish dialects. Compare Klaproth, page 121. They are the ancestors of the Usbeck Turks. These Ogors were of the same Finnish race with the Huns ; and the 20,000 families which fled toward the west, after the Turkish invasion, were of the same race with those which remained to the east of the Volga, the true Avars of Theophylact.—M.

River Til, which derived the epithet of Black from its dark water or gloomy forests.[31] The khan of the Ogors was slain with three hundred thousand of his subjects, and their bodies were scattered over the space of four days' journey : their surviving countrymen acknowledged the strength and mercy of the Turks ; and a small portion, about twenty thousand warriors, preferred exile to servitude. They followed the well-known road of the Volga, cherished the error of the nations who confounded them with the AVARS, and spread the terror of that false though famous appellation, which had not, however, saved its lawful proprietors from the yoke of the Turks.[32] After a long and victorious march, the new Avars arrived at the foot of Mount Caucasus, in the country of the Alani[33] and Circassians, where they first heard of the splendor and weakness of the Roman empire. They humbly requested their confederate, the prince of the Alani, to lead them to this source of riches ; and their ambassador, with the permission of the governor of Lazica, was transported by the Euxine Sea to Constantinople. The whole city was poured forth to behold with curiosity and terror the aspect of a strange people : their long hair, which hung in tresses down their backs, was gracefully bound with ribbons, but the rest of their habit appeared to imitate the fashion of the Huns. When they were admitted to the audience of Justinian, Candish, the first of the ambassadors, addressed the Roman emperor in these terms : " You see before you, O mighty prince, the representatives of the strongest and most populous of nations, the invincible, the irresistible Avars. We are willing to devote ourselves to your service : we are able to vanquish and destroy all the enemies who now disturb your repose. But we expect, as the price of our alliance, as the reward of our valor, precious gifts, annual subsidies, and fruitful possessions." At the time of this embassy, Justinian had reigned above thirty, he had lived above seventy-five years : his mind, as well as his body, was feeble and languid ; and the conqueror of Africa and Italy, careless of the permanent interest of his people, aspired only to end his days in the bosom even of inglorious peace. In a studied oration, he imparted to the senate his resolution to dissemble the insult, and to purchase the friendship of the Avars ; and the whole senate, like the mandarins of China, applauded the incomparable wisdom and foresight of their sovereign. The instruments of luxury were immediately prepared to captivate the barbarians ; silken garments, soft and splendid beds, and chains and collars incrusted with gold. The ambassadors, content with such liberal reception, departed from Constantinople, and Valentin, one of the emperor's guards, was sent with a similar character to their camp at the foot of Mount Caucasus. As their destruction or their success must be alike advantageous to the empire, he persuaded them to invade the enemies of Rome : and they were easily tempted, by gifts and promises, to gratify their ruling inclinations. These fugitives, who fled before the Turkish arms, passed the Tanais and Borysthenes, and boldly advanced into the heart of Poland and Germany, violating the law of nations, and abusing the rights of victory. Before ten years had elapsed, their camps were seated on the Danube and the Elbe, many Bulgarian and Sclavonian names were obliterated from the earth, and the remainder of their tribes are found, as tributaries and vassals, under the standard of the Avars. The chagan, the peculiar title of their king, still affected to cultivate the friendship of the emperor ; and Justinian entertained some thoughts of fixing them in Pannonia, to balance the prevailing power of the Lombards. But the virtue or treachery of an Avar betrayed the secret enmity and ambitious designs of their countrymen ; and they loudly complained of the timid, though jealous policy, of detaining their ambassadors, and denying the arms which they had been allowed to purchase in the capital of the empire.[34]

Perhaps the apparent change in the dispositions of the emperors may be ascribed to the embassy which was received from the conquerors of the Avars.[35] The immense distance which eluded their arms could not extinguish their resentment : the Turkish ambassadors pursued the footsteps of the vanquished to the Jaik, the Volga, Mount Caucasus, the Euxine, and Constantinople, and at length appeared before the successor of Constantine, to request that he would not espouse the cause of rebels and fugitives. Even commerce had some share in this remarkable negotiation : and the Sogdoites, who were now the tributaries of the Turks, embraced the fair occasion of opening, by the north of the Caspian, a new road for the importation of Chinese silk into the Roman empire. The Persian, who preferred the navigation of Ceylon, had stopped the caravans of Bochara and Samarcand : their silk was contemptuously burnt : some Turkish ambassadors died in Persia, with a suspicion of poison ; and the great khan permitted his faithful vassal Maniach, the prince of the Sogdoites, to propose, at the Byzantine court, a treaty of alliance against their common enemies. Their splendid apparel and rich presents, the fruit of Oriental luxury, distinguished Maniach and his colleagues from the rude savages of the North : their letters, in the Scythian character and language, announced a people who had attained the rudiments of science :[36] they enumerated the conquests, they offered the friendship and military aid of the Turks; and their sincerity was attested by direful imprecations (if they were guilty of falsehood) against their own head, and the head of Disabul their master. The Greek prince entertained with hospitable regard the ambassadors of a remote and powerful monarch: the sight of silk-worms and looms disappointed the hopes of the Sogdoites; the emperor renounced, or seemed to renounce, the fugitive Avars, but he accepted the alliance of the Turks; and the ratification of the treaty was carried by a Roman minister to the foot of Mount Altai. Under the successors of Justinian, the friendship of the two nations was cultivated by frequent and cordial intercourse; the most favored vassals were permitted to imitate the example of the great khan, and one hundred and six Turks, who, on various occasions, had visited Constantinople, departed at the same time for their native country. The duration and length of the journey from the Byzantine court to Mount Altai are not specified: it might have been difficult to mark a road through the nameless deserts, the mountains, rivers, and morasses of Tartary; but a curious account has been preserved of the reception of the Roman ambassadors at the royal camp. After they had been purified with fire and incense, according to a rite still practised under the sons of Zingis,* they were introduced to the presence of Disabul. In a valley of the Golden Mountain, they found the great khan in his tent, seated in a chair with wheels, to which a horse might be occasionally harnessed. As soon as they had delivered their presents, which were received by the proper officers, they exposed, in a florid oration, the wishes of the Roman emperor, that victory might attend the arms of the Turks, that their reign might be long and prosperous, and that a strict alliance, without envy or deceit, might forever be maintained between the two most powerful nations of the earth. The answer of Disabul corresponded with these friendly professions, and the ambassadors were seated by his side, at a banquet which

---

* This rite is so curious, that I have subjoined the description of it:

When these (the exorcisers, the Shamans) approached Zemarchus, they took all our baggage and placed it in the centre. Then, kindling a fire with branches of frankincense, lowly murmuring certain barbarous words in the Scythian language, beating on a kind of bell (a gong) and a drum, they passed over the baggage the leaves of the frankincense, crackling with the fire, and at the same time themselves becoming frantic, and violently leaping about, seemed to exorcise the evil spirits. Having thus, as they thought, averted all evil, they led Zemarchus himself through the fire. Menander, in Niebuhr's Byzant. Hist. p. 381. Compare Carpini's Travels. The princes of the race of Zingis Khan condescended to receive the ambassadors of the king of France, at the end of the 13th century, without their submitting to this humiliating rite. See Correspondence published by Abel Remusat, Nouv. Mém. de l'Acad. des Inscrip. vol. vii. On the embassy of Zemarchus, compare Klaproth, Tableaux de l'Asie, p. 116.—M.

lasted the greatest part of the day : the tent was surrounded with silk hangings, and a Tartar liquor was served on the table, which possessed at least the intoxicating qualities of wine. The entertainment of the succeeding day was more sumptuous ; the silk hangings of the second tent were embroidered in various figures ; and the royal seat, the cups, and the vases, were of gold. A third pavilion was supported by columns of gilt wood ; a bed of pure and massy gold was raised on four peacocks of the same metal : and before the entrance of the tent, dishes, basins, and statues of solid silver, and admirable art, were ostentatiously piled in wagons, the monuments of valor rather than of industry. When Disabul led his armies against the frontiers of Persia, his Roman allies followed many days the march of the Turkish camp, nor were they dismissed till they had enjoyed their precedency over the envoy of the great king, whose loud and intemperate clamors interrupted the silence of the royal banquet. The power and ambition of Chosroes cemented the union of the Turks and Romans, who touched his dominions on either side : but those distant nations, regardless of each other, consulted the dictates of interest, without recollecting the obligations of oaths and treaties. While the successor of Disabul celebrated his father's obsequies, he was saluted by the ambassadors of the emperor Tiberius, who proposed an invasion of Persia, and sustained, with firmness, the angry and perhaps the just reproaches of that haughty barbarian. "You see my ten fingers," said the great khan, and he applied them to his mouth. "You Romans speak with as many tongues, but they are tongues of deceit and perjury. To me you hold one language, to my subjects another ; and the nations are successively deluded by your perfidious eloquence. You precipitate your allies into war and danger, you enjoy their labors, and you neglect your benefactors. Hasten your return, inform your master that a Turk is incapable of uttering or forgiving falsehood, and that he shall speedily meet the punishment which he deserves. While he solicits my friendship with flattering and hollow words, he is sunk to a confederate of my fugitive Varchonites. If I condescend to march against those contemptible slaves, they will tremble at the sound of our whips ; they will be trampled, like a nest of ants, under the feet of my innumerable cavalry. I am not ignorant of the road which they have followed to invade your empire ; nor can I be deceived by the vain pretence, that Mount Caucasus is the impregnable barrier of the Romans. I know the course of the Niester, the Danube, and the Hebrus ; the most warlike nations have yielded to the arms of the Turks ; and from the rising to the setting sun, the earth is my inheritance." Notwithstanding this menace, a sense of mutual advantage soon renewed the alliance of the Turks and Romans : but the pride of the great khan survived his resentment ; and when he announced an important conquest to his friend the emperor Maurice, he styled himself the master of the seven races, and the lord of the seven climates of the world.[37]

Disputes have often arisen between the sovereigns of Asia for the title of king of the world ; while the contest has proved that it could not belong to either of the competitors. The kingdom of the Turks was bounded by the Oxus or Gihon ; and *Touran* was separated by that great river from the rival monarchy of *Iran*, or Persia, which in a smaller compass contained perhaps a larger measure of power and population. The Persians, who alternately invaded and repulsed the Turks and the Romans, were still ruled by the house of Sassan, which ascended the throne three hundred years before the accession of Justinian. His contemporary, Cabades, or Kobad, had been successful in war against the emperor Anastasius ; but the reign of that prince was distracted by civil and religious troubles. A prisoner in the hands of his subjects, an exile among the enemies of Persia, he recovered his liberty by prostituting the honor of his wife, and regained his kingdom with the dangerous and mercenary aid of the barbarians, who had slain his father. His nobles were suspicious that Kobad never forgave the authors of his expulsion, or even those of his restoration. The people was deluded and inflamed by the fanaticism of Mazdak,[38] who asserted the community of women,[39] and the equality of mankind, whilst he appropriated the richest lands and most beautiful females to the use of his sectaries. The view of these disorders, which had been fomented by his laws and example,[40] imbittered the declining age of the Persian monarch ; and his fears were increased by the consciousness of his design to reverse the natural and customary order of succession, in favor of his third and most favored son, so famous under the names of Chosroes and Nushirvan. To render the youth more illustrious in the eyes of the nations, Kobad was desirous that he should be adopted by the emperor Justin : * the hope of peace inclined the Byzantine court to accept this singular proposal ; and Chosroes might have acquired a specious claim to the inheritance of his

---

* St. Martin questions this adoption : he argues its improbability ; and supposes that Procopius, perverting some popular traditions, or the remembrance of some fruitless negotiations which took place at that time, has mistaken, for a treaty of adoption, some treaty of guaranty or protection for the purpose of insuring the crown, after the death of Kobad, to his favorite son Chosroes, vol. viii. p. 82. Yet the Greek historians seem unanimous as to the proposal : the Persians might be expected to maintain silence on such a subject.—M.

Roman parent. But the future mischief was diverted by the advice of the quæstor Proclus : a difficulty was started, whether the adoption should be performed as a civil or military rite ; [41] the treaty was abruptly dissolved ; and the sense of this indignity sunk deep into the mind of Chosroes, who had already advanced to the Tigris on his road to Constantinople. His father did not long survive the disappointment of his wishes : the testament of their deceased sovereign was read in the assembly of the nobles ; and a powerful faction, prepared for the event, and regardless of the priority of age, exalted Chosroes to the throne of Persia. He filled that throne during a prosperous period of forty-eight years ; [42] and the JUSTICE of Nushirvan is celebrated as the theme of immortal praise by the nations of the East.

But the justice of kings is understood by themselves, and even by their subjects, with an ample indulgence for the gratification of passion and interest. The virtue of Chosroes was that of a conqueror, who, in the measures of peace and war, is excited by ambition, and restrained by prudence ; who confounds the greatness with the happiness of a nation, and calmly devotes the lives of thousands to the fame, or even the amusement, of a single man. In his domestic administration, the just Nushirvan would merit in our feelings the appellation of a tyrant. His two elder brothers had been deprived of their fair expectations of the diadem : their future life, between the supreme rank and the condition of subjects, was anxious to themselves and formidable to their master : fear as well as revenge might tempt them to rebel ; the slightest evidence of a conspiracy satisfied the author of their wrongs ; and the repose of Chosroes was secured by the death of these unhappy princes, with their families and adherents. One guiltless youth was saved and dismissed by the compassion of a veteran general ; and this act of humanity, which was revealed by his son, overbalanced the merit of reducing twelve nations to the obedience of Persia. The zeal and prudence of Mebodes had fixed the diadem on the head of Chosroes himself ; but he delayed to attend the royal summons, till he had performed the duties of a military review ; he was instantly commanded to repair to the iron tripod, which stood before the gate of the palace, [43] where it was death to relieve or approach the victim ; and Mebodes languished several days before his sentence was pronounced, by the inflexible pride and calm ingratitude of the son of Kobad. But the people, more especially in the East, is disposed to forgive, and even to applaud, the cruelty which strikes at the loftiest heads ; at the slaves of ambition, whose voluntary choice has exposed them to live in the smiles, and to perish by the frown, of a capricious monarch. In the execution of the laws which he had no temptation to violate ; in the punishment of crimes which attacked his own dignity as well as the happiness of individuals ; Nushirvan, or Chosroes, deserved the appellation of *just*. His government was firm, rigorous, and impartial. It was the first labor of his reign to abolish the dangerous theory of common or equal possessions : the lands and women which the sectaries of Mazdak had usurped were restored to their lawful owners ; and the temperate * chastisement of the fanatics or impostors confirmed the domestic rights of society. Instead of listening with blind confidence to a favorite minister, he established four viziers over the four great provinces of his empire, Assyria, Media, Persia, and Bactriana. In the choice of judges, præfects, and counsellors, he strove to remove the mask which is always worn in the presence of kings : he wished to substitute the natural order of talents for the accidental distinctions of birth and fortune ; he professed, in specious language, his intention to prefer those men who carried the poor in their bosoms, and to banish corruption from the seat of justice, as dogs were excluded from the temples of the Magi. The code of laws of the first Artaxerxes was revived and published as the rule of the magistrates ; but the assurance of speedy punishment was the best security of their virtue. Their behavior was inspected by a thousand eyes, their words were overheard by a thousand ears, the secret or public agents of the throne ; and the provinces, from the Indian to the Arabian confines, were enlightened by the frequent visits of a sovereign, who affected to emulate his celestial brother in his rapid and salutary career. Education and agriculture he viewed as the two objects most deserving of his care. In every city of Persia, orphans, and the children of the poor, were maintained and instructed at the public expense ; the daughters were given in marriage to the richest citizens of their own rank, and the sons, according to their different talents, were employed in mechanic trades, or promoted to more honorable service. The deserted villages were relieved by his bounty ; to the peasants and farmers who were found incapable of cultivating their lands, he distributed cattle, seed, and the instruments of husbandry ; and the rare and inestimable treasure of fresh water was parsimoniously managed, and skilfully dis-

---

* This is a strange term. Nushirvan employed a stratagem similar to that of Jehu, 2 Kings, x. 18–28, to separate the followers of Mazdak from the rest of his subjects, and with a body of his troops to cut them all in pieces. The Greek writers concur with the Persian in this representation of Nushirvan's *temperate* conduct. Theophanes, p. 146. Mirkhond, p. 362. Eutychius, Ann. vol. ii. p. 179. Abulfeda, in an unedited part, consulted by St. Martin, as well as in a passage formerly cited. Le Beau, vol. viii. p. 38. Malcolm, vol. i. p. 109.—M.

persed over the arid territory of Persia.[44] The prosperity of that kingdom was the effect and evidence of his virtues : his vices are those of Oriental despotism ; but in the long competition between Chosroes and Justinian, the advantage both of merit and fortune is almost always on the side of the barbarian.[45]

To the praise of justice Nushirvan united the reputation of knowledge ; and the seven Greek philosophers, who visited his court, were invited and deceived by the strange assurance, that a disciple of Plato was seated on the Persian throne. Did they expect, that a prince, strenuously exercised in the toils of war and government, should agitate, with dexterity like their own, the abstruse and profound questions which amused the leisure of the schools of Athens ? Could they hope that the precepts of philosophy should direct the life, and control the passions, of a despot, whose infancy had been taught to consider *his* absolute and fluctuating will as the only rule of moral obligation ?[46] The studies of Chosroes were ostentatious and superficial : but his example awakened the curiosity of an ingenious people, and the light of science was diffused over the dominions of Persia.[47] At Gondi Sapor, in the neighborhood of the royal city of Susa, an academy of physic was founded, which insensibly became a liberal school of poetry, philosophy, and rhetoric.[48] The annals of the monarchy[49] were composed ; and while recent and authentic history might afford some useful lessons both to the prince and people, the darkness of the first ages was embellished by the giants, the dragons, and the fabulous heroes of Oriental romance.[50] Every learned or confident stranger was enriched by the bounty, and flattered by the conversation, of the monarch : he nobly rewarded a Greek physician,[51] by the deliverance of three thousand captives ; and the sophists, who contended for his favor, were exasperated by the wealth and insolence of Uranius, their more successful rival. Nushirvan believed, or at least respected, the religion of the Magi ; and some traces of persecution may be discovered in his reign.[52] Yet he allowed himself freely to compare the tenets of the various sects ; and the theological disputes, in which he frequently presided, diminished the authority of the priest, and enlightened the minds of the people. At his command, the most celebrated writers of Greece and India were translated into the Persian language ; a smooth and elegant idiom, recommended by Mahomet to the use of paradise ; though it is branded with the epithets of savage and unmusical, by the ignorance and presumption of Agathias.[53] Yet the Greek historian might reasonably wonder that it should be found possible to execute an entire version of Plato and Aristotle in a foreign dialect, which had not been framed to express the spirit of freedom and the subtilties of philosophic disquisition. And, if the reason of the Stagyrite might be equally dark, or equally intelligible in every tongue, the dramatic art and verbal argumentation of the disciple of Socrates,[54] appear to be indissolubly mingled with the grace and perfection of his Attic style. In the search of universal knowledge, Nushirvan was informed, that the moral and political fables of Pilpay, an ancient Brachman, were preserved with jealous reverence among the treasures of the kings of India. The physician Perozes was secretly despatched to the banks of the Ganges, with instructions to procure, at any price, the communication of this valuable work. His dexterity obtained a transcript, his learned diligence accomplished the translation; and the fables of Pilpay[55] were read and admired in the assembly of Nushirvan and his nobles. The Indian original, and the Persian copy, have long since disappeared; but this venerable monument has been saved by the curiosity of the Arabian caliphs, revived in the modern Persic, the Turkish, the Syriac, the Hebrew, and the Greek idioms, and transfused through successive versions into the modern languages of Europe. In their present form, the peculiar character, the manners and religion of the Hindoos, are completely obliterated; and the intrinsic merit of the fables of Pilpay is far inferior to the concise elegance of Phædrus, and the native graces of La Fontaine. Fifteen moral and political sentences are illustrated in a series of apologues: but the composition is intricate, the narrative prolix, and the precept obvious and barren. Yet the Brachman may assume the merit of *inventing* a pleasing fiction, which adorns the nakedness of truth, and alleviates, perhaps, to a royal ear, the harshness of instruction. With a similar design, to admonish kings that they are strong only in the strength of their subjects, the same Indians invented the game of chess, which was likewise introduced into Persia under the reign of Nushirvan.[56]

The son of Kobad found his kingdom involved in a war with the successor of Constantine; and the anxiety of his domestic situation inclined him to grant the suspension of arms, which Justinian was impatient to purchase. Chosroes saw the Roman ambassadors at his feet. He accepted eleven thousand pounds of gold, as the price of an *endless* or indefinite peace;[57] some mutual exchanges were regulated; the Persian assumed the guard of the gates of Caucasus, and the demolition of Dara was suspended, on condition that it should never be made the residence of the general of the East. This interval of repose had been solicited, and was diligently improved, by the ambition of the emperor: his African conquests were the first fruits of the Persian treaty; and the

avarice of Chosroes was soothed by a large portion of the spoils of
Carthage, which his ambassadors required in a tone of pleasantry,
and under the color of friendship.[58]   But the trophies of Belisarius
disturbed the slumbers of the great king ; and he heard with
astonishment, envy, and fear, that Sicily, Italy, and Rome itself,
had been reduced, in three rapid campaigns, to the obedience of
Justinian.   Unpractised in the art of violating treaties, he secretly
excited his bold and subtle vassal Almondar.   That prince of
the Saracens, who resided at Hira,[59] had not been included in the
general peace, and still waged an obscure war against his rival
Arethas, the chief of the tribe of Gassan, and confederate of the
empire.   The subject of their dispute was an extensive sheep-walk
in the desert to the south of Palmyra.   An immemorial tribute for
the license of pasture appeared to attest the rights of Almondar,
while the Gassanite appealed to the Latin name of strata, a paved
road, as an unquestionable evidence of the sovereignty and labors
of the Romans.[60]   Tne two monarchs supported the cause of their
respective vassals ; and the Persian Arab, without expecting the
event of a slow and doubtful arbitration, enriched his flying camp
with the spoil and captives of Syria.   Instead of repelling the
arms, Justinian attempted to seduce the fidelity of Almondar,
while he called from the extremities of the earth the nations of
Æthiopia and Scythia to invade the dominions of his rival.   But the
aid of such allies was distant and precarious, and the discovery of
this hostile correspondence justified the complaints of the Goths
and Armenians, who implored, almost at the same time, the protection of Chosroes.   The descendants of Arsaces, who were still
numerous in Armenia, had been provoked to assert the last relics
of national freedom and hereditary rank ; and the ambassadors of
Vitiges had secretly traversed the empire to expose the instant,
and almost inevitable, danger of the kingdom of Italy.   Their
representations were uniform, weighty, and effectual.   " We stand
before your throne, the advocates of your interest as well as of our
own.   The ambitious and faithless Justinian aspires to be the sole
master of the world.   Since the endless peace, which betrayed the
common freedom of mankind, that prince, your ally in words, your
enemy in actions, has alike insulted his friends and foes, and
has filled the earth with blood and confusion.   Has he not violated
the privileges of Armenia, the independence of Colchos, and the
wild liberty of the Tzanian mountains ?   Has he not usurped,
with equal avidity, the city of Bosphorus on the frozen Mæotis, and
the vale of palm-trees on the shores of the Red Sea ?   The Moors,
the Vandals, the Goths, have been successively oppressed, and
each nation has calmly remained the spectator of their neighbor's

ruin. Embrace, O king! the favorable moment; the East is left without defence, while the armies of Justinian and his renowned general are detained in the distant regions of the West. If you hesitate and delay, Belisarius and his victorious troops will soon return from the Tyber to the Tigris, and Persia may enjoy the wretched consolation of being the last devoured.'' [61] By such arguments, Chosroes was easily persuaded to imitate the example which he condemned: but the Persian, ambitious of military fame, disdained the inactive warfare of a rival, who issued his sanguinary commands from the secure station of the Byzantine palace.

Whatever might be the provocations of Chosroes, he abused the confidence of treaties; and the just reproaches of dissimulation and falsehood could only be concealed by the lustre of his victories. [62] The Persian army, which had been assembled in the plains of Babylon, prudently declined the strong cities of Mesopotamia, and followed the western bank of the Euphrates, till the small, though populous, town of Dura* presumed to arrest the progress of the great king. The gates of Dura, by treachery and surprise, were burst open; and as soon as Chosroes had stained his cimeter with the blood of the inhabitants, he dismissed the ambassador of Justinian to inform his master in what place he had left the enemy of the Romans. The conqueror still affected the praise of humanity and justice; and as he beheld a noble matron with her infant rudely dragged along the ground, he sighed, he wept, and implored the divine justice to punish the author of these calamities. Yet the herd of twelve thousand captives was ransomed for two hundred pounds of gold; the neighboring bishop of Sergiopolis pledged his faith for the payment: and in the subsequent year the unfeeling avarice of Chosroes exacted the penalty of an obligation which it was generous to contract and impossible to discharge. He advanced into the heart of Syria; but a feeble enemy, who vanished at his approach, disappointed him of the honor of victory; and as he could not hope to establish his dominion, the Persian king displayed in this inroad the mean and rapacious vices of a robber. Hierapolis, Berrhæa or Aleppo, Apamea and Chalcis, were successively besieged: they redeemed their safety by a ransom of gold or silver, proportioned to their respective strength and opulence; and their new master enforced, without observing, the terms of capitulation. Educated in the religion of the Magi, he exercised, without remorse, the lucrative trade of sacrilege; and, after stripping of its gold and gems a piece of the true cross, he generously restored the naked relic to the devotion of the Chris-

---

* It is *Sura* in Procopius. Is it a misprint in Gibbon'?—M.

tians of Apamea. No more than fourteen years had elapsed since Antioch was ruined by an earthquake ; † but the queen of the East, the new Theopolis, had been raised from the ground by the liberality of Justinian ; and the increasing greatness of the buildings and the people already erased the memory of this recent disaster. On one side, the city was defended by the mountain, on the other by the River Orontes ; but the most accessible part was commanded by a superior eminence : the proper remedies were rejected, from the despicable fear of discovering its weakness to the enemy ; and Germanus, the emperor's nephew, refused to trust his person and dignity within the walls of a besieged city. The people of Antioch had inherited the vain and satirical genius of their ancestors : they were elated by a sudden re-enforcement of six thousand soldiers ; they disdained the offers of an easy capitulation ; and their intemperate clamors insulted from the ramparts the majesty of the great king. Under his eye the Persian myriads mounted with scaling-ladders to the assault ; the Roman mercenaries fled through the opposite gate of Daphne ; and the generous assistance of the youth of Antioch served only to aggravate the miseries of their country. As Chosroes, attended by the ambassadors of Justinian, was descending from the mountain, he affected, in a plaintive voice, to deplore the obstinacy and ruin of that unhappy people ; but the slaughter still raged with unrelenting fury ; and the city, at the command of a barbarian, was delivered to the flames. The cathedral of Antioch was indeed preserved by the avarice, not the piety, of the conqueror : a more honorable exemption was granted to the church of St. Julian, and the quarter of the town where the ambassadors resided ; some distant streets were saved by the shifting of the wind, and the walls still subsisted to protect, and soon to betray, their new inhabitants. Fanaticism had defaced the ornaments of Daphne, but Chosroes breathed a purer air amidst her groves and fountains ; and some idolaters in his train might sacrifice with impunity to the nymphs of that elegant retreat. Eighteen miles below Antioch, the River Orontes falls into the Mediterranean. The haughty Persian visited the term of his conquests ; and, after bathing alone in the sea, he offered a solemn sacrifice of thanksgiving to the sun, or rather to the Creator of the sun, whom the Magi adored. If this act of superstition offended the prejudices of the Syrians, they were pleased by the courteous and even eager attention with which he assisted at the games of the circus ; and as Chosroes had heard that the *blue*

---

† Joannes Lydus a'tributes the easy capture of Antioch to the want of fortifications, which had not been restored since the earthquake, l. iii. c. 54, p. 246.—M.

faction was espoused by the emperor, his peremptory command secured the victory of the *green* charioteer. From the discipline of his camp the people derived more solid consolation ; and they interceded in vain for the life of a soldier who had too faithfully copied the rapine of the just Nushirvan. At length, fatigued, though unsatiated, with the spoil of Syria,[*] he slowly moved to the Euphrates, formed a temporary bridge in the neighborhood of Barbalissus, and defined the space of three days for the entire passage of his numerous host. After his return, he founded, at the distance of one day's journey from the palace of Ctesiphon, a new city, which perpetuated the joint names of Chosroes and of Antioch. The Syrian captives recognized the form and situation of their native abodes : baths and a stately circus were constructed for their use ; and a colony of musicians and charioteers revived in Assyria the pleasures of a Greek capital. By the munificence of the royal founder, a liberal allowance was assigned to these fortunate exiles ; and they enjoyed the singular privilege of bestowing freedom on the slaves whom they acknowledged as their kinsmen. Palestine, and the holy wealth of Jerusalem, were the next objects that attracted the ambition, or rather the avarice, of Chosroes. Constantinople, and the palace of the Cæsars, no longer appeared impregnable or remote ; and his aspiring fancy already covered Asia Minor with the troops, and the Black Sea with the natives, of Persia.

These hopes might have been realized, if the conqueror of Italy had not been seasonably recalled to the defence of the East.[63] While Chosroes pursued his ambitious designs on the coast of the Euxine, Belisarius, at the head of an army without pay or discipline, encamped beyond the Euphrates, within six miles of Nisibis. He meditated, by a skilful operation, to draw the Persians from their impregnable citadel, and improving his advantage in the field, either to intercept their retreat, or perhaps to enter the gates with the flying barbarians. He advanced one day's journey on the territories of Persia, reduced the fortress of Sisaurane, and sent the governor, with eight hundred chosen horsemen, to serve the emperor in his Italian wars. He detached Arethas and his Arabs, supported by twelve hundred Romans, to pass the Tigris, and to ravage the harvests of Assyria, a fruitful province, long exempt from the calamities of war. But the plans of Belisarius were disconcerted by the untractable spirit of Arethas, who neither returned to the camp, nor sent any intelligence of his motions.

---

[*] Lydus asserts that he carried away all the statues, pictures, and marbles which adorned the city, l. iii. c. 54, p. 246.—M.

The Roman general was fixed in anxious expectation to the same spot ; the time of action elapsed, the ardent sun of Mesopotamia inflamed with fevers the blood of his European soldiers ; and the stationary troops and officers of Syria affected to tremble for the safety of their defenceless cities.   Yet this diversion had already succeeded in forcing Chosroes to return with loss and precipitation ; and if the skill of Belisarius had been seconded by discipline and valor, his success might have satisfied the sanguine wishes of the public, who required at his hands the conquest of Ctesiphon, and the deliverance of the captives of Antioch.   At the end of the campaign, he was recalled to Constantinople by an ungrateful court, but the dangers of the ensuing spring restored his confidence and command ; and the hero, almost alone, was despatched, with the speed of post-horses, to repel, by his name and presence, the invasion of Syria.   He found the Roman generals, among whom was a nephew of Justinian, imprisoned by their fears in the fortifications of Hierapolis.   But instead of listening to their timid counsels, Belisarius commanded them to follow him to Europus, where he had resolved to collect his forces, and to execute whatever God should inspire him to achieve against the enemy.   His firm attitude on the banks of the Euphrates restrained Chosroes from advancing towards Palestine ; and he received with art and dignity the ambassadors, or rather spies, of the Persian monarch. The plain between Hierapolis and the river was covered with the squadrons of cavalry, six thousand hunters, tall and robust, who pursued their game without the apprehension of an enemy.   On the opposite bank the ambassadors descried a thousand Armenian horse, who appeared to guard the passage of the Euphrates.   The tent of Belisarius was of the coarsest linen, the simple equipage of a warrior who disdained the luxury of the East.   Around his tent, the nations who marched under his standard were arranged with skilful confusion.   The Thracians and Illyrians were posted in the front, the Heruli and Goths in the centre ; the prospect was closed by the Moors and Vandals, and their loose array seemed to multiply their numbers.   Their dress was light and active ; one soldier carried a whip, another a sword, a third a bow, a fourth, perhaps, a battle-axe, and the whole picture exhibited the intrepidity of the troops and the vigilance of the general.   Chosroes was deluded by the address, and awed by the genius, of the lieutenant of Justinian.   Conscious of the merit, and ignorant of the force, of his antagonist, he dreaded a decisive battle in a distant country, from whence not a Persian might return to relate the melancholy tale.   The great king hastened to repass the Euphrates ; and Belisarius pressed his retreat, by affecting to oppose a measure so salutary to the empire, and which could scarcely have been prevented by an army of a hundred thousand men. Envy might suggest to ignorance and pride, that the public enemy had been suffered to escape : but the African and Gothic triumphs are less glorious than this safe and bloodless victory, in which neither fortune, nor the valor of the soldiers, can subtract any part of the general's renown. The second removal of Belisarius from the Persian to the Italian war revealed the extent of his personal merit, which had corrected or supplied the want of discipline and courage. Fifteen generals, without concert or skill, led through the mountains of Armenia an army of thirty thousand Romans, inattentive to their signals, their ranks, and their ensigns. Four thousand Persians, intrenched in the camp of Dubis, vanquished, almost without a combat, this disorderly multitude ; their useless arms were scattered along the road, and their horses sunk under the fatigue of their rapid flight. But the Arabs of the Roman party prevailed over their brethren ; the Armenians returned to their allegiance ; the cities of Dara and Edessa resisted a sudden assault and a regular siege, and the calamities of war were suspended by those of pestilence. A tacit or formal agreement between the two sovereigns protected the tranquillity of the Eastern frontier, and the arms of Chosroes were confined to the Colchian or Lazic war, which has been too minutely described by the historians of the times.[64]

The extreme length of the Euxine Sea,[65] from Constantinople to the mouth of the Phasis, may be computed as a voyage of nine days, and a measure of seven hundred miles. From the Iberian Caucasus, the most lofty and craggy mountains of Asia, that river descends with such oblique vehemence, that in a short space it is traversed by one hundred and twenty bridges. Nor does the stream become placid and navigable, till it reaches the town of Sarapana, five days' journey from the Cyrus, which flows from the same hills, but in a contrary direction to the Caspian Lake. The proximity of these rivers has suggested the practice, or at least the idea, of wafting the precious merchandise of India down the Oxus, over the Caspian, up the Cyrus, and with the current of the Phasis into the Euxine and Mediterranean Seas. As it successively collects the streams of the plain of Colchos, the Phasis moves with diminished speed, though accumulated weight. At the mouth it is sixty fathom deep, and half a league broad, but a small woody island is interposed in the midst of the channel ; the water, so soon as it has deposited an earthy or metallic sediment, floats on the surface of the waves, and is no longer susceptible of corruption. In a course of one hundred miles, forty of which are navigable for large vessels, the Phasis divides the celebrated region of Colchos,[66] or Mingrelia,[67] which, on three sides, is fortified by the Iberian and Armenian mountains, and whose maritime coast extends about two hundred miles from the neighborhood of Trebizond to Dioscurias and the confines of Circassia. Both the soil and climate are relaxed by excessive moisture : twenty-eight rivers, besides the Phasis and his dependent streams, convey their waters to the sea ; and the hollowness of the ground appears to indicate the subterraneous channels between the Euxine and the Caspian. In the fields where wheat or barley is sown, the earth is too soft to sustain the action of the plough ; but the *gom*, a small grain, not unlike the millet or coriander seed, supplies the ordinary food of the people ; and the use of bread is confined to the prince and his nobles. Yet the vintage is more plentiful than the harvest ; and the bulk of the stems, as well as the quality of the wine, display the unassisted powers of nature. The same powers continually tend to overshadow the face of the country with thick forests ; the timber of the hills, and the flax of the plains, contribute to the abundance of naval stores ; the wild and tame animals, the horse, the ox, and the hog, are remarkably prolific, and the name of the pheasant is expressive of his native habitation on the banks of the Phasis. The gold mines to the south of Trebizond, which are still worked with sufficient profit, were a subject of national dispute between Justinian and Chosroes ; and it is not unreasonable to believe, that a vein of precious metal may be equally diffused through the circle of the hills, although these secret treasures are neglected by the laziness, or concealed by the prudence, of the Mingrelians. The waters, impregnated with particles of gold, are carefully strained through sheep-skins or fleeces ; but this expedient, the groundwork perhaps of a marvellous fable, affords a faint image of the wealth extracted from a virgin earth by the power and industry of ancient kings. Their silver palaces and golden chambers surpass our belief ; but the fame of their riches is said to have excited the enterprising avarice of the Argonauts.[68] Tradition has affirmed, with some color of reason, that Egypt planted on the Phasis a learned and polite colony,[69] which manufactured linen, built navies, and invented geographical maps. The ingenuity of the moderns has peopled, with flourishing cities and nations, the isthmus between the Euxine and the Caspian ;[70] and a lively writer, observing the resemblance of climate, and, in his apprehension, of trade, has not hesitated to pronounce Colchos the Holland of antiquity.[71]

But the riches of Colchos shine only through the darkness of conjecture or tradition ; and its genuine history presents a uniform scene of rudeness and poverty. If one hundred and thirty languages were spoken in the market of Dioscurias,[72] they were the imperfect idioms of so many savage tribes or families, sequestered from each other in the valleys of Mount Caucasus; and their separation, which diminished the importance, must have multiplied the number, of their rustic capitals. In the present state of Mingrelia, a village is an assemblage of huts within a wooden fence; the fortresses are seated in the depths of forests; the princely town of Cyta, or Cotatis, consists of two hundred houses, and a stone edifice appertains only to the magnificence of kings. Twelve ships from Constantinople, and about sixty barks, laden with the fruits of industry, annually cast anchor on the coast; and the list of Colchian exports is much increased, since the natives had only slaves and hides to offer in exchange for the corn and salt which they purchased from the subjects of Justinian. Not a vestige can be found of the art, the knowledge, or the navigation, of the ancient Colchians: few Greeks desired or dared to pursue the footsteps of the Argonauts; and even the marks of an Egyptian colony are lost on a nearer approach. The rite of circumcision is practised only by the Mahometans of the Euxine; and the curled hair and swarthy complexion of Africa no longer disfigure the most perfect of the human race. It is in the adjacent climates of Georgia, Mingrelia, and Circassia, that nature has placed, at least to our eyes, the model of beauty in the shape of the limbs, the color of the skin, the symmetry of the features, and the expression of the countenance.[73] According to the destination of the two sexes, the men seemed formed for action, the women for love; and the perpetual supply of females from Mount Caucasus has purified the blood, and improved the breed, of the southern nations of Asia. The proper district of Mingrelia, a portion only of the ancient Colchos, has long sustained an exportation of twelve thousand slaves. The number of prisoners or criminals would be inadequate to the annual demand; but the common people are in a state of servitude to their lords; the exercise of fraud or rapine is unpunished in a lawless community; and the market is continually replenished by the abuse of civil and paternal authority. Such a trade,[74] which reduces the human species to the level of cattle, may tend to encourage marriage and population, since the multitude of children enriches their sordid and inhuman parent. But this source of impure wealth must inevitably poison the national manners, obliterate the sense of honor and virtue, and almost extinguish the instincts of nature: the *Christians* of Georgia and Mingrelia are the most dissolute of mankind; and their children, who, in a tender age, are sold into foreign slavery, have already learned to imitate the rapine of the father and the prostitution of the mother. Yet, amidst the rudest ignorance, the untaught natives discover a singular dexterity both of mind and hand ; and although the want of union and discipline exposes them to their more powerful neighbors, a bold and intrepid spirit has animated the Colchians of every age. In the host of Xerxes, they served on foot ; and their arms were a dagger or a javelin, a wooden casque, and a buckler of raw hides. But in.their own country the use of cavalry has more generally prevailed : the meanest of the peasants disdained to walk ; the martial nobles are possessed, perhaps, of two hundred horses ; and about five thousand are numbered in the train of the prince of Mingrelia. The Colchian government has been always a pure and hereditary kingdom ; and the authority of the sovereign is only restrained by the turbulence of his subjects. Whenever they were obedient, he could lead a numerous army into the field ; but some faith is requisite to believe, that the single tribe of the Suanians was composed of two hundred thousand soldiers, or that the population of Mingrelia now amounts to four millions of inhabitants.[75] It was the boast of the Colchians, that their ancestors had checked the victories of Sesostris ; and the defeat of the Egyptian is less incredible than his successful progress as far as the foot of Mount Caucasus. They sunk without any memorable effort, under the arms of Cyrus ; followed in distant wars the standard of the great king, and presented him every fifth year with one hundred boys, and as many virgins, the fairest produce of the land.[76] Yet he accepted this *gift* like the gold and ebony of India, the frankincense of the Arabs, or the negroes and ivory of Æthiopia : the Colchians were not subject to the dominion of a satrap, and they continued to enjoy the name as well as substance of national independence.[77] After the fall of the Persian empire, Mithridates, king of Pontus, added Colchos to the wide circle of his dominions on the Euxine ; and when the natives presumed to request that his son might reign over them, he bound the ambitious youth in chains of gold, and delegated a servant in his place. In pursuit of Mithridates, the Romans advanced to the banks of the Phasis, and their galleys ascended the river till they reached the camp of Pompey and his legions.[78] But the senate, and afterwards the emperors, disdained to reduce that distant and useless conquest into the form of a province. The family of a Greek rhetorician was permitted to reign in Colchos and the adjacent kingdoms from the time of Mark Antony to that of Nero ; and after the race of Polemo [79] was extinct, the eastern Pontus, which preserved his name, extended no farther than the neighborhood of Trebizond.

Beyond these limits the fortifications of Hyssus, of Apsarus, of the Phasis, of Dioscurias or Sebastopolis, and of Pityus, were guarded by sufficient detachments of horse and foot ; and six princes of Colchos received their diadems from the lieutenants of Cæsar. One of these lieutenants, the eloquent and philosophic Arrian, surveyed, and has described, the Euxine coast, under the reign of Hadrian. The garrison which he reviewed at the mouth of the Phasis consisted of four hundred chosen legionaries ; the brick walls and towers, the double ditch, and the military engines on the rampart, rendered this place inaccessible to the barbarians : but the new suburbs which had been built by the merchants and veterans, required, in the opinion of Arrian, some external defence.[80] As the strength of the empire was gradually impaired, the Romans stationed on the Phasis were neither withdrawn nor expelled ; and the tribe of the Lazi,[81] whose posterity speak a foreign dialect, and inhabit the sea-coast of Trebizond, imposed their name and dominion on the ancient kingdom of Colchos. Their independence was soon invaded by a formidable neighbor, who had acquired, by arms and treaties, the sovereignty of Iberia. The dependent king of Lazica received his sceptre at the hands of the Persian monarch, and the successors of Constantine acquiesced in this injurious claim, which was proudly urged as a right of immemorial prescription. In the beginning of the sixth century, their influence was restored by the introduction of Christianity, which the Mingrelians still profess with becoming zeal, without understanding the doctrines, or observing the precepts, of their religion. After the decease of his father, Zathus was exalted to the regal dignity by the favor of the great king ; but the pious youth abhorred the ceremonies of the Magi, and sought, in the palace of Constantinople, an orthodox baptism, a noble wife, and the alliance of the emperor Justin. The king of Lazica was solemnly invested with the diadem, and his cloak and tunic of white silk, with a gold border, displayed, in rich embroidery, the figure of his new patron ; who soothed the jealousy of the Persian court, and excused the revolt of Colchos, by the venerable names of hospitality and religion. The common interest of both empires imposed on the Colchians the duty of guarding the passes of Mount Caucasus, where a wall of sixty miles is now defended by the monthly service of the musketeers of Mingrelia.[82]

But this honorable connection was soon corrupted by the avarice and ambition of the Romans. Degraded from the rank of allies, the Lazi were incessantly reminded, by words and actions, of their dependent state. At the distance of a day's journey beyond the Apsarus, they beheld the rising fortress of Petra,[83] which

commanded the maritime country to the south of the Phasis.
Instead of being protected by the valor, Colchos was insulted by
the licentiousness, of foreign mercenaries; the benefits of commerce
were converted into base and vexatious monopoly ; and Gubazes,
the native prince, was reduced to a pageant of royalty, by the
superior influence of the officers of Justinian. Disappointed in
their expectations of Christian virtue, the indignant Lazi reposed
some confidence in the justice of an unbeliever. After a private
assurance that their ambassadors should not be delivered to the
Romans, they publicly solicited the friendship and aid of Chosroes. The sagacious monarch instantly discerned the use and
importance of Colchos ; and meditated a plan of conquest, which
was renewed at the end of a thousand years by Shah Abbas, the
wisest and most powerful of his successors.[84] His ambition was
fired by the hope of launching a Persian navy from the Phasis,
of commanding the trade and navigation of the Euxine Sea, of
desolating the coast of Pontus and Bithynia, of distressing, perhaps of attacking, Constantinople, and of persuading the barbarians of Europe to second his arms and counsels against the
common enemy of mankind. Under the pretence of a Scythian
war, he silently led his troops to the frontiers of Iberia ; the
Colchian guides were prepared to conduct them through the
woods and along the precipices of Mount Caucasus ; and a narrow
path was laboriously formed into a safe and spacious highway, for
the march of cavalry, and even of elephants. Gubazes laid his
person and diadem at the feet of the king of Persia ; his Colchians
imitated the submission of their prince ; and after the walls of
Petra had been shaken, the Roman garrison prevented, by a
capitulation, the impending fury of the last assault. But the Lazi
soon discovered, that their impatience had urged them to choose
an evil more intolerable than the calamities which they strove to
escape. The monopoly of salt and corn was effectually removed
by the loss of those valuable commodities. The authority of a
Roman legislator was succeeded by the pride of an Oriental despot,
who beheld, with equal disdain, the slaves whom he had exalted,
and the kings whom he had humbled before the footstool of his
throne. The adoration of fire was introduced into Colchos by the
zeal of the Magi : their intolerant spirit provoked the fervor of a
Christian people ; and the prejudice of nature or education was
wounded by the impious practice of exposing the dead bodies of
their parents, on the summit of a lofty tower, to the crows and
vultures of the air.[85] Conscious of the increasing hatred, which
retarded the execution of his great designs, the just Nushirvan
had secretly given orders to assassinate the king of the Lazi, to

transplant the people into some distant land, and to fix a faithful and warlike colony on the banks of the Phasis. The watchful jealousy of the Colchians foresaw and averted the approaching ruin. Their repentance was accepted at Constantinople by the prudence, rather than the clemency, of Justinian ; and he commanded Dagisteus, with seven thousand Romans, and one thousand of the Zani,* to expel the Persians from the coast of the Euxine.

The siege of Petra, which the Roman general, with the aid of the Lazi, immediately undertook, is one of the most remarkable actions of the age. The city was seated on a craggy rock, which hung over the sea, and communicated by a steep and narrow path with the land. Since the approach was difficult, the attack might be deemed impossible : the Persian conqueror had strengthened the fortifications of Justinian ; and the places least inaccessible were covered by additional bulwarks. In this important fortress, the vigilance of Chosroes had deposited a magazine of offensive and defensive arms, sufficient for five times the number, not only of the garrison, but of the besiegers themselves. The stock of flour and salt provisions was adequate to the consumption of five years ; the want of wine was supplied by vinegar, and of grain from whence a strong liquor was extracted ; and a triple aqueduct eluded the diligence, and even the suspicions, of the enemy. But the firmest defence of Petra was placed in the valor of fifteen hundred Persians, who resisted the assaults of the Romans, whilst, in a softer vein of earth, a mine was secretly perforated. The wall, supported by slender and temporary props, hung tottering in the air ; but Dagisteus delayed the attack till he had secured a specific recompense ; and the town was relieved before the return of his messenger from Constantinople. The Persian garrison was reduced to four hundred men, of whom no more than fifty were exempt from sickness or wounds ; yet such had been their inflexable perseverance, that they concealed their losses from the enemy, by enduring, without a murmur, the sight and putrefying stench of the dead bodies of their eleven hundred companions. After their deliverance, the breaches were hastily stopped with sand bags ; the mine was replenished with earth ; a new wall was erected on a frame of substantial timber ; and a fresh garrison of three thousand men was stationed at Petra to sustain the labors of a second siege. The operations, both of the attack and defence, were conducted with skilful obstinacy ; and each party derived useful lessons from the experience of their past faults. A battering-ram was invented, of light construction and powerful effect :

---

* These seem the same people called Suanians.—M.

it was transported and worked by the hands of forty soldiers ; and as the stones were loosened by its repeated strokes, they were torn with long iron hooks from the wall. From those walls, a shower of darts was incessantly poured on the heads of the assailants ; but they were most dangerously annoyed by a fiery composition of sulphur and bitumen, which in Colchos might with some propriety be named the oil of Medea. Of six thousand Romans who mounted the scaling-ladders, their general Bessas was the first, a gallant veteran of seventy years of age : the courage of their leader, his fall, and extreme danger, animated the irresistible effort of his troops ; and their prevailing numbers oppressed the strength, without subduing the spirit, of the Persian garrison. The fate of these valiant men deserves to be more distinctly noticed. Seven hundred had perished in the siege, two thousand three hundred survived to defend the breach. One thousand and seventy were destroyed with fire and sword in the last assault ; and if seven hundred and thirty were made prisoners, only eighteen among them were found without the marks of honorable wounds. The remaining five hundred escaped into the citadel, which they maintained without any hopes of relief, rejecting the fairest terms of capitulation and service, till they were lost in the flames. They died in obedience to the commands of their prince ; and such examples of loyalty and valor might excite their countrymen to deeds of equal despair and more prosperous event. The instant demolition of the works of Petra confessed the astonishment and apprehension of the conqueror.

A Spartan would have praised and pitied the virtue of these heroic slaves ; but the tedious warfare and alternate success of the Roman and Persian arms cannot detain the attention of posterity at the foot of Mount Caucasus. The advantages obtained by the troops of Justinian were more frequent and splendid ; but the forces of the great king were continually supplied, till they amounted to eight elephants and seventy thousand men, including twelve thousand Scythian allies, and above three thousand Dilemites, who descended by their free choice from the hills of Hyrcania, and were equally formidable in close or in distant combat. The siege of Archæopolis, a name imposed or corrupted by the Greeks, was raised with some loss and precipitation ; but the Persians occupied the passes of Iberia : Colchos was enslaved by their forts and garrisons ; they devoured the scanty sustenance of the people ; and the prince of the Lazi fled into the mountains. In the Roman camp, faith and discipline were unknown ; and the independent leaders, who were invested with equal power, disputed with each other the pre-eminence of vice and corruption. The

Persians followed, without a murmur, the commands of a single chief, who implicitly obeyed the instructions of their supreme lord. Their general was distinguished among the heroes of the East by his wisdom in council, and his valor in the field. The advanced age of Mermeroes, and the lameness of both his feet, could not diminish the activity of his mind, or even of his body; and, whilst he was carried in a litter in the front of battle, he inspired terror to the enemy, and a just confidence to the troops, who, under his banners, were always successful. After his death, the command devolved to Nacoragan, a proud satrap, who, in a conference with the Imperial chiefs, had presumed to declare that he disposed of victory as absolutely as of the ring on his finger. Such presumption was the natural cause and forerunner of a shameful defeat. The Romans had been gradually repulsed to the edge of the sea-shore; and their last camp, on the ruins of the Grecian colony of Phasis, was defended on all sides by strong intrenchments, the river, the Euxine, and a fleet of galleys. Despair united their counsels and invigorated their arms: they withstood the assault of the Persians; and the flight of Nacoragan preceded or followed the slaughter of ten thousand of his bravest soldiers. He escaped from the Romans to fall into the hands of an unforgiving master, who severely chastised the error of his own choice: the unfortunate general was flayed alive, and his skin, stuffed into the human form, was exposed on a mountain: a dreadful warning to those who might hereafter be intrusted with the fame and fortune of Persia.[86] Yet the prudence of Chosroes insensibly relinquished the prosecution of the Colchian war, in the just persuasion, that it is impossible to reduce, or, at least, to hold a distant country against the wishes and efforts of its inhabitants. The fidelity of Gubazes sustained the most rigorous trials. He patiently endured the hardships of a savage life, and rejected, with disdain, the specious temptations of the Persian court.* The king of the Lazi had been educated in the Christian religion; his mother was the daughter of a senator; during his youth, he had served ten years a silentiary of the Byzantine palace,[87] and the arrears of an unpaid salary were a motive of attachment as well as of complaint. But the long continuance of his sufferings extorted from him a naked representation of the truth; and truth was an unpardonable libel on the lieutenants of Justinian, who, amidst the delays of a ruinous war, had spared his enemies and trampled on his allies. Their malicious information persuaded

---

* According to Agathias, the death of Gubazes preceded the defeat of Nacoragan. The trial took place after the battle.—M.

the emperor that his faithless vassal already meditated a second defection : an order was surprised to send him prisoner to Constantinople ; a treacherous clause was inserted, that he might be lawfully killed in case of resistance ; and Gubazes, without arms, or suspicion of danger, was stabbed in the security of a friendly interview. In the first moments of rage and despair, the Colchians would have sacrificed their country and religion to the gratification of revenge. But the authority and eloquence of the wiser few obtained a salutary pause : the victory of the Phasis restored the terror of the Roman arms, and the emperor was solicitous to absolve his own name from the imputation of so foul a murder. A judge of senatorial rank was commissioned to inquire into the conduct and death of the king of the Lazi. He ascended a stately tribunal, encompassed by the ministers of justice and punishment : in the presence of both nations, this extraordinary cause was pleaded, according to the forms of civil jurisprudence, and some satisfaction was granted to an injured people, by the sentence and execution of the meaner criminals.[88]

In peace, the king of Persia continually sought the pretences of a rupture : but no sooner had he taken up arms, than he expressed his desire of a safe and honorable treaty. During the fiercest hostilities, the two monarchs entertained a deceitful negotiation ; and such was the superiority of Chosroes, that whilst he treated the Roman ministers with insolence and contempt, he obtained the most unprecedented honors for his own ambassadors at the Imperial court. The successor of Cyrus assumed the majesty of the Eastern sun, and graciously permitted his younger brother Justinian to reign over the West, with the pale and reflected splendor of the moon. This gigantic style was supported by the pomp and eloquence of Isdigune, one of the royal chamberlains. His wife and daughters, with a train of eunuchs and camels, attended the march of the ambassador : two satraps with golden diadems were numbered among his followers : he was guarded by five hundred horse, the most valiant of the Persians ; and the Roman governor of Dara wisely refused to admit more than twenty of this martial and hostile caravan. When Isdigune had saluted the emperor, and delivered his presents, he passed ten months at Constantinople without discussing any serious affairs. Instead of being confined to his palace, and receiving food and water from the hands of his keepers, the Persian ambassador, without spies or guards, was allowed to visit the capital ; and the freedom of conversation and trade enjoyed by his domestics, offended the prejudices of an age which rigorously practised the law of nations, without confidence or courtesy.[89] By an unexampled indulgence, his interpreter, a servant below the notice of a Roman magistrate, was seated, at the table of Justinian, by the side of his master : and one thousand pounds of gold might be assigned for the expense of his journey and entertainment. Yet the repeated labors of Isdigune could procure only a partial and imperfect truce, which was always purchased with the treasures, and renewed at the solicitation, of the Byzantine court. Many years of fruitless desolation elapsed before Justinian and Chosroes were compelled, by mutual lassitude, to consult the repose of their declining age. At a conference held on the frontier, each party, without expecting to gain credit, displayed the power, the justice, and the pacific intentions, of their respective sovereigns ; but necessity and interest dictated the treaty of peace, which was concluded for a term of fifty years, diligently composed in the Greek and Persian languages, and attested by the seals of twelve interpreters. The liberty of commerce and religion was fixed and defined ; the allies of the emperor and the great king were included in the same benefits and obligations ; and the most scrupulous precautions were provided to prevent or determine the accidental disputes that might arise on the confines of two hostile nations. After twenty years of destructive though feeble war, the limits still remained without alteration ; and Chosroes was persuaded to renounce his dangerous claim to the possession or sovereignty of Colchos and its dependent states. Rich in the accumulated treasures of the East, he extorted from the Romans an annual payment of thirty thousand pieces of gold ; and the smallness of the sum revealed the disgrace of a tribute in its naked deformity. In a previous debate, the chariot of Sesostris, and the wheel of fortune, were applied by one of the ministers of Justinian, who observed that the reduction of Antioch, and some Syrian cities, had elevated beyond measure the vain and ambitious spirit of the barbarian. "You are mistaken," replied the modest Persian : "the king of kings, the lord of mankind, looks down with contempt on such petty acquisitions ; and of the ten nations, vanquished by his invincible arms, he esteems the Romans as the least formidable." [90] According to the Orientals, the empire of Nushirvan extended from Ferganah, in Transoxiana, to Yemen, or Arabia Fœlix. He subdued the rebels of Hyrcania, reduced the provinces of Cabul and Zablestan on the banks of the Indus, broke the power of the Euthalites, terminated by an honorable treaty the Turkish war, and admitted the daughter of the great khan into the number of his lawful wives. Victorious and respected among the princes of Asia, he gave audience, in his palace of Madain, or Ctesiphon, to the ambassadors of the world. Their gifts or tributes, arms, rich garments, gems, slaves or aromatics, were humbly presented at the foot of his throne ; and he condescended to accept from the king of India ten quintals of the wood of aloes, a maid seven cubits in height, and a carpet softer than silk, the skin, as it was reported, of an extraordinary serpent.[91]

Justinian had been reproached for his alliance with the Æthiopians, as if he attempted to introduce a people of savage negroes into the system of civilized society. But the friends of the Roman empire, the Axumites, or Abyssinians, may be always distinguished from the original natives of Africa.[92] The hand of nature has flattered the noses of the negroes, covered their heads with shaggy wool, and tinged their skin with inherent and indelible blackness. But the olive complexion of the Abyssinians, their hair, shape, and features, distinctly mark them as a colony of Arabs ; and this descent is confirmed by the resemblance of language and manners, the report of an ancient emigration, and the narrow interval between the shores of the Red Sea. Christianity had raised that nation above the level of African barbarism :[93] their intercourse with Egypt, and the successors of Constantine,[94] had communicated the rudiments of the arts and sciences ; their vessels traded to the Isle of Ceylon,[95] and seven kingdoms obeyed the Negus or supreme prince of Abyssinia. The independence of the Homerites,* who reigned in the rich and happy Arabia, was first violated by an Æthiopian conqueror : he drew his hereditary claim from the queen of Sheba,[96] and his ambition was sanctified by religious zeal. The Jews, powerful and active in exile, had seduced the mind of Dunaan, prince of the Homerites. They urged him to retaliate the persecution inflicted by the Imperial laws on their unfortunate brethren : some Roman merchants were injuriously treated ; and several Christians of Negra[97] were honored with the crown of martyrdom.[98] The churches of Arabia implored the protection of the Abyssinian monarch. The Negus passed the Red Sea with a fleet and army, deprived the Jewish proselyte of his kingdom and life, and extinguished a race of princes, who had ruled above two thousand years the sequestered region of myrrh and frankincense. The conqueror immediately announced the victory of the gospel, requested an orthodox patriarch, and so warmly professed his friendship to the Roman empire, that Justinian was flattered by the hope of diverting the silk

---

* It appears by the important inscription discovered by Mr. Salt at Axoum, and from a law of Constantius (16th Jan., 356, inserted in the Theodosian Code, l. 12. c. 12), that in the middle of the fourth century of our era the princes of the Axumites joined to their titles that of king of the Homerites. The conquests which they made over the Arabs in the sixth century were only a restoration of the ancient order of things. St. Martin, vol. viii. p. 46.—M.

trade through the channel of Abyssinia, and of exciting the forces of Arabia against the Persian king. Nonnosus, descended from a family of ambassadors, was named by the emperor to execute this important commission. He wisely declined the shorter, but more dangerous road, through the sandy deserts of Nubia ; ascended the Nile, embarked on the Red Sea, and safely landed at the African port of Adulis. From Adulis to the royal city of Axume is no more than fifty leagues, in a direct line ; but the winding passes of the mountains detained the ambassador fifteen days ; and as he traversed the forests, he saw, and vaguely computed, about five thousand wild elephants. The capital, according to his report, was large and populous ; and the *village* of Axume is still conspicuous by the regal coronations, by the ruins of a Christian temple, and by sixteen or seventeen obelisks inscribed with Grecian characters.[99] But the Negus * gave audience in the open field seated on a lofty chariot, which was drawn by four elephants, superbly caparisoned, and surrounded by his nobles and musicians. He was clad in a linen garment and cap, holding in his hand two javelins and a light shield ; and, although his nakedness was imperfectly covered, he displayed the barbaric pomp of gold chains, collars, and bracelets, richly adorned with pearls and precious stones. The ambassador of Justinian knelt ; the Negus raised him from the ground, embraced Nonnosus, kissed the seal, perused the letter, accepted the Roman alliance, and brandishing his weapons, denounced implacable war against the worshippers of fire. But the proposal of the silk trade was eluded ; and notwithstanding the assurances, and perhaps the wishes, of the Abyssinians, these hostile menaces evaporated without effect. The Homerites were unwilling to abandon their aromatic groves, to explore a sandy desert, and to encounter, after all their fatigues, a formidable nation from whom they had never received any personal injuries. Instead of enlarging his conquests, the king of Æthiopia was incapable of defending his possessions. Abrahah,† the slave of a Roman merchant of Adulis, assumed the sceptre of the Homerites ; the troops of Africa were

---

* The Negus is differently called Elesbaan, Elesboas, Elisthæus, probably the same name, or rather appellation. See St. Martin, vol. viii. p. 49.—M.

† According to the Arabian authorities (Johannsen, Hist. Yemanæ, p. 94, Bonn, 1828), Abrahah was an Abyssinian, the rival of Ariathus, the brother of the Abyssinian king ; he surprised and slew Ariathus, and by his craft appeased the resentment of Nadjash, the Abyssinian king. Abrahah was a Christian ; be built a magnificent church at Sana, and dissuaded his subjects from their accustomed pilgrimages to Mecca. The church was defiled, it was supposed, by the Koreishites, and Abrahah took up arms to revenge himself on the temple at Mecca. He was repelled by miracle: his elephant would not advance, but knelt down before the sacred place ; Abrahah fled, discomfited and mortally wounded, to Sana.—M.

seduced by the luxury of the climate ; and Justinian solicited the friendship of the usurper, who honored with a slight tribute the supremacy of his prince.   After a long series of prosperity, the power of Abrahah was overthrown before the gates of Mecca ; his children were despoiled by the Persian conqueror ; and the Æthiopians were finally expelled from the continent of Asia. This narrative of obscure and remote events is not foreign to the decline and fall of the Roman empire.   If a Christian power had been maintained in Arabia, Mahomet must have been crushed in his cradle, and Abyssinia would have prevented a revolution which has changed the civil and religious state of the world.[100] *

CHAPTER XLIII.

REBELLIONS OF AFRICA. — RESTORATION OF THE GOTHIC KINGDOM BY TOTILA. — LOSS AND RECOVERY OF ROME. — FINAL CONQUEST OF ITALY BY NARSES. — EXTINCTION OF THE OSTROGOTHS. — DEFEAT OF THE FRANKS AND ALEMANNI. — LAST VICTORY, DISGRACE, AND DEATH OF BELISARIUS. — DEATH AND CHARACTER OF JUSTINIAN. — COMET, EARTHQUAKES, AND PLAGUE.

THE review of the nations from the Danube to the Nile has exposed, on every side, the weakness of the Romans ; and our wonder is reasonably excited that they should presume to enlarge an empire whose ancient limits they were incapable of defending. But the wars, the conquests, and the triumphs of Justinian, are the feeble and pernicious efforts of old age, which exhaust the remains of strength, and accelerate the decay of the powers of life. He exulted in the glorious act of restoring Africa and Italy to the republic ; but the calamities which followed the departure of Belisarius betrayed the impotence of the conqueror, and accomplished the ruin of those unfortunate countries.

From his new acquisitions, Justinian expected that his avarice, as well as pride, should be richly gratified.   A rapacious minister of the finances closely pursued the footsteps of Belisarius ; and as the old registers of tribute had been burnt by the Vandals, he indulged his fancy in a liberal calculation and arbitrary assessment of the wealth of Africa.[1]   The increase of taxes, which were

---

* A period of sixty-seven years is assigned by most of the Arabian authorities to the Abyssinian kingdom in Homeritis.—M.

drawn away by a distant sovereign, and a general resumption of the patrimony or crown lands, soon dispelled the intoxication of the public joy : but the emperor was insensible to the modest complaints of the people, till he was awakened and alarmed by the clamors of military discontent. Many of the Roman soldiers had married the widows and daughters of the Vandals. As their own, by the double right of conquest and inheritance, they claimed the estates which Genseric had assigned to his victorious troops. They heard with disdain the cold and selfish representations of their officers, that the liberality of Justinian had raised them from a savage or servile condition ; that they were already enriched by the spoils of Africa, the treasure, the slaves, and the movables of the vanquished barbarians ; and that the ancient and lawful patrimony of the emperors would be applied only to the support of that government on which their own safety and reward must ultimately depend. The mutiny was secretly inflamed by a thousand soldiers, for the most part Heruli, who had imbibed the doctrines, and were instigated by the clergy, of the Arian sect ; and the cause of perjury and rebellion was sanctified by the dispensing powers of fanaticism. The Arians deplored the ruin of their church, triumphant above a century in Africa ; and they were justly provoked by the laws of the conqueror, which interdicted the baptism of their children, and the exercise of all religious worship. Of the Vandals chosen by Belisarius, the far greater part, in the honors of the Eastern service, forgot their country and religion. But a generous band of four hundred obliged the mariners, when they were in sight of the Isle of Lesbos, to alter their course : they touched on Peloponnesus, ran ashore on a desert coast of Africa, and boldly erected, on Mount Aurasius, the standard of independence and revolt. While the troops of the province disclaimed the commands of their superiors, a conspiracy was formed at Carthage against the life of Solomon, who filled with honor the place of Belisarius ; and the Arians had piously resolved to sacrifice the tyrant at the foot of the altar, during the awful mysteries of the festival of Easter. Fear or remorse restrained the daggers of the assassins, but the patience of Solomon emboldened their discontent ; and, at the end of ten days, a furious sedition was kindled in the Circus, which desolated Africa above ten years. The pillage of the city, and the indiscriminate slaughter of its inhabitants, were suspended only by darkness, sleep, and intoxication : the governor, with seven companions, among whom was the historian Procopius, escaped to Sicily : two thirds of the army were involved in the guilt of treason ; and eight thousand insurgents, assembling in the field of elected Stoza for their chief, a private soldier, who possessed in a superior degree the virtues of a rebel. Under the mask of freedom, his eloquence could lead, or at least impel, the passions of his equals. He raised himself to a level with Belisarius, and the nephew of the emperor, by daring to encounter them in the field; and the victorious generals were compelled to acknowledge that Stoza deserved a purer cause, and a more legitimate command. Vanquished in battle, he dexterously employed the arts of negotiation; a Roman army was seduced from their allegiance, and the chiefs who had trusted to his faithless promise were murdered by his order in a church of Numidia. When every resource, either of force or perfidy, was exhausted, Stoza, with some desperate Vandals, retired to the wilds of Mauritania, obtained the daughter of a barbarian prince, and eluded the pursuit of his enemies, by the report of his death. The personal weight of Belisarius, the rank, the spirit, and the temper, of Germanus, the emperor's nephew, and the vigor and success of the second administration of the eunuch Solomon, restored the modesty of the camp, and maintained for a while the tranquillity of Africa. But the vices of the Byzantine court were felt in that distant province; the troops complained that they were neither paid nor relieved, and as soon as the public disorders were sufficiently mature, Stoza was again alive, in arms, and at the gates of Carthage. He fell in a single combat, but he smiled in the agonies of death, when he was informed that his own javelin had reached the heart of his antagonist.* The example of Stoza, and the assurance that a fortunate soldier had been the first king, encouraged the ambition of Gontharis, and he promised, by a private treaty, to divide Africa with the Moors, if, with their dangerous aid, he should ascend the throne of Carthage. The feeble Areobindus, unskilled in the affairs of peace and war, was raised, by his marriage with the niece of Justinian, to the office of exarch. He was suddenly oppressed by a sedition of the guards, and his abject supplica-

---

* Corippus gives a different account of the death of Stoza; he was transfixed by an arrow from the hand of John (not the hero of his poem), who broke desperately through the victorious troops of the enemy. Stoza repented, says the poet, of his treasonous rebellion, and anticipated—another Catiline—eternal torments as his punishment.

> Reddam, improba, poenas
> Quas merui. Furiis socius Catilina cruentis
> Exagitatus adest. Video jam Tartara, fundo
> Flammarumque globos, et clara incendia volvi.
>
> Johannidos, book iv. line 211.

All the other authorities confirm Gibbon's account of the death of John by the hand of Stoza. This poem of Corippus, unknown to Gibbon, was first published by Mazzuchelli during the present century, and is reprinted in the new edition of the Byzantine writers.—M.

tions, which provoked the contempt, could not move the pity, of the inexorable tyrant. After a reign of thirty days, Gontharis himself was stabbed at a banquet by the hand of Artaban; * and it is singular enough, that an Armenian prince, of the royal family of Arsaces, should re-establish at Carthage the authority of the Roman empire. In the conspiracy which unsheathed the dagger of Brutus against the life of Cæsar, every circumstance is curious and important to the eyes of posterity; but the guilt or merit of these loyal or rebellious assassins could interest only the contemporaries of Procopius, who, by their hopes and fears, their friendship or resentment, were personally engaged in the revolutions of Africa.[2]

That country was rapidly sinking into the state of barbarism from whence it had been raised by the Phœnician colonies and Roman laws; and every step of intestine discord was marked by some deplorable victory of savage man over civilized society. The Moors,[3] though ignorant of justice, were impatient of oppression: their vagrant life and boundless wilderness disappointed the arms, and eluded the chains, of a conqueror; and experience had shown, that neither oaths nor obligations could secure the fidelity of their attachment. The victory of Mount Auras had awed them into momentary submission; but if they respected the character of Solomon, they hated and despised the pride and luxury of his two nephews, Cyrus and Sergius, on whom their unclehad imprudently bestowed the provincial governments of Tripoli and Pentapolis. A Moorish tribe encamped under the walls of Leptis, to renew their alliance, and receive from the governor the customary gifts. Fourscore of their deputies were introduced as friends into the city; but on the dark suspicion of a conspiracy, they were massacred at the table of Sergius, and the clamor of arms and revenge was re-echoed through the valleys of Mount Atlas from both the Syrtes to the Atlantic Ocean. A personal injury, the unjust execution or murder of his brother, rendered Antalas the enemy of the Romans. The defeat of the Vandals had formerly signalized his valor; the rudiments of justice and prudence were still more conspicuous in a Moor; and while he laid Adrumetum in ashes, he calmly admonished the emperor that the peace of Africa might be secured by the recall of Solomon and his unworthy nephews. The exarch led forth his troops from Carthage: but, at the distance of six days' journey, in the neighbor-

---

* This murder was prompted to the Armenian (according to Corippus) by the *good* Athanasius (then præfect of Africa).

Hunc placidus canâ gravitate coegit
Immitem mactare virum,—Corippus, vol. iv. p. 237.—M.

hood of Tebeste,[4] he was astonished by the superior numbers and fierce aspect of the barbarians. He proposed a treaty; solicited a reconciliation; and offered to bind himself by the most solemn oaths. "By what oaths can he bind himself?" interrupted the indignant Moors. "Will he swear by the Gospels, the divine books of the Christians? It was on those books that the faith of his nephew Sergius was pledged to eighty of our innocent and unfortunate brethren. Before we trust them a second time, let us try their efficacy in the chastisement of perjury and the vindication of their own honor." Their honor was vindicated in the field of Tebeste, by the death of Solomon, and the total loss of his army.* The arrival of fresh troops and more skilful commanders soon checked the insolence of the Moors: seventeen of their princes were slain in the same battle; and the doubtful and transient submission of their tribes was celebrated with lavish applause by the people of Constantinople. Successive inroads had reduced the province of Africa to one third of the measure of Italy; yet the Roman emperors continued to reign above a century over Carthage and the fruitful coast of the Mediterranean. But the victories and the losses of Justinian were alike pernicious to mankind; and such was the desolation of Africa, that in many parts a stranger might wander whole days without meeting the face either of a friend or an enemy. The nation of the Vandals had disappeared: they once amounted to a hundred and sixty thousand warriors, without including the children, the women, or the slaves. Their numbers were infinitely surpassed by the number of the Moorish families extirpated in a relentless war; and the same destruction was retaliated on the Romans and their allies, who perished by the climate, their mutual quarrels, and the rage of the barbarians. When Procopius first landed, he admired the populousness of the cities and country, strenuously exercised in the labors of commerce and agriculture. In less than twenty years, that busy scene was converted into a silent solitude; the wealthy citizens escaped to Sicily and Constantinople; and the secret historian has confidently affirmed, that five millions of Africans were consumed by the wars and government of the emperor Justinian.[5]

The jealousy of the Byzantine court had not permitted Belisarius to achieve the conquest of Italy; and his abrupt departure revived the courage of the Goths,[6] who respected his genius, his virtue, and even the laudable motive which had urged the servant

---

* Corippus (Johannidos, lib. iii. 417-441) describes the defeat and death of Solomon.—M.

of Justinian to deceive and reject them. They had lost their king (an inconsiderable loss), their capital, their treasures, the provinces from Sicily to the Alps, and the military force of two hundred thousand barbarians, magnificently equipped with horses and arms. Yet all was not lost, as long as Pavia was defended by one thousand Goths, inspired by a sense of honor, the love of freedom, and the memory of their past greatness. The supreme command was unanimously offered to the brave Uraias; and it was in his eyes alone that the disgrace of his uncle Vitiges could appear as a reason of exclusion. His voice inclined the election in favor of Hildibald, whose personal merit was recommended by the vain hope that his kinsman Theudes, the Spanish monarch, would support the common interest of the Gothic nation. The success of his arms in Liguria and Venetia seemed to justify their choice; but he soon declared to the world that he was incapable of forgiving or commanding his benefactor. The consort of Hildibald was deeply wounded by the beauty, the riches, and the pride, of the wife of Uraias; and the death of that virtuous patriot excited the indignation of a free people. A bold assassin executed their sentence by striking off the head of Hildibald in the midst of a banquet; the Rugians, a foreign tribe, assumed the privilege of election; and Totila,* the nephew of the late king, was tempted, by revenge, to deliver himself and the garrison of Trevigo into the hands of the Romans. But the gallant and accomplished youth was easily persuaded to prefer the Gothic throne before the service of Justinian; and as soon as the palace of Pavia had been purified from the Rugian usurper, he reviewed the national force of five thousand soldiers, and generously undertook the restoration of the kingdom of Italy.

The successors of Belisarius, eleven generals of equal rank, neglected to crush the feeble and disunited Goths, till they were roused to action by the progress of Totila and the reproaches of Justinian. The gates of Verona were secretly opened to Artabazus, at the head of one hundred Persians in the service of the empire. The Goths fled from the city. At the distance of sixty furlongs the Roman generals halted to regulate the division of the spoil. While they disputed, the enemy discovered the real number of the victors: the Persians were instantly overpowered, and it was by leaping from the wall that Artabazus preserved a life which he lost in a few days by the lance of a barbarian, who had defied him to single combat. Twenty thousand Romans en-

---

* His real name, as appears by medals, was Baduilla or Badiula. Totila signifies immortal; tod (in German) is death. Todilas, deathless. Compare St. Martin, vol. ix. p. 37.—M.

countered the forces of Totila, near Faenza, and on the hills of Mugello, of the Florentine territory. The ardor of freedmen, who fought to regain their country, was opposed to the languid temper of mercenary troops, who were even destitute of the merits of strong and well-disciplined servitude. On the first attack, they abandoned their ensigns, threw down their arms, and dispersed on all sides with an active speed, which abated the loss, whilst it aggravated the shame, of their defeat. The king of the Goths, who blushed for the baseness of his enemies, pursued with rapid steps the path of honor and victory. Totila passed the Po,* traversed the Apennine, suspended the important conquest of Ravenna, Florence, and Rome, and marched through the heart of Italy, to form the siege, or rather the blockade, of Naples. The Roman chiefs, imprisoned in their respective cities, and accusing each other of the common disgrace, did not presume to disturb his enterprise. But the emperor, alarmed by the distress and danger of his Italian conquests, despatched to the relief of Naples a fleet of galleys and a body of Thracian and Armenian soldiers. They landed in Sicily, which yielded its copious stores of provisions ; but the delays of the new commander, an unwarlike magistrate, protracted the sufferings of the besieged ; and the succors, which he dropped with a timid and tardy hand, were successively intercepted by the armed vessels stationed by Totila in the Bay of Naples. The principal officer of the Romans was dragged, with a rope round his neck, to the foot of the wall, from whence, with a trembling voice, he exhorted the citizens to implore, like himself, the mercy of the conqueror. They requested a truce, with a promise of surrendering the city, if no effectual relief should appear at the end of thirty days. Instead of *one* month, the audacious barbarian granted them *three*, in the just confidence that famine would anticipate the term of their capitulation. After the reduction of Naples and Cumæ, the provinces of Lucania, Apulia, and Calabria, submitted to the king of the Goths. Totila led his army to the gates of Rome, pitched his camp at Tibur, or Tivoli, within twenty miles of the capital, and calmly exhorted the senate and people to compare the tyranny of the Greeks with the blessings of the Gothic reign.

The rapid success of Totila may be partly ascribed to the revolution which three years' experience had produced in the sentiments of the Italians. At the command, or at least in the name, of a Catholic emperor, the pope,[7] their spiritual father, had been

---

* This is not quite correct ; he had crossed the Po before the battle of Faenza. —M.

torn from the Roman church, and either starved, or murdered, on a desolate island.[8] The virtues of Belisarius were replaced by the various or uniform vices of eleven chiefs, at Rome, Ravenna, Florence, Perugia, Spoleto, etc., who abused their authority for the indulgence of lust or avarice. The improvement of the revenue was committed to Alexander, a subtle scribe, long practised in the fraud and oppression of the Byzantine schools, and whose name of *Psalliction*, the *scissors*,[9] was drawn from the dexterous artifice with which he reduced the size, without defacing the figure, of the gold coin. Instead of expecting the restoration of peace and industry, he imposed a heavy assessment on the fortunes of the Italians. Yet his present or future demands were less odious than a prosecution of arbitrary rigor against the persons and property of all those who, under the Gothic kings, had been concerned in the receipt and expenditure of the public money. The subjects of Justinian, who escaped these partial vexations, were oppressed by the irregular maintenance of the soldiers, whom Alexander defrauded and despised ; and their hasty sallies in quest of wealth, or subsistence, provoked the inhabitants of the country to await or implore their deliverance from the virtues of a barbarian. Totila [10] was chaste and temperate ; and none were deceived, either friends or enemies, who depended on his faith or his clemency. To the husbandmen of Italy the Gothic king issued a welcome proclamation, enjoining them to pursue their important labors, and to rest assured, that, on the payment of the ordinary taxes, they should be defended by his valor and discipline from the injuries of war. The strong towns he successively attacked ; and as soon as they had yielded to his arms, he demolished the fortifications ; to save the people from the calamities of a future siege, to deprive the Romans of the arts of defence, and to decide the tedious quarrel of the two nations, by an equal and honorable conflict in the field of battle. The Roman captives and deserters were tempted to enlist in the service of a liberal and courteous adversary ; the slaves were attracted by the firm and faithful promise, that they should never be delivered to their masters ; and from the thousand warriors of Pavia, a new people, under the same appellation of Goths, was insensibly formed in the camp of Totila. He sincerely accomplished the articles of capitulation, without seeking or accepting any sinister advantage from ambiguous expressions or unforeseen events : the garrison of Naples had stipulated, that they should be transported by sea ; the obstinacy of the winds prevented their voyage, but they were generously supplied with horses, provisions, and a safe-conduct to the gates of Rome. The wives of the senators, who had been surprised in the villas of Campania, were restored, without a ransom, to their husbands ; the violation of female chastity was inexorably chastised with death ; and in the salutary regulation of the edict of the famished Neapolitans, the conqueror assumed the office of a humane and attentive physician. The virtues of Totila are equally laudable, whether they proceeded from true policy, religious principle, or the instinct of humanity : he often harangued his troops ; and it was his constant theme, that national vice and ruin are inseparably connected ; that victory is the fruit of moral as well as military virtue ; and that the prince, and even the people, are responsible for the crimes which they neglect to punish.

The return of Belisarius to save the country which he had subdued, was pressed with equal vehemence by his friends and enemies ; and the Gothic war was imposed as a trust or an exile on the veteran commander. A hero on the banks of the Euphrates, a slave in the palace of Constantinople, he accepted with reluctance the painful task of supporting his own reputation, and retrieving the faults of his successors. The sea was open to the Romans : the ships and soldiers were assembled at Salona, near the palace of Diocletian : he refreshed and reviewed his troops at Pola in Istria, coasted round the head of the Adriatic, entered the port of Ravenna, and despatched orders rather than supplies to the subordinate cities. His first public oration was addressed to the Goths and Romans, in the name of the emperor, who had suspended for a while the conquest of Persia, and listened to the prayers of his Italian subjects. He gently touched on the causes and the authors of the recent disasters ; striving to remove the fear of punishment for the past, and the hope of impunity for the future, and laboring, with more zeal than success, to unite all the members of his government in a firm league of affection and obedience. Justinian, his gracious master, was inclined to pardon and reward ; and it was their interest, as well as duty, to reclaim their deluded brethren, who had been seduced by the arts of the usurper. Not a man was tempted to desert the standard of the Gothic king. Belisarius soon discovered that he was sent to remain the idle and impotent spectator of the glory of a young barbarian ; and his own epistle exhibits a genuine and lively picture of the distress of a noble mind. "Most excellent prince, we are arrived in Italy, destitute of all the necessary implements of war, men, horses, arms, and money. In our late circuit through the villages of Thrace and Illyricum, we have collected, with extreme difficulty, about four thousand recruits, naked, and unskilled in the use of weapons and the exercises of the camp.

The soldiers already stationed in the province are discontented, fearful, and dismayed ; at the sound of an enemy, they dismiss their horses, and cast their arms on the ground. No taxes can be raised, since Italy is in the hands of the barbarians ; the failure of payment has deprived us of the right of command, or even of admonition. Be assured, dread Sir, that the greater part of your troops have already deserted to the Goths. If the war could be achieved by the presence of Belisarius alone, your wishes are satisfied ; Belisarius is in the midst of Italy. But if you desire to conquer, far other preparations are requisite : without a military force, the title of general is an empty name. It would be expedient to restore to my service my own veterans and domestic guards. Before I can take the field, I must receive an adequate supply of light and heavy armed troops ; and it is only with ready money that you can procure the indispensable aid of a powerful body of the cavalry of the Huns." [11] An officer in whom Belisarius confided was sent from Ravenna to hasten and conduct the succors ; but the message was neglected, and the messenger was detained at Constantinople by an advantageous marriage. After his patience had been exhausted by delay and disappointment, the Roman general repassed the Adriatic, and expected at Dyrrachium the arrival of the troops, which were slowly assembled among the subjects and allies of the empire. His powers were still inadequate to the deliverance of Rome, which was closely besieged by the Gothic king. The Appian way, a march of forty days, was covered by the barbarians ; and as the prudence of Belisarius declined a battle, he preferred the safe and speedy navigation of five days from the coast of Epirus to the mouth of the Tyber.

After reducing, by force, or treaty, the towns of inferior note in the midland provinces of Italy, Totila proceeded, not to assault, but to encompass and starve, the ancient capital. Rome was afflicted by the avarice, and guarded by the valor, of Bessas, a veteran chief of Gothic extraction, who filled, with a garrison of three thousand soldiers, the spacious circle of her venerable walls. From the distress of the people he extracted a profitable trade, and secretly rejoiced in the continuance of the siege. It was for his use that the granaries had been replenished ; the charity of Pope Vigilius had purchased and embarked an ample supply of Sicilian corn ; but the vessels which escaped the barbarians were seized by a rapacious governor, who imparted a scanty sustenance to the soldiers, and sold the remainder to the wealthy Romans. The medimnus, or fifth part of the quarter of wheat, was exchanged for seven pieces of gold ; fifty pieces were given for an ox, a rare and accidental prize ; the progress of famine enhanced this exorbitant value, and the mercenaries were tempted to deprive themselves of the allowance which was scarcely sufficient for the support of life. A tasteless and unwholesome mixture, in which the bran thrice exceeded the quantity of flour, appeased the hunger of the poor ; they were gradually reduced to feed on dead horses, dogs, cats, and mice, and eagerly to snatch the grass, and even the nettles, which grew among the ruins of the city. A crowd of spectres, pale and emaciated, their bodies oppressed with disease, and their minds with despair, surrounded the palace of the governor, urged, with unavailing truth, that it was the duty of a master to maintain his slaves, and humbly requested that he would provide for their subsistence, permit their flight, or command their immediate execution. Bessas replied, with unfeeling tranquillity, that it was impossible to feed, unsafe to dismiss, and unlawful to kill, the subjects of the emperor. Yet the example of a private citizen might have shown his countrymen that a tyrant cannot withhold the privilege of death. Pierced by the cries of five children, who vainly called on their father for bread, he ordered them to follow his steps, advanced with calm and silent despair to one of the bridges of the Tyber, and, covering his face, threw himself headlong into the stream, in the presence of his family and the Roman people. To the rich and pusillanimous, Bessas [12] sold the permission of departure ; but the greatest part of the fugitives expired on the public highways, or were intercepted by the flying parties of barbarians. In the mean while, the artful governor soothed the discontent, and revived the hopes, of the Romans, by the vague reports of the fleets and armies which were hastening to their relief from the extremities of the East. They derived more rational comfort from the assurance that Belisarius had landed at the *port ;* and, without numbering his forces, they firmly relied on the humanity, the courage, and the skill of their great deliverer.

The foresight of Totila had raised obstacles worthy of such an antagonist. Ninety furlongs below the city, in the narrowest part of the river, he joined the two banks by strong and solid timbers in the form of a bridge, on which he erected two lofty towers, manned by the bravest of his Goths, and profusely stored with missile weapons and engines of offence. The approach of the bridge and towers was covered by a strong and massy chain of iron ; and the chain, at either end, on the opposite sides of the Tyber, was defended by a numerous and chosen detachment of archers. But the enterprise of forcing these barriers, and relieving the capital, displays a shining example of the boldness and conduct of Belisarius. His cavalry advanced from the port along the public road, to awe the motions, and distract the attention of the enemy. His infantry and provisions were distributed in two hundred large boats; and each boat was shielded by a high rampart of thick planks, pierced with many small holes for the discharge of missile weapons. In the front, two large vessels were linked together to sustain a floating castle, which commanded the towers of the bridge, and contained a magazine of fire, sulphur, and bitumen. The whole fleet, which the general led in person, was laboriously moved against the current of the river. The chain yielded to their weight, and the enemies who guarded the banks were either slain or scattered. As soon as they touched the principal barrier, the fire-ship was instantly grappled to the bridge; one of the towers, with two hundred Goths, was consumed by the flames; the assailants shouted victory; and Rome was saved, if the wisdom of Belisarius had not been defeated by the misconduct of his officers. He had previously sent orders to Bessas to second his operations by a timely sally from the town; and he had fixed his lieutenant, Isaac, by a peremptory command, to the station of the port. But avarice rendered Bessas immovable; while the youthful ardor of Isaac delivered him into the hands of a superior enemy. The exaggerated rumor of his defeat was hastily carried to the ears of Belisarius: he paused; betrayed in that single moment of his life some emotions of surprise and perplexity; and reluctantly sounded a retreat to save his wife Antonina, his treasures, and the only harbor which he possessed on the Tuscan coast. The vexation of his mind produced an ardent and almost mortal fever; and Rome was left without protection to the mercy or indignation of Totila. The continuance of hostilities had embittered the national hatred: the Arian clergy was ignominiously driven from Rome; Pelagius, the archdeacon, returned without success from an embassy to the Gothic camp; and a Sicilian bishop, the envoy or nuncio of the pope, was deprived of both his hands, for daring to utter falsehoods in the service of the church and state.

Famine had relaxed the strength and discipline of the garrison of Rome. They could derive no effectual service from a dying people; and the inhuman avarice of the merchant at length absorbed the vigilance of the governor. Four Isaurian sentinels, while their companions slept, and their officers were absent, descended by a rope from the wall, and secretly proposed to the Gothic king to introduce his troops into the city. The offer was entertained with coldness and suspicion; they returned in safety; they twice repeated their visit; the place was twice examined; the conspiracy was known and disregarded; and no sooner had

Totila consented to the attempt, than they unbarred the Asinarian gate, and gave admittance to the Goths. Till the dawn of day, they halted in order of battle, apprehensive of treachery or ambush; but the troops of Bessas, with their leader, had already escaped; and when the king was pressed to disturb their retreat, he prudently replied, that no sight could be more grateful than that of a flying enemy. The patricians, who were still possessed of horses, Decius, Basilius, etc., accompanied the governor; their brethren, among whom Olybrius, Orestes, and Maximus, are named by the historian, took refuge in the church of St. Peter: but the assertion, that only five hundred persons remained in the capital, inspires some doubt of the fidelity either of his narrative or of his text. As soon as daylight had displayed the entire victory of the Goths, their monarch devoutly visited the tomb of the prince of the apostles; but while he prayed at the altar, twenty-five soldiers, and sixty citizens, were put to the sword in the vestibule of the temple. The archdeacon Pelagius [13] stood before him, with the Gospels in his hand. "O Lord, be merciful to your servant." "Pelagius," said Totila, with an insulting smile, "your pride now condescends to become a suppliant." "I *am* a suppliant," replied the prudent archdeacon; "God has now made us your subjects, and as your subjects, we are entitled to your clemency." At his humble prayer, the lives of the Romans were spared; and the chastity of the maids and matrons was preserved inviolate from the passions of the hungry soldiers. But they were rewarded by the freedom of pillage, after the most precious spoils had been reserved for the royal treasury. The houses of the senators were plentifully stored with gold and silver; and the avarice of Bessas had labored with so much guilt and shame for the benefit of the conqueror. In this revolution, the sons and daughters of Roman consuls tasted the misery which they had spurned or relieved, wandered in tattered garments through the streets of the city, and begged their bread, perhaps without success, before the gates of their hereditary mansions. The riches of Rusticiana, the daughter of Symmachus and widow of Boethius, had been generously devoted to alleviate the calamities of famine. But the barbarians were exasperated by the report, that she had prompted the people to overthrow the statues of the great Theodoric; and the life of that venerable matron would have been sacrificed to his memory, if Totila had not respected her birth, her virtues, and even the pious motive of her revenge. The next day he pronounced two orations, to congratulate and admonish his victorious Goths, and to reproach the senate, as the vilest of slaves, with their perjury, folly, and ingratitude; sternly declaring, that their estates and honors were justly forfeited to the companions of his arms. Yet he consented to forgive their revolt ; and the senators repaid his clemency by despatching circular letters to their tenants and vassals in the provinces of Italy, strictly to enjoin them to desert the standard of the Greeks, to cultivate their lands in peace, and to learn from their masters the duty of obedience to a Gothic sovereign. Against the city which had so long delayed the course of his victories, he appeared inexorable : one third of the walls, in different parts, were demolished by his command ; fire and engines prepared to consume or subvert the most stately works of antiquity ; and the world was astonished by the fatal decree, that Rome should be changed into a pasture for cattle. The firm and temperate remonstrance of Belisarius suspended the execution ; he warned the barbarian not to sully his fame by the destruction of those monuments which were the glory of the dead, and the delight of the living ; and Totila was persuaded, by the advice of an enemy, to preserve Rome as the ornament of his kingdom, or the fairest pledge of peace and reconciliation. When he had signified to the ambassadors of Belisarius his intention of sparing the city, he stationed an army at the distance of one hundred and twenty furlongs, to observe the motions of the Roman general. With the remainder of his forces he marched into Lucania and Apulia, and occupied on the summit of Mount Garganus [14] o1e of the camps of Hannibal. [15] The senators were dragged in his train, and afterwards confined in the fortresses of Campania : the citizens, with their wives and children, were dispersed in exile ; and during forty days Rome was abandoned to desolate and dreary solitude. [16]

The loss of Rome was speedily retrieved by an action, to which, according to the event, the public opinion would apply the names of rashness or heroism. After the departure of Totila, the Roman general sallied from the port at the head of a thousand horse, cut in pieces the enemy who opposed his progress, and visited with pity and reverence the vacant space of the *eternal* city. Resolved to maintain a station so conspicuous in the eyes of mankind, he summoned the greatest part of his troops to the standard which he erected on the Capitol : the old inhabitants were recalled by the love of their country and the hopes of food ; and the keys of Rome were sent a second time to the emperor Justinian. The walls, as far as they had been demolished by the Goths, were repaired with rude and dissimilar materials ; the ditch was restored ; iron spikes [17] were profusely scattered in the highways to annoy the feet of the horses ; and as new gates could not suddenly be procured, the entrance was guarded by a Spartan rampart of his bravest soldiers.

At the expiration of twenty-five days, Totila returned by hasty marches from Apulia to avenge the injury and disgrace. Belisarius expected his approach. The Goths were thrice repulsed in three general assaults; they lost the flower of their troops; the royal standard had almost fallen into the hands of the enemy, and the fame of Totila sunk, as it had risen, with the fortune of his arms. Whatever skill and courage could achieve, had been performed by the Roman general: it remained only that Justinian should terminate, by a strong and seasonable effort, the war which he had ambitiously undertaken. The indolence, perhaps the impotence, of a prince who despised his enemies, and envied his servants, protracted the calamities of Italy. After a long silence, Belisarius was commanded to leave a sufficient garrison at Rome, and to transport himself into the province of Lucania, whose inhabitants, inflamed by Catholic zeal, had cast away the yoke of their Arian conquerors. In this ignoble warfare, the hero, invincible against the power of the barbarians, was basely vanquished by the delay, the disobedience, and the cowardice of his own officers. He reposed in his winter quarters of Crotona, in the full assurance, that the two passes of the Lucanian hills were guarded by his cavalry. They were betrayed by treachery or weakness; and the rapid march of the Goths scarcely allowed time for the escape of Belisarius to the coast of Sicily. At length a fleet and army were assembled for the relief of Ruscianum, or Rossano,[18] a fortress sixty furlongs from the ruins of Sybaris, where the nobles of Lucania had taken refuge. In the first attempt, the Roman forces were dissipated by a storm. In the second, they approached the shore; but they saw the hills covered with archers, the landing-place defended by a line of spears, and the king of the Goths impatient for battle. The conqueror of Italy retired with a sigh, and continued to languish, inglorious and inactive, till Antonina, who had been sent to Constantinople to solicit succors, obtained, after the death of the empress, the permission of his return.

The last five campaigns of Belisarius might abate the envy of his competitors, whose eyes had been dazzled and wounded by the blaze of his former glory. Instead of delivering Italy from the Goths, he had wandered like a fugitive along the coast, without daring to march into the country, or to accept the bold and repeated challenge of Totila. Yet, in the judgment of the few who could discriminate counsels from events, and compare the instruments with the execution, he appeared a more consummate master of the art of war, than in the season of his prosperity, when he presented two captive kings before the throne of Justinian. The valor of Belisarius was not chilled by age: his prudence was matured by experience ; but the more noble virtues of humanity and justice seem to have yielded to the hard necessity of the times. The parsimony or poverty of the emperor compelled him to deviate from the rule of conduct which had deserved the love and confidence of the Italians. The war was maintained by the oppression of Ravenna, Sicily, and all the faithful subjects of the empire ; and the rigorous prosecution of Herodian provoked that injured or guilty officer to deliver Spoleto into the hands of the enemy. The avarice of Antonina, which had been sometimes diverted by love, now reigned without a rival in her breast. Belisarius himself had always understood, that riches, in a corrupt age, are the support and ornament of personal merit. And it cannot be presumed that he should stain his honor for the public service, without applying a part of the spoil to his private emolument. The hero had escaped the sword of the barbarians. But the dagger of conspiracy [19] awaited his return. In the midst of wealth and honors, Artaban, who had chastised the African tyrant, complained of the ingratitude of courts. He aspired to Præjecta, the emperor's niece, who wished to reward her deliverer ; but the impediment of his previous marriage was asserted by the piety of Theodora. The pride of royal descent was irritated by flattery ; and the service in which he gloried had proved him capable of bold and sanguinary deeds. The death of Justinian was resolved, but the conspirators delayed the execution till they could surprise Belisarius disarmed, and naked, in the palace of Constantinople. Not a hope could be entertained of shaking his long-tried fidelity ; and they justly dreaded the revenge, or rather the justice, of the veteran general, who might speedily assemble an army in Thrace to punish the assassins, and perhaps to enjoy the fruits of their crime. Delay afforded time for rash communications and honest confessions : Artaban and his accomplices were condemned by the senate, but the extreme clemency of Justinian detained them in the gentle confinement of the palace, till he pardoned their flagitious attempt against his throne and life. If the emperor forgave his enemies, he must cordially embrace a friend whose victories were alone remembered, and who was endeared to his prince by the recent circumstance of their common danger. Belisarius reposed from his toils, in the high station of general of the East and count of the domestics ; and the older consuls and patricians respectfully yielded the precedency of rank to the peerless merit of the first of the Romans. [20] The first of the Romans still submitted to be the slave of his wife ; but the servitude of habit and affection became less disgraceful when the death of Theodora had removed the baser influence of fear. Joannina,

their daughter, and the sole heiress of their fortunes, was betrothed
to Anastasius, the grandson, or rather the nephew, of the empress, [21]
whose kind interposition forwarded the consummation of their
youthful loves. But the power of Theodora expired, the parents
of Joannina returned, and her honor, perhaps her happiness,
were sacrificed to the revenge of an unfeeling mother, who dissolved the imperfect nuptials before they had been ratified by the
ceremonies of the church. [22]

Before the departure of Belisarius, Perusia was besieged, and
few cities were impregnable to the Gothic arms. Ravenna,
Ancona, and Crotona, still resisted the barbarians ; and when
Totila asked in marriage one of the daughters of France, he was
stung by the just reproach that the king of Italy was unworthy of
his title till it was acknowledged by the Roman people. Three
thousand of the bravest soldiers had been left to defend the
capital. On the suspicion of a monopoly, they massacred the
governor, and announced to Justinian, by a deputation of the
clergy, that unless their offence was pardoned, and their arrears
were satisfied, they should instantly accept the tempting offers
of Totila. But the officer who succeeded to the command (his
name was Diogenes) deserved their esteem and confidence ; and
the Goths, instead of finding an easy conquest, encountered a
vigorous resistance from the soldiers and people, who patiently
endured the loss of the port and of all maritime supplies. The
siege of Rome would perhaps have been raised, if the liberality
of Totila to the Isaurians had not encouraged some of their venal
countrymen to copy the example of treason. In a dark night,
while the Gothic trumpets sounded on another side, they silently
opened the gate of St. Paul : the barbarians rushed into the city ;
and the flying garrison was intercepted before they could reach
the harbor of Centumcellæ. A soldier trained in the school of
Belisarius, Paul of Cilicia, retired with four hundred men to the
mole of Hadrian. They repelled the Goths ; but they felt the
approach of famine ; and their aversion to the taste of horse-flesh
confirmed their resolution to risk the event of a desperate and
decisive sally. But their spirit insensibly stooped to the offers of
capitulation ; they retrieved their arrears of pay, and preserved
their arms and horses, by enlisting in the service of Totila ;
their chiefs, who pleaded a laudable attachment to their wives and
children in the East, were dismissed with honor ; and above four
hundred enemies, who had taken refuge in the sanctuaries, were
saved by the clemency of the victor. He no longer entertained a
wish of destroying the edifices of Rome, [23] which he now respected
as the seat of the Gothic kingdom : the senate and people were

restored to their country ; the means of subsistence were liberally provided ; and Totila, in the robe of peace, exhibited the equestrian games of the circus. Whilst he amused the eyes of the multitude, four hundred vessels were prepared for the embarkation of his troops. The cities of Rhegium and Tarentum were reduced : he passed into Sicily, the object of his implacable resentment ; and the island was stripped of its gold and silver, of the fruits of the earth, and of an infinite number of horses, sheep, and oxen. Sardinia and Corsica obeyed the fortune of Italy ; and the seacoast of Greece was visited by a fleet of three hundred galleys.[24] The Goths were landed in Corcyra and the ancient continent of Epirus ; they advanced as far as Nicopolis, the trophy of Augustus, and Dodona,[25] once famous by the oracle of Jove. In every step of his victories, the wise barbarian repeated to Justinian the desire of peace, applauded the concord of their predecessors, and offered to employ the Gothic arms in the service of the empire.

Justinian was deaf to the voice of peace ; but he neglected the prosecution of war ; and the indolence of his temper disappointed, in some degree, the obstinacy of his passions. From his salutary slumber the emperor was awakened by the pope Vigilius and the patrician Cethegus, who appeared before his throne, and adjured him, in the name of God and the people, to resume the conquest and deliverance of Italy. In the choice of the generals, caprice, as well as judgment, was shown. A fleet and army sailed for the relief of Sicily, under the conduct of Liberius ; but his youth* and want of experience were afterwards discovered, and before he touched the shores of the island he was overtaken by his successor. In the place of Liberius, the conspirator Artaban was raised from a prison to military honors ; in the pious presumption, that gratitude would animate his valor and fortify his allegiance. Belisarius reposed in the shade of his laurels, but the command of the principal army was reserved for Germanus,[26] the emperor's nephew, whose rank and merit had been long depressed by the jealousy of the court. Theodora had injured him in the rights of a private citizen, the marriage of his children, and the testament of his brother ; and although his conduct was pure and blameless, Justinian was displeased that he should be thought worthy of the confidence of the malcontents. The life of Germanus

---

* This is a singular mistake. Procopius calls him εσχατογέρως. Gibbon must have hastily caught at his inexperience, and concluded that it must have been from youth. Lord Mahon has pointed out this error, p. 401. I should add that in the last 4to edition, corrected by Gibbon, it stands "want of youth and experience ;" but Gibbon can scarcely have intended such a phrase.—M.

was a lesson of implicit obedience : he nobly refused to prostitute his name and character in the factions of the circus : the gravity of his manners was tempered by innocent cheerfulness ; and his riches were lent without interest to indigent or deserving friends. His valor had formerly triumphed over the Sclavonians of the Danube and the rebels of Africa : the first report of his promotion revived the hopes of the Italians ; and he was privately assured, that a crowd of Roman deserters would abandon, on his approach, the standard of Totila. His second marriage with Malasontha, the granddaughter of Theodoric, endeared Germanus to the Goths themselves ; and they marched with reluctance against the father of a royal infant, the last offspring of the line of Amali.[27] A splendid allowance was assigned by the emperor : the general contributed his private fortune ; his two sons were popular and active ; and he surpassed, in the promptitude and success of his levies, the expectation of mankind. He was permitted to select some squadrons of Thracian cavalry : the veterans, as well as the youth of Constantinople and Europe, engaged their voluntary service ; and as far as the heart of Germany, his fame and liberality attracted the aid of the barbarians.* The Romans advanced to Sardica ; an army of Sclavonians fled before their march ; but within two days of their final departure, the designs of Germanus were terminated by his malady and death. Yet the impulse which he had given to the Italian war still continued to act with energy and effect. The maritime towns, Ancona, Crotona, Centumcellæ, resisted the assaults of Totila. Sicily was reduced by the zeal of Artaban, and the Gothic navy was defeated near the coast of the Adriatic. The two fleets were almost equal, forty-seven to fifty galleys : the victory was decided by the knowledge and dexterity of the Greeks ; but the ships were so closely grappled, that only twelve of the Goths escaped from this unfortunate conflict. They affected to depreciate an element in which they were unskilled ; but their own experience confirmed the truth of a maxim, that the master of the sea will always acquire the dominion of the land.[28]

After the loss of Germanus, the nations were provoked to smile, by the strange intelligence, that the command of the Roman armies was given to a eunuch. But the eunuch Narses[29] is ranked among the few who have rescued that unhappy name from the contempt and hatred of mankind. A feeble, diminutive body concealed the soul of a statesman and a warrior. His youth had been employed in the management of the loom and distaff, in the cares of the household, and the service of female luxury ; but while his hands

---

* See note 31, p. 189.—M.

were busy, he secretly exercised the faculties of a vigorous and discerning mind. A stranger to the schools and the camp, he studied in the palace to dissemble, to flatter, and to persuade ; and as soon as he approached the person of the emperor, Justinian listened with surprise and pleasure to the manly counsels of his chamberlain and private treasurer.[30] The talents of Narses were tried and improved in frequent embassies : he led an arffiy into Italy, acquired a practical knowledge of the war and the country, and presumed to strive with the genius of Belisarius. Twelve years after his return, the eunuch was chosen to achieve the conquest which had been left imperfect by the first of the Roman generals. Instead of being dazzled by vanity or emulation, he seriously declared that, unless he were armed with an adequate force, he would never consent to risk his own glory and that of his sovereign. Justinian granted to the favorite what he might have denied to the hero : the Gothic war was rekindled from its ashes, and the preparations were not unworthy of the ancient majesty of the empire. The key of the public treasure was put into his hand, to collect magazines, to levy soldiers, to purchase arms and horses, to discharge the arrears of pay, and to tempt the fidelity of the fugitives and deserters. The troops of Germanus were still in arms ; they halted at Salona in the expectation of a new leader ; and legions of subjects and allies were created by the well-known liberality of the eunuch Narses. The king of the Lombards[31] satisfied or surpassed the obligations of a treaty, by lending two thousand two hundred of his bravest warriors,* who were followed by three thousand of their martial attendants. Three thousand Heruli fought on horseback under Philemuth, their native chief ; and the noble Aratus, who adopted the manners and discipline of Rome, conducted a band of veterans of the same nation. Dagistheus was released from prison to command the Huns ; and Kobad, the grandson and nephew of the great king, was conspicuous by the regal tiara at the head of his faithful Persians, who had devoted themselves to the fortunes of their prince.[32] Absolute in the exercise of his authority, more absolute in the affection of his troops, Narses led a numerous and gallant army from Philippopolis to Salona, from whence he coästed

---

* Gibbon has blindly followed the translation of Maltretus : Bis mille ducentos—while the original Greek says expressly πεντακοσίους τε καὶ δισχελιους, (Goth. lib. iv. c. 26). In like manner (p. 188) he draws volunteers from Germany, on the authority of Cousin, who, in one place, has mistakén Germanus for Germania. Yet only a few pages further we find Gibbon loudly condemning the French and Latin readers of Procopius. Lord Mahon, p. 403. The first of these errors remains uncorrected in the new edition of the Byzantines.—M.

the eastern side of the Adriatic as far as the confines of Italy.
His progress was checked. The East could not supply vessels
capable of transporting such multitudes of men and horses. The
Franks, who, in the general confusion had usurped the greater
part of the Venetian province, refused a free passage to the friends
of the Lombards. The station of Verona was occupied by Teias,
with the flower of the Gothic forces ; and that skilful commander
had overspread the adjacent country with the fall of woods and
the inundation of waters.[33] In this perplexity, an officer of experience proposed a measure, secure by the appearance of rashness ;
that the Roman army should cautiously advance along the sea-shore,
while the fleet preceded their march, and successively cast a
bridge of boats over the mouths of the rivers, the Timavus, the
Brenta, the Adige, and the Po, that fall into the Adriatic to the
north of Ravenna. Nine days he reposed in the city, collected
the fragments of the Italian army, and marched towards Rimini
to meet the defiance of an insulting enemy.

The prudence of Narses impelled him to speedy and decisive
action. His powers were the last effort of the state ; the cost of
each day accumulated the enormous account ; and the nations,
untrained to discipline or fatigue, might be rashly provoked
to turn their arms against each other, or against their benefactor.
The same considerations might have tempered the ardor of Totila.
But he was conscious that the clergy and people of Italy aspired
to a second revolution : he felt or suspected the rapid progress of
treason ; and he resolved to risk the Gothic kingdom on the
chance of a day, in which the valiant would be animated by
instant danger, and the disaffected might be awed by mutual
ignorance. In his march from Ravenna, the Roman general
chastised the garrison of Rimini, traversed in a direct line the
hills of Urbino, and re-entered the Flaminian way, nine miles
beyond the perforated rock, an obstacle of art and nature which
might have stopped or retarded his progress.[34] The Goths were
assembled in the neighborhood of Rome ; they advanced without
delay to seek a superior enemy, and the two armies approached each
other at the distance of one hundred furlongs, between Tagina [35]
and the sepulchres of the Gauls.[36] The haughty message of Narses
was an offer, not of peace, but of pardon. The answer of the
Gothic king declared his resolution to die or conquer. "What
day," said the messenger, "will you fix for the combat ?" "The
eighth day," replied Totila ; but early the next morning he
attempted to surprise a foe, suspicious of deceit, and prepared for
battle. Ten thousand Heruli and Lombards, of approved valor
and doubtful faith, were placed in the centre. Each of the wings

was composed of eight thousand Romans ; the right was guarded by the cavalry of the Huns, the left was covered by fifteen hundred chosen horse, destined, according to the emergencies of action, to sustain the retreat of their friends, or to encompass the flank of the enemy. From his proper station at the head of the right wing, the eunuch rode along the line, expressing by his voice and countenance the assurance of victory ; exciting the soldiers of the emperor to punish the guilt and madness of a band of robbers ; and exposing to their view gold chains, collars, and bracelets, the rewards of military virtue. From the event of a single combat they drew an omen of success ; and they beheld with pleasure the courage of fifty archers, who maintained a small eminence against three successive attacks of the Gothic cavalry. At the distance only of two bow-shots, the armies spent the morning in dreadful suspense, and the Romans tasted some necessary food, without unloosing the cuirass from their breast, or the bridle from their horses. Narses awaited the charge ; and it was delayed by Totila till he had received his last succors of two thousand Goths. While he consumed the hours in fruitless treaty, the king exhibited in a narrow space the strength and agility of a warrior. His armor was enchased with gold ; his purple banner floated with the wind : he cast his lance into the air ; caught it with the right hand ; shifted it to the left ; threw himself backwards ; recovered his seat ; and managed a fiery steeed in all the paces and evolutions of the equestrian school. As soon as the succors had arrived, he retired to his tent, assumed the dress and arms of a private soldier, and gave the signal of battle. The first line of cavalry advanced with more courage than discretion, and left behind them the infantry of the second line. They were soon engaged between the horns of a crescent, into which the adverse wings had been insensibly curved, and were saluted from either side by the volleys of four thousand archers. Their ardor, and even their distress, drove them forwards to a close and unequal conflict, in which they could only use their lances against an enemy equally skilled in all the instruments of war. A generous emulation inspired the Romans and their barbarian allies ; and Narses, who calmly viewed and directed their efforts, doubted to whom he should adjudge the prize of superior bravery. The Gothic cavalry was astonished and disordered, pressed and broken ; and the line of infantry, instead of presenting their spears, or opening their intervals, were trampled under the feet of the flying horse. Six thousand of the Goths were slaughtered without mercy in the field of Tagina. Their prince, with five attendants, was overtaken by Asbad, of the race of the Gepidæ. " Spare the king of Italy," * cried a loyal voice, and Asbad struck his lance through the body of Totila. The blow was instantly revenged by the faithful Goths: they transported their dying monarch seven miles beyond the scene of his disgrace; and his last moments were not imbittered by the presence of an enemy. Compassion afforded him the shelter of an obscure tomb; but the Romans were not satisfied of their victory, till they beheld the corpse of the Gothic king. His hat, enriched with gems, and his bloody robe, were presented to Justinian by the messengers of triumph.[37]

As soon as Narses had paid his devotions to the Author of victory, and the blessed Virgin, his peculiar patroness,[38] he praised, rewarded, and dismissed the Lombards. The villages had been reduced to ashes by these valiant savages; they ravished matrons and virgins on the altar; their retreat was diligently watched by a strong detachment of regular forces, who prevented a repetition of the like disorders. The victorious eunuch pursued his march through Tuscany, accepted the submission of the Goths, heard the acclamations, and often the complaints, of the Italians, and encompassed the walls of Rome with the remainder of his formidable host. Round the wide circumference, Narses assigned to himself, and to each of his lieutenants, a real or a feigned attack, while he silently marked the place of easy and unguarded entrance. Neither the fortifications of Hadrian's mole, nor of the port, could long delay the progress of the conqueror; and Justinian once more received the keys of Rome, which, under his reign, had been *five* times taken and recovered.[39] But the deliverance of Rome was the last calamity of the Roman people. The barbarian allies of Narses too frequently confounded the privileges of peace and war. The despair of the flying Goths found some consolation in sanguinary revenge; and three hundred youths of the noblest families, who had been sent as hostages beyond the Po, were inhumanly slain by the successor of Totila. The fate of the senate suggests an awful lesson of the vicissitude of human affairs. Of the senators whom Totila had banished from their country, some were rescued by an officer of Belisarius, and transported from Campania to Sicily; while others were too guilty to confide in the clemency of Justinian, or too poor to provide horses for their escape to the sea-shore. Their brethren languished five years in a state of indigence and exile: the victory of Narses revived their hopes; but their premature return to the metropolis was prevented by the furious Goths; and all the fortresses of Campania were

---

* " Dog, wilt thou strike thy Lord ?" was the more characteristic expression of the Gothic youth. Procop. lib. iv. p. 32.—M.

stained with patrician [40] blood. After a period of thirteen centuries, the institution of Romulus expired ; and if the nobles of Rome still assumed the title of senators, few subsequent traces can be discovered of a public council, or constitutional order. Ascend six hundred years, and contemplate the kings of the earth soliciting an audience, as the slaves or freedmen of the Roman senate ! [41]

The Gothic war was yet alive. The bravest of the nation retired beyond the Po ; and Teias was unanimously chosen to succeed and revenge their departed hero. The new king immediately sent ambassadors to implore, or rather to purchase, the aid of the Franks, and nobly lavished, for the public safety, the riches which had been deposited in the palace of Pavia. The residue of the royal treasure was guarded by his brother Aligern, at Cumæa, in Campania ; but the strong castle which Totila had fortified was closely besieged by the arms of Narses. From the Alps to the foot of Mount Vesuvius, the Gothic king, by rapid and secret marches, advanced to the relief of his brother, eluded the vigilance of the Roman chiefs, and pitched his camp on the banks of the Sarnus or *Draco*, [42] which flows from Nuceria into the Bay of Naples. The river separated the two armies : sixty days were consumed in distant and fruitless combats, and Teias maintained this important post till he was deserted by his fleet and the hope of subsistence. With reluctant steps he ascended the *Lactarian* mount, where the physicians of Rome, since the time of Galen, had sent their patients for the benefit of the air and the milk. [43] But the Goths soon embraced a more generous resolution : to descend the hill, to dismiss their horses, and to die in arms, and in the possession of freedom. The king marched at their head, bearing in his right hand a lance, and an ample buckler in his left : with the one he struck dead the foremost of the assailants ; with the other he received the weapons which every hand was ambitious to aim against his life. After the combat of many hours, his left arm was fatigued by the weight of twelve javelins which hung from his shield. Without moving from his ground, or suspending his blows, the hero called aloud on his attendants for a fresh buckler ; but in the moment while his side was uncovered, it was pierced by a mortal dart. He fell ; and his head, exalted on a spear, proclaimed to the nations that the Gothic kingdom was no more. But the example of his death served only to animate the companions who had sworn to perish with their leader. They fought till darkness descended on the earth. They reposed on their arms. The combat was renewed with the return of light, and maintained with unabated vigor till the evening of the second day. The repose of a second night, the want of water, and the loss of their bravest champions, determined the surviving Goths to accept the fair capitulation which the prudence of Narses was inclined to propose. They embraced the alternative of residing in Italy, as the subjects and soldiers of Justinian, or departing with a portion of their private wealth in search of some independent country.[44] Yet the oath of fidelity or exile was alike rejected by one thousand Goths, who broke away before the treaty was signed, and boldly effected their retreat to the walls of Pavia. The spirit, as well as the situation, of Aligern prompted him to imitate rather than to bewail his brother ; a strong and dexterous archer, he transpierced with a single arrow the armor and breast of his antagonist ; and his military conduct defended Cumæ [45] above a year against the forces of the Romans. Their industry had scooped the Sibyl's cave [46] into a prodigious mine ; combustible materials were introduced to consume the temporary props : the wall and the gate of Cumæ sunk into the cavern, but the ruins formed a deep and inaccessible precipice. On the fragment of a rock Aligern stood alone and unshaken, till he calmly surveyed the hopeless condition of his country, and judged it more honorable to be the friend of Narses, than the slave of the Franks. After the death of Teias, the Roman general separated his troops to reduce the cities of Italy : Lucca sustained a long and vigorous siege : and such was the humanity or the prudence of Narses, that the repeated perfidy of the inhabitants could not provoke him to exact the forfeit lives of their hostages. These hostages were dismissed in safety ; and their grateful zeal at length subdued the obstinacy of their countrymen.[47]

Before Lucca had surrendered, Italy was overwhelmed by a new deluge of barbarians. A feeble youth, the grandson of Clovis, reigned over the Austrasians or oriental Franks. The guardians of Theodebald entertained with coldness and reluctance the magnificent promises of the Gothic ambassadors. But the spirit of a martial people outstripped the timid counsels of the court : two brothers, Lothaire and Buccelin,[48] the dukes of the Alemanni, stood forth as the leaders of the Italian war ; and seventy-five thousand Germans descended in the autumn from the Rhætian Alps into the plain of Milan. The vanguard of the Roman army was stationed near the Po, under the conduct of Fulcaris, a bold Herulian, who rashly conceived that personal bravery was the sole duty and merit of a commander. As he marched without order or precaution along the Æmilian way, an ambuscade of Franks suddenly rose from the amphitheatre of Parma ; his troops were surprised and routed ; but their leader refused to fly ; declaring, to the last moment, that death was less terrible than the angry countenance of Narses.* The death of Fulcaris, and the retreat of the surviving chiefs, decided the fluctuating and rebellious temper of the Goths; they flew to the standard of their deliverers, and admitted them into the cities which still resisted the arms of the Roman general. The conqueror of Italy opened a free passage to the irresistible torrent of barbarians. They passed under the walls of Cesena, and answered by threats and reproaches the advice of Aligern,† that the Gothic treasures could no longer repay the labor of an invasion. Two thousand Franks were destroyed by the skill and valor of Narses himself, who sailed from Rimini at the head of three hundred horse, to chastise the licentious rapine of their march. On the confines of Samnium the two brothers divided their forces. With the right wing, Buccelin assumed the spoil of Campania, Lucania, and Bruttium; with the left, Lothaire accepted the plunder of Apulia and Calabria. They followed the coast of the Mediterranean and the Adriatic, as far as Rhegium and Otranto, and the extreme lands of Italy were the term of their destructive progress. The Franks, who were Christians and Catholics, contented themselves with simple pillage and occasional murder. But the churches which their piety had spared, were stripped by the sacrilegious hands of the Alemanni, who sacrificed horses' heads to their native deities of the woods and rivers: [49] they melted or profaned the consecrated vessels, and the ruins of shrines and altars were stained with the blood of the faithful. Buccelin was actuated by ambition, and Lothaire by avarice. The former aspired to restore the Gothic kingdom; the latter, after a promise to his brother of speedy succors, returned by the same road to deposit his treasure beyond the Alps. The strength of their armies was already wasted by the change of climate and contagion of disease: the Germans revelled in the vintage of Italy; and their own intemperance avenged, in some degree, the miseries of a defenceless people.‡

At the entrance of the spring, the Imperial troops, who had guarded the cities, assembled, to the number of eighteen thousand men, in the neighborhood of Rome. Their winter hours had not been consumed in idleness. By the command, and after the example, of Narses, they repeated each day their military exercise

---

* . . . τὴν γλῶτταν Ναρσοῦ μεμφομένην μοι τῆς ἀβουλίας. Agathias.

† Aligern, after the surrender of Cumæ, had been sent to Cesena by Narses. Agathias.—M.

‡ A body of Lothaire's troops was defeated near Fano, some were driven down precipices into the sea, others fled to the camp; many prisoners seized the opportunity of making their escape; and the barbarians lost most of their booty in their precipitate retreat. Agathias.—M.

on foot and on horseback, accustomed their ear to obey the sound
of the trumpet, and practised the steps and evolutions of the Pyr-
rhic dance. From the Straits of Sicily, Buccelin, with thirty
thousand Franks and Alemanni, slowly moved towards Capua, occupied with a wooden tower the bridge of Casilinum, covered his
right by the stream of the Vulturnus, and secured the rest of his
encampment by a rampart of sharp stakes, and a circle of wagons,
whose wheels were buried in the earth. He impatiently expected
the return of Lothaire ; ignorant, alas ! that his brother could
never return, and that the chief and his army had been swept
away by a strange disease [50] on the banks of the Lake Benacus,
between Trent and Verona. The banners of Narses soon approached the Vulturnus, and the eyes of Italy were anxiously fixed
on the event of this final contest. Perhaps the talents of the Roman general were most conspicuous in the calm operations which
precede the tumult of a battle. His skilful movements intercepted the subsistence of the barbarian, deprived him of the advantage of the bridge and river, and in the choice of the ground and
moment of action reduced him to comply with the inclination of
his enemy. On the morning of the important day, when the
ranks were already formed, a servant, for some trivial fault, was
killed by his master, one of the leaders of the Heruli. The justice or passion of Narses was awakened : he summoned the offender
to his presence, and without listening to his excuses, gave the signal to the minister of death. If the cruel master had not infringed
the laws of his nation, this arbitrary execution was not less unjust
than it appears to have been imprudent. The Heruli felt the indignity ; they halted : but the Roman general, without soothing
their rage, or expecting their resolution, called aloud, as the
trumpets sounded, that unless they hastened to occupy their
place, they would lose the honor of the victory. His troops were
disposed [51] in a long front, the cavalry on the wings ; in the centre, the heavy-armed foot ; the archers and slingers in the rear.
The Germans advanced in a sharp-pointed column, of the form of
a triangle or solid wedge. They pierced the feeble centre of
Narses, who received them with a smile into the fatal snare, and
directed his wings of cavalry insensibly to wheel on their flanks
and encompass their rear. The host of the Franks and Alemanni
consisted of infantry : a sword and buckler hung by their side ;
and they used, as their weapons of offence, a weighty hatchet and
a hooked javelin, which were only formidable in close combat, or
at a short distance. The flower of the Roman archers, on horseback, and in complete armor, skirmished without peril round this
immovable phalanx ; supplied by active speed the deficiency of

number ; and aimed their arrows against a crowd of barbarians, who, instead of a cuirass and helmet, were covered by a loose garment of fur or linen. They paused, they trembled, their ranks were confounded, and in the decisive moment the Heruli, preferring glory to revenge, charged with rapid violence the head of the column. Their leader, Sinbal, and Aligern, the Gothic prince, deserved the prize of superior valor ; and their example incited the victorious troops to achieve with swords and spears the destruction of the enemy. Buccelin, and the greatest part of his army, perished on the field of battle, in the waters of the Vulturnus, or by the hands of the enraged peasants : but it may seem incredible, that a victory,[52] which no more than five of the Alemanni survived, could be purchased with the loss of fourscore Romans. Seven thousand Goths, the relics of the war, defended the fortress of Campsa till the ensuing spring ; and every messenger of Narses announced the reduction of the Italian cities, whose names were corrupted by the ignorance or vanity of the Greeks.[53] After the battle of Casilinum, Narses entered the capital ; the arms and treasures of the Goths, the Franks, and the Alemanni, were displayed ; his soldiers, with garlands in their hands, chanted the praises of the conqueror ; and Rome, for the last time, beheld the semblance of a triumph.

After a reign of sixty years, the throne of the Gothic kings was filled by the exarchs of Ravenna, the representatives in peace and war of the emperor of the Romans. Their jurisdiction was soon reduced to the limits of a narrow province ; but Narses himself, the first and most powerful of the exarchs, administered above fifteen years the entire kingdom of Italy. Like Belisarius, he had deserved the honors of envy, calumny, and disgrace : but the favorite eunuch still enjoyed the confidence of Justinian ; or the leader of a victorious army awed and repressed the ingratitude of a timid court. Yet it was not by weak and mischievous indulgence that Narses secured the attachment of his troops. Forgetful of the past, and regardless of the future, they abused the present hour of prosperity and peace. The cities of Italy resounded with the noise of drinking and dancing : the spoils of victory were wasted in sensual pleasures ; and nothing (says Agathias) remained unless to exchange their shields and helmets for the soft lute and the capacious hogshead.[54] In a manly oration, not unworthy of a Roman censor, the eunuch reproved these disorderly vices, which sullied their fame, and endangered their safety. The soldiers blushed and obeyed ; discipline was confirmed ; the fortifications were restored ; a *duke* was stationed for the defence and military command of each of the principal cities ; [55] and the eye of Narses pervaded the ample prospect from Calabria to the Alps. The remains of the Gothic nation evacuated the country, or mingled with the people ; the Franks, instead of revenging the death of Buccelin, abandoned, without a struggle, their Italian conquests ; and the rebellious Sinbal, chief of the Heruli, was subdued, taken and hung on a lofty gallows by the inflexible justice of the exarch. [56]   The civil state of Italy, after the agitation of a long tempest, was fixed by a pragmatic sanction, which the emperor promulgated at the request of the pope. Justinian introduced his own jurisprudence into the schools and tribunals of the West : he ratified the acts of Theodoric and his immediate successors, but every deed was rescinded and abolished which force had extorted, or fear had subscribed, under the usurpation of Totila. A moderate theory was framed to reconcile the rights of property with the safety of prescription, the claims of the state with the poverty of the people, and the pardon of offences with the interest of virtue and order of society. Under the exarchs of Ravenna, Rome was degraded to the second rank. Yet the senators were gratified by the permission of visiting their estates in Italy, and of approaching, without obstacle, the throne of Constantinople : the regulation of weights and measures was delegated to the pope and senate ; and the salaries of lawyers and physicians, of orators and grammarians, were destined to preserve, or rekindle, the light of science in the ancient capital. Justinian might dictate benevolent edicts, [57] and Narses might second his wishes by the restoration of cities, and more especially of churches. But the power of kings is most effectual to destroy ; and the twenty years of the Gothic war had consummated the distress and depopulation of Italy. As early as the fourth campaign, under the discipline of Belisarius himself, fifty thousand laborers died of hunger [58] in the narrow region of Picenum ; [59] and a strict interpretation of the evidence of Procopius would swell the loss of Italy above the total sum of her present inhabitants. [60]

I desire to believe, but I dare not affirm, that Belisarius sincerely rejoiced in the triumph of Narses. Yet the consciousness of his own exploits might teach him to esteem without jealousy the merit of a rival ; and the repose of the aged warrior was crowned by a last victory, which saved the emperor and the capital. The barbarians, who annually visited the provinces of Europe, were less discouraged by some accidental defeats, than they were excited by the double hope of spoil and of subsidy. In the thirty-second winter of Justinian's reign, the Danube was deeply frozen : Zabergan led the cavalry of the Bulgarians, and his standard was followed by a promiscuous multitude of Sclavonians.* The savage chief passed, without opposition, the river and the mountains, spread his troops over Macedonia and Thrace, and advanced with no more than seven thousand horse to the long wall, which should have defended the territory of Constantinople. But the works of man are impotent against the assaults of nature : a recent earthquake had shaken the foundations of the wall ; and the forces of the empire were employed on the distant frontiers of Italy, Africa, and Persia. The seven *schools*,[61] or companies of the guards or domestic troops, had been augmented to the number of five thousand five hundred men, whose ordinary station was in the peaceful cities of Asia. But the places of the brave Armenians were insensibly supplied by lazy citizens, who purchased an exemption from the duties of civil life, without being exposed to the dangers of military service. Of such soldiers, few could be tempted to sally from the gates ; and none could be persuaded to remain in the field, unless they wanted strength and speed to escape from the Bulgarians. The report of the fugitives exaggerated the numbers and fierceness of an enemy, who had polluted holy virgins, and abandoned new-born infants to the dogs and vultures ; a crowd of rustics, imploring food and protection, increased the consternation of the city, and the tents of Zabergan were pitched at the distance of twenty miles,[62] on the banks of a small river, which encircles Melanthias, and afterwards falls into the Propontis.[63] Justinian trembled : and those who had only seen the emperor in his old age, were pleased to suppose, that he had *lost* the alacrity and vigor of his youth. By his command the vessels of gold and silver were removed from the churches in the neighborhood, and even the suburbs, of Constantinople ; the ramparts were lined with trembling spectators ; the golden gate was crowded with useless generals and tribunes, and the senate shared the fatigues and the apprehensions of the populace.

But the eyes of the prince and people were directed to a feeble veteran, who was compelled by the public danger to resume the armor in which he had entered Carthage and defended Rome. The horses of the royal stables, of private citizens, and even of the circus, were hastily collected ; the emulation of the old and young was roused by the name of Belisarius, and his first encampment was in the presence of a victorious enemy. His prudence, and the labor of the friendly peasants, secured, with a ditch and rampart, the repose of the night ; innumerable fires, and clouds of

---

* Zabergan was king of the Cutrigours, a tribe of Huns, who were nei·her Bulgarians nor Sclavonians. St. Martin, vol. ix. p. 408-420.—M.

dust, were artfully contrived to magnify the opinion of his
strength ; his soldiers suddenly passed from despondency to presumption ; and, while ten thousand voices demanded the battle,
Belisarius dissembled his knowledge, that in the hour of trial he
must depend on the firmness of three hundred veterans. The
next morning the Bulgarian cavalry advanced to the charge. But
they heard the shouts of multitudes, they beheld the arms and
discipline of the front ; they were assaulted on the flanks by two
ambuscades which rose from the woods ; their foremost warriors
fell by the hand of the aged hero and his guards ; and the swiftness of their evolutions was rendered useless by the close attack
and rapid pursuit of the Romans. In this action (so speedy was
their flight) the Bulgarians lost only four hundred horse ; but
Constantinople was saved ; and Zabergan, who felt the hand of a
master, withdrew to a respectful distance. But his friends were
numerous in the councils of the emperor, and Belisarius obeyed
with reluctance the commands of envy and Justinian, which forbade him to achieve the deliverance of his country. On his return to the city, the people, still conscious of their danger, accompanied his triumph with acclamations of joy and gratitude, which
were imputed as a crime to the victorious general. But when he
entered the palace, the courtiers were silent, and the emperor,
after a cold and thankless embrace, dismissed him to mingle with
the train of slaves. Yet so deep was the impression of his glory
on the minds of men, that Justinian, in the seventy-seventh year
of his age, was encouraged to advance near forty miles from the
capital, and to inspect in person the restoration of the long wall.
The Bulgarians wasted the summer in the plains of Thrace ; but
they were inclined to peace by the failure of their rash attempts
on Greece and the Chersonesus. A menace of killing their prisoners quickened the payment of heavy ransoms ; and the departure of Zabergan was hastened by the report, that double-prowed
vessels were built on the Danube to intercept his passage. The
danger was soon forgotten ; and a vain question, whether their
sovereign had shown more wisdom or weakness, amused the idleness of the city.[64]

About two years after the last victory of Belisarius, the emperor returned from a Thracian journey of health, or business, or
devotion. Justinian was afflicted by a pain in his head ; and his
private entry countenanced the rumor of his death. Before the
third hour of the day, the bakers' shops were plundered of their
bread, the houses were shut, and every citizen, with hope or terror, prepared for the impending tumult. The senators themselves, fearful and suspicious, were convened at the ninth hour ;

and the præfect received their commands to visit every quarter of the city, and proclaim a general illumination for the recovery of the emperor's health. The ferment subsided ; but every accident betrayed the impotence of the government, and the factious temper of the people : the guards were disposed to mutiny as often as their quarters were changed, or their pay was withheld : the frequent calamities of fires and earthquakes afforded the opportunities of disorder ; the disputes of the blues and greens, of the orthodox and heretics, degenerated into bloody battles ; and.in the presence of the Persian ambassador, Justinian blushed for himself and for his subjects. Capricious pardon and arbitrary punishment imbittered the irksomeness and discontent of a long reign : a conspiracy was formed in the palace ; and, unless we are deceived by the names of Marcellus and Sergius, the most virtuous and the most profligate of the courtiers were associated in the same designs. They had fixed the time of the execution ; their rank gave them access to the royal banquet ; and their black slaves [65] were stationed in the vestibule and porticos, to announce the death of the tyrant, and to excite a sedition in the capital: But the indiscretion of an accomplice saved the poor remnant of the days of Justinian. The conspirators were detected and seized, with daggers hidden under their garments : Marcellus died by his own hand, and Sergius was dragged from the sanctuary. [66] Pressed by remorse, or tempted by the hopes of safety, he accused two officers of the household of Belisarius ; and torture forced them to declare, that they had acted according to the secret instructions of their patron. [67] Posterity will not hastily believe that a hero who, in the vigor of life, had disdained the fairest offers of ambition and revenge, should stoop to the murder of his prince, whom he could not long expect to survive. His followers were impatient to fly ; but flight must have been supported by rebellion, and he had lived enough for nature and for glory. Belisarius appeared before the council with less fear than indignation : after forty years' service, the emperor had prejudged his guilt ; and injustice was sanctified by the presence and authority of the patriarch. The life of Belisarius was graciously spared ; but his fortunes were sequestered, and, from December to July, he was guarded as a prisoner in his own palace. At length his innocence was acknowledged ; his freedom and honors were restored ; and death, which might be hastened by resentment and grief, removed him from the world about eight months after his deliverance. The name of Belisarius can never die : but instead of the funeral, the monuments, the statues, so justly due to his memory, I only read, that his treasures, the spoils of the Goths and Vandals, were immediately confiscated by the emperor. Some decent portion was reserved, however, for the use of his widow : and as Antonina had much to repent, she devoted the last remains of her life and fortune to the foundation of a convent. Such is the simple and genuine narrative of the fall of Belisarius and the ingratitude of Justinian.[68] That he was deprived of his eyes, and reduced by envy to beg his bread,* "Give a penny to Belisarius the general!" is a fiction of later times,[69] which has obtained credit, or rather favor, as a strange example of the vicissitudes of fortune.[70]

If the emperor could rejoice in the death of Belisarius, he enjoyed the base satisfaction only eight months, the last period of a reign of thirty-eight years, and a life of eighty-three years. It would be difficult to trace the character of a prince who is not the most conspicuous object of his own times : but the confessions of an enemy may be received as the safest evidence of his virtues. The resemblance of Justinian to the bust of Domitian, is maliciously urged ;[71] with the acknowledgment, however, of a well-proportioned figure, a ruddy complexion, and a pleasing countenance. The emperor was easy of access, patient of hearing, courteous and affable in discourse, and a master of the angry passions which rage with such destructive violence in the breast of a despot. Procopius praises his temper to reproach him with calm and deliberate cruelty : but in the conspiracies which attacked his authority and person, a more candid judge will approve the justice, or admire the clemency, of Justinian. He excelled in the private virtues of chastity and temperance : but the impartial love of beauty would have been less mischievous than his conjugal tenderness for Theodora ; and his abstemious diet was regulated, not by the prudence of a philosopher, but the superstition of a monk. His repasts were short and frugal : on solemn fasts, he contented himself with water and vegetables ; and such was his strength, as well as fervor, that he frequently passed two days, and as many nights, without tasting any food. The measure of his sleep was not less rigorous : after the repose of a single hour, the body was awakened by the soul, and, to the astonishment of his chamberlains, Justinian walked or studied till the morning light. Such restless application prolonged his time for the acquisition of knowledge[72] and the despatch of business, and he might

---

* Le Beau, following Alemannus, conceives that Belisarius was confounded with John of Cappadocia, who was thus reduced to beggary (vol. ix. p. 58, 449). Lord Mahon has, with considerable learning, and on the authority of a yet unquoted writer of the eleventh century, endeavored to re-establish the old tradition. I cannot acknowledge that I have been convinced, and am inclined to subscribe to the theory of Le Beau.—M.

seriously deserve the reproach of confounding, by minute and preposterous diligence, the general order of his administration. The emperor professed himself a musician and architect, a poet and philosopher, a lawyer and theologian ; and if he failed in the enterprise of reconciling the Christian sects, the review of the Roman jurisprudence is a noble monument of his spirit and industry. In the government of the empire, he was less wise, or less successful : the age was unfortunate ; the people was oppressed and discontented ; Theodora abused her power ; a succession of bad ministers disgraced his judgment ; and Justinian was neither beloved in his life, nor regretted at his death. The love of fame was deeply implanted in his breast, but he condescended to the poor ambition of titles, honors, and contemporary praise ; and while he labored to fix the admiration, he forfeited the esteem and affection, of the Romans. The design of the African and Italian wars was boldly conceived and executed ; and his penetration discovered the talents of Belisarius in the camp, of Narses in the palace. But the name of the emperor is eclipsed by the names of his victorious generals ; and Belisarius still lives, to upbraid the envy and ingratitude of his sovereign. The partial favor of mankind applauds the genius of a conqueror, who leads and directs his subjects in the exercise of arms. The characters of Philip the Second and of Justinian are distinguished by the cold ambition which delights in war, and declines the dangers of the field. Yet a colossal statue of bronze represented the emperor on horseback, preparing to march against the Persians in the habit and armor of Achilles. In the great square before the church of St. Sophia, this monument was raised on a brass column and a stone pedestal of seven steps ; and the pillar of Theodosius, which weighed seven thousand four hundred pounds of silver, was removed from the same place by the avarice and vanity of Justinian. Future princes were more just or indulgent to *his* memory ; the elder Andronicus, in the beginning of the fourteenth century, repaired and beautified his equestrian statue : since the fall of the empire it has been melted into cannon by the victorious Turks.[73]

I shall conclude this chapter with the comets, the earthquakes, and the plague, which astonished or afflicted the age of Justinian.

I. In the fifth year of his reign, and in the month of September, a comet [74] was seen during twenty days in the western quarter of the heavens, and which shot its rays into the north. Eight years afterwards, while the sun was in Capricorn, another comet appeared to follow in the Sagittary ; the size was gradually increasing ; the head was in the east, the tail in the west, and it remained visible above forty days. The nations, who gazed with astonishment, expected wars and calamities from their baleful influence; and these expectations were abundantly fulfilled. The astronomers dissembled their ignorance of the nature of these blazing stars, which they affected to represent as the floating meteors of the air; and few among them embraced the simple notion of Seneca and the Chaldeans, that they are only planets of a longer period and more eccentric motion.[75] Time and science have justified the conjectures and predictions of the Roman sage: the telescope has opened new worlds to the eyes of astronomers;[76] and, in the narrow space of history and fable, one and the same comet is already found to have revisited the earth in *seven* equal revolutions of five hundred and seventy-five years. The *first*,[77] which ascends beyond the Christian æra one thousand seven hundred and sixty-seven years, is coeval with Ogyges, the father of Grecian antiquity. And this appearance explains the tradition which Varro has preserved, that under his reign the planet Venus changed her color, size, figure, and course; a prodigy without example either in past or succeeding ages.[78] The *second* visit, in the year eleven hundred and ninety-three, is darkly implied in the fable of Electra, the seventh of the Pleiads, who have been reduced to six since the time of the Trojan war. That nymph, the wife of Dardanus, was unable to support the ruin of her country: she abandoned the dances of her sister orbs, fled from the zodiac to the north pole, and obtained, from her dishevelled locks, the name of the *comet*. The *third* period expires in the year six hundred and eighteen, a date that exactly agrees with the tremendous comet of the Sibyl, and perhaps of Pliny, which arose in the west two generations before the reign of Cyrus. The *fourth* apparition, forty-four years before the birth of Christ, is of all others the most splendid and important. After the death of Cæsar, a long-haired star was conspicuous to Rome and to the nations, during the games which were exhibited by young Octavian in honor of Venus and his uncle. The vulgar opinion, that it conveyed to heaven the divine soul of the dictator, was cherished and consecrated by the piety of a statesman; while his secret superstition referred the comet to the glory of his own times.[79] The *fifth* visit has been already ascribed to the fifth year of Justinian, which coincides with the five hundred and thirty-first of the Christian æra. And it may deserve notice, that in this, as in the preceding instance, the comet was followed, though at a longer interval, by a remarkable paleness of the sun. The *sixth* return, in the year eleven hundred and six, is recorded by the chronicles of Europe and China: and in the first fervor of the crusades, the Christians and the Mahometans might surmise, with equal reason, that it portended the destruction of the Infidels. The *seventh* phenomenon, of one thousand six hundred and eighty, was presented to the eyes of an enlightened age.[80] The philosophy of Bayle dispelled a prejudice which Milton's muse had so recently adorned, that the comet, "from its horrid hair shakes pestilence and war."[81] Its road in the heavens was observed with exquisite skill by Flamstead and Cassini; and the mathematical science of Bernoulli, Newton,* and Halley, investigated the laws of its revolutions. At the *eighth* period, in the year two thousand three hundred and fifty-five, their calculations may perhaps be verified by the astronomers of some future capital in the Siberian or American wilderness.

II. The near approach of a comet may injure or destroy the globe which we inhabit; but the changes on its surface have been hitherto produced by the action of volcanoes and earthquakes.[82] The nature of the soil may indicate the countries most exposed to these formidable concussions, since they are caused by subterraneous fires, and such fires are kindled by the union and fermentation of iron and sulphur. But their times and effects appear to lie beyond the reach of human curiosity; and the philosopher will discreetly abstain from the prediction of earthquakes, till he has counted the drops of water that silently filtrate on the inflammable mineral, and measured the caverns which increase by resistance the explosion of the imprisoned air. Without assigning the cause, history will distinguish the periods in which these calamitous events have been rare or frequent, and will observe, that this fever of the earth raged with uncommon violence during the reign of Justinian.[83] Each year is marked by the repetition of earthquakes, of such duration, that Constantinople has been shaken above forty days; of such extent, that the shock has been communicated to the whole surface of the globe, or at least of the Roman empire. An impulsive or vibratory motion was felt: enormous chasms were opened, huge and heavy bodies were discharged into the air, the sea alternately advanced and retreated beyond its ordinary bounds, and a mountain was torn from Libanus,[84] and cast into the waves, where it protected, as a mole, the new harbor of Botrys[85] in Phœnicia. The stroke that agitates an ant-hill may crush the insect-myriads in the dust; yet truth must extort confession that man has industriously labored for his own destruction. The institution of great cities, which include a nation within the limits of a wall, almost realizes the wish of Caligula, that the Roman people had but one neck. Two hundred and

* Compare Pingrè, Histoire des Comêtes.—M.

fifty thousand persons are said to have perished in the earthquake of Antioch, whose domestic multitudes were swelled by the conflux of strangers to the festival of the Ascension. The loss of Berytus [86] was of smaller account, but of much greater value. That city, on the coast of Phœnicia, was illustrated by the study of the civil law, which opened the surest road to wealth and dignity : the schools of Berytus were filled with the rising spirits of the age, and many a youth was lost in the earthquake, who might have lived to be the scourge or the guardian of his country. In these disasters, the architect becomes the enemy of mankind. The hut of a savage, or the tent of an Arab, may be thrown down without injury to the inhabitant ; and the Peruvians had reason to deride the folly of their Spanish conquerors, who with so much cost and labor erected their own sepulchres. The rich marbles of a patrician are dashed on his own head : a whole people is buried under the ruins of public and private edifices, and the conflagration is kindled and propagated by the innumerable fires which are necessary for the subsistence and manufactures of a great city. Instead of the mutual sympathy which might comfort and assist the distressed, they dreadfully experience the vices and passions which are released from the fear of punishment : the tottering houses are pillaged by intrepid avarice ; revenge embraces the moment, and selects the victim ; and the earth often swallows the assassin, or the ravisher, in the consummation of their crimes. Superstition involves the present danger with invisible terrors ; and if the image of death may sometimes be subservient to the virtue or repentance of individuals, an affrighted people is more forcibly moved to expect the end of the world, or to deprecate with servile homage the wrath of an avenging Deity.

III. Æthiopia and Egypt have been stigmatized, in every age, as the original source and seminary of the plague. [87] In a damp, hot, stagnating air, this African fever is generated from the putrefaction of animal substances, and especially from the swarms of locusts, not less destructive to mankind in their death than in their lives. The fatal disease which depopulated the earth in the time of Justinian and his successors, [88] first appeared in the neighborhood of Pelusium, between the Serbonian bog and the eastern channel of the Nile. From thence, tracing as it were a double path, it spread to the East, over Syria, Persia, and the Indies, and penetrated to the West, along the coast of Africa, and over the continent of Europe. In the spring of the second year, Constantinople, during three or four months, was visited by the pestilence ; and Procopius, who observed its progress and symptoms with the eyes of a physician, [89] has emulated the skill and diligence of Thucydides in the description of the plague of Athens.[90] The infection was sometimes announced by the visions of a distempered fancy, and the victim despaired as soon as he had heard the menace and felt the stroke of an invisible spectre. But the greater number, in their beds, in the streets, in their usual occupation, were surprised by a slight fever; so slight, indeed, that neither the pulse nor the color of the patient gave any signs of the approaching danger. The same, the next, or the succeeding day, it was declared by the swelling of the glands, particularly those of the groin, of the armpits, and under the ear; and when these buboes or tumors were opened, they were found to contain a *coal*, or black substance, of the size of a lentil. If they came to a just swelling and suppuration, the patient was saved by this kind and natural discharge of the morbid humor. But if they continued hard and dry, a mortification quickly ensued, and the fifth day was commonly the term of his life. The fever was often accompanied with lethargy or delirium; the bodies of the sick were covered with black pustules or carbuncles, the symptoms of immediate death; and in the constitutions too feeble to produce an irruption, the vomiting of blood was followed by a mortification of the bowels. To pregnant women the plague was generally mortal: yet one infant was drawn alive from its dead mother, and three mothers survived the loss of their infected fœtus. Youth was the most perilous season; and the female sex was less susceptible than the male: but every rank and profession was attacked with indiscriminate rage, and many of those who escaped were deprived of the use of their speech, without being secure from a return of the disorder.[91] The physicians of Constantinople were zealous and skilful; but their art was baffled by the various symptoms and pertinacious vehemence of the disease: the same remedies were productive of contrary effects, and the event capriciously disappointed their prognostics of death or recovery. The order of funerals, and the right of sepulchres, were confounded: those who were left without friends or servants, lay unburied in the streets, or in their desolate houses; and a magistrate was authorized to collect the promiscuous heaps of dead bodies, to transport them by land or water, and to inter them in deep pits beyond the precincts of the city. Their own danger, and the prospect of public distress, awakened some remorse in the minds of the most vicious of mankind; the confidence of health again revived their passions and habits; but philosophy must disdain the observation of Procopius, that the lives of such men were guarded by the peculiar favor of fortune or Providence. He forgot, or perhaps he secretly recollected, that the plague had

touched the person of Justinian himself ; but the abstemious diet
of the emperor may suggest, as in the case of Socrates, a more
rational and honorable cause for his recovery.[92]   During his sickness, the public consternation was expressed in the habits of the
citizens ; and their idleness and despondence occasioned a general
scarcity in the capital of the East.

Contagion is the inseparable symptom of the plague ; which, by
mutual respiration, is transfused from the infected persons to the
lungs and stomach of those who approach them.   While philosophers believe and tremble, it is singular, that the existence of a
real danger should have been denied by a people most prone to
vain and imaginary terrors.[93]   Yet the fellow-citizens of Procopius
were satisfied, by some short and partial experience, that the infection could not be gained by the closest conversation : [94] and
this persuasion might support the assiduity of friends or physicians in the care of the sick, whom inhuman prudence would
have condemned to solitude and despair.   But the fatal security,
like the predestination of the Turks, must have aided the progress of the contagion ; and those salutary precautions to which
Europe is indebted for her safety, were unknown to the government of Justinian.   No restraints were imposed on the free and
frequent intercourse of the Roman provinces : from Persia to
France, the nations were mingled and infected by wars and emigrations ; and the pestilential odor which lurks for years in a bale
of cotton was imported, by the abuse of trade, into the most distant regions.   The mode of its propagation is explained by the
remark of Procopius himself, that it always spread from the sea-
coast to the inland country : the most sequestered islands and
mountains were successively visited ; the places which had
escaped the fury of its first passage were alone exposed to the
contagion of the ensuing year.   The winds might diffuse that
subtile venom ; but unless the atmosphere be previously disposed
for its reception, the plague would soon expire in the cold or temperate climates of the earth.   Such was the universal corruption
of the air, that the pestilence which burst forth in the fifteenth
year of Justinian was not checked or alleviated by any difference
of the seasons.   In time, its first malignity was abated and dispersed, the disease alternately languished and revived ; but it was
not till the end of a calamitous period of fifty-two years, that
mankind recovered their health, or the air resumed its pure and
salubrious quality.   No facts have been preserved to sustain an
account, or even a conjecture, of the numbers that perished in this
extraordinary mortality.   I only find, that during three months,
five, and at length ten, thousand persons died each day at Con-

stantinople; that many cities of the East were left vacant, and that in several districts of Italy the harvest and the vintage withered on the ground. The triple scourge of war, pestilence, and famine, afflicted the subjects of Justinian; and his reign is disgraced by a visible decrease of the human species, which has never been repaired in some of the fairest countries of the globe.[95]

CHAPTER XLIV.*

IDEA OF THE ROMAN JURISPRUDENCE.—THE LAWS OF THE KINGS.—THE TWELVE TABLES OF THE DECEMVIRS.—THE LAWS OF THE PEOPLE.—THE DECREES OF THE SENATE.—THE EDICTS OF THE MAGISTRATES AND EMPERORS.—AUTHORITY OF THE CIVILIANS.—CODE, PANDECTS, NOVELS, AND INSTITUTES OF JUSTINIAN:—I. RIGHTS OF PERSONS.—II. RIGHTS OF THINGS.—III. PRIVATE INJURIES AND ACTIONS.—IV. CRIMES AND PUNISHMENTS.

THE vain titles of the victories of Justinian are crumbled into dust; but the name of the legislator is inscribed on a fair and everlasting monument. Under his reign, and by his care, the civil jurisprudence was digested in the immortal works of the CODE, the PANDECTS, and the INSTITUTES:[1] the public reason of the Romans has been silently or studiously transfused into the domestic institutions of Europe,[2] and the laws of Justinian still command the respect or obedience of independent nations. Wise or fortunate is the prince who connects his own reputation with the honor and interest of a perpetual order of men. The defence of their founder is the first cause, which in every age has exercised the zeal and industry of the civilians. They piously commemorate his virtues; dissemble or deny his failings; and fiercely chastise the guilt or folly of the rebels, who presume to sully the

* In the notes to this important chapter, which is received as the text-book on Civil Law in some of the foreign universities, I have consulted, I. The newly discovered Institutes of Gains (Gaii Institutiones, ed. Goeschen, Berlin, 1824), with some other fragments of the Roman law (Codicis Theodosiani Fragmenta inedita, ab Amadeo Peyron, Turin, 1824). II. The History of the Roman Law, by Professor Hugo, in the French translation of M. Jourdan, Paris, 1825. III. Savigny, Geschichte des Römischen Rechts im Mittelalter, 6 bände, Heidelberg, 1815. IV. Walther, Römische Rechts-Geschichte, Bonn, 1834. But I am particularly indebted to an edition of the French translation of this chapter, with additional notes, by one of the most learned civilians of Europe, Professor Warnkönig, published at Liege, 1821. I have inserted almost the whole of these notes, which are distinguished by the letter W.—M.

majesty of the purple. The idolatry of love has provoked, as it usually happens, the rancor of opposition; the character of Justinian has been exposed to the blind vehemence of flattery and invective; and the injustice of a sect (the *Anti-Tribonians*) has refused all praise and merit to the prince, his ministers, and his laws.[3] Attached to no party, interested only for the truth and candor of history, and directed by the most temperate and skilful guides,[4] I enter with just diffidence on the subject of civil law, which has exhausted so many learned lives, and clothed the walls of such spacious libraries. In a single, if possible in a short, chapter, I shall trace the Roman jurisprudence from Romulus to Justinian,[5] appreciate the labors of that emperor, and pause to contemplate the principles of a science so important to the peace and happiness of society. The laws of a nation form the most instructive portion of its history; and, although I have devoted myself to write the annals of a declining monarchy, I shall embrace the occasion to breathe the pure and invigorating air of the republic.

The primitive government of Rome [6] was composed, with some political skill, of an elective king, a council of nobles, and a general assembly of the people. War and religion were administered by the supreme magistrate; and he alone proposed the laws, which were debated in the senate, and finally ratified or rejected by a majority of votes in the thirty *curiæ* or parishes of the city. Romulus, Numa, and Servius Tullius, are celebrated as the most ancient legislators; and each of them claims his peculiar part in the threefold division of jurisprudence.[7] The laws of marriage, the education of children, and the authority of parents, which may seem to draw their origin from *nature* itself, are ascribed to the untutored wisdom of Romulus. The law of *nations* and of religious worship, which Numa introduced, was derived from his nocturnal converse with the nymph Egeria. The *civil* law is attributed to the experience of Servius: he balanced the rights and fortunes of the seven classes of citizens; and guarded, by fifty new regulations, the observance of contracts and the punishment of crimes. The state, which he had inclined towards a democracy, was changed by the last Tarquin into a lawless despotism; and when the kingly office was abolished, the patricians engrossed the benefits of freedom. The royal laws became odious or obsolete; the mysterious deposit was silently preserved by the priests and nobles; and, at the end of sixty years, the citizens of Rome still complained that they were ruled by the arbitrary sentence of the magistrates. Yet the positive institutions of the kings had blended themselves with the public and private manners of the city ; some fragments of that venerable jurisprudence [6] were compiled by the diligence of antiquarians,[9] and above twenty texts still speak the rudeness of the Pelasgic idiom of the Latins.[10]

I shall not repeat the well-known story of the Decemvirs,[11] who sullied by their actions the honor of inscribing on brass, or wood, or ivory, the TWELVE TABLES of the Roman laws.[12] They were dictated by the rigid and jealous spirit of an aristocracy, which had yielded with reluctance to the just demands of the people. But the substance of the Twelve Tables was adapted to the state of the city ; and the Romans had emerged from barbarism, since they were capable of studying and embracing the institutions of their more enlightened neighbors.* A wise Ephesian was driven by envy from his native country : before he could reach the shores of Latium, he had observed the various forms of human nature and civil society : he imparted his knowledge to the legislators of Rome, and a statue was erected in the forum to the perpetual memory of Hermodorus.[13] The names and divisions of the copper money, the sole coin of the infant state, were of Dorian origin : [14] the harvests of Campania and Sicily relieved the wants of a people whose agriculture was often interrupted by war and faction ; and since the trade was established,[15] the deputies who sailed from the Tyber might return from the same harbors with a more precious cargo of political wisdom. The colonies of Great Greece had transported and improved the arts of their mother country. Cumæ and Rhegium, Crotona and Tarentum, Agrigentum and Syracuse, were in the rank of the most flourishing cities. The disciples of Pythagoras applied philosophy to the use of government ; the unwritten laws of Charondas accepted the aid of poetry and music,[16] and Zaleucus framed the republic of the Locrians, which stood without alteration above two hundred years.[17] From a similar motive of national pride, both Livy and Dionysius are willing to believe, that the deputies of Rome visited Athens under the wise and splendid administration of Pericles ; and the laws of Solon were transfused into the twelve tables. If such an embassy had indeed been received from the barbarians of Hesperia, the Roman name would have been familiar to the Greeks before the reign of Alexander ; [18] and the faintest evidence would have been explored and celebrated by the curiosity of succeeding times. But the Athenian monuments are silent ; nor will it seem credible that the patricians should undertake a long and perilous navigation to copy the purest model of a democracy. In the comparison of the tables of Solon with those of the Decemvirs, some

* Compare Niebuhr, vol. ii, p. 349, etc.—M.

casual resemblance may be found ; some rules which nature and
reason have revealed to every society ; some proofs of a common
descent from Egypt or Phœnicia.[19] But in all the great lines of
public and private jurisprudence, the legislators of Rome and
Athens appear to be strangers or adverse at each other.

Whatever might be the origin or the merit of the Twelve
Tables,[20] they obtained among the Romans that blind and partial
reverence which the lawyers of every country delight to bestow
on their municipal institutions. The study is recommended by
Cicero[21] as equally pleasant and instructive. " They amuse the
mind by the remembrance of old words and the portrait of ancient
manners ; they inculcate the soundest principles of government
and morals ; and I am not afraid to affirm, that the brief composition of the Decemvirs surpasses in genuine value the libraries of
Grecian philosophy. How admirable," says Tully, with honest
or affected prejudice, " is the wisdom of our ancestors ! We alone
are the masters of civil prudence, and our superiority is the more
conspicuous, if we deign to cast our eyes on the rude and almost
ridiculous jurisprudence of Draco, of Solon, and of Lycurgus."
The Twelve Tables were committed to the memory of the young
and meditation of the old ; they were transcribed and illustrated
with learned diligence ; they had escaped the flames of the Gauls,
they subsisted in the age of Justinian, and their subsequent loss
has been imperfectly restored by the labors of modern critics.[22]
But although these venerable monuments were considered as the
rule of right and the fountain of justice,[23] they were overwhelmed
by the weight and variety of new laws, which, at the end of five
centuries, became a grievance more intolerable than the vices of
the city.[24] Three thousand brass plates, the acts of the senate of
the people, were deposited in the Capitol :[25] and some of the acts,
as the Julian law against extortion, surpassed the number of a
hundred chapters.[26] The Decemvirs had neglected to import the
sanction of Zaleucus, which so long maintained the integrity of
his republic. A Locrian, who proposed any new law, stood forth
in the assembly of the people with a cord round his neck, and if
the law was rejected, the innovator was instantly strangled.

The Decemvirs had been named, and their tables were approved, by an assembly of the *centuries*, in which riches prepon-
derated against numbers. To the first class of Romans, the proprietors of one hundred thousand pounds of copper,[27] ninety-eight
votes were assigned, and only ninety-five were left for the six inferior classes, distributed according to their substance by the artful policy of Servius. But the tribunes soon established a more
specious and popular maxim, that every citizen has an equal right

to enact the laws which he is bound to obey. Instead of the *centuries*, they convened the *tribes;* and the patricians, after an impotent struggle, submitted to the decrees of an assembly, in which their votes were confounded with those of the meanest plebeians. Yet as long as the tribes successively passed over narrow *bridges*,[28] and gave their voices aloud, the conduct of each citizen was exposed to the eyes and ears of his friends and countrymen. The insolvent debtor consulted the wishes of his creditor ; the client would have blushed to oppose the views of his patron ; the general was followed by his veterans, and the aspect of a grave magistrate was a living lesson to the multitude. A new method of secret ballot abolished the influence of fear and shame, of honor and interest, and the abuse of freedom accelerated the progress of anarchy and despotism.[29] The Romans had aspired to be equal ; they were levelled by the equality of servitude ; and the dictates of Augustus were patiently ratified by the formal consent of the tribes or centuries. Once, and once only, he experienced a sincere and strenuous opposition. His subjects had resigned all political liberty ; they defended the freedom of domestic life. A law which enforced the obligation, and strengthened the bonds, of marriage, was clamorously rejected ; Propertius, in the arms of Delia, applauded the victory of licentious love ; and the project of reform was suspended till a new and more tractable generation had arisen in the world.[30] Such an example was not necessary to instruct a prudent usurper of the mischief of popular assemblies ; and their abolition, which Augustus had silently prepared, was accomplished without resistance, and almost without notice, on the accession of his successor.[31] Sixty thousand plebeian legislators, whom numbers made formidable, and poverty secure, were supplanted by six hundred senators, who held their honors, their fortunes, and their lives, by the clemency of the emperor. The loss of executive power was alleviated by the gift of legislative authority ; and Ulpian might assert, after the practice of two hundred years, that the decrees of the senate obtained the force and validity of laws. In the times of freedom, the resolves of the people had often been dictated by the passion or error of the moment : the Cornelian, Pompeian, and Julian laws were adapted by a single hand to the prevailing disorders ; but the senate, under the reign of the Cæsars, was composed of magistrates and lawyers, and in questions of private jurisprudence, the integrity of their judgment was seldom perverted by fear or interest.[32]

The silence or ambiguity of the laws was supplied by the occasional EDICTS * of those magistrates who were invested with the

---

† There is a curious passage from Aurelius, a writer on Law, on the Prætorian

honors of the state.[33]   This ancient prerogative of the Roman kings was transferred in their respective offices, to the consuls and dictators, the censors and prætors ; and a similar right was assumed by the tribunes of the people, the ediles, and the proconsuls.   At Rome, and in the provinces, the duties of the subject, and the intentions of the governor, were proclaimed ; and the civil jurisprudence was reformed by the annual edicts of the supreme judge, the prætor of the city.*   As soon as he ascended his tribunal, he announced by the voice of the crier, and afterwards inscribed on a white wall, the rules which he proposed to follow in the decision of doubtful cases, and the relief which his equity would afford from the precise rigor of ancient statutes.   A principle of discretion more congenial to monarchy was introduced into the republic : the art of respecting the name, and eluding the efficacy, of the laws, was improved by successive prætors ; subtleties and fictions were invented to defeat the plainest meaning of the Decemvirs, and where the end was salutary, the means were frequently absurd.   The secret or probable wish of the dead was suffered to prevail over the order of succession and the forms of testaments ; and the claimant, who was excluded from the character of heir, accepted with equal pleasure from an indulgent prætor the possession of the goods of his late kinsman or benefactor.   In the redress of private wrongs, compensations and fines were substituted to the obsolete rigor of the Twelve Tables ; time and space were annihilated by fanciful suppositions and the plea of youth, or fraud, or violence, annulled the obligation, or excused the performance, of an inconvenient contract.   A jurisdiction thus vague and arbitrary was exposed to the most dangerous abuse : the substance, as well as the form, of justice were often sacrificed to the prejudices of virtue, the bias of laudable affection, and the grosser seductions of interest or resentment.   But the errors or vices of each prætor expired with his annual office ; such maxims alone as had been approved by reason and practice were copied by succeeding judges ; the rule of proceeding was defined by the solution of new cases ; and the temptations of injustice were removed

---

Præfect, quoted in Lydus de Magistratibus, p. 32, edit. Hase.   The Prætorian præfect was to the emperor what the master of the horse was to the dictator under the Republic.   He was the delegate, therefore, of the full Imperial authority ; and no appeal could be made or exception taken against his edicts.   I had not observed this passage, when the second volume, where it would have been more appropriately placed, passed through the press.—M.

   * Compare throughout the brief but admirable sketch of the progress and growth of the Roman jurisprudence, the necessary operation of the jus gentium, when Rome became the sovereign of nations, upon the jus civile of the citizens of Rome, in the first chapter of Savigny.   Geschichte des Römischen Rechts im Mittelalter.—M.

by the Cornelian law, which compelled the prætor of the year to adhere to the letter and spirit of his first proclamation.[34] It was reserved for the curiosity and learning of Adrian, to accomplish the design which had been conceived by the genius of Cæsar ; and the prætorship of Salvius Julian, an eminent lawyer, was immortalized by the composition of the PERPETUAL EDICT. This well-digested code was ratified by the emperor and the senate ; the long divorce of law and equity was at length reconciled ; and, instead of the Twelve Tables, the perpetual edict was fixed as the invariable standard of civil jurisprudence.[35]

From Augustus to Trajan, the modest Cæsars were content to promulgate their edicts in the various characters of a Roman magistrate ; * and, in the decrees of the senate, the *epistles* and *orations* of the prince were respectfully inserted. Adrian[36] appears to have been the first who assumed, without disguise, the plenitude of legislative power. And this innovation, so agreeable to his active mind, was countenanced by the patience of the times, and his long absence from the seat of government. The same policy was embraced by succeeding monarchs, and, according to the harsh metaphor of Tertullian, " the gloomy and intricate forest of ancient laws was cleared away by the axe of royal mandates and *constitutions*."[37] During four centuries, from Adrian to Justinian, the public and private jurisprudence was moulded by the will of the sovereign ; and few institutions, either human or divine, were permitted to stand on their former basis. The origin of Imperial legislation was concealed by the darkness of ages and the terrors of armed despotism ; and a double fiction was propagated by the servility, or perhaps the ignorance, of the civilians, who basked in the sunshine of the Roman and Byzantine courts. 1. To the prayer of the ancient Cæsars, the people or the senate had sometimes granted a personal exemption from the obligation and penalty of particular statutes ; and each indulgence was an act of jurisdiction exercised by the republic over the first of her citizens. His humble privilege was at length transformed into the prerogative of a tyrant ; and the Latin expression of " released from the laws"[38] was supposed to exalt the emperor above *all* human restraints, and to leave his conscience and reason as the sacred measure of his conduct. 2. A similar dependence was im-

---

* It is an important question in what manner the emperors were invested with this legislative power. The newly discovered Gaius distinctly states that it was in virtue of a law—Nec unquam dubitatum est, quin id legis vicem obtineat, cum ipse imperator per *legem* imperium accipiat. But it is still uncertain whether this was a general law, passed on the transition of the government from a republican to a monarchical form, or a law passed on the accession of each emperor. Compare Hugo, Hist. du Droit Romain (French translation), vol. ii. p. 8.—M.

plied in the decrees of the senate, which, in every reign, defined the titles and powers of an elective magistrate. But it was not before the ideas, and even the language, of the Romans had been corrupted, that a *royal* law,[39] and an irrevocable gift of the people, were created by the fancy of Ulpian, or more probably of Tribonian himself ;[40] and the origin of Imperial power, though false in fact, and slavish in its consequence, was supported on a principle of freedom and justice. "The pleasure of the emperor has the vigor and effect of law, since the Roman people, by the royal law, have transferred to their prince the full extent of their own power and sovereignty."[41] The will of a single man, of a child perhaps, was allowed to prevail over the wisdom of ages and the inclinations of millions ; and the degenerate Greeks were proud to declare, that in his hands alone the arbitrary exercise of legislation could be safely deposited. "What interest or passion," exclaims Theophilus in the court of Justinian, "can reach the calm and sublime elevation of the monarch ? He is already master of the lives and fortunes of his subjects ; and those who have incurred his displeasure are already numbered with the dead."[42] Disdaining the language of flattery, the historian may confess, that in questions of private jurisprudence, the absolute sovereign of a great empire can seldom be influenced by any personal considerations. Virtue, or even reason, will suggest to his impartial mind, that he is the guardian of peace and equity, and that the interest of society is inseparably connected with his own. Under the weakest and most vicious reign, the seat of justice was filled by the wisdom and integrity of Papinian and Ulpian ;[43] and the purest materials of the Code and Pandects are inscribed with the names of Caracalla and his ministers.[44] The tyrant of Rome was sometimes the benefactor of the provinces. A dagger terminated the crimes of Domitian ; but the prudence of Nerva confirmed his acts, which, in the joy of their deliverance, had been rescinded by an indignant senate.[45] Yet in the *rescripts*,[46] replies to the consultations of the magistrates, the wisest of princes might be deceived by a partial exposition of the case. And this abuse, which placed their hasty decisions on the same level with mature and deliberate acts of legislation, was ineffectually condemned by the sense and example of Trajan. The *rescripts* of the emperor, his *grants* and *decrees*, his *edicts* and *pragmatic sanctions*, were subscribed in purple ink,[47] and transmitted to the provinces as general or special laws, which the magistrates were bound to execute, and the people to obey. But as their number continually multiplied, the rule of obedience became each day more doubtful and obscure, till the will of the sovereign was fixed and ascertained in the Gregorian, the Hermogenian, and the Theodosian codes.* The two first, of which some fragments have escaped, were framed by two private lawyers, to preserve the constitutions of the Pagan emperors from Adrian to Constantine. The third, which is still extant, was digested in sixteen books by the order of the younger Theodosius to consecrate the laws of the Christian princes from Constantine to his own reign. But the three codes obtained an equal authority in the tribunals ; and any act which was not included in the sacred deposit might be disregarded by the judge as spurious or obsolete.[48]

Among savage nations, the want of letters is imperfectly supplied by the use of visible signs, which awaken attention, and perpetuate the remembrance of any public or private transaction. The jurisprudence of the first Romans exhibited the scenes of a pantomime ; the words were adapted to the gestures, and the slightest error or neglect in the *forms* of proceeding was sufficient to annul the *substance* of the fairest claim. The communion of the marriage-life was denoted by the necessary elements of fire and water ;[49] and the divorced wife resigned the bunch of keys, by the delivery of which she had been invested with the government of the family. The manumission of a son, or a slave, was performed by turning him round with a gentle blow on the cheek ; a work was prohibited by the casting of a stone ; prescription was interrupted by the breaking of a branch ; the clinched fist was the symbol of a pledge or deposit ; the right hand was the gift of faith and confidence. The indenture of covenants was a broken straw ; weights and scales were introduced into every payment, and the heir who accepted a testament was sometimes obliged to snap his fingers, to cast away his garments, and to leap and dance with real or affected transport.[50] If a citizen pursued any stolen goods into a neighbor's house, he concealed his nakedness with a linen towel, and hid his face with a mask or basin, lest he should encounter the eyes of a virgin or a

---

* Savigny states the following as the authorities for the Roman law at the commencement of the fifth century :

1. The writings of the jurists, according to the regulations of the Constitution of Valentinian III., first promulgated in the West, but by its admission into the Theodosian Code established likewise in the East. (This Constitution established the authority of the five great jurists, Papinian, Paulus, Caius, Ulpian, and Modestinus, as interpreters of the ancient law. . . . In case of difference of opinion among these five, a majority decided the case ; where they were equal, the opinion of Papinian ; where he was silent, the judge ; but see p. 40, and Hugo, vol. ii. p. 89.)

2. The Gregorian and Hermogenian Collection of the Imperial Rescripts.

3. The Code of Theodosius II.

4. The particular Novellæ, as additions and supplements to this Code. Savigny, vol. i. p. 10.—M.

matron.[51] In a civil action the plaintiff touched the ear of h[?]s witness, seized his reluctant adversary by the neck, and implored, in solemn lamentation, the aid of his fellow-citizens. The two competitors grasped each other's hand as if they stood prepared for combat before the tribunal of the prætor ; he commanded them to produce the object of the dispute ; they went, they returned with measured steps, and a clod of earth was cast at his feet to represent the field for which they contended. This occult science of the words and actions of law was the inheritance of the pontiffs and patricians. Like the Chaldean astrologers, they announced to their clients the days of business and repose ; these important trifles were interwoven with the religion of Numa ; and after the publication of the Twelve Tables, the Roman people was still enslaved by the ignorance of judicial proceedings. The treachery of some plebeian officers at length revealed the profitable mystery : in a more enlightened age, the legal actions were derided and observed ; and the same antiquity which sanctified the practice, obliterated the use and meaning, of this primitive language.[52] A more liberal art was cultivated, however, by the sages of Rome, who, in a stricter sense, may be considered as the authors of the civil law. The alteration of the idiom and manners of the Romans rendered the style of the Twelve Tables less familiar to each rising generation, and the doubtful passages were imperfectly explained by the study of legal antiquarians. To define the ambiguities, to circumscribe the latitude, to apply the principles, to extend the consequences, to reconcile the real or apparent contradictions, was a much nobler and more important task ; and the province of legislation was silently invaded by the expounders of ancient statutes. Their subtle interpretations concurred with the equity of the prætor, to reform the tyranny of the darker ages : however strange or intricate the means, it was the aim of artificial jurisprudence to restore the simple dictates of nature and reason, and the skill of private citizens was usefully employed to undermine the public institutions of their country.* The revolution of almost one thousand years, from the Twelve Tables to the reign to Justinian, may be divided into three periods, almost equal in duration, and distinguished from each other by the mode of instruction and the character of the civilians.[53] Pride and ignorance contributed, during the first period, to confine within narrow limits the science of the Roman law. On the public days of market or assembly, the masters of the art were seen walking in the forum

---

* Compare, on the Responsa Prudentum, Warnkönig, Histoire Externe du Droit Romain, Bruxelles, 1836, p. 122.—M.

ready to impart the needful advice to the meanest of their fellow-citizens, from whose votes, on a future occasion, they might solicit a grateful return. As their years and honors increased, they seated themselves at home on a chair or throne, to expect with patient gravity the visits of their clients, who at the dawn of day, from the town and country, began to thunder at their door. The duties of social life, and the incidents of judicial proceeding, were the ordinary subject of these consultations, and the verbal or written opinion of the *juris-consults* was framed according to the rules of prudence and law. The youths of their own order and family were permitted to listen ; their children enjoyed the benefit of more private lessons, and the Mucian race was long renowned for the hereditary knowledge of the civil law. The second period, the learned and splendid age of jurisprudence, may be extended from the birth of Cicero to the reign of Severus Alexander. A system was formed, schools were instituted, books were composed, and both the living and the dead became subservient to the instruction of the student. The *tripartite* of Ælius Pætus, surnamed Catus, or the Cunning, was preserved as the oldest work of jurisprudence. Cato the Censor derived some additional fame from his legal studies and those of his son : the kindred appellation of Mucius Scævola was illustrated by three sages of the law ; but the perfection of the science was ascribed to Servius Sulpicius, their disciple, and the friend of Tully ; and the long succession, which shone with equal lustre under the republic and under the Cæsars, is finally closed by the respectable characters of Papinian, of Paul, and of Ulpian. Their names, and the various titles of their productions, have been minutely preserved, and the example of Labeo may suggest some idea of their diligence and fecundity. That eminent lawyer of the Augustan age divided the year between the city and country, between business and composition ; and four hundred books are enumerated as the fruit of his retirement. Of the collection of his rival Capito, the two hundred and fifty-ninth book is expressly quoted ; and few teachers could deliver their opinions in less than a century of volumes. In the third period, between the reigns of Alexander and Justinian, the oracles of jurisprudence were almost mute. The measure of curiosity had been filled : the throne was occupied by tyrants and barbarians, the active spirits were diverted by religious disputes, and the professors of Rome, Constantinople, and Berytus, were humbly content to repeat the lessons of their more enlightened predecessors. From the slow advances and rapid decay of these legal studies, it may be inferred, that they require a state of peace and refinement. From the multitude of voluminous civilians who fill the intermediate space, it is evident that such studies may be pursued, and such works may be performed, with a common share of judgment, experience, and industry. The genius of Cicero and Virgil was more sensibly felt, as each revolving age had been found incapable of producing a similar or a second : but the most eminent teachers of the law were assured of leaving disciples equal or superior to themselves in merit and reputation.

The jurisprudence which had been grossly adapted to the wants of the first Romans, was polished and improved in the seventh century of the city, by the alliance of Grecian philosophy. The Scævolas had been taught by use and experience ; but Servius Sulpicius * was the first civilian who established his art on a certain and general theory.[54] For the discernment of truth and falsehood he applied, as an infallible rule, the logic of Aristotle and the Stoics, reduced particular cases to general principles, and diffused over the shapeless mass the light of order and eloquence. Cicero, his contemporary and friend, declined the reputation of a professed lawyer ; but the jurisprudence of his country was adorned by his incomparable genius, which converts into gold every object that it touches. After the example of Plato, he composed a republic ; and, for the use of his republic, a treatise of laws ; in which he labors to deduce from a celestial origin, the wisdom and justice of the Roman constitution. The whole universe, according to his sublime hypothesis, forms one immense commonwealth : gods and men, who participate of the same essence, are members of the same community ; reason prescribes the law of nature and nations ; and all positive institutions, however modified by accident or custom, are drawn from the rule of right, which the Deity has inscribed on every virtuous mind. From these philosophical mysteries, he mildly excludes the Sceptics who refuse to believe, and the Epicureans who are unwilling to act. The latter disdain the care of the republic : he advises them to slumber in their shady gardens. But he humbly entreats that the new academy would be silent, since her bold objections would too soon destroy the fair and well-ordered structure of his lofty system.[55] Plato, Aristotle, and Zeno, he represents as the only teachers who arm and instruct a citizen for the duties of social life. Of these, the armor of the Stoics[56] was found to be of the firmest temper ; and it was chiefly worn, both for use and ornament, in the schools of jurisprudence. From the portico, the

---

* M. Hugo thinks that the ingenious system of the Institutes adopted by a great number of the ancient lawyers, and by Justinian himself, dates from Severus Sulpicius. Hist. du Droit Romain, vol. ii. p. 119.—W.

Roman civilians learned to live, to reason, and to die : but they imbibed in some degree the prejudices of the sect ; the love of paradox, the pertinacious habits of dispute, and a minute attachment to words and verbal distinctions. The superiority of *form* to *matter* was introduced to ascertain the right of property : and the equality of crimes is countenanced by an opinion of Trebatius,[57] that he who touches the ear, touches the whole body ; and that he who steals from a heap of corn, or a hogshead of wine, is guilty of the entire theft.[58]

Arms, eloquence, and the study of the civil law, promoted a citizen to the honors of the Roman state ; and the three professions were sometimes more conspicuous by their union in the same character. In the composition of the edict, a learned prætor gave a sanction and preference to his private sentiments ; the opinion of a censor, or a consul, was entertained with respect ; and a doubtful interpretation of the laws might be supported by the virtues or triumphs of the civilian. The patrician arts were long protected by the veil of mystery ; and in more enlightened times, the freedom of inquiry established the general principles of jurisprudence. Subtile and intricate cases were elucidated by the disputes of the forum : rules, axioms, and definitions,[59] were admitted as the genuine dictates of reason ; and the consent of the legal professors was interwoven into the practice of the tribunals. But these interpreters could neither enact nor execute the laws of the republic ; and the judges might disregard the authority of the Scævolas themselves, which was often overthrown by the violence or sophistry of an ingenious pleader.[60] Augustus and Tiberius were the first to adopt, as a useful engine, the science of the civilians ; and their servile labors accommodated the old system to the spirit and views of despotism. Under the fair pretence of securing the dignity of the art, the privilege of subscribing legal and valid opinions was confined to the sages of senatorian or equestrian rank, who had been previously approved by the judgment of the prince ; and this monopoly prevailed, till Adrian restored the freedom of the profession to every citizen conscious of his abilities and knowledge. The discretion of the prætor was now governed by the lessons of his teachers ; the judges were enjoined to obey the comment as well as the text of the law ; and the use of codicils was a memorable innovation, which Augustus ratified by the advice of the civilians.[61] *

---

* The author here follows the then generally received opinion of Heineccius. The proofs which appear to confirm it are l. 2, § 47, D. I. 2, and § 8. Instit. I. 2. The first of these passages speaks expressly of a privilege granted to certain lawyers, until the time of Adrian, publice respondendi jus ante Augusti tempora non

The most absolute mandate could only require that the judges should agree with the civilians, if the civilians agreed among themselves. But positive institutions are often the result of custom and prejudice ; laws and language are ambiguous and arbitrary ; where reason is incapable of pronouncing, the love of argument is inflamed by the envy of rivals, the vanity of masters, the blind attachment of their disciples ; and the Roman jurisprudence was divided by the once famous sects of the *Proculians* and *Sabinians*.[62] Two sages of the law, Ateius Capito and Antistius Labeo,[63] adorned the peace of the Augustan age ; the former distinguished by the favor of his sovereign ; the latter more illustrious by his contempt of that favor, and his stern though harmless opposition to the tyrant of Rome. Their legal studies were influenced by the various colors of their temper and principles. Labeo was attached to the form of the old republic ; his rival embraced the more profitable substance of the rising monarchy. But the disposition of a courtier is tame and submissive ; and Capito seldom presumed to deviate from the sentiments, or at least from the words, of his predecessors ; while the bold republican pursued his

---

dabatur. Primus Divus Augustus, ut major juris auctoritas haberetur, constituit, ut ex auctoritate•ejus responderent. The passage of the Institutes speaks of the different opinions of those, quibus est permissum jura condere. It is true that the first of these passages does not say that the opinion of these privileged lawyers had the force of a law for the judges. For this reason M. Hugo altogether rejects the opinion adopted by Heineccius, by Bach, and in general by all the writers who preceded him. He conceives that the § 8 of the Institutes referred to the constitution of Valentinian III., which regulated the respective authority to be ascribed to the different writings of the great civilians, But we have now the following passage in the Institutes of Gaius : Responsa prudentum sunt sententiæ et opiniones eorum, quibus permissum est jura condere ; quorum omnium si in unum sententiæ concurrunt, id quod ita sentiunt, legis vicem obtinet, si vero dissentiunt, judici licet, quam velit sententiam sequi, idque rescripto Divi Hadriani significatur. I do not know how, in opposition to this passage, the opinion of M. Hugo can be maintained. We must add to this the passage quoted from Pomponius ; and from such strong proofs it seems incontestable that the emperors had granted some kind of privilege to certain civilians, quibus permissum erat jura condere. Their opinion had sometimes the force of law, legis vicem. M. Hugo, endeavoring to reconcile this phrase with his system, gives it a forced interpretation, which quite alters the sense ; he supposes that the passage contains no more than what is evident of itself, that the authority of the civilians was to be respected, thus making a privilege of that which was free to all the world. It appears to me almost indisputable that the emperors had sanctioned certain provisions relative to the authority of these civilians, consulted by the judges. But how far was their advice to be respected ? This is a question which it is impossible to answer precisely, from the want of historic evidence.

Is it not possible that the emperors established an authority to be consulted by the judges ? and in this case this authority must have emanated from certain civilians named for this purpose by the emperors. See Hugo. Moreover, may not the passage of Suetonius in the Life of Caligula, where he says that the emperor would no longer permit the civilians to give their advice, mean that Caligula entertained the design of suppressing this institution ? See on this passage the Themis, vol. xi. p. 17, 36. Our author, not being acquainted with the opinions opposed to Heineccius, has not gone to the bottom of the subject. —W.

independent ideas without fear of paradox or innovations. The freedom of Labeo was enslaved, however, by the rigor of his own conclusions, and he decided, according to the letter of the law, the same questions which his indulgent competitor resolved with a latitude of equity more suitable to the common sense and feelings of mankind. If a fair exchange had been substituted to the payment of money, Capito still considered the transaction as a legal sale ; [64] and he consulted nature for the age of puberty, without confining his definition to the precise period of twelve or fourteen years. [65] This opposition of sentiments was propagated in the writings and lessons of the two founders ; the schools of Capito and Labeo maintained their inveterate conflict from the age of Augustus to that of Adrian ; [66] and the two sects derived their appellations from Sabinus and Proculus, their most celebrated teachers. The names of *Cassians* and *Pegasians* were likewise applied to the same parties ; but, by a strange reverse, the popular cause was in the hands of Pegasus, [67] a timid slave of Domitian, while the favorite of the Cæsars was represented by Cassius, [68] who gloried in his descent from the patriot assassin. By the perpetual edict, the controversies of the sects were in a great measure determined. For that important work, the emperor Adrian preferred the chief of the Sabinians : the friends of monarchy prevailed ; but the moderation of Salvius Julian insensibly reconciled the victors and the vanquished. Like the contemporary philosophers, the lawyers of the age of the Antonines disclaimed the authority of a master, and adopted from every system the most probable doctrines. [69] But their writings would have been less voluminous, had their choice been more unanimous. The conscience of the judge was perplexed by the number and weight of discordant testimonies, and every sentence that his passion or interest might pronounce was justified by the sanction of some venerable name. An indulgent edict of the younger Theodosius excused him from the labor of comparing and weighing their arguments. Five civilians, Caius, Papinian, Paul, Ulpian, and Modestinus, were established as the oracles of jurisprudence : a majority was decisive : but if their opinions were equally divided, a casting vote was ascribed to the superior wisdom of Papinian. [70]

When Justinian ascended the throne, the reformation of the Roman jurisprudence was an arduous but indispensable task. In the space of ten centuries, the infinite variety of laws and legal opinions had filled many thousand volumes, which no fortune could purchase and no capacity could digest. Books could not easily be found ; and the judges, poor in the midst of riches, were

reduced to the exercise of their illiterate discretion. The subjects of the Greek provinces were ignorant of the language that
disposed of their lives and properties ; and the *barbarous* dialect
of the Latins was imperfectly studied in the academies of Berytus and Constantinople. As an Illyrian soldier, that idiom was
familiar to the infancy of Justinian ; his youth had been instructed by the lessons of jurisprudence, and his Imperial choice
selected the most learned civilians of the East, to labor with their
sovereign in the work of reformation.[71] The theory of professors
was assisted by the practice of advocates, and the experience of
magistrates ; and the whole undertaking was animated by the
spirit of Tribonian.[72] This extraordinary man, the object of so
much praise and censure, was a native of Side in Pamphylia ; and
his genius, like that of Bacon, embraced, as his own, all the business and knowledge of the age. Tribonian composed, both in
prose and verse, on a strange diversity of curious and abstruse
subjects :[73] a double panegyric of Justinian and the life of the
philosopher Theodotus ; the nature of happiness and the duties of
government ; Homer's catalogue and the four-and-twenty sorts of
metre ; the astronomical canon of Ptolemy ; the changes of the
months ; the houses of the planets ; and the harmonic system of
the world. To the literature of Greece he added the use of the
Latin tongue ; the Roman civilians were deposited in his library
and in his mind ; and he most assiduously cultivated those arts
which opened the road of wealth and preferment. From the bar
of the Prætorian præfects, he raised himself to the honors of quæstor, of consul, and of master of the offices : the council of Justinian listened to his eloquence and wisdom ; and envy was mitigated by the gentleness and affability of his manners. The reproaches of impiety and avarice have stained the virtues or the
reputation of Tribonian. In a bigoted and persecuting court, the
principal minister was accused of a secret aversion to the Christian faith, and was supposed to entertain the sentiments of an
Atheist and a Pagan, which have been imputed, inconsistently
enough, to the last philosophers of Greece. His avarice was more
clearly proved and more sensibly felt. If he were swayed by gifts
in the administration of justice, the example of Bacon will again
occur, nor can the merit of Tribonian atone for his baseness, if he
degraded the sanctity of his profession ; and if laws were every
day enacted, modified, or repealed, for the base consideration of
his private emolument. In the sedition of Constantinople, his removal was granted to the clamors, perhaps to the just indignation, of the people : but the quæstor was speedily restored, and,
till the hour of his death, he possessed, above twenty years, the

favor and confidence of the emperor. His passive and dutiful submission has been honored with the praise of Justinian himself, whose vanity was incapable of discerning how often that submission degenerated into the grossest adulation. Tribonian adored the virtues of his gracious master : the earth was unworthy of such a prince ; and he affected a pious fear, that Justinian, like Elijah or Romulus, would be snatched into the air, and translated alive to the mansions of celestial glory.[74]

If Cæsar had achieved the reformation of the Roman law, his creative genius, enlightened by reflection and study, would have given to the world a pure and original system of jurisprudence. Whatever flattery might suggest, the emperor of the East was afraid to establish his private judgment as the standard of equity : in the possession of legislative power, he borrowed the aid of time and opinion ; and his laborious compilations are guarded by the sages and legislators of past times. Instead of a statue cast in a simple mould by the hand of an artist, the works of Justinian represent a tessellated pavement of antique and costly, but too often of incoherent, fragments. In the first year of his reign, he directed the faithful Tribonian, and nine learned associates, to revise the ordinances of his predecessors, as they were contained, since the time of Adrian, in the Gregorian, Hermogenian, and Theodosian codes ; to purge the errors and contradictions, to retrench whatever was obsolete or superfluous, and to select the wise and salutary laws best adapted to the practice of the tribunals and the use of his subjects. The work was accomplished in fourteen months ; and the twelve books or *tables*, which the new decemvirs produced, might be designed to imitate the labors of their Roman predecessors. The new CODE of Justinian was honored with his name, and confirmed by his royal signature : authentic transcripts were multiplied by the pens of notaries and scribes ; they were transmitted to the magistrates of the European, the Asiatic, and afterwards the African provinces ; and the law of the empire was proclaimed on solemn festivals at the doors of churches. A more arduous operation was still behind—to extract the spirit of jurisprudence from the decisions and conjectures, the questions and disputes, of the Roman civilians. Seventeen lawyers, with Tribonian at their head, were appointed by the emperor to exercise an absolute jurisdiction over the works of their predecessors. If they had obeyed his commands in ten years, Justinian would have been satisfied with their diligence ; and the rapid composition of the DIGEST or PANDECTS,[75] in three years, will deserve praise or censure, according to the merit of the execution. From the library of Tribonian, they chose forty, the most eminent civilians of former times : [76] two thousand treatises were comprised in an abridgment of fifty books ; and it has been carefully recorded, that three millions of lines or sentences, [77] were reduced, in this abstract, to the moderate number of one hundred and fifty thousand. The edition of this great work was delayed a month after that of the INSTITUTES ; and it seemed reasonable that the elements should precede the digest of the Roman law. As soon as the emperor had approved their labors, he ratified, by his legislative power, the speculations of these private citizens : their commentaries, on the Twelve Tables, the perpetual edict, the laws of the people, and the decrees of the senate, succeeded to the authority of the text ; and the text was abandoned, as a useless, though venerable, relic of antiquity. The *Code*, the *Pandects*, and the *Institutes*, were declared to be the legitimate system of civil jurisprudence ; they alone were admitted in the tribunals, and they alone were taught in the academies of Rome, Constantinople, and Berytus. Justinian addressed to the senate and provinces his *eternal oracles ;* and his pride, under the mask of piety, ascribed the consummation of this great design to the support and inspiration of the Deity.

Since the emperor declined the fame and envy of original composition, we can only require, at his hands, method, choice, and fidelity, the humble, though indispensable, virtues of a compiler. Among the various combinations of ideas, it is difficult to assign any reasonable preference ; but as the order of Justinian is different in his three works, it is possible that all may be wrong ; and it is certain that two cannot be right. In the selection of ancient laws, he seems to have viewed his predecessors without jealousy, and with equal regard : the series could not ascend above the reign of Adrian, and the narrow distinction of Paganism and Christianity, introduced by the superstition of Theodosius, had been abolished by the consent of mankind. But the jurisprudence of the Pandects is circumscribed, within a period of a hundred years, from the perpetual edict, to the death of Severus Alexander : the civilians who lived under the first Cæsars are seldom permitted to speak, and only three names can be attributed to the age of the republic. The favorite of Justinian (it has been fiercely urged) was fearful of encountering the light of freedom and the gravity of Roman sages. Tribonian condemned to oblivion the genuine and native wisdom of Cato, the Scævolas, and Sulpicius ; while he invoked spirits more congenial to his own, the Syrians, Greeks, and Africans, who flocked to the Imperial court to study Latin as a foreign tongue, and jurisprudence as a lucrative profession. But the ministers of Justinian [78] were instructed to labor, not for the curiosity of antiquarians, but for the immediate benefit of the subjects. It was their duty to select the useful and practical parts of the Roman law ; and the writings of the old republicans, however curious or excellent, were no longer suited to the new system of manners, religion, and government. Perhaps, if the preceptors and friends of Cicero were still alive, our candor would acknowledge, that, except in purity of language,[79] their intrinsic merit was excelled by the school of Papinian and Ulpian. The science of the laws is the slow growth of time and experience, and the advantage both of method and materials, is naturally assumed by the most recent authors. The civilians of the reign of the Antonines had studied the works of their predecessors : their philosophic spirit had mitigated the rigor of antiquity, simplified the forms of proceeding, and emerged from the jealousy and prejudice of the rival sects. The choice of the authorities that compose the Pandects depended on the judgment of Tribonian : but the power of his sovereign could not absolve him from the sacred obligations of truth and fidelity. As the legislator of the empire, Justinian might repeal the acts of the Antonines, or condemn, as seditious, the free principles which were maintained by the last of the *Roman* lawyers.[80] But the existence of past facts is placed beyond the reach of despotism ; and the emperor was guilty of fraud and forgery, when he corrupted the integrity of their text, inscribed with their venerable names the words and ideas of his servile reign,[81] and suppressed, by the hand of power, the pure and authentic copies of their sentiments. The changes and interpolations of Tribonian and his colleagues are excused by the pretence of uniformity : but their cares have been insufficient, and the *antinomies*, or contradictions of the Code and Pandects, still exercise the patience and subtilty of modern civilians.[82]

A rumor devoid of evidence has been propagated by the enemies of Justinian ; that the jurisprudence of ancient Rome was reduced to ashes by the author of the Pandects, from the vain persuasion, that it was now either false or superfluous. Without usurping an office so invidious, the emperor might safely commit to ignorance and time the accomplishment of this destructive wish. Before the invention of printing and paper, the labor and the materials of writing could be purchased only by the rich ; and it may reasonably be computed, that the price of books was a hundred fold their present value.[83] Copies were slowly multiplied and cautiously renewed : the hopes of profit tempted the sacrilegious scribes to erase the characters of antiquity,* and Sophocles or

---

* Among the works which have been recovered, by the persevering and successful

Tacitus were obliged to resign the parchment to missals, homilies, and the golden legend.[84] If such was the fate of the most beautiful compositions of genius, what stability could be expected from the dull and barren works of an obsolete science ? The books of jurisprudence were interesting to few, and entertaining to none : their value was connected with present use, and they sunk forever as soon as that use was superseded by the innovations of fashion, superior merit, or public authority. In the age of peace and learning, between Cicero and the last of the Antonines, many losses had been already sustained, and some luminaries of the school, or forum, were known only to the curious by tradition and report. Three hundred and sixty years of disorder and decay accelerated the progress of oblivion ; and it may fairly be presumed, that of the writings, which Justinian is accused of neglecting, many were no longer to be found in the libraries of the East.[85] The copies of Papinian, or Ulpian, which the reformer had proscribed, were deemed unworthy of future notice : the Twelve Tables and prætorian edicts insensibly vanished, and the monuments of ancient Rome were neglected or destroyed by the envy and ignorance of the Greeks. Even the Pandects themselves have escaped with difficulty and danger from the common shipwreck, and criticism has pronounced that *all* the editions and manuscripts of the West are derived from *one* original.[86] It was transcribed at Constantinople in the beginning of the seventh century,[87] was successively transported by the accidents of war and commerce to Amalphi,[88] Pisa,[89] and Florence,[90] and is now deposited as a sacred relic [91] in the ancient palace of the republic.[92]

It is the first care of a reformer to prevent any future reformation. To maintain the text of the Pandects, the Institutes, and the Code, the use of ciphers and abbreviations was rigorously proscribed ; and as Justinian recollected, that the perpetual edict had been buried under the weight of commentators, he denounced the punishment of forgery against the rash civilians who should presume to interpret or pervert the will of their sovereign. The scholars of Accursius, of Bartolus, of Cujacius, should blush for their accumulated guilt, unless they dare to dispute his right of binding the authority of his successors, and the native freedom of the mind. But the emperor was unable to fix his own inconstancy ; and while he boasted of renewing the exchange of Diomede, of transmuting brass into gold,[93] discovered the necessity of purify-

---

endeavors of M. Mai and his followers to trace the imperfectly erased characters of the ancient writers on these Palimpsests, Gibbon at this period of his labors would have hailed with delight the recovery of the Institutes of Gaius, and the fragments of the Theodosian Code, published by M. Peyron of Turin.—M.

ing his gold from the mixture of baser alloy. Six years had not elapsed from the publication of the Code, before he condemned the imperfect attempt, by a new and more accurate edition of the same work ; which he enriched with two hundred of his own laws, and fifty decisions of the darkest and most intricate points of jurisprudence. Every year, or, according to Procopius, each day, of his long reign, was marked by some legal innovation. Many of his acts were rescinded by himself ; many were rejected by his successors ; many have been obliterated by time ; but the number of sixteen EDICTS, and one hundred and sixty-eight NOVELS,[94] has been admitted into the authentic body of the civil jurisprudence. In the opinion of a philosopher superior to the prejudices of his profession, these incessant, and, for the most part, trifling alterations, can be only explained by the venal spirit of a prince, who sold without shame his judgments and his laws.[95] The charge of the secret historian is indeed explicit and vehement ; but the sole instance, which he produces, may be ascribed to the devotion as well as to the avarice of Justinian. A wealthy bigot had bequeathed his inheritance to the church of Emesa ; and its value was enchanced by the dexterity of an artist, who subscribed confessions of debt and promises of payment with the names of the richest Syrians. They pleaded the established prescription of thirty or forty years ; but their defence was overruled by a retrospective edict, which extended the claims of the church to the term of a century ; an edict so pregnant with injustice and disorder, that, after serving this occasional purpose, it was prudently abolished in the same reign.[96] If candor will acquit the emperor himself, and transfer the corruption to his wife and favorites, the suspicion of so foul a vice must still degrade the majesty of his laws ; and the advocates of Justinian may acknowledge, that such levity, whatsoever be the motive, is unworthy of a legislator and a man.

Monarchs seldom condescend to become the preceptors of their subjects ; and some praise is due to Justinian, by whose command an ample system was reduced to a short and elementary treatise. Among the various institutes of the Roman law,[97] those of Caius[98] were the most popular in the East and West ; and their use may be considered as an evidence of their merit. They were selected by the Imperial delegates, Tribonian, Theophilus, and Dorotheus, and the freedom and purity of the Antonines was intrusted with the coarser materials of a degenerate age. The same volume which introduced the youth of Rome, Constantinople, and Berytus, to the gradual study of the Code and Pandects, is still precious to the historian, the philosopher, and the magistrate. The

INSTITUTES of Justinian are divided into four books : they proceed, with no contemptible method, from, I. *Persons*, to, II. *Things*, and from things, to, III. *Actions ;* and the article IV., of *Private Wrongs*, is terminated by the principles of *Criminal Law.**

The distinction of ranks and *persons* is the firmest basis of a mixed and limited government. In France, the remains of liberty are kept alive by the spirit, the honors, and even the prejudices, of fifty thousand nobles.⁹⁹ Two hundred families † supply, in lineal descent, the second branch of the English legislature, which maintains, between the king and commons, the balance of the constitution. A gradation of patricians and plebeians, of strangers and subjects, has supported the aristocracy of Genoa, Venice, and ancient Rome. The perfect equality of men is the point in which the extremes of democracy and despotism are confounded ; since the majesty of the prince or people would be offended, if any heads were exalted above the level of their fellow-slaves or fellow-citizens. In the decline of the Roman empire, the proud distinctions of the republic were gradually abolished, and the reason or instinct of Justinian completed the simple form of an absolute monarchy. The emperor could not eradicate the popular reverence which always waits on the possession of hereditary wealth, or the memory of famous ancestors. He delighted to honor, with titles and emoluments, his generals, magistrates, and senators ; and his precarious indulgence communicated some rays of their glory to the persons of their wives and children. But in the eye of the law, all Roman citizens were equal, and all subjects of the empire were citizens of Rome. That inestimable character was degraded to an obsolete and empty name. The voice of a Roman could no longer enact his laws or create the annual ministers of his power : his constitutional rights might have checked the arbitrary will of a master : and the bold adventurer from Germany or Arabia was admitted, with equal favor, to the civil and military command, which the citizen alone had been once entitled to assume over the conquests of his fathers. The first Cæsars had scrupulously guarded the distinction of *ingenuous* and *servile* birth, which was decided by the condition of the mother ; and the candor of the laws were satisfied, if *her* freedom could be ascertained, during a single moment between the conception and the delivery. The slaves, who were liberated by a generous master, immediately

---

* Gibbon, dividing the Institutes into four parts, considers the appendix of the criminal law in the last title as a fourth part.—W.

† Since the time of Gibbon, the House of Peers has been more than doubled : it is above 400, exclusive of the spiritual peers—a wise policy, to increase the patrician order in proportion to the general increase of the nation.—M.

entered into the middle class of *libertines* or freedmen ; but they could never be enfranchised from the duties of obedience and gratitude : whatever were the fruits of their industry, their patron and his family inherited the third part ; or even the whole of their fortune, if they died without children and without a testament. Justinian respected the rights of patrons ; but his indulgence removed the badge of disgrace from the two inferior orders of freedmen : whoever ceased to be a slave, obtained, without reserve or delay, the station of a citizen ; and at length the dignity of an ingenuous birth, which nature had refused, was created, or supposed, by the omnipotence of the emperor. Whatever restraints of age, or forms, or numbers, had been formerly introduced to check the abuse of manumissions, and the too rapid increase of vile and indigent Romans, he finally abolished ; and the spirit of his laws promoted the extinction of domestic servitude. Yet the Eastern provinces were filled, in the time of Justinian, with multitudes of slaves, either born or purchased for the use of their masters ; and the price, from ten to seventy pieces of gold, was determined by their age, their strength, and their education.[109] But the hardships of this dependent state were continually diminished by the influence of government and religion ; and the pride of a subject was no longer elated by his absolute dominion over the life and happiness of his bondsman.[101]

The law of nature instructs most animals to cherish and educate their infant progeny. The law of reason inculcates to the human species the returns of filial piety. But the exclusive, absolute, and perpetual dominion of the father over his children, is peculiar to the Roman jurisprudence,[102] and seems to be coeval with the foundation of the city.[103] The paternal power was instituted or confirmed by Romulus himself, and, after the practice of three centuries, it was inscribed on the fourth table of the Decemvirs. In the forum, the senate, or the camp, the adult son of a Roman citizen enjoyed the public and private rights of a *person :* in his father's house he was a mere *thing ;* * confounded by the laws with the movables, the cattle, and the slaves, whom the capricious master might alienate or destroy, without being responsible to any earthly tribunal. The hand which bestowed the daily sustenance might resume the voluntary gift, and whatever was acquired by the labor or fortune of the son was·immediately lost in the property

---

* This parental power was strictly confined to the Roman citizen. The foreigner, or he who had only jus Latii, did not possess it. If a Roman citizen unknowingly married a Latin or a foreign wife, he did not possess this power over his son, because the son, following the legal condition of the mother, was not a Roman citizen. A man, however, alleging sufficient cause for his ignorance, might raise both mother and child to the rights of citizenship. Gaius, p. 30.—M.

of the father. His stolen goods (his oxen or his children) might be recovered by the same action of theft ; [104] and if either had been guilty of a trespass, it was in his own option to compensate the damage, or resign to the injured party the obnoxious animal. At the call of indigence or avarice, the master of a family could dispose of his children or his slaves. But the condition of the slave was far more advantageous, since he regained, by the first manumission, his alienated freedom : the son was again restored to his unnatural father ; he might be condemned to servitude a second and a third time, and it was not till after the third sale and deliverance, [105] that he was enfranchised from the domestic power which had been so repeatedly abused. According to his discretion, a father might chastise the real or imaginary faults of his children, by stripes, by imprisonment, by exile, by sending them to the country to work in chains among the meanest of his servants. The majesty of a parent was armed with the power of life and death ; [106] and the examples of such bloody executions, which were sometimes praised and never punished, may be traced in the annals of Rome beyond the times of Pompey and Augustus. Neither age, nor rank, nor the consular office, nor the honors of a triumph, could exempt the most illustrious citizen from the bonds of filial subjection : [107] his own descendants were included in the family of their common ancestor ; and the claims of adoption were not less sacred or less rigorous than those of nature. Without fear, though not without danger of abuse, the Roman legislators had reposed an unbounded confidence in the sentiments of paternal love ; and the oppression was tempered by the assurance, that each generation must succeed in its turn to the awful dignity of parent and master.

The first limitation of paternal power is ascribed to the justice and humanity of Numa ; and the maid who, with *his* father's consent, had espoused a freeman, was protected from the disgrace of becoming the wife of a slave. In the first ages, when the city was pressed, and often famished, by her Latin and Tuscan neighbors, the sale of children might be a frequent practice ; but as a Roman could not legally purchase the liberty of his fellow-citizen, the market must gradually fail, and the trade would be destroyed by the conquests of the republic. An imperfect right of property was at length communicated to sons ; and the threefold distinction of *profectitious*, *adventitious*, and *professional* was ascertained by the jurisprudence of the Code and Pandects. [108] Of all that proceeded from the father, he imparted only the use, and reserved the absolute dominion ; yet if his goods were sold, the filial portion was excepted, by a favorable interpretation, from the demands of the creditors. In whatever accrued by marriage, gift, or collateral succession, the property was secured to the son ; but the father, unless he had been specially excluded, enjoyed the usufruct during his life. As a just and prudent reward of military virtue, the spoils of the enemy were acquired, possessed, and bequeathed by the soldier alone ; and the fair analogy was extended to the emoluments of any liberal profession, the salary of public service, and the sacred liberality of the emperor or empress. The life of a citizen was less exposed than his fortune to the abuse of paternal power. Yet his life might be adverse to the interest or passions of an unworthy father : the same crimes that flowed from the corruption, were more sensibly felt by the humanity, of the Augustan age ; and the cruel Erixo, who whipped his son till he expired, was saved by the emperor from the just fury of the multitude.[109] The Roman father, from the license of servile dominion, was reduced to the gravity and moderation of a judge. The presence and opinion of Augustus confirmed the sentence of exile pronounced against an intentional parricide by the domestic tribunal of Arius. Ardian transported to an island the jealous parent who, like a robber, had seized the opportunity of hunting, to assassinate a youth, the incestuous lover of his step-mother.[110] A private jurisdiction is repugnant to the spirit of monarchy ; the parent was again reduced from a judge to an accuser ; and the magistrates were enjoined by Severus Alexander to hear his complaints and execute his sentence. He could no longer take the life of a son without incurring the guilt and punishment of murder ; and the pains of parricide, from which he had been excepted by the Pompeian law, were finally inflicted by the justice of Constantine.[111] The same protection was due to every period of existence ; and reason must applaud the humanity of Paulus, for imputing the crime of murder to the father who strangles, or starves, or abandons his new-born infant ; or exposes him in a public place to find the mercy which he himself had denied. But the exposition of children was the prevailing and stubborn vice of antiquity : it was sometimes prescribed, often permitted, almost always practised with impunity, by the nations who never entertained the Roman ideas of paternal power ; and the dramatic poets, who appeal to the human heart, represent with indifference a popular custom which was palliated by the motives of economy and compassion.[112] If the father could subdue his own feelings, he might escape, though not the censure, at least the chastisement, of the laws ; and the Roman empire was stained with the blood of infants, till such murders were included, by Valentinian and his colleagues, in the letter and spirit of the Cornelian law.

The lessons of jurisprudence[113] and Christianity had been insufficient to eradicate this inhuman practice, till their gentle influence was fortified by the terrors of capital punishment.[114]

Experience has proved, that savages are the tyrants of the female sex, and that the condition of women is usually softened by the refinements of social life. In the hope of a robust progeny, Lycurgus had delayed the season of marriage : it was fixed by Numa at the tender age of twelve years, that the Roman husband might educate to his will a pure and obedient virgin.[115] According to the custom of antiquity, he bought his bride of her parents, and she fulfilled the *coemption* by purchasing, with three pieces of copper, a just introduction to his house and household deities. A sacrifice of fruits was offered by the pontiffs in the presence of ten witnesses ; the contracting parties were seated on the same sheep-skin ; they tasted a salt cake of *far* or rice ; and this *confarreation*,[116] which denoted the ancient food of Italy, served as an emblem of their mystic union of mind and body. But this union on the side of the woman was rigorous and unequal : and she renounced the name and worship of her father's house, to embrace a new servitude, decorated only by the title of adoption, a fiction of the law, neither rational nor elegant, bestowed on the mother of a family[117] (her proper appellation) the strange characters of sister to her own children, and of daughter to her husband or master, who was invested with the plenitude of paternal power. By his judgment or caprice her behavior was approved, or censured, or chastised ; he exercised the jurisdiction of life and death ; and it was allowed, that in the cases of adultery or drunkenness,[118] the sentence might be properly inflicted. She acquired and inherited for the sole profit of her lord ; and so clearly was woman defined, not as a *person*, but as a *thing*, that, if the original title were deficient, she might be claimed, like other movables, by the *use* and possession of an entire year. The inclination of the Roman husband discharged or withheld the conjugal debt, so scrupulously exacted by the Athenian and Jewish laws :[119] but as polygamy was unknown, he could never admit to his bed a fairer or more favored partner.

After the Punic triumphs, the matrons of Rome aspired to the common benefits of a free and opulent republic : their wishes were gratified by the indulgence of fathers and lovers, and their ambition was unsuccessfully resisted by the gravity of Cato the Censor.[120] They declined the solemnities of the old nuptials ; defeated the annual prescription by an absence of three days ; and, without losing their name or independence, subscribed the liberal and definite terms of a marriage contract. Of their private fortunes, they communicated the use, and secured the property : the estates of a wife could neither be alienated nor mortgaged by a prodigal husband ; their mutual gifts were prohibited by the jealousy of the laws ; and the misconduct of either party might afford, under another name, a future subject for an action of theft. To this loose and voluntary compact, religious and civil rights were no longer essential ; and, between persons of a similar rank, the apparent community of life was allowed as sufficient evidence of their nuptials. The dignity of marriage was restored by the Christians, who derived all spiritual grace from the prayers of the faithful and the benediction of the priest or bishop. The origin, validity, and duties of the holy institution were regulated by the tradition of the synagogue ; the precepts of the gospel, and the canons of general or provincial synods ; [121] and the conscience of the Christians was awed by the decrees and censures of their ecclesiastical rulers. Yet the magistrates of Justinian were not subject to the authority of the church : the emperor consulted the unbelieving civilians of antiquity, and the choice of matrimonial laws in the Code and Pandects, is directed by the earthly motives of justice, policy, and the natural freedom of both sexes. [122]

Besides the agreement of the parties, the essence of every rational contract, the Roman marriage required the previous approbation of the parents. A father might be forced by some recent laws to supply the wants of a mature daughter ; but even his insanity was not generally allowed to supersede the necessity of his consent. The causes of the dissolution of matrimony have varied among the Romans ; [123] but the most solemn sacrament, the confarreation itself, might always be done away by rites of a contrary tendency. In the first ages, the father of a family might sell his children, and his wife was reckoned in the number of his children : the domestic judge might pronounce the death of the offender, or his mercy might expel her from his bed and house ; but the slavery of the wretched female was hopeless and perpetual, unless he asserted for his own convenience the manly prerogative of divorce.* The warmest applause has been lavished on the virtue of the Romans, who abstained from the exercise of this tempting privilege above five hundred years : [124] but the same fact evinces the unequal terms of a connection in which the slave was unable to renounce her tyrant, and the tyrant was unwilling to relinquish his slave. When the Roman matrons became the equal and voluntary companions of their lords, a new jurisprudence was introduced, that marriage,

---

* Montesquieu relates and explains this fact in a different manner. Esprit des Loix, l. xvi. c. 16.—G.

like other partnerships, might be dissolved by the abdication of
one of the associates. In three centuries of prosperity and corruption, this principle was enlarged to frequent practice and
pernicious abuse. Passion, interest, or caprice, suggested daily
motives for the dissolution of marriage ; a word, a sign, a message,
a letter, the mandate of a freedman, declared the separation ; the
most tender of human connections was degraded to a transient
society of profit or pleasure. According to the various conditions
of life, both sexes alternately felt the disgrace and injury : an
inconstant spouse transferred her wealth to a new family,
abandoning a numerous, perhaps a spurious, progeny to the
parental authority and care of her late husband ; a beautiful virgin
might be dismissed to the world, old, indigent, and friendless ;
but the reluctance of the Romans, when they were pressed to
marriage by Augustus, sufficiently marks, that the prevailing
institutions were least favorable to the males. A specious theory
is confuted by this free and perfect experiment, which demon-
strates, that the liberty of divorce does not contribute to happiness
and virtue. The facility of separation would destroy all mutual
confidence, and inflame every trifling dispute : the minute difference between a husband and a stranger, which might so easily
be removed, might still more easily be forgotten ; and the matron,
who in five years can submit to the embraces of eight husbands,
must cease to reverence the chastity of her own person.[125]

Insufficient remedies followed with distant and tardy steps the
rapid progress of the evil. The ancient worship of the Romans
afforded a peculiar goddess to hear and reconcile the complaints
of a married life ; but her epithet of *Viriplaca*,[126] the appeaser of
husbands, too clearly indicates on which side submission and
repentance were always expected. Every act of a citizen was
subject to the judgment of the *censors ;* the first who used the
privilege of divorce assigned, at their command, the motives of
his conduct ;[127] and a senator was expelled for dismissing his
virgin spouse without the knowledge or advice of his friends.
Whenever an action was instituted for the recovery of a marriage
portion, the *prætor*, as the guardian of equity, examined the cause
and the characters, and gently inclined the scale in favor of the
guiltless and injured party. Augustus, who united the powers of
both magistrates, adopted their different modes of repressing or
chastising the license of divorce.[128] The presence of seven Roman
witnesses was required for the validity of this solemn and
deliberate act : if any adequate provocation had been given by
the husband, instead of the delay of two years, he was compelled
to refund immediately, or in the space of six months ; but if he

could arraign the manners of his wife, her guilt or levity was expiated by the loss of the sixth or eighth part of her marriage portion. The Christian princes were the first who specified the just causes of a private divorce; their institutions, from Constantine to Justinian, appear to fluctuate between the custom of the empire and the wishes of the church,[129] and the author of the Novels too frequently reforms the jurisprudence of the Code and Pandects. In the most rigorous laws, a wife was condemned to support a gamester, a drunkard, or a libertine, unless he was guilty of homicide, poison, or sacrilege, in which cases the marriage, as it should seem, might have been dissolved by the hand of the executioner. But the sacred right of the husband was invariably maintained, to deliver his name and family from the disgrace of adultery: the list of *mortal* sins, either male or female, was curtailed and enlarged by successive regulations, and the obstacles of incurable impotence, long absence, and monastic profession, were allowed to rescind the matrimonial obligation. Whoever transgressed the permission of the law, was subject to various and heavy penalties. The woman was stripped of her wealth and ornaments, without excepting the bodkin of her hair: if the man introduced a new bride into his bed, *her* fortune might be lawfully seized by the vengeance of his exiled wife. Forfeiture was sometimes commuted to a fine; the fine was sometimes aggravated by transportation to an island, or imprisonment in a monastery; the injured party was released from the bonds of marriage; but the offender, during life, or a term of years, was disabled from the repetition of nuptials. The successor of Justinian yielded to the prayers of his unhappy subjects, and restored the liberty of divorce by mutual consent: the civilians were unanimous,[130] the theologians were divided,[131] and the ambiguous word, which contains the precepts of Christ, is flexible to any interpretation that the wisdom of a legislator can demand.

The freedom of love and marriage was restrained among the Romans by natural and civil impediments. An instinct, almost innate and universal, appears to prohibit the incestuous commerce[132] of parents and children in the infinite series of ascending and descending generations. Concerning the oblique and collateral branches, nature is indifferent, reason mute, and custom various and arbitrary. In Egypt, the marriage of brothers and sisters was admitted without scruple or exception: a Spartan might espouse the daughter of his father, an Athenian, that of his mother; and the nuptials of an uncle with his niece were applauded at Athens as a happy union of the dearest relations. The profane lawgivers of Rome were never tempted by interest or superstition to multiply the forbidden degrees : but they inflexibly condemned the marriage of sisters and brothers, hesitated whether first cousins should be touched by the same interdict ; revered the parental character of aunts and uncles,* and treated affinity and adoption as a just imitation of the ties of blood. According to the proud maxims of the republic, a legal marriage could only be contracted by free citizens ; an honorable, at least an ingenuous birth, was required for the spouse of a senator : but the blood of kings could never mingle in legitimate nuptials with the blood of a Roman ; and the name of Stranger degraded Cleopatra and Berenice,[133] to live the *concubines* of Mark Antony and Titus.[134] This appellation, indeed, so injurious to the majesty, cannot without indulgence be applied to the manners, of these Oriental queens. A concubine, in the strict sense of the civilians, was a woman of servile or plebeian extraction, the sole and faithful companion of a Roman citizen, who continued in a state of celibacy. Her modest station, below the honors of a wife, above the infamy of a prostitute, was acknowledged and approved by the laws : from the age of Augustus to the tenth century, the use of this secondary marriage prevailed both in the West and East ; and the humble virtues of a concubine were often preferred to the pomp and insolence of a noble matron. In this connection, the two Antonines, the best of princes and of men, enjoyed the comforts of domestic love : the example was imitated by many citizens impatient of celibacy, but regardful of their families. If at any time they desired to legitimate their natural children, the conversion was instantly performed by the celebration of their nuptials with a partner whose fruitfulness and fidelity they had already tried.† By this epithet of *natural*, the offspring of the concubine were distinguished from the spurious brood of adultery, prostitution, and incest, to whom Justinian reluctantly grants the necessary aliments of life ; and these natural children alone were capable of succeeding to a sixth part of the inheritance of their reputed father. According to the rigor of law, bastards were entitled only to the name and condition of their mother, from whom they might derive the character of a slave, a stranger, or a citizen. The

* According to the earlier law (Gaii Instit. p. 27), a man might marry his niece on the brother's, not on the sister's side. The emperor Claudius set the example of the former. In the Institutes, this distinction was abolished, and both declared illegal.—M.

† The edict of Constantine first conferred this right ; for Augustus had prohibited the taking as a concubine a woman who might be taken as a wife ; and if marriage took place afterwards, this marriage made no change in the rights of the children born before it ; recourse was then had to adoption, properly called arrogation.—G.

outcasts of every family were adopted without reproach as the children of the state.[155] *

The relation of guardian and ward, or, in Roman words, of *tutor* and *pupil*, which covers so many titles of the Institutes and Pandects,[136] is of a very simple and uniform nature. The person and property of an orphan must always be trusted to the custody of some discreet friend. If the deceased father had not signified his choice, the *agnats*, or paternal kindred of the nearest degree, were compelled to act as the natural guardians : the Athenians were apprehensive of exposing the infant to the power of those most interested in his death ; but an axiom of Roman jurisprudence has pronounced that the charge of tutelage should constantly attend the emolument of succession. If the choice of the father, and the line of consanguinity, afforded no efficient guardian, the failure was supplied by the nomination of the prætor of the city, or the president of the province. But the person whom they named to this *public* office might be legally excused by insanity or blindness, by ignorance or inability, by previous enmity or adverse interest, by the number of children or guardianships with which he was already burdened, and by the immunities which were granted to the useful labors of magistrates, lawyers, physicians, and professors. Till the infant could speak, and think, he was represented by the tutor, whose authority was finally determined by the age of puberty. Without his consent, no act of the pupil could bind himself to his own prejudice, though it might oblige others for his personal benefit. It is needless to observe, that the tutor often gave security, and always rendered an account, and that the want of diligence or integrity exposed him to a civil and almost criminal action for the violation of his sacred trust. The

---

* See, however, the two fragments of laws in the newly discovered extracts from the Theodosian Code, published by M. A. Peyron, at Turin. By the first law of Constantine, the legitimate offspring could alone inherit ; where there were no near legitimate relatives, the inheritance went to the fiscus. The son of a certain Licinianus, who had inherited his father's property under the supposition that he was legitimate, and had been promoted to a place of dignity, was to be degraded, his property confiscated, himself punished with stripes and imprisonment. By the second, all persons, even of the highest rank, senators, perfectissimi, decemvirs, were to be declared infamous, and out of the protection of the Roman law, if born ex ancillâ, vel ancillæ filiâ, vel libertâ, vel libertæ filiâ, sive Romanâ factâ, seu Latinâ, vel scœnicæ filiâ, vel ex tabernariâ, vel ex tabernariæ filiâ, vel humili vel abjectâ, vel lenonis, aut arenarii filiâ, vel quæ mercimoniis publicis præfuit. Whatever a fond father had conferred on such children was revoked, and either restored to the legitimate children, or confiscated to the state; the mothers, who were guilty of thus *poisoning* the minds of the fathers, were to be put to the torture (tormentis subjici jubemus). The unfortunate son of Licinianus, it appears from this second law, having fled, had been taken, and was ordered to be kept in chains to work in the Gynæceum at Carthage. Cod. Theodos. ab. A. Peyron, 87-90.—M.

age of puberty had been rashly fixed by the civilians at fourteen ; *
but as the faculties of the mind ripen more slowly than those of
the body, a *curator* was interposed to guard the fortunes of a Roman
youth from his own inexperience and headstrong passions. Such
a trustee had been first instituted by the prætor, to save a family
from the blind havoc of a prodigal or madman ; and the minor
was compelled, by the laws, to solicit the same protection, to give
validity to his acts till he accomplished the full period of twenty-
five years. Women were condemned to the perpetual tutelage of
parents, husbands, or guardians : a sex created to please and obey
was never supposed to have attained the age of reason and
experience. Such, at least, was the stern and haughty spirit of
the ancient law, which had been insensibly mollified before the
time of Justinian.

II. The original right of property can only be justified by the
accident or merit of prior occupancy ; and on this foundation it is
wisely established by the philosophy of the civilians.[137] The
savage who hollows a tree, inserts a sharp stone into a wooden
handle, or applies a string to an elastic branch, becomes in a state
of nature the just proprietor of the canoe, the bow, or the hatchet.
The materials were common to all ; the new form, the produce of
his time and simple industry, belongs solely to himself. His
hungry brethren cannot, without a sense of their own injustice,
extort from the hunter the game of the forest overtaken or slain
by his personal strength and dexterity. If his provident care
preserves and multiplies the tame animals, whose nature is tractable
to the arts of education, he acquires a perpetual title to the use
and service of their numerous progeny, which derives its existence
from him alone. If he encloses and cultivates a field for their
sustenance and his own, a barren waste is converted into a fertile
soil ; the seed, the manure, the labor, create a new value, and the
rewards of harvest are painfully earned by the fatigues of the
revolving year. In the successive states of society, the hunter,
the shepherd, the husbandman, may defend their possessions by
two reasons which forcibly appeal to the feelings of the human
mind: that whatever they enjoy is the fruit of their own industry ;
and that every man who envies their felicity, may purchase similar
acquisitions by the exercise of similar diligence. Such, in truth,
may be the freedom and plenty of a small colony cast on a fruitful

---

* Gibbon accuses the civilians of having "rashly fixed the age of puberty at
twelve or fourteen years." It was not so ; before Justinian, no law existed on this
subject. Ulpian relates the discussions which took place on this point among the
different sects of civilians. See the Institutes, l. i. tit. 22, and the fragments of
Ulpian. Nor was the curatorship obligatory for all minors.—W.

island. But the colony multiplies, while the space still continues the same ; the common rights, the equal inheritance of mankind, are engrossed by the bold and crafty ; each field and forest is circumscribed by the landmarks of a jealous master ; and it is the peculiar praise of the Roman jurisprudence, that it asserts the claim of the first occupant to the wild animals of the earth, the air, and the waters. In the progress from primitive equity to final injustice, the steps are silent, the shades are almost imperceptible, and the absolute monopoly is guarded by positive laws and artificial reason. The active, insatiate principle of self-love can alone supply the arts of life and the wages of industry ; and as soon as civil government and exclusive property have been introduced, they become necessary to the existence of the human race. Except in the singular institutions of Sparta, the wisest legislators have disapproved an agrarian law as a false and dangerous innovation. Among the Romans, the enormous disproportion of wealth surmounted the ideal restraints of a doubtful tradition, and an obsolete statute ; a tradition that the poorest follower of Romulus had been endowed with the perpetual inheritance of two *jugera ;* [138] a statute which confined the richest citizen to the measure of five hundred jugera, or three hundred and twelve acres of land. The original territory of Rome consisted only of some miles of wood and meadow along the banks of the Tyber ; and domestic exchange could add nothing to the national stock. But the goods of an alien or enemy were lawfully exposed to the first hostile occupier ; the city was enriched by the profitable trade of war ; and the blood of her sons was the only price that was paid for the Volscian sheep, the slaves of Britain, or the gems and gold of Asiatic kingdoms. In the language of ancient jurisprudence, which was corrupted and forgotten before the age of Justinian, these spoils were distinguished by the name of *manceps* or *mancipium,* taken with the hand ; and whenever they were sold or *emancipated,* the purchaser required some assurance that they had been the property of an enemy, and not of a fellow-citizen. [139] A citizen could only forfeit his rights by apparent dereliction, and such dereliction of a valuable interest could not easily be presumed. Yet, according to the Twelve Tables, a prescription of one year for movables, and of two years for immovables, abolished the claim of the ancient master, if the actual possessor had acquired them by a fair transaction from the person whom he believed to be the lawful proprietor. [140] Such conscientious injustice, without any mixture of fraud or force, could seldom injure the members of a small republic ; but the various periods of three, of ten, or of twenty years, determined by Justinian, are more

suitable to the latitude of a great empire.   It is only in the term
of prescription that the distinction of real and personal fortune
has been remarked by the civilians ; and their general idea of
property is that of simple, uniform, and absolute dominion.   The
subordinate exceptions of *use*, of *usufruct*,[141] of *servitude*,[142]
imposed for the benefit of a neighbor on lands and houses, are
abundantly explained by the professors of jurisprudence.   The
claims of property, as far as they are altered by the mixture, the
division, or the transformation of substances, are investigated
with metaphysical subtility by the same civilians.

The personal title of the first proprietor must be determined by
his death : but the possession, without any appearance of change,
is peaceably continued in his children, the associates of his toil,
and the partners of his wealth.   This natural inheritance has been
protected by the legislators of every climate and age, and the
father is encouraged to persevere in slow and distant improvements, by the tender hope, that a long posterity will enjoy the
fruits of his labor.   The *principle* of hereditary succession is universal ; but the *order* has been variously established by convenience or caprice, by the spirit of national institutions, or by some
partial example which was originally decided by fraud or violence.   The jurisprudence of the Romans appears to have deviated from the equality of nature much less than the Jewish,[143] the
Athenian,[144] or the English institutions.[145]   On the death of a
citizen, all his descendants, unless they were already freed from
his paternal power, were called to the inheritance of his possessions.   The insolent prerogative of primogeniture was unknown ;
the two sexes were placed on a just level ; all the sons and daughters were entitled to an equal portion of the patrimonial estate ;
and if any of the sons had been intercepted by a premature death,
his person was represented, and his share was divided, by his surviving children.   On the failure of the direct line, the right of
succession must diverge to the collateral branches.   The degrees
of kindred [146] are numbered by the civilians, ascending from the
last possessor to a common parent, and descending from the common parent to the next heir : my father stands in the first degree, my brother in the second, his children in the third, and the
remainder of the series may be conceived by fancy, or pictured in
a genealogical table.   In this computation, a distinction was
made, essential to the laws and even the constitution of Rome ;
the *agnats*, or persons connected by a line of males, were called, as
they stood in the nearest degree, to an equal partition ; but a
female was incapable of transmitting any legal claims ; and the
cognats of every rank, without excepting the dear relation of a

mother and a son, were disinherited by the Twelve Tables, as strangers and aliens. Among the Romans, *agens* or lineage was united by a common *name* and domestic rites ; the various *cognomens* or *surnames* of Scipio, or Marcellus, distinguishd from each other the subordinate branches or families of the Cornelian or Claudian race : the default of the *agnats*, of the same surname, was supplied by the larger denomination of *gentiles ;* and the vigilance of the laws maintained, in the same name, the perpetual descent of religion and property. A similar principle dictated the Voconian law,[147] which abolished the right of female inheritance. As long as virgins were given or sold in marriage, the adoption of the wife extinguished the hopes of the daughter. But the equal succession of independent matrons supported their pride and luxury, and might transport into a foreign house the riches of their fathers. While the maxims of Cato[148] were revered, they tended to perpetuate in each family a just and virtuous mediocrity : till female blandishments insensibly triumphed ; and every salutary restraint was lost in the dissolute greatness of the republic. The rigor of the decemvirs was tempered by the equity of the prætors. Their edicts restored and emancipated posthumous children to the rights of nature ; and upon the failure of the *agnats*, they preferred the blood of the *cognats* to the name of the gentiles, whose title and character were insensibly covered with oblivion. The reciprocal inheritance of mothers and sons was established in the Tertullian and Orphitian decrees by the humanity of the senate. A new and more impartial order was introduced by the Novels of Justinian, who affected to revive the jurisprudence of the Twelve Tables. The lines of masculine and female kindred were confounded : the descending, ascending, and collateral series was accurately defined ; and each degree, according to the proximity of blood and affection, succeeded to the vacant possessions of a Roman citizen.[149]

The order of succession is regulated by nature, or at least by the general and permanent reason of the lawgiver : but this order is frequently violated by the arbitrary and partial *wills*, which prolong the dominion of the testator beyond the grave.[150] In the simple state of society, this last use or abuse of the right of property is seldom indulged : it was introduced at Athens by the laws of Solon ; and the private testaments of the father of a family are authorized by the Twelve Tables. Before the time of the decemvirs,[151] a Roman citizen exposed his wishes and motives to the assembly of the thirty curiæ or parishes, and the general law of inheritance was suspended by an occasional act of the legislature. After the permission of the decemvirs, each private lawgiver pro-

mulgated his verbal or written testament in the presence of five
citizens, who represented the five classes of the Roman people; a
sixth witness attested their concurrence; a seventh weighed the
copper money, which was paid by an imaginary purchaser; and
the estate was emancipated by a fictitious sale and immediate re-
lease. This singular ceremony,[152] which excited the wonder of
the Greeks, was still practised in the age of Severus; but the prætors had already approved a more simple testament, for which
they required the seals and signatures of seven witnesses, free
from all legal exception, and purposely summoned for the execution of that important act. A domestic monarch, who reigned
over the lives and fortunes of his children, might distribute their
respective shares according to the degrees of their merit or his
affection; his arbitrary displeasure chastised an unworthy son by
the loss of his inheritance, and the mortifying preference of a
stranger. But the experience of unnatural parents recommended
some limitations of their testamentary powers. A son, or, by the
laws of Justinian, even a daughter, could no longer be disinherited by their silence: they were compelled to name the criminal,
and to specify the offence; and the justice of the emperor enumerated the sole causes that could justify such a violation of the first
principles of nature and society.[153] Unless a legitimate portion, a
fourth part, had been reserved for the children, they were entitled to institute an action or complaint of *inofficious* testament; to
suppose that their father's understanding was impaired by sickness or age; and respectfully to appeal from his rigorous sentence
to the deliberate wisdom of the magistrate. In the Roman jurisprudence, an essential distinction was admitted between the inheritance and the legacies. The heirs who succeeded to the entire
unity, or to any of the twelve fractions of the substance of the
testator, represented his civil and religious character, asserted his
rights, fulfilled his obligations, and discharged the gifts of friendship or liberality, which his last will had bequeathed under the
name of legacies. But as the imprudence or prodigality of a dying man might exhaust the inheritance, and leave only risk and
labor to his successor, he was empowered to retain the *Falcidian*
portion; to deduct, before the payment of the legacies, a clear
fourth for his own emolument. A reasonable time was allowed
to examine the proportion between the debts and the estate, to
decide whether he should accept or refuse the testament; and if
he used the benefit of an inventory, the demands of the creditors
could not exceed the valuation of the effects. The last will of a
citizen might be altered during his life, or rescinded after his
death: the persons whom he named might die before him, or re-

ject the inheritance, or be exposed to some legal disqualification. In the contemplation of these events, he was permitted to substitute second and third heirs, to replace each other according to the order of the testament ; and the incapacity of a madman or an infant to bequeath his property might be supplied by a similar substitution.[154] But the power of the testator expired with the acceptance of the testament : each Roman of mature age and discretion acquired the absolute dominion of his inheritance, and the simplicity of the civil law was never clouded by the long and intricate entails which confine the happiness and freedom of unborn generations.

Conquest and the formalities of law established the use of *codicils*. If a Roman was surprised by death in a remote province of the empire, he addressed a short epistle to his legitimate or testamentary heir ; who fulfilled with honor, or neglected with impunity, this last request, which the judges before the age of Augustus were not authorized to enforce. A codicil might be expressed in any mode, or in any language ; but the subscription of five witnesses must declare that it was the genuine composition of the author. His intention, however laudable, was sometimes illegal ; and the invention of *fidei-commissa*, or trusts, arose from the struggle between natural justice and positive jurisprudence. A stranger of Greece or Africa might be the friend or benefactor of a childless Roman, but none, except a fellow-citizen, could act as his heir. The Voconian law, which abolished female succession, restrained the legacy or inheritance of a woman to the sum of one hundred thousand sesterces,[155] and an only daughter was condemned almost as an alien in her father's house. The zeal of friendship, and parental affection, suggested a liberal artifice : a qualified citizen was named in the testament, with a prayer or injunction that he would restore the inheritance to the person for whom it was truly intended. Various was the conduct of the trustees in this painful situation : they had sworn to observe the laws of their country, but honor prompted them to violate their oath ; and if they preferred their interest under the mask of patriotism, they forfeited the esteem of every virtuous mind. The declaration of Augustus relieved their doubts, gave a legal sanction to confidential testaments and codicils, and gently unravelled the forms and restraints of the republican jurisprudence.[156] But as the new practice of trusts degenerated into some abuse, the trustee was enabled, by the Trebellian and Pegasian decrees, to reserve one fourth of the estate, or to transfer on the head of the real heir all the debts and actions of the succession. The interpretation of testaments was strict and literal ; but the language of *trusts* and codicils was delivered from the minute and technical accuracy of the civilians.[157]

III. The general duties of mankind are imposed by their public and private relations : but their specific *obligations* to each other can only be the effect of, 1, a promise, 2, a benefit, or 3, an injury : and when these obligations are ratified by law, the interested party may compel the performance by a judicial *action*. On this principle, the civilians of every country have erected a similar jurisprudence, the fair conclusion of universal reason and justice.[158]

1. The goddess of *faith* (of human and social faith) was worshipped, not only in her temples, but in the lives of the Romans ; and if that nation was deficient in the more amiable qualities of benevolence and generosity, they astonished the Greeks by their sincere and simple performance of the most burdensome engagements.[159] Yet among the same people, according to the rigid maxims of the patricians and decemvirs, a *naked pact*, a promise, or even an oath, did not create any civil obligation, unless it was confirmed by the legal form of a *stipulation*. Whatever might be the etymology of the Latin word, it conveyed the idea of a firm and irrevocable contract, which was always expressed in the mode of a question and answer. Do you promise to pay me one hundred pieces of gold ? was the solemn interrogation of Seius. I do promise, was the reply of Sempronius. The friends of Sempronius, who answered for his ability and inclination, might be separately used at the option of Seius ; and the benefit of partition, or order of reciprocal actions, insensibly deviated from the strict theory of stipulation. The most cautious and deliberate consent was justly required to sustain the validity of a gratuitous promise ; and the citizen who might have obtained a legal security, incurred the suspicion of fraud, and paid the forfeit of his neglect. But the ingenuity of the civilians successfully labored to convert simple engagements into the form of solemn stipulations. The prætors, as the guardians of social faith, admitted every rational evidence of a voluntary and deliberate act, which in their tribunal produced an equitable obligation, and for which they gave an action and a remedy.[160]

2. The obligations of the second class, as they were contracted by the delivery of a thing, are marked by the civilians with the epithet of real.[161] A grateful return is due to the author of a benefit ; and whoever is intrusted with the property of another, has bound himself to the sacred duty of restitution. In the case of a friendly loan, the merit of generosity is on the side of the lender only ; in a deposit, on the side of the receiver ; but in a *pledge*, and the rest of the selfish commerce of ordinary life, the

benefit is compensated by an equivalent, and the obligation to restore is variously modified by the nature of the transaction. The Latin language very happily expresses the fundamental difference between the *commodatum* and the *mutuum*, which our poverty is reduced to confound under the vague and common appellation of a loan. In the former, the borrower was obliged to restore the same individual thing with which he had been *accommodated* for the temporary supply of his wants ; in the latter, it was destined for his use and consumption, and he discharged this *mutual* engagement, by substituting the same specific value according to a just estimation of number, of weight, and of measure. In the contract of *sale*, the absolute dominion is transferred to the purchaser, and he repays the benefit with an adequate sum of gold or silver, the price and universal standard of all earthly possessions. The obligation of another contract, that of *location*, is of a more complicated kind. Lands or houses, labor or talents, may be hired for a definite term ; at the expiration of the time, the thing itself must be restored to the owner, with an additional reward for the beneficial occupation and employment. In these lucrative contracts, to which may be added those of partnership and commissions, the civilians sometimes imagine the delivery of the object, and sometimes presume the consent of the parties. The substantial pledge has been refined into the invisible rights of a mortgage or *hypotheca ;* and the agreement of sale, for a certain price, imputes, from that moment, the chances of gain or loss to the account of the purchaser. It may be fairly supposed, that every man will obey the dictates of his interest ; and if he accepts the benefit, he is obliged to sustain the expense, of the transaction. In this boundless subject, the historian will observe the *location* of land and money, the rent of the one and the interest of the other, as they materially affect the prosperity of agriculture and commerce. The landlord was often obliged to advance the stock and instruments of husbandry, and to content himself with a partition of the fruits. If the feeble tenant was oppressed by accident, contagion, or hostile violence, he claimed a proportionable relief from the equity of the laws : five years were the customary term, and no solid or costly improvements could be expected from a farmer, who, at each moment, might be ejected by the sale of the estate.[162] Usury,[163] the inveterate grievance of the city, had been discouraged by the Twelve Tables,[164] and abolished by the clamors of the people. It was revived by their wants and idleness, tolerated by the discretion of the prætors, and finally determined by the Code of Justinian. Persons of illustrious rank were confined to the moderate profit of *four per cent. ;* six was pronounced to be the ordinary and legal standard of interest ; eight was allowed for the convenience of manufacturers and merchants ; twelve was granted to nautical insurance, which the wiser ancients had not attempted to define ; but, except in this perilous adventure, the practice of exorbitant usury was severely restrained.[165] The most simple interest was condemned by the clergy of the East and West ;[166] but the sense of mutual benefit, which had triumphed over the laws of the republic, has resisted with equal firmness the decrees of the church, and even the prejudices of mankind.[167]

3. Nature and society impose the strict obligation of repairing an injury ; and the sufferer by private injustice acquires a personal right and a legitimate action. If the property of another be intrusted to our care, the requisite degree of care may rise and fall according to the benefit which we derive from such temporary possession ; we are seldom made responsible for inevitable accident, but the consequences of a voluntary fault must always be imputed to the author.[168] A Roman pursued and recovered his stolen goods by a civil action of theft ; they might pass through a succession of pure and innocent hands, but nothing less than a prescription of thirty years could extinguish his original claim. They were restored by the sentence of the prætor, and the injury was compensated by double, or threefold, or even quadruple damages, as the deed had been perpetrated by secret fraud or open rapine, as the robber had been surprised in the fact, or detected by a subsequent research. The Aquilian law [169] defended the living property of a citizen, his slaves and cattle, from the stroke of malice or negligence : the highest price was allowed that could be ascribed to the domestic animal at any moment of the year preceding his death ; a similar latitude of thirty days was granted on the destruction of any other valuable effects. A personal injury is blunted or sharpened by the manners of the times and the sensibility of the individual : the pain or the disgrace of a word or blow cannot easily be appreciated by a pecuniary equivalent. The rude jurisprudence of the decemvirs had confounded all hasty insults, which did not amount to the fracture of a limb, by condemning the aggressor to the common penalty of twenty-five *asses*. But the same denomination of money was reduced, in three centuries, from a pound to the weight of half an ounce : and the insolence of a wealthy Roman indulged himself in the cheap amusement of breaking and satisfying the law of the Twelve Tables. Veratius ran through the streets striking on the face the inoffensive passengers, and his attendant purse-bearer immediately silenced their clamors by the legal tender of twenty-five

pieces of copper, about the value of one shilling.[170] The equity of the prætors examined and estimated the distinct merits of each particular complaint. In the adjudication of civil damages, the magistrate assumed a right to consider the various circumstances of time and place, of age and dignity, which may aggravate the shame and sufferings of the injured person : but if he admitted the idea of a fine, a punishment, an example, he invaded the province, though, perhaps, he supplied the defects, of the criminal law.

The execution of the Alban dictator, who was dismembered by eight horses, is represented by Livy as the first and the last instance of Roman cruelty in the punishment of the most atrocious crimes.[171] But this act of justice, or revenge, was inflicted on a foreign enemy in the heat of victory, and at the command of a single man. The Twelve Tables afford a more decisive proof of the national spirit, since they were framed by the wisest of the senate, and accepted by the free voices of the people ; yet these laws, like the statutes of Draco,[172] are written in characters of blood.[173] They approve the inhuman and unequal principle of retaliation ; and the forfeit of an eye for an eye, a tooth for a tooth, a limb for a limb, is rigorously exacted, unless the offender can redeem his pardon by a fine of three hundred pounds of copper. The decemvirs distributed with much liberality the slighter chastisements of flagellation and servitude ; and nine crimes of a very different complexion are adjudged worthy of death. 1. Any act of *treason* against the state, or of correspondence with the public enemy. The mode of execution was painful and ignominious : the head of the degenerate Roman was shrouded in a veil, his hands were tied behind his back, and after he had been scourged by the lictor, he was suspended in the midst of the forum on a cross, or inauspicious tree. 2. Nocturnal meetings in the city ; whatever might be the pretence of pleasure, or religion, or the public good. 3. The murder of a citizen ; for which the common feelings of mankind demand the blood of the murderer. Poison is still more odious than the sword or dagger ; and we are surprised to discover, in two flagitious events, how early such subtle wickedness had infected the simplicity of the republic, and the chaste virtues of the Roman matrons.[174] The parricide, who violated the duties of nature and gratitude, was cast into the river or the sea, enclosed in a sack ; and a cock, a viper, a dog, and a monkey, were successively added, as the most suitable companions.[175] Italy produces no monkeys ; but the want could never be felt, till the middle of the sixth century first revealed the guilt of a parricide.[176] 4. The malice of an *incendiary*. After the previous

ceremony of whipping, he himself was delivered to the flames ;
and in this example alone our reason is tempted to applaud the
justice of retaliation. 5. *Judicial perjury.* The corrupt or malicious witness was thrown headlong from the Tarpeian rock, to expiate his falsehood, which was rendered still more fatal by the
severity of the penal laws, and the deficiency of written evidence.
6. The corruption of a judge, who accepted bribes to pronounce
an iniquitous sentence. 7. Libels and satires, whose rude strains
sometimes disturbed the peace of an illiterate city. The author
was beaten with clubs, a worthy chastisement, but it is not cer-.
tain that he was left to expire under the blows of the executioner.[177] 8. The nocturnal mischief of damaging or destroying a
neighbor's corn. The criminal was suspended as a grateful victim to Ceres. But the sylvan deities were less implacable, and
the extirpation of a more valuable tree was compensated by the
moderate fine of twenty-five pounds of copper. 9. Magical in-
cantations ; which had power, in the opinion of the Latian shepherds, to exhaust the strength of an enemy, to extinguish his life,
and to remove from their seats his deep-rooted plantations. The
cruelty of the Twelve Tables against insolvent debtors still remains
to be told ; and I shall dare to prefer the literal sense of antiquity
to the specious refinements of modern criticism.[178] * After the
judicial proof or confession of the debt, thirty days of grace were
allowed before a Roman was delivered into the power of his fellow-citizen. In this private prison, twelve ounces of rice were his
daily food ; he might be bound with a chain of fifteen pounds
weight ; and his misery was thrice exposed in the market-place,
to solicit the compassion of his friends and countrymen. At the
expiration of sixty days, the debt was discharged by the loss of
liberty or life ; the insolvent debtor was either put to death, or
sold in foreign slavery beyond the Tyber : but, if several creditors
were alike obstinate and unrelenting, they might legally dismem-
ber his body, and satiate their revenge by this horrid partition.
The advocates for this savage law have insisted, that it must
strongly operate in deterring idleness and fraud from contracting
debts which they were unable to discharge ; but experience would
dissipate this salutary terror, by proving that no creditor could be
found to exact this unprofitable penalty of life or limb. As the
manners of Rome were insensibly polished, the criminal code of
the decemvirs was abolished by the humanity of accusers, witnesses,
and judges ; and impunity became the consequence of immoderate
rigor. The Porcian and Valerian laws prohibited the magistrates

* Hugo (Histoire du Droit Romain, tom. i. p. 234) concurs with Gibbon. See Niebuhr, vol. ii. p. 313.—M.

from inflicting on a free citizen any capital, or even corporal, punishment ; and the obsolete statutes of blood were artfully, and perhaps truly, ascribed to the spirit, not of patrician, but of regal, tyranny.

In the absence of penal laws, and the insufficiency of civil actions, the peace and justice of the city were imperfectly maintained by the private jurisdiction of the citizens. The malefactors who replenish our jails are the outcasts of society, and the crimes for which they suffer may be commonly ascribed to ignorance, poverty, and brutal appetite. For the perpetration of similar enormities, a vile plebeian might claim and abuse the sacred character of a member of the republic : but, on the proof or suspicion of guilt, the slave, or the stranger, was nailed to a cross ; and this strict and summary justice might be exercised without restraint over the greatest part of the populace of Rome. Each family contained a domestic tribunal, which was not confined, like that of the prætor, to the cognizance of external actions : virtuous principles and habits were inculcated by the discipline of education ; and the Roman father was accountable to the state for the manners of his children, since he disposed, without appeal, of their life, their liberty, and their inheritance. In some pressing emergencies, the citizen was authorized to avenge his private or public wrongs. The consent of the Jewish, the Athenian, and the Roman laws approved the slaughter of the noctural thief ; though in open daylight a robber could not be slain without some previous evidence of danger and complaint. Whoever surprised an adulterer in his nuptial bed might freely exercise his revenge ; [179] the most bloody and wanton outrage was excused by the provocation ; [180] nor was it before the reign of Augustus that the husband was reduced to weigh the rank of the offender, or that the parent was condemned to sacrifice his daughter with her guilty seducer. After the expulsion of the kings, the ambitious Roman, who should dare to assume their title or imitate their tyranny, was devoted to the infernal gods : each of his fellowcitizens was armed with the sword of justice ; and the act of Brutus, however repugnant to gratitude or prudence, had been already sanctified by the judgment of his country. [181] The barbarous practice of wearing arms in the midst of peace, [182] and the bloody maxims of honor, were unknown to the Romans ; and, during the two purest ages, from the establishment of equal freedom to the end of the Punic wars, the city was never disturbed by sedition, and rarely polluted with atrocious crimes. The failure of penal laws was more sensibly felt, when every vice was inflamed by faction at home and dominion abroad. In the time of

Cicero, each private citizen enjoyed the privilege of anarchy ; each minister of the republic was exalted to the temptations of regal power, and their virtues are entitled to the warmest praise, as the spontaneous fruits of nature or philosophy.   After a triennial indulgence of lust, rapine, and cruelty, Verres, the tyrant of Sicily, could only be sued for the pecuniary restitution of three hundred thousand pounds sterling ; and such was the temper of the laws, the judges, and perhaps the accuser himself, [183] that, on refunding a thirteenth part of his plunder, Verres could retire to an easy and luxurious exile. [184]

The first imperfect attempt to restore the proportion of crimes and punishments was made by the dictator Sylla, who, in the midst of his sanguinary triumph, aspired to restrain the license, rather than to oppress the liberty, of the Romans.   He gloried in the arbitrary proscription of four thousand seven hundred citizens. [185]   But, in the character of a legislator, he respected the prejudices of the times ; and, instead of pronouncing a sentence of death against the robber or assassin, the general who betrayed an army, or the magistrate who ruined a province, Sylla was content to aggravate the pecuniary damages by the penalty of exile, or, in more constitutional language, by the interdiction of fire and water.   The Cornelian, and afterwards the Pompeian and Julian, laws introduced a new system of criminal jurisprudence ; [186] and the emperors, from Augustus to Justinian, disguised their increasing rigor under the names of the original authors.   But the invention and frequent use of *extraordinary pains* proceeded from the desire to extend and conceal the progress of despotism.   In the condemnation of illustrious Romans, the senate was always prepared to confound, at the will of their masters, the judicial and legislative powers.   It was the duty of the governors to maintain the peace of their province, by the arbitrary and rigid administration of justice ; the freedom of the city evaporated in the extent of empire, and the Spanish malefactor, who claimed the privilege of a Roman, was elevated by the command of Galba on a fairer and more lofty cross. [187]   Occasional rescripts issued from the throne to decide the questions which, by their novelty or importance, appeared to surpass the authority and discernment of a proconsul.   Transportation and beheading were reserved for honorable persons ; meaner criminals were either hanged, or burnt, or buried in the mines, or exposed to the wild beasts of the amphitheatre.   Armed robbers were pursued and extirpated as the enemies of society ; the driving away horses or cattle was made a capital offence ; [188] but simple theft was uniformly considered as a mere civil and private injury.   The degrees of guilt, and the modes of punishment, were too often determined by the discretion of the rulers, and the subject was left in ignorance of the legal danger which he might incur by every action of his life.

A sin, a vice, a crime, are the objects of theology, ethics, and jurisprudence. Whenever their judgments agree, they corroborate each other ; but, as often as they differ, a prudent legislator appreciates the guilt and punishment according to the measure of social injury. On this principle, the most daring attack on the life and property of a private citizen is judged less atrocious than the crime of treason or rebellion, which invades the *majesty* of the republic : the obsequious civilians unanimously pronounced, that the republic is contained in the person of its chief ; and the edge of the Julian law was sharpened by the incessant diligence of the emperors. The licentious commerce of the sexes may be tolerated as an impulse of nature, or forbidden as a source of disorder and corruption ; but the fame, the fortunes, the family of the husband, are seriously injured by the adultery of the wife. The wisdom of Augustus, after curbing the freedom of revenge, applied to this domestic offence the animadversion of the laws : and the guilty parties, after the payment of heavy forfeitures and fines, were condemned to long or perpetual exile in two separate islands.[189] Religion pronounces an equal censure against the infidelity of the husband ; but, as it is not accompanied by the same civil effects, the wife was never permitted to vindicate her wrongs ;[190] and the distinction of simple or double adultery, so familiar and so important in the canon law, is unknown to the jurisprudence of the Code and the Pandects. I touch with reluctance, and despatch with impatience, a more odious vice, of which modesty rejects the name, and nature abominates the idea. The primitive Romans were infected by the example of the Etruscans[191] and Greeks :[192] in the mad abuse of prosperity and power, every pleasure that is innocent was deemed insipid ; and the Scatinian law,[193] which had been extorted by an act of violence, was insensibly abolished by the lapse of time and the multitude of criminals. By this law, the rape, perhaps the seduction, of an ingenuous youth, was compensated, as a personal injury, by the poor damages of ten thousand sesterces, or fourscore pounds ; the ravisher might be slain by the resistance or revenge of chastity ; and I wish to believe, that at Rome, as in Athens, the voluntary and effeminate deserter of his sex was degraded from the honors and the rights of a citizen.[194] But the practice of vice was not discouraged by the severity of opinion : the indelible stain of manhood was confounded with the more venal transgressions of fornication and adultery, nor was the licentious lover exposed to

the same dishonor which he impressed on the male or female partner of his guilt. From Catullus to Juvenal,[195] the poets accuse
and celebrate the degeneracy of the times ; and the reformation
of manners was feebly attempted by the reason and authority of
the civilians till the most virtuous of the Cæsars proscribed the
sin against nature as a crime against society-[196]

A new spirit of legislation, respectable even in its error, arose
in the empire with the religion of Constantine.[197] The laws of
Moses were received as the divine original of justice, and the
Christian princes adapted their penal statutes to the degrees of
moral and religious turpitude. Adultery was first declared to be
a capital offence : the frailty of the sexes was assimilated to poison or assassination, to sorcery or parricide ; the same penalties
were inflicted on the passive and active guilt of pæderasty ; and
all criminals of free or servile condition were either drowned or
beheaded, or cast alive into the avenging flames. The adulterers
were spared by the common sympathy of mankind ; but the lovers
of their own sex were pursued by general and pious indignation :
the impure manners of Greece still prevailed in the cities of Asia,
and every vice was fomented by the celibacy of the monks and
clergy. Justinian relaxed the punishment at least of female infidelity : the guilty spouse was only condemned to solitude and
penance, and at the end of two years she might be recalled to the
arms of a forgiving husband. But the same emperor declared
himself the implacable enemy of unmanly lust, and the cruelty of
his persecution can scarcely be excused by the purity of his motives.[198] In defiance of every principle of justice, he stretched to
past as well as future offences the operations of his edicts, with
the previous allowance of a short respite for confession and pardon. A painful death was inflicted by the amputation of the sinful instrument, or the insertion of sharp reeds into the pores and
tubes of most exquisite sensibility ; and Justinian defended the
propriety of the execution, since the criminals would have lost
their hands, had they been convicted of sacrilege. In this state
of disgrace and agony, two bishops, Isaiah of Rhodes and Alexander of Diospolis, were dragged through the streets of Constantinople, while their brethren were admonished, by the voice of a
crier, to observe this awful lesson, and not to pollute the sanctity
of their character. Perhaps these prelates were innocent. A sentence of death and infamy was often founded on the slight and
suspicious evidence of a child or a servant : the guilt of the green
faction, of the rich, and of the enemies of Theodora, was presumed by the judges, and pæderasty became the crime of those to
whom no crime could be imputed. A French philosopher[199] has

dared to remark that whatever is secret must be doubtful, and that our natural horror of vice may be abused as an engine of tyranny. But the favorable persuasion of the same writer, that a legislator may confide in the taste and reason of mankind, is impeached by the unwelcome discovery of the antiquity and extent of the disease.[200]

The free citizens of Athens and Rome enjoyed, in all criminal cases, the invaluable privilege of being tried by their country.[201] 1. The administration of justice is the most ancient office of a prince : it was exercised by the Roman kings, and abused by Tarquin ; who alone, without law or council, pronounced his arbitrary judgments. The first consuls succeeded to this regal prerogative ; but the sacred right of appeal soon abolished the jurisdiction of the magistrates, and all public causes were decided by the supreme tribunal of the people. But a wild democracy, superior to the forms, too often disdains the essential principles, of justice : the pride of despotism was envenomed by plebeian envy, and the heroes of Athens might sometimes applaud the happiness of the Persian, whose fate depended on the caprice of a *single* tyrant. Some salutary restraints, imposed by the people on their own passions, were at once the cause and effect of the gravity and temperance of the Romans. The right of accusation was confined to the magistrates. A vote of the thirty-five tribes could inflict a fine ; but the cognizance of all capital crimes was reserved by a fundamental law to the assembly of the centuries, in which the weight of influence and property was sure to preponderate. Repeated proclamations and adjournments were interposed, to allow time for prejudice and resentment to subside : the whole proceeding might be annulled by a seasonable omen, or the opposition of a tribune ; and such popular trials were commonly less formidable to innocence than they were favorable to guilt. But this union of the judicial and legislative powers left it doubtful whether the accused party was pardoned or acquitted ; and, in the defence of an illustrious client, the orators of Rome and Athens address their arguments to the policy and benevolence, as well as to the justice, of their sovereign. 2. The task of convening the citizens for the trial of each offender became more difficult, as the citizens and the offenders continually multiplied ; and the ready expedient was adopted of delegating the jurisdiction of the people to the ordinary magistrates, or to extraordinary *inquisitors*. In the first ages these questions were rare and occasional. In the beginning of the seventh century of Rome they were made perpetual : four prætors were annually empowered to sit in judgment on the state offences of treason, extortion, peculation, and bribery ;

and Sylla added new prætors and new questions for those crimes which more directly injure the safety of individuals. By these *inquisitors* the trial was prepared and directed ; but they could only pronounce the sentence of the majority of *judges*, who with some truth, and more prejudice, have been compared to the English juries.[202] To discharge this important, though burdensome office, an annual list of ancient and respectable citizens was formed by the prætor. After many constitutional struggles, they were chosen in equal numbers from the senate, the equestrian order, and the people ; four hundred and fifty were appointed for single questions ; and the various rolls or *decuries* of judges must have contained the names of some thousand Romans, who represented the judicial authority of the state. In each particular cause, a sufficient number was drawn from the urn ; their integrity was guarded by an oath ; the mode of ballot secured their independence ; the suspicion of partiality was removed by the mutual challenges of the accuser and defendant ; and the judges of Milo, by the retrenchment of fifteen on each side, were reduced to fifty-one voices or tablets, of acquittal, of condemnation, or of favorable doubt.[203] 3. In his civil jurisdiction, the prætor of the city was truly a judge, and almost a legislator ; but, as soon as he had prescribed the action of law, he often referred to a delegate the determination of the fact. With the increase of legal proceedings, the tribunal of the centumvirs, in which he presided, acquired more weight and reputation. But whether he acted alone, or with the advice of his council, the most absolute powers might be trusted to a magistrate who was annually chosen by the votes of the people. The rules and precautions of freedom have required some explanation ; the order of despotism is simple and inanimate. Before the age of Justinian, or perhaps of Diocletian, the decuries of Roman judges had sunk to an empty title : the humble advice of the assessors might be accepted or despised ; and in each tribunal the civil and criminal jurisdiction was administered by a single magistrate, who was raised and disgraced by the will of the emperor.

A Roman accused of any capital crime might prevent the sentence of the law by voluntary exile, or death. Till his guilt had been legally proved, his innocence was presumed, and his person was free : till the votes of the last *century* had been counted and declared, he might peaceably secede to any of the allied cities of Italy, or Greece, or Asia.[204] His fame and fortunes were preserved, at least to his children, by this civil death ; and he might still be happy in every rational and sensual enjoyment, if a mind accustomed to the ambitious tumult of Rome could support the uniformity and silence of Rhodes or Athens. A bolder effort was required to escape from the tyranny of the Cæsars ; but this effort was rendered familiar by the maxims of the Stoics, the example of the bravest Romans, and the legal encouragements of suicide. The bodies of condemned criminals were exposed to public ignominy, and their children, a more serious evil, were reduced to poverty by the confiscation of their fortunes. But, if the victims of Tiberius and Nero anticipated the decree of the prince or senate, their courage and despatch were recompensed by the applause of the public, the decent honors of burial, and the validity of their testaments.[205] The exquisite avarice and cruelty of Domitian appear to have deprived the unfortunate of this last consolation, and it was still denied even by the clemency of the Antonines. A voluntary death, which, in the case of a capital offence, intervened between the accusation and the sentence, was admitted as a confession of guilt, and the spoils of the deceased were seized by the inhuman claims of the treasury.[206] Yet the civilians have always respected the natural right of a citizen to dispose of his life ; and the posthumous disgrace invented by Tarquin,[207] to check the despair of his subjects, was never revived or imitated by succeeding tyrants. The powers of this world have indeed lost their dominion over him who is resolved on death ; and his arm can only be restrained by the religious apprehension of a future state. Suicides are enumerated by Virgil among the unfortunate, rather than the guilty ;[208] and the poetical fables of the infernal shades could not seriously influence the faith or practice of mankind. But the precepts of the gospel, or the church, have at length imposed a pious servitude on the minds of Christians, and condemn them to expect, without a murmur, the last stroke of disease or the executioner.

The penal statutes form a very small proportion of the sixty-two books of the Code and Pandects ; and in all judicial proceeding, the life or death of a citizen is determined with less caution or delay than the most ordinary question of covenant or inheritance. This singular distinction, though something may be allowed for the urgent necessity of defending the peace of society, is derived from the nature of criminal and civil jurisprudence. Our duties to the state are simple and uniform : the law by which he is condemned is inscribed not only on brass or marble, but on the conscience of the offender, and his guilt is commonly proved by the testimony of a single fact. But our relations to each other are various and infinite ; our obligations are created, annulled, and modified, by injuries, benefits, and promises ; and the interpretation of voluntary contracts and testaments, which are often dictated by fraud or ignorance, affords a long and laborious exercise to the sagacity of the judge. The business of life is multiplied by the extent of commerce and dominion, and the residence of the parties in the distant provinces of an empire is productive of doubt, delay, and inevitable appeals from the local to the supreme magistrate. Justinian, the Greek emperor of Constantinople and the East, was the legal successor of the Latian shepherd who had planted a colony on the banks of the Tyber. In a period of thirteen hundred years, the laws had reluctantly followed the changes of government and manners ; and the laudable desire of conciliating ancient names with recent institutions destroyed the harmony and swelled the magnitude of the obscure and irregular system. The laws which excuse, on any occasions, the ignorance of their subjects, confess their own imperfections : the civil jurisprudence, as it was abridged by Justinian, still continued a mysterious science, and a profitable trade, and the innate perplexity of the study was involved in tenfold darkness by the private industry of the practitioners. The expense of the pursuit sometimes exceeded the value of the prize, and the fairest rights were abandoned by the poverty or prudence of the claimants. Such costly justice might tend to abate the spirit of litigation, but the unequal pressure serves only to increase the influence of the rich, and to aggravate the misery of the poor. By these dilatory and expensive proceedings, the wealthy pleader obtains a more certain advantage than he could hope from the accidental corruption of his judge. The experience of an abuse, from which our own age and country are not perfectly exempt, may sometimes provoke a generous indignation, and extort the hasty wish of exchanging our elaborate jurisprudence for the simple and summary decrees of a Turkish cadhi. Our calmer reflection will suggest, that such form and delays are necessary to guard the person and property of the citizen ; that the discretion of the judge is the first engine of tyranny ; and that the laws of a free people should foresee and determine every question that may probably arise in the exercise of power and the transactions of industry. But the government of Justinian united the evils of liberty and servitude ; and the Romans were oppressed at the same time by the multiplicity of their laws and the arbitrary will of their master.

CHAPTER XLV.

REIGN OF THE YOUNGER JUSTIN.—EMBASSY OF THE AVARS.—THEIR SETTLEMENT ON THE DANUBE.—CONQUEST OF ITALY BY THE LOMBARDS.—ADOPTION AND REIGN OF TIBERIUS.—OF MAURICE.—STATE OF ITALY UNDER THE LOMBARDS AND THE EXARCHS.—OF RAVENNA.—DISTRESS OF ROME.—CHARACTER AND PONTIFICATE OF GREGORY THE FIRST.

DURING the last years of Justinian, his infirm mind was devoted to heavenly contemplation, and he neglected the business of the lower world. His subjects were impatient of the long continuance of his life and reign : yet all who were capable of reflection apprehended the moment of his death, which might involve the capital in tumult, and the empire in civil war. Seven nephews [1] of the childless monarch, the sons or grandsons of his brother and sister, had been educated in the splendor of a princely fortune ; they had been shown in high commands to the provinces and armies ; their characters were known, their followers were zealous, and, as the jealousy of age postponed the declaration of a successor, they might expect with equal hopes the inheritance of their uncle. He expired in his palace, after a reign of thirty-eight years ; and the decisive opportunity was embraced by the friends of Justin, the son of Vigilantia. [2] At the hour of midnight, his domestics were awakened by an importunate crowd, who thundered at his door, and obtained admittance by revealing themselves to be the principal members of the senate. These welcome deputies announced the recent and momentous secret of the emperor's decease ; reported, or perhaps invented, his dying choice of the best beloved and most deserving of his nephews, and conjured Justin to prevent the disorders of the multitude, if they should perceive, with the return of light, that they were left without a master. After composing his countenance to surprise, sorrow, and decent modesty, Justin, by the advice of his wife Sophia, submitted to the authority of the senate. He was conducted with speed and silence to the palace ; the guards saluted their new sovereign ; and the martial and religious rites of his coronation were diligently accomplished. By the hands of the proper officers he was invested with the Imperial garments, the red buskins, white tunic, and purple robe. A fortunate soldier, whom he instantly promoted to the rank of tribune, encircled his neck with a military collar ; four robust youths exalted him on a shield; he stood firm and erect to receive the adoration of his subjects; and their choice was sanctified by the benediction of the patriarch, who imposed the diadem on the head of an orthodox prince. The hippodrome was already filled with innumerable multitudes; and no sooner did the emperor appear on his throne, than the voices of the blue and the green factions were confounded in the same loyal acclamations. In the speeches which Justin addressed to the senate and people, he promised to correct the abuses which had disgraced the age of his predecessor, displayed the maxims of a just and beneficent government, and declared that, on the approaching calends of January,[3] he would revive in his own person the name and liberty of a Roman consul. The immediate discharge of his uncle's debts exhibited a solid pledge of his faith and generosity: a train of porters, laden with bags of gold, advanced into the midst of the hippodrome, and the hopeless creditors of Justinian accepted this equitable payment as a voluntary gift. Before the end of three years, his example was imitated and surpassed by the empress Sophia, who delivered many indigent citizens from the weight of debt and usury: an act of benevolence the best entitled to gratitude, since it relieves the most intolerable distress; but in which the bounty of a prince is the most liable to be abused by the claims of prodigality and fraud.[4]

On the seventh day of his reign, Justin gave audience to the ambassadors of the Avars, and the scene was decorated to impress the barbarians with astonishment, veneration, and terror. From the palace gate, the spacious courts and long porticos were lined with the lofty crests and gilt bucklers of the guards, who presented their spears and axes with more confidence than they would have shown in a field of battle. The officers who exercised the power, or attended the person, of the prince, were attired in their richest habits, and arranged according to the military and civil order of the hierarchy. When the veil of the sanctuary was withdrawn, the ambassadors beheld the emperor of the East on his throne, beneath a canopy, or dome, which was supported by four columns, and crowned with a winged figure of Victory. In the first emotions of surprise, they submitted to the servile adoration of the Byzantine court; but as soon as they rose from the ground, Targetius, the chief of the embassy, expressed the freedom and pride of a barbarian. He extolled, by the tongue of his interpreter, the greatness of the chagan, by whose clemency the kingdoms of the South were permitted to exist, whose victorious subjects had traversed the frozen rivers of Scythia, and who now covered the banks of the Danube with innumerable tents. The late emperor had cultivated, with annual and costly gifts, the friendship of a grateful monarch, and the enemies of Rome had respected the allies of the Avars. The same prudence would instruct the nephew of Justinian to imitate the liberality of his uncle, and to purchase the blessings of peace from an invincible people, who delighted and excelled in the exercise of war. The reply of the emperor was delivered in the same strain of haughty defiance, and he derived his confidence from the God of the Christians, the ancient glory of Rome, and the recent triumphs of Justinian. "The empire," said he, "abounds with men and horses, and arms sufficient to defend our frontiers, and to chastise the barbarians. You offer aid, you threaten hostilities: we despise your enmity and your aid. The conquerors of the Avars solicit our alliance; shall we dread their fugitives and exiles?[5] The bounty of our uncle was granted to your misery, to your humble prayers. From us you shall receive a more important obligation, the knowledge of your own weakness. Retire from our presence: the lives of ambassadors are safe; and, if you return to implore our pardon, perhaps you will taste of our benevolence."[6] On the report of his ambassadors, the chagan was awed by the apparent firmness of a Roman emperor of whose character and resources he was ignorant. Instead of executing his threats against the Eastern empire, he marched into the poor and savage countries of Germany, which were subject to the dominion of the Franks. After two doubtful battles, he consented to retire, and the Austrasian king relieved the distress of his camp with an immediate supply of corn and cattle.[7] Such repeated disappointments had chilled the spirit of the Avars, and their power would have dissolved away in the Sarmatian desert, if the alliance of Alboin, king of the Lombards, had not given a new object to their arms, and a lasting settlement to their wearied fortunes.

While Alboin served under his father's standard, he encountered in battle, and transpierced with his lance, the rival prince of the Gepidæ. The Lombards, who applauded such early prowess, requested his father, with unanimous acclamations, that the heroic youth, who had shared the dangers of the field, might be admitted to the feast of victory. "You are not unmindful," replied the inflexible Audoin, "of the wise customs of our ancestors. Whatever may be his merit, a prince is incapable of sitting at table with his father till he has received his arms from a foreign and royal hand." Alboin bowed with reverence to the institutions of his country, selected forty companions, and boldly visited the court of Turisund, king of the Gepidæ, who embraced and entertained, according to the laws of hospitality, the murderer of his son. At the banquet, whilst Alboin occupied the seat of the youth whom he had slain, a tender remembrance arose in the mind of Turisund. "How dear is that place! how hateful is that person!" were the words that escaped, with a sigh, from the indignant father. His grief exasperated the national resentment of the Gepidæ; and Cunimund, his surviving son, was provoked by wine, or fraternal affection, to the desire of vengeance. "The Lombards," said the rude barbarian, "resemble, in figure and in smell, the mares of our Sarmatian plains." And this insult was a coarse allusion to the white bands which enveloped their legs. "Add another resemblance," replied an audacious Lombard; "you have felt how strongly they kick. Visit the plain of Asfield, and seek for the bones of thy brother: they are mingled with those of the vilest animals." The Gepidæ, a nation of warriors, started from their seats, and the fearless Alboin, with his forty companions, laid their hands on their swords. The tumult was appeased by the venerable interposition of Turisund. He saved his own honor, and the life of his guest; and, after the solemn rites of investiture, dismissed the stranger in the bloody arms of his son; the gift of a weeping parent. Alboin returned in triumph; and the Lombards, who celebrated his matchless intrepidity, were compelled to praise the virtues of an enemy.[8] In this extraordinary visit he had probably seen the daughter of Cunimund, who soon after ascended the throne of the Gepidæ. Her name was Rosamond, an appellation expressive of female beauty, and which our own history or romance has consecrated to amorous tales. The king of the Lombards (the father of Alboin no longer lived) was contracted to the granddaughter of Clovis; but the restraints of faith and policy soon yielded to the hope of possessing the fair Rosamond, and of insulting her family and nation. The arts of persuasion were tried without success; and the impatient lover, by force and stratagem, obtained the object of his desires. War was the consequence which he foresaw and solicited; but the Lombards could not long withstand the furious assault of the Gepidæ, who were sustained by a Roman army. And, as the offer of marriage was rejected with contempt, Alboin was compelled to relinquish his prey, and to partake of the disgrace which he had inflicted on the house of Cunimund.[9]

When a public quarrel is envenomed by private injuries, a blow that is not mortal or decisive can be productive only of a short truce, which allows the unsuccessful combatant to sharpen his arms for a new encounter. The strength of Alboin had been found unequal to the gratification of his love, ambition, and revenge: he condescended to implore the formidable aid of the chagan ; and the arguments that he employed are expressive of the art and policy of the barbarians. In the attack of the Gepidæ, he had been prompted by the just desire of extirpating a people whom their alliance with the Roman empire had rendered the common enemies of the nations, and the personal adversaries of the chagan. If the forces of the Avars and the Lombards should unite in this glorious quarrel, the victory was secure, and the reward inestimable : the Danube, the Hebrus, Italy, and Constantinople, would be exposed, without a barrier, to their invincible arms. But, if they hesitated or delayed to prevent the malice of the Romans, the same spirit which had insulted would pursue the Avars to the extremity of the earth. These specious reasons were heard by the chagan with coldness and disdain : he detained the Lombard ambassadors in his camp, protracted the negotiation, and by turns alleged his want of inclination, or his want of ability, to undertake this important enterprise. At length he signified the ultimate price of his alliance, that the Lombards should immediately present him with a tithe of their cattle ; that the spoils and captives should be equally divided ; but that the lands of the Gepidæ should become the sole patrimony of the Avars. Such hard conditions were eagerly accepted by the passions of Alboin ; and, as the Romans were dissatisfied with the ingratitude and perfidy of the Gepidæ, Justin abandoned that incorrigible people to their fate, and remained the tranquil spectator of this unequal conflict. The despair of Cunimund was active and dangerous. He was informed that the Avars had entered his confines ; but, on the strong assurance that, after the defeat of the Lombards, these foreign invaders would easily be repelled, he rushed forward to encounter the implacable enemy of his name and family. But the courage of the Gepidæ could secure them no more than an honorable death. The bravest of the nation fell in the field of battle ; the king of the Lombards contemplated with delight the head of Cunimund ; and his skull was fashioned into a cup to satiate the hatred of the conqueror, or, perhaps, to comply with the savage custom of his country.[10] After this victory, no further obstacle could impede the progress of the confederates, and they faithfully executed the terms of their agreement.[11] The fair countries of Wallachia, Moldavia, Transylvania, and the other parts of Hungary beyond the Danube, were occupied, without resistance, by a new colony of Scythians ; and the Dacian empire of the chagans subsisted with splendor above two hundred and thirty years. The nation of the Gepidæ was dissolved ; but, in the distribution of the captives, the slaves of the Avars were less fortunate than the companions of the Lombards, whose generosity adopted a valiant foe, and whose freedom was incompatible with cool and deliberate tyranny. One moiety of the spoil introduced into the camp of Alboin more wealth than a barbarian could readily compute. The fair Rosamond was persuaded, or compelled, to acknowledge the rights of her victorious lover ; and the daughter of Cunimund appeared to forgive those crimes which might be imputed to her own irresistible charms.

The destruction of a mighty kingdom established the fame of Alboin. In the days of Charlemagne, the Bavarians, the Saxons, and the other tribes of the Teutonic language, still repeated the songs which described the heroic virtues, the valor, liberality, and fortune of the king of the Lombards.[12] But his ambition was yet unsatisfied ; and the conqueror of the Gepidæ turned his eye from the Danube to the richer banks of the Po and the Tyber. Fifteen years had not elapsed, since his subjects, the confederates of Narses, had visited the pleasant climate of Italy : the mountains, the rivers, the highways, were familiar to their memory : the report of their success, perhaps the view of their spoils, had kindled in the rising generation the flame of emulation and enterprise. Their hopes were encouraged by the spirit and eloquence of Alboin ; and it is affirmed, that he spoke to their senses, by producing, at the royal feast, the fairest and most exquisite fruits that grew spontaneously in the garden of the world. No sooner had he erected his standard, than the native strength of the Lombards was multiplied by the adventurous youth of Germany and Scythia. The robust peasantry of Noricum and Pannonia had resumed the manners of barbarians ; and the names of the Gepidæ, Bulgarians, Sarmatians, and Bavarians, may be distinctly traced in the provinces of Italy.[13] Of the Saxons, the old allies of the Lombards, twenty thousand warriors, with their wives and children, accepted the invitation of Alboin. Their bravery contributed to his success ; but the accession or the absence of their numbers was not sensibly felt in the magnitude of his host. Every mode of religion was freely practised by its respective votaries. The king of the Lombards had been educated in the Arian heresy ; but the Catholics, in their public worship, were allowed to pray for his conversion ; while the more stubborn barbarians sacrificed a she-goat, or perhaps a captive, to the gods of their fathers.[14] The Lombards, and their confederates, were united by their common attachment to a chief, who excelled in all the virtues and vices of a savage hero ; and the vigilance of Alboin provided an ample magazine of offensive and defensive arms for the use of the expedition. The portable wealth of the Lombards attended the march : their lands they cheerfully relinquished to the Avars, on the solemn promise, which was made and accepted without a smile, that if they failed in the conquest of Italy, these voluntary exiles should be reinstated in their former possessions.

They might have failed, if Narses had been the antagonist of the Lombards ; and the veteran warriors, the associates of his Gothic victory, would have encountered with reluctance an enemy whom they dreaded and esteemed. But the weakness of the Byzantine court was subservient to the barbarian cause ; and it was for the ruin of Italy, that the emperor once listened to the complaints of his subjects. The virtues of Narses were stained with avarice ; and, in his provincial reign of fifteen years, he accumulated a treasure of gold and silver which surpassed the modesty of a private fortune. His government was oppressive or unpopular, and the general discontent was expressed with freedom by the deputies of Rome. Before the throne of Justin they boldly declared, that their Gothic servitude had been more tolerable than the despotism of a Greek eunuch ; and that, unless their tyrant were instantly removed, they would consult their own happiness in the choice of a master. The apprehension of a revolt was urged by the voice of envy and detraction, which had so recently triumphed over the merit of Belisarius. A new exarch, Longinus, was appointed to supersede the conqueror of Italy, and the base motives of his recall were revealed in the insulting mandate of the empress Sophia, " that he should leave to *men* the exercise of arms, and return to his proper station among the maidens of the palace, where a distaff should be again placed in the hand of the eunuch." " I will spin her such a thread as she shall not easily unravel !" is said to have been the reply which indignation and conscious virtue extorted from the hero. Instead of attending, a slave and a victim, at the gate of the Byzantine palace, he retired to Naples, from whence (if any credit is due to the belief of the times) Narses invited the Lombards to chastise the ingratitude of the prince and people.[15] But the passions of the people are furious and changeable, and the Romans soon recollected the merits, or dreaded the resentment, of their victorious general. By the mediation of the pope, who undertook a special pilgrimage to Naples, their repentance was accepted ; and Narses, assuming a milder aspect and a more dutiful language, consented to fix his residence in the Capitol. His death,[16] though in the extreme period of old age, was unseasonable and premature, since *his* genius alone could have repaired the last and fatal error of his life. The reality, or the suspicion, of a conspiracy disarmed and disunited the Italians. The soldiers resented the disgrace, and bewailed the loss, of their general. They were ignorant of their new exarch ;

and Longinus was himself ignorant of the state of the army and the province. In the preceding years Italy had been desolated by pestilence and famine, and a disaffected people ascribed the calamities of nature to the guilt or folly of their rulers.[17]

Whatever might be the grounds of his security, Alboin neither expected nor encountered a Roman army in the field. He ascended the Julian Alps, and looked down with contempt and desire on the fruitful plains to which his victory communicated the perpetual appellation of LOMBARDY. A faithful chieftain, and a select band, were stationed at Forum Julii, the modern Friuli, to guard the passes of the mountains. The Lombards respected the strength of Pavia, and listened to the prayers of the Trevisans : their slow and heavy multitudes proceeded to occupy the palace and city of Verona ; and Milan, now rising from her ashes, was invested by the powers of Alboin five months after his departure from Pannonia. Terror preceded his march : he found everywhere, or he left, a dreary solitude ; and the pusillanimous Italians presumed, without a trial, that the stranger was invincible. Escaping to lakes, or rocks, or morasses, the affrighted crowds concealed some fragments of the wealth, and delayed the moment of their servitude. Paulinus, the patriarch of Aquileia, removed his treasures, sacred and profane, to the Isle of Grado,[18] and his successors were adopted by the infant republic of Venice, which was continually enriched by the public calamities. Honoratus, who filled the chair of St. Ambrose, had creduously accepted the faithless offers of a capitulation ; and the archbishop, with the clergy and nobles of Milan, were driven by the perfidy of Alboin to seek a refuge in the less accessible ramparts of Genoa. Along the maritime coast, the courage of the inhabitants was supported by the facility of supply, the hopes of relief, and the power of escape ; but from the Trentine hills to the gates of Ravenna and Rome, the inland regions of Italy became, without a battle or a siege, the lasting patrimony of the Lombards. The submission of the people invited the barbarian to assume the character of a lawful sovereign, and the helpless exarch was confined to the office of announcing to the emperor Justin the rapid and irretrievable loss of his provinces and cities.[19] One city, which had been diligently fortified by the Goths, resisted the arms of a new invader ; and, while Italy was subdued by the flying detachments of the Lombards, the royal camp was fixed above three years before the western gate of Ticinum, or Pavia. The same courage which obtains the esteem of a civilized enemy provokes the fury of a savage, and the impatient besieger had bound himself by a tremendous oath, that age, and sex, and dignity, should be confounded in a general massacre. The aid of famine at length enabled him to execute his bloody vow ; but, as Alboin entered the gate, his horse stumbled, fell, and could not be raised from the ground. One of his attendants was prompted by compassion, or piety, to interpret this miraculous sign of the wrath of Heaven : the conqueror paused and relented ; he sheathed his sword, and peacefully reposing himself in the palace of Theodoric, proclaimed to the trembling multitude that they should live and obey. Delighted with the situation of a city which was endeared to his pride by the difficulty of the purchase, the prince of the Lombards disdained the ancient glories of Milan ; and Pavia, during some ages, was respected as the capital of the kingdom of Italy.²⁰

The reign of the founder was splendid and transient ; and, before he could regulate his new conquests, Alboin fell a sacrifice to domestic treason and female revenge. In a palace near Verona, which had not been erected for the barbarians, he feasted the companions of his arms ; intoxication was the reward of valor, and the king himself was tempted by appetite or vanity to exceed the ordinary measure of his intemperance. After draining many capacious bowls of Rhætian or Falernian wine, he called for the skull of Cunimund, the noblest and most precious ornament of his sideboard. The cup of victory was accepted with horrid applause by the circle of the Lombard chiefs. "Fill it again with wine," exclaimed the inhuman conqueror ; "fill it to the brim : carry this goblet to the queen, and request in my name that she would rejoice with her father." In an agony of grief and rage, Rosamond had strength to utter, "Let the will of my lord be obeyed !" and, touching it with her lips, pronounced a silent imprecation, that the insult should be washed away in the blood of Alboin. Some indulgence might be due to the resentment of a daughter, if she had not already violated the duties of a wife. Implacable in her enmity, or inconstant in her love, the queen of Italy had stooped from the throne to the arms of a subject, and Helmichis, the king's armor-bearer, was the secret minister of her pleasure and revenge. Against the proposal of the murder, he could no longer urge the scruples of fidelity or gratitude ; but Helmichis trembled when he revolved the danger as well as the guilt, when he recollected the matchless strength and intrepidity of a warrior whom he had so often attended in the field of battle. He pressed and obtained, that one of the bravest champions of the Lombards should be associated to the enterprise ; but no more than a promise of secrecy could be drawn from the gallant Peredeus, and the mode of seduction employed by Rosamond betrays her shameless insensibility both to honor and love. She supplied the place of one of her female attendants who was beloved by Peredeus, and contrived some excuse for darkness and silence, till she could inform her companion that he had enjoyed the queen of the Lombards, and that his own death, or the death of Alboin, must be the consequence of such treasonable adultery. In this alternative he chose rather to be the accomplice than the victim of Rosamond,[21] whose undaunted spirit was incapable of fear or remorse. She expected and soon found a favorable moment, when the king, oppressed with wine, had retired from the table to his afternoon slumbers. His faithless spouse was anxious for his health and repose : the gates of the palace were shut, the arms removed, the attendants dismissed, and Rosamond, after lulling him to rest by her tender caresses, unbolted the chamber door, and urged the reluctant conspirators to the instant execution of the deed. On the first alarm, the warrior started from his couch : his sword, which he attempted to draw, had been fastened to the scabbard by the hand of Rosamond ; and a small stool, his only weapon, could not long protect him from the spears of the assassins. The daughter of Cunimund smiled in his fall : his body was buried under the staircase of the palace ; and the grateful posterity of the Lombards revered the tomb and the memory of their victorious leader.

The ambitious Rosamond aspired to reign in the name of her lover ; the city and palace of Verona were awed by her power ; and a faithful band of her native Gepidæ was prepared to applaud the revenge, and to second the wishes, of their sovereign. But the Lombard chiefs, who fled in the first moments of consternation and disorder, had resumed their courage and collected their powers ; and the nation, instead of submitting to her reign, demanded, with unanimous cries, that justice should be executed on the guilty spouse and the murderers of their king. She sought a refuge among the enemies of her country ; and a criminal who deserved the abhorrence of mankind was protected by the selfish policy of the exarch. With her daughter, the heiress of the Lombard throne, her two lovers, her trusty Gepidæ, and the spoils of the palace of Verona, Rosamond descended the Adige and the Po, and was transported by a Greek vessel to the safe harbor of Ravenna. Longinus beheld with delight the charms and the treasures of the widow of Alboin : her situation and her past conduct might justify the most licentious proposals ; and she readily listened to the passion of a minister, who, even in the decline of the empire, was respected as the equal of kings. The death of a jealous lover was an easy and grateful sacrifice ; and, as Helmichis issued from the bath, he received the deadly potion from the hand of his mistress. The taste of the liquor, its speedy operation, and his experience of the character of Rosamond, convinced him that he was poisoned : he pointed his dagger to her breast, compelled her to drain the remainder of the cup, and expired in a few minutes, with the consolation that she could not survive to enjoy the fruits of her wickedness. The daughter of Alboin and Rosamond, with the richest spoils of the Lombards, was embarked for Constantinople : the surprising strength of Peredeus amused and terrified the Imperial court : * his blindness and revenge exhibited an imperfect copy of the adventures of Samson. By the free suffrage of the nation, in the assembly of Pavia, Clepho, one of their noblest chiefs, was elected as the successor of Alboin. Before the end of eighteen months, the throne was polluted by a second murder : Clepho was stabbed by the hand of a domestic ; the regal office was suspended above ten years during the minority of his son Autharis ; and Italy was divided and oppressed by a ducal aristocracy of thirty tyrants.[22]

When the nephew of Justinian ascended the throne, he proclaimed a new æra of happiness and glory. The annals of the second Justin[23] are marked with disgrace abroad and misery at home. In the West, the Roman empire was afflicted by the loss of Italy, the desolation of Africa, and the conquests of the Persians. Injustice prevailed both in the capital and the provinces : the rich trembled for their property, the poor for their safety, the ordinary magistrates were ignorant or venal, the occasional remedies appear to have been arbitrary and violent, and the complaints of the people could no longer be silenced by the splendid names of a legislator and a conqueror. The opinion which imputes to the prince all the calamities of his times may be countenanced by the historian as a serious truth or a salutary prejudice. Yet a candid suspicion will arise, that the sentiments of Justin were pure and benevolent, and that he might have filled his station without reproach, if the faculties of his mind had not been impaired by disease, which deprived the emperor of the use of his feet, and confined him to the palace, a stranger to the complaints of the people and the vices of the government. The tardy knowledge of his own impotence determined him to lay down the weight of the diadem ; and, in the choice of a worthy substitute, he showed some symptoms of a discerning and even magnanimous spirit. The only son of Justin and Sophia died in his infancy ; their daughter Arabia was the wife of Baduarius,[24] superintendent of the palace,

---

* He killed a lion. His eyes were put out by the timid Justin. Peredeus requesting an interview, Justin substituted two patricians, whom the blinded barbarian stabbed to the heart with two concealed daggers. See Le Beau, vol. x. p. 99.— M.

and afterwards commander of the Italian armies, who vainly aspired to confirm the rights of marriage by those of adoption. While the empire appeared an object of desire, Justin was accustomed to behold with jealousy and hatred his brothers and cousins, the rivals of his hopes; nor could he depend on the gratitude of those who would accept the purple as a restitution, rather than a gift. Of these competitors, one had been removed by exile, and afterwards by death; and the emperor himself had inflicted such cruel insults on another, that he must either dread his resentment or despise his patience. This domestic animosity was refined into a generous resolution of seeking a successor, not in his family, but in the republic; and the artful Sophia recommended Tiberius,[25] his faithful captain of the guards, whose virtues and fortune the emperor might cherish as the fruit of his judicious choice. The ceremony of his elevation to the rank of Cæsar, or Augustus, was performed in the portico of the palace, in the presence of the patriarch and the senate. Justin collected the remaining strength of his mind and body; but the popular belief that his speech was inspired by the Deity betrays a very humble opinion both of the man and of the times.[26] "You behold," said the emperor, "the ensigns of supreme power. You are about to receive them, not from my hand, but from the hand of God. Honor them, and from them you will derive honor. Respect the empress your mother: you are now her son; before, you were her servant. Delight not in blood; abstain from revenge; avoid those actions by which I have incurred the public hatred; and consult the experience, rather than the example, of your predecessor. As a man, I have sinned; as a sinner, even in this life, I have been severely punished: but these servants (and he pointed to his ministers), who have abused my confidence, and inflamed my passions, will appear with me before the tribunal of Christ. I have been dazzled by the splendor of the diadem: be thou wise and modest; remember what you have been, remember what you are. You see around us your slaves, and your children: with the authority, assume the tenderness, of a parent. Love your people like yourself; cultivate the affections, maintain the discipline, of the army; protect the fortunes of the rich, relieve the necessities of the poor."[27] The assembly, in silence and in tears, applauded the counsels, and sympathized with the repentance, of their prince: the patriarch rehearsed the prayers of the church; Tiberius received the diadem on his knees; and Justin, who in his abdication appeared most worthy to reign, addressed the new monarch in the following words: "If you consent, I live; if you command, I die: may the God of heaven and earth infuse into your heart whatever I have neglected or forgotten." The four last years of the emperor Justin were passed in tranquil obscurity : his conscience was no longer tormented by the remembrance of those duties which he was incapable of discharging ; and his choice was justified by the filial reverence and gratitude of Tiberius.

Among the virtues of Tiberius, [28] his beauty (he was one of the tallest and most comely of the Romans) might introduce him to the favor of Sophia ; and the widow of Justin was persuaded, that she should preserve her station and influence under the reign of a second and more youthful husband. But, if the ambitious candidate had been tempted to flatter and dissemble, it was no longer in his power to fulfil her expectations, or his own promise. The factions of the hippodrome demanded, with some impatience, the name of their new empress : both the people and Sophia were astonished by the proclamation of Anastasia, the secret, though lawful, wife of the emperor Tiberius. Whatever could alleviate the disappointment of Sophia, Imperial honors, a stately palace, a numerous household, was liberally bestowed by the piety of her adopted son ; on solemn occasions he attended and consulted the widow of his benefactor ; but her ambition disdained the vain semblance of royalty, and the respectful appellation of mother served to exasperate, rather than appease, the rage of an injured woman. While she accepted, and repaid with a courtly smile, the fair expressions of regard and confidence, a secret alliance was concluded between the dowager empress and her ancient enemies ; and Justinian, the son of Germanus, was employed as the instrument of her revenge. The pride of the reigning house supported, with reluctance, the dominion of a stranger : the youth was deservedly popular ; his name, after the death of Justin, had been mentioned by a tumultuous faction ; and his own submissive offer of his head, with a treasure of sixty thousand pounds, might be interpreted as an evidence of guilt, or at least of fear. Justinian received a free pardon, and the command of the eastern army. The Persian monarch fled before his arms ; and the acclamations which accompanied his triumph declared him worthy of the purple. His artful patroness had chosen the month of the vintage, while the emperor, in a rural solitude, was permitted to enjoy the pleasures of a subject. On the first intelligence of her designs, he returned to Constantinople, and the conspiracy was suppressed by his presence and firmness. From the pomp and honors which she had abused, Sophia was reduced to a modest allowance : Tiberius dismissed her train, intercepted her correspondence, and committed to a faithful guard the custody of her person. But the services of Justinian were not considered by that excellent prince as an aggravation of his offences : after a mild reproof, his treason and ingratitude were forgiven ; and it was commonly believed, that the emperor entertained some thoughts of contracting a double alliance with the rival of his throne. The voice of an angel (such a fable was propagated) might reveal to the emperor, that he should always triumph over his domestic foes ; but Tiberius derived a firmer assurance from the innocence and generosity of his own mind.

With the odious name of Tiberius, he assumed the more popular appellation of Constantine, and imitated the purer virtues of the Antonines. After recording the vice or folly of so many Roman princes, it is pleasing to repose, for a moment, on a character conspicuous by the qualities of humanity, justice, temperance, and fortitude ; to contemplate a sovereign affable in his palace, pious in the church, impartial on the seat of judgment, and victorious, at least by his generals, in the Persian war. The most glorious trophy of his victory consisted in a multitude of captives, whom Tiberius entertained, redeemed, and dismissed to their native homes with the charitable spirit of a Christian hero. The merit or misfortunes of his own subjects had a dearer claim to his beneficence, and he measured his bounty not so much by their expectations as by his own dignity. This maxim, however dangerous in a trustee of the public wealth, was balanced by a principle of humanity and justice, which taught him to abhor, as of the basest alloy, the gold which was extracted from the tears of the people. For their relief, as often as they had suffered by natural or hostile calamities, he was impatient to remit the arrears of the past, or the demands of future taxes : he sternly rejected the servile offerings of his ministers, which were compensated by tenfold oppression ; and the wise and equitable laws of Tiberius excited the praise and regret of succeeding times. Constantinople believed that the emperor had discovered a treasure : but his genuine treasure consisted in the practise of liberal economy, and the contempt of all vain and superfluous expense. The Romans of the East would have been happy, if the best gift of Heaven, a patriot king, had been confirmed as a proper and permanent blessing. But in less than four years after the death of Justin, his worthy successor sunk into a mortal disease, which left him only sufficient time to restore the diadem, according to the tenure by which he held it, to the most deserving of his fellow-citizens. He selected Maurice from the crowd, a judgment more precious than the purple itself : the patriarch and senate were summoned to the bed of the dying prince : he bestowed his daughter and the empire ; and his last advice was solemnly delivered by the voice of the quæstor. Tiberius expressed his hope that the virtues of his son and successor would erect the noblest mausoleum to his memory. His memory was embalmed by the public affliction ; but the most sincere grief evaporates in the tumult of a new reign, and the eyes and acclamations of mankind were speedily directed to the rising sun.

The emperor Maurice derived his origin from ancient Rome ; [29] but his immediate parents were settled at Arabissus in Cappadocia, and their singular felicity preserved them alive to behold and partake the fortune of their *august* son. The youth of Maurice was spent in the profession of arms : Tiberius promoted him to the command of a new and favorite legion of twelve thousand confederates ; his valor and conduct were signalized in the Persian war ; and he returned to Constantinople to accept, as his just reward, the inheritance of the empire. Maurice ascended the throne at the mature age of forty-three years ; and he reigned above twenty years over the East and over himself ; [30] expelling from his mind the wild democracy of passions, and establishing (according to the quaint expression of Evagrius) a perfect aristocracy of reason and virtue. Some suspicion will degrade the testimony of a subject, though he protests that his secret praise should never reach the ear of his sovereign, [31] and some failings seem to place the character of Maurice below the purer merit of his predecessor. His cold and reserved demeanor might be imputed to arrogance ; his justice was not always exempt from cruelty, nor his clemency from weakness ; and his rigid economy too often exposed him to the reproach of avarice. But the rational wishes of an absolute monarch must tend to the happiness of his people : Maurice was endowed with sense and courage to promote that happiness, and his administration was directed by the principles and example of Tiberius. The pusillanimity of the Greeks had introduced so complete a separation between the offices of king and of general, that a private soldier, who had deserved and obtained the purple, seldom or never appeared at the head of his armies. Yet the emperor Maurice enjoyed the glory of restoring the Persian monarch to his throne ; his lieutenants waged a doubtful war against the Avars of the Danube ; and he cast an eye of pity, of ineffectual pity, on the abject and distressful state of his Italian provinces.

From Italy the emperors were incessantly tormented by tales of misery and demands of succor, which extorted the humiliating confession of their own weakness. The expiring dignity of Rome was only marked by the freedom and energy of her complaints :

"If you are incapable," she said, "of delivering us from the sword of the Lombards, save us at least from the calamity of famine." Tiberius forgave the reproach, and relieved the distress: a supply of corn was transported from Egypt to the Tyber; and the Roman people, invoking the name, not of Camillus, but of St. Peter, repulsed the barbarians from their walls. But the relief was accidental, the danger was perpetual and pressing; and the clergy and senate, collecting the remains of their ancient opulence, a sum of three thousand pounds of gold, despatched the patrician Pamphronius to lay their gifts and their complaints at the foot of the Byzantine throne. The attention of the court, and the forces of the East, were diverted by the Persian war: but the justice of Tiberius applied the subsidy to the defence of the city; and he dismissed the patrician with his best advice, either to bribe the Lombard chiefs or to purchase the aid of the kings of France. Notwithstanding this weak invention, Italy was still afflicted, Rome was again besieged, and the suburb of Classe, only three miles from Ravenna, was pillaged and occupied by the troops of a simple duke of Spoleto. Maurice gave audience to a second deputation of priests and senators: the duties and the menaces of religion were forcibly urged in the letters of the Roman pontiff; and his nuncio, the deacon Gregory, was alike qualified to solicit the powers either of heaven or of the earth. The emperor adopted, with stronger effect, the measures of his predecessor: some formidable chiefs were persuaded to embrace the friendship of the Romans; and one of them, a mild and faithful barbarian, lived and died in the service of the exarch: the passes of the Alps were delivered to the Franks; and the pope encouraged them to violate, without scruple, their oaths and engagements to the misbelievers. Childebert, the great-grandson of Clovis, was persuaded to invade Italy by the payment of fifty thousand pieces: but, as he had viewed with delight some Byzantine coin of the weight of one pound of gold, the king of Austrasia might stipulate, that the gift should be rendered more worthy of his acceptance, by a proper mixture of these respectable medals. The dukes of the Lombards had provoked by frequent inroads their powerful neighbors of Gaul. As soon as they were apprehensive of a just retaliation, they renounced their feeble and disorderly independence: the advantages of regal government, union, secrecy, and vigor, were unanimously confessed; and Autharis, the son of Clepho, had already attained the strength and reputation of a warrior. Under the standard of their new king, the conquerors of Italy withstood three successive invasions, one of which was led by Childebert himself, the last of the Merovingian race who descended from the Alps. The first expedition was defeated by the jealous animosity of the Franks and Alemanni. In the second they were vanquished in a bloody battle, with more loss and dishonor than they had sustained since the foundation of their monarchy. Impatient for revenge, they returned a third time with accumulated force, and Autharis yielded to the fury of the torrent. The troops and treasures of the Lombards were distributed in the walled towns between the Alps and the Apennine. A nation, less sensible of danger than of fatigue and delay, soon murmured against the folly of their twenty commanders ; and the hot vapors of an Italian sun infected with disease those tramontane bodies which had already suffered the vicissitudes of intemperance and famine. The powers that were inadequate to the conquest, were more than sufficient for the desolation, of the country ; nor could the trembling natives distinguish between their enemies and their deliverers. If the junction of the Merovingian and Imperial forces had been effected in the neighborhood of Milan, perhaps they might have subverted the throne of the Lombards ; but the Franks expected six days the signal of a flaming village, and the arms of the Greeks were idly employed in the reduction of Modena and Parma, which were torn from them after the retreat of their transalpine allies. The victorious Autharis asserted his claim to the dominion of Italy. At the foot of the Rhætian Alps, he subdued the resistance, and rifled the hidden treasures, of a sequestered island in the Lake of Comum. At the extreme point of the Calabria, he touched with his spear a column on the sea-shore of Rhegium,[52] proclaiming that ancient landmark to stand the immovable boundary of his kingdom.[33]

During a period of two hundred years, Italy was unequally divided between the kingdom of the Lombards and the exarchate of Ravenna. The offices and professions, which the jealousy of Constantine had separated, were united by the indulgence of Justinian ; and eighteen successive exarchs were invested, in the decline of the empire, with the full remains of civil, of military, and even of ecclesiastical, power. Their immediate jurisdiction, which was afterwards consecrated as the patrimony of St. Peter, extended over the modern Romagna, the marshes or valleys of Ferrara and Commachio,[34] five maritime cities from Rimini to Ancona, and a second inland Pentapolis, between the Adriatic coast and the hills of the Apennine. Three subordinate provinces of Rome, of Venice, and of Naples, which were divided by hostile lands from the palace of Ravenna, acknowledged, both in peace and war, the supremacy of the exarch. The duchy of Rome appears to have included the Tuscan, Sabine, and Latin conquests, of the first four hundred years of the city, and the limits may be distinctly traced along the coast, from Civita Vecchia to Terracina, and with the course of the Tyber from Ameria and Narni to the port of Ostia. The numerous islands from Grado to Chiozza composed the infant dominion of Venice: but the more accessible towns on the Continent were overthrown by the Lombards, who beheld with impotent fury a new capital rising from the waves. The power of the dukes of Naples was circumscribed by the bay and the adjacent isles, by the hostile territory of Capua, and by the Roman colony of Amalphi,[35] whose industrious citizens, by the invention of the mariner's compass, have unveiled the face of the globe. The three islands of Sardinia, Corsica, and Sicily, still adhered to the empire; and the acquisition of the farther Calabria removed the landmark of Autharis from the shore of Rhegium to the Isthmus of Consentia. In Sardinia, the savage mountaineers preserved the liberty and religion of their ancestors; but the husbandmen of Sicily were chained to their rich and cultivated soil. Rome was oppressed by the iron sceptre of the exarchs, and a Greek, perhaps a eunuch, insulted with impunity the ruins of the Capitol. But Naples soon acquired the privilege of electing her own dukes:[36] the independence of Amalphi was the fruit of commerce; and the voluntary attachment of Venice was finally ennobled by an equal alliance with the Eastern empire. On the map of Italy, the measure of the exarchate occupies a very inadequate space, but it included an ample proportion of wealth, industry, and population. The most faithful and valuable subjects escaped from the barbarian yoke; and the banners of Pavia and Verona, of Milan and Padua, were displayed in their respective quarters by the new inhabitants of Ravenna. The remainder of Italy was possessed by the Lombards; and from Pavia, the royal seat, their kingdom was extended to the east, the north, and the west, as far as the confines of the Avars, the Bavarians, and the Franks of Austrasia and Burgundy. In the language of modern geography, it is now represented by the Terra Firma of the Venetian republic, Tyrol, the Milanese, Piedmont, the coast of Genoa, Mantua, Parma, and Modena, the grand duchy of Tuscany, and a large portion of the ecclesiastical state from Perugia to the Adriatic. The dukes, and at length the princes, of Beneventum, survived the monarchy, and propagated the name of the Lombards. From Capua to Tarentum, they reigned near five hundred years over the greatest part of the present kingdom of Naples.[37]

In comparing the proportion of the victorious and the vanquished people, the change of language will afford the most probable inference. According to this standard, it will appear, that the Lombards of Italy, and the Visigoths of Spain, were less numerous than the Franks or Burgundians; and the conquerors of Gaul must yield, in their turn, to the multitude of Saxons and Angles who almost eradicated the idioms of Britain. The modern Italian has been insensibly formed by the mixture of nations: the awkwardness of the barbarians in the nice management of declensions and conjugations reduced them to the use of articles and auxiliary verbs; and many new ideas have been expressed by Teutonic appellations. Yet the principal stock of technical and familiar words is found to be of Latin derivation; [38] and, if we were sufficiently conversant with the obsolete, the rustic, and the municipal dialects of ancient Italy, we should trace the origin of many terms which might, perhaps, be rejected by the classic purity of Rome. A numerous army constitutes but a small nation, and the powers of the Lombards were soon diminished by the retreat of twenty thousand Saxons, who scorned a dependent situation, and returned, after many bold and perilous adventures, to their native country. [39] The camp of Alboin was of formidable extent, but the extent of a camp would be easily circumscribed within the limits of a city; and its martial inhabitants must be thinly scattered over the face of a large country. When Alboin descended from the Alps, he invested his nephew, the first duke of Friuli, with the command of the province and the people: but the prudent Gisulf would have declined the dangerous office, unless he had been permitted to choose, among the nobles of the Lombards, a sufficient number of families [40] to form a perpetual colony of soldiers and subjects. In the progress of conquest, the same option could not be granted to the dukes of Brescia or Bergamo, of Pavia or Turin, of Spoleto or Beneventum; but each of these, and each of their colleagues, settled in his appointed district with a band of followers, who resorted to his standard in war and his tribunal in peace. Their attachment was free and honorable: resigning the gifts and benefits which they had accepted, they might emigrate with their families into the jurisdiction of another duke; but their absence from the kingdom was punished with death, as a crime of military desertion. [41] The posterity of the first conquerors struck a deeper root into the soil, which, by every motive of interest and honor, they were bound to defend. A Lombard was born the soldier of his king and his duke; and the civil assemblies of the nation displayed the banners, and assumed the appellation, of a regular army. Of this army, the pay and the rewards were drawn from the conquered provinces; and the distribution, which was not effected till after the death of Alboin, is disgraced by the foul marks of injustice and rapine. Many of the most wealthy Italians were slain or banished ; the remainder were divided among the strangers, and a tributary obligation was imposed (under the name of hospitality) of paying to the Lombards a third part of the fruits of the earth. Within less than seventy years, this artificial system was abolished by a more simple and solid tenure.[42] Either the Roman landlord was expelled by his strong and insolent guest, or the annual payment, a third of the produce, was exchanged by a more equitable transaction for an adequate proportion of landed property. Under these foreign masters, the business of agriculture, in the cultivation of corn, vines, and olives, was exercised with degenerate skill and industry by the labor of the slaves and natives. But the occupations of a pastoral life were more pleasing to the idleness of the barbarians. In the rich meadows of Venetia, they restored and improved the breed of horses, for which that province had once been illustrious ;[43] and the Italians beheld with astonishment a foreign race of oxen or buffaloes.[44] The depopulation of Lombardy, and the increase of forests, afforded an ample range for the pleasures of the chase.[45] That marvellous art which teaches the birds of the air to acknowledge the voice, and execute the commands, of their master, had been unknown to the ingenuity of the Greeks and Romans.[46] Scandinavia and Scythia produce the boldest and most tractable falcons :[47] they were tamed and educated by the roving inhabitants, always on horseback and in the field. This favorite amusement of our ancestors was introduced by the barbarians into the Roman provinces : and the laws of Italy esteem the sword and the hawk as of equal dignity and importance in the hands of a noble Lombard.[48]

So rapid was the influence of climate and example, that the Lombards of the fourth generation surveyed with curiosity and affright the portraits of their savage forefathers.[49] Their heads were shaven behind, but the shaggy locks hung over their eyes and mouth, and a long beard represented the name and character of the nation. Their dress consisted of loose linen garments, after the fashion of the Anglo-Saxons, which were decorated, in their opinion, with broad stripes or variegated colors. The legs and feet were clothed in long hose, and open sandals ; and even in the security of peace a trusty sword was constantly girt to their side. Yet this strange apparel, and horrid aspect, often concealed a gentle and generous disposition ; and as soon as the rage of battle had subsided, the captives and subjects were sometimes surprised by the humanity of the victor. The vices of the

Lombards were the effect of passion, of ignorance, of intoxication ; their virtues are the more laudable, as they were not affected by the hypocrisy of social manners, nor imposed by the rigid constraint of laws and education. I should not be apprehensive of deviating from my subject, if it were in my power to delineate the private life of the conquerors of Italy ; and I shall relate with pleasure the adventurous gallantry of Autharis, which breathes the true spirit of chivalry and romance.[50] After the loss of his promised bride, a Merovingian princess, he sought in marriage the daughter of the king of Bavaria ; and Garribald accepted the alliance of the Italian monarch. Impatient of the slow progress of negotiation, the ardent lover escaped from his palace, and visited the court of Bavaria in the train of his own embassy. At the public audience, the unknown stranger advanced to the throne, and informed Garribald that the ambassador was indeed the minister of state, but that he alone was the friend of Autharis, who had trusted him with the delicate commission of making a faithful report of the charms of his spouse. Theudelinda was summoned to undergo this important examination ; and, after a pause of silent rapture, he hailed her as the queen of Italy, and humbly requested that, according to the custom of the nation, she would present a cup of wine to the first of her new subjects. By the command of her father she obeyed : Autharis received the cup in his turn, and, in restoring it to the princess, he secretly touched her hand, and drew his own finger over his face and lips. In the evening, Theudelinda imparted to her nurse the indiscreet familiarity of the stranger, and was comforted by the assurance, that such boldness could proceed only from the king her husband, who, by his beauty and courage, appeared worthy of her love. The ambassadors were dismissed : no sooner did they reach the confines of Italy, than Autharis, raising himself on his horse, darted his battle-axe against a tree with incomparable strength and dexterity. " Such," said he to the astonished Bavarians, " such are the strokes of the king of the Lombards." On the approach of a French army, Garribald and his daughter took refuge in the dominions of their ally ; and the marriage was consummated in the palace of Verona. At the end of one year, it was dissolved by the death of Autharis : but the virtues of Theudelinda[51] had endeared her to the nation, and she was permitted to bestow, with her hand, the sceptre of the Italian kingdom.

From this fact, as well as from similar events,[52] it is certain that the Lombards possessed freedom to elect their sovereign, and sense to decline the frequent use of that dangerous privilege. The public revenue arose from the produce of land and the profits of justice. When the independent dukes agreed that Autharis should ascend the throne of his father, they endowed the regal office with a fair moiety of their respective domains. The proudest nobles aspired to the honors of servitude near the person of their prince : he rewarded the fidelity of his vassals by the precarious gift of pensions and *benefices ;* and atoned for the injuries of war by the rich foundation of monasteries and churches. In peace a judge, a leader in war, he never usurped the powers of a sole and absolute legislator. The king of Italy convened the national assemblies in the palace, or more probably in the fields, of Pavia : his great council was composed of the persons most eminent by their birth and dignities ; but the validity, as well as the execution, of their decrees depended on the approbation of the *faithful* people, the *fortunate* army of the Lombards. About fourscore years after the conquest of Italy, their traditional customs were transcribed in Teutonic Latin,[53] and ratified by the consent of the prince and people : some new regulations were introduced. more suitable to their present condition ; the example of Rotharis was imitated by the wisest of his successors ; and the laws of the Lombards have been esteemed the least imperfect of the barbaric codes.[54] Secure by their courage in the possession of liberty, these rude and hasty legislators were incapable of balancing the powers of the constitution, or of discussing the nice theory of political government. Such crimes as threatened the life of the sovereign, or the safety of the state, were adjudged worthy of death ; but their attention was principally confined to the defence of the person and property of the subject. According to the strange jurisprudence of the times, the guilt of blood might be redeemed by a fine ; yet the high price of nine hundred pieces of gold declares a just sense of the value of a simple citizen. Less atrocious injuries, a wound, a fracture, a blow, an opprobrious word, were measured with scrupulous and almost ridiculous diligence ; and the prudence of the legislator encouraged the ignoble practice of bartering honor and revenge for a pecuniary compensation. The ignorance of the Lombards in the state of Paganism or Christianity gave implicit credit to the malice and mischief of witchcraft ; but the judges of the seventeenth century might have been instructed and confounded by the wisdom of Rotharis, who derides the absurd superstition and protects the wretched victims of popular or judicial cruelty.[55] The same spirit of a legislator, superior to his age and country, may be ascribed to Luitprand, who condemns, while he tolerates, the impious and inveterate abuse of duels,[56] observing, from his own experience, that the juster cause had often been oppressed by successful violence.

Whatever merit may be discovered in the laws of the Lombards, they are the genuine fruit of the reason of the barbarians, who never admitted the bishops of Italy to a seat in their legislative councils. But the succession of their kings is marked with virtue and ability ; the troubled series of their annals is adorned with fair intervals of peace, order, and domestic happiness ; and the Italians enjoyed a milder and more equitable government than any of the other kingdoms which had been founded on the ruins of the Western empire.[57]

Amidst the arms of the Lombards, and under the despotism of the Greeks, we again inquire into the fate of Rome,[58] which had reached, about the close of the sixth century, the lowest period of her depression. By the removal of the seat of empire, and the successive loss of the provinces, the sources of public and private opulence were exhausted : the lofty tree, under whose shade the nations of the earth had reposed, was deprived of its leaves and branches, and the sapless trunk was left to wither on the ground. The ministers of command, and the messengers of victory, no longer met on the Appian or Flaminian way ; and the hostile approach of the Lombards was often felt, and continually feared. The inhabitants of a potent and peaceful capital who visit without an anxious thought the garden of the adjacent country, will faintly picture in their fancy the distress of the Romans : they shut or opened their gates with a trembling hand, beheld from the walls the flames of their houses, and heard the lamentations of their brethren, who were coupled together like dogs, and dragged away into distant slavery beyond the sea and the mountains. Such incessant alarms must annihilate the pleasures and interrupt the labors of a rural life ; and the Campagna of Rome was speedily reduced to the state of a dreary wilderness, in which the land is barren, the waters are impure, and the air is infectious. Curiosity and ambition no longer attracted the nations to the capital of the world : but, if chance or necessity directed the steps of a wandering stranger, he contemplated with horror the vacancy and solitude of the city, and might be tempted to ask, Where is the senate, and where are the people ? In a season of excessive rains, the Tyber swelled above its banks, and rushed with irresistible violence into the valleys of the seven hills. A pestilential disease arose from the stagnation of the deluge, and so rapid was the contagion, that fourscore persons expired in an hour in the midst of a solemn procession, which implored the mercy of Heaven.[59] A society in which marriage is encouraged and industry prevails soon repairs the accidental losses of pestilence and war : but, as the far greater part of the Romans was condemned to hopeless indigence and celibacy, the depopulation was constant and visible, and the gloomy enthusiasts might expect the approaching failure of the human race.[60] Yet the number of citizens still exceeded the measure of subsistence : their precarious food was supplied from the harvests of Sicily or Egypt ; and the frequent repetition of famine betrays the inattention of the emperor to a distant province. The edifices of Rome were exposed to the same ruin and decay : the mouldering fabrics were easily overthrown by inundations, tempests, and earthquakes ; and the monks, who had occupied the most advantageous stations, exulted in their base triumph over the ruins of antiquity.[61] It is commonly believed, that Pope Gregory the First attacked the temples and mutilated the statues of the city ; that, by the command of the barbarian, the Palatine library was reduced to ashes, and that the history of Livy was the peculiar mark of his absurd and mischievous fanaticism. The writings of Gregory himself reveal his implacable aversion to the monuments of classic genius ; and he points his severest censure against the profane learning of a bishop, who taught the art of grammar, studied the Latin poets, and pronounced with the same voice the praises of Jupiter and those of Christ. But the evidence of his destructive rage is doubtful and recent : the Temple of Peace, or the theatre of Marcellus, have been demolished by the slow operation of ages, and a formal proscription would have multiplied the copies of Virgil and Livy in the countries which were not subject to the ecclesiastical dictator.[62]

Like Thebes, or Babylon, or Carthage, the name of Rome might have been erased from the earth, if the city had not been animated by a vital principle, which again restored her to honor and dominion. A vague tradition was embraced, that two Jewish teachers, a tent-maker and a fisherman, had formerly been executed in the circus of Nero, and at the end of five hundred years, their genuine or fictitious relics were adored as the Palladium of Christian Rome. The pilgrims of the East and West resorted to the holy threshold ; but the shrines of the apostles were guarded by miracles and invisible terrors ; and it was not without fear that the pious Catholic approached the object of his worship. It was fatal to touch, it was dangerous to behold, the bodies of the saints ; and those who, from the purest motives, presumed to disturb the repose of the sanctuary, were affrighted by visions, or punished with sudden death. The unreasonable request of an empress, who wished to deprive the Romans of their sacred treasure, the head of St. Paul, was rejected with the deepest abhorrence ; and the pope asserted, most probably with truth, that a linen which had been sanctified in the neighborhood of his body, or the filings of his chain, which it was sometimes easy and sometimes impossible to obtain, possessed an equal degree of miraculous virtue.[63] But the power as well as virtue of the apostles resided with living energy in the breast of their successors ; and the chair of St. Peter was filled under the reign of Maurice by the first and greatest of the name of Gregory.[64] His grandfather Felix had himself been pope, and as the bishops were already bound by the law of celibacy, his consecration must have been preceded by the death of his wife. The parents of Gregory, Sylvia, and Gordian, were the noblest of the senate, and the most pious of the church of Rome ; his female relations were numbered among the saints and virgins ; and his own figure, with those of his father and mother, were represented near three hundred years in a family portrait,[65] which he offered to the monastery of St. Andrew. The design and coloring of this picture afford an honorable testimony, that the art of painting was cultivated by the Italians of the sixth century ; but the most abject ideas must be entertained of their taste and learning, since the epistles of Gregory, his sermons, and his dialogues, are the work of a man who was second in erudition to none of his contemporaries : [66] his birth and abilities had raised him to the office of præfect of the city, and he enjoyed the merit of renouncing the pomps and vanities of this world. His ample patrimony was dedicated to the foundation of seven monasteries,[67] one in Rome,[68] and six in Sicily ; and it was the wish of Gregory that he might be unknown in this life, and glorious only in the next. Yet his devotion (and it might be sincere) pursued the path which would have been chosen by a crafty and ambitious statesman. The talents of Gregory, and the splendor which accompanied his retreat, rendered him dear and useful to the church ; and implicit obedience has been always inculcated as the first duty of a monk. As soon as he had received the character of deacon, Gregory was sent to reside at the Byzantine court, the nuncio or minister of the apostolic see ; and he boldly assumed, in the name of St. Peter, a tone of independent dignity, which would have been criminal and dangerous in the most illustrious layman of the empire. He returned to Rome with a just increase of reputation, and, after a short exercise of the monastic virtues, he was dragged from the cloister to the papal throne, by the unanimous voice of the clergy, the senate, and the people. He alone resisted, or seemed to resist, his own elevation ; and his humble petition, that Maurice would be pleased to reject the choice of the Romans, could only serve to exalt his character in the eyes of the emperor and the public. When the fatal mandate was proclaimed, Gregory solic-

ited the aid of some friendly merchants to convey him in a basket
beyond the gates of Rome, and modestly concealed himself some
days among the woods and mountains, till his retreat was discovered, as it is said, by a celestial light.

The pontificate of Gregory the *Great*, which lasted thirteen
years, six months, and ten days, is one of the most edifying periods of the history of the church. His virtues, and even his faults,
a singular mixture of simplicity and cunning, of pride and humility, of sense and superstition, were happily suited to his station
and to the temper of the times. In his rival, the patriarch of
Constantinople, he condemned the anti-Christian title of universal bishop, which the successor of St. Peter was too haughty to
concede, and too feeble to assume ; and the ecclesiastical jurisdiction of Gregory was confined to the triple character of Bishop of
Rome, Primate of Italy, and Apostle of the West. He frequently
ascended the pulpit, and kindled, by his rude, though pathetic,
eloquence, the congenial passions of his audience : the language
of the Jewish prophets was interpreted and applied ; and the
minds of a people, depressed by their present calamities, were
directed to the hopes and fears of the invisible world. His precepts and example defined the model of the Roman liturgy ; [69] the
distribution of the parishes, the calendar of festivals, the order of
processions, the service of the priests and deacons, the variety and
change of sacerdotal garments. Till the last days of his life, he
officiated in the canon of the mass, which continued above
three hours : the Gregorian chant [70] has preserved the vocal and
instrumental music of the theatre, and the rough voices of the
barbarians attempted to imitate the melody of the Roman
school. [71] Experience had shown him the efficacy of these solemn
and pompous rites, to soothe the distress, to confirm the faith, to
mitigate the fierceness, and to dispel the dark enthusiasm of the
vulgar, and he readily forgave their tendency to promote the reign
of priesthood and superstition. The bishops of Italy and the adjacent islands acknowledged the Roman pontiff as their special
metropolitan. Even the existence, the union, or the translation
of episcopal seats was decided by his absolute discretion : and his
successful inroads into the provinces of Greece, of Spain, and of
Gaul, might countenance the more lofty pretensions of succeeding
popes. He interposed to prevent the abuses of popular elections ;
his jealous care maintained the purity of faith and discipline ;
and the apostolic shepherd assiduously watched over the faith and
discipline of the subordinate pastors. Under his reign, the Arians
of Italy and Spain were reconciled to the Catholic church, and the
conquest of Britain reflects less glory on the name of Cæsar than

on that of Gregory the First. Instead of six legions, forty monks were embarked for that distant island, and the pontiff lamented the austere duties which forbade him to partake the perils of their spiritual warfare. In less than two years, he could announce to the archbishop of Alexandria, that they had baptized the king of Kent with ten thousand of his Anglo-Saxons, and that the Roman missionaries, like those of the primitive church, were armed only with spiritual and supernatural powers. The credulity or the prudence of Gregory was always disposed to confirm the truths of religion by the evidence of ghosts, miracles, and resurrections ;[72] and posterity has paid to *his* memory the same tribute which he freely granted to the virtue of his own or the preceding generation. The celestial honors have been liberally bestowed by the authority of the popes, but Gregory is the last of their own order whom they have presumed to inscribe in the calendar of saints.

Their temporal power insensibly arose from the calamities of the times : and the Roman bishops, who have deluged Europe and Asia with blood, were compelled to reign as the ministers of charity and peace. I. The church of Rome, as it has been formerly observed, was endowed with ample possessions in Italy, Sicily, and the more distant provinces ; and her agents, who were commonly sub-deacons, had acquired a civil, and even criminal, jurisdiction over their tenants and husbandmen. The successor of St. Peter administered his patrimony with the temper of a vigilant and moderate landlord ;[73] and the epistles of Gregory are filled with salutary instructions to abstain from doubtful or vexatious lawsuits ; to preserve the integrity of weights and measures ; to grant every reasonable delay ; and to reduce the capitation of the slaves of the glebe, who purchased the right of marriage by the payment of an arbitrary fine.[74] The rent or the produce of these estates was transported to the mouth of the Tyber, at the risk and expense of the pope : in the use of wealth he acted like a faithful steward of the church and the poor, and liberally applied to their wants the inexhaustible resources of abstinence and order. The voluminous account of his receipts and disbursements was kept above three hundred years in the Lateran, as the model of Christian economy. On the four great festivals, he divided their quarterly allowance to the clergy, to his domestics, to the monasteries, the churches, the places of burial, the alms-houses, and the hospitals of Rome, and the rest of the diocese. On the first day of every month, he distributed to the poor, according to the season, their stated portion of corn, wine, cheese, vegetables, oil, fish, fresh provisions, clothes, and money ; and his treasurers were continually summoned to satisfy, in his name, the extraordinary demands of indigence and merit. The instant distress of the sick and helpless, of strangers and pilgrims, was relieved by the bounty of each day, and of every hour; nor would the pontiff indulge himself in a frugal repast, till he had sent the dishes from his own table to some objects deserving of his compassion. The misery of the times had reduced the nobles and matrons of Rome to accept, without a blush, the benevolence of the church: three thousand virgins received their food and raiment from the hand of their benefactor; and many bishops of Italy escaped from the barbarians to the hospitable threshold of the Vatican. Gregory might justly be styled the Father of his Country; and such was the extreme sensibility of his conscience, that, for the death of a beggar who had perished in the streets, he interdicted himself during several days from the exercise of sacerdotal functions. II. The misfortunes of Rome involved the apostolical pastor in the business of peace and war; and it might be doubtful to himself, whether piety or ambition prompted him to supply the place of his absent sovereign. Gregory awakened the emperor from a long slumber; exposed the guilt or incapacity of the exarch and his inferior ministers; complained that the veterans were withdrawn from Rome for the defence of Spoleto; encouraged the Italians to guard their cities and altars; and condescended, in the crisis of danger, to name the tribunes, and to direct the operations, of the provincial troops. But the martial spirit of the pope was checked by the scruples of humanity and religion: the imposition of tribute, though it was employed in the Italian war, he freely condemned as odious and oppressive; whilst he protected, against the Imperial edicts, the pious cowardice of the soldiers who deserted a military for a monastic life. If we may credit his own declarations, it would have been easy for Gregory to exterminate the Lombards by their domestic factions, without leaving a king, a duke, or a count, to save that unfortunate nation from the vengeance of their foes. As a Christian bishop, he preferred the salutary offices of peace; his mediation appeased the tumult of arms: but he was too conscious of the arts of the Greeks, and the passions of the Lombards, to engage his sacred promise for the observance of the truce. Disappointed in the hope of a general and lasting treaty, he presumed to save his country without the consent of the emperor or the exarch. The sword of the enemy was suspended over Rome; it was averted by the mild eloquence and seasonable gifts of the pontiff, who commanded the respect of heretics and barbarians. The merits of Gregory were treated by the Byzantine court with reproach and insult ; but in the attachment of a grateful people, he found the purest reward of a citizen, and the best right of a sovereign.[75]

CHAPTER XLVI.

REVOLUTIONS OF PERSIA AFTER THE DEATH OF CHOSROES OR NUSHIRVAN.—HIS SON HORMOUZ, A TYRANT, IS DEPOSED.— USURPATION OF BAHARAM.—FLIGHT AND RESTORATION OF CHOSROES II.—HIS GRATITUDE TO THE ROMANS.—THE CHAGAN OF THE AVARS.—REVOLT OF THE ARMY AGAINST MAURICE.— HIS DEATH.—TYRANNY OF PHOCAS.—ELEVATION OF HERACLIUS. —THE PERSIAN WAR.—CHOSROES SUBDUES SYRIA, EGYPT, AND ASIA MINOR.—SIEGE OF CONSTANTINOPLE BY THE PERSIANS AND AVARS.—PERSIAN EXPEDITIONS.—VICTORIES AND TRIUMPH OF HERACLIUS.

THE conflict of Rome and Persia was prolonged from the death of Crassus to the reign of Heraclius. An experience of seven hundred years might convince the rival nations of the impossibility of maintaining their conquests beyond the fatal limits of the Tigris and Euphrates. Yet the emulation of Trajan and Julian was awakened by the trophies of Alexander, and the sovereigns of Persia indulged the ambitious hope of restoring the empire of Cyrus.[1] Such extraordinary efforts of power and courage will always command the attention of posterity ; but the events by which the fate of nations is not materially changed, leave a faint impression on the page of history, and the patience of the reader would be exhausted by the repetition of the same hostilities, undertaken without cause, prosecuted without glory, and terminated without effect. The arts of negotiation, unknown to the simple greatness of the senate and the Cæsars, were assiduously cultivated by the Byzantine princes ; and the memorials of their perpetual embassies[2] repeat, with the same uniform prolixity, the language of falsehood and declamation, the insolence of the barbarians, and the servile temper of the tributary Greeks. Lamenting the barren superfluity of materials, I have studied to compress the narrative of these uninteresting transactions : but the just Nushirvan is still applauded as the model of Oriental kings, and the ambition of his grandson Chosroes prepared the revolution of the East, which was speedily accomplished by the arms and the religion of the successors of Mahomet.

In the useless altercations, that precede and justify the quarrels of princes, the Greeks and the barbarians accused each other of violating the peace which had been concluded between the two empires about four years before the death of Justinian. The sovereign of Persia and India aspired to reduce under his obedience the province of Yemen or Arabia [3] Felix ; the distant land of myrrh and frankincense, which had escaped, rather than opposed, the conquerors of the East. After the defeat of Abrahah under the walls of Mecca, the discord of his sons and brothers gave an easy entrance to the Persians : they chased the strangers of Abyssinia beyond the Red Sea ; and a native prince of the ancient Homerites was restored to the throne as the vassal or viceroy of the great Nushirvan. [4] But the nephew of Justinian declared his resolution to avenge the injuries of his Christian ally the prince of Abyssinia, as they suggested a decent pretence to discontinue the annual *tribute*, which was poorly disguised by the name of pension. The churches of Persarmenia were oppressed by the intolerant spirit of the Magi ; * they secretly invoked the protector of the Christians, and, after the pious murder of their satraps, the rebels were avowed and supported as the brethren and subjects of the Roman emperor. The complaints of Nushirvan were disregarded by the Byzantine court ; Justin yielded to the importunities of the Turks, who offered an alliance against the common enemy ; and the Persian monarchy was threatened at the same instant by the united forces of Europe, of Æthiopia, and of Scythia. At the age of fourscore the sovereign of the East would perhaps have chosen the peaceful enjoyment of his glory and greatness ; but as soon as war became inevitable, he took the field with the alacrity of youth, whilst the aggressor trembled in

---

* Persarmenia was long maintained in peace by the tolerant administration of Mejej, prince of the Gnounians. On his death he was succeeded by a persecutor, a Persian, named Ten-Schahpour, who attempted to propagate Zoroastrianism by violence. Nushirvan, on an appeal to the throne by the Armenian clergy, replaced Ten-Schahpour, in 552, by Veschnas-Vahram. The new marzban, or governor, was instructed to repress the bigoted Magi in their persecutions of the Armenians, but the Persian converts to Christianity were still exposed to cruel sufferings. The most distinguished of them, Izdbouzid, was crucified at Dovin in the presence of a vast multitude. The fame of this martyr spread to the West. Menander, the historian, not only, as appears by a fragment published by Mai, related this event in his history, but, according to M. St. Martin, wrote a tragedy on the subject. This, however, is an unwarrantable inference from the phrase τραγῳδίαν θέμενος, which merely means that he related the tragic event in his history. An epigram on the same subject, preserved in the Anthology, Jacob's Anth. Palat. '. 27, belongs to the historian. Yet Armenia remained in peace under the government of Veschnas-Vahram, and his successor, Varazdat. The tyranny of his successor, Surena, led to the insurrection under Vartan, the Mamigonian, who revenged the death of his brother on the marzban Surena, surprised Dovin, and put to the sword the governor, the soldiers, and the Magians. From St. Martin, vol. x. p. 79-89.—M.

the palace of Constantinople. Nushirvan, or Chosroes, conducted in person the siege of Dara ; and although that important fortress had been left destitute of troops and magazines, the valor of the inhabitants resisted above five months the archers, the elephants, and the military engines of the Great King. In the mean while his general Adarman advanced from Babylon, traversed the desert, passed the Euphrates, insulted the suburbs of Antioch, reduced to ashes the city of Apamea, and laid the spoils of Syria at the feet of his master, whose perseverance in the midst of winter at length subverted the bulwark of the East. But these losses, which astonished the provinces and the court, produced a salutary effect in the repentance and abdication of the emperor Justin : a new spirit arose in the Byzantine councils ; and a truce of three years was obtained by the prudence of Tiberius. That seasonable interval was employed in the preparations of war ; and the voice of rumor proclaimed to the world, that from the distant countries of the Alps and the Rhine, from Scythia, Mæsia, Pannonia, Illyricum, and Isauria, the strength of the Imperial cavalry was re-enforced with one hundred and fifty thousand soldiers. Yet the king of Persia, without fear, or without faith, resolved to prevent the attack of the enemy ; again passed the Euphrates, and dismissing the ambassadors of Tiberius, arrogantly commanded them to await his arrival at Cæsarea, the metropolis of the Cappadocian provinces. The two armies encountered each other in the battle of Melitene : * the barbarians, who darkened the air with a cloud of arrows, prolonged their line, and extended their wings across the plain ; while the Romans, in deep and solid bodies, expected to prevail in closer action, by the weight of their swords and lances. A Scythian chief, who commanded their right wing, suddenly turned the flank of the enemy, attacked their rear-guard in the presence of Chosroes, penetrated to the midst of the camp, pillaged the royal tent, profaned the eternal fire, loaded a train of camels with the spoils of Asia, cut his way through the Persian host, and returned with songs of victory to his friends, who had consumed the day in single combats, or ineffectual skirmishes. The darkness of the night, and the separation of the Romans, afforded the Persian monarch an opportunity of revenge ; and one of their camps was swept away by a rapid and impetuous assault. But the review of his loss, and the consciousness of his danger, determined Chosroes to a speedy retreat : he burnt, in his passage, the vacant town of Melitene ; and, without consulting the safety of his troops, boldly swam the

---

* Malathiah.   It was in the Lesser Armenia.—M.

Euphrates on the back of an elephant. After this unsuccessful campaign, the want of magazines, and perhaps some inroad of the Turks, obliged him to disband or divide his forces ; the Romans were left masters of the field, and their general Justinian, advancing to the relief of the Persarmenian rebels, erected his standard on the banks of the Araxes. The great Pompey had formerly halted within three days' march of the Caspian : [5] that inland sea was explored, for the first time, by a hostile fleet, [6] and seventy thousand captives were transplanted from Hyrcania to the Isle of Cyprus. On the return of spring, Justinian descended into the fertile plains of Assyria ; the flames of war approached the residence of Nushirvan ; the indignant monarch sunk into the grave ; and his last edict restrained his successors from exposing their person in battle against the Romans.* Yet the memory of this transient affront was lost in the glories of a long reign ; and his formidable enemies, after indulging their dream of conquest, again solicited a short respite from the calamities of war. [7]

The throne of Chosroes Nushirvan was filled by Hormouz, or Hormisdas, the eldest or the most favored of his sons. With the kingdoms of Persia and India, he inherited the reputation and example of his father, the service, in every rank, of his wise and valiant officers, and a general system of administration, harmonized by time and political wisdom to promote the happiness of the prince and people. But the royal youth enjoyed a still more valuable blessing, the friendship of a sage who had presided over his education, and who always preferred the honor to the interest of his pupil, his interest to his inclination. In a dispute with the Greek and Indian philosophers, Buzurg [8] had once maintained that the most grievous misfortune of life is old age without the remembrance of virtue ; and our candor will presume that the same principle compelled him, during three years, to direct the councils of the Persian empire. His zeal was rewarded by the gratitude and docility of Hormouz, who acknowledged himself more indebted to his preceptor than to his parent : but when age and labor had impaired the strength, and perhaps the faculties, of this prudent counsellor, he retired from court, and abandoned the youthful monarch to his own passions and those of his favorites. By the fatal vicissitude of human affairs, the same scenes were renewed at Ctesiphon, which had been exhibited at Rome after the death of Marcus Antoninus. The ministers of flattery and corruption, who had been banished by the father, were re-

* This circumstance rests on the statements of Evagrius and Theophylact Simocatta. They are not of sufficient authority to establish a fact so improbable. St. Martin, vol. x. p. 140.—M.

called and cherished by the son ; the disgrace and exile of the friends of Nushirvan established their tyranny ; and virtue was driven by degrees from the mind of Hormouz, from his palace, and from the government of the state. The faithful agents, the eyes and ears of the king, informed him of the progress of disorder, that the provincial governors flew to their prey with the fierceness of lions and eagles, and that their rapine and injustice would teach the most loyal of his subjects to abhor the name and authority of their sovereign. The sincerity of this advice was punished with death ; the murmurs of the cities were despised, their tumults were quelled by military execution : the intermediate powers between the throne and the people were abolished ; and the childish vanity of Hormouz, who affected the daily use of the tiara, was fond of declaring, that he alone would be the judge as well as the master of his kingdom. In every word, and in every action, the son of Nushirvan degenerated from the virtues of his father. His avarice defrauded the troops ; his jealous caprice degraded the satraps ; the palace, the tribunals, the waters of the Tigris, were stained with the blood of the innocent, and the tyrant exulted in the sufferings and execution of thirteen thousand victims. As the excuse of his cruelty, he sometimes condescended to observe, that the fears of the Persians would be productive of hatred, and that their hatred must terminate in rebellion ; but he forgot that his own guilt and folly had inspired the sentiments which he deplored, and prepared the event which he so justly apprehended. Exasperated by long and hopeless oppression, the provinces of Babylon, Susa, and Carmania, erected the standard of revolt ; and the princes of Arabia, India, and Scythia, refused the customary tribute to the unworthy successor of Nushirvan. The arms of the Romans, in slow sieges and frequent inroads, afflicted the frontiers of Mesopotamia and Assyria : one of their generals professed himself the disciple of Scipio ; and the soldiers were animated by a miraculous image of Christ, whose mild aspect should never have been displayed in the front of battle.[9] At the same time, the eastern provinces of Persia were invaded by the great khan, who passed the Oxus at the head of three or four hundred thousand Turks. The imprudent Hormouz accepted their perfidious and formidable aid ; the cities of Khorassan or Bactriana were commanded to open their gates : the march of the barbarians towards the mountains of Hyrcania revealed the correspondence of the Turkish and Roman arms ; and their union must have subverted the throne of the house of Sassan.

Persia had been lost by a king ; it was saved by a hero. After his revolt, Varanes or Bahram is stigmatized by the son of Hor-

mouz as an ungrateful slave ; the proud and ambiguous reproach
of despotism, since he was truly descended from the ancient
princes of Rei,[10] one of the seven families whose splendid, as well
as substantial, prerogatives exalted them above the heads of the
Persian nobility.[11]   At the siege of Dara, the valor of Bahram was
signalized under the eyes of Nushirvan, and both the father
and son successively promoted him to the command of armies, the
government of Media, and the superintendence of the palace.
The popular prediction which marked him as the deliverer of Persia, might be inspired by his past victories and extraordinary
figure : the epithet *Giubin* * is expressive of the quality of *dry
wood :* he had the strength and stature of a giant ; and his savage
countenance was fancifully compared to that of a wild cat.
While the nation trembled, while Hormouz disguised his terror by
the name of suspicion, and his servants concealed their disloyalty
under the mask of fear, Bahram alone displayed his undaunted
courage and apparent fidelity : and as soon as he found that no
more than twelve thousand soldiers would follow him against the
enemy, he prudently declared, that to this fatal number Heaven
had reserved the honors of the triumph.†   The steep and narrow
descent of the Pule Rudbar,[12] or Hyrcanian rock, is the only pass
through which an army can penetrate into the territory of Rei and
the plains of Media.   From the commanding heights, a band of
resolute men might overwhelm with stones and darts the myriads
of the Turkish host : their emperor and his son were transpierced
with arrows ; and the fugitives were left, without counsel or provisions, to the revenge of an injured people.   The patriotism of
the Persian general was stimulated by his affection for the city of
his forefathers ; in the hour of victory, every peasant became a
soldier, and every soldier a hero ; and their ardor was kindled by
the gorgeous spectacle of beds, and thrones, and tables of massy
gold, the spoils of Asia, and the luxury of the hostile camp.   A
prince of a less malignant temper could not easily have forgiven
his benefactor ; and the secret hatred of Hormouz was envenomed
by a malicious report, that Bahram had privately retained the
most precious fruits of his Turkish victory.   But the approach of
a Roman army on the side of the Araxes compelled the implacable tyrant to smile and to applaud ; and the toils of Bahram were
rewarded with the permission of encountering a new enemy, by

---

* He is generally called Baharam Choubeen. Baharam *the stick-like*, probably
from his appearance.   Malcolm, vol. i. p. 120.—M.

† The Persian historians say that Hormouz entreated his general to increase his
numbers ; but Baharam replied that experience had taught him that it was the
quality, not the numbers of soldiers, which gave success. . . . No man in his army
was under forty years, and none above fifty.   Malcolm, vol. i. p. 121.—M.

their skill and discipline more formidable than a Scythian multitude. Elated by his recent success, he despatched a herald with a bold defiance to the camp of the Romans, requesting them to fix a day of battle, and to choose whether they would pass the river themselves, or allow a free passage to the arms of the great king. The lieutenant of the emperor Maurice preferred the safer alternative ; and this local circumstance, which would have enhanced the victory of the Persians, rendered their defeat more bloody and their escape more difficult. But the loss of his subjects, and the danger of his kingdom, were overbalanced in the mind of Hormouz by the disgrace of his personal enemy ; and no sooner had Bahram collected and reviewed his forces, than he received from a royal messenger the insulting gift of a distaff, a spinning-wheel, and a complete suit of female apparel. Obedient to the will of his sovereign, he showed himself to the soldiers in this unworthy disguise : they resented his ignominy and their own ; a shout of rebellion ran through the ranks ; and the general accepted their oath of fidelity and vows of revenge. A second messenger, who had been commanded to bring the rebel in chains, was trampled under the feet of an elephant, and manifestoes were diligently circulated, exhorting the Persians to assert their freedom against an odious and contemptible tyrant. The defection was rapid and universal ; his loyal slaves were sacrificed to the public fury ; the troops deserted to the standard of Bahram ; and the provinces again saluted the deliverer of his country.

As the passes were faithfully guarded, Hormouz could only compute the number of his enemies by the testimony of a guilty conscience, and the daily defection of those who, in the hour of his distress, avenged their wrongs, or forgot their obligations. He proudly displayed the ensigns of royalty ; but the city and palace of Modain had already escaped from the hand of the tyrant. Among the victims of his cruelty, Bindoes, a Sassanian prince, had been cast into a dungeon ; his fetters were broken by the zeal and courage of a brother ; and he stood before the king at the head of those trusty guards, who had been chosen as the ministers of his confinement, and perhaps of his death. Alarmed by the hasty intrusion and bold reproaches of the captive, Hormouz looked round, but in vain, for advice or assistance ; discovered that his strength consisted in the obedience of others ; and patiently yielded to the single arm of Bindoes, who dragged him from the throne to the same dungeon in which he himself had been so lately confined. At the first tumult, Chosroes, the eldest of the sons of Hormouz, escaped from the city ; he was persuaded to return by the pressing and friendly invitation of Bindoes, who

promised to seat him on his father's throne, and who expected to
reign under the name of an inexperienced youth. In the just
assurance, that his accomplices could neither forgive nor hope to
be forgiven, and that every Persian might be trusted as the judge
and enemy of the tyrant, he instituted a public trial, without a
precedent and without a copy in the annals of the East. The son
of Nushirvan, who had requested to plead in his own defence,
was introduced as a criminal into the full assembly of the nobles
and satraps.[13] He was heard with decent attention as long as he
expatiated on the advantages of order and obedience, the danger
of innovation, and the inevitable discord of those who had
encouraged each other to trample on their lawful and hereditary
sovereign. By a pathetic appeal to their humanity, he extorted
that pity which is seldom refused to the fallen fortunes of a king ;
and while they beheld the abject posture and squalid appearance
of the prisoner, his tears, his chains, and the marks of ignominious stripes, it was impossible to forget how recently they had
adored the divine splendor of his diadem and purple. But an
angry murmur arose in the assembly as soon as he presumed to
vindicate his conduct, and to applaud the victories of his reign.
He defined the duties of a king, and the Persian nobles listened
with a smile of contempt ; they were fired with indignation when
he dared to vilify the character of Chosroes ; and by the indiscreet offer of resigning the sceptre to the second of his sons, he
subscribed his own condemnation, and sacrificed the life of his innocent favorite. The mangled bodies of the boy and his mother
were exposed to the people ; the eyes of Hormouz were pierced
with a hot needle ; and the punishment of the father was succeeded by the coronation of his eldest son. Chosroes had ascended the throne without guilt, and his piety strove to alleviate
the misery of the abdicated monarch ; from the dungeon he
removed Hormouz to an apartment of the palace, supplied with
liberality the consolations of sensual enjoyment, and patiently
endured the furious sallies of his resentment and despair. He
might despise the resentment of a blind and unpopular tyrant,
but the tiara was trembling on his head, till he could subvert the
power, or acquire the friendship, of the great Bahram, who sternly
denied the justice of a revolution, in which himself and his soldiers, the true representatives of Persia, had never been consulted.
The offer of a general amnesty, and of the second rank in his
kingdom, was answered by an epistle from Bahram, friend of the
gods, conqueror of men, and enemy of tyrants, the satrap of
satraps, general of the Persian armies, and a prince adorned with
the title of eleven virtues.[14] He commands Chosroes, the son of

Hormouz, to shun the example and fate of his father, to confine the traitors who had been released from their chains, to deposit in some holy place the diadem which he had usurped, and to accept from his gracious benefactor the pardon of his faults and the government of a province. The rebel might not be proud, and the king most assuredly was not humble ; but the one was conscious of his strength, the other was sensible of his weakness ; and even the modest language of his reply still left room for treaty and reconciliation. Chosroes led into the field the slaves of the palace and the populace of the capital : they beheld with terror the banners of a veteran army ; they were encompassed and surprised by the evolutions of the general ; and the satraps who had deposed Hormouz received the punishment of their revolt, or expiated their first treason by a second and more criminal act of disloyalty. The life and liberty of Chosroes were saved, but he was reduced to the necessity of imploring aid or refuge in some foreign land ; and the implacable Bindoes, anxious to secure an unquestionable title, hastily returned to the palace, and ended, with a bowstring, the wretched existence of the son of Nushirvan.[15]

While Chosroes despatched the preparations of his retreat, he deliberated with his remaining friends,[16] whether he should lurk in the valleys of Mount Caucasus, or fly to the tents of the Turks, or solicit the protection of the emperor. The long emulation of the successors of Artaxerxes and Constantine increased his reluctance to appear as a suppliant in a rival court ; but he weighed the forces of the Romans, and prudently considered, that the neighborhood of Syria would render his escape more easy and their succors more effectual. Attended only by his concubines, and a troop of thirty guards, he secretly departed from the capital, followed the banks of the Euphrates, traversed the desert, and halted at the distance of ten miles from Circesium. About the third watch of the night, the Roman præfect was informed of his approach, and he introduced the royal stranger to the fortress at the dawn of day. From thence the king of Persia was conducted to the more honorable residence of Hierapolis ; and Maurice dissembled his pride, and displayed his benevolence, at the reception of the letters and ambassadors of the grandson of Nushirvan. They humbly represented the vicissitudes of fortune and the common interest of princes, exaggerated the ingratitude of Bahram, the agent of the evil principle, and urged, with specious argument, that it was for the advantage of the Romans themselves to support the two monarchies which balance the world, the two great luminaries by whose salutary influence it is vivified and

adorned. The anxiety of Chosroes was soon relieved by the assurance that the emperor had espoused the cause of justice and
royalty ; but Maurice prudently declined the expense and delay of
his useless visit to Constantinople. In the name of his generous
benefactor, a rich diadem was presented to the fugitive prince,
with an inestimable gift of jewels and gold ; a powerful army was
assembled on the frontiers of Syria and Armenia, under the command of the valiant and faithful Narses,[17] and this general, of his
own nation, and his own choice, was directed to pass the Tigris,
and never to sheathe his sword till he had restored Chosroes to
the throne of his ancestors.* The enterprise, however splendid,
was less arduous than it might appear. Persia had already repented of her fatal rashness, which betrayed the heir of the house
of Sassan to the ambition of a rebellious subject : and the bold
refusal of the Magi to consecrate his usurpation, compelled Bahram to assume the sceptre, regardless of the laws and prejudices
of the nation. The palace was soon distracted with conspiracy,
the city with tumult, the provinces with insurrection ; and the
cruel execution of the guilty and the suspected served to irritate
rather than subdue the public discontent. No sooner did the
grandson of Nushirvan display his own and the Roman banners
beyond the Tigris, than he was joined, each day, by the increasing multitudes of the nobility and people ; and as he advanced,
he received from every side the grateful offerings of the keys of
his cities and the heads of his enemies. As soon as Modain was
freed from the presence of the usurper, the loyal inhabitants
obeyed the first summons of Mebodes at the head of only two
thousand horse, and Chosroes accepted the sacred and precious
ornaments of the palace as the pledge of their truth and the presage of his approaching success. After the junction of the Imperial troops, which Bahram vainly struggled to prevent, the contest was decided by two battles on the banks of the Zab, and the
confines of Media. The Romans, with the faithful subjects of
Persia, amounted to sixty thousand, while the whole force of the
usurper did not exceed forty thousand men : the two generals
signalized their valor and ability ; but the victory was finally determined by the prevalence of numbers and discipline. With the
remnant of a broken army, Bahram fled towards the eastern provinces of the Oxus ; the enmity of Persia reconciled him to the
Turks ; but his days were shortened by poison, perhaps the most
incurable of poisons, the stings of remorse and despair, and the
bitter remembrance of lost glory. Yet the modern Persians still

---

* The Armenians adhered to Chosroes. St. Martin, vol. x. p. 312.—M.

commemorate the exploits of Bahram ; and some excellent laws have prolonged the duration of his troubled and transitory reign.*

The restoration of Chosroes was celebrated with feasts and executions ; and the music of the royal banquet was often disturbed by the groans of dying or mutilated criminals. A general pardon might have diffused comfort and tranquillity through a country which had been shaken by the late revolutions ; yet before the sanguinary temper of Chosroes is blamed, we should learn whether the Persians had not been accustomed either to dread the rigor, or to despise the weakness, of their sovereign. The revolt of Bahram, and the conspiracy of the satraps, were impartially punished by the revenge or justice of the conqueror ; the merits of Bindoes himself could not purify his hand from the guilt of royal blood : and the son of Hormouz was desirous to assert his own innocence, and to vindicate the sanctity of kings. During the vigor of the Roman power, several princes were seated on the throne of Persia by the arms and the authority of the first Cæsars. But their new subjects were soon disgusted with the vices or virtues which they had imbibed in a foreign land ; the instability of their dominion gave birth to a vulgar observation, that the choice of Rome was solicited and rejected with equal ardor by the capricious levity of Oriental slaves.[18] But the glory of Maurice was conspicuous in the long and fortunate reign of his *son* and his ally. A band of a thousand Romans, who continued to guard the person of Chosroes, proclaimed his confidence in the fidelity of the strangers ; his growing strength enabled him to dismiss this unpopular aid, but he steadily professed the same gratitude and reverence to his adopted father ; and till the death of Maurice, the peace and alliance of the two empires were faithfully maintained. Yet the mercenary friendship of the Roman prince had been purchased with costly and important gifts ; the strong cities of Martyropolis and Dara† were restored, and the Persarmenians became the willing subjects of an empire, whose eastern limit was extended, beyond the example of former times, as far as the banks of the Araxes, and the neighborhood of the Caspian. A pious hope was indulged, that the church as well as the state might triumph in this revolution ; but if Chosroes had sincerely listened to the

---

* According to Mirkhond and the Oriental writers, Bahram received the daughter of the Khakan in marriage, and commanded a body of Turks in an invasion of Persia. Some say that he was assassinated ; Malcolm adopts the opinion that he was poisoned. His sister Gourdieh, the companion of his flight, is celebrated in the Shah Nameh. She was afterwards one of the wives of Chosroes. St. Martin, vol. x. p. 331.—M.

† Concerning Nisibis, see St. Martin and his Armenian authorities vol. x. p. 332, and Mémoires sur l'Arménie, tom. i. p. 25.—M.

Christian bishops, the impression was erased by the zeal and eloquence of the Magi : if he was armed with philosophic indifference, he accommodated his belief, or rather his professions, to the
various circumstances of an exile and a sovereign. The imaginary
conversion of the king of Persia was reduced to a local and superstitious veneration for Sergius,[19] one of the saints of Antioch, who
heard his prayers and appeared to him in dreams ; he enriched the
shrine with offerings of gold and silver, and ascribed to this invisible patron the success of his arms, and the pregnancy of Sira, a
devout Christian, and the best beloved of his wives.[20] The beauty
of Sira, or Schirin,[21] her wit, her musical talents, are still famous
in the history, or rather in the romances, of the East : her own
name is expressive, in the Persian tongue, of sweetness and grace ;
and the epithet of *Parviz* alludes to the charms of her royal lover.
Yet Sira never shared the passion which she inspired, and the
bliss of Chosroes was tortured by a jealous doubt, that whilst he
possessed her person, she had bestowed her affections on a meaner
favorite.[22]

While the majesty of the Roman name was revived in the East,
the prospect of Europe is less pleasing and less glorious. By the
departure of the Lombards and the ruin of the Gepidæ, the balance
of power was destroyed on the Danube ; and the Avars spread
their permanent dominion from the foot of the Alps to the sea-
coast of the Euxine. The reign of Baian is the brightest æra of
their monarchy ; their chagan, who occupied the rustic palace of
Attila, appears to have imitated his character and policy ;[23] but
as the same scenes were repeated in a smaller circle, a minute representation of the copy would be devoid of the greatness and
novelty of the original. The pride of the second Justin, of Tiberius, and Maurice, was humbled by a proud barbarian, more
prompt to inflict than exposed to suffer the injuries of war ; and
as often as Asia was threatened by the Persian arms, Europe was
oppressed by the dangerous inroads, or costly friendship, of the
Avars. When the Roman envoys approached the presence of the
chagan, they were commanded to wait at the door of his tent, till,
at the end perhaps of ten or twelve days, he condescended to admit them. If the substance or the style of their message was offensive to his ear, he insulted, with real or affected fury, their own
dignity, and that of their prince ; their baggage was plundered,
and their lives were only saved by the promise of a richer present
and a more respectful address. But *his* sacred ambassadors enjoyed and abused an unbounded license in the midst of Constantinople : they urged, with importunate clamors, the increase of
tribute, or the restitution of captives and deserters : and the maj-

esty of the empire was almost equally degraded by a base compliance, or by the false and fearful excuses with which they eluded such insolent demands. The chagan had never seen an elephant ; and his curiosity was excited by the strange, and perhaps fabulous, portrait of that wonderful animal. At his command, one of the largest elephants of the Imperial stables was equipped with stately caparisons, and conducted by a numerous train to the royal village in the plains of Hungary. He surveyed the enormous beast with surprise, with disgust, and possibly with terror ; and smiled at the vain industry of the Romans, who, in search of such useless rarities, could explore the limits of the land and sea. He wished, at the expense of the emperor, to repose in a golden bed. The wealth of Constantinople, and the skilful diligence of her artists, were instantly devoted to the gratification of his caprice ; but when the work was finished, he rejected with scorn a present so unworthy the majesty of a great king.[24] These were the casual sallies of his pride ; but the avarice of the chagan was a more steady and tractable passion : a rich and regular supply of silk apparel, furniture, and plate introduced the rudiments of art and luxury among the tents of the Scythians ; their appetite was stimulated by the pepper and cinnamon of India ;[25] the annual subsidy or tribute was raised from fourscore to one hundred and twenty thousand pieces of gold ; and after each hostile interruption, the payment of the arrears, with exorbitant interest, was always made the first condition of the new treaty. In the language of a barbarian, without guile, the prince of the Avars affected to complain of the insincerity of the Greeks ;[26] yet he was not inferior to the most civilized nations in the refinements of dissimulation and perfidy. As the successor of the Lombards, the chagan asserted his claim to the important city of Sirmium, the ancient bulwark of the Illyrian provinces.[27] The plains of the Lower Hungary were covered with the Avar horse ; and a fleet of large boats was built in the Hercynian wood, to descend the Danube, and to transport into the Save the materials of a bridge. But as the strong garrison of Singidunum, which commanded the conflux of the two rivers, might have stopped their passage and baffled his designs, he dispelled their apprehensions by a solemn oath that his views were not hostile to the empire. He swore by his sword, the symbol of the god of war, that he did not, as the enemy of Rome, construct a bridge upon the Save. "If I violate my oath," pursued the intrepid Baian, "may I myself, and the last of my nation, perish by the sword ! May the heavens, and fire, the deity of the heavens, fall upon our heads ! May the forests and mountains bury us in their ruins ! and the Save, returning against the laws

of nature, to his source, overwhelm us in his angry waters!''
After this barbarous imprecation, he calmly inquired what oath
was most sacred and venerable among the Christians, what guilt or
perjury it was most dangerous to incur. The bishop of Singidunum
presented the gospel, which the chagan received with devout reverence. ''I swear,'' said he, ''by the God who has spoken in
this holy book, that I have neither falsehood on my tongue, nor
treachery in my heart.'' As soon as he rose from his knees he
accelerated the labor of the bridge, and despatched an envoy to
proclaim what he no longer wished to conceal. ''Inform the emperor,'' said the perfidious Baian, that Sirmium is invested on
every side. Advise his prudence to withdraw the citizens and
their effects, and to resign a city which it is now impossible to
relieve or defend.'' Without the hope of relief, the defence of
Sirmium was prolonged above three years : the walls were still
untouched ; but famine was enclosed within the walls, till a merciful capitulation allowed the escape of the naked and hungry inhabitants. Singidunum, at the distance of fifty miles, experienced
a more cruel fate : the buildings were razed, and the vanquished
people was condemned to servitude and exile. Yet the ruins of
Sirmium are no longer visible ; the advantageous situation of
Singidunum soon attracted a new colony of Sclavonians, and the
conflux of the Save and Danube is still guarded by the fortifications of Belgrade, or the *White City*, so often and so obstinately
disputed by the Christian and Turkish arms.[28] From Belgrade to
the walls of Constantinople a line may be measured of six hundred
miles : that line was marked with flames and with blood ; the
horses of the Avars were alternately bathed in the Euxine and the
Adriatic ; and the Roman pontiff, alarmed by the approach of a
more savage enemy,[29] was reduced to cherish the Lombards, as
the protectors of Italy. The despair of a captive, whom his country refused to ransom, disclosed to the Avars the invention and
practice of military engines.[30] But in the first attempts they were
rudely framed, and awkwardly managed ; and the resistance of
Diocletianopolis and Beræa, of Philippopolis and Adrianople, soon
exhausted the skill and patience of the besiegers. The warfare
of Baian was that of a Tartar ; yet his mind was susceptible of a
humane and generous sentiment : he spared Anchialus, whose salutary waters had restored the health of the best beloved of his
wives ; and the Romans confessed, that their starving army was
fed and dismissed by the liberality of a foe. His empire extended
over Hungary, Poland, and Prussia, from the mouth of the Danube to that of the Oder ;[31] and his new subjects were divided and
transplanted by the jealous policy of the conqueror.[32] The east-

ern regions of Germany, which had been left vacant by the emigration of the Vandals, were replenished with Sclavonian colonists ; the same tribes are discovered in the neighborhood of the Adriatic and of the Baltic, and with the name of Baian himself, the Illyrian cities of Neyss and Lissa are again found in the heart of Silesia. In the disposition both of his troops and provinces the chagan exposed the vassals, whose lives he disregarded,[33] to the first assault ; and the swords of the enemy were blunted before they encountered the native valor of the Avars.

The Persian alliance restored the troops of the East to the defence of Europe : and Maurice, who had supported ten years the insolence of the chagan, declared his resolution to march in person against the barbarians. In the space of two centuries none of the successors of Theodosius had appeared in the field : their lives were supinely spent in the palace of Constantinople ; and the Greeks could no longer understand, that the name of *emperor*, in its primitive sense, denoted the chief of the armies of the republic. The martial ardor of Maurice was opposed by the grave flattery of the senate, the timid superstition of the patriarch, and the tears of the empress Constantina ; and they all conjured him to devolve on some meaner general the fatigues and perils of a Scythian campaign. Deaf to their advice and entreaty, the emperor boldly advanced[34] seven miles from the capital ; the sacred ensign of the cross was displayed in the front ; and Maurice reviewed, with conscious pride, the arms and numbers of the veterans who had fought and conquered beyond the Tigris. Anchialus was the last term of his progress by sea and land ; he solicited, without success, a miraculous answer to his nocturnal prayers ; his mind was confounded by the death of a favorite horse, the encounter of a wild boar, a storm of wind and rain, and the birth of a monstrous child ; and he forgot, that the best of omens is to unsheathe our sword in the defence of our country.[35] Under the pretence of receiving the ambassadors of Persia, the emperor returned to Constantinople, exchanged the thoughts of war for those of devotion, and disappointed the public hope by his absence and the choice of his lieutenants. The blind partiality of fraternal love might excuse the promotion of his brother Peter, who fled with equal disgrace from the barbarians, from his own soldiers, and from the inhabitants of a Roman city. That city, if we may credit the resemblance of name and character, was the famous Azimuntium,[36] which had alone repelled the tempest of Attila. The example of her warlike youth was propagated to succeeding generations ; and they obtained, from the first or the second Justin, an honorable privilege, that their valor should be always reserved

for the defence of their native country.   The brother of Maurice
attempted to violate this privilege, and to mingle a patriot band
with the mercenaries of his camp ; they retired to the church ; he
was not awed by the sanctity of the place ; the people rose in
their cause, the gates were shut, the ramparts were manned ; and
the cowardice of Peter was found equal to his arrogance and injustice.   The military fame of Commentiolus [37] is the object of
satire or comedy rather than of serious history, since he was even
deficient in the vile and vulgar qualification of personal courage.
His solemn councils, strange evolutions, and secret orders, always supplied an apology for flight or delay.   If he marched
against the enemy, the pleasant valleys of Mount Hæmus opposed
an insuperable barrier ; but in his retreat, he explored, with fearless curiosity, the most difficult and obsolete paths, which had
almost escaped the memory of the oldest native.   The only blood
which he lost was drawn, in a real or affected malady, by the
lancet of a surgeon ; and his health, which felt with exquisite
sensibility the approach of the barbarians, was uniformly restored
by the repose and safety of the winter season.   A prince who
could promote and support this unworthy favorite must derive no
glory from the accidental merit of his colleague Priscus. [38]   In five
successive battles, which seem to have been conducted with skill
and resolution, seventeen thousand two hundred barbarians were
made prisoners : near sixty thousand, with four sons of the chagan,
were slain : the Roman general surprised a peaceful district of the
Gepidæ, who slept under the protection of the Avars ; and his
last trophies were erected on the banks of the Danube and the
Teyss.   Since the death of Trajan, the arms of the empire had not
penetrated so deeply into the old Dacia : yet the success of Priscus was transient and barren ; and he was soon recalled by the
apprehension that Baian, with dauntless spirit and recruited
forces, was preparing to avenge his defeat under the walls of Constantinople. [39]

The theory of war was not more familiar to the camps of Cæsar
and Trajan, than to those of Justinian and Maurice. [40]   The iron
of Tuscany or Pontus still received the keenest temper from the
skill of the Byzantine workmen.   The magazines were plentifully
stored with every species of offensive and defensive arms.   In the
construction and use of ships, engines, and fortifications, the barbarians admired the superior ingenuity of a people whom they so
often vanquished in the field.   The science of tactics, the order,
evolutions, and stratagems of antiquity, was transcribed and
studied in the books of the Greeks and Romans.   But the solitude
or degeneracy of the provinces could no longer supply a race of

men to handle those weapons, to guard those walls, to navigate those ships, and to reduce the theory of war into bold and successful practice. The genius of Belisarius and Narses had been formed without a master, and expired without a disciple. Neither honor nor patriotism, nor generous superstition, could animate the lifeless bodies of slaves and strangers, who had succeeded to the honors of the legions : it was in the camp alone that the emperor should have exercised a despotic command ; it was only in the camps that his authority was disobeyed and insulted : he appeased and inflamed with gold the licentiousness of the troops ; but their vices were inherent, their victories were accidental, and their costly maintenance exhausted the substance of a state which they were unable to defend. After a long and pernicious indulgence, the cure of this inveterate evil was undertaken by Maurice ; but the rash attempt, which drew destruction on his own head, tended only to aggravate the disease. A reformer should be exempt from the suspicion of interest, and he must possess the confidence and esteem of those whom he proposes to reclaim. The troops of Maurice might listen to the voice of a victorious leader ; they disdained the admonitions of statesmen and sophists ; and, when they received an edict, which deducted from their pay the price of their arms and clothing, they execrated the avarice of a prince insensible of the dangers and fatigues from which he had escaped. The camps both of Asia and Europe were agitated with frequent and furious seditions ; [41] the enraged soldiers of Edessa pursued with reproaches, with threats, with wounds, their trembling generals ; they overturned the statues of the emperor, cast stones against the miraculous image of Christ, and either rejected the yoke of all civil and military laws, or instituted a dangerous model of voluntary subordination. The monarch, always distant, and often deceived, was incapable of yielding, or persisting, according to the exigence of the moment. But the fear of a general revolt induced him too readily to accept any act of valor, or any expression of loyalty, as an atonement for the popular offence ; the new reform was abolished as hastily as it had been announced, and the troops, instead of punishment and restraint, were agreeably surprised by a gracious proclamation of immunities and rewards. But the soldiers accepted without gratitude the tardy and reluctant gifts of the emperor : their insolence was elated by the discovery of his weakness and their own strength ; and their mutual hatred was inflamed beyond the desire of forgiveness or the hope of reconciliation. The historians of the times adopt the vulgar suspicion, that Maurice conspired to destroy the troops whom he had labored to reform ; the misconduct and favor of

Commentiolus are imputed to this malevolent design ; and every age must condemn the inhumanity or avarice [42] of a prince, who, by the trifling ransom of six thousand pieces of gold, might have prevented the massacre of twelve thousand prisoners in the hands of the chagan. In the just fervor of indignation, an order was signified to the army of the Danube, that they should spare the magazines of the province, and establish their winter quarters in the hostile country of the Avars. The measure of their grievances was full : they pronounced Maurice unworthy to reign, expelled or slaughtered his faithful adherents, and, under the command of Phocas, a simple centurion, returned by hasty marches to the neighborhood of Constantinople. After a long series of legal succession, the military disorders of the third century were again revived ; yet such was the novelty of the enterprise, that the insurgents were awed by their own rashness. They hesitated to invest their favorite with the vacant purple ; and while they rejected all treaty with Maurice himself, they held a friendly correspondence with his son Theodosius, and with Germanus, the father-in-law of the royal youth. So obscure had been the former condition of Phocas, that the emperor was ignorant of the name and character of his rival ; but as soon as he learned that the centurion, though bold in sedition, was timid in the face of danger, " Alas !" cried the desponding prince, " if he is a coward, he will surely be a murderer."

Yet if Constantinople had been firm and faithful, the murderer might have spent his fury against the walls ; and the rebel army would have been gradually consumed or reconciled by the prudence of the emperor. In the games of the Circus, which he repeated with unusual pomp, Maurice disguised, with smiles of confidence, the anxiety of his heart, condescended to solicit the applause of the *factions*, and flattered their pride by accepting from their respective tribunes a list of nine hundred *blues* and fifteen hundred *greens*, whom he affected to esteem as the solid pillars of his throne. Their treacherous or languid support betrayed his weakness and hastened his fall : the green faction were the secret accomplices of the rebels, and the blues recommended lenity and moderation in a contest with their Roman brethren. The rigid and parsimonious virtues of Maurice had long since alienated the hearts of his subjects : as he walked barefoot in a religious procession, he was rudely assaulted with stones, and his guards were compelled to present their iron maces in the defence of his person. A fanatic monk ran through the streets with a drawn sword, denouncing against him the wrath and the sentence of God ; and a vile plebeian, who represented his countenance and apparel, was seated on an ass, and pursued by the imprecations of the multitude.[43] The emperor suspected the popularity of Germanus with the soldiers and citizens : he feared, he threatened, but he delayed to strike ; the patrician fled to the sanctuary of the church ; the people rose in his defence, the walls were deserted by the guards, and the lawless city was abandoned to the flames and rapine of a nocturnal tumult. In a small bark, the unfortunate Maurice, with his wife and nine children, escaped to the Asiatic shore ; but the violence of the wind compelled him to land at the church of St. Autonomus,[44] near Chalcedon, from whence he despatched Theodosius, his eldest son, to implore the gratitude and friendship of the Persian monarch. For himself, he refused to fly : his body was tortured with sciatic pains,[45] his mind was enfeebled by superstition ; he patiently awaited the event of the revolution, and addressed a fervent and public prayer to the Almighty, that the punishment of his sins might be inflicted in this world rather than in a future life. After the abdication of Maurice the two factions disputed the choice of an emperor ; but the favorite of the blues was rejected by the jealousy of their antagonists, and Germanus himself was hurried along by the crowds who rushed to the palace of Hebdomon, seven miles from the city, to adore the majesty of Phocas the centurion. A modest wish of resigning the purple to the rank and merit of Germanus was opposed by *his* resolution, more obstinate and equally sincere ; the senate and clergy obeyed his summons ; and, as soon as the patriarch was assured of his orthodox belief, he consecrated the successful usurper in the church of St. John the Baptist. On the third day, amidst the acclamations of a thoughtless people, Phocas made his public entry in a chariot drawn by four white horses : the revolt of the troops was rewarded by a lavish donative ; and the new sovereign, after visiting the palace, beheld from his throne the games of the hippodrome. In a dispute of precedency between the two factions, his partial judgment inclined in favor of the greens. " Remember that Maurice is still alive," resounded from the opposite side ; and the indiscreet clamor of the blues admonished and stimulated the cruelty of the tyrant. The ministers of death were despatched to Chalcedon : they dragged the emperor from his sanctuary ; and the five sons of Maurice were successively murdered before the eyes of their agonizing parent. At each stroke, which he felt in his heart, he found strength to rehearse a pious ejaculation : " Thou art just, O Lord ! and thy judgments are righteous." And such, in the last moments, was his rigid attachment to truth and justice, that he revealed to the soldiers the pious falsehood of a nurse who presented her own child in the place of a royal infant.[46] The tragic scene was finally closed by the execution of the emperor himself, in the twentieth year of his reign, and the sixty-third of his age. The bodies of the father and his five sons were cast into the sea ; their heads were exposed at Constantinople to the insults or pity of the multitude ; and it was not till some signs of putrefaction had appeared, that Phocas connived at the private burial of these venerable remains. In that grave the faults and errors of Maurice were kindly interred. His fate alone was remembered ; and at the end of twenty years, in the recital of the history of Theophylact, the mournful tale was interrupted by the tears of the audience.[47]

Such tears must have flowed in secret, and such compassion would have been criminal, under the reign of Phocas, who was peaceably acknowledged in the provinces of the East and West. The images of the emperor and his wife Leontia were exposed in the Lateran to the veneration of the clergy and senate of Rome, and afterwards deposited in the palace of the Cæsars, between those of Constantine and Theodosius. As a subject and a Christian, it was the duty of Gregory to acquiesce in the established government ; but the joyful applause with which he salutes the fortune of the assassin, has sullied, with indelible disgrace, the character of the saint. The successor of the apostles might have inculcated with decent firmness the guilt of blood, and the necessity of repentance ; he is content to celebrate the deliverance of the people and the fall of the oppressor ; to rejoice that the piety and benignity of Phocas have been raised by Providence to the Imperial throne ; to pray that his hands may be strengthened against all his enemies ; and to express a wish, perhaps a prophecy, that, after a long and triumphant reign, he may be transferred from a temporal to an everlasting kingdom.[48] I have already traced the steps of a revolution so pleasing, in Gregory's opinion, both to heaven and earth ; and Phocas does not appear less hateful in the exercise than in the acquisition of power. The pencil of an impartial historian has delineated the portrait of a monster :[49] his diminutive and deformed person, the closeness of his shaggy eyebrows, his red hair, his beardless chin, and his cheek disfigured and discolored by a formidable scar. Ignorant of letters, of laws, and even of arms, he indulged in the supreme rank a more ample privilege of lust and drunkenness ; and his brutal pleasures were either injurious to his subjects or disgraceful to himself. Without assuming the office of a prince, he renounced the profession of a soldier, and the reign of Phocas afflicted Europe with ignominious peace, and Asia with desolating war. His savage temper was inflamed by passion, hardened by fear, and exasperated by resistance or reproach. The flight of Theodosius to the Persian court had been intercepted by a rapid pursuit, or a deceitful message : he was beheaded at Nice, and the last hours of the young prince were soothed by the comforts of religion and the consciousness of innocence. Yet his phantom disturbed the repose of the usurper : a whisper was circulated through the East, that the son of Maurice was still alive : the people expected their avenger, and the widow and daughters of the late emperor would have adopted as their son and brother the vilest of mankind. In the massacre of the Imperial family,[50] the mercy, or rather the discretion, of Phocas had spared these unhappy females, and they were decently confined to a private house. But the spirit of the empress Constantina, still mindful of her father, her husband, and her sons, aspired to freedom and revenge. At the dead of night she escaped to the sanctuary of St. Sophia ; but her tears and the gold of her associate Germanus, were insufficient to provoke an insurrection. Her life was forfeited to revenge, and even to justice : but the patriarch obtained and pledged an oath for her safety : a monastery was allotted for her prison, and the widow of Maurice accepted and abused the lenity of his assassin. The discovery or the suspicion of a second conspiracy, dissolved the engagements, and rekindled the fury, of Phocas. A matron who commanded the respect and pity of mankind, the daughter, wife, and mother, of emperors, was tortured like the vilest malefactor, to force a confession of her designs and associates ; and the empress Constantina, with her three innocent daughters, was beheaded at Chalcedon, on the same ground which had been stained with the blood of her husband and five sons. After such an example, it would be superfluous to enumerate the names and sufferings of meaner victims. Their condemnation was seldom preceded by the forms of trial, and their punishment was imbittered by the refinements of cruelty : their eyes were pierced, their tongues were torn from the root, the hands and feet were amputated ; some expired under the lash, others in the flames, others again were transfixed with arrows ; and a simple speedy death was mercy which they could rarely obtain. The hippodrome, the sacred asylum of the pleasures and the liberty of the Romans, was polluted with heads and limbs, and mangled bodies ; and the companions of Phocas were the most sensible, that neither his favor, nor their services, could protect them from a tyrant, the worthy rival of the Caligulas and Domitians of the first age of the empire.[51]

A daughter of Phocas, his only child, was given in marriage to

the patrician Crispus,[52] and the *royal* images of the bride and
bridegroom were indiscreetly placed in the Circus, by the side of
the emperor. The father must desire that his posterity should
inherit the fruit of his crimes, but the monarch was offended by
this premature and popular association : the tribunes of the green
faction, who accused the officious error of their sculptors, were
condemned to instant death : their lives were granted to the
prayers of the people ; but Crispus might reasonably doubt,
whether a jealous usurper could forget and pardon his involuntary
competition. The green faction was alienated by the ingratitude of Phocas and the loss of their privileges ; every province of
the empire was ripe for rebellion ; and Heraclius, exarch of
Africa, persisted above two years in refusing all tribute and obedience to the centurion who disgraced the throne of Constantinople. By the secret emissaries of Crispus and the senate, the independent exarch was solicited to save and to govern his country ;
but his ambition was chilled by age, and he resigned the dangerous enterprise to his son Heraclius, and to Nicetas, the son of
Gregory, his friend and lieutenant. The powers of Africa were
armed by the two adventurous youths ; they agreed that the one
should navigate the fleet from Carthage to Constantinople, that
the other should lead an army through Egypt and Asia, and that
the Imperial purple should be the reward of diligence and success. A faint rumor of their undertaking was conveyed to the
ears of Phocas, and the wife and mother of the younger Heraclius
were secured as the hostages of his faith : but the treacherous
heart of Crispus extenuated the distant peril, the means of defence were neglected or delayed, and the tyrant supinely slept
till the African navy cast anchor in the Hellespont. Their standard was joined at Abidus by the fugitives and exiles who thirsted
for revenge ; the ships of Heraclius, whose lofty masts were
adorned with the holy symbols of religion,[53] steered their triumphant course through the Propontis ; and Phocas beheld from the
windows of the palace his approaching and inevitable fate. The
green faction was tempted, by gifts and promises, to oppose a feeble and fruitless resistance to the landing of the Africans : but the
people, and even the guards, were determined by the well-timed
defection of Crispus ; and the tyrant was seized by a private enemy, who boldly invaded the solitude of the palace. Stripped of
the diadem and purple, clothed in a vile habit, and loaded with
chains, he was transported in a small boat to the Imperial galley
of Heraclius, who reproached him with the crimes of his abominable reign. " Wilt thou govern better ?" were the last words
of the despair of Phocas. After suffering each variety of insult

and torture, his head was severed from his body, the mangled trunk was cast into the flames, and the same treatment was inflicted on the statues of the vain usurper, and the seditious banner of the green faction. The voice of the clergy, the senate, and the people, invited Heraclius to ascend the throne which he had purified from guilt and ignominy; after some graceful hesitation, he yielded to their entreaties. His coronation was accompanied by that of his wife Eudoxia; and their posterity, till the fourth generation, continued to reign over the empire of the East. The voyage of Heraclius had been easy and prosperous; the tedious march of Nicetas was not accomplished before the decision of the contest: but he submitted without a murmur to the fortune of his friend, and his laudable intentions were rewarded with an equestrian statue, and a daughter of the emperor. It was more difficult to trust the fidelity of Crispus, whose recent services were recompensed by the command of the Cappadocian army. His arrogance soon provoked, and seemed to excuse, the ingratitude of his new sovereign. In the presence of the senate, the son-in-law of Phocas was condemned to embrace the monastic life; and the sentence was justified by the weighty observation of Heraclius, that the man who had betrayed his father could never be faithful to his friend.[54]

Even after his death the republic was afflicted by the crimes of Phocas, which armed with a pious cause the most formidable of her enemies. According to the friendly and equal forms of the Byzantine and Persian courts, he announced his exaltation to the throne; and his ambassador Lilius, who had presented him with the heads of Maurice and his sons, was the best qualified to describe the circumstances of the tragic scene.[55] However it might be varnished by fiction or sophistry, Chosroes turned with horror from the assassin, imprisoned the pretended envoy, disclaimed the usurper, and declared himself the avenger of his father and benefactor. The sentiments of grief and resentment, which humanity would feel, and honor would dictate, promoted on this occasion the interest of the Persian king; and his interest was powerfully magnified by the national and religious prejudices of the Magi and satraps. In a strain of artful adulation, which assumed the language of freedom, they presumed to censure the excess of his gratitude and friendship for the Greeks; a nation with whom it was dangerous to conclude either peace or alliance; whose superstition was devoid of truth and justice, and who must be incapable of any virtue, since they could perpetrate the most atrocious of crimes, the impious murder of their sovereign.[56] For the crime of an ambitious centurion, the nation which he oppressed was chastised with the calamities of war ; and the same calamities, at the end of twenty years, were retaliated and redoubled on the heads of the Persians.[57] The general who had restored Chosroes to the throne still commanded in the East ; and the name of Narses was the formidable sound with which the Assyrian mothers were accustomed to terrify their infants. It is not improbable, that a native subject of Persia should encourage his master and his friend to deliver and possess the provinces of Asia. It is still more probable that Chosroes should animate his troops by the assurance that the sword which they dreaded the most would remain it its scabbard, or be drawn in their favor. The hero could not depend on the faith of a tyrant ; and the tyrant was conscious how little he deserved the obedience of a hero. Narses was removed from his military command ; he reared an independent standard at Hierapolis, in Syria : he was betrayed by fallacious promises, and burnt alive in the market-place of Constantinople. Deprived of the only chief whom they could fear or esteem, the bands which he had led to victory were twice broken by the cavalry, trampled by the elephants, and pierced by the arrows of the barbarians ; and a great number of the captives were beheaded on the field of battle by the sentence of the victor, who might justly condemn these seditious mercenaries as the authors or accomplices of the death of Maurice. Under the reign of Phocas, the fortifications of Merdin, Dara, Amida, and Edessa, were successively besieged, reduced, and destroyed by the Persian monarch : he passed the Euphrates, occupied the Syrian cities, Hierapolis, Chalcis, and Berrhæa or Aleppo, and soon encompassed the walls of Antioch with his irresistible arms. The rapid tide of success discloses the decay of the empire, the incapacity of Phocas, and the disaffection of his subjects ; and Chosroes provided a decent apology for their submission or revolt, by an impostor, who attended his camp as the son of Maurice[58] and the lawful heir of the monarchy.

The first intelligence from the East which Heraclius received,[59] was that of the loss of Antioch ; but the aged metropolis, so often overturned by earthquakes, and pillaged by the enemy, could supply but a small and languid stream of treasure and blood. The Persians were equally successful, and more fortunate, in the sack of Cæsarea, the capital of Cappadocia ; and as they advanced beyond the ramparts of the frontier, the boundary of ancient war, they found a less obstinate resistance and a more plentiful harvest. The pleasant vale of Damascus has been adorned in every age with a royal city : her obscure felicity has hitherto escaped the historian of the Roman empire : but Chosroes reposed his troops in the paradise of Damascus before he ascended the hills of Libanus, or invaded the cities of the Phœnician coast. The conquest of Jerusalem,[60] which had been meditated by Nushirvan, was achieved by the zeal and avarice of his grandson ; the ruin of the proudest monument of Christianity was vehemently urged by the intolerant spirit of the Magi ; and he could enlist for this holy warfare with an army of six-and-twenty thousand Jews, whose furious bigotry might compensate, in some degree, for the want of valor and discipline.* After the reduction of Galilee, and the region beyond the Jordan, whose resistance appears to have delayed the fate of the capital, Jerusalem itself was taken by assault. The sepulchre of Christ, and the stately churches of Helena and Constantine, were consumed, or at least damaged, by the flames ; the devout offerings of three hundred years were rifled in one sacrilegious day ; the Patriarch Zachariah, and the *true cross*, were transported into Persia ; and the massacre of ninety thousand Christians is imputed to the Jews and Arabs, who swelled the disorder of the Persian march. The fugitives of Palestine were entertained at Alexandria by the charity of John the Archbishop, who is distinguished among a crowd of saints by the epithet of *almsgiver :* [61] and the revenues of the church, with a treasure of three hundred thousand pounds, were restored to the true proprietors, the poor of every country and every denomination. But Egypt itself, the only province which had been exempt, since the time of Diocletian, from foreign and domestic war, was again subdued by the successors of Cyrus. Pelusium, the key of that impervious country, was surprised by the cavalry of the Persians : they passed, with impunity, the innumerable channels of the Delta, and explored the long valley of the Nile, from the pyramids of Memphis to the confines of Æthiopia. Alexandria might have been relieved by a naval force, but the archbishop and the præfect embarked for Cyprus ; and Chosroes entered the second city of the empire, which still preserved a wealthy remnant of industry and commerce. His western trophy was erected, not on the walls of Carthage,[62] but in the neighborhood of Tripoli : the Greek colonies of Cyrene were finally extirpated ; and the conqueror, treading in the footsteps of Alexander, returned in triumph through the sands of the Libyan desert. In the same campaign another army advanced from the Euphrates to the Thracian Bosphorus ; Chalcedon surrendered after a long siege, and a Persian camp was maintained above ten years in the presence of Constantinople. The sea-coast of Pontus, the city of

---

* See Hist. of Jews, vol. iii. p. 240.—M.

Ancyra, and the Isle of Rhodes, are enumerated among the last conquests of the great king; and if Chosroes had possessed any maritime power, his boundless ambition would have spread slavery and desolation over the provinces of Europe.

From the long-disputed banks of the Tigris and Euphrates, the reign of the grandson of Nushirvan was suddenly extended to the Hellespont and the Nile, the ancient limits of the Persian monarchy. But the provinces, which had been fashioned by the habits of six hundred years to the virtues and vices of the Roman government, supported with reluctance the yoke of the barbarians. The idea of a republic was kept alive by the institutions, or at least by the writings, of the Greeks and Romans, and the subjects of Heraclius had been educated to pronounce the words of liberty and law. But it has always been the pride and policy of Oriental princes to display the titles and attributes of their omnipotence; to upbraid a nation of slaves with their true name and abject condition, and to enforce, by cruel and insolent threats, the rigor of their absolute commands. The Christians of the East were scandalized by the worship of fire, and the impious doctrine of the two principles: the Magi were not less intolerant than the bishops; and the martyrdom of some native Persians, who had deserted the religion of Zoroaster,[63] was conceived to be the prelude of a fierce and general persecution. By the oppressive laws of Justinian, the adversaries of the church were made the enemies of the state; the alliance of the Jews, Nestorians, and Jacobites, had contributed to the success of Chosroes, and his partial favor to the sectaries provoked the hatred and fears of the Catholic clergy. Conscious of their fear and hatred, the Persian conqueror governed his new subjects with an iron sceptre; and, as if he suspected the stability of his dominion, he exhausted their wealth by exorbitant tributes and licentious rapine; despoiled or demolished the temples of the East; and transported to his hereditary realms the gold, the silver, the precious marbles, the arts, and the artists of the Asiatic cities. In the obscure picture of the calamities of the empire,[64] it is not easy to discern the figure of Chosroes himself, to separate his actions from those of his lieutenants, or to ascertain his personal merit in the general blaze of glory and magnificence. He enjoyed with ostentation the fruits of victory, and frequently retired from the hardships of war to the luxury of the palace. But in the space of twenty-four years, he was deterred by superstition or resentment from approaching the gates of Ctesiphon: and his favorite residence of Artemita, or Dastagerd, was situate beyond the Tigris, about sixty miles to the north of the capital.[65] The adjacent pastures were covered with flocks and herds: the paradise or park was replenished with pheasants, peacocks, ostriches, roebucks, and wild boars, and the noble game of lions and tigers was sometimes turned loose for the bolder pleasures of the chase. Nine hundred and sixty elephants were maintained for the use or splendor of the great king : his tents and baggage were carried into the field by twelve thousand great camels and eight thousand of a smaller size ; [66] and the royal stables were filled with six thousand mules and horses, among whom the names of Shebdiz and Barid are renowned for their speed or beauty.* Six thousand guards successively mounted before the palace gate ; the service of the interior apartments was performed by twelve thousand slaves, and in the number of three thousand virgins, the fairest of Asia, some happy concubine might console her master for the age or the indifference of Sira. The various treasures of gold, silver, gems, silks, and aromatics, were deposited in a hundred subterraneous vaults ; and the chamber *Badaverd* denoted the accidental gift of the winds which had wafted the spoils of Heraclius into one of the Syrian harbors of his rival. The vice of flattery, and perhaps of fiction, is not ashamed to compute the thirty thousand rich hangings that adorned the walls ; the forty thousand columns of silver, or more probably of marble, and plated wood, that supported the roof ; and the thousand globes of gold suspended in the dome, to imitate the motions of the planets and the constellations of the zodiac. [67] While the Persian monarch contemplated the wonders of his art and power, he received an epistle from an obscure citizen of Mecca, inviting him to acknowledge Mahomet as the apostle of God. He rejected the invitation, and tore the epistle. "It is thus," exclaimed the Arabian prophet, "that God will tear the kingdom, and reject the supplications of Chosroes." [68] † Placed on the verge of the two great empires of the East, Mahomet observed with secret joy the progress of their mutual destruction ; and in the midst of the Persian triumphs, he

---

* The ruins of these scenes of Khoosroo's magnificence have been visited by Sir R. K. Porter. At the ruins of T'okhtai Bostan he saw a gorgeous picture of a hunt, singularly illustrative of this passage. Travels, vol. ii. p. 204. Kisra Shirene, which he afterwards examined, appears to have been the palace of Dastagerd. Vol. ii. p. 173-175.—M.

† Khoosroo Purvcez was encamped on the banks of the Karasoo River when he received the letter of Mahomed. He tore the letter and threw it into the Karasoo. For this action the moderate author of the Zeenut-ul-Tuarikh calls him a wretch, and rejoices in all his subsequent misfortunes. These impressions still exist. I remarked to a Persian, when encamped near the Karasoo, in 1800, that the banks were very high, which must make it difficult to apply its waters to irrigation. "It once fertilized the whole country," said the zealous Mahomedan, "but its channel sunk with horror from its banks, when that madman, Khoosroo, threw our holy Prophet's letter into its stream ; which has ever since been accursed and useless." Malcolm's Persia, vol. i. p. 126.—M.

ventured to foretell, that before many years should elapse, victory would again return to the banners of the Romans.[69]

At the time when this prediction is said to have been delivered, no prophecy could be more distant from its accomplishment, since the first twelve years of Heraclius announced the approaching dissolution of the empire. If the motives of Chosroes had been pure and honorable, he must have ended the quarrel with the death of Phocas, and he would have embraced, as his best ally, the fortunate African who had so generously avenged the injuries of his benefactor Maurice. The prosecution of the war revealed the true character of the barbarian ; and the suppliant embassies of Heraclius to beseech his clemency, that he would spare the innocent, accept a tribute, and give peace to the world, were rejected with contemptuous silence or insolent menace. Syria, Egypt, and the provinces of Asia, were subdued by the Persian arms, while Europe, from the confines of Istria to the long wall of Thrace, was oppressed by the Avars, unsatiated with the blood and rapine of the Italian war. They had coolly massacred their male captives in the sacred field of Pannonia ; the women and children were reduced to servitude, and the noblest virgins were abandoned to the promiscuous lust of the barbarians. The amorous matron who opened the gates of Friuli, passed a short night in the arms of her royal lover ; the next evening, Romilda was condemned to the embraces of twelve Avars, and the third day the Lombard princess was impaled in the sight of the camp, while the chagan observed, with a cruel smile, that such a husband was the fit recompense of her lewdness and perfidy.[70] By these implacable enemies, Heraclius, on either side, was insulted and besieged : and the Roman empire was reduced to the walls of Constantinople, with the remnant of Greece, Italy, and Africa, and some maritime cities, from Tyre to Trebizond, of the Asiatic coast. After the loss of Egypt, the capital was afflicted by famine and pestilence ; and the emperor, incapable of resistance, and hopeless of relief, had resolved to transfer his person and government to the more secure residence of Carthage. His ships were already laden with the treasures of the palace ; but his flight was arrested by the patriarch, who armed the powers of religion in the defence of his country ; led Heraclius to the altar of St. Sophia, and extorted a solemn oath, that he would live and die with the people whom God had intrusted to his care. The chagan was encamped in the plains of Thrace ; but he dissembled his perfidious designs, and solicited an interview with the emperor near the town of Heraclea. Their reconciliation was celebrated with equestrian games ; the senate and people, in their gayest apparel, resorted to the festival of peace ; and the Avars beheld, with envy and desire, the spectacle of Roman luxury. On a sudden the hippodrome was encompassed by the Scythian cavalry, who had pressed their secret and nocturnal march : the tremendous sound of the chagan's whip gave the signal of the assault, and Heraclius, wrapping his diadem round his arm, was saved with extreme hazard, by the fleetness of his horse. So rapid was the pursuit, that the Avars almost entered the golden gate of Constantinople with the flying crowds : [71] but the plunder of the suburbs rewarded their treason, and they transported beyond the Danube two hundred and seventy thousand captives. On the shore of Chalcedon, the emperor held a safer conference with a more honorable foe, who, before Heraclius descended from his galley, saluted with reverence and pity the majesty of the purple. The friendly offer of Sain, the Persian general, to conduct an embassy to the presence of the great king, was accepted with the warmest gratitude, and the prayer for pardon and peace was humbly presented by the Prætorian præfect, the præfect of the city, and one of the first ecclesiastics of the patri- archal church. [72] But the lieutenant of Chosroes had fatally mis- taken the intentions of his master. "It was not an embassy," said the tyrant of Asia, "it was the person of Heraclius, bound in chains, that he should have brought to the foot of my throne. I will never give peace to the emperor of Rome, till he has abjured his crucified God, and embraced the worship of the sun." Sain was flayed alive, according to the inhuman practice of his country ; and the separate and rigorous confinement of the ambassadors violated the law of nations, and the faith of an express stipula- tion. Yet the experience of six years at length persuaded the Persian monarch to renounce the conquest of Constantinople, and to specify the annual tribute or ransom of the Roman empire ; a thousand talents of gold, a thousand talents of silver, a thousand silk robes, a thousand horses, and a thousand virgins. Heraclius subscribed these ignominious terms ; but the time and space which he obtained to collect such treasures from the poverty of the East, was industriously employed in the preparations of a bold and desperate attack.

Of the characters conspicuous in history, that of Heraclius is one of the most extraordinary and inconsistent. In the first and last years of a long reign, the emperor appears to be the slave of sloth, of pleasure, or of superstition, the careless and impotent spectator of the public calamities. But the languid mists of the morning and evening are separated by the brightness of the meridian sun : the Arcadius of the palace arose the Cæsar of the camp ; and the honor of Rome and Heraclius was gloriously retrieved by the exploits and trophies of six adventurous campaigns. It was the duty of the Byzantine historians to have revealed the causes of his slumber and vigilance. At this distance we can only conjecture, that he was endowed with more personal courage than political resolution ; that he was detained by the charms, and perhaps the arts, of his niece Martina, with whom, after the death of Eudocia, he contracted an incestuous marriage ;[73] and that he yielded to the base advice of the counsellors, who urged, as a fundamental law, that the life of the emperor should never be exposed in the field.[74] Perhaps he was awakened by the last insolent demand of the Persian conqueror ; but at the moment when Heraclius assumed the spirit of a hero, the only hopes of the Romans were drawn from the vicissitudes of fortune, which might threaten the proud prosperity of Chosroes, and must be favorable to those who had attained the lowest period of depression.[75] To provide for the expenses of war, was the first care of the emperor ; and for the purpose of collecting the tribute, he was allowed to solicit the benevolence of the eastern provinces. But the revenue no longer flowed in the usual channels ; the credit of an arbitrary prince is annihilated by his power ; and the courage of Heraclius was first displayed in daring to borrow the consecrated wealth of churches, under the solemn vow of restoring, with usury, whatever he had been compelled to employ in the service of religion and of the empire. The clergy themselves appear to have sympathized with the public distress ; and the discreet patriarch of Alexandria, without admitting the precedent of sacrilege, assisted his sovereign by the miraculous or seasonable revelation of a secret treasure.[76] Of the soldiers who had conspired with Phocas, only two were found to have survived the stroke of time and of the barbarians ;[77] the loss, even of these seditious veterans, was imperfectly supplied by the new levies of Heraclius, and the gold of the sanctuary united, in the same camp, the names, and arms, and languages of the East and West. He would have been content with the neutrality of the Avars ; and his friendly entreaty, that the chagan would act, not as the enemy, but as the guardian, of the empire, was accompanied with a more persuasive donative of two hundred thousand pieces of gold. Two days after the festival of Easter, the emperor, exchanging his purple for the simple garb of a penitent and warrior,[78] gave the signal of his departure. To the faith of the people Heraclius recommended his children ; the civil and military powers were vested in the most deserving hands, and the discretion of the patriarch and senate was authorized to save or surrender the city, if they should be oppressed in his absence by the superior forces of the enemy.

The neighboring heights of Chalcedon were covered with tents and arms : but if the new levies of Heraclius had been rashly led to the attack, the victory of the Persians in the sight of Constantinople might have been the last day of the Roman empire. As imprudent would it have been to advance into the provinces of Asia, leaving their innumerable cavalry to intercept his convoys, and continually to hang on the lassitude and disorder of his rear. But the Greeks were still masters of the sea ; a fleet of galleys, transports, and store-ships, was assembled in the harbor ; the barbarians consented to embark ; a steady wind carried them through the Hellespont ; the western and southern coast of Asia Minor lay on their left hand ; the spirit of their chief was first displayed in a storm ; and even the eunuchs of his train were excited to suffer and to work by the example of their master. He landed his troops on the confines of Syria and Cilicia, in the Gulf of Scanderoon, where the coast suddenly turns to the south ;[79] and his discernment was expressed in the choice of this important post.[80] From all sides, the scattered garrisons of the maritime cities and the mountains might repair with speed and safety to his Imperial standard. The natural fortifications of Cilicia protected, and even concealed, the camp of Heraclius, which was pitched near Issus, on the same ground where Alexander had vanquished the host of Darius. The angle which the emperor occupied was deeply indented into a vast semicircle of the Asiatic, Armenian, and Syrian provinces ; and to whatsoever point of the circumference he should direct his attack, it was easy for him to dissemble his own motions, and to prevent those of the enemy. In the camp of Issus, the Roman general reformed the sloth and disorder of the veterans, and educated the new recruits in the knowledge and practice of military virtue. Unfolding the miraculous image of Christ, he urged them to *revenge* the holy altars which had been profaned by the worshippers of fire ; addressing them by the endearing appellations of sons and brethren, he deplored the public and private wrongs of the republic. The subjects of a monarch were persuaded that they fought in the cause of freedom ; and a similar enthusiasm was communicated to the foreign mercenaries, who must have viewed with equal indifference the interest of Rome and of Persia. Heraclius himself, with the skill and patience of a centurion, inculcated the lessons of the school of tactics, and the soldiers were assiduously trained in the use of their weapons, and the exercises and evolutions of the field. The cavalry and infantry in light or heavy armor were divided into two parties ; the trumpets were fixed in the centre, and their signals directed the march, the charge, the retreat or pursuit ; the direct or oblique

order, the deep or extended phalanx ; to represent in fictitious
combat the operations of genuine war. Whatever hardships the
emperor imposed on the troops, he inflicted with equal severity on
himself ; their labor, their diet, their sleep, were measured by
the inflexible rules of discipline ; and, without despising the
enemy, they were taught to repose an implicit confidence in their
own valor and the wisdom of their leader. Cilicia was soon
encompassed with the Persian arms ; but their cavalry hesitated
to enter the defiles of Mount Taurus, till they were circumvented
by the evolutions of Heraclius, who insensibly gained their rear,
whilst he appeared to present his front in order of battle. By a
false motion, which seemed to threaten Armenia, he drew them,
against their wishes, to a general action. They were tempted by
the artful disorder of his camp ; but when they advanced to combat, the ground, the sun, and the expectation of both armies,
were unpropitious to the barbarians ; the Romans successfully
repeated their tactics in a field of battle,[81] and the event of the
day declared to the world, that the Persians were not invincible,
and that a hero was invested with the purple. Strong in victory
and fame, Heraclius boldly ascended the heights of Mount Taurus,
directed his march through the plains of Cappadocia, and established his troops, for the winter season, in safe and plentiful
quarters on the banks of the River Halys.[82] His soul was superior
to the vanity of entertaining Constantinople with an imperfect
triumph ; but the presence of the emperor was indispensably
required to soothe the restless and rapacious spirit of the Avars.

Since the days of Scipio and Hannibal, no bolder enterprise has
been attempted than that which Heraclius achieved for the deliverance of the empire.[83] He permitted the Persians to oppress for a
while the provinces, and to insult with impunity the capital of
the East ; while the Roman emperor explored his perilous way
through the Black Sea,[84] and the mountains of Armenia, penetrated into the heart of Persia,[85] and recalled the armies of the
great king to the defence of their bleeding country. With a select
band of five thousand soldiers, Heraclius sailed from Constantinople to Trebizond ; assembled his forces which had wintered in
the Pontic regions ; and, from the mouth of the Phasis to the
Caspian Sea, encouraged his subjects and allies to march with the
successor of Constantine under the faithful and victorious banner
of the cross. When the legions of Lucullus and Pompey first
passed the Euphrates, they blushed at their easy victory over the
natives of Armenia. But the long experience of war had hardened
the minds and bodies of that effeminate people ; their zeal and
bravery were approved in the service of a declining empire ;

they abhorred and feared the usurpation of the house of Sassan, and the memory of persecution envenomed their pious hatred of the enemies of Christ. The limits of Armenia, as it had been ceded to the emperor Maurice, extended as far as the Araxes: the river submitted to the indignity of a bridge,[66] and Heraclius, in the footsteps of Mark Antony, advanced towards the city of Tauris or Gandzaca,[87] the ancient and modern capital of one of the provinces of Media. At the head of forty thousand men, Chosroes himself had returned from some distant expedition to oppose the progress of the Roman arms; but he retreated on the approach of Heraclius, declining the generous alternative of peace or of battle. Instead of half a million of inhabitants, which have been ascribed to Tauris under the reign of the Sophys, the city contained no more than three thousand houses; but the value of the royal treasures was enhanced by a tradition, that they were the spoils of Croesus, which had been transported by Cyrus from the citadel of Sardes. The rapid conquests of Heraclius were suspended only by the winter season; a motive of prudence, or superstition,[88] determined his retreat into the province of Albania, along the shores of the Caspian; and his tents were most probably pitched in the plains of Mogan,[89] the favorite encampment of Oriental princes. In the course of this successful inroad, he signalized the zeal and revenge of a Christian emperor: at his command, the soldiers extinguished the fire, and destroyed the temples, of the Magi; the statues of Chosroes, who aspired to divine honors, were abandoned to the flames; and the ruins of Thebarma or Ormia,[90] which had given birth to Zoroaster himself, made some atonement for the injuries of the holy sepulchre. A purer spirit of religion was shown in the relief and deliverance of fifty thousand captives. Heraclius was rewarded by their tears and grateful acclamations; but this wise measure, which spread the fame of his benevolence, diffused the murmurs of the Persians against the pride and obstinacy of their own sovereign.

Amidst the glories of the succeeding campaign, Heraclius is almost lost to our eyes, and to those of the Byzantine historians.[91] From the spacious and fruitful plains of Albania, the emperor appears to follow the chain of Hyrcanian Mountains, to descend into the province of Media or Irak, and to carry his victorious arms as far as the royal cities of Casbin and Ispahan, which had never been approached by a Roman conqueror. Alarmed by the danger of his kingdom, the powers of Chosroes were already recalled from the Nile and the Bosphorus, and three formidable armies surrounded, in a distant and hostile land, the camp of the emperor. The Colchian allies prepared to desert his standard;

and the fears of the bravest veterans were expressed, rather than concealed, by their desponding silence. " Be not terrified," said the intrepid Heraclius, " by the multitude of your foes. With the aid of Heaven, one Roman may triumph over a thousand barbarians. But if we devote our lives for the salvation of our brethren, we shall obtain the crown of martyrdom, and our immortal reward will be liberally paid by God and posterity." These magnanimous sentiments were supported by the vigor of his actions. He repelled the threefold attack of the Persians, improved the divisions of their chiefs, and, by a well-concerted train of marches, retreats, and successful actions, finally chased them from the field into the fortified cities of Media and Assyria. In the severity of the winter season, Sarbaraza deemed himself secure in the walls of Salban : he was surprised by the activity of Heraclius, who divided his troops, and performed a laborious march in the silence of the night. The flat roofs of the houses were defended with useless valor against the darts and torches of the Romans : the satraps and nobles of Persia, with their wives and children, and the flower of their martial youth, were either slain or made prisoners. The general escaped by a precipitate flight, but his golden armor was the prize of the conqueror ; and the soldiers of Heraclius enjoyed the wealth and repose which they had so nobly deserved. On the return of spring, the emperor traversed in seven days the mountains of Curdistan, and passed without resistance the rapid stream of the Tigris. Oppressed by the weight of their spoils and captives, the Roman army halted under the walls of Amida ; and Heraclius informed the senate of Constantinople of his safety and success, which they had already felt by the retreat of the besiegers. The bridges of the Euphrates were destroyed by the Persians ; but as soon as the emperor had discovered a ford, they hastily retired to defend the banks of the Sarus,[92] in Cilicia. That river, an impetuous torrent, was about three hundred feet broad ; the bridge was fortified with strong turrets ; and the banks were lined with barbarian archers. After a bloody conflict, which continued till the evening, the Romans prevailed in the assault ; and a Persian of gigantic size was slain and thrown into the Sarus by the hand of the emperor himself. The enemies were dispersed and dismayed ; Heraclius pursued his march to Sebaste in Cappadocia ; and at the expiration of three years, the same coast of the Euxine applauded his return from a long and victorious expedition.[93]

Instead of skirmishing on the frontier, the two monarchs who disputed the empire of the East aimed their desperate strokes at the heart of their rival. The military force of Persia was wasted by the marches and combats of twenty years, and many of the veterans, who had survived the perils of the sword and the climate, were still detained in the fortresses of Egypt and Syria. But the revenge and ambition of Chosroes exhausted his kingdom; and the new levies of subjects, strangers, and slaves, were divided into three formidable bodies.[94] The first army of fifty thousand men, illustrious by the ornament and title of the *golden spears*, was destined to march against Heraclius; the second was stationed to prevent his junction with the troops of his brother Theodorus; and the third was commanded to besiege Constantinople, and to second the operations of the chagan, with whom the Persian king had ratified a treaty of alliance and partition. Sarbar, the general of the third army, penetrated through the provinces of Asia to the well-known camp of Chalcedon, and amused himself with the destruction of the sacred and profane buildings of the Asiatic suburbs, while he impatiently waited the arrival of his Scythian friends on the opposite side of the Bosphorus. On the twenty-ninth of June, thirty thousand barbarians, the vanguard of the Avars, forced the long wall, and drove into the capital a promiscuous crowd of peasants, citizens, and soldiers. Fourscore thousand[95] of his native subjects, and of the vassal tribes of Gepidæ, Russians, Bulgarians, and Sclavonians, advanced under the standard of the chagan; a month was spent in marches and negotiations, but the whole city was invested on the thirty-first of July, from the suburbs of Pera and Galata to the Blachernæ and seven towers; and the inhabitants descried with terror the flaming signals of the European and Asiatic shores. In the mean while, the magistrates of Constantinople repeatedly strove to purchase the retreat of the chagan; but their deputies were rejected and insulted; and he suffered the patricians to stand before his throne, while the Persian envoys, in silk robes, were seated by his side. "You see," said the haughty barbarian, "the proofs of my perfect union with the great king; and his lieutenant is ready to send into my camp a select band of three thousand warriors. Presume no longer to tempt your master with a partial and inadequate ransom: your wealth and your city are the only presents worthy of my acceptance. For yourselves, I shall permit you to depart, each with an undergarment and a shirt; and, at my entreaty, my friend Sarbar will not refuse a passage through his lines. Your absent prince, even now a captive or a fugitive, has left Constantinople to its fate; nor can you escape the arms of the Avars and Persians, unless you could soar into the air like birds, unless like fishes you could dive into the waves."[96] During ten successive days, the capital was assaulted by the Avars, who had made some progress in the science of attack ; they advanced to sap or batter the wall, under the cover of the impenetrable tortoise ; their engines discharged a perpetual volley of stones and darts ; and twelve lofty towers of wood exalted the combatants to the height of the neighboring ramparts.   But the senate and people were animated by the spirit of Heraclius, who had detached to their relief a body of twelve thousand cuirassiers ; the powers of fire and mechanics were used with superior art and success in the defence of Constantinople ; and the galleys, with two and three ranks of oars, commanded the Bosphorus, and rendered the Persians the idle spectators of the defeat of their allies.   The Avars were repulsed ; a fleet of Sclavonian canoes was destroyed in the harbor ; the vassals of the chagan threatened to desert, his provisions were exhausted, and, after burning his engines, he gave the signal of a slow and formidable retreat.   The devotion of the Romans ascribed this signal deliverance to the Virgin Mary ; but the mother of Christ would surely have condemned their inhuman murder of the Persian envoys, who were entitled to the rights of humanity, if they were not protected by the laws of nations.[97]

After the division of his army, Heraclius prudently retired to the banks of the Phasis, from whence he maintained a defensive war against the fifty thousand gold spears of Persia.   His anxiety was relieved by the deliverance of Constantinople ; his hopes were confirmed by a victory of his brother Theodorus ; and to the hostile league of Chosroes with the Avars, the Roman emperor opposed the useful and honorable alliance of the Turks.   At his liberal invitation, the horde of Chozars[98] transported their tents from the plains of the Volga to the mountains of Georgia ; Heraclius received them in the neighborhood of Teflis, and the khan with his nobles dismounted from their horses, if we may credit the Greeks, and fell prostrate on the ground, to adore the purple of the Cæsars.   Such voluntary homage and important aid were entitled to the warmest acknowledgments ; and the emperor, taking off his own diadem, placed it on the head of the Turkish prince, whom he saluted with a tender embrace and the appellation of son.   After a sumptuous banquet, he presented Ziebel with the plate and ornaments, the gold, the gems, and the silk, which had been used at the Imperial table, and, with his own hand, distributed rich jewels and ear-rings to his new allies.   In a secret interview, he produced the portrait of his daughter Eudocia,[99] condescended to flatter the barbarian with the promise of a fair and *august* bride ; obtained an immediate succor of forty thousand horse, and negotiated a strong diversion of the Turkish arms on the side of the Oxus.[100]   The Persians in their turn retreated with precipitation ; in the camp of Edessa, Heraclius reviewed an army of seventy thousand Romans and strangers ; and some months were successfully employed in the recovery of the cities of Syria, Mesopotamia, and Armenia, whose fortifications had been imperfectly restored. Sarbar still maintained the important station of Chalcedon ; but the jealousy of Chosroes, or the artifice of Heraclius, soon alienated the mind of that powerful satrap from the service of his king and country. A messenger was intercepted with a real or fictitious mandate to the cadarigan, or second in command, directing him to send, without delay, to the throne, the head of a guilty or unfortunate general. The despatches were transmitted to Sarbar himself ; and as soon as he read the sentence of his own death, he dexterously inserted the names of four hundred officers, assembled a military council, and asked the *cadarigan* whether he was prepared to execute the commands of their tyrant. The Persians unanimously declared, that Chosroes had forfeited the sceptre ; a separate treaty was concluded with the government of Constantinople ; and if some considerations of honor or policy restrained Sarbar from joining the standard of Heraclius, the emperor was assured that he might prosecute, without interruption, his designs of victory and peace.

Deprived of his firmest support, and doubtful of the fidelity of his subjects, the greatness of Chosroes was still conspicuous in its ruins. The number of five hundred thousand may be interpreted as an Oriental metaphor, to describe the men and arms, the horses and elephants, that covered Media and Assyria against the invasion of Heraclius. Yet the Romans boldly advanced from the Araxes to the Tigris, and the timid prudence of Rhazates was content to follow them by forced marches through a desolate country, till he received a peremptory mandate to risk the fate of Persia in a decisive battle. Eastward of the Tigris, at the end of the bridge of Mosul, the great Nineveh had formerly been erected :[101] the city, and even the ruins of the city, had long since disappeared :[102] the vacant space afforded a spacious field for the operations of the two armies. But these operations are neglected by the Byzantine historians, and, like the authors of epic poetry and romance, they ascribe the victory, not to the military conduct, but to the personal valor, of their favorite hero. On this memorable day, Heraclius, on his horse Phallas, surpassed the bravest of his warriors : his lip was pierced with a spear ; the steed was wounded in the thigh ; but he carried his master safe and victorious through the triple phalanx of the barbarians. In the heat of the action, three valiant chiefs were successively slain by the sword and lance of the emperor : among these was Rhazates himself ; he fell like a soldier, but the sight of his head scattered grief and despair through the fainting ranks of the Persians. His armor of pure and massy gold, the shield of one hundred and twenty plates, the sword and belt, the saddle and cuirass, adorned the triumph of Heraclius ; and if he had not been faithful to Christ, and his mother, the champion of Rome might have offered the fourth *opime* spoils to the Jupiter of the Capitol.[103] In the battle of Nineveh, which was fiercely fought from daybreak to the eleventh hour, twenty-eight standards, besides those which might have been broken or torn, were taken from the Persians ; the greatest part of their army was cut in pieces, and the victors, concealing their own loss, passed the night on the field. They acknowledged, that on this occasion it was less difficult to kill than to discomfit the soldiers of Chosroes ; amidst the bodies of their friends, no more than two bow-shot from the enemy, the remnant of the Persian cavalry stood firm till the seventh hour of the night ; about the eighth hour they retired to their unrifled camp, collected their baggage, and dispersed on all sides, from the want of orders rather than of resolution. The diligence of Heraclius was not less admirable in the use of victory ; by a march of forty-eight miles in four-and-twenty hours, his vanguard occupied the bridges of the great and the lesser Zab ; and the cities and palaces of Assyria were open for the first time to the Romans. By a just gradation of magnificent scenes, they penetrated to the royal seat of Dastagerd,* and, though much of the treasure had been removed, and much had been expended, the remaining wealth appears to have exceeded their hopes, and even to have satiated their avarice. Whatever could not be easily transported, they consumed with fire, that Chosroes might feel the anguish of those wounds which he had so often inflicted on the provinces of the empire : and justice might allow the excuse, if the desolation had been confined to the works of regal luxury, if national hatred, military license, and religious zeal, had not wasted with equal rage the habitations and the temples of the guiltless subject. The recovery of three hundred Roman standards, and the deliverance of the numerous captives of Edessa and Alexandria, reflect a purer glory on the arms of Heraclius. From the palace of Dastagerd, he pursued his march within a few miles of Modain or Ctesiphon, till he was stopped, on the banks of the Arba, by the difficulty of the passage, the rigor of the season, and perhaps the fame of an impregnable

---

* Macdonald Kinneir places Dastagerd at Kasr e Shirin, the palace of Sira on the banks of the Diala, between Holwan and Kanabee. Kinneir Geograph. Mem. p. 306.—M.

capital. The return of the emperor is marked by the modern name of the city of Sherhzour : he fortunately passed Mount Zara, before the snow, which fell incessantly thirty-four days ; and the citizens of Gandzca, or Tauris, were compelled to entertain his soldiers and their horses with a hospitable reception.[104]

When the ambition of Chosroes was reduced to the defence of his hereditary kingdom, the love of glory, or even the sense of shame, should have urged him to meet his rival in the field. In the battle of Nineveh his courage might have taught the Persians to vanquish, or he might have fallen with honor by the lance of a Roman emperor. The successor of Cyrus chose rather, at a secure distance, to expect the event, to assemble the relics of the defeat, and to retire, by measured steps, before the march of Heraclius, till he beheld with a sigh the once loved mansions of Dastagerd. Both his friends and enemies were persuaded, that it was the intention of Chosroes to bury himself under the ruins of the city and palace : and as both might have been equally adverse to his flight, the monarch of Asia, with Sira,* and three concubines, escaped through a hole in the wall nine days before the arrival of the Romans. The slow and stately procession in which he showed himself to the prostrate crowd, was changed to a rapid and secret journey ; and the first evening he lodged in the cottage of a peasant, whose humble door would scarcely give admittance to the great king.[105] His superstition was subdued by fear : on the third day he entered with joy the fortifications of Ctesiphon ; yet he still doubted of his safety till he had opposed the River Tigris to the pursuit of the Romans. The discovery of his flight agitated with terror and tumult, the palace, the city, and the camp of Dastagerd : the satraps hesitated whether they had most to fear from their sovereign or the enemy ; and the females of the harem were astonished and pleased by the sight of mankind, till the jealous husband of three thousand wives again confined them to a more distant castle. At his command the army of Dastagerd retreated to a new camp : the front was covered by the Arba, and a line of two hundred elephants ; the troops of the more distant provinces successively arrived, and the vilest domestics of the king and satraps were enrolled for the last defence of the throne. It was still in the power of Chosroes to obtain a reasonable peace ; and he was repeatedly pressed by the messengers of Heraclius to spare the blood of his subjects, and to relieve a hu-

* The Schirin of Persian poetry. The love of Chosru and Schirin rivals in Persian romance that of Joseph with Zuleika, the wife of Potiphar, of Solomon with the Queen of Sheba, and that of Mejnoun and Leila. The number of Persian poems on the subject may be seen in M. von Hammer's preface to his poem of Schirin.—M.

mane conqueror from the painful duty of carrying fire and sword through the fairest countries of Asia. But the pride of the Persian had not yet sunk to the level of his fortune; he derived a momentary confidence from the retreat of the emperor; he wept with impotent rage over the ruins of his Assyrian palaces, and disregarded too long the rising murmurs of the nation, who complained that their lives and fortunes were sacrificed to the obstinacy of an old man. That unhappy old man was himself tortured with the sharpest pains both of mind and body; and, in the consciousness of his approaching end, he resolved to fix the tiara on the head of Merdaza, the most favored of his sons. But the will of Chosroes was no longer revered, and Siroes,* who gloried in the rank and merit of his mother Sira, had conspired with the malcontents to assert and anticipate the rights of primogeniture.[106] Twenty-two satraps (they styled themselves patriots) were tempted by the wealth and honors of a new reign: to the soldiers, the heir of Chosroes promised an increase of pay; to the Christians the free exercise of their religion; to the captives, liberty and rewards; and to the nation, instant peace and reduction of taxes. It was determined by the conspirators, that Siroes, with the ensigns of royalty, should appear in the camp; and if the enterprise should fail, his escape was contrived to the Imperial court. But the new monarch was saluted with unanimous acclamations; the flight of Chosroes (yet where could he have fled?) was rudely arrested, eighteen sons were massacred† before his face, and he was thrown into a dungeon, where he expired on the fifth day. The Greeks and modern Persians minutely describe how Chosroes was insulted, and famished, and tortured by the command of an inhuman son, who so far surpassed the example of his father: but at the time of his death, what tongue would relate the story of the parricide? what eye could penetrate into the *tower of darkness?* According to the faith and mercy of his Christian enemies, he sunk without hope into a still deeper abyss;[107] and it will not be denied, that tyrants of every age and sect are the best entitled to such infernal abodes. The glory of the house of Sassan ended with the life of Chosroes: his unnatural son enjoyed only eight months the fruit of his crimes: and in the space of four years,

---

* His name was Kabad (as appears from an official letter in the Paschal Chronicle, p. 402). St. Martin considers the name Siroes, Schiroüïeh or Schirwev, derived from the word schir, royal. St. Martin, xi. 153.—M.

† According to Le Beau, this massacre was perpetrated at Mahuza, in Babylonia, not in the presence of Chosroes. The Syrian historian, Thomas of Maraga, gives Chosroes twenty-four sons; Mirkhond (translated by De Sacy), fifteen; the inedited Modjmel-alte-warikh, agreeing with Gibbon, eighteen, with their names. Le Beau and St. Martin, xi. 146.—M.

the regal title was assumed by nine candidates, who disputed, with the sword or dagger, the fragments of an exhausted monarchy. Every province, and each city of Persia, was the scene of independence, of discord, and of blood ; and the state of anarchy prevailed about eight years longer,* till the factions were silenced and united under the common yoke of the Arabian caliphs.[108]

As soon as the mountains became passable, the emperor received the welcome news of the success of the conspiracy, the death of Chosroes, and the elevation of his eldest son to the throne of Persia. The authors of the revolution, eager to display their merits in the court or camp of Tauris, preceded the ambassadors of Siroes, who delivered the letters of their master to his *brother* the emperor of the Romans.[169] In the language of the usurpers of every age, he imputes his own crimes to the Deity, and, without degrading his equal majesty, he offers to reconcile the long discord of the two nations, by a treaty of peace and alliance more durable than brass or iron. The conditions of the treaty were easily defined and faithfully executed. In the recovery of the standards and prisoners which had fallen into the hands of the Persians, the emperor imitated the example of Augustus : their care of the national dignity was celebrated by the poets of the times, but the decay of genius may be measured by the distance between Horace and George of Pisidia : the subjects and brethren of Heraclius were redeemed from persecution, slavery, and exile ; but, instead of the Roman eagles, the true wood of the holy cross was restored to the importunate demands of the successor of Constantine. The victor was not ambitious of enlarging the weakness of the empire ; the son of Chosroes abandoned without regret the conquests of his father ; the Persians who evacuated the cities of Syria and Egypt were honorably conducted to the frontier, and a war which had wounded the vitals of the two monarchies, produced no change in their external and relative situation. The return of Heraclius from Tauris to Constantinople was a perpetual triumph ; and after the exploits of six glorious campaigns, he peaceably enjoyed the Sabbath of his toils. After a long impatience, the senate, the clergy, and the people, went forth to meet their hero, with tears and acclamations, with olive branches and innumerable lamps : he entered the capital in a chariot drawn by four elephants ; and as soon as the emperor could disengage himself from the tumult of public joy, he tasted

---

* Yet Gibbon himself places the flight and death of Yesdegird III., the last king of Persia, in 651. The famous era of Yesdegird dates from his accession, June 16, 632.—M.

more genuine satisfaction in the embraces of his mother and his son.[110]

The succeeding year was illustrated by a triumph of a very different kind, the restitution of the true cross to the holy sepulchre. Heraclius performed in person the pilgrimage of Jerusalem, the identity of the relic was verified by the discreet patriarch,[111] and this august ceremony has been commemorated by the annual festival of the exaltation of the cross. Before the emperor presumed to tread the consecrated ground, he was instructed to strip himself of the diadem and purple, the pomp and vanity of the world : but in the judgment of his clergy, the persecution of the Jews was more easily reconciled with the precepts of the gospel.* He again ascended his throne to receive the congratulations of the ambassadors of France and India : and the fame of Moses, Alexander, and Hercules,[112] was eclipsed, in the popular estimation, by the superior merit and glory of the great Heraclius. Yet the deliverer of the East was indigent and feeble. Of the Persian spoils, the most valuable portion had been expended in the war, distributed to the soldiers, or buried, by an unlucky tempest, in the waves of the Euxine. The conscience of the emperor was oppressed by the obligation of restoring the wealth of the clergy, which he had borrowed for their own defence : a perpetual fund was required to satisfy these inexorable creditors ; the provinces, already wasted by the arms and avarice of the Persians, were compelled to a second payment of the same taxes ; and the arrears of a simple citizen, the treasurer of Damascus, were commuted to a fine of one hundred thousand pieces of gold. The loss of two hundred thousand soldiers[113] who had fallen by the sword, was of less fatal importance than the decay of arts, agriculture, and population, in this long and destructive war : and although a victorious army had been formed under the standard of Heraclius, the unnatural effort appears to have exhausted rather than exercised their strength. While the emperor triumphed at Constantinople or Jerusalem, an obscure town on the confines of Syria was pillaged by the Saracens, and they cut in pieces some troops who advanced to its relief ; an ordinary and trifling occurrence, had it not been the prelude of a mighty revolution. These robbers were

---

* If the clergy imposed upon the kneeling and penitent emperor the persecution of the Jews, it must be acknowledged that provocation was not wanting ; for how many of them had been eye-witnesses of, perhaps sufferers in, the horrible atrocities committed on the capture of the city ! Yet we have no authentic account of great severities exercised by Heraclius. The law of Hadrian was re-enacted, which prohibited the Jews from approaching within three miles of the city—a law which, in the present exasperated state of the Christians, might be a measure of security or mercy, rather than of oppression. Milman, Hist. of Jews, iii. 242.—M.

the apostles of Mahomet ; their fanatic valor had emerged from the desert ; and in the last eight years of his reign, Heraclius lost to the Arabs the same provinces which he had rescued from the Persians.

CHAPTER XLVII.

THEOLOGICAL HISTORY OF THE DOCTRINE OF THE INCARNATION.—THE HUMAN AND DIVINE NATURE OF CHRIST.—ENMITY OF THE PATRIARCHS OF ALEXANDRIA AND CONSTANTINOPLE.—ST. CYRIL AND NESTORIUS.—THIRD GENERAL COUNCIL OF EPHESUS.—HERESY OF EUTYCHES.—FOURTH GENERAL COUNCIL OF CHALCEDON.—CIVIL AND ECCLESIASTICAL DISCORD.—INTOLERANCE OF JUSTINIAN.—THE THREE CHAPTERS.—THE MONOTHELITE CONTROVERSY.—STATE OF THE ORIENTAL SECTS :—I. THE NESTORIANS.—II. THE JACOBITES.—III. THE MARONITES.—IV. THE ARMENIANS.—V. THE COPTS AND ABYSSINIANS.

AFTER the extinction of Paganism, the Christians in peace and piety might have enjoyed their solitary triumph. But the principle of discord was alive in their bosom, and they were more solicitous to explore the nature, than to practise the laws, of their founder. I have already observed that the disputes of the TRINITY were succeeded by those of the INCARNATION ; alike scandalous to the church, alike pernicious to the state, still more minute in their origin, still more durable in their effects. It is my design to comprise in the present chapter a religious war of two hundred and fifty years, to represent the ecclesiastical and political schism of the Oriental sects, and to introduce their clamorous or sanguinary contests, by a modest inquiry into the doctrines of the primitive church.[1]

I. A laudable regard for the honor of the first proselytes has countenanced the belief, the hope, the wish, that the Ebionites, or at least the Nazarenes, were distinguished only by their obstinate perseverance in the practice of the Mosaic rites. Their churches have disappeared, their books are obliterated ; their obscure freedom might allow a latitude of faith, and the softness of their infant creed would be variously moulded by the zeal or prudence of three hundred years. Yet the most charitable criticism must refuse these sectaries any knowledge of the pure and proper divinity of Christ. Educated in the school of Jewish prophecy and prejudice, they had never been taught to elevate their

hopes above a human and temporal Messiah.[2] If they had courage
to hail their king when he appeared in a plebeian garb, their grosser apprehensions were incapable of discerning their God, who had
studiously disguised his cœlestial character under the name and
person of a mortal.[3] The familiar companions of Jesus of Nazareth conversed with their friend and countryman, who, in all the
actions of rational and animal life, appeared of the same species
with themselves. His progress from infancy to youth and manhood was marked by a regular increase in stature and wisdom ;
and after a painful agony of mind and body, he expired on the
cross. He lived and died for the service of mankind : but the
life and death of Socrates had likewise been devoted to the cause
of religion and justice ; and although the stoic or the hero may
disdain the humble virtues of Jesus, the tears which he shed over
his friend and country may be esteemed the purest evidence of his
humanity. The miracles of the gospel could not astonish a people
who held with intrepid faith the more splendid prodigies of the
Mosaic law. The prophets of ancient days had cured diseases,
raised the dead, divided the sea, stopped the sun, and ascended
to heaven in a fiery chariot. And the metaphorical style of the
Hebrews might ascribe to a saint and martyr the adopted title of
Son of God.

Yet in the insufficient creed of the Nazarenes and the Ebionites, a distinction is faintly noticed between the heretics, who
confounded the generation of Christ in the common order of nature, and the less guilty schismatics, who revered the virginity of
his mother, and excluded the aid of an earthly father. The in-
credulity of the former was countenanced by the visible circumstances of his birth, the legal marriage of the reputed parents,
Joseph and Mary, and his lineal claim to the kingdom of David
and the inheritance of Judah. But the secret and authentic history has been recorded in several copies of the Gospel according
to St. Matthew,[4] which these sectaries long preserved in the original Hebrew,[5] as the sole evidence of their faith. The natural
suspicions of the husband, conscious of his own chastity, were
dispelled by the assurance (in a dream) that his wife was pregnant
of the Holy Ghost : and as this distant and domestic prodigy
could not fall under the personal observation of the historian, he
must have listened to the same voice which dictated to Isaiah the
future conception of a virgin. The son of a virgin, generated by
the ineffable operation of the Holy Spirit, was a creature without
example or resemblance, superior in every attribute of mind and
body to the children of Adam. Since the introduction of the
Greek or Chaldean philosophy,[6] the Jews[7] were persuaded of the

pre-existence, transmigration, and immortality of souls ; and providence was justified by a supposition, that they were confined in their earthly prisons to expiate the stains which they had contracted in a former state.[8] But the degrees of purity and corruption are almost immeasurable. It might be fairly presumed that the most sublime and virtuous of human spirits was infused in the offspring of Mary and the Holy Ghost ;[9] that his abasement was the result of his voluntary choice ; and that the object of his mission was to purify, not his own, but the sins of the world. On his return to his native skies, he received the immense reward of his obedience ; the everlasting kingdom of the Messiah, which had been darkly foretold by the prophets, under the carnal images of peace, of conquest, and of dominion. Omnipotence could enlarge the human faculties of Christ to the extent of his cœlestial office. In the language of antiquity, the title of God has not been severely confined to the first parent, and his incomparable minister, his only-begotten Son, might claim, without presumption, the religious, though secondary, worship of a subject world.

II. The seeds of the faith, which had slowly arisen in the rocky and ungrateful soil of Judea, were transplanted, in full maturity, to the happier climes of the Gentiles ; and the strangers of Rome or Asia, who never beheld the manhood, were the more readily disposed to embrace the divinity, of Christ. The polytheist and the philosopher, the Greek and the barbarian, were alike accustomed to conceive a long succession, an infinite chain of angels or dæmons, or deities, or æons, or emanations, issuing from the throne of light. Nor could it seem strange or incredible, that the first of these æons, the *Logos*, or Word of God, of the same substance with the Father, should descend upon earth, to deliver the human race from vice and error, and to conduct them in the paths of life and immortality. But the prevailing doctrine of the eternity and inherent pravity of matter infected the primitive churches of the East. Many among the Gentile proselytes refused to believe that a cœlestial spirit, an undivided portion of the first essence, had been personally united with a mass of impure and contaminated flesh ; and, in their zeal for the divinity, they piously abjured the humanity, of Christ. While his blood was still recent on Mount Calvary,[10] the *Docetes*, a numerous and learned sect of Asiatics, invented the *phantastic* system, which was afterwards propagated by the Marcionites, the Manichæans, and the various names of the Gnostic heresy.[11] They denied the truth and authenticity of the Gospels, as far as they relate the conception of Mary, the birth of Christ, and the thirty years that preceded the exercise of his ministry. He first appeared on the banks of the Jordan in the form of perfect manhood ; but it was a form only, and not a substance ; a human figure created by the hand of Omnipotence to imitate the faculties and actions of a man, and to impose a perpetual illusion on the senses of his friends and enemies. Articulate sounds vibrated on the ears of the disciples ; but the image which was impressed on their optic nerve eluded the more stubborn evidence of the touch ; and they enjoyed the spiritual, not the corporeal, presence of the Son of God. The rage of the Jews was idly wasted against an impassive phantom ; and the mystic scenes of the passion and death, the resurrection and ascension, of Christ were represented on the theatre of Jerusalem for the benefit of mankind. If it were urged, that such ideal mimicry, such incessant deception, was unworthy of the God of truth, the Docetes agreed with too many of their orthodox brethren in the justification of pious falsehood. In the system of the Gnostics, the Jehovah of Israel, the Creator of this lower world, was a rebellious, or at least an ignorant, spirit. The Son of God descended upon earth to abolish his temple and his law ; and, for the accomplishment of this salutary end, he dexterously transferred to his own person the hope and prediction of a temporal Messiah.

One of the most subtile disputants of the Manichæan school has pressed the danger and indecency of supposing, that the God of the Christians, in the state of a human fœtus, emerged at the end of nine months from a female womb. The pious horror of his antagonists provoked them to disclaim all sensual circumstances of conception and delivery ; to maintain that the divinity passed through Mary like a sunbeam through a plate of glass ; and to assert that the seal of her virginity remained unbroken even at the moment when she became the mother of Christ. But the rashness of these concessions has encouraged a milder sentiment of those of the Docetes, who taught, not that Christ was a phantom, but that he was clothed with an impassible and incorruptible body. Such, indeed, in the more orthodox system, he has acquired since his resurrection, and such he must have always possessed, if it were capable of pervading, without resistance or injury, the density of intermediate matter. Devoid of its most essential properties, it might be exempt from the attributes and infirmities of the flesh. A fœtus that could increase from an invisible point to its full maturity ; a child that could attain the stature of perfect manhood without deriving any nourishment from the ordinary sources, might continue to exist without repairing a daily waste by a daily supply of external matter. Jesus might share the repasts of his disciples without being subject to the calls of thirst or hunger ; and his virgin purity was never sullied by the involuntary stains of sensual concupiscence. Of a body thus singularly constituted, a question would arise, by what means, and of what materials, it was originally framed ; and our sounder theology is startled by an answer which was not peculiar to the Gnostics, that both the form and the substance proceeded from the divine essence. The idea of pure and absolute spirit is a refinement of modern philosophy : the incorporeal essence, ascribed by the ancients to human souls, cœlestial beings, and even the Deity himself, does not exclude the notion of extended space ; and their imagination was satisfied with a subtile nature of air, or fire, or æther, incomparably more perfect than the grossness of the material world. If we define the place, we must describe the figure, of the Deity. Our experience, perhaps our vanity, represents the powers of reason and virtue under a human form. The Anthropomorphites, who swarmed among the monks of Egypt and the Catholics of Africa, could produce the express declaration of Scripture, that man was made after the image of his Creator.[12] The venerable Serapion, one of the saints of the Nitrian deserts, relinquished, with many a tear, his darling prejudice ; and bewailed, like an infant, his unlucky conversion, which had stolen away his God, and left his mind without any visible object of faith or devotion.[13]

III. Such were the fleeting shadows of the Docetes. A more substantial, though less simple, hypothesis, was contrived by Cerinthus of Asia,[14] who dared to oppose the last of the apostles. Placed on the confines of the Jewish and Gentile world, he labored to reconcile the Gnostic with the Ebionite, by confessing in the same Messiah the supernatural union of a man and a God ; and this mystic doctrine was adopted with many fanciful improvements by Carpocrates, Basilides, and Valentine,[15] the heretics of the Egyptian school. In their eyes, JESUS of Nazareth was a mere mortal, the legitimate son of Joseph and Mary : but he was the best and wisest of the human race, selected as the worthy instrument to restore upon earth the worship of the true and supreme Deity. When he was baptized in the Jordan, the CHRIST, the first of the æons, the Son of God himself, descended on Jesus in the form of a dove, to inhabit his mind, and direct his actions during the allotted period of his ministry. When the Messiah was delivered into the hands of the Jews, the Christ, an immortal and impassible being, forsook his earthly tabernacle, flew back to the *pleroma* or world of spirits, and left the solitary Jesus to suffer, to complain, and to expire. But the justice and generosity of such a desertion are strongly questionable ; and the fate of an innocent martyr, at first impelled, and at length abandoned, by his divine companion, might provoke the pity and indignation of the profane. Their murmurs were variously silenced by the sectaries who espoused and modified the double system of Cerinthus. It was alleged, that when Jesus was nailed to the cross, he was endowed with a miraculous apathy of mind and body, which rendered him insensible of his apparent sufferings. It was affirmed that these momentary, though real, pangs would be abundantly repaid by the temporal reign of a thousand years reserved for the Messiah in his kingdom of the new Jerusalem. It was insinuated, that if he suffered, he deserved to suffer; that human nature is never absolutely perfect; and that the cross and passion might serve to expiate the venial transgressions of the Son of Joseph before his mysterious union with the Son of God.[16]

IV. All those who believe the immateriality of the soul, a specious and noble tenet, must confess, from their present experience, the incomprehensible union of mind and matter. A similar union is not inconsistent with a much higher, or even with the highest, degree of mental faculties; and the incarnation of an æon or archangel, the most perfect of created spirits, does not involve any positive contradiction or absurdity. In the age of religious freedom, which was determined by the council of Nice, the dignity of Christ was measured by private judgment according to the indefinite rule of Scripture, or reason, or tradition. But when his pure and proper divinity had been established on the ruins of Arianism, the faith of the Catholics trembled on the edge of a precipice where it was impossible to recede, dangerous to stand, dreadful to fall; and the manifold inconveniences of their creed were aggravated by the sublime character of their theology. They hesitated to pronounce; that God himself, the second person of an equal and consubstantial trinity, was manifested in the flesh;[17] that a being who pervades the universe, had been confined in the womb of Mary; that his eternal duration had been marked by the days and months, and years of human existence; that the Almighty had been scourged and crucified; that his impassible essence had felt pain and anguish; that his omniscience was not exempt from ignorance; and that the source of life and immortality expired on Mount Calvary. These alarming consequences were affirmed with unblushing simplicity by Apollinaris,[18] bishop of Laodicea, and one of the luminaries of the church. The son of a learned grammarian, he was skilled in all the sciences of Greece; eloquence, erudition, and philosophy, conspicuous in the volumes of Apollinaris, were humbly devoted to the service of religion. The worthy friend of Athanasius, the worthy antagonist of Julian, he bravely wrestled with the Arians and Polytheists, and though he affected the rigor of geometrical demonstration, his commentaries revealed the literal and allegorical sense of the Scriptures. A mystery, which had long floated in the looseness of popular belief, was defined by his perverse diligence in a technical form ; and he first proclaimed the memorable words, " One incarnate nature of Christ," which are still re-echoed with hostile clamors in the churches of Asia, Egypt, and Æthiopia. He taught that the Godhead was united or mingled with the body of a man ; and that the *Logos*, the eternal wisdom, supplied in the flesh the place and office of a human soul. Yet as the profound doctor had been terrified at his own rashness, Apollinaris was heard to mutter some faint accents of excuse and explanation. He acquiesced in the old distinction of the Greek philosophers between the rational and sensitive soul of man ; that he might reserve the *Logos* for intellectual functions, and employ the subordinate human principle in the meaner actions of animal life. With the moderate Docetes, he revered Mary as the spiritual, rather than as the carnal, mother of Christ, whose body either came from heaven, impassible and incorruptible, or was absorbed, and as it were transformed, into the essence of the Deity. The system of Apollinaris was strenuously encountered by the Asiatic and Syrian divines, whose schools are honored by the names of Basil, Gregory, and Chrysostom, and tainted by those of Diodorus, Theodore, and Nestorius. But the person of the aged bishop of Laodicea, his character and dignity, remained inviolate ; and his rivals, since we may not suspect him of the weakness of toleration, were astonished, perhaps, by the novelty of the argument, and diffident of the final sentence of the Catholic church. Her judgment at length inclined in their favor ; the heresy of Apollinaris was condemned, and the separate congregations of his disciples were proscribed by the Imperial laws. But his principles were secretly entertained in the monasteries of Egypt, and his enemies felt the hatred of Theophilus and Cyril, the successive patriarchs of Alexandria.

V. The grovelling Ebionite, and the fantastic Docetes, were rejected and forgotten : the recent zeal against the errors of Apollinaris reduced the Catholics to a seeming agreement with the double nature of Cerinthus. But instead of a temporary and occasional alliance, *they* established, and *we* still embrace, the substantial, indissoluble, and everlasting union of a perfect God with a perfect man, of the second person of the trinity with a reasonable soul and human flesh. In the beginning of the fifth century, the *unity* of the *two natures* was the prevailing doctrine of the

church.   On all sides, it was confessed, that the mode of their co-
existence could neither be represented by our ideas, nor expressed
by our language.   Yet a secret and incurable discord was cherished, between those who were most apprehensive of confounding, and those who were most fearful of separating the divinity,
and the humanity, of Christ.   Impelled by religious frenzy, they
fled with adverse haste from the error which they mutually deemed most destructive of truth and salvation.   On either hand, they
were anxious to guard, they were jealous to defend, the union
and the distinction of the two natures, and to invent such forms
of speech, such symbols of doctrine, as were least susceptible of
doubt or ambiguity.   The poverty of ideas and language tempted
them to ransack art and nature for every possible comparison,
and- each comparison misled their fancy in the explanation of an
incomparable mystery.   In the polemic microscope, an atom is
enlarged to a monster, and each party was skilful to exaggerate
the absurd or impious conclusions that might be extorted from
the principles of their adversaries.   To escape from each other,
they wandered through many a dark and devious thicket, till they
were astonished by the horrid phantoms of Cerinthus and Apollinaris, who guarded the opposite issues of the theological labyrinth.   As soon as they beheld the twilight of sense and heresy,
they started, measured back their steps, and were again involved
in the gloom of impenetrable orthodoxy.   To purge themselves
from the guilt or reproach of damnable error, they disavowed
their consequences, explained their principles, excused their in-
discretions, and unanimously pronounced the sounds of concord and
faith.   Yet a latent and almost invisible spark still lurked among
the embers of controversy : by the breath of prejudice and passion, it was quickly kindled to a mighty flame, and the verbal
disputes [19] of the Oriental sects have shaken the pillars of the
church and state.

The name of CYRIL of Alexandria is famous in controversial
story, and the title of *saint* is a mark that his opinions and his
party have finally prevailed.   In the house of his uncle, the archbishop Theophilus, he imbibed the orthodox lessons of zeal and
dominion, and five years of his youth were profitably spent in the
adjacent monasteries of Nitria.   Under the tuition of the abbot
Serapion, he applied himself to ecclesiastical studies with such indefatigable ardor, that in the course of *one* sleepless night, he
has perused the four Gospels, the Catholic Epistles, and the Epistle
to the Romans.   Origen he detested ; but the writings of Clemens
and Dionysius, of Athanasius and Basil, were continually in his
hands : by the theory and practice of dispute, his faith was con-

firmed and his wit was sharpened ; he extended round his cell the cobwebs of scholastic theology, and meditated the works of allegory and metaphysics, whose remains, in seven verbose folios, now peaceably slumber by the side of their rivals.[20] Cyril prayed and fasted in the desert, but his thoughts (it is the reproach of a friend)[21] were still fixed on the world ; and the call of Theophilus, who summoned him to the tumult of cities and synods, was too readily obeyed by the aspiring hermit. With the approbation of his uncle, he assumed the office, and acquired the fame, of a popular preacher. His comely person adorned the pulpit ; the harmony of his voice resounded in the cathedral ; his friends were stationed to lead or second the applause of the congregation ;[22] and the hasty notes of the scribes preserved his discourses, which, in their effect, though not in their composition, might be compared with those of the Athenian orators. The death of Theophilus expanded and realized the hopes of his nephew. The clergy of Alexandria was divided ; the soldiers and their general supported the claims of the archdeacon ; but a resistless multitude, with voices and with hands, asserted the cause of their favorite ; and after a period of thirty-nine years, Cyril was seated on the throne of Athanasius.[23]

The prize was not unworthy of his ambition. At a distance from the court, and at the head of an immense capital, the patriarch, as he was now styled, of Alexandria, had gradually usurped the state and authority of a civil magistrate. The public and private charities of the city were managed by his discretion ; his voice inflamed or appeased the passions of the multitude ; his commands were blindly obeyed by his numerous and fanatic *parabolani*,[24] familiarized in their daily office with scenes of death ; and the præfects of Egypt were awed or provoked by the temporal power of these Christian pontiffs. Ardent in the prosecution of heresy, Cyril auspiciously opened his reign by oppressing the Novatians, the most innocent and harmless of the sectaries. The interdiction of their religious worship appeared in his eyes a just and meritorious act ; and he confiscated their holy vessels, without apprehending the guilt of sacrilege. The toleration, and even the privileges of the Jews, who had multiplied to the number of forty thousand, were secured by the laws of the Cæsars and Ptolemies, and a long prescription of seven hundred years since the foundation of Alexandria. Without any legal sentence, without any royal mandate, the patriarch, at the dawn of day, led a seditious multitude to the attack of the synagogues. Unarmed and unprepared, the Jews were incapable of resistance ; their houses of prayer were levelled with the ground, and the episcopal warrior, after rewarding his troops with the plunder of their goods, expelled from the city the remnant of the unbelieving nation. Perhaps he might plead the insolence of their prosperity, and their deadly hatred of the Christians, whose blood they had recently shed in a malicious or accidental tumult. Such crimes would have deserved the animadversion of the magistrate ; but in this promiscuous outrage, the innocent were confounded with the guilty, and Alexandria was impoverished by the loss of a wealthy and industrious colony. The zeal of Cyril exposed him to the penalties of the Julian law ; but in a feeble government and a superstitious age, he was secure of impunity and even of praise. Orestes complained ; but his just complaints were too quickly forgotten by the ministers of Theodosius, and too deeply remembered by a priest who affected to pardon, and continued to hate, the præfect of Egypt. As he passed through the streets, his chariot was assaulted by a band of five hundred of the Nitrian monks ; his guards fled from the wild beasts of the desert ; his protestations that he was a Christian and a Catholic were answered by a volley of stones, and the face of Orestes was covered with blood. The loyal citizens of Alexandria hastened to his rescue ; he instantly satisfied his justice and revenge against the monk by whose hand he had been wounded, and Ammonius expired under the rod of the lictor. At the command of Cyril, his body was raised from the ground, and transported, in solemn procession, to the cathedral ; the name of Ammonius was changed to that of Thaumasius the *wonderful ;* his tomb was decorated with the trophies of martyrdom, and the patriarch ascended the pulpit to celebrate the magnanimity of an assassin and a rebel. Such honors might incite the faithful to combat and die under the banners of the saint ; and he soon prompted, or accepted, the sacrifice of a virgin, who professed the religion of the Greeks, and cultivated the friendship of Orestes. Hypatia, the daughter of Theon the mathematician,[25] was initiated in her father's studies ; her learned comments have elucidated the geometry of Apollonius and Diophantus, and she publicly taught, both at Athens and Alexandria, the philosophy of Plato and Aristotle. In the bloom of beauty and in the maturity of wisdom, the modest maid refused her lovers and instructed her disciples ; the persons most illustrious for their rank or merit were impatient to visit the female philosopher ; and Cyril beheld, with a jealous eye, the gorgeous train of horses and slaves who crowded the door of her academy. A rumor was spread among the Christians that the daughter of Theon was the only obstacle to the reconciliation of the præfect and the archbishop ; and that obstacle was speedily removed. On a fatal day, in the holy season of Lent, Hypatia was torn from her chariot, stripped naked, dragged to the church, and inhumanly butchered by the hands of Peter the reader, and a troop of savage and merciless fanatics : her flesh was scraped from her bones with sharp oyster shells, [26] and her quivering limbs were delivered to the flames. The just progress of inquiry and punishment was stopped by seasonable gifts ; but the murder of Hypatia has imprinted an indelible stain on the character and religion of Cyril of Alexandria. [27]

Superstition, perhaps, would more gently expiate the blood of a virgin, than the banishment of a saint ; and Cyril had accompanied his uncle to the iniquitous synod of the Oak. When the memory of Chrysostom was restored and consecrated, the nephew of Theophilus, at the head of a dying faction, still maintained the justice of his sentence ; nor was it till after a tedious delay and an obstinate resistance, that he yielded to the consent of the Catholic world. [28] His enmity to the Byzantine pontiffs [29] was a sense of interest, not a sally of passion : he envied their fortunate station in the sunshine of the Imperial court ; and he dreaded their upstart ambition, which oppressed the metropolitans of Europe and Asia, invaded the provinces of Antioch and Alexandria, and measured their diocese by the limits of the empire. The long moderation of Atticus, the mild usurper of the throne of Chrysostom, suspended the animosities of the Eastern patriarchs ; but Cyril was at length awakened by the exaltation of a rival more worthy of his esteem and hatred. After the short and troubled reign of Sisinnius, bishop of Constantinople, the factions of the clergy and people were appeased by the choice of the emperor, who, on this occasion, consulted the voice of fame, and invited the merit of a stranger. Nestorius, [30] a native of Germanicia, and a monk of Antioch, was recommended by the austerity of his life, and the eloquence of his sermons ; but the first homily which he preached before the devout Theodosius betrayed the acrimony and impatience of his zeal. " Give me, O Cæsar ! " he exclaimed, " give me the earth purged of heretics, and I will give you in exchange the kingdom of heaven. Exterminate with me the heretics ; and with you I will exterminate the Persians." On the fifth day, as if the treaty had been already signed, the patriarch of Constantinople discovered, surprised, and attacked a secret conventicle of the Arians : they preferred death to submission ; the flames that were kindled by their despair, soon spread to the neighboring houses, and the triumph of Nestorius was clouded by the name of *incendiary.* On either side of the Hellespont his episcopal vigor imposed a rigid formulary of faith and discipline ; a chronological error concerning the festival of Easter was punished as an offence against the church and state. Lydia and Caria, Sardes and Miletus, were purified with the blood of the obstinate Quartodecimans; and the edict of the emperor, or rather of the patriarch, enumerates three-and-twenty degrees and denominations in the guilt and punishment of heresy.[31] But the sword of persecution which Nestorius so furiously wielded was soon turned against his own breast. Religion was the pretence; but, in the judgment of a contemporary saint, ambition was the genuine motive of episcopal warfare.[32]

In the Syrian school, Nestorius had been taught to abhor the confusion of the two natures, and nicely to discriminate the humanity of his *master* Christ from the divinity of the *word* Jesus.[33] The Blessed Virgin he revered as the mother of Christ, but his ears were offended with the rash and recent title of mother of God,[34] which had been insensibly adopted since the origin of the Arian controversy. From the pulpit of Constantinople, a friend of the patriarch, and afterwards the patriarch himself, repeatedly preached against the use, or the abuse, of a word[35] unknown to the apostles, unauthorized by the church, and which could only tend to alarm the timorous, to mislead the simple, to amuse the profane, and to justify, by a seeming resemblance, the old genealogy of Olympus.[36] In his calmer moments Nestorius confessed, that it might be tolerated or excused by the union of the two natures, and the communication of their *idioms:*[37] but he was exasperated, by contradiction, to disclaim the worship of a new-born, an infant Deity, to draw his inadequate similes from the conjugal or civil partnerships of life, and to describe the manhood of Christ as the robe, the instrument, the tabernacle of his Godhead. At these blasphemous sounds, the pillars of the sanctuary were shaken. The unsuccessful competitors of Nestorius indulged their pious or personal resentment, the Byzantine clergy were secretly displeased with the intrusion of a stranger: whatever is superstitious or absurd, might claim the protection of the monks; and the people was interested in the glory of their virgin patroness.[38] The sermons of the archbishop, and the service of the altar, were disturbed by seditious clamor; his authority and doctrine were renounced by separate congregations; every wind scattered round the empire the leaves of controversy; and the voice of the combatants on a sonorous theatre re-echoed in the cells of Palestine and Egypt. It was the duty of Cyril to enlighten the zeal and ignorance of his innumerable monks: in the school of Alexandria, he had imbibed and professed the incarnation of one nature; and the successor of Athanasius consulted his pride and ambition, when he rose in arms against another Arius, more formidable and more guilty, on the second throne of the hierarchy. After a short correspondence, in which the rival prelates disguised their hatred in the hollow language of respect and charity, the patriarch of Alexandria denounced to the prince and people, to the East and to the West, the damnable errors of the Byzantine pontiff. From the East, more especially from Antioch, he obtained the ambiguous counsels of toleration and silence, which were addressed to both parties while they favored the cause of Nestorius. But the Vatican received with open arms the messengers of Egypt. The vanity of Celestine was flattered by the appeal ; and the partial version of a monk decided the faith of the pope, who with his Latin clergy was ignorant of the language, the arts, and the theology of the Greeks. At the head of an Italian synod, Celestine weighed the merits of the cause, approved the creed of Cyril, condemned the sentiments and person of Nestorius, degraded the heretic from his episcopal dignity, allowed a respite of ten days for recantation and penance, and delegated to his enemy the execution of this rash and illegal sentence. But the patriarch of Alexandria, whilst he darted the thunders of a god, exposed the errors and passions of a mortal ; and his twelve anathemas [39] still torture the orthodox slaves, who adore the memory of a saint, without forfeiting their allegiance to the synod of Chalcedon. These bold assertions are indelibly tinged with the colors of the Apollinarian heresy ; but the serious, and perhaps the sincere professions of Nestorius have satisfied the wiser and less partial theologians of the present times. [40]

Yet neither the emperor nor the primate of the East were disposed to obey the mandate of an Italian priest ; and a synod of the Catholic, or rather of the Greek church, was unanimously demanded as the sole remedy that could appease or decide this ecclesiastical quarrel. [41] Ephesus, on all sides accessible by sea and land, was chosen for the place, the festival of Pentecost for the day, of the meeting ; a writ of summons was despatched to each metropolitan, and a guard was stationed to protect and confine the fathers till they should settle the mysteries of heaven, and the faith of the earth. Nestorius appeared not as a criminal, but as a judge ; he depended on the weight rather than the number of his prelates, and his sturdy slaves from the baths of Zeuxippus were armed for every service of injury or defence. But his adversary Cyril was more powerful in the weapons both of the flesh and of the spirit. Disobedient to the letter, or at least to the meaning, of the royal summons, he was attended by fifty Egyptian bishops, who expected from their patriarch's nod the inspiration of the Holy Ghost. He had contracted an intimate alliance with

Memnon, bishop of Ephesus. The despotic primate of Asia disposed of the ready succors of thirty or forty episcopal votes : a crowd of peasants, the slaves of the church, was poured into the city to support with blows and clamors a metaphysical argument ; and the people zealously asserted the honor of the Virgin, whose body reposed within the walls of Ephesus.[42] The fleet which had transported Cyril from Alexandria was laden with the riches of Egypt ; and he disembarked a numerous body of mariners, slaves, and fanatics, enlisted with blind obedience under the banner of St. Mark and the mother of God. The fathers, and even the guards, of the council were awed by this martial array ; the adversaries of Cyril and Mary were insulted in the streets, or threatened in their houses ; his eloquence and liberality made a daily increase in the number of his adherents ; and the Egyptian soon computed that he might command the attendance and the voices of two hundred bishops.[43] But the author of the twelve anathemas foresaw and dreaded the opposition of John of Antioch, who, with a small, but respectable, train of metropolitans and divines, was advancing by slow journeys from the distant capital of the East. Impatient of a delay, which he stigmatized as voluntary and culpable,[44] Cyril announced the opening of the synod sixteen days after the festival of Pentecost. Nestorius, who depended on the near approach of his Eastern friends, persisted, like his predecessor Chrysostom, to disclaim the jurisdiction, and to disobey the summons, of his enemies : they hastened his trial, and his accuser presided in the seat of judgment. Sixty-eight bishops, twenty-two of metropolitan rank, defended his cause by a modest and temperate protest : they were excluded from the councils of their brethren. Candidian, in the emperor's name, requested a delay of four days : the profane magistrate was driven with outrage and insult from the assembly of the saints. The whole of this momentous transaction was crowded into the compass of a summer's day : the bishops delivered their separate opinions ; but the uniformity of style reveals the influence or the hand of a master, who has been accused of corrupting the public evidence of their acts and subscriptions.[45] Without a dissenting voice, they recognized in the epistles of Cyril the Nicene creed and the doctrine of the fathers : but the partial extracts from the letters and homilies of Nestorius were interrupted by curses and anathemas : and the heretic was degraded from his episcopal and ecclesiastical dignity. The sentence, maliciously inscribed to the new Judas, was affixed and proclaimed in the streets of Ephesus : the weary prelates, as they issued from the church of the mother of God, were saluted as her champions ;

and her victory was celebrated by the illuminations, the songs, and the tumult of the night.

On the fifth day, the triumph was clouded by the arrival and indignation of the Eastern bishops. In a chamber of the inn, before he had wiped the dust from his shoes, John of Antioch gave audience to Candidian, the Imperial minister; who related his ineffectual efforts to prevent or to annul the hasty violence of the Egyptian. With equal haste and violence, the Oriental synod of fifty bishops degraded Cyril and Memnon from their episcopal honors, condemned, in the twelve anathemas, the purest venom of the Apollinarian heresy, and described the Alexandrian primate as a monster, born and educated for the destruction of the church.[46] *His* throne was distant and inaccessible; but they instantly resolved to bestow on the flock of Ephesus the blessing of a faithful shepherd. By the vigilance of Memnon, the churches were shut against them, and a strong garrison was thrown into the cathedral. The troops, under the command of Candidian, advanced to the assault; the outguards were routed and put to the sword, but the place was impregnable: the besiegers retired; their retreat was pursued by a vigorous sally; they lost their horses, and many of the soldiers were dangerously wounded with clubs and stones. Ephesus, the city of the Virgin, was defiled with rage and clamor, with sedition and blood; the rival synods darted anathemas and excommunications from their spiritual engines; and the court of Theodosius was perplexed by the adverse and contradictory narratives of the Syrian and Egyptian factions. During a busy period of three months, the emperor tried every method, except the most effectual means of indifference and contempt, to reconcile this theological quarrel. He attempted to remove or intimidate the leaders by a common sentence of acquittal or condemnation; he invested his representatives at Ephesus with ample power and military force; he summoned from either party eight chosen deputies to a free and candid conference in the neighborhood of the capital, far from the contagion of popular frenzy. But the Orientals refused to yield, and the Catholics, proud of their numbers and of their Latin allies, rejected all terms of union or toleration. The patience of the meek Theodosius was provoked; and he dissolved in anger this episcopal tumult, which at the distance of thirteen centuries assumes the venerable aspect of the third oecumenical council.[47] "God is my witness," said the pious prince, "that I am not the author of this confusion. His providence will discern and punish the guilty. Return to your provinces, and may your private virtues repair the mischief and scandal of your meeting." They returned to their provinces; but the same passions which had distracted the synod of Ephesus were diffused over the Eastern world. After three obstinate and equal campaigns, John of Antioch and Cyril of Alexandria condescended to explain and embrace : but their seeming reunion must be imputed rather to prudence than to reason, to the mutual lassitude rather than to the Christian charity of the patriarchs.

The Byzantine pontiff had instilled into the royal ear a baleful prejudice against the character and conduct of his Egyptian rival. An epistle of menace and invective,[48] which accompanied the summons, accused him as a busy, insolent, and envious priest, who perplexed the simplicity of the faith, violated the peace of the church and state, and, by his artful and separate addresses to the wife and sister of Theodosius, presumed to suppose, or to scatter, the seeds of discord in the imperial family. At the stern command of his sovereign, Cyril had repaired to Ephesus, where he was resisted, threatened, and confined, by the magistrates in the interest of Nestorius and the Orientals ; who assembled the troops of Lydia and Ionia to suppress the fanatic and disorderly train of the patriarch. Without expecting the royal license, he escaped from his guards, precipitately embarked, deserted the imperfect synod, and retired to his episcopal fortress of safety and independence. But his artful emissaries, both in the court and city, successfully labored to appease the resentment, and to conciliate the favor, of the emperor. The feeble son of Arcadius was alternately swayed by his wife and sister, by the eunuchs and women of the palace : superstition and avarice were their ruling passions ; and the orthodox chiefs were assiduous in their endeavors to alarm the former and to gratify the latter. Constantinople and the suburbs were sanctified with frequent monasteries, and the holy abbots, Dalmatius and Eutyches,[49] had devoted their zeal and fidelity to the cause of Cyril, the worship of Mary, and the unity of Christ. From the first moment of their monastic life, they had never mingled with the world or trod the profane ground of the city. But in this awful moment of the danger of the church, their vow was superseded by a more sublime and indispensable duty. At the head of a long order of monks and hermits, who carried burning tapers in their hands, and chanted litanies to the mother of God, they proceeded from their monasteries to the palace. The people was edified and inflamed by this extraordinary spectacle, and the trembling monarch listened to the prayers and adjurations of the saints, who boldly pronounced, that none could hope for salvation, unless they embraced the person and the creed of the orthodox successor of Athanasius. At the same time, every avenue of the throne was assaulted with gold. Under the decent names of *eulogies* and *benedictions*, the courtiers of both sexes were bribed according to the measure of their power and rapaciousness. But their incessant demands despoiled the sanctuaries of Constantinople and Alexandria ; and the authority of the patriarch was unable to silence the just murmur of his clergy, that a debt of sixty thousand pounds had already been contracted to support the expense of this scandalous corruption.[50] Pulcheria, who relieved her brother from the weight of an empire, was the firmest pillar of orthodoxy ; and so intimate was the alliance between the thunders of the synod and the whispers of the court, that Cyril was assured of success if he could displace one eunuch, and substitute another in the favor of Theodosius. Yet the Egyptian could not boast of a glorious or decisive victory. The emperor, with unaccustomed firmness, adhered to his promise of protecting the innocence of the Oriental bishops ; and Cyril softened his anathemas, and confessed, with ambiguity and reluctance, a twofold nature of Christ, before he was permitted to satiate his revenge against the unfortunate Nestorius.[51]

The rash and obstinate Nestorius, before the end of the synod, was oppressed by Cyril, betrayed by the court, and faintly supported by his Eastern friends. A sentiment of fear or indignation prompted him, while it was yet time, to affect the glory of a voluntary abdication :[52] his wish, or at least his request, was readily granted ; he was conducted with honor from Ephesus to his old monastery of Antioch ; and, after a short pause, his successors, Maximian and Proclus, were acknowledged as the lawful bishops of Constantinople. But in the silence of his cell, the degraded patriarch could no longer resume the innocence and security of a private monk. The past he regretted, he was discontented with the present, and the future he had reason to dread : the Oriental bishops successively disengaged their cause from his unpopular name, and each day decreased the number of the schismatics who revered Nestorius as the confessor of the faith. After a residence at Antioch of four years, the hand of Theodosius subscribed an edict,[53] which ranked him with Simon the magician, proscribed his opinions and followers, condemned his writings to the flames, and banished his person first to Petra, in Arabia, and at length to Oasis, one of the *islands* of the Libyan desert.[54] Secluded from the church and from the world, the exile was still pursued by the rage of bigotry and war. A wandering tribe of the Blemmyes or Nubians invaded his solitary prison : in their retreat they dismissed a crowd of useless captives ; but no sooner had Nestorius reached the banks of the Nile, than he would gladly have escaped from a Roman and orthodox city, to the milder servitude of the savages.

His flight was punished as a new crime : the soul of the patriarch inspired the civil and ecclesiastical powers of Egypt ; the magistrates, the soldiers, the monks, devoutly tortured the enemy of Christ and St. Cyril ; and, as far as the confines of Æthiopia, the heretic was alternately dragged and recalled, till his aged body was broken by the hardships and accidents of these reiterated journeys. Yet his mind was still independent and erect ; the president of Thebais was awed by his pastoral letters ; he survived the Catholic tyrant of Alexandria, and, after sixteen years' banishment, the synod of Chalcedon would perhaps have restored him to the honors, or at least to the communion of the church. The death of Nestorius prevented his obedience to their welcome summons ;[55] and his disease might afford some color to the scandalous report, that his tongue, the organ of blasphemy, had been eaten by the worms. He was buried in a city of Upper Egypt, known by the names of Chemnis or Panopolis, or Akmim ;[56] but the immortal malice of the Jacobites has persevered for ages to cast stones against his sepulchre, and to propagate the foolish tradition, that it was never watered by the rain of heaven, which equally descends on the righteous and the ungodly.[57] Humanity may drop a tear on the fate of Nestorius ; yet justice must observe, that he suffered the persecution which he had approved and inflicted.[58]

The death of the Alexandrian primate, after a reign of thirty-two years, abandoned the Catholics to the intemperance of zeal and the abuse of victory.[59] The *monophysite* doctrine (one incarnate nature) was rigorously preached in the churches of Egypt and the monasteries of the East ; the primitive creed of Apollinarius was protected by the sanctity of Cyril ; and the name of EUTYCHES, his venerable friend, has been applied to the sect most adverse to the Syrian heresy of Nestorius. His rival Eutyches was the abbot, or archimandrite, or superior of three hundred monks, but the opinions of a simple and illiterate recluse might have expired in the cell, where he had slept above seventy years, if the resentment or discretion of Flavian, the Byzantine pontiff, had not exposed the scandal to the eyes of the Christian world. His domestic synod was instantly convened, their proceedings were sullied with clamor and artifice, and the aged heretic was surprised into a seeming confession that Christ had not derived his body from the substance of the Virgin Mary. From their partial decree, Eutyches appealed to a general council ; and his cause was vigorously asserted by his godson Chrysaphius, the reigning eunuch of the palace, and his accomplice Dioscorus, who had succeeded to the throne, the creed, the talents, and the vices, of the nephew of Theophilus. By the special summons of Theodosius, the second synod of Ephesus was judiciously composed of ten metropolitans and ten bishops from each of the six dioceses of the Eastern empire : some exceptions of favor or merit enlarged the number to one hundred and thirty-five ; and the Syrian Barsumas, as the chief and representative of the monks, was invited to sit and vote with the successors of the apostles. But the despotism of the Alexandrian patriarch again oppressed the freedom of debate : the same spiritual and carnal weapons were again drawn from the arsenals of Egypt : the Asiatic veterans, a band of archers, served under the orders of Dioscorus ; and the more formidable monks, whose minds were inaccessible to reason or mercy, besieged the doors of the cathedral. The general, and, as it should seem, the unconstrained voice of the fathers, accepted the faith and even the anathemas of Cyril ; and the heresy of the two natures was formally condemned in the persons and writings of the most learned Orientals. " May those who divide Christ be divided with the sword, may they be hewn in pieces, may they be burned alive !" were the charitable wishes of a Christian synod.[69] The innocence and sanctity of Eutyches were acknowledged without hesitation ; but the prelates, more especially those of Thrace and Asia, were unwilling to depose their patriarch for the use or even the abuse of his lawful jurisdiction. They embraced the knees of Dioscorus, as he stood with a threatening aspect on the footstool of his throne, and conjured him to forgive the offences, and to respect the dignity, of his brother. " Do you mean to raise a sedition ?" exclaimed the relentless tyrant. " Where are the officers ?" At these words a furious multitude of monks and soldiers, with staves, and swords, and chains, burst into the church : the trembling bishops hid themselves behind the altar, or under the benches, and as they were not inspired with the zeal of martyrdom, they successively subscribed a blank paper, which was afterwards filled with the condemnation of the Byzantine pontiff. Flavian was instantly delivered to the wild beasts of this spiritual amphitheatre : the monks were stimulated by the voice and example of Barsumas to avenge the injuries of Christ : it is said that the patriarch of Alexandria reviled, and buffeted, and kicked, and trampled his brother of Constantinople :[61] it is certain, that the victim, before he could reach the place of his exile, expired on the third day of the wounds and bruises which he had received at Ephesus. This second synod has been justly branded as a gang of robbers and assassins ; yet the accusers of Dioscorus would magnify his violence, to alleviate the cowardice and inconstancy of their own behavior.

The faith of Egypt had prevailed : but the vanquished party was supported by the same pope who encountered without fear the hostile rage of Attila and Genseric. The theology of Leo, his famous *tome* or epistle on the mystery of the incarnation, had been disregarded by the synod of Ephesus : his authority, and that of the Latin church, was insulted in his legates, who escaped from slavery and death to relate the melancholy tale of the tyranny of Dioscorus and the martyrdom of Flavian. His provincial synod annulled the irregular proceedings of Ephesus ; but as this step was itself irregular, he solicited the convocation of a general council in the free and orthodox provinces of Italy. From his independent throne, the Roman bishop spoke and acted without danger, as the head of the Christians, and his dictates were obsequiously transcribed by Placidia and her son Valentinian ; who addressed their Eastern colleague to restore the peace and unity of the church. But the pageant of Oriental royalty was moved with equal dexterity by the hand of the eunuch ; and Theodosius could pronounce, without hesitation, that the church was already peaceful and triumphant, and that the recent flame had been extinguished by the just punishment of the Nestorians. Perhaps the Greeks would be still involved in the heresy of the Monophysites, if the emperor's horse had not fortunately stumbled ; Theodosius expired ; his orthodox sister, Pulcheria, with a nominal husband, succeeded to the throne ; Chrysaphius was burnt, Dioscorus was disgraced, the exiles were recalled, and the *tome* of Leo was subscribed by the Oriental bishops. Yet the pope was disappointed in his favorite project of a Latin council : he disdained to preside in the Greek synod, which was speedily assembled at Nice in Bithynia ; his legates required in a peremptory tone the presence of the emperor ; and the weary fathers were transported to Chalcedon under the immediate eye of Marcian and the senate of Constantinople. A quarter of a mile from the Thracian Bosphorus, the church of St. Euphemia was built on the summit of a gentle though lofty ascent : the triple structure was celebrated as a prodigy of art, and the boundless prospect of the land and sea might have raised the mind of a sectary to the contemplation of the God of the universe. Six hundred and thirty bishops were ranged in order in the nave of the church ; but the patriarchs of the East were preceded by the legates, of whom the third was a simple priest ; and the place of honor was reserved for twenty laymen of consular or senatorian rank. The gospel was ostentatiously displayed in the centre, but the rule of faith was defined by the Papal and Imperial ministers, who moderated the thirteen sessions of the council of Chalcedon.[62] Their partial interposition silenced the intemperate shouts and execrations, which degraded the episcopal gravity ; but, on the formal accusation of the legates, Dioscorus was compelled to descend from his throne to the rank of a criminal already condemned in the opinion of his judges. The Orientals, less adverse to Nestorius than to Cyril, accepted the Romans as their deliverers : Thrace, and Pontus, and Asia, were exasperated against the murderer of Flavian, and the new patriarchs of Constantinople and Antioch secured their places by the sacrifice of their benefactor. The bishops of Palestine, Macedonia, and Greece, were attached to the faith of Cyril ; but in the face of the synod, in the heat of the battle, the leaders, with their obsequious train, passed from the right to the left wing, and decided the victory by this seasonable desertion. Of the seventeen suffragans who sailed from Alexandria, four were tempted from their allegiance, and the thirteen, falling prostrate on the ground, implored the mercy of the council, with sighs and tears, and a pathetic declaration, that, if they yielded, they should be massacred, on their return to Egypt, by the indignant people. A tardy repentance was allowed to expiate the guilt or error of the accomplices of Dioscorus : but their sins were accumulated on his head ; he neither asked nor hoped for pardon, and the moderation of those who pleaded for a general amnesty was drowned in the prevailing cry of victory and revenge. To save the reputation of his late adherents, some *personal* offences were skilfully detected ; his rash and illegal excommunication of the pope, and his contumacious refusal (while he was detained a prisoner) to attend the summons of the synod. Witnesses were introduced to prove the special facts of his pride, avarice, and cruelty ; and the fathers heard with abhorrence, that the alms of the church were lavished on the female dancers, that his palace, and even his bath, was open to the prostitutes of Alexandria, and that the infamous Pansophia, or Irene, was publicly entertained as the concubine of the patriarch.[63]

For these scandalous offences, Dioscorus was deposed by the synod, and banished by the emperor ; but the purity of his faith was declared in the presence, and with the tacit approbation, of the fathers. Their prudence supposed rather than pronounced the heresy of Eutyches, who was never summoned before their tribunal ; and they sat silent and abashed, when a bold Monophysite, casting at their feet a volume of Cyril, challenged them to anathematize in his person the doctrine of the saint. If we fairly peruse the acts of Chalcedon as they are recorded by the orthodox party,[64] we shall find that a great majority of the bishops embraced the simple unity of Christ ; and the ambiguous concession that

he was formed OF or FROM two natures, might imply either their
previous existence, or their subsequent confusion, or some dangerous interval between the conception of the man and the assumption
of the God. The Roman theology, more positive and precise, adopted the term most offensive to the ears of the Egyptians, that Christ
existed IN two natures ; and this momentous particle [65] (which the
memory, rather than the understanding, must retain) had almost
produced a schism among the Catholic bishops. The *tome* of Leo
had been respectfully, perhaps sincerely, subscribed ; but they
protested, in two successive debates, that it was neither expedient
nor lawful to transgress the sacred landmarks which had been
fixed at Nice, Constantinople, and Ephesus, according to the rule
of Scripture and tradition. At length they yielded to the importunities of their masters ; but their infallible decree, after it
had been ratified with deliberate votes and vehement acclamations,
was overturned in the next session by the opposition of the legates
and their Oriental friends. It was in vain that a multitude of
episcopal voices repeated in chorus, " The definition of the fathers
is orthodox and immutable ! The heretics are now discovered !
Anathema to the Nestorians ! Let them depart from the synod !
Let them repair to Rome." [66] The legates threatened, the emperor
was absolute, and a committee of eighteen bishops prepared a
new decree, which was imposed on the reluctant assembly. In
the name of the fourth general council, the Christ in one person,
but *in* two natures, was announced to the Catholic world : an
invisible line was drawn between the heresy of Apollinaris and the
faith of St. Cyril ; and the road to paradise, a bridge as sharp as
a razor, was suspended over the abyss by the master hand of the
theological artist. During ten centuries of blindness and servitude,
Europe received her religious opinions from the oracle of the
Vatican ; and the same doctrine, already varnished with the rust
of antiquity, was admitted without dispute into the creed of the
reformers, who disclaimed the supremacy of the Roman pontiff.
The synod of Chalcedon still triumphs in the Protestant churches ;
but the ferment of controversy has subsided, and the most pious
Christians of the present day are ignorant, or careless, of their
own belief concerning the mystery of the incarnation.

Far different was the temper of the Greeks and Egyptians under
the orthodox reigns of Leo and Marcian. Those pious emperors
enforced with arms and edicts the symbol of their faith ; [67] and
it was declared by the conscience or honor of five hundred bishops,
that the decrees of the synod of Chalcedon might be lawfully
supported, even with blood. The Catholics observed with satisfaction, that the same synod was odious both to the Nestorians

and the Monophysites ; [68] but the Nestorians were less angry, or less powerful, and the East was distracted by the obstinate and sanguinary zeal of the Monophysites. Jerusalem was occupied by an army of monks ; in the name of the one incarnate nature, they pillaged, they burnt, they murdered ; the sepulchre of Christ was defiled with blood ; and the gates of the city were guarded in tumultuous rebellion against the troops of the emperor. After the disgrace and exile of Dioscorus, the Egyptians still regretted their spiritual father ; and detested the usurpation of his successor, who was introduced by the fathers of Chalcedon. The throne of Proterius was supported by a guard of two thousand soldiers : he waged a five years' war against the people of Alexandria ; and on the first intelligence of the death of Marcian, he became the victim of their zeal. On the third day before the festival of Easter, the patriarch was besieged in the cathedral, and murdered in the baptistery. The remains of his mangled corpse were delivered to the flames, and his ashes to the wind ; and the deed was inspired by the vision of a pretended angel : an ambitious monk, who, under the name of Timothy the Cat, [69] succeeded to the place and opinion of Dioscorus. This deadly superstition was inflamed, on either side, by the principle and the practice of retaliation : in the pursuit of a metaphysical quarrel, many thousands [70] were slain, and the Christians of every degree were deprived of the substantial enjoyments of social life, and of the invisible gifts of baptism and the holy communion. Perhaps an extravagant fable of the times may conceal an allegorical picture of these fanatics, who tortured each other and themselves. "Under the consulship of Venantius and Celer," says a grave bishop, "the people of Alexandria, and all Egypt, were seized with a strange and diabolical frenzy : great and small, slaves and freedmen, monks and clergy, the natives of the land, who opposed the synod of Chalcedon, lost their speech and reason, barked like dogs, and tore, with their own teeth, the flesh from their hands and arms."

The disorders of thirty years at length produced the famous HENOTICON [72] of the emperor Zeno, which in his reign, and in that of Anastasius, was signed by all the bishops of the East, under the penalty of degradation and exile, if they rejected or infringed this salutary and fundamental law. The clergy may smile or groan at the presumption of a layman who defines the articles of faith ; yet if he stoops to the humiliating task, his mind is less infected by prejudice or interest, and the authority of the magistrate can only be maintained by the concord of the people. It is in ecclesiastical story, that Zeno appears less contemptible ;

and I am not able to discern any Manichæan or Eutychian guilt in
the generous saying of Anastasius, That it was unworthy of an
emperor to persecute the worshippers of Christ and the citizens of
Rome. The Henoticon was most pleasing to the Egyptians; yet
the smallest blemish has not been descried by the jealous, and
even jaundiced eyes of our orthodox schoolmen, and it accurately
represents the Catholic faith of the incarnation, without adopting
or disclaiming the peculiar terms or tenets of the hostile sects. A
solemn anathema is pronounced against Nestorius and Eutyches;
against all heretics by whom Christ is divided, or confounded, or
reduced to a phantom. Without defining the number or the article
of the word *nature*, the pure system of St. Cyril, the faith of Nice,
Constantinople, and Ephesus, is respectfully confirmed; but,
instead of bowing at the name of the fourth council, the subject
is dismissed by the censure of all contrary doctrines, *if* any such
have been taught either elsewhere or at Chalcedon. Under this
ambiguous expression, the friends and the enemies of the last
synod might unite in a silent embrace. The most reasonable
Christians acquiesced in this mode of toleration; but their reason
was feeble and inconstant, and their obedience was despised as
timid and servile by the vehement spirit of their brethren. On a
subject which engrossed the thought and discourses of men, it
was difficult to preserve an exact neutrality; a book, a sermon, a
prayer, rekindled the flame of controversy; and the bonds of
communion were alternately broken and renewed by the private
animosity of the bishops. The space between Nestorius and
Eutyches was filled by a thousand shades of language and opinion;
the *acephali* [73] of Egypt, and the Roman pontiffs, of equal valor,
though of unequal strength, may be found at the two extremities
of the theological scale. The acephali, without a king or a bishop,
were separated above three hundred years from the patriarchs of
Alexandria, who had accepted the communion of Constantinople,
without exacting a formal condemnation of the synod of Chalcedon.
For accepting the communion of Alexandria, without a formal
approbation of the same synod, the patriarchs of Constantinople
were anathematized by the popes. Their inflexible despotism
involved the most orthodox of the Greek churches in this spiritual
contagion, denied or doubted the validity of their sacraments, [74]
and fomented, thirty-five years, the schism of the East and West,
till they finally abolished the memory of four Byzantine
pontiffs, who had dared to oppose the supremacy of St. Peter. [75]
Before that period, the precarious truce of Constantinople and
Egypt had been violated by the zeal of the rival prelates.
Macedonius, who was suspected of the Nestorian heresy, asserted,

in disgrace and exile, the synod of Chalcedon, while the successor of Cyril would have purchased its overthrow with a bribe of two thousand pounds of gold.

In the fever of the times, the sense, or rather the sound of a syllable, was sufficient to disturb the peace of an empire. The TRISAGION [76] (thrice holy), "Holy, holy, holy, Lord God of Hosts !" is supposed, by the Greeks, to be the identical hymn which the angels and cherubim eternally repeat before the throne of God, and which, about the middle of the fifth century, was miraculously revealed to the church of Constantinople. The devotion of Antioch soon added, "who was crucified for us !" and this grateful address, either to Christ alone, or to the whole Trinity, may be justified by the rules of theology, and has been gradually adopted by the Catholics of the East and West. But it had been imagined by a Monophysite bishop ; [77] the gift of an enemy was at first rejected as a dire and dangerous blasphemy, and the rash innovation had nearly cost the emperor Anastasius his throne and his life. [78] The people of Constantinople was devoid of any rational principles of freedom ; but they held, as a lawful cause of rebellion, the color of a livery in the races, or the color of a mystery in the schools. The Trisagion, with and without this obnoxious addition, was chanted in the cathedral by two adverse choirs, and when their lungs were exhausted, they had recourse to the more solid arguments of sticks and stones ; the aggressors were punished by the emperor, and defended by the patriarch ; and the crown and mitre were staked on the event of this momentous quarrel. The streets were instantly crowded with innumerable swarms of men, women, and children ; the legions of monks, in regular array, marched, and shouted, and fought at their head, "Christians ! this is the day of martyrdom : let us not desert our spiritual father ; anathema to the Manichæan tyrant ! he is unworthy to reign." Such was the Catholic cry ; and the galleys of Anastasius lay upon their oars before the palace, till the patriarch had pardoned his penitent, and hushed the waves of the troubled multitude. The triumph of Macedonius was checked by a speedy exile ; but the zeal of his flock was again exasperated by the same question, "Whether one of the Trinity had been crucified ?" On this momentous occasion, the blue and green factions of Constantinople suspended their discord, and the civil and military powers were annihilated in their presence. The keys of the city, and the standards of the guards, were deposited in the forum of Constantine, the principal station and camp of the faithful. Day and night they were incessantly busied either in singing hymns to the honor of their God, or in pillaging and murdering the servants of their prince.   The head of his favorite monk, the friend, as they styled him, of the enemy of the Holy Trinity, was borne aloft on a spear ; and the firebrands, which had been darted against heretical structures, diffused the undistinguishing flames over the most orthodox buildings.   The statues of the emperor were broken, and his person was concealed in a suburb, till, at the end of three days, he dared to implore the mercy of his subjects.   Without his diadem, and in the posture of a suppliant, Anastasius appeared on the throne of the circus.   The Catholics, before his face, rehearsed their genuine Trisagion ; they exulted in the offer, which he proclaimed by the voice of a herald, of abdicating the purple ; they listened to the admonition, that, since *all* could not reign, they should previously agree in the choice of a sovereign ; and they accepted the blood of two unpopular ministers, whom their master, without hesitation, condemned to the lions.   These furious but transient seditions were encouraged by the success of Vitalian, who, with an army of Huns and Bulgarians, for the most part idolaters, declared himself the champion of the Catholic faith.   In this pious rebellion he depopulated Thrace, besieged Constantinople, exterminated sixty-five thousand of his fellow-Christians, till he obtained the recall of the bishops, the satisfaction of the pope, and the establishment of the council of Chalcedon, an orthodox treaty, reluctantly signed by the dying Anastasius, and more faithfully performed by the uncle of Justinian.   And such was the event of the *first* of the religious wars which have been waged in the name, and by the disciples, of the God of peace.[73]

Justinian has been already seen in the various lights of a prince, a conqueror, and a lawgiver : the theologian [83] still remains, and it forms an unfavorable prejudice that his theology should form a very prominent feature of his portrait.   The sovereign sympathized with his subjects in their superstitious reverence for living and departed saints : his Code, and more especially his Novels, confirm and enlarge the privileges of the clergy ; and in every dispute between a monk and a layman, the partial judge was inclined to pronounce, that truth, and innocence, and justice, were always on the side of the church.   In his public and private devotions, the emperor was assiduous and exemplary ; his prayers, vigils, and fasts, displayed the austere penance of a monk ; his fancy was amused by the hope, or belief, of personal inspiration ; he had secured the patronage of the Virgin and St. Michael the archangel ; and his recovery from a dangerous disease was ascribed to the miraculous succor of the holy martyrs Cosmas and Damian.   The capital and the provinces of the East were decorated with the monuments of his religion ; [81] and though the far greater part of these costly structures may be attributed to his taste or ostentation, the zeal of the royal architect was probably quickened by a genuine sense of love and gratitude towards his invisible benefactors. Among the titles of Imperial greatness, the name of *Pious* was most pleasing to his ear ; to promote the temporal and spiritual interest of the church was the serious business of his life ; and the duty of father of his country was often sacrificed to that of defender of the faith. The controversies of the times were congenial to his temper and understanding ; and the theological professors must inwardly deride the diligence of a stranger, who cultivated their art and neglected his own. " What can ye fear," said a bold conspirator to his associates, "from your bigoted tyrant ? Sleepless and unarmed, he sits whole nights in his closet, debating with reverend graybeards, and turning over the pages of ecclesiastical volumes." [82] The fruits of these lucubrations were displayed in many a conference, where Justinian might shine as the loudest and most subtile of the disputants ; in many a sermon, which, under the name of edicts and epistles, proclaimed to the empire the theology of their master. While the barbarians invaded the provinces, while the victorious legions marched under the banners of Belisarius and Narses, the successor of Trajan, unknown to the camp, was content to vanquish at the head of a synod. Had he invited to these synods a disinterested and rational spectator, Justinian might have learned, " *that* religious controversy is the offspring of arrogance and folly ; *that* true piety is most laudably expressed by silence and submission ; *that* man, ignorant of his own nature, should not presume to scrutinize the nature of his God ; and *that* it is sufficient for us to know, that power and benevolence are the perfect attributes of the Deity." [83]

Toleration was not the virtue of the times, and indulgence to rebels has seldom been the virtue of princes. But when the prince descends to the narrow and peevish character of a disputant, he is easily provoked to supply the defect of argument by the plenitude of power, and to chastise without mercy the perverse blindness of those who wilfully shut their eyes against the light of demonstration. The reign of Justinian was a uniform yet various scene of persecution ; and he appears to have surpassed his indolent predecessors, both in the contrivance of his laws and the rigor of their execution. The insufficient term of three months was assigned for the conversion or exile of all heretics ; [84] and if he still connived at their precarious stay, they were deprived, under his iron yoke, not only of the benefits of society, but of the common birthright of men and Christians. At the end of four hundred years, the Montanists of Phrygia [85] still breathed the wild enthusiasm of perfection and prophecy which they had imbibed from their male and female apostles, the special organs of the Paraclete. On the approach of the Catholic priests and soldiers, they grasped with alacrity the crown of martyrdom ; the conventicle and the congregation perished in the flames, but these primitive fanatics were not extinguished three hundred years after the death of their tyrant. Under the protection of the Gothic confederates, the church of the Arians at Constantinople had braved the severity of the laws : their clergy equalled the wealth and magnificence of the senate ; and the gold and silver which were seized by the rapacious hand of Justinian might perhaps be claimed as the spoils of the provinces, and the trophies of the barbarians. A secret remnant of Pagans, who still lurked in the most refined and most rustic conditions of mankind, excited the indignation of the Christians, who were perhaps unwilling that any strangers should be the witnesses of their intestine quarrels. A bishop was named as the inquisitor of the faith, and his diligence soon discovered, in the court and city, the magistrates, lawyers, physicians, and sophists, who still cherished the superstition of the Greeks. They were sternly informed that they must choose without delay between the pleasure of Jupiter or Justinian, and that their aversion to the gospel could no longer be disguised under the scandalous mask of indifference or impiety. The patrician Photius, perhaps, alone was resolved to live and die like his ancestors ; he enfranchised himself with the stroke of a dagger, and left his tyrant the poor consolation of exposing with ignominy the lifeless corpse of the fugitive. His weaker brethren submitted to their earthly monarch, underwent the ceremony of baptism, and labored, by their extraordinary zeal, to erase the suspicion, or to expiate the guilt, of idolatry. The native country of Homer, and the theatre of the Trojan war, still retained the last sparks of his mythology : by the care of the same bishop, seventy thousand Pagans were detected and converted in Asia, Phrygia, Lydia, and Caria ; ninety-six churches were built for the new proselytes ; and linen vestments, Bibles, and liturgies, and vases of gold and silver, were supplied by the pious munificence of Justinian. [86] The Jews, who had been gradually stripped of their immunities, were opposed by a vexatious law, which compelled them to observe the festival of Easter the same day on which it was celebrated by the Christians. [87] And they might complain with the more reason, since the Catholics themselves did not agree with the astronomical calculations of their sovereign : the people of Constantinople delayed the beginning of their Lent a whole week after it had been ordained by authority ; and they had the pleasure of fasting seven days, while meat was exposed for sale by the command of the emperor. The Samaritans of Palestine [88] were a motley race, an ambiguous set, rejected as Jews by the Pagans, by the Jews as schismatics, and by the Christians as idolaters. The abomination of the cross had already been planted on their holy mount of Garizim,[89] but the persecution of Justinian offered only the alternative of baptism or rebellion. They chose the latter : under the standard of a desperate leader, they rose in arms, and retaliated their wrongs on the lives, the property, and the temples, of a defenceless people. The Samaritans were finally subdued by the regular forces of the East : twenty thousand were slain, twenty thousand were sold by the Arabs to the infidels of Persia and India, and the remains of that unhappy nation atoned for the crime of treason by the sin of hypocrisy. It has been computed that one hundred thousand Roman subjects were extirpated in the Samaritan war,[90] which converted the once fruitful province into a desolate and smoking wilderness. But in the creed of Justinian, the guilt of murder could not be applied to the slaughter of unbelievers ; and he piously labored to establish with fire and sword the unity of the Christian faith.[91]

With these sentiments, it was incumbent on him, at least to be always in the right. In the first years of his administration, he signalized his zeal as the disciple and patron of orthodoxy : the reconciliation of the Greeks and Latins established the *tome* of St. Leo as the creed of the emperor and the empire ; the Nestorians and Eutychians were exposed, on either side, to the double edge of persecution ; and the four synods of Nice, Constantinople, Ephesus, and *Chalcedon*, were ratified by the code of a Catholic lawgiver.[92] But while Justinian strove to maintain the uniformity of faith and worship, his wife Theodora, whose vices were not incompatible with devotion, had listened to the Monophysite teachers ; and the open or clandestine enemies of the church revived and multiplied at the smile of their gracious patroness. The capital, the palace, the nuptial bed, were torn by spiritual discord ; yet so doubtful was the sincerity of the royal consorts that their seeming disagreement was imputed by many to a secret and mischievous confederacy against the religion and happiness of their people.[93] The famous dispute of the THREE CHAPTERS,[94] which has filled more volumes than it deserves lines, is deeply marked with this subtile and disingenuous spirit. It was now three hundred years since the body of Origen [95] had been eaten by the worms : his soul, of which he held the pre-existence, was in the hands of its Creator ; but his writings were eagerly perused by the monks of Palestine.

In these writings, the piercing eye of Justinian descried more than ten metaphysical errors; and the primitive doctor, in the company of Pythagoras and Plato, was devoted by the clergy to the *eternity* of hell-fire, which he presumed to deny. Under the cover of this precedent, a treacherous blow was aimed at the council of Chalcedon. The fathers had listened without impatience to the praise of Theodore of Mopsuestia; [96] and their justice or indulgence had restored both Theodoret of Cyrrhus, and Ibas of Edessa, to the communion of the church. But the characters of these Oriental bishops were tainted with the reproach of heresy; the first had been the master, the two others were the friends, of Nestorius: their most suspicious passages were accused under the title of the *three chapters;* and the condemnation of their memory must involve the honor of a synod, whose name was pronounced with sincere or affected reverence by the Catholic world. If these bishops, whether innocent or guilty, were annihilated in the sleep of death, they would not probably be awakened by the clamor which, after a hundred years, was raised over their grave. If they were already in the fangs of the dæmon, their torments could neither be aggravated nor assuaged by human industry. If in the company of saints and angels they enjoyed the rewards of piety, they must have smiled at the idle fury of the theological insects who still crawled on the surface of the earth. The foremost of these insects, the emperor of the Romans, darted his sting, and distilled his venom, perhaps without discerning the true motives of Theodora and her ecclesiastical faction. The victims were no longer subject to his power, and the vehement style of his edicts could only proclaim their damnation, and invite the clergy of the East to join in a full chorus of curses and anathemas. The East, with some hesitation, consented to the voice of her sovereign: the fifth general council, of three patriarchs and one hundred and sixty-five bishops, was held at Constantinople; and the authors, as well as the defenders, of the three chapters were separated from the communion of the saints, and solemnly delivered to the prince of darkness. But the Latin churches were more jealous of the honor of Leo and the synod of Chalcedon: and if they had fought as they usually did under the standard of Rome, they might have prevailed in the cause of reason and humanity. But their chief was a prisoner in the hands of the enemy; the throne of St. Peter, which had been disgraced by the simony, was betrayed by the cowardice of Vigilius, who yielded, after a long and inconsistent struggle, to the despotism of Justinian and the sophistry of the Greeks. His apostasy provoked the indignation of the Latins, and no more than two bishops could be found who would impose their hands on his deacon and successor Pelagius. Yet the perseverance of the popes insensibly transferred to their adversaries the appellation of schismatics ; the Illyrian, African, and Italian churches were oppressed by the civil and ecclesiastical powers, not without some effort of military force ; [97] the distant barbarians transcribed the creed of the Vatican, and, in the period of a century, the schism of the three chapters expired in an obscure angle of the Venetian province. [98] But the religious discontent of the Italians had already prompted the conquests of the Lombards, and the Romans themselves were accustomed to suspect the faith and to detest the government of their Byzantine tyrant.

Justinian was neither steady nor consistent in the nice process of fixing his volatile opinions and those of his subjects. In his youth he was offended by the slightest deviation from the orthodox line ; in his old age he transgressed the measure of temperate heresy, and the Jacobites, not less than the Catholics, were scandalized by his declaration, that the body of Christ was incorruptible, and that his manhood was never subject to any wants and infirmities, the inheritance of our mortal flesh. This *fantastic* opinion was announced in the last edicts of Justinian ; and at the moment of his seasonable departure, the clergy had refused to subscribe, the prince was prepared to persecute, and the people were resolved to suffer or resist. A bishop of Treves, secure beyond the limits of his power, addressed the monarch of the East in the language of authority and affection. "Most gracious Justinian, remember your baptism and your creed. Let not your gray hairs be defiled with heresy. Recall your fathers from exile, and your followers from perdition. You cannot be ignorant that Italy and Gaul, Spain and Africa, already deplore your fall, and anathematize your name. Unless without delay you destroy what you have taught ; unless you exclaim with a loud voice, I have erred, I have sinned, anathema to Nestorius, anathema to Eutyches, you deliver your soul to the same flames in which *they* eternally burn." He died and made no sign. [99] His death restored in some degree the peace of the church, and the reigns of his four successors, Justin, Tiberius, Maurice, and Phocas, are distinguished by a rare, though fortunate, vacancy in the ecclesiastical history of the East. [100]

The faculties of sense and reason are least capable of acting on themselves ; the eye is most inaccessible to the sight, the soul to the thought ; yet we think, and even feel, that *one will*, a sole principle of action, is essential to a rational and conscious being. When Heraclius returned from the Persian war, the orthodox hero consulted his bishops, whether the Christ whom he adored, of one person, but of two natures, was actuated by a single or a double will. They replied in the singular, and the emperor was encouraged to hope that the Jacobites of Egypt and Syria might be reconciled by the profession of a doctrine, most certainly harmless, and most probably true, since it was taught even by the Nestorians themselves.[101] The experiment was tried without effect, and the timid or vehement Catholics condemned even the semblance of a retreat in the presence of a subtle and audacious enemy. The orthodox (the prevailing) party devised new modes of speech and argument and interpretation : to either nature of Christ they speciously applied a proper and distinct energy ; but the difference was no longer visible when they allowed that the human and the divine will were invariably the same.[102] The disease was attended with the customary symptoms : but the Greek clergy, as if satiated with the endless controversy of the incarnation, instilled a healing counsel into the ear of the prince and people. They declared themselves MONOTHELITES (asserters of the unity of will), but they treated the words as new, the questions as superfluous ; and recommended a religious silence as the most agreeable to the prudence and charity of the Gospel. This law of silence was successively imposed by the *ecthesis* or exposition of Heraclius, the *type* or model of his grandson Constans ;[103] and the Imperial edicts were subscribed with alacrity or reluctance by the four patriarchs of Rome, Constantinople, Alexandria, and Antioch. But the bishop and monks of Jerusalem sounded the alarm : in the language, or even in the silence, of the Greeks, the Latin churches detected a latent heresy ; and the obedience of Pope Honorius to the commands of his sovereign was retracted and censured by the bolder ignorance of his successors. They condemned the execrable and abominable heresy of the Monothelites, who revived the errors of Manes, Apollinaris, Eutyches, etc.; they signed the sentence of excommunication on the tomb of St. Peter ; the ink was mingled with the sacramental wine, the blood of Christ ; and no ceremony was omitted that could fill the superstitious mind with horror and affright. As the representative of the Western church, Pope Martin and his Lateran synod anathematized the perfidious and guilty silence of the Greeks : one hundred and five bishops of Italy, for the most part the subjects of Constans, presumed to reprobate his wicked *type*, and the impious *ecthesis* of his grandfather ; and to confound the authors and their adherents with the twenty-one notorious heretics, the apostates from the church, and the organs of the devil. Such an insult, under the tamest reign, could not pass with impunity. Pope Martin ended his days on the inhospitable shore of the Tauric Chersonesus, and his oracle, the abbot Maximus, was inhumanly chastised by the amputation of his tongue and his right hand.[104] But the same invincible spirit survived in their successors ; and the triumph of the Latins avenged their recent defeat, and obliterated the disgrace of the three chapters. The synods of Rome were confirmed by the sixth general council of Constantinople, in the palace and the presence of a new Constantine, a descendant of Heraclius. The royal convert converted the Byzantine pontiff and a majority of the bishops ;[105] the dissenters, with their chief, Macarius of Antioch, were condemned to the spiritual and temporal pains of heresy ; the East condescended to accept the lessons of the West ; and the creed was finally settled, which teaches the Catholics of every age, that two wills or energies are harmonized in the person of Christ. The majesty of the pope and the Roman synod was represented by two priests, one deacon, and three bishops ; but these obscure Latins had neither arms to compel, nor treasures to bribe, nor language to persuade ; and I am ignorant by what arts they could determine the lofty emperor of the Greeks to abjure the catechism of his infancy, and to persecute the religion of his fathers. Perhaps the monks and people of Constantinople[106] were favorable to the Lateran creed, which is indeed the least reasonable of the two : and the suspicion is countenanced by the unnatural moderation of the Greek clergy, who appear in this quarrel to be conscious of their weakness. While the synod debated, a fanatic proposed a more summary decision, by raising a dead man to life : the prelates assisted at the trial ; but the acknowledged failure may serve to indicate that the passions and prejudices of the multitude were not enlisted on the side of the Monothelites. In the next generation, when the son of Constantine was deposed and slain by the disciple of Macarius, they tasted the feast of revenge and dominion : the image or monument of the sixth council was defaced, and the original acts were committed to the flames. But in the second year their patron was cast headlong from the throne, the bishops of the East were released from their occasional conformity, the Roman faith was more firmly replanted by the orthodox successors of Bardanes, and the fine problems of the incarnation were forgotten in the more popular and visible quarrel of the worship of images.[107]

Before the end of the seventh century, the creed of the incarnation, which had been defined at Rome and Constantinople, was uniformly preached in the remote islands of Britain and Ireland ;[108] the same ideas were entertained, or rather the same words were repeated, by all the Christians whose liturgy was performed in the Greek or the Latin tongue. Their numbers and visible splendor bestowed an imperfect claim to the appellation of Catholics ; but

in the East they were marked with the less honorable name of
Melchites, or Royalists ;[109] of men whose faith, instead of resting
on the basis of Scripture, reason, or tradition, had been established, and was still maintained, by the arbitrary power of a temporal monarch. Their adversaries might allege the words of the
fathers of Constantinople, who profess themselves the slaves of
the king ; and they might relate with malicious joy how the decrees of Chalcedon had been inspired and reformed by the emperor
Marcian and his virgin bride. The prevailing faction will naturally inculcate the duty of submission, nor is it less natural that
dissenters should feel and assert the principles of freedom.
Under the rod of persecution, the Nestorians and Monophysites
degenerated into rebels and fugitives ; and the most ancient and
useful allies of Rome were taught to consider the emperor not as
the chief, but as the enemy of the Christians. Language, the leading principle which unites or separates the tribes of mankind,
soon discriminated the sectaries of the East, by a peculiar and
perpetual badge, which abolished the means of intercourse and
the hope of reconciliation. The long dominion of the Greeks,
their colonies, and, above all, their eloquence, had propagated a
language doubtless the most perfect that has been contrived by
the art of man. Yet the body of the people, both in Syria and
Egypt, still persevered in the use of their national idioms ; with
this difference, however, that the Coptic was confined to the rude
and illiterate peasants of the Nile, while the Syriac,[110] from the
mountains of Assyria to the Red Sea, was adapted to the higher
topics of poetry and argument. Armenia and Abyssinia were infected by the speech or learning of the Greeks ; and their barbaric tongues, which have been revived in the studies of modern
Europe, were unintelligible to the inhabitants of the Roman
empire. The Syriac and the Coptic, the Armenian and the Æthiopic, are consecrated in the service of their respective churches ;
and their theology is enriched by domestic versions[111] both of the
Scriptures and of the most popular fathers. After a period of
thirteen hundred and sixty years, the spark of controversy, first
kindled by a sermon of Nestorius, still burns in the bosom of the
East, and the hostile communions still maintain the faith and discipline of their founders. In the most abject state of ignorance,
poverty, and servitude, the Nestorians and Monophysites reject
the spiritual supremacy of Rome, and cherish the toleration of
their Turkish masters, which allows them to anathematize, on
the one hand, St. Cyril and the synod of Ephesus : on the other,
Pope Leo and the council of Chalcedon. The weight which they
cast into the downfall of the Eastern empire demands our notice,

and the reader may be amused with the various prospect of, I. The Nestorians ; II. The Jacobites ;[112] III. The Maronites ; IV. The Armenians ; V. The Copts ; and, VI. The Abyssinians. To the three former the Syriac is common ; but of the latter each is discriminated by the use of a national idiom. Yet the modern natives of Armenia and Abyssinia would be incapable of conversing with their ancestors ; and the Christians of Egypt and Syria, who reject the religion, have adopted the language, of the Arabians. The lapse of time has seconded the sacerdotal arts ; and in the East, as well as in the West, the Deity is addressed in an obsolete tongue, unknown to the majority of the congregation.

I. Both in his native and his episcopal province, the heresy of the unfortunate Nestorius was speedily obliterated. The Oriental bishops, who at Ephesus had resisted to his face the arrogance of Cyril, were mollified by his tardy concessions. The same prelates, or their successors, subscribed, not without a murmur, the decrees of Chalcedon ; the power of the Monophysites reconciled them with the Catholics in the conformity of passion, of interest, and, insensibly, of belief ; and their last reluctant sigh was breathed in the defence of the three chapters. Their dissenting brethren, less moderate, or more sincere, were crushed by the penal laws ; and, as early as the reign of Justinian, it became difficult to find a church of Nestorians within the limits of the Roman empire. Beyond those limits they had discovered a new world, in which they might hope for liberty, and aspire to conquest. In Persia, notwithstanding the resistance of the Magi, Christianity had struck a deep root, and the nations of the East reposed under its salutary shade. The *catholic*, or primate, resided in the capital : in *his* synods, and in *their* dioceses, his metropolitans, bishops, and clergy, represented the pomp and order of a regular hierarchy : they rejoiced in the increase of proselytes, who were converted from the Zendavesta to the Gospel, from the secular to the monastic life ; and their zeal was stimulated by the presence of an artful and formidable enemy. The Persian church had been founded by the missionaries of Syria, and their language, discipline, and doctrine, were closely interwoven with its original frame. The *catholics* were elected and ordained by their own suffragans ; but their filial dependence on the patriarchs of Antioch is attested by the canons of the Oriental church.[113] In the Persian school of Edessa,[114] the rising generations of the faithful imbibed their theological idiom : they studied in the Syriac version the ten thousand volumes of Theodore of Mopsuestia ; and they revered the apostolic faith and holy martyrdom of his disciple Nestorius, whose person and language were equally unknown to the nations beyond the Tigris. The first indelible lesson of Ibas, bishop of Edessa, taught them to execrate the *Egyptians*, who, in the synod of Ephesus, had impiously confounded the two natures of Christ. The flight of the masters and scholars, who were twice expelled from the Athens of Syria, dispersed a crowd of missionaries inflamed by the double zeal of religion and revenge. And the rigid unity of the Monophysites, who, under the reigns of Zeno and Anastasius, had invaded the thrones of the East, provoked their antagonists, in a land of freedom, to avow a moral, rather than a physical, union of the two persons of Christ. Since the first preaching of the Gospel, the Sassanian kings beheld with an eye of suspicion a race of aliens and apostates who had embraced the religion, and who might favor the cause, of the hereditary foes of their country. The royal edicts had often prohibited their dangerous correspondence with the Syrian clergy : the progress of the schism was grateful to the jealous pride of Pezores, and he listened to the eloquence of an artful prelate, who painted Nestorius as the friend of Persia, and urged him to secure the fidelity of his Christian subjects, by granting a just preference to the victims and enemies of the Roman tyrant. The Nestorians composed a large majority of the clergy and people : they were encouraged by the smile, and armed with the sword, of despotism ; yet many of their weaker brethren were startled at the thought of breaking loose from the communion of the Christian world, and the blood of seven thousand seven hundred Monophysites, or Catholics, confirmed the uniformity of faith and discipline in the churches of Persia.[115] Their ecclesiastical institutions are distinguished by a liberal principle of reason, or at least of policy ; the austerity of the cloister was relaxed and gradually forgotten ; houses of charity were endowed for the education of orphans and foundlings ; the law of celibacy, so forcibly recommended to the Greeks and Latins, was disregarded by the Persian clergy ; and the number of the elect was multiplied by the public and reiterated nuptials of the priests, the bishops, and even the patriarch himself. To this standard of natural and religious freedom, myriads of fugitives resorted from all the provinces of the Eastern empire ; the narrow bigotry of Justinian was punished by the emigration of his most industrious subjects ; they transported into Persia the arts both of peace and war : and those who deserved the favor were promoted in the service of a discerning monarch. The arms of Nushirvan, and his fiercer grandson, were assisted, with advice, and money, and troops, by the desperate sectaries who still lurked in their native cities of the East ; their zeal was rewarded with the gift of the Catholic churches ; but when those cities and churches were recovered by Heraclius, their open profession of treason and heresy compelled them to seek a refuge in the realm of their foreign ally. But the seeming tranquillity of the Nestorians was often endangered, and sometimes overthrown. They were involved in the common evils of Oriental despotism ; their enmity to Rome could not always atone for their attachment to the Gospel : and a colony of three hundred thousand Jacobites, the captives of Apamea and Antioch, was permitted to erect a hostile altar in the face of the *catholic*, and in the sunshine of the court. In his last treaty, Justinian introduced some conditions which tended to enlarge and fortify the toleration of Christianity in Persia. The emperor, ignorant of the rights of conscience, was incapable of pity or esteem for the heretics who denied the authority of the holy synods : but he flattered himself that they would gradually perceive the temporal benefits of union with the empire and the church of Rome ; and if he failed in exciting their gratitude, he might hope to provoke the jealousy of their sovereign. In a later age the Lutherans have been burnt at Paris, and protected in Germany, by the superstition and policy of the most Christian king.

The desire of gaining souls for God and subjects for the church has excited in every age the diligence of the Christian priests. From the conquest of Persia, they carried their spiritual arms to the north, the east, and the south ; and the simplicity of the Gospel was fashioned and painted with the colors of the Syriac theology. In the sixth century, according to the report of a Nestorian traveller,[116] Christianity was successfully preached to the Bactrians, the Huns, the Persians, the Indians, the Persarmenians, the Medes, and the Elamites : the Barbaric churches, from the Gulf of Persia to the Caspian Sea, were almost infinite ; and their recent faith was conspicuous in the number and sanctity of their monks and martyrs. The pepper coast of Malabar, and the isles of the ocean, Socotora and Ceylon, were peopled with an increasing multitude of Christians ; and the bishops and clergy of those sequestered regions derived their ordination from the Catholic of Babylon. In a subsequent age the zeal of the Nestorians overleaped the limits which had confined the ambition and curiosity both of the Greeks and Persians. The missionaries of Balch and Samarcand pursued without fear the footsteps of the roving Tartar, and insinuated themselves into the camps of the valleys of Imaus and the banks of the Selinga. They exposed a metaphysical creed to those illiterate shepherds : to those sanguinary warriors they recommended humanity and repose. Yet a khan, whose power they vainly magnified, is said to have received at

their hands the rites of baptism, and even of ordination ; and the
fame of *Prester* or *Presbyter* John [117] has long amused the credulity
of Europe. The royal convert was indulged in the use of a portable altar ; but he despatched an embassy to the patriarch, to inquire how, in the season of Lent, he should abstain from animal
food, and how he might celebrate the Eucharist in a desert that
produced neither corn nor wine. In their progress by sea and
land, the Nestorians entered China by the port of Canton and the
northern residence of Sigan. Unlike the senators of Rome, who
assumed with a smile the characters of priests and augurs, the
mandarins, who affect in public the reason of philosophers, are
devoted in private to every mode of popular superstition. They
cherished and they confounded the gods of Palestine and of
India ; but the propagation of Christianity awakened the jealousy
of the state, and, after a short vicissitude of favor and persecution, the foreign sect expired in ignorance and oblivion. [118] Under
the reign of the caliphs, the Nestorian church was diffused from
China to Jerusalem and Cyprus ; and their numbers, with those
of the Jacobites, were computed to surpass the Greek and Latin
communions. [119] Twenty-five metropolitans or archbishops composed their hierarchy ; but several of these were dispensed, by the
distance and danger of the way, from the duty of personal attendance, on the easy condition that every six years they should testify their faith and obedience to the *catholic* or patriarch of Babylon, a vague appellation which has been successively applied to
the royal seats of Seleucia, Ctesiphon, and Bagdad. These remote branches are long since withered ; and the old patriarchal
trunk [120] is now divided by the *Elijahs* of Mosul, the representatives almost in lineal descent of the genuine and primitive succession ; the *Josephs* of Amida, who are reconciled to the church of
Rome ; [121] and the *Simeons* of Van or Ormia, whose revolt, at the
head of forty thousand families, was promoted in the sixteenth
century by the Sophis of Persia. The number of three hundred
thousand is allowed for the whole body of the Nestorians, who,
under the name of Chaldeans or Assyrians, are confounded
with the most learned or the most powerful nation of Eastern antiquity.

According to the legend of antiquity the Gospel was preached in
India by St. Thomas. [122] At the end of the ninth century, his
shrine, perhaps in the neighborhood of Madras, was devoutly
visited by the ambassadors of Alfred ; and their return with a
cargo of pearls and spices rewarded the zeal of the English monarch, who entertained the largest projects of trade and discovery. [123]
When the Portuguese first opened the navigation of India, the

Christians of St. Thomas had been seated for ages on the coast of Malabar, and the difference of their character and color attested the mixture of a foreign race. In arms, in arts, and possibly in virtue, they excelled the natives of Hindostan ; the husbandmen cultivated the palm-tree, the merchants were enriched by the pepper trade, the soldiers preceded the *nairs* or nobles of Malabar, and their hereditary privileges were respected by the gratitude or the fear of the king of Cochin and the Zamorin himself. They acknowledged a Gentoo sovereign, but they were governed, even in temporal concerns, by the bishop of Angamala. He still asserted his ancient title of metropolitan of India, but his real jurisdiction was exercised in fourteen hundred churches, and he was intrusted with the care of two hundred thousand souls. Their religion would have rendered them the firmest and most cordial allies of the Portuguese ; but the inquisitors soon discerned in the Christians of St. Thomas the unpardonable guilt of heresy and schism. Instead of owning themselves the subjects of the Roman pontiff, the spiritual and temporal monarch of the globe, they adhered, like their ancestors, to the communion of the Nestorian patriarch ; and the bishops whom he ordained at Mosul traversed the dangers of the sea and land to reach their diocese on the coast of Malabar. In their Syriac liturgy the names of Theodore and Nestorius were piously commemorated : they united their adoration of the two persons of Christ ; the title of Mother of God was offensive to their ear, and they measured, with scrupulous avarice, the honors of the Virgin Mary, whom the superstition of the Latins had *almost* exalted to the rank of a goddess. When her image was first presented to the disciples of St. Thomas, they indignantly exclaimed, " We are Christians, not idolaters !" and their simple devotion was content with the veneration of the cross. Their separation from the Western world had left them in ignorance of the improvements, or corruptions, of a thousand years ; and their conformity with the faith and practice of the fifth century would equally disappoint the prejudices of a Papist or a Protestant. It was the first care of the ministers of Rome to intercept all correspondence with the Nestorian patriarch, and several of his bishops expired in the prisons of the holy office. The flock, without a shepherd, was assaulted by the power of the Portuguese, the arts of the Jesuits, and the zeal of Alexis de Menezes, archbishop of Goa, in his personal visitation of the coast of Malabar. The synod of Diamper, at which he presided, consummated the pious work of the reunion ; and rigorously imposed the doctrine and discipline of the Roman church, without forgetting auricular confession, the strongest engine of ecclesiastical torture. The memory of Theodore and Nestorius was condemned, and Malabar was reduced under the dominion of the pope, of the primate, and of the Jesuits who invaded the see of Angamala or Cranganor. Sixty years of servitude and hypocrisy were patiently endured ; but as soon as the Portuguese empire was shaken by the courage and industry of the Dutch, the Nestorians asserted, with vigor and effect, the religion of their fathers. The Jesuits were incapable of defending the power which they had abused ; the arms of forty thousand Christians were pointed against their falling tyrants ; and the Indian archdeacon assumed the character of bishop, till a fresh supply of episcopal gifts and Syriac missionaries could be obtained from the patriarch of Babylon. Since the expulsion of the Portuguese, the Nestorian creed is freely professed on the coast of Malabar. The trading companies of Holland and England are the friends of toleration ; but if oppression be less mortifying than contempt, the Christians of St. Thomas have reason to complain of the cold and silent indifference of their brethren of Europe.[124]

II. The history of the Monophysites is less copious and interesting than that of the Nestorians. Under the reigns of Zeno and Anastasius, their artful leaders surprised the ear of the prince, usurped the thrones of the East, and crushed on its native soil the school of the Syrians. The rule of the Monophysite faith was defined with exquisite discretion by Severus, patriarch of Antioch : he condemned, in the style of the Henoticon, the adverse heresies of Nestorius ; and Eutyches maintained against the latter the reality of the body of Christ, and constrained the Greeks to allow that he was a liar who spoke truth.[125] But the approximation of ideas could not abate the vehemence of passion ; each party was the more astonished that their blind antagonist could dispute on so trifling a difference ; the tyrant of Syria enforced the belief of his creed, and his reign was polluted with the blood of three hundred and fifty monks, who were slain, not perhaps without provocation or resistance, under the walls of Apamea.[126] The successor of Anastasius replanted the orthodox standard in the East ; Severus fled into Egypt ; and his friend, the eloquent Xenaias,[127] who had escaped from the Nestorians of Persia, was suffocated in his exile by the Melchites of Paphlagonia. Fifty-four bishops were swept from their thrones, eight hundred ecclesiastics were cast into prison,[128] and notwithstanding the ambiguous favor of Theodora, the Oriental flocks, deprived of their shepherds, must insensibly have been either famished or poisoned. In this spiritual distress, the expiring faction was revived and united and perpetuated by the labors of a monk ; and the name of James Baradæus [129] has been preserved in the appellation of *Jacobites*, a familiar sound, which may startle the ear of an English reader. From the holy confessors in their prison of Constantinople, he received the powers of bishop of Edessa and apostle of the East, and the ordination of fourscore thousand bishops, priests, and deacons, is derived from the same inexhaustible source. The speed of the zealous missionary was promoted by the fleetest dromedaries of a devout chief of the Arabs ; the doctrine and discipline of the Jacobites were secretly established in the dominions of Justinian ; and each Jacobite was compelled to violate the laws and to hate the Roman legislator. The successors of Severus, while they lurked in convents or villages, while they sheltered their proscribed heads in the caverns of hermits, or the tents of the Saracens, still asserted, as they now assert, their indefeasible right to the title, the rank, and the prerogatives of patriarch of Antioch : under the milder yoke of the infidels, they reside about a league from Merdin, in the pleasant monastery of Zapharan, which they have embellished with cells, aqueducts, and plantations. The secondary, though honorable, place is filled by the *maphrian*, who, in his station at Mosul itself, defies the Nestorian *catholic* with whom he contests the primacy of the East. Under the patriarch and the maphrian, one hundred and fifty archbishops and bishops have been counted in the different ages of the Jacobite church ; but the order of the hierarchy is relaxed or dissolved, and the greater part of their dioceses is confined to the neighborhood of the Euphrates and the Tigris. The cities of Aleppo and Amida, which are often visited by the patriarch, contain some wealthy merchants and industrious mechanics, but the multitude derive their scanty sustenance from their daily labor : and poverty, as well as superstition, may impose their excessive fasts : five annual lents, during which both the clergy and laity abstain not only from flesh or eggs, but even from the taste of wine, of oil, and of fish. Their present numbers are esteemed from fifty to fourscore thousand souls, the remnant of a populous church, which has gradually decreased under the oppression of twelve centuries. Yet in that long period, some strangers of merit have been converted to the Monophysite faith, and a Jew was the father of Abulpharagius, [130] primate of the East, so truly eminent both in his life and death. In his life, he was an elegant writer of the Syriac and Arabic tongues, a poet, physician, and historian, a subtile philosopher, and a moderate divine. In his death his funeral was attended by his rival, the Nestorian patriarch, with a train of Greeks and Armenians, who forgot their disputes and mingled their tears over the grave of an enemy. The sect which was honored by the virtues of Abul-pharagius appears, however, to sink below the level of their Nestorian brethren. The superstition of the Jacobites is more abject, their fasts more rigid,[131] their intestine divisions are more numerous, and their doctors (as far as I can measure the degrees of nonsense) are more remote from the precincts of reason. Something may possibly be allowed for the rigor of the Monophysite theology ; much more for the superior influence of the monastic order. In Syria, in Egypt, in Æthiopia, the Jacobite monks have ever been distinguished by the austerity of their penance and the absurdity of their legends. Alive or dead, they are worshipped as the favorites of the Deity ; the croiser of bishop and patriarch is reserved for their venerable hands ; and they assume the government of men, while they are yet reeking with the habits and prejudices of the cloister.[132]

III. In the style of the Oriental Christians, the Monothelites of every age are described under the appellation of *Maronites*,[133] a name which has been insensibly transferred from a hermit to a monastery, from a monastery to a nation. Maron, a saint or savage of the fifth century, displayed his religious madness in Syria ; the rival cities of Apamea and Emesa disputed his relics, a stately church was erected on his tomb, and six hundred of his disciples united their solitary cells on the banks of the Orontes. In the controversies of the incarnation, they nicely threaded the orthodox line between the sects of Nestorius and Eutyches ; but the unfortunate question of *one will* or operation in the two natures of Christ was generated by their curious leisure. Their proselyte, the emperor Heraclius, was rejected as a Maronite from the walls of Emesa ; he found a refuge in the monastery of his brethren ; and their theological lessons were repaid with the gift of a spacious and wealthy domain. The name and doctrine of this venerable school were propagated among the Greeks and Syrians, and their zeal is expressed by Macarius, patriarch of Antioch, who declared before the synod of Constantinople that, sooner than subscribe the *two wills* of Christ, he would submit to be hewn piecemeal and cast into the sea.[134] A similar or a less cruel mode of persecution soon converted the unresisting subjects of the plain, while the glorious title of *Mardaites*,[135] or rebels, was bravely maintained by the hardy natives of Mount Libanus. John Maron, one of the most learned and popular of the monks, assumed the character of patriarch of Antioch ; his nephew, Abraham, at the head of the Maronites, defended their civil and religious freedom against the tyrants of the East. The son of the orthodox Constantine pursued with pious hatred a people of soldiers, who might have stood the bulwark of his empire against the common foes of Christ and of Rome. An army of Greeks invaded Syria ; the monastery of St. Maron was destroyed with fire ; the bravest chieftains were betrayed and murdered, and twelve thousand of their followers were transplanted to the distant frontiers of Armenia and Thrace. Yet the humble nation of the Maronites had survived the empire of Constantinople, and they still enjoy, under their Turkish masters, a free religion and a mitigated servitude. Their domestic governors are chosen among the ancient nobility ; the patriarch, in his monastery of Canobin, still fancies himself on the throne of Antioch ; nine bishops composed his synod, and one hundred and fifty priests, who retain the liberty of marriage, are intrusted with the care of one hundred thousand souls. Their country extends from the ridge of Mount Libanus to the shores of Tripoli ; and the gradual descent affords, in a narrow space, each variety of soil and climate, from the Holy Cedars, erect under the weight of snow,[136] to the vine, the mulberry, and the olive-trees of the fruitful valley. In the twelfth century, the Maronites, abjuring the Monothelite error, were reconciled to the Latin churches of Antioch and Rome,[137] and the same alliance has been frequently renewed by the ambition of the popes and the distress of the Syrians. But it may reasonably be questioned, whether their union has ever been perfect or sincere ; and the learned Maronites of the college of Rome have vainly labored to absolve their ancestors from the guilt of heresy and schism.[138]

IV. Since the age of Constantine, the ARMENIANS[139] had signalized their attachment to the religion and empire of the Christians.* The disorders of their country, and their ignorance of the Greek tongue, prevented their clergy from assisting at the synod of Chalcedon, and they floated eighty-four years[140] in a state of indifference or suspense, till their vacant faith was finally occupied by the missionaries of Julian of Halicarnassus,[141] who in Egypt, their common exile, had been vanquished by the arguments or the influence of his rival Severus, the Monophysite patriarch of Antioch. The Armenians alone are the pure disciples of Eutyches, an unfortunate parent, who has been renounced by the greater part of his spiritual progeny. They alone persevere in the opinion that the manhood of Christ was created, or existed, without creation, of a divine and incorruptible substance. Their adversaries reproach them with the adoration of a phantom ; and they retort the accusation, by deriding or execrating the blasphemy of the Jacobites, who impute to the Godhead the vile in-

---

* See vol. i. ch. xx. p. 612.—M.

firmities of the flesh, even the natural effects of nutrition and digestion. The religion of Armenia could not derive much glory from the learning or the power of its inhabitants. The royalty expired with the origin of their schism ; and their Christian kings, who arose and fell in the thirteenth century on the confines of Cilicia, were the clients of the Latins and the vassals of the Turkish sultan of Iconium. The helpless nation has seldom been permitted to enjoy the tranquillity of servitude. From the earliest period to the present hour, Armenia has been the theatre of perpetual war : the lands between Tauris and Erivan were dispeopled by the cruel policy of the Sophis ; and myriads of Christian families were transplanted, to perish or to propagate in the distant provinces of Persia. Under the rod of oppression the zeal of the Armenians is fervent and intrepid ; they have often preferred the crown of martyrdom to the white turban of Mahomet ; they devoutly hate the error and idolatry of the Greeks ; and their transient union with the Latins is not less devoid of truth than the thousand bishops, whom their patriarch offered at the feet of the Roman pontiff.[142] The *catholic*, or patriarch, of the Armenians, resides in the monastery of Ekmiasin, three leagues from Erivan. Forty-seven archbishops, each of whom may claim the obedience of four or five suffragans, are consecrated by his hand ; but the far greater part are only titular prelates, who dignify with their presence and service the simplicity of his court. As soon as they have performed the liturgy, they cultivate the garden ; and our bishops will hear with surprise, that the austerity of their life increases in just proportion to the elevation of their rank. In the fourscore thousand towns or villages of his spiritual empire, the patriarch receives a small and voluntary tax from each person above the age of fifteen ; but the annual amount of six hundred thousand crowns is insufficient to supply the incessant demands of charity and tribute. Since the beginning of the last century, the Armenians have obtained a large and lucrative share of the commerce of the East : in their return from Europe, the caravan usually halts in the neighborhood of Erivan, the altars are enriched with the fruits of their patient industry, and the faith of Eutyches is preached in their recent congregations of Barbary and Poland.[143]

V. In the rest of the Roman empire, the despotism of the prince might eradicate or silence the sectaries of an obnoxious creed. But the stubborn temper of the Egyptians maintained their opposition to the synod of Chalcedon, and the policy of Justinian condescended to expect and to seize the opportunity of discord. The Monophysite church of Alexandria[144] was torn by the disputes of the *corruptibles* and *incorruptibles*, and on the death of the patri-arch, the two factions upheld their respective candidates.[145] Gaian was the disciple of Julian, Theodosius had been the pupil of Severus : the claims of the former were supported by the con-sent of the monks and senators, the city and the province ; the latter depended on the priority of his ordination, the favor of the empress Theodora, and the arms of the eunuch Narses, which might have been used in more honorable warfare. The exile of the popular candidate to Carthage and Sardinia inflamed the ferment of Alexandria ; and after a schism of one hundred and seventy years, the *Gaianites* still revered the memory and doctrine of their founder. The strength of numbers and of discipline was tried in a desperate and bloody conflict ; the streets were filled with the dead bodies of citizens and soldiers ; the pious women, ascending the roofs of their houses, showered down every sharp or ponderous utensil on the heads of the enemy ; and the final victory of Narses was owing to the flames, with which he wasted the third capital of the Roman world. But the lieutenant of Jus-tinian had not conquered in the cause of a heretic ; Theodosius himself was speedily, though gently, removed ; and Paul of Tanis, an orthodox monk, was raised to the throne of Athanasius. The powers of government were strained in his support ; he might appoint or displace the dukes and tribunes of Egypt ; the allow-ance of bread, which Diocletian had granted, was suppressed, the churches were shut, and a nation of schismatics was deprived at once of their spiritual and carnal food. In his turn the tyrant was excommunicated by the zeal and revenge of the people : and none except his servile Melchites would salute him as a man, a Christian, or a bishop. Yet such is the blindness of ambition, that, when Paul was expelled on a charge of murder, he solicited, with a bribe of seven hundred pounds of gold, his restoration to the same station of hatred and ignominy. His successor Apolli-naris entered the hostile city in military array, alike qualified for prayer or for battle. His troops, under arms, were distributed through the streets ; the gates of the cathedral were guarded, and a chosen band was stationed in the choir, to defend the per-son of their chief. He stood erect on his throne, and throwing aside the upper garment of a warrior, suddenly appeared before the eyes of the multitude in the robes of patriarch of Alexandria. Astonishment held them mute ; but no sooner had Apollinaris be-gun to read the tome of St. Leo than a volley of curses and invec-tives and stones assaulted the odious minister of the emperor and the synod. A charge was instantly sounded by the successor of the apostles ; the soldiers waded to their knees in blood ; and two hundred thousand Christians are said to have fallen by the sword : an incredible account, even if it be extended from the slaughter of a day to the eighteen years of the reign of Apollinaris. Two succeeding patriarchs, Eulogius,[146] and John,[147] labored in the conversion of heretics, with arms and arguments more worthy of their evangelical profession. The theological knowledge of Eulogius was displayed in many a volume, which magnified the errors of Eutyches and Severus, and attempted to reconcile the ambiguous language of St. Cyril with the orthodox creed of Pope Leo and the fathers of Chalcedon. The bounteous alms of John the eleemosynary were dictated by superstition, or benevolence, or policy. Seven thousand five hundred poor were maintained at his expense ; on his accession, he found eight thousand pounds of gold in the treasury of the church ; he collected ten thousand from the liberality of the faithful ; yet the primate could boast in his testament that he left behind him no more than the third part of the smallest of the silver coins. The churches of Alexandria were delivered to the Catholics, the religion of the Monophysites was proscribed in Egypt, and a law was revived which excluded the natives from the honors and emoluments of the state.

A more important conquest still remained, of the patriarch, the oracle and leader of the Egyptian church. Theodosius had resisted the threats and promises of Justinian with the spirit of an apostle or an enthusiast. "Such," replied the patriarch, "were the offers of the tempter when he showed the kingdoms of the earth. But my soul is far dearer to me than life or dominion. The churches are in the hands of a prince who can kill the body ; but my conscience is my own ; and in exile, poverty, or chains, I will steadfastly adhere to the faith of my holy predecessors, Athanasius, Cyril, and Dioscorus. Anathema to the tome of Leo and the synod of Chalcedon ! Anathema to all who embrace their creed ! Anathema to them now and forevermore ! Naked came I out of my mother's womb, naked shall I descend into the grave. Let those who love God follow me and seek their salvation." After comforting his brethren, he embarked for Constantinople, and sustained, in six successive interviews, the almost irresistible weight of the royal presence. His opinions were favorably entertained in the palace and the city ; the influence of Theodora assured him a safe conduct and honorable dismission ; and he ended his days, though not on the throne, yet in the bosom, of his native country. On the news of his death, Apollinaris indecently feasted the nobles and the clergy ; but his joy was checked by the intelligence of a new election ; and while he enjoyed the wealth of Alexandria, his rivals reigned in the monasteries of

Thebais, and were maintained by the voluntary oblations of the people. A perpetual succession of patriarchs arose from the ashes of Theodosius ; and the Monophysite churches of Syria and Egypt were united by the name of Jacobites and the communion of the faith. But the same faith, which has been confined to a narrow sect of the Syrians, was diffused over the mass of the Egyptian or Coptic nation ; who, almost unanimously, rejected the decrees of the synod of Chalcedon. A thousand years were now elapsed since Egypt had ceased to be a kingdom, since the conquerors of Asia and Europe had trampled on the ready necks of a people, whose ancient wisdom and power ascend beyond the records of history. The conflict of zeal and persecution rekindled some sparks of their national spirit. They abjured, with a foreign heresy, the manners and language of the Greeks : every Melchite, in their eyes, was a stranger, every Jacobite a citizen ; the alliance of marriage, the offices of humanity, were condemned as a deadly sin ; the natives renounced all allegiance to the emperor ; and his orders, at a distance from Alexandria, were obeyed only under the pressure of military force. A generous effort might have redeemed the religion and liberty of Egypt, and her six hundred monasteries might have poured forth their myriads of holy warriors, for whom death should have no terrors, since life had no comfort or delight. But experience has proved the distinction of active and passive courage ; the fanatic who endures without a groan the torture of the rack or the stake, would tremble and fly before the face of an armed enemy. The pusillanimous temper of the Egyptians could only hope for a change of masters ; the arms of Chosroes depopulated the land, yet under his reign the Jacobites enjoyed a short and precarious respite. The victory of Heraclius renewed and aggravated the persecution, and the patriarch again escaped from Alexandria to the desert. In his flight, Benjamin was encouraged by a voice, which bade him expect, at the end of ten years, the aid of a foreign nation, marked, like the Egyptians themselves, with the ancient rite of circumcision. The character of these deliverers, and the nature of the deliverance, will be hereafter explained ; and I shall step over the interval of eleven centuries to observe the present misery of the Jacobites of Egypt. The populous city of Cairo affords a residence, or rather a shelter, for their indigent patriarch, and a remnant of ten bishops ; forty monasteries have survived the inroads of the Arabs ; and the progress of servitude and apostasy has reduced the Coptic nation to the despicable number of twenty-five or thirty thousand families ;[148] a race of illiterate beggars, whose only consolation is derived from the superior wretchedness of the Greek patriarch and his diminutive congregation.[149]

VI. The Coptic patriarch, a rebel to the Cæsars, or a slave to the khalifs, still gloried in the filial obedience of the kings of Nubia and Æthiopia. He repaid their homage by magnifying their greatness ; and it was boldly asserted that they could bring into the field a hundred thousand horse, with an equal number of camels ;[150] that their hand could pour out or restrain the waters of the Nile ;[151] and the peace and plenty of Egypt was obtained, even in this world, by the intercession of the patriarch. In exile at Constantinople, Theodosius recommended to his patroness the conversion of the black nations of Nubia, from the Tropic of Cancer to the confines of Abyssinia.[152] Her design was suspected and emulated by the more orthodox emperor. The rival missionaries, a Melchite and a Jacobite, embarked at the same time ; but the empress, from a motive of love or fear, was more effectually obeyed ; and the Catholic priest was detained by the president of Thebais, while the king of Nubia and his court were hastily baptized in the faith of Dioscorus. The tardy envoy of Justinian was received and dismissed with honor : but when he accused the heresy and treason of the Egyptians, the negro convert was instructed to reply that he would never abandon his brethren, the true believers, to the persecuting ministers of the synod of Chalcedon.[153] During several ages, the bishops of Nubia were named and consecrated by the Jacobite patriarch of Alexandria : as late as the twelfth century, Christianity prevailed ; and some rites, some ruins, are still visible in the savage towns of Sennaar and Dongola.[154] But the Nubians at length executed their threats of returning to the worship of idols ; the climate required the indulgence of polygamy, and they have finally preferred the triumph of the Koran to the abasement of the Cross. A metaphysical religion may appear too refined for the capacity of the negro race : yet a black or a parrot might be taught to repeat the *words* of the Chalcedonian or Monophysite creed.

Christianity was more deeply rooted in the Abyssinian empire ; and, although the correspondence has been sometimes interrupted above seventy or a hundred years, the mother-church of Alexandria retains her colony in a state of perpetual pupilage. Seven bishops once composed the Æthiopic synod : had their number amounted to ten, they might have elected an independent primate ; and one of their kings was ambitious of promoting his brother to the ecclesiastical throne. But the event was foreseen, the increase was denied ; the episcopal office has been gradually confined to the *abuna*,[155] the head and author of the Abyssinian priesthood ; the patriarch supplies each vacancy with an Egyptian monk ; and the character of a stranger appears more venerable in the eyes of the people, less dangerous in those of the monarch. In the sixth century, when the schism of Egypt was confirmed, the rival chiefs, with their patrons, Justinian and Theodora, strove to outstrip each other in the conquest of a remote and independent province. The industry of the empress was again victorious, and the pious Theodora has established in that sequestered church the faith and discipline of the Jacobites.[156] Encompassed on all sides by the enemies of their religion, the Æthiopians slept near a thousand years, forgetful of the world, by whom they were forgotten. They were awakened by the Portuguese, who, turning the southern promontory of Africa, appeared in India and the Red Sea, as if they had descended through the air from a distant planet. In the first moments of their interview, the subjects of Rome and Alexandria observed the resemblance, rather than the difference, of their faith ; and each nation expected the most important benefits from an alliance with their Christian brethren. In their lonely situation, the Æthiopians had almost relapsed into the savage life. Their vessels, which had traded to Ceylon, scarcely presumed to navigate the rivers of Africa ; the ruins of Axume were deserted, the nation was scattered in villages, and the emperor, a pompous name, was content, both in peace and war, with the immovable residence of a camp. Conscious of their own indigence, the Abyssinians had formed the rational project of importing the arts and ingenuity of Europe ; [157] and their ambassadors at Rome and Lisbon were instructed to solicit a colony of smiths, carpenters, tilers, masons, printers, surgeons, and physicians, for the use of their country. But the public danger soon called for the instant and effectual aid of arms and soldiers, to defend an unwarlike people from the barbarians who ravaged the inland country, and the Turks and Arabs who advanced from the sea-coast in more formidable array. Æthiopia was saved by four hundred and fifty Portuguese, who displayed in the field the native valor of Europeans, and the artificial power of the musket and cannon. In a moment of terror, the emperor had promised to reconcile himself and his subjects to the Catholic faith ; a Latin patriarch represented the supremacy of the pope : [158] the empire, enlarged in a tenfold proportion, was supposed to contain more gold than the mines of America ; and the wildest hopes of avarice and zeal were built on the willing submission of the Christians of Africa.

But the vows which pain had extorted were forsworn on the return of health. The Abyssinians still adhered with unshaken

constancy to the Monophysite faith ; their languid belief was inflamed by the exercise of dispute ; they branded the Latins with
the names of Arians and Nestorians, and imputed the adoration of
four gods to those who separated the two natures of Christ. Fre-
mona, a place of worship, or rather of exile, was assigned to the
Jesuit missionaries. Their skill in the liberal and mechanic arts,
their theological learning, and the decency of their manners, inspired a barren esteem ; but they were not endowed with the gift
of miracles,[159] and they vainly solicited a re-enforcement of European troops. The patience and dexterity of forty years at length
obtained a more favorable audience, and two emperors of Abyssinia were persuaded that Rome could insure the temporal and
everlasting happiness of her votaries. The first of these royal
converts lost his crown and his life ; and the rebel army was sanctified by the *abuna*, who hurled an anathema at the apostate, and
absolved his subjects from their oath of fidelity. The fate of
Zadenghel was revenged by the courage and fortune of Susneus,
who ascended the throne under the name of Segued, and more
vigorously prosecuted the pious enterprise of his kinsman. After
the amusement of some unequal combats between the Jesuits and
his illiterate priests, the emperor declared himself a proselyte to
the synod of Chalcedon, presuming that his clergy and people
would embrace without delay the religion of their prince. The
liberty of choice was succeeded by a law, which imposed, under
pain of death, the belief of the two natures of Christ : the Abyssinians were enjoined to work and to play on the Sabbath ; and
Segued, in the face of Europe and Africa, renounced his connection with the Alexandrian church. A Jesuit, Alphonso Mendez,
the Catholic patriarch of Æthiopia, accepted, in the name of
Urban VIII., the homage and abjuration of his penitent. "I confess," said the emperor on his knees, "I confess that the pope is
the vicar of Christ, the successor of St. Peter, and the sovereign
of the world. To him I swear true obedience, and at his feet I
offer my person and kingdom." A similar oath was repeated by
his son, his brother, the clergy, the nobles, and even the ladies of
the court : the Latin patriarch was invested with honors and
wealth ; and his missionaries erected their churches or citadels in
the most convenient stations of the empire. The Jesuits themselves deplore the fatal indiscretion of their chief, who forgot the
mildness of the Gospel and the policy of his order, to introduce
with hasty violence the liturgy of Rome and the inquisition of
Portugal. He condemned the ancient practice of circumcision,
which health, rather than superstition, had first invented in the
climate of Æthiopia.[160] A new baptism, a new ordination, was

inflicted on the natives ; and they trembled with horror when the most holy of the dead were torn from their graves, when the most illustrious of the living were excommunicated by a foreign priest. In the defence of their religion and liberty the Abyssinians rose in arms, with desperate but unsuccessful zeal. Five rebellions were extinguished in the blood of the insurgents : two abunas were slain in battle, whole legions were slaughtered in the field, or suffocated in their caverns ; and neither merit, nor rank, nor sex, could save from an ignominious death the enemies of Rome. But the victorious monarch was finally subdued by the constancy of the nation, of his mother, of his son, and of his most faithful friends. Segued listened to the voice of pity, of reason, perhaps of fear : and his edict of liberty of conscience instantly revealed the tyranny and weakness of the Jesuits. On the death of his father, Basilides expelled the Latin patriarch, and restored to the wishes of the nation the faith and the discipline of Egypt. The Monophysite churches resounded with a song of triumph, " that the sheep of Æthiopia were now delivered from the hyænas of the West ; " and the gates of that solitary realm were forever shut against the arts, the science, and the fanaticism of Europe.[161]

CHAPTER XLVIII.

PLAN OF THE LAST TWO VOLUMES.—SUCCESSION AND CHARACTERS OF THE GREEK EMPERORS OF CONSTANTINOPLE, FROM THE TIME OF HERACLIUS TO THE LATIN CONQUEST.

I HAVE now deduced from Trajan to Constantine, from Constantine to Heraclius, the regular series of the Roman emperors ; and faithfully exposed the prosperous and adverse fortunes of their reigns. Five centuries of the decline and fall of the empire have already elapsed ; but a period of more than eight hundred years still separates me from the term of my labors, the taking of Constantinople by the Turks. Should I persevere in the same course, should I observe the same measure, a prolix and slender thread would be spun through many a volume, nor would the patient reader find an adequate reward of instruction or amusement. At every step, as we sink deeper in the decline and fall of the Eastern empire, the annals of each succeeding reign would impose a more ungrateful and melancholy task. These annals must continue to repeat a tedious and uniform tale of weakness and mis-

ery ; the natural connection of causes and events would be broken
by frequent and hasty transitions, and a minute accumulation of
circumstances must destroy the light and effect of those general
pictures which compose the use and ornament of a remote history.
From the time of Heraclius, the Byzantine theatre is contracted
and darkened : the line of empire, which had been defined by the
laws of Justinian and the arms of Belisarius, recedes on all sides
from our view ; the Roman name, the proper subject of our inquiries, is reduced to a narrow corner of Europe, to the lonely
suburbs of Constantinople ; and the fate of the Greek empire has
been compared to that of the Rhine, which loses itself in the
sands, before its waters can mingle with the ocean. The scale of
dominion is diminished to our view by the distance of time and
place ; nor is the loss of external splendor compensated by the
nobler gifts of virtue and genius. In the last moments of her decay, Constantinople was doubtless more opulent and populous
than Athens at her most flourishing æra, when a scanty sum of
six thousand talents, or twelve hundred thousand pounds sterling, was possessed by twenty-one thousand male citizens of an
adult age. But each of these citizens was a freeman, who dared
to assert the liberty of his thoughts, words, and actions ; whose
person and property were guarded by equal law ; and who exercised his independent vote in the government of the republic.
Their numbers seem to be multiplied by the strong and various
discriminations of character ; under the shield of freedom, on the
wings of emulation and vanity, each Athenian aspired to the level
of the national dignity ; from this commanding eminence some
chosen spirits soared beyond the reach of a vulgar eye ; and the
chances of superior merit in a great and populous kingdom, as the
are proved by experience, would excuse the computation of imaginary millions. The territories of Athens, Sparta, and their allies,
do not exceed a moderate province of France or England ; but
after the trophies of Salamis and Platea, they expand in our
fancy to the gigantic size of Asia, which had been trampled under
the feet of the victorious Greeks. But the subjects of the Byzantine empire, who assume and dishonor the names both of Greeks
and Romans, present a dead uniformity of abject vices, which are
neither softened by the weakness of humanity, nor animated by
the vigor of memorable crimes. The freemen of antiquity might
repeat with generous enthusiasm the sentence of Homer, "that
on the first day of his servitude, the captive is deprived of one
half of his manly virtue." But the poet had only seen the effects
of civil or domestic slavery, nor could he foretell that the second
moiety of manhood must be annihilated by the spiritual despotism

which shackles not only the actions, but even the thoughts, of the prostrate votary. By this double yoke, the Greeks were oppressed under the successors of Heraclius; the tyrant, a law of eternal justice, was degraded by the vices of his subjects; and on the throne, in the camp, in the schools, we search, perhaps with fruitless diligence, the names and characters that may deserve to be rescued from oblivion. Nor are the defects of the subject compensated by the skill and variety of the painters. Of a space of eight hundred years, the four first centuries are overspread with a cloud interrupted by some faint and broken rays of historic light: in the lives of the emperors, from Maurice to Alexius, Basil the Macedonian has alone been the theme of a separate work; and the absence, or loss, or imperfection of contemporary evidence, must be poorly supplied by the doubtful authority of more recent compilers. The four last centuries are exempt from the reproach of penury; and with the Comnenian family, the historic muse of Constantinople again revives, but her apparel is gaudy, her motions are without elegance or grace. A succession of priests, or courtiers, treads in each other's footsteps in the same path of servitude and superstition: their views are narrow, their judgment is feeble or corrupt: and we close the volume of copious barrenness, still ignorant of the causes of events, the characters of the actors, and the manners of the times which they celebrate or deplore. The observation which has been applied to a man may be extended to a whole people, that the energy of the sword is communicated to the pen; and it will be found by experience that the tone of history will rise or fall with the spirit of the age.

From these considerations, I should have abandoned without regret the Greek slaves and their servile historians, had I not reflected that the fate of the Byzantine monarchy is *passively* connected with the most splendid and important revolutions which have changed the state of the world. The space of the lost provinces was immediately replenished with new colonies and rising kingdoms: the active virtues of peace and war deserted from the vanquished to the victorious nations; and it is in their origin and conquests, in their religion and government, that we must explore the causes and effects of the decline and fall of the Eastern empire. Nor will this scope of narrative, the riches and variety of these materials, be incompatible with the unity of design and composition. As, in his daily prayers, the Mussulman of Fez or Delhi still turns his face towards the temple of Mecca, the historian's eye shall be always fixed on the city of Constantinople. The excursive line may embrace the wilds of Arabia and Tartary, but the circle will be ultimately reduced to the decreasing limit of the Roman monarchy.

On this principle I shall now establish the plan of the last two volumes of the present work. The first chapter will contain, in a regular series, the emperors who reigned at Constantinople during a period of six hundred years, from the days of Heraclius to the Latin conquest ; a rapid abstract, which may be supported by a *general* appeal to the order and text of the original historians. In this introduction I shall confine myself to the revolutions of the throne, the succession of families, the personal characters of the Greek princes, the mode of their life and death, the maxims and influence of their domestic government, and the tendency of their reign to accelerate or suspend the downfall of the Eastern empire. Such a chronological review will serve to illustrate the various argument of the subsequent chapters ; and each circumstance of the eventful story of the barbarians will adapt itself in a proper place to the Byzantine annals. The internal state of the empire, and the dangerous heresy of the Paulicians, which shook the East and enlightened the West, will be the subject of two separate chapters ; but these inquiries must be postponed till our further progress shall have opened the view of the world in the ninth and tenth centuries of the Christian æra. . After this foundation of Byzantine history, the following nations will pass before our eyes, and each will occupy the space to which it may be entitled by greatness or merit, or the degree of connection with the Roman world and the present age. I. The FRANKS ; a general appellation which includes all the barbarians of France, Italy, and Germany, who were united by the sword and sceptre of Charlemagne. The persecution of images and their votaries separate Rome and Italy from the Byzantine throne, and prepared the restoration of the Roman empire in the West. II. The ARABS or SARACENS. Three ample chapters will be devoted to this curious and interesting object. In the first, after a picture of the country and its inhabitants, I shall investigate the character of Mahomet ; the character, religion, and success of the prophet. In the second, I shall lead the Arabs to the conquest of Syria, Egypt, and Africa, the provinces of the Roman empire ; nor can I check their victorious career till they have overthrown the monarchies of Persia and Spain. In the third, I shall inquire how Constantinople and Europe were saved by the luxury and arts, the division and decay, of the empire of the caliphs. A single chapter will include, III. The BULGARIANS, IV. HUNGARIANS, and, V. RUSSIANS, who assaulted by sea or by land the provinces and the capital ; but the last of these, so important in their present greatness, will excite some curiosity in their origin and infancy. VI. The NORMANS ; or rather the private adventurers of that warlike people, who founded a powerful kingdom in Apulia and Sicily, shook the throne of Constantinople, displayed the trophies of chivalry, and almost realized the wonders of romance. VII. The LATINS ; the subjects of the pope, the nations of the West who enlisted under the banner of the cross for the recovery or relief of the holy sepulchre. The Greek emperors were terrified and preserved by the myriads of pilgrims who marched to Jerusalem with Godfrey of Bouillon and the peers of Christendom. The second and third crusades trod in the footsteps of the first : Asia and Europe were mingled in a sacred war of two hundred years ; and the Christian powers were bravely resisted, and finally expelled, by Saladin and the Mamelukes of Egypt. In these memorable crusades, a fleet and army of French and Venetians were diverted from Syria to the Thracian Bosphorus : they assaulted the capital, they subverted the Greek monarchy ; and a dynasty of Latin princes was seated near threescore years on the throne of Constantine. VIII. The GREEKS themselves, during this period of captivity and exile, must be considered as a foreign nation ; the enemies, and again the sovereigns of Constantinople. Misfortune had rekindled a spark of national virtue ; and the Imperial series may be continued with some dignity from their restoration to the Turkish conquest. IX. The MOGULS and TARTARS. By the arms of Zingis and his descendants, the globe was shaken from China to Poland and Greece : the sultans were overthrown : the caliphs fell, and the Cæsars trembled on their throne. The victories of Timour suspended above fifty years the final ruin of the Byzantine empire. X. I have already noticed the first appearance of the TURKS ; and the names of the fathers, of *Seljuk* and *Othman*, discriminate the two successive dynasties of the nation, which emerged in the eleventh century from the Scythian wilderness. The former established a potent and splendid kingdom from the banks of the Oxus to Antioch and Nice ; and the first crusade was provoked by the violation of Jerusalem and the danger of Constantinople. From an humble origin the *Ottomans* arose, the scourge and terror of Christendom. Constantinople was besieged and taken by Mahomet II., and his triumph annihilates the remnant, the image, the title, of the Roman empire in the East. The schism of the Greeks will be connected with their last calamities, and the restoration of learning in the Western world. I shall return from the captivity of the new to the ruins of ancient ROME ; and the venerable name, the interesting theme, will shed a ray of glory on the conclusion of my labors.

THE emperor Heraclius had punished a tyrant and ascended his throne ; and the memory of his reign is perpetuated by the transient conquest, and irreparable loss, of the Eastern provinces. After the death of Eudocia, his first wife, he disobeyed the patriarch, and violated the laws, by his second marriage with his niece Martina ; and the superstition of the Greeks beheld the judgment of Heaven in the diseases of the father and the deformity of his offspring. But the opinion of an illegitimate birth is sufficient to distract the choice, and loosen the obedience, of the people : the ambition of Martina was quickened by maternal love, and perhaps by the envy of a step-mother ; and the aged husband was too feeble to withstand the arts of conjugal allurements. Constantine, his eldest son, enjoyed in a mature age the title of Augustus ; but the weakness of his constitution required a colleague and a guardian, and he yielded with secret reluctance to the partition of the empire. The senate was summoned to the palace to ratify or attest the association of Heracleonas, the son of Martina : the imposition of the diadem was consecrated by the prayer and blessing of the patriarch ; the senators and patricians adored the majesty of the great emperor and the partners of his reign ; and as soon as the doors were thrown open, they were hailed by the tumultuary but important voice of the soldiers. After an interval of five months, the pompous ceremonies which formed the essence of the Byzantine state were celebrated in the cathedral and the hippodrome : the concord of the royal brothers was affectedly displayed by the younger leaning on the arm of the elder ; and the name of Martina was mingled in the reluctant or venal acclamations of the people. Heraclius survived this association about two years : his last testimony declared his two sons the equal heirs of the Eastern empire, and commanded them to honor his widow Martina as their mother and their sovereign.

When Martina first appeared on the throne with the name and attributes of royalty, she was checked by a firm, though respectful, opposition ; and the dying embers of freedom were kindled by the breath of superstitious prejudice. " We reverence," exclaimed the voice of a citizen, " we reverence the mother of our princes ; but to those princes alone our obedience is due ; and Constantine, the elder emperor, is of an age to sustain, in his own hands, the weight of the sceptre. Your sex is excluded by nature from the toils of government. How could you combat, how could you answer, the barbarians, who, with hostile or friendly intentions, may approach the royal city ? May Heaven avert from the Roman republic this national disgrace, which would provoke the patience of the slaves of Persia !" Martina descended from the throne with indignation, and sought a refuge in the female apartment of the palace. The reign of Constantine the Third lasted only one hundred and three days : he expired in the thirtieth year of his age, and, although his life had been a long malady, a belief was entertained that poison had been the means, and his cruel step-mother the author of his untimely fate. Martina reaped indeed the harvest of his death, and assumed the government in the name of the surviving emperor ; but the incestuous widow of Heraclius was universally abhorred ; the jealousy of the people was awakened, and the two orphans whom Constantine had left became the objects of the public care. It was in vain that the son of Martina, who was no more than fifteen years of age, was taught to declare himself the guardian of his nephews, one of whom he had presented at the baptismal font : it was in vain that he swore on the wood of the true cross to defend them against all their enemies. On his death-bed, the late emperor had despatched a trusty servant to arm the troops and provinces of the East in the defence of his helpless children : the eloquence and liberality of Valentin had been successful, and from his camp of Chalcedon he boldly demanded the punishment of the assassins, and the restoration of the lawful heir. The license of the soldiers, who devoured the grapes and drank the wine of their Asiatic vineyards, provoked the citizens of Constantinople against the domestic authors of their calamities, and the dome of St. Sophia re-echoed, not with prayers and hymns, but with the clamors and imprecations of an enraged multitude. At their imperious command, Heracleonas appeared in the pulpit with the eldest of the royal orphans ; Constans alone was saluted as emperor of the Romans, and a crown of gold, which had been taken from the tomb of Heraclius, was placed on his head, with the solemn benediction of the patriarch. But in the tumult of joy and indignation, the church was pillaged, the sanctuary was polluted by a promiscuous crowd of Jews and barbarians, and the Monothelite Pyrrhus, a creature of the empress, after dropping a protestation on the altar, escaped by a prudent flight from the zeal of the Catholics. A more serious and bloody task was reserved for the senate, who derived a temporary strength from the consent of the soldiers and people. The spirit of Roman freedom revived the ancient and awful examples of the judgment of tyrants, and the Imperial culprits were deposed and condemned as the authors of the death of Constantine. But the severity of the conscript fathers was stained by the indiscriminate punishment of the innocent and the guilty : Martina and Heracleonas were sentenced to the amputation, the former of her tongue, the latter of his nose ;

and after this cruel execution, they consumed the remainder of their days in exile and oblivion. The Greeks who were capable of reflection might find some consolation for their servitude by observing the abuse of power when it was lodged for a moment in the hands of an aristocracy.

We shall imagine ourselves transported five hundred years backwards to the age of the Antonines, if we listen to the oration which Constans II. pronounced in the twelfth year of his age before the Byzantine senate. After returning his thanks for the just punishment of the assassins, who had intercepted the fairest hopes of his father's reign, "By the divine Providence," said the young emperor, "and by your righteous decree, Martina and her incestuous progeny have been cast headlong from the throne. Your majesty and wisdom have prevented the Roman state from degenerating into lawless tyranny. I therefore exhort and beseech you to stand forth as the counsellors and judges of the common safety." The senators were gratified by the respectful address and liberal donative of their sovereign; but these servile Greeks were unworthy and regardless of freedom; and in his mind, the lesson of an hour was quickly erased by the prejudices of the age and the habits of despotism. He retained only a jealous fear lest the senate or people should one day invade the right of primogeniture, and seat his brother Theodosius on an equal throne. By the imposition of holy orders, the grandson of Heraclius was disqualified for the purple; but this ceremony, which seemed to profane the sacraments of the church, was insufficient to appease the suspicions of the tyrant, and the death of the deacon Theodosius could alone expiate the crime of his royal birth.* His murder was avenged by the imprecations of the people, and the assassin, in the fulness of power, was driven from his capital into voluntary and perpetual exile. Constans embarked for Greece; and, as if he meant to retort the abhorrence which he deserved, he is said, from the Imperial galley, to have spit against the walls of his native city. After passing the winter at Athens, he sailed to Tarentum in Italy, visited Rome,† and concluded a long pilgrimage of disgrace and sacrilegious rapine, by fixing his residence at Syracuse. But if Constans could fly from his people, he could not fly from himself. The remorse of his conscience created a phantom who pursued him by land and sea, by day and by night; and

---

* His soldiers (according to Abulfaradji. Chron. Syr. p. 112) called him another Cain. St. Martin, t. xi. p. 379.—M.

† He was received in Rome, and pillaged the churches. He carried off the brass roof of the Pantheon to Syracuse, or, as Schlosser conceives, to Constantinople. Schlosser, Geschichte der bilder-stürmenden. Kaiser, p. 80.—M.

the visionary Theodosius, presenting to his lips a cup of blood, said, or seemed to say, "Drink, brother, drink," a sure emblem of the aggravation of his guilt, since he had received from the hands of the deacon the mystic cup of the blood of Christ. Odious to himself and to mankind, Constans perished by domestic, perhaps by episcopal, treason, in the capital of Sicily. A servant who waited in the bath, after pouring warm water on his head, struck him violently with the vase. He fell, stunned by the blow, and suffocated by the water; and his attendants, who wondered at the tedious delay, beheld with indifference the corpse of their lifeless emperor. The troops of Sicily invested with the purple an obscure youth, whose inimitable beauty eluded, and it might easily elude, the declining art of the painters and sculptors of the age.

Constans had left in the Byzantine palace three sons, the eldest of whom had been clothed in his infancy with the purple. When the father summoned them to attend his person in Sicily, these precious hostages were detained by the Greeks, and a firm refusal informed him that they were the children of the state. The news of his murder was conveyed with almost supernatural speed from Syracuse to Constantinople; and Constantine, the eldest of his sons, inherited his throne without being the heir of the public hatred. His subjects contributed, with zeal and alacrity, to chastise the guilt and presumption of a province which had usurped the rights of the senate and people; the young emperor sailed from the Hellespont with a powerful fleet; and the legions of Rome and Carthage were assembled under his standard in the harbor of Syracuse. The defeat of the Sicilian tyrant was easy, his punishment just, and his beauteous head was exposed in the hippodrome: but I cannot applaud the clemency of a prince, who, among a crowd of victims, condemned the son of a patrician, for deploring with some bitterness the execution of a virtuous father. The youth was castrated: he survived the operation, and the memory of this indecent cruelty is preserved by the elevation of Germanus to the rank of a patriarch and saint. After pouring this bloody libation on his father's tomb, Constantine returned to his capital; and the growth of his young beard during the Sicilian voyage was announced, by the familiar surname of Pogonatus, to the Grecian world. But his reign, like that of his predecessor, was stained with fraternal discord. On his two brothers, Heraclius and Tiberius, he had bestowed the title of Augustus; an empty title, for they continued to languish, without trust or power, in the solitude of the palace. At their secret instigation, the troops of the Anatolian *theme* or province approached the city on the Asiatic side, demanded for the royal brothers the partition or exercise of sovereignty, and supported their seditious claim by a theological argument. They were Christians (they cried), and orthodox Catholics ; the sincere votaries of the holy and undivided Trinity. Since there are three equal persons in heaven, it is reasonable there should be three equal persons upon earth. The emperor invited these learned divines to a friendly conference, in which they might propose their arguments to the senate : they obeyed the summons, but the prospect of their bodies hanging on the gibbet in the suburb of Galata reconciled their companions to the unity of the reign of Constantine. He pardoned his brothers, and their names were still pronounced in the public acclamations : but on the repetition or suspicion of a similar offence, the obnoxious princes were deprived of their titles and noses,* in the presence of the Catholic bishops who were assembled at Constantinople in the sixth general synod. In the close of his life, Pogonatus was anxious only to establish the right of primogeniture : the heir of his two sons, Justinian and Heraclius, was offered on the shrine of St. Peter, as a symbol of their spiritual adoption by the pope ; but the elder was alone exalted to the rank of Augustus, and the assurance of the empire.

After the decease of his father, the inheritance of the Roman world devolved to Justinian II. ; and the name of a triumphant lawgiver was dishonored by the vices of a boy, who imitated his namesake only in the expensive luxury of building. His passions were strong ; his understanding was feeble ; and he was intoxicated with a foolish pride, that his birth had given him the command of millions, of whom the smallest community would not have chosen him for their local magistrate. His favorite ministers were two beings the least susceptible of human sympathy, a eunuch and a monk : to the one he abandoned the palace, to the other the finances ; the former corrected the emperor's mother with a scourge, the latter suspended the insolvent tributaries, with their heads downwards, over a slow and smoky fire. Since the days of Commodus and Caracalla, the cruelty of the Roman princes had most commonly been the effect of their fear ; but Justinian, who possessed some vigor of character, enjoyed the sufferings, and braved the revenge, of his subjects, about ten years, till the measure was full, of his crimes, and of their patience. In a

---

* Schlosser (Geschichte der bilder-stürmenden. Kaiser, p. 90) supposes that the young princes were mutilated after the first insurrection ; that after this the acts were still inscribed with their names, the princes being closely secluded in the palace. The improbability of this circumstance may be weighed against Gibbon's want of authority for his statement.—M.

dark dangeon, Leontius, a general of reputation, had groaned above three years, with some of the noblest and most deserving of the patricians : he was suddenly drawn forth to assume the government of Greece ; and this promotion of an injured man was a mark of the contempt rather than of the confidence of his prince. As he was followed to the port by the kind offices of his friends, Leontius observed, with a sigh, that he was a victim adorned for sacrifice, and that inevitable death would pursue his footsteps. They ventured to reply that glory and empire might be the recompense of a generous resolution ; that every order of men abhorred the reign of a monster ; and that the hands of two hundred thousand patriots expected only the voice of a leader. The night was chosen for their deliverance ; and in the first effort of the conspirators the præfect was slain, and the prisons were forced open : the emissaries of Leontius proclaimed in every street, " Christians, to St. Sophia !" and the seasonable text of the patriarch, " This is the day of the Lord !" was the prelude of an inflammatory sermon. From the church the people adjourned to the hippodrome : Justinian, in whose cause not a sword had been drawn, was dragged before these tumultuary judges, and their clamors demanded the instant death of the tyrant. But Leontius, who was already clothed with the purple, cast an eye of pity on the prostrate son of his own benefactor and of so many emperors. The life of Justinian was spared ; the amputation of his nose, perhaps of his tongue, was imperfectly performed : the happy flexibility of the Greek language could impose the name of Rhinotmetus ; and the mutilated tyrant was banished to Chersonæ in Crim-Tartary, a lonely settlement, where corn, wine, and oil, were imported as foreign luxuries.

On the edge of the Scythian wilderness, Justinian still cherished the pride of his birth, and the hope of his restoration. After three years' exile, he received the pleasing intelligence that his injury was avenged by a second revolution, and that Leontius in his turn had been dethroned and mutilated by the rebel Apsimar, who assumed the more respectable name of Tiberius. But the claim of lineal succession was still formidable to a plebeian usurper ; and his jealousy was stimulated by the complaints and charges of the Chersonites, who beheld the vices of the tyrant in the spirit of the exile. With a band of followers, attached to his person by common hope or common despair, Justinian fled from the inhospitable shore to the horde of the Chozars, who pitched their tents between the Tanais and Borysthenes. The khan entertained with pity and respect the royal suppliant : Phanagoria, once an opulent city, on the Asiatic side of the Lake Mœotis, was

assigned for his residence ; and every Roman prejudice was stifled
in his marriage with the sister of the barbarian, who seems, however, from the name of Theodora, to have received the sacrament
of baptism. But the faithless Chozar was soon tempted by the
gold of Constantinople : and had not the design been revealed by
the conjugal love of Theodora, her husband must have been assassinated or betrayed into the power of his enemies. After stran-
gling, with his own hands, the two emissaries of the khan, Justinian sent back his wife to her brother, and embarked on the Euxine in search of new and more faithful allies. His vessel was assaulted by a violent tempest ; and one of his pious companions
advised him to deserve the mercy of God by a vow of general forgiveness, if he should be restored to the throne. "Of forgiveness ?" replied the intrepid tyrant : "may I perish this instant—
may the Almighty whelm me in the waves—if I consent to spare
a single head of my enemies !" He survived this impious menace, sailed into the mouth of the Danube, trusted his person in
the royal village of the Bulgarians, and purchased the aid of Terbelis, a pagan conqueror, by the promise of his daughter and a
fair partition of the treasures of the empire. The Bulgarian kingdom extended to the confines of Thrace ; and the two princes besieged Constantinople at the head of fifteen thousand horse. Apsimar was dismayed by the sudden and hostile apparition of his
rival, whose head had been promised by the Chozar, and of whose
evasion he was yet ignorant. After an absence of ten years, the
crimes of Justinian were faintly remembered, and the birth and
misfortunes of their hereditary sovereign excited the pity of the
multitude, ever discontented with the ruling powers ; and by the
active diligence of his adherents, he was introduced into the city
and palace of Constantine.

In rewarding his allies, and recalling his wife, Justinian displayed some sense of honor and gratitude ; * and Terbelis retired,
after sweeping away a heap of gold coin, which he measured with
his Scythian whip. But never was vow more religiously performed than the sacred oath of revenge which he had sworn
amidst the storms of the Euxine. The two usurpers (for I must
reserve the name of tyrant for the conqueror) were dragged into
the hippodrome, the one from his prison, the other from his palace. Before their execution, Leontius and Apsimar were cast
prostrate in chains beneath the throne of the emperor ; and Justinian, planting a foot on each of their necks, contemplated above

---

* Of fear, rather than of more generous motives. Compare Le Beau, vol. xii.
p 64.—M.

an hour the chariot-race, while the inconstant people shouted, in the words of the Psalmist, "Thou shalt trample on the asp and basilisk, and on the lion and dragon shalt thou set thy foot!" The universal defection which he had once experienced might provoke him to repeat the wish of Caligula, that the Roman people had but one head. Yet I shall presume to observe that such a wish is unworthy of an ingenious tyrant, since his revenge and cruelty would have been extinguished by a single blow, instead of the slow variety of tortures which Justinian inflicted on the victims of his anger. His pleasures were inexhaustible : neither private virtue nor public service could expiate the guilt of active, or even passive, obedience to an established government ; and, during the six years of his new reign, he considered the axe, the cord, and the rack, as the only instruments of royalty. But his most implacable hatred was pointed against the Chersonites, who had insulted his exile and violated the laws of hospitality. Their remote situation afforded some means of defence, or at least of escape ; and a grievous tax was imposed on Constantinople, to supply the preparations of a fleet and army. "All are guilty, and all must perish," was the mandate of Justinian ; and the bloody execution was intrusted to his favorite Stephen, who was recommended by the epithet of the savage. Yet even the savage Stephen imperfectly accomplished the intentions of his sovereign. The slowness of his attack allowed the greater part of the inhabitants to withdraw into the country ; and the minister of vengeance contented himself with reducing the youth of both sexes to a state of servitude, with roasting alive seven of the principal citizens, with drowning twenty in the sea, and with reserving forty-two in chains to receive their doom from the mouth of the emperor. In their return, the fleet was driven on the rocky shores of Anatolia ; and Justinian applauded the obedience of the Euxine, which had involved so many thousands of his subjects and enemies in a common shipwreck : but the tyrant was still insatiate of blood ; and a second expedition was commanded to extirpate the remains of the proscribed colony. In the short interval, the Chersonites had returned to their city, and were prepared to die in arms ; the khan of the Chozars had renounced the cause of his odious brother ; the exiles of every province were assembled in Tauris ; and Bardanes, under the name of Philippicus, was invested with the purple. The Imperial troops, unwilling and unable to perpetrate the revenge of Justinian, escaped his displeasure by abjuring his allegiance : the fleet, under their new sovereign, steered back a more auspicious course to the harbors of Sinope and Constantinople, and every tongue was prompt to pronounce, every hand to execute, the death of the tyrant. Destitute of friends, he was deserted by his barbarian guards ; and the stroke of the assassin was praised as an act of patriotism and Roman virtue. His son Tiberius had taken refuge in a church ; his aged grandmother guarded the door ; and the innocent youth, suspending round his neck the most formidable relics, embraced with one hand the altar, with the other the wood of the true cross. But the popular fury that dares to trample on superstition is deaf to the cries of humanity ; and the race of Heraclius was extinguished after a reign of one hundred years.

Between the fall of the Heraclian and the rise of the Isaurian dynasty, a short interval of six years is divided into three reigns. Bardanes, or Philippicus, was hailed at Constantinople as a hero who had delivered his country from a tyrant ; and he might taste some moments of happiness in the first transports of sincere and universal joy. Justinian had left behind him an ample treasure, the fruit of cruelty and rapine : but this useful fund was soon and idly dissipated by his successor. On the festival of his birthday, Philippicus entertained the multitude with the games of the hippodrome ; from thence he paraded through the streets with a thousand banners and a thousand trumpets ; refreshed himself in the baths of Zeuxippus, and returning to the palace, entertained his nobles with a sumptuous banquet. At the meridian hour he withdrew to his chamber, intoxicated with flattery and wine, and forgetful that his example had made every subject ambitious, and that every ambitious subject was his secret enemy. Some bold conspirators introduced themselves in the disorder of the feast ; and the slumbering monarch was surprised, bound, blinded, and deposed, before he was sensible of his danger. Yet the traitors were deprived of their reward ; and the free voice of the senate and people promoted Artemius from the office of secretary to that of emperor : he assumed the title of Anastasius the Second, and displayed in a short and troubled reign the virtues both of peace and war. But after the extinction of the Imperial line, the rule of obedience was violated, and every change diffused the seeds of new revolutions. In a mutiny of the fleet, an obscure and reluctant officer of the revenue was forcibly invested with the purple : after some months of a naval war, Anastasius resigned the sceptre ; and the conqueror, Theodosius the Third, submitted in his turn to the superior ascendant of Leo, the general and emperor of the Oriental troops. His two predecessors were permitted to embrace the ecclesiastical profession : the restless impatience of Anastasius tempted him to risk and to lose his life in a treasonable enterprise ; but the last days of Theodosius were honorable and secure. The single sublime word, "HEALTH," which he inscribed on his tomb, expresses the confidence of philosophy or religion; and the fame of his miracles was long preserved among the people of Ephesus. This convenient shelter of the church might sometimes impose a lesson of clemency; but it may be questioned whether it is for the public interest to diminish the perils of unsuccessful ambition.

I have dwelt on the fall of a tyrant; I shall briefly represent the founder of a new dynasty, who is known to posterity by the invectives of his enemies, and whose public and private life is involved in the ecclesiastical story of the Iconoclasts. Yet, in spite of the clamors of superstition, a favorable prejudice for the character of Leo the Isaurian may be reasonably drawn from the obscurity of his birth, and the duration of his reign.—I. In an age of manly spirit, the prospect of an Imperial reward would have kindled every energy of the mind, and produced a crowd of competitors as deserving as they were desirous to reign. Even in the corruption and debility of the modern Greeks, the elevation of a plebeian from the last to the first rank of society, supposes some qualifications above the level of the multitude. He would probably be ignorant and disdainful of speculative science; and, in the pursuit of fortune, he might absolve himself from the obligations of benevolence and justice; but to his character we may ascribe the useful virtues of prudence and fortitude, the knowledge of mankind, and the important art of gaining their confidence and directing their passions. It is agreed that Leo was a native of Isauria, and that Conon was his primitive name. The writers, whose awkward satire is praise, describe him as an itinerant pedler, who drove an ass with some paltry merchandise to the country fairs; and foolishly relate that he met on the road some Jewish fortune-tellers, who promised him the Roman empire, on condition that he should abolish the worship of idols. A more probable account relates the migration of his father from Asia Minor to Thrace, where he exercised the lucrative trade of a grazier; and he must have acquired considerable wealth, since the first introduction of his son was procured by a supply of five hundred sheep to the Imperial camp. His first service was in the guards of Justinian, where he soon attracted the notice, and by degrees the jealousy, of the tyrant. His valor and dexterity were conspicuous in the Colchian war: from Anastasius he received the command of the Anatolian legions, and by the suffrage of the soldiers he was raised to the empire with the general applause of the Roman world.—II. In this dangerous elevation, Leo the Third supported himself against the envy of his equals, the discontent of a powerful faction, and the assaults of his foreign and domestic enemies. The Catholics, who accuse his religious innovations, are obliged to confess that they were undertaken with temper and conducted with firmness. Their silence respects the wisdom of his administration and the purity of his manners. After a reign of twenty-four years, he peaceably expired in the palace of Constantinople ; and the purple which he had acquired was transmitted by the right of inheritance to the third generation.*

In a long reign of thirty-four years, the son and successor of Leo, Constantine the Fifth, surnamed Copronymus, attacked with less temperate zeal the images or idols of the church. Their votaries have exhausted the bitterness of religious gall, in their portrait of this spotted panther, this antichrist, this flying dragon of the serpent's seed, who surpassed the vices of Elagabalus and Nero. His reign was a long butchery of whatever was most noble, or holy, or innocent, in his empire. In person, the emperor assisted at the execution of his victims, surveyed their agonies, listened to their groans, and indulged, without satiating, his appetite for blood ; a plate of noses was accepted as a grateful offering, and his domestics were often scourged or mutilated by the royal hand. His surname was derived from his pollution of his baptismal font. The infant might be excused ; but the manly pleasures of Copronymus degraded him below the level of a brute ; his lust confounded the eternal distinctions of sex and species, and he seemed to extract some unnatural delight from the objects most offensive to human sense. In his religion the Iconoclast was a Heretic, a Jew, a Mahometan, a Pagan, and an Atheist ; and his belief of an invisible power could be discovered only in his magic rites, human victims, and nocturnal sacrifices to Venus and the dæmons of antiquity. His life was stained with the most opposite vices, and the ulcers which covered his body, anticipated before his death the sentiment of hell-tortures. Of these accusations, which I have so patiently copied, a part is refuted by its own absurdity ; and in the private anecdotes of the life of princes, the lie is more easy as the detection is more difficult. Without adopting the pernicious maxim, that where much is alleged something must be true, I can, however, discern that Constantine the Fifth was dissolute and cruel. Calumny is more

---

* During the latter part of his reign, the hostilities of the Saracens, who invested a Pergamenian, named Tiberius, with the purple, and proclaimed him as the son of Justinian, and an earthquake, which destroyed the walls of Constantinople, compelled Leo greatly to increase the burden of taxation upon his subjects. A twelfth was exacted in addition to every aureus (νομισμα) as a wall tax. Theophanes, p. 275. Schlosser, Bilder-stürmend. Kaiser, p. 197.—M.

prone to exaggerate than to invent ; and her licentious tongue is checked in some measure by the experience of the age and country to which she appeals. Of the bishops and monks, the generals and magistrates, who are said to have suffered under his reign, the numbers are recorded, the names were conspicuous, the execution was public, the mutilation visible and permanent.* The Catholics hated the person and government of Copronymus ; but even their hatred is a proof of their oppression. They dissembled the provocations which might excuse or justify his rigor, but even these provocations must gradually inflame his resentment and harden his temper in the use or the abuse of despotism. Yet the character of the fifth Constantine was not devoid of merit, nor did his government always deserve the curses or the contempt of the Greeks. From the confession of his enemies, I am informed of the restoration of an ancient aqueduct, of the redemption of two thousand five hundred captives, of the uncommon plenty of the times, and of the new colonies with which he repeopled Constantinople, and the Thracian cities. They reluctantly praise his activity and courage ; he was on horseback in the field at the head of his legions ; and, although the fortune of his arms was various, he triumphed by sea and land, on the Euphrates and the Danube, in civil and barbarian war. Heretical praise must be cast into the scale to counterbalance the weight of orthodox invective. The Iconoclasts revered the virtues of the prince : forty years after his death they still prayed before the tomb of the saint. A miraculous vision was propagated by fanaticism or fraud : and the Christian hero appeared on a milk-white steed, brandishing his lance against the Pagans of Bulgaria : " An absurd fable," says the Catholic historian, " since Copronymus is chained with the dæmons in the abyss of hell."

Leo the Fourth, the son of the fifth and the father of the sixth Constantine, was of a feeble constitution both of mind † and body, and the principal care of his reign was the settlement of the succession. The association of the young Constantine was urged by the officious zeal of his subjects ; and the emperor, conscious of his decay, complied, after a prudent hesitation, with their unanimous wishes. The royal infant, at the age of five years, was

* He is accused of burning the library of Constantinople, founded by Julian, with its president and twelve professors. This eastern Sorbonne had discomfited the Imperial theologians on the great question of image-worship. Schlosser observes that this accidental fire took place six years after the emperor had laid the question of image-worship before the professors. Bilder-stürmend. Kaiser, p. 264. Compare Le Beau, vol. xii. p. 156.—M.

† Schlosser thinks more highly of Leo's mind ; but his only proof of his superiority is the successes of his generals against the Saracens. Schlosser, p. 256.—M.

crowned with his mother Irene ; and the national consent was ratified by every circumstance of pomp and solemnity that could dazzle the eyes or bind the conscience of the Greeks. An oath of fidelity was administered in the palace, the church, and the hippodrome, to the several orders of the state, who adjured the holy names of the Son, and mother of God. "Be witness, O Christ ! that we will watch over the safety of Constantine the son of Leo, expose our lives in his service, and bear true allegiance to his person and posterity." They pledged their faith on the wood of the true cross, and the act of their engagement was deposited on the altar of St. Sophia. The first to swear, and the first to violate their oath, were the five sons of Copronymus by a second marriage ; and the story of these princes is singular and tragic. The right of primogeniture excluded them from the throne ; the injustice of their elder brother defrauded them of a legacy of about two millions sterling ; some vain titles were not deemed a sufficient compensation for wealth and power ; and they repeatedly conspired against their nephew, before and after the death of his father. Their first attempt was pardon ; for the second offence * they were condemned to the ecclesiastical state ; and for the third treason, Nicephorus, the eldest and most guilty, was deprived of his eyes, and his four brothers, Christopher, Nicetas, Anthemeus, and Eudoxas, were punished, as a milder sentence, by the amputation of their tongues. After five years' confinement, they escaped to the church of St. Sophia, and displayed a pathetic spectacle to the people. "Countrymen and Christians," cried Nicephorus for himself and his mute brethren, "behold the sons of your emperor, if you can still recognize our features in this miserable state. A life, an imperfect life, is all that the malice of our enemies has spared. It is now threatened, and we now throw ourselves on your compassion." The rising murmur might have produced a revolution, had it not been checked by the presence of a minister, who soothed the unhappy princes with flattery and hope, and gently drew them from the sanctuary to the palace. They were speedily embarked for Greece, and Athens was allotted for the place of their exile. In this calm retreat, and in their helpless condition, Nicephorus and his brothers were tormented by the thirst of power, and tempted by a Sclavonian chief, who offered to break their prison, and to lead them in arms, and in the purple, to the gates of Constantinople. But the Athenian people, ever zealous in the cause of Irene, prevented her justice or cruelty ;

---

* The second offence was on the accession of the young Constantine.—M.

and the five sons of Copronymus were plunged in eternal darkness and oblivion.

For himself, that emperor had chosen a barbarian wife, the daughter of the khan of the Chozars ; but in the marriage of his heir he preferred an Athenian virgin, an orphan, seventeen years old, whose sole fortune must have consisted in her personal accomplishments. The nuptials of Leo and Irene were celebrated with royal pomp ; she soon acquired the love and confidence of a feeble husband, and in his testament he declared the empress guardian of the Roman world, and of their son Constantine the Sixth, who was no more than ten years of age. During his childhood, Irene most ably and assiduously discharged, in her public administration, the duties of a faithful mother ; and her zeal in the restoration of images has deserved the name and honors of a saint, which she still occupies in the Greek calendar. But the emperor attained the maturity of youth ; the maternal yoke became more grievous ; and he listened to the favorites of his own age, who shared his pleasures, and were ambitious of sharing his power. Their reasons convinced him of his right, their praises of his ability, to reign ; and he consented to reward the services of Irene by a perpetual banishment to the Isle of Sicily. But her vigilance and penetration easily disconcerted their rash projects : a similar, or more severe, punishment was retaliated on themselves and their advisers ; and Irene inflicted on the ungrateful prince the chastisement of a boy. After this contest, the mother and the son were at the head of two domestic factions ; and instead of mild influence and voluntary obedience, she held in chains a captive and an enemy. The empress was overthrown by the abuse of victory ; the oath of fidelity, which she exacted to herself alone, was pronounced with reluctant murmurs ; and the bold refusal of the Armenian guards encouraged a free and general declaration, that Constantine the Sixth was the lawful emperor of the Romans. In this character he ascended his hereditary throne, and dismissed Irene to a life of solitude and repose. But her haughty spirit condescended to the arts of dissimulation : she flattered the bishops and eunuchs, revived the filial tenderness of the prince, regained his confidence, and betrayed his credulity. The character of Constantine was not destitute of sense or spirit ; but his education had been studiously neglected ; and his ambitious mother exposed to the public censure the vices which she had nourished, and the actions which she had secretly advised : his divorce and second marriage offended the prejudices of the clergy, and by his imprudent rigor he forfeited the attachment of the Armenian guards. A powerful conspiracy was formed for the restoration of Irene ; and the secret, though widely diffused, was faithfully kept above eight months, till the emperor, suspicious of his danger, escaped from Constantinople, with the design of appealing to the provinces and armies. By this hasty flight, the empress was left on the brink of the precipice ; yet before she implored the mercy of her son, Irene addressed a private epistle to the friends whom she had placed about his person, with a menace, that unless *they* accomplished, *she* would reveal, their treason. Their fear rendered them intrepid ; they seized the emperor on the Asiatic shore, and he was transported to the porphyry apartment of the palace, where he had first seen the light. In the mind of Irene, ambition had stifled every sentiment of humanity and nature ; and it was decreed in her bloody council that Constantine should be rendered incapable of the throne : her emissaries assaulted the sleeping prince, and stabbed their daggers with such violence and precipitation into his eyes as if they meant to execute a mortal sentence. An ambiguous passage of Theophanes persuaded the annalist of the church that death was the immediate consequence of this barbarous execution. The Catholics have been deceived or subdued by the authority of Baronius ; and Protestant zeal has re-echoed the words of a cardinal, desirous, as it should seem, to favor the patroness of images.* Yet the blind son of Irene survived many years, oppressed by the court and forgotten by the world ; the Isaurian dynasty was silently extinguished ; and the memory of Constantine was recalled only by the nuptials of his daughter Euphrosyne with the emperor Michael the Second.

The most bigoted orthodoxy has justly execrated the unnatural mother, who may not easily be paralleled in the history of crimes. To her bloody deed superstition has attributed a subsequent darkness of seventeen days, during which many vessels in midday were driven from their course, as if the sun, a globe of fire so vast and so remote, could sympathize with the atoms of a revolving planet. On earth, the crime of Irene was left five years unpunished ; her reign was crowned with external splendor ; and if she could silence the voice of conscience, she neither heard nor regarded the reproaches of mankind. The Roman world bowed to the government of a female ; and as she moved through the streets of Constantinople, the reins of four milk-white steeds were held by as many patricians, who marched on foot before the golden chariot of their queen. But these patricians were for the

---

* Gibbon has been attacked on account of this statement, but is successfully defended by Schlosser. B. S. Kaiser, p. 327. Compare Le Beau, c. xii. p. 372.—M.

most part eunuchs ; and their black ingratitude justified on this occasion the popular hatred and contempt. Raised, enriched, intrusted with the first dignities of the empire, they basely conspired against their benefactress ; the great treasurer Nicephorus was secretly invested with the purple ; her successor was introduced into the palace, and crowned at St. Sophia by the venal patriarch. In their first interview, she recapitulated with dignity the revolutions of her life, gently accused the perfidy of Nicephorus, insinuated that he owed his life to her unsuspicious clemency, and for the throne and treasures which she resigned, solicited a decent and honorable retreat. His avarice refused this modest compensation ; and, in her exile of the Isle of Lesbos, the empress earned a scanty subsistence by the labors of her distaff.

Many tyants have reigned undoubtedly more criminal than Nicephorus, but none perhaps have more deeply incurred the universal abhorrence of their people. His character was stained with the three odious vices of hypocrisy, ingratitude, and avarice : his want of virtue was not redeemed by any superior talents, nor his want of talents by any pleasing qualifications. Unskilful and unfortunate in war, Nicephorus was vanquished by the Saracens, and slain by the Bulgarians ; and the advantage of his death overbalanced, in the public opinion, the destruction of a Roman army.* His son and heir Stauracius escaped from the field with a mortal wound ; yet six months of an expiring life were sufficient to refute his indecent, though popular declaration, that he would in all things avoid the example of his father. On the near prospect of his decease, Michael, the great master of the palace, and the husband of his sister Procopia, was named by every person of the palace and city, except by his envious brother. Tenacious of a sceptre now falling from his hand, he conspired against the life of his successor, and cherished the idea of changing to a democracy the Roman empire. But these rash projects served only to inflame the zeal of the people and to remove the scruples of the candidate : Michael the First accepted the purple, and before he sunk into the grave, the son of Nicephorus implored the clemency of his new sovereign. Had Michael in an age of peace ascended an hereditary throne, he might have reigned and died the father of his people : but his mild virtues were adapted to the shade of private life, nor was he capable of controlling the ambition of his equals, or of resisting the arms of the victorious Bulgarians. While his want of ability and success

* The Syrian historian, Aboulfaradj. Chron. Syr. p. 133, 139, speaks of him as a brave, prudent, and pious prince, formidable to the Arabs. St. Martin, c. xii. p. 402. Compare Schlosser, p. 350.—M.

exposed him to the contempt of the soldiers, the masculine spirit of his wife Procopia awakened their indignation. Even the Greeks of the ninth century were provoked by the insolence of a female, who, in the front of the standards, presumed to direct their discipline and animate their valor ; and their licentious clamors advised the new Semiramis to reverence the majesty of a Roman camp. After an unsuccessful campaign, the emperor left, in their winter-quarters of Thrace, a disaffected army under the command of his enemies ; and their artful eloquence persuaded the soldiers to break the dominion of the eunuchs, to degrade the husband of Procopia, and to assert the right of a military election. They marched towards the capital : yet the clergy, the senate, and the people of Constantinople, adhered to the cause of Michael ; and the troops and treasures of Asia might have protracted the mischiefs of civil war. But his humanity (by the ambitious it will be termed his weakness) protested that not a drop of Christian blood should be shed in his quarrel, and his messengers presented the conquerors with the keys of the city and the palace. They were disarmed by his innocence and submission ; his life and his eyes were spared ; and the Imperial monk enjoyed the comforts of solitude and religion above thirty-two years after he had been stripped of the purple and separated from his wife.

A rebel, in the time of Nicephorus, the famous and unfortunate Bardanes, had once the curiosity to consult an Asiatic prophet, who, after prognosticating his fall, announced the fortunes of his three principal officers, Leo the Armenian, Michael the Phrygian, and Thomas the Cappadocian, the successive reigns of the two former, the fruitless and fatal enterprise of the third. This prediction was verified, or rather was produced, by the event. Ten years afterwards, when the Thracian camp rejected the husband of Procopia, the crown was presented to the same Leo, the first in military rank and the secret author of the mutiny. As he affected to hesitate, " with this sword," said his companion Michael, " I will open the gates of Constantinople to your Imperial sway ; or instantly plunge it into your bosom, if you obstinately resist the just desires of your fellow-soldiers." The compliance of the Armenian was rewarded with the empire, and he reigned seven years and a half under the name of Leo the Fifth. Educated in a camp, and ignorant both of laws and letters, he introduced into his civil government the rigor and even cruelty of military discipline ; but if his severity was sometimes dangerous to the innocent, it was always formidable to the guilty. His religious inconstancy was taxed by the epithet of Chameleon, but the Catholics have acknowledged by the voice of a saint and confessors, that the life of the Iconoclast was useful to the republic. The zeal of his companion Michael was repaid with riches, honors, and military command ; and his subordinate talents were beneficially employed in the public service. Yet the Phrygian was dissatisfied at receiving as a favor a scanty portion of the Imperial prize which he had bestowed on his equal ; and his discontent, which sometimes evaporated in hasty discourse, at length assumed a more threatening and hostile aspect against a prince whom he represented as a cruel tyrant. That tyrant, however, repeatedly detected, warned, and dismissed the old companion of his arms, till fear and resentment prevailed over gratitude ; and Michael, after a scrutiny into his actions and designs, was convicted of treason, and sentenced to be burnt alive in the furnace of the private baths. The devout humanity of the empress Theophano was fatal to her husband and family. A solemn day, the twenty-fifth of December, had been fixed for the execution : she urged, that the anniversary of the Saviour's birth would be profaned by this inhuman spectacle, and Leo consented with reluctance to a decent respite. But on the vigil of the feast, his sleepless anxiety prompted him to visit at the dead of night the chamber in which his enemy was confined : he beheld him released from his chain, and stretched on his jailer's bed in a profound slumber. Leo was alarmed at these signs of security and intelligence ; but though he retired with silent steps, his entrance and departure were noticed by a slave who lay concealed in a corner of the prison. Under the pretence of requesting the spiritual aid of a confessor, Michael informed the conspirators that their lives depended on his discretion, and that a few hours were left to assure their own safety, by the deliverance of their friend and country. On the great festivals, a chosen band of priests and chanters was admitted into the palace by a private gate to sing matins in the chapel ; and Leo, who regulated with the same strictness the discipline of the choir and of the camp, was seldom absent from these early devotions. In the ecclesiastical habit, but with swords under their robes, the conspirators mingled with the procession, lurked in the angles of the chapel, and expected, as the signal of murder, the intonation of the first psalm by the emperor himself. The imperfect light, and the uniformity of dress, might have favored his escape, whilst their assault was pointed against a harmless priest, but they soon discovered their mistake, and encompassed on all sides the royal victim. Without a weapon and without a friend, he grasped a weighty cross, and stood at bay against the hunters of his life ; but as he asked for mercy, " This is the hour, not of mercy, but of vengeance," was the inexorable reply. The stroke of a well-aimed sword separated from his body the right arm and the cross, and Leo the Armenian was slain at the foot of the altar.

A memorable reverse of fortune was displayed in Michael the Second, who from a defect in his speech was surnamed the Stammerer. He was snatched from the fiery furnace to the sovereignty of an empire; and as in the tumult a smith could not readily be found, the fetters remained on his legs several hours after he was seated on the throne of the Cæsars. The royal blood which had been the price of his elevation was unprofitably spent: in the purple he retained the ignoble vices of his origin; and Michael lost his provinces with as supine indifference as if they had been the inheritance of his fathers. His title was disputed by Thomas, the last of the military triumvirate, who transported into Europe fourscore thousand barbarians from the banks of the Tigris and the shores of the Caspian. He formed the siege of Constantinople; but the capital was defended with spiritual and carnal weapons; a Bulgarian king assaulted the camp of the Orientals, and Thomas had the misfortune, or the weakness, to fall alive into the power of the conqueror. The hands and feet of the rebel were amputated; he was placed on an ass, and, amidst the insults of the people, was led through the streets, which he sprinkled with his blood. The depravation of manners, as savage as they were corrupt, is marked by the presence of the emperor himself. Deaf to the lamentations of a fellow-soldier, he incessantly pressed the discovery of more accomplices, till his curiosity was checked by the question of an honest or guilty minister: "Would you give credit to an enemy against the most faithful of your friends?" After the death of his first wife, the emperor, at the request of the senate, drew from her monastery Euphrosyne, the daughter of Constantine the Sixth. Her august birth might justify a stipulation in the marriage-contract, that her children should equally share the empire with their elder brother. But the nuptials of Michael and Euphrosyne were barren; and she was content with the title of mother of Theophilus, his son and successor.

The character of Theophilus is a rare example in which religious zeal has allowed, and perhaps magnified, the virtues of a heretic and a persecutor. His valor was often felt by the enemies, and his justice by the subjects, of the monarchy; but the valor of Theophilus was rash and fruitless, and his justice arbitrary and cruel. He displayed the banner of the cross against the Saracens; but his five expeditions were concluded by a signal overthrow: Amorium, the native city of his ancestors, was levelled with the ground, and from his military toils he derived only the surname of the Unfortunate. The wisdom of a sovereign is comprised in the institution of laws and the choice of magistrates, and while he seems without action, his civil government revolves round his centre with the silence and order of the planetary system. But the justice of Theophilus was fashioned on the model of the Oriental despots, who, in personal and irregular acts of authority, consult the reason or passion of the moment, without measuring the sentence by the law, or the penalty by the offence. A poor woman threw herself at the emperor's feet to complain of a powerful neighbor, the brother of the empress, who had raised his palace wall to such an inconvenient height, that her humble dwelling was excluded from light and air ! On the proof of the fact, instead of granting, like an ordinary judge, sufficient or ample damages to the plaintiff, the sovereign adjudged to her use and benefit the palace and the ground. Nor was Theophilus content with this extravagant satisfaction : his zeal converted a civil trespass into a criminal act ; and the unfortunate patrician was stripped and scourged in the public place of Constantinople. For some venial offences, some defect of equity or vigilance, the principal ministers, a præfect, a quæstor, a captain of the guards, were banished or mutilated, or scalded with boiling pitch, or burnt alive in the hippodrome : and as these dreadful examples might be the effects of error or caprice, they must have alienated from his service the best and wisest of the citizens. But the pride of the monarch was flattered in the exercise of power, or, as he thought, of virtue ; and the people, safe in their obscurity, applauded the danger and debasement of their superiors. This extraordinary rigor was justified, in some measure, by its salutary consequences ; since, after a scrutiny of seventeen days, not a complaint or abuse could be found in the court or city ; and it might be alleged that the Greeks could be ruled only with a rod of iron, and that the public interest is the motive and law of the supreme judge. Yet in the crime, or the suspicion, of treason, that judge is of all others the most credulous and partial. Theophilus might inflict a tardy vengeance on the assassins of Leo and the saviors of his father ; but he enjoyed the fruits of their crime ; and his jealous tyranny sacrificed a brother and a prince to the future safety of his life. A Persian of the race of the Sassanides died in poverty and exile at Constantinople, leaving an only son, the issue of a plebeian marriage. At the age of twelve years, the royal birth of Theophobus was revealed, and his merit was not unworthy of his birth. He was educated in the Byzantine palace, a Christian and a soldier ; advanced with rapid steps in the career of fortune and glory; received the hand of the emperor's sister; and was promoted to the command of thirty thousand Persians, who, like his father, had fled from the Mahometan conquerors. These troops, doubly infected with mercenary and fanatic vices, were desirous of revolting against their benefactor, and erecting the standard of their native king: but the loyal Theophobus rejected their offers, disconcerted their schemes, and escaped from their hands to the camp or palace of his royal brother. A generous confidence might have secured a faithful and able guardian for his wife and his infant son, to whom Theophilus, in the flower of his age, was compelled to leave the inheritance of the empire. But his jealousy was exasperated by envy and disease; he feared the dangerous virtues which might either support or oppress their infancy and weakness; and the dying emperor demanded the head of the Persian prince. With savage delight he recognized the familiar features of his brother: "Thou art no longer Theophobus," he said; and, sinking on his couch, he added, with a faltering voice, "Soon, too soon, I shall be no more Theophilus!"

The Russians, who have borrowed from the Greeks the greatest part of their civil and ecclesiastical policy, preserved, till the last century, a singular institution in the marriage of the Czar. They collected, not the virgins of every rank and of every province, a vain and romantic idea, but the daughters of the principal nobles, who awaited in the palace the choice of their sovereign. It is affirmed, that a similar method was adopted in the nuptials of Theophilus. With a golden apple in his hand, he slowly walked between two lines of contending beauties: his eye was detained by the charms of Icasia, and in the awkwardness of a first declaration, the prince could only observe, that, in this world, women had been the cause of much evil; "And surely, sir," she pertly replied, "they have likewise been the occasion of much good." This affectation of unseasonable wit displeased the Imperial lover: he turned aside in disgust; Icasia concealed her mortification in a convent; and the modest silence of Theodora was rewarded with the golden apple. She deserved the love, but did not escape the severity, of her lord. From the palace garden he beheld a vessel deeply laden, and steering into the port: on the discovery that the precious cargo of Syrian luxury was the property of his wife, he condemned the ship to the flames, with a sharp reproach, that her avarice had degraded the character of an empress into that of a merchant. Yet his last choice intrusted her with the guardianship of the empire and her son Michael, who was left an orphan in the fifth year of his age. The restoration of images, and the final extirpation of the Iconoclasts, has endeared her name to the devotion of the Greeks ; but in the fervor of religious zeal, Theodora entertained a grateful regard for the memory and salvation of her husband. After thirteen years of a prudent and frugal administration, she perceived the decline of her influence ; but the second Irene imitated only the virtues of her predecessor. Instead of conspiring against the life or government of her son, she retired, without a struggle, though not without a murmur, to the solitude of private life, deploring the ingratitude, the vices, and the inevitable ruin, of the worthless youth.

Among the successors of Nero and Elagabalus, we have not hitherto found the imitation of their vices, the character of a Roman prince who considered pleasure as the object of life, and virtue as the enemy of pleasure. Whatever might have been the maternal care of Theodora in the education of Michael the Third, her unfortunate son was a king before he was a man. If the ambitious mother labored to check the progress of reason, she could not cool the ebullition of passion ; and her selfish policy was justly repaid by the contempt and ingratitude of the headstrong youth. At the age of eighteen he rejected her authority, without feeling his own incapacity to govern the empire and himself. With Theodora all gravity and wisdom retired from the court ; their place was supplied by the alternate dominion of vice and folly ; and it was impossible, without forfeiting the public esteem, to acquire or preserve the favor of the emperor. The millions of gold and silver which had been accumulated for the service of the state, were lavished on the vilest of men, who flattered his passions and shared his pleasures ; and in a reign of thirteen years the richest of sovereigns was compelled to strip the palace and the churches of their precious furniture. Like Nero, he delighted in the amusements of the theatre, and sighed to be surpassed in the accomplishments in which he should have blushed to excel. Yet the studies of Nero in music and poetry betrayed some symptoms of a liberal taste ; the more ignoble arts of the son of Theophilus were confined to the chariot race of the hippodrome. The four factions which had agitated the peace, still amused the idleness, of the capital : for himself, the emperor assumed the blue livery ; the three rival colors were distributed to his favorites, and in the vile though eager contention he forgot the dignity of his person and the safety of his dominions. He silenced the messenger of an invasion, who presumed to divert his attention in the most critical moment of the race ; and by his command the importunate beacons were extinguished, that too frequently spread the alarm from Tarsus to Constantinople. The most skilful charioteers obtained the first place in his confidence and esteem ; their merit was profusely rewarded : the emperor feasted in their houses, and presented their children at the baptismal font ; and while he applauded his own popularity, he affected to blame the cold and stately reserve of his predecessors. The unnatural lusts which had degraded even the manhood of Nero, were banished from the world ; yet the strength of Michael was consumed by the indulgence of love and intemperance.* In his midnight revels, when his passions were inflamed by wine, he was provoked to issue the most sanguinary commands ; and if any feelings of humanity were left, he was reduced, with the return of sense, to approve the salutary disobedience of his servants. But the most extraordinary feature in the character of Michael, is the profane mockery of the religion of his country. The superstition of the Greeks might indeed excite the smile of a philosopher ; but his smile would have been rational and temperate, and he must have condemned the ignorant folly of a youth who insulted the objects of public veneration. A buffoon of the court was invested in the robes of the patriarch : his twelve metropolitans, among whom the emperor was ranked, assumed their ecclesiastical garments : they used or abused the sacred vessels of the altar ; and in their bacchanalian feasts, the holy communion was administered in a nauseous compound of vingear and mustard. Nor were these impious spectacles concealed from the eyes of the city. On the day of a solemn festival, the emperor, with his bishops or buffoons, rode on asses through the streets, encountered the true patriarch at the head of his clergy ; and by their licentious shouts and obscene gestures, disordered the gravity of the Christian procession. The devotion of Michael appeared only in some offence to reason or piety : he received his theatrical crowns from the statue of the Virgin ; and an Imperial tomb was violated for the sake of burning the bones of Constantine the Iconoclast. By this extravagant conduct, the son of Theophilus became as contemptible as he was odious : every citizen was impatient for the deliverance of his country ; and even the favorites of the moment were apprehensive that a caprice might snatch away what a caprice had bestowed. In the thirtieth year of his age, and in the hour of intoxication and sleep, Michael the Third was murdered in his chamber by the founder of a new dynasty, whom the emperor had raised to an equality of rank and power.

The genealogy of Basil the Macedonian (if it be not the spuri-

---

* In a campaign against the Saracens he betrayed both imbecility and cowardice. Genesius, c. iv. p. 94.—M.

ous offspring of pride and flattery) exhibits a genuine picture of the revolution of the most illustrious families. The Arsacides, the rivals of Rome, possessed the sceptre of the East near four hundred years : a younger branch of these Parthian kings continued to reign in Armenia ; and their royal descendants survived the partition and servitude of that ancient monarchy. Two of these, Artabanus and Chlienes, escaped or retired to the court of Leo the First : his bounty seated them in a safe and hospitable exile, in the province of Macedonia : Adrianople was their final settlement. During several generations they maintained the dignity of their birth ; and their Roman patriotism rejected the tempting offers of the Persian and Arabian powers, who recalled them to their native country. But their splendor was insensibly clouded by time and poverty ; and the father of Basil was reduced to a small farm, which he cultivated with his own hands : yet he scorned to disgrace the blood of the Arsacides by a plebeian alliance : his wife, a widow of Adrianople, was pleased to count among her ancestors the great Constantine ; and their royal infant was connected by some dark affinity of lineage or country with the Macedonian Alexander. No sooner was he born, than the cradle of Basil, his family, and the city, were swept away by an inundation of the Bulgarians : he was educated a slave in a foreign land ; and in this severe discipline he acquired the hardiness of body and flexibility of mind which promoted his future elevation. In the age of youth or manhood he shared the deliverance of the Roman captives, who generously broke their fetters, marched through Bulgaria to the shores of the Euxine, defeated two armies of barbarians, embarked in the ships which had been stationed for their reception, and returned to Constantinople, from whence they were distributed to their respective homes. But the freedom of Basil was naked and destitute : his farm was ruined by the calamities of war ; after his father's death, his manual labor, or service, could no longer support a family of orphans ; and he resolved to seek a more conspicuous theatre, in which every virtue and every vice may lead to the paths of greatness. The first night of his arrival at Constantinople, without friends or money, the weary pilgrim slept on the steps of the church of St. Diomede : he was fed by the casual hospitality of a monk ; and was introduced to the service of a cousin and namesake of the emperor Theophilus ; who, though himself of a diminutive person, was always followed by a train of tall and handsome domestics. Basil attended his patron to the government of Pelopennesus ; eclipsed, by his personal merit, the birth and dignity of Theophilus, and formed a useful connection with a wealthy and charitable matron of Patras. Her spiritual or carnal love embraced the young adventurer, whom she adopted as her son. Danielis presented him with thirty slaves ; and the produce of her bounty was expended in the support of his brothers, and the purchase of some large estates in Macedonia. His gratitude or ambition still attached him to the service of Theophilus ; and a lucky accident recommended him to the notice of the court. A famous wrestler in the train of the Bulgarian ambassadors, had defied, at the royal banquet, the boldest and most robust of the Greeks. The strength of Basil was praised ; he accepted the challenge ; and the barbarian champion was overthrown at the first onset. A beautiful but vicious horse was condemned to be hamstrung : it was subdued by the dexterity and courage of the servant of Theophilus ; and his conqueror was promoted to an honorable rank in the Imperial stables. But it was impossible to obtain the confidence of Michael, without complying with his vices ; and his new favorite, the great chamberlain of the palace, was raised and supported by a disgraceful marriage with a royal concubine, and the dishonor of his sister, who succeeded to her place. The public administration had been abandoned to the Cæsar Bardas, the brother and enemy of Theodora ; but the arts of female influence persuaded Michael to hate and to fear his uncle : he was drawn from Constantinople, under the pretense of a Cretan expedition, and stabbed in the tent of audience, by the sword of the chamberlain, and in the presence of the emperor. About a month after this execution, Basil was invested with the title of Augustus and the government of the empire. He supported this unequal association till his influence was fortified by popular esteem. His life was in danger by the caprice of the emperor ; and his dignity was profaned by a second colleague, who had rowed in the galleys. Yet the murder of his benefactor must be condemned as an act of ingratitude and treason ; and the churches which he dedicated to the name of St. Michael were a poor and puerile expiation of his guilt.

The different ages of Basil the First may be compared with those of Augustus. The situation of the Greek did not allow him in his earliest youth to lead an army against his country, or to proscribe the noblest of her sons ; but his aspiring genius stooped to the arts of a slave ; he dissembled his ambition and even his virtues, and grasped, with the bloody hand of an assassin, the empire which he ruled with the wisdom and tenderness of a parent. A private citizen may feel his interest repugnant to his duty ; but it must be from a deficiency of sense or courage, that an absolute monarch can separate his happiness from his glory, or his glory from the public welfare. The life or panegyric of Basil has indeed been composed and published under the long reign of his descendants; but even their stability on the throne may be justly ascribed to the superior merit of their ancestor. In his character, his grandson Constantine has attempted to delineate a perfect image of royalty: but that feeble prince, unless he had copied a real model, could not easily have soared so high above the level of his own conduct or conceptions. But the most solid praise of Basil is drawn from the comparison of a ruined and a flourishing monarchy, that which he wrested from the dissolute Michael, and that which he bequeathed to the Macedonian dynasty. The evils which had been sanctified by time and example, were corrected by his master hand; and he revived, if not the national spirit, at least the order and majesty of the Roman empire. His application was indefatigable, his temper cool, his understanding vigorous and decisive; and in his practice he observed that rare and salutary moderation, which pursues each virtue, at an equal distance between the opposite vices. His military service had been confined to the palace; nor was the emperor endowed with the spirit or the talents of a warrior. Yet under his reign the Roman arms were again formidable to the barbarians. As soon as he had formed a new army by discipline and exercise, he appeared in person on the banks of the Euphrates, curbed the pride of the Saracens, and suppressed the dangerous though just revolt of the Manichæans. His indignation against a rebel who had long eluded his pursuit, provoked him to wish and to pray, that, by the grace of God, he might drive three arrows into the head of Chrysochir. That odious head, which had been obtained by treason rather than by valor, was suspended from a tree, and thrice exposed to the dexterity of the Imperial archer; a base revenge against the dead, more worthy of the times than of the character of Basil. But his principal merit was in the civil administration of the finances and of the laws. To replenish an exhausted treasury, it was proposed to resume the lavish and ill-placed gifts of his predecessor: his prudence abated one moiety of the restitution; and a sum of twelve hundred thousand pounds was instantly procured to answer the most pressing demands, and to allow some space for the mature operations of economy. Among the various schemes for the improvement of the revenue, a new mode was suggested of capitation, or tribute, which would have too much depended on the arbitrary discretion of the assessors. A sufficient list of honest and able agents was instantly produced by the minister; but on the more careful scrutiny of Basil himself, only two could be found, who might be safely intrusted with such dangerous powers ; and they justified his esteem by declining his confidence. But the serious and successful diligence of the emperor established, by degrees, an equitable balance of property and payment, of receipt and expenditure ; a peculiar fund was appropriated to each service ; and a public method secured the interest of the prince and the property of the people. After reforming the luxury, he assigned two patrimonial estates to supply the decent plenty of the Imperial table : the contributions of the subject were reserved for his defence ; and the residue was employed in the embellishment of the capital and provinces. A taste for building, however costly, may deserve some praise and much excuse : from thence industry is fed, art is encouraged, and some object is attained of public emolument or pleasure ; the use of a road, an aqueduct, or a hospital, is obvious and solid ; and the hundred churches that arose by the command of Basil were consecrated to the devotion of the age. In the character of a judge he was assiduous and impartial ; desirous to save, but not afraid to strike : the oppressors of the people were severely chastised ; but his personal foes, whom it might be unsafe to pardon, were condemned, after the loss of their eyes, to a life of solitude and repentance. The change of language and manners demanded a revision of the obsolete jurisprudence of Justinian : the voluminous body of his Institutes, Pandects, Code, and Novels, was digested under forty titles, in the Greek idiom ; and the *Basilics*, which were improved and completed by his son and grandson, must be referred to the original genius of the founder of their race. This glorious reign was terminated by an accident in the chase. A furious stag entangled his horns in the belt of Basil, and raised him from his horse : he was rescued by an attendant, who cut the belt and slew the animal ; but the fall, or the fever, exhausted the strength of the aged monarch, and he expired in the palace amidst the tears of his family and people. If he struck off the head of the faithful servant for presuming to draw his sword against his sovereign, the pride of despotism—which had lain dormant in his life, revived in the last moments of despair, when he no longer wanted or valued the opinion of mankind.

Of the four sons of the emperor, Constantine died before his father, whose grief and credulity were amused by a flattering impostor and a vain apparition. Stephen, the youngest, was content with the honors of a patriarch and a saint ; both Leo and Alexander were alike invested with the purple, but the powers of government were solely exercised by the elder brother. The name of Leo the Sixth has been dignified with the title of *philosopher ;* and the union of the prince and the sage, of the active and speculative virtues, would indeed constitute the perfection of human nature. But the claims of Leo are far short of this ideal excellence. Did he reduce his passions and appetites under the dominion of reason ? His life was spent in the pomp of the palace, in the society of his wives and concubines ; and even the clemency which he showed, and the peace which he strove to preserve, must be imputed to the softness and indolence of his character. Did he subdue his prejudices and those of his subjects ? His mind was tinged with the most puerile superstition ; the influence of the clergy and the errors of the people, were consecrated by his laws ; and the oracles of Leo, which reveal, in prophetic style, the fates of the empire, are founded on the arts of astrology and divination. If we still inquire the reason of his sage appellation, it can only be replied, that the son of Basil was less ignorant than the greater part of his contemporaries in church and state ; that his education had been directed by the learned Photius ; and that several books of profane and ecclesiastical science were composed by the pen, or in the name, of the Imperial *philosopher*. But the reputation of his philosophy and religion was overthrown by a domestic vice, the repetition of his nuptials. The primitive ideas of the merit and holiness of celibacy were preached by the monks and entertained by the Greeks. Marriage was allowed as a necessary means for the propagation of mankind ; after the death of either party, the survivor might satisfy, by a *second* union, the weakness or the strength of the flesh : but a *third* marriage was censured as a state of legal fornication ; and a *fourth* was a sin or scandal as yet unknown to the Christians of the East. In the beginning of his reign, Leo himself had abolished the state of concubines, and condemned, without annulling, third marriages : but his patriotism and love soon compelled him to violate his own laws, and to incur the penance, which in a similar case he had imposed on his subjects. In his three first alliances, his nuptial bed was unfruitful ; the emperor required a female companion, and the empire a legitimate heir. The beautiful Zoe was introduced into the palace as a concubine ; and after a trial of her fecundity, and the birth of Constantine, her lover declared his intention of legitimating the mother and the child, by the celebration of his fourth nuptials. But the patriarch Nicholas refused his blessing : the Imperial baptism of the young prince was obtained by a promise of separation ; and the contumacious husband of Zoe was excluded from the communion of the faithful. Neither the fear of exile, nor the desertion of his brethren, nor the authority of the Latin church, nor the danger of failure or doubt in the succession to the empire, could bend the spirit of the inflexible monk. After the death of Leo, he was recalled from exile to the civil and ecclesiastical administration ; and the edict of union which was promulgated in the interest of Constantine, condemned the future scandal of fourth marriages, and left a tacit imputation on his own birth.

In the Greek language, *purple* and *porphyry* are the same word : and as the colors of nature are invariable, we may learn that a dark deep red was the Tyrian dye which stained the purple of the ancients. An apartment of the Byzantine palace was lined with porphyry : it was reserved for the use of the pregnant empresses ; and the royal birth of their children was expressed by the appellation of *porphyrogenite*, or born in purple. Several of the Roman princes had been blessed with an heir ; but this peculiar surname was first applied to Constantine the Seventh. His life and titular reign were of equal duration ; but of fifty-four years, six had elapsed before his father's death ; and the son of Leo was ever the voluntary or reluctant subject of those who oppressed his weakness or abused his confidence. His uncle Alexander, who had long been invested with the title of Augustus, was the first colleague and governor of the young prince : but in a rapid career of vice and folly, the brother of Leo already emulated the reputation of Michael ; and when he was extinguished by a timely death, he entertained a project of castrating his nephew, and leaving the empire to a worthless favorite. The succeeding years of the minority of Constantine were occupied by his mother Zoe, and a succession or council of seven regents, who pursued their interest, gratified their passions, abandoned the republic, supplanted each other, and finally vanished in the presence of a soldier. From an obscure origin, Romanus Lecapenus had raised himself to the command of the naval armies ; and in the anarchy of the times had deserved, or at least had obtained, the national esteem. With a victorious and affectionate fleet, he sailed from the mouth of the Danube into the harbor of Constantinople, and was hailed as the deliverer of the people and the guardian of the prince. His supreme office was at first defined by the new appellation of father of the emperor ; but Romanus soon disdained the subordinate powers of a minister, and assumed, with the titles of Cæsar and Augustus, the full independence of royalty, which he held near five-and-twenty years. His three sons, Christopher, Stephen, and Constantine, were successively adorned with the same honors, and the lawful emperor was degraded from the first to the fifth rank in this college of princes. Yet in the preservation of his life and crown, he might still applaud his own fortune and the clemency of the usurper. The examples of ancient and modern history would have excused the ambition of Romanus : the powers and the laws of the empire were in his hand ; the spurious birth of Constantine would have justified his exclusion ; and the grave or the monastery was open to receive the son of the concubine. But Lecapenus does not appear to have possessed either the virtues or the vices of a tyrant. The spirit and activity of his private life dissolved away in the sunshine of the throne ; and in his licentious pleasures he forgot the safety both of the republic and of his family. Of a mild and religious character, he respected the sanctity of oaths, the innocence of the youth, the memory of his parents, and the attachment of the people. The studious temper and retirement of Constantine disarmed the jealousy of power : his books and music, his pen and his pencil, were a constant source of amusement ; and if he could improve a scanty allowance by the sale of his pictures, if their price was not enhanced by the name of the artist, he was endowed with a personal talent which few princes could employ in the hour of adversity.

The fall of Romanus was occasioned by his own vices and those of his children. After the decease of Christopher, his eldest son, the two surviving brothers quarrelled with each other and conspired against their father. At the hour of noon, when all strangers were regularly excluded from the palace, they entered his apartment with an armed force, and conveyed him, in the habit of a monk, to a small island in the Propontis, which was peopled by a religious community. The rumor of this domestic revolution excited a tumult in the city ; but Porphyrogenitus alone, the true and lawful emperor, was the object of the public care ; and the sons of Lecapenus were taught, by tardy experience, that they had achieved a guilty and perilous enterprise for the benefit of their rival. Their sister Helena, the wife of Constantine, revealed, or supposed, their treacherous design of assassinating her husband at the royal banquet. His loyal adherents were alarmed, and the two usurpers were prevented, seized, degraded from the purple, and embarked for the same island and monastery where their father had been so lately confined. Old Romanus met them on the beach with a sarcastic smile, and, after a just reproach of their folly and ingratitude, presented his Imperial colleagues with an equal share of his water and vegetable diet. In the fortieth year of his reign, Constantine the Seventh obtained the possession of the Eastern world, which he ruled, or seemed to rule, near fifteen years. But he was devoid of that energy of character which could emerge into a life of action and glory ; and the studies which

had amused and dignified his leisure, were incompatible with the
serious duties of a sovereign. The emperor neglected the practice to instruct his son Romanus in the theory of government ;
while he indulged the habits of intemperance and sloth, he
dropped the reins of the administration into the hands of Helena
his wife ; and in the shifting scene of her favor and caprice, each
minister was regretted in the promotion of a more worthless successor. Yet the birth and misfortunes of Constantine had endeared him to the Greeks ; they excused his failings ; they respected his learning, his innocence, and charity, his love of justice ; and the ceremony of his funeral was mourned with the un
feigned tears of his subjects. The body, according to ancient
custom, lay in state in the vestibule of the palace ; and the civil
and military officers, the patricians, the senate, and the clergy
approached in due order to adore and kiss the inanimate corpse
of their sovereign. Before the procession moved towards the Imperial sepulchre, a herald proclaimed this awful admonition :
" Arise, O king of the world, and obey the summons of the King
of kings !"

The death of Constantine was imputed to poison ; and his son
Romanus, who derived that name from his maternal grandfather,
ascended the throne of Constantinople. A prince, who, at the
age of twenty, could be suspected of anticipating his inheritance,
must have been already lost in the public esteem ; yet Romanus
was rather weak than wicked ; and the largest share of the guilt
was transferred to his wife, Theophano, a woman of base origin,
masculine spirit, and flagitious manners. The sense of personal
glory and public happiness, the true pleasures of royalty, were unknown to the son of Constantine ; and, while the two brothers,
Nicephorus and Leo, triumphed over the Saracens, the hours
which the emperor owed to his people were consumed in strenuous
idleness. In the morning he visited the circus ; at noon he
feasted the senators ; the greater part of the afternoon he spent
in the *sphæristerium*, or tennis-court, the only theatre of his victories ; from thence he passed over to the Asiatic side of the Bosphorus, hunted and killed four wild boars of the largest size, and
returned to the palace, proudly content with the labors of the
day. In strength and beauty he was conspicuous above his
equals : tall and straight as a young cypress, his complexion was
fair and florid, his eyes sparkling, his shoulders broad, his nose
long and aquiline. Yet even these perfections were insufficient
to fix the love of Theophano ; and, after a reign of four * years,

---

* Three years and five months. Leo Diaconus in Niebuhr. Byz. Hist. p. 30.—M

she mingled for her husband the same deadly draught which she had composed for his father.

By his marriage with this imperious woman, Romanus the younger left two sons, Basil the Second and Constantine the Ninth, and two daughters, Theophano and Anne. The eldest sister was given to Otho the Second, emperor of the West; the younger became the wife of Wolodomir, great duke and apostle of Russia, and, by the marriage of her granddaughter with Henry the First, king of France, the blood of the Macedonians, and perhaps of the Arsacides, still flows in the veins of the Bourbon line. After the death of her husband, the empress aspired to reign in the name of her sons, the elder of whom was five, and the younger only two years of age; but she soon felt the instability of a throne which was supported by a female who could not be esteemed, and two infants who could not be feared. Theophano looked around for a protector, and threw herself into the arms of the bravest soldier; her heart was capricious; but the deformity of the new favorite rendered it more than probable that interest was the motive and excuse of her love. Nicephorus Phocus united, in the popular opinion, the double merit of a hero and a saint. In the former character, his qualifications were genuine and splendid: the descendant of a race illustrious by their military exploits, he had displayed in every station and in every province the courage of a soldier and the conduct of a chief; and Nicephorus was crowned with recent laurels, from the important conquest of the Isle of Crete. His religion was of a more ambiguous cast; and his hair-cloth, his fasts, his pious idiom, and his wish to retire from the business of the world, were a convenient mask for his dark and dangerous ambition. Yet he imposed on a holy patriarch, by whose influence, and by a decree of the senate, he was intrusted, during the minority of the younger princes, with the absolute and independent command of the Oriental armies. As soon as he had secured the leaders and the troops, he boldly marched to Constantinople, trampled on his enemies, avowed his correspondence with the empress, and without degrading her sons, assumed, with the title of Augustus, the pre-eminence of rank and the plenitude of power. But his marriage with Theophano was refused by the same patriarch who had placed the crown on his head; by his second nuptials he incurred a year of canonical penance;* a bar of spiritual affinity was opposed to their celebration; and some

---

* The canonical objection to the marriage was his relation of *Godfather* to her sons. Leo Diac. p. 50.—M.

evasion and perjury were required to silence the scruples of the clergy and people. The popularity of the emperor was lost in the purple : in a reign of six years he provoked the hatred of strangers and subjects : and the hypocrisy and avarice of the first Nicephorus were revived in his successor. Hypocrisy I shall never justify or palliate ; but I will dare to observe, that the odious vice of avarice is of all others most hastily arraigned, and most unmercifully condemned. In a private citizen, our judgment seldom expects an accurate scrutiny into his fortune and expense ; and in a steward of the public treasure, frugality is always a virtue, and the increase of taxes too often an indispensable duty. In the use of his patrimony, the generous temper of Nicephorus had been proved ; and the revenue was strictly applied to the service of the state : each spring the emperor marched in person against the Saracens ; and every Roman might compute the employment of his taxes in triumphs, conquests, and the security of the Eastern barrier.[*]

Among the warriors who promoted his elevation, and served under his standard, a noble and valiant Armenian had deserved and obtained the most eminent rewards. The stature of John Zimisces was below the ordinary standard : but his diminutive body was endowed with strength, beauty, and the soul of a hero. By the jealousy of the emperor's brother, he was degraded from the office of general of the East, to that of director of the posts, and his murmurs were chastised with disgrace and exile. But Zimisces was ranked among the numerous lovers of the empress : on her intercession he was permitted to reside at Chalcedon, in the neighborhood of the capital : her bounty was repaid in his clandestine and amorous visits to the palace ; and Theophano consented, with alacrity, to the death of an ugly and penurious husband. Some bold and trusty conspirators were concealed in her most private chambers : in the darkness of a winter night, Zimisces, with his principal companions, embarked in a small boat, traversed the Bosphorus, landed at the palace stairs, and silently ascended a ladder of ropes, which was cast down by the female attendants. Neither his own suspicions, nor the warnings of his friends, nor the tardy aid of his brother Leo, nor the fortress which he had erected in the palace, could protect Nicephorus from a domestic foe, at whose voice every door was opened to the assassins. As he slept on a bear-skin on the ground, he was roused by their noisy intrusion, and thirty daggers glittered be-

---

[*] He retook Antioch, and brought home as a trophy the sword of "the most unholy and impious Mahomet." Leo Diac. p. 76.—M.

fore his eyes.   It is doubtful whether Zimisces imbrued his hands
in the blood of his sovereign ; but he enjoyed the inhuman spectacle of revenge.*   The murder was protracted by insult and
cruelty : and as soon as the head of Nicephorus was shown from
the window, the tumult was hushed, and the Armenian was
emperor of the East.   On the day of his coronation, he was stopped on the threshold of St. Sophia, by the intrepid patriarch ;
who charged his conscience with the deed of treason and blood ;
and required, as a sign of repentance, that he should separate
himself from his more criminal associate.   This sally of apostolic
zeal was not offensive to the prince, since he could neither love
nor trust a woman who had repeatedly violated the most sacred
obligations ; and Theophano, instead of sharing his Imperial
fortune, was dismissed with ignominy from his bed and palace.
In their last interview, she displayed a frantic and impotent rage ; accused the ingratitude of her lover ; assaulted with
words and blows her son Basil, as he stood silent and submissive
in the presence of a superior colleague ; and avowed her own
prostitution in proclaiming the illegitimacy of his birth.   The
public indignation was appeased by her exile, and the punishment
of the meaner accomplices : the death of an unpopular prince was
forgiven ; and the guilt of Zimisces was forgotten in the splendor
of his virtues.   Perhaps his profusion was less useful to the state
than the avarice of Nicephorus ; but his gentle and generous behavior delighted all who approached his person ; and it was only
in the paths of victory that he trod in the footsteps of his predecessor.   The greatest part of his reign was employed in the
camp and the field : his personal valor and activity were signalized on the Danube and the Tigris, the ancient boundaries of the
Roman world ; and by his double triumph over the Russians and
the Saracens, he deserved the titles of savior of the empire, and
conqueror of the East.   In his last return from Syria, he observed
that the most fruitful lands of his new provinces were possessed
by the eunuchs.   " And is it for them," he exclaimed, with
honest indignation, " that we have fought and conquered ?   Is it
for them that we shed our blood, and exhaust the treasures of
our people ?"   The complaint was re-echoed to the palace, and
the death of Zimisces is strongly marked with the suspicion of
poison.

---

* According to Leo Diaconus, Zimisces, after ordering the wounded emperor to
be dragged to his feet, and heaping him with insult, to which the miserable man
only replied by invoking the name of the "mother of God," with his own hand
plucked his beard, while his accomplices beat out his teeth with the hilts of their
swords, and then trampling him to the ground, drove his sword into his skull.   Leo
Diac. in Niebuhr. Byz. Hist. l. vii. c. 8, p. 88.—M.

Under this usurpation, or regency, of twelve years, the two lawful emperors, Basil and Constantine, had silently grown to the age of manhood. Their tender years had been incapable of dominion : the respectful modesty of their attendance and salutation was due to the age and merit of their guardian ; the childless ambition of those guardians had no temptation to violate their right of succession : their patrimony was ably and faithfully administered ; and the premature death of Zimisces was a loss, rather than a benefit, to the sons of Romanus. Their want of experience detained them twelve years longer the obscure and voluntary pupils of a minister, who extended his reign by persuading them to indulge the pleasures of youth, and to disdain the labors of government. In this silken web, the weakness of Constantine was forever entangled ; but his elder brother felt the impulse of genius and the desire of action ; he frowned, and the minister was no more. Basil was the acknowledged sovereign of Constantinople and the provinces of Europe ; but Asia was oppressed by two veteran generals, Phocas and Sclerus, who, alternately friends and enemies, subjects and rebels, maintained their independence, and labored to emulate the example of successful usurpation. Against these domestic enemies the son of Romanus first drew his sword, and they trembled in the presence of a lawful and high-spirited prince. The first, in the front of battle, was thrown from his horse, by the stroke of poison or an arrow ; the second, who had been twice loaded with chains,* and twice invested with the purple, was desirous of ending in peace the small remainder of his days. As the aged suppliant approached the throne, with dim eyes and faltering steps, leaning on his two attendants, the emperor exclaimed, in the insolence of youth and power, " And is this the man who has so long been the object of our terror ?" After he had confirmed his own authority and the peace of the empire, the trophies of Nicephorus and Zimisces would not suffer their royal pupil to sleep in the palace. His long and frequent expeditions against the Saracens were rather glorious than useful to the empire ; but the final destruction of the kingdom of Bulgaria appears, since the time of Belisarius, the most important triumph of the Roman arms. Yet, instead of applauding their victorious prince, his subjects detested the rapacious and rigid avarice of Basil ; and in the imperfect narrative of his exploits, we can only discern the courage, patience, and ferociousness of a soldier. A vicious education, which could not subdue his spirit,

* Once by the caliph, once by his rival, Phocas. Compare Le Beau, l. xiv. p. 176
—M.

had clouded his mind ; he was ignorant of every science ; and the remembrance of his learned and feeble grandsire might encourage his real or affected contempt of laws and lawyers, of artists and arts. Of such a character, in such an age, superstition took a firm and lasting possession ; after the first license of his youth, Basil the Second devoted his life, in the palace and the camp, to the penance of a hermit, wore the monastic habit under his robes and armor, observed a vow of continence, and imposed on his appetites a perpetual abstinence from wine and flesh. In the sixty-eighth year of his age, his martial spirit urged him to embark in person for a holy war against the Saracens of Sicily ; he was prevented by death, and Basil, surnamed the Slayer of the Bulgarians, was dismissed from the world with the blessings of the clergy and the curses of the people. After his decease, his brother Constantine enjoyed, about three years, the power, or rather the pleasures, of royalty ; and his only care was the settlement of the succession. He had enjoyed sixty-six years the title of Augustus ; and the reign of the two brothers is the longest and most obscure of the Byzantine history.

A lineal succession of five emperors, in a period of one hundred and sixty years, had attached the loyalty of the Greeks to the Macedonian dynasty, which had been thrice respected by the usurpers of their power. After the death of Constantine the Ninth, the last male of the royal race, a new and broken scene presents itself, and the accumulated years of twelve emperors do not equal the space of his single reign. His elder brother had preferred his private chastity to the public interest, and Constantine himself had only three daughters ; Eudocia, who took the veil, and Zoe and Theodora, who were preserved till a mature age in a state of ignorance and virginity. When their marriage was discussed in the council of their dying father, the cold or pious Theodora refused to give an heir to the empire, but her sister Zoe presented herself a willing victim at the altar. Romanus Argyrus, a patrician of a graceful person and fair reputation, was chosen for her husband, and, on his declining that honor, was informed that blindness or death was the second alternative. The motive of his reluctance was conjugal affection, but his faithful wife sacrificed her own happiness to his safety and greatness ; and her entrance into a monastery removed the only bar to the Imperial nuptials. After the decease of Constantine, the sceptre devolved to Romanus the Third ; but his labors at home and abroad were equally feeble and fruitless ; and the mature age, the forty-eight years of Zoe, were less favorable to the hopes of pregnancy than to the indulgence of pleasure. Her favorite chamberlain was a handsome Paphlagonian of the name of Michael, whose first trade had been that of a money-changer ; and Romanus, either from gratitude or equity, connived at their criminal intercourse, or accepted a slight assurance of their innocence. But Zoe soon justified the Roman maxim, that every adulteress is capable of poisoning her husband ; and the death of Romanus was instantly followed by the scandalous marriage and elevation of Michael the Fourth. The expectations of Zoe were, however, disappointed : instead of a vigorous and grateful lover, she had placed in her bed a miserable wretch, whose health and reason were impaired by epileptic fits, and whose conscience was tormented by despair and remorse. The most skilful physicians of the mind and body were summoned to his aid ; and his hopes were amused by frequent pilgrimages to the baths, and to the tombs of the most popular saints ; the monks applauded his penance, and, except restitution (but to whom should he have restored ?), Michael sought every method of expiating his guilt. While he groaned and prayed in sackcloth and ashes, his brother, the eunuch John, smiled at his remorse, and enjoyed the harvest of a crime of which himself was the secret and most guilty author. His administration was only the art of satiating his avarice, and Zoe became a captive in the palace of her fathers and in the hands of her slaves. When he perceived the irretrievable decline of his brother's health, he introduced his nephew, another Michael, who derived his surname of Calaphates from his father's occupation in the careening of vessels : at the command of the eunuch, Zoe adopted for her son the son of a mechanic ; and this fictitious heir was invested with the title and purple of the Cæsars, in the presence of the senate and clergy. So feeble was the character of Zoe, that she was oppressed by the liberty and power which she recovered by the death of the Paphlagonian ; and at the end of four days she placed the crown on the head of Michael the Fifth, who had protested, with tears and oaths, that he should ever reign the first and most obedient of her subjects. The only act of his short reign was his base ingratitude to his benefactors, the eunuch and the empress. The disgrace of the former was pleasing to the public : but the murmurs, and at length the clamors, of Constantinople deplored the exile of Zoe, the daughter of so many emperors ; her vices were forgotten, and Michael was taught, that there is a period in which the patience of the tamest slaves rises into fury and revenge. The citizens of every degree assembled in a formidable tumult which lasted three days ; they besieged the palace, forced the gates, recalled their *mothers*, Zoe from her prison, Theodora from her monastery, and condemned the son of Calaphates to the loss of his eyes or of his life. For the first time the Greeks beheld with surprise the two royal sisters seated on the same throne, presiding in the senate, and giving audience to the ambassadors of the nations. But this singular union subsisted no more than two months; the two sovereigns, their tempers, interests, and adherents, were secretly hostile to each other; and as Theodora was still averse to marriage, the indefatigable Zoe, at the age of sixty, consented, for the public good, to sustain the embraces of a third husband, and the censures of the Greek church. His name and number were Constantine the Tenth, and the epithet of *Monomachus*, the single combatant, must have been expressive of his valor and victory in some public or private quarrel. But his health was broken by the tortures of the gout, and his dissolute reign was spent in the alternative of sickness and pleasure. A fair and noble widow had accompanied Constantine in his exile to the Isle of Lesbos, and Sclerena gloried in the appellation of his mistress. After his marriage and elevation, she was invested with the title and pomp of *Augusta*, and occupied a contiguous apartment in the palace. The lawful consort (such was the delicacy or corruption of Zoe) consented to this strange and scandalous partition; and the emperor appeared in public between his wife and his concubine. He survived them both; but the last measures of Constantine to change the order of succession were prevented by the more vigilant friends of Theodora; and after his decease, she resumed, with the general consent, the possession of her inheritance. In her name, and by the influence of four eunuchs, the Eastern world was peaceably governed about nineteen months; and as they wished to prolong their dominion, they persuaded the aged princess to nominate for her successor Michael the Sixth. The surname of *Stratioticus* declares his military profession; but the crazy and decrepit veteran could only see with the eyes, and execute with the hands, of his ministers. Whilst he ascended the throne, Theodora sunk into the grave; the last of the Macedonian or Basilian dynasty. I have hastily reviewed, and gladly dismiss, this shameful and destructive period of twenty-eight years, in which the Greeks, degraded below the common level of servitude, were transferred like a herd of cattle by the choice or caprice of two impotent females.

From this night of slavery, a ray of freedom, or at least of spirit, begins to emerge: the Greeks either preserved or revived the use of surnames, which perpetuate the fame of hereditary virtue: and we now discern the rise, succession, and alliances of the last dynasties of Constantinople and Trebizond. The *Comneni*, who

upheld for a while the fate of the sinking empire, assumed the
honor of a Roman origin : but the family had been long since
transported from Italy to Asia. Their patrimonial estate was situate in the district of Castamona, in the neighborhood of the
Euxine ; and one of their chiefs, who had already entered the
paths of ambition, revisited with affection, perhaps with regret,
the modest though honorable dwelling of his fathers. The first
of their line was the illustrious Manuel, who in the reign of the
second Basil, contributed by war and treaty to appease the
troubles of the East : he left, in a tender age, two sons, Isaac and
John, whom, with the consciousness of desert, he bequeathed to
the gratitude and favor of his sovereign. The noble youths were
carefully trained in the learning of the monastery, the arts of the
palace, and the exercises of the camp : and from the domestic
service of the guards they were rapidly promoted to the command of provinces and armies. Their fraternal union doubled
the force and reputation of the Comneni, and their ancient nobility was illustrated by the marriage of the two brothers, with a
captive princess of Bulgaria, and the daughter of a patrician, who
had obtained the name of *Charon* from the number of enemies
whom he had sent to the infernal shades. The soldiers had
served with reluctant loyalty a series of effeminate masters ; the
elevation of Michael the Sixth was a personal insult to the more
deserving generals : and their discontent was inflamed by the parsimony of the emperor and the insolence of the eunuchs. They
secretly assembled in the sanctuary of St. Sophia, and the votes
of the military synod would have been unanimous in favor of the
old and valiant Catacalon, if the patriotism or modesty of the
veteran had not suggested the importance of birth as well as
merit in the choice of a sovereign. Isaac Comnenus was approved by general consent, and the associates separated without
delay to meet in the plains of Phrygia at the head of their respective squadrons and detachments. The cause of Michael was defended in a single battle by the mercenaries of the Imperial guard,
who were aliens to the public interest, and animated only by a
principle of honor and gratitude. After their defeat, the fears of
the emperor solicited a treaty, which was almost accepted by the
moderation of the Comnenian. But the former was betrayed by
his ambassadors, and the latter was prevented by his friends.
The solitary Michael submitted to the voice of the people ; the
patriarch annulled their oath of allegiance ; and as he shaved the
head of the royal monk, congratulated his beneficial exchange of
temporal royalty for the kingdom of heaven ; an exchange, however, which the priest, on his own account, would probably have

declined. By the hands of the same patriarch, Isaac Comnenus was solemnly crowned ; the sword which he inscribed on his coins might be an offensive symbol, if it implied his title by conquest ; but this sword would have been drawn against the foreign and domestic enemies of the state. The decline of his health and vigor suspended the operation of active virtue ; and the prospect of approaching death determined him to interpose some moments between life and eternity. But instead of leaving the empire as the marriage portion of his daughter, his reason and inclination concurred in the preference of his brother John, a soldier, a patriot, and the father of five sons, the future pillars of an hereditary succession. His first modest reluctance might be the natural dictates of discretion and tenderness, but his obstinate and successful perseverance, however it may dazzle with the show of virtue, must be censured as a criminal desertion of his duty, and a rare offence against his family and country. The purple which he had refused was accepted by Constantine Ducas, a friend of the Comnenian house, and whose noble birth was adorned with the experience and reputation of civil policy. In the monastic habit, Isaac recovered his health, and survived two years his voluntary abdication. At the command of his abbot, he observed the rule of St. Basil, and executed the most servile offices of the convent : but his latent vanity was gratified by the frequent and respectful visits of the reigning monarch, who revered in his person the character of a benefactor and a saint.

If Constantine the Eleventh were indeed the subject most worthy of empire, we must pity the debasement of the age and nation in which he was chosen. In the labor of puerile declamations he sought, without obtaining, the crown of eloquence, more precious, in his opinion, than that of Rome ; and in the subordinate functions of a judge, he forgot the duties of a sovereign and a warrior. Far from imitating the patriotic indifference of the authors of his greatness, Ducas was anxious only to secure, at the expense of the republic, the power and prosperity of his children. His three sons, Michael the Seventh, Andronicus the First, and Constantine the Twelfth, were invested, in a tender age, with the equal title of Augustus ; and the succession was speedily opened by their father's death. His widow, Eudocia, was intrusted with the administration ; but experience had taught the jealousy of the dying monarch to protect his sons from the danger of her second nuptials ; and her solemn engagement, attested by the principal senators, was deposited in the hands of the patriarch. Before the end of seven months, the wants of Eudocia, or those of the state, called aloud for the male virtues of a soldier ;

and her heart had already chosen Romanus Diogenes, whom she raised from the scaffold to the throne. The discovery of a treasonable attempt had exposed him to the severity of the laws : his beauty and valor absolved him in the eyes of the empress ; and Romanus, from a mild exile, was recalled on the second day to the command of the Oriental armies. Her royal choice was yet unknown to the public ; and the promise which would have betrayed her falsehood and levity, was stolen by a dexterous emissary from the ambition of the patriarch. Xiphilin at first alleged the sanctity of oaths and the sacred nature of a trust ; but a whisper, that his brother was the future emperor, relaxed his scruples, and forced him to confess that the public safety was the supreme law. He resigned the important paper ; and when his hopes were confounded by the nomination of Romanus, he could no longer regain his security, retract his declarations, nor oppose the second nuptials of the empress. Yet a murmur was heard in the palace ; and the barbarian guards had raised their battle-axes in the cause of the house of Ducas, till the young princes were soothed by the tears of their mother and the solemn assurances of the fidelity of their guardian, who filled the Imperial station with dignity and honor. Hereafter I shall relate his valiant, but unsuccessful, efforts to resist the progress of the Turks. His defeat and captivity inflicted a deadly wound on the Byzantine monarchy of the East ; and after he was released from the chains of the sultan, he vainly sought his wife and his subjects. His wife had been thrust into a monastery, and the subjects of Romanus had embraced the rigid maxim of the civil law, that a prisoner in the hands of the enemy is deprived, as by the stroke of death, of all the public and private rights of a citizen. In the general consternation, the Cæsar John asserted the indefeasable right of his three nephews : Constantinople listened to his voice : and the Turkish captive was proclaimed in the capital and received on the frontier, as an enemy of the republic. Romanus was not more fortunate in domestic than in foreign war : the loss of two battles compelled him to yield, on the assurance of fair and honorable treatment ; but his enemies were devoid of faith or humanity ; and, after the cruel extinction of his sight, his wounds were left to bleed and corrupt, till in a few days he was relieved from a state of misery. Under the triple reign of the house of Ducas, the two younger brothers were reduced to the vain honors of the purple ; but the eldest, the pusillanimous Michael, was incapable of sustaining the Roman sceptre ; and his surname of *Parapinaces* denotes the reproach which he shared with an avaricious favorite, who enhanced the price, and diminished the measure, of wheat.

In the school of Psellus, and after the example of his mother, the son of Eudocia made some proficiency in philosophy and rhetoric; but his character was degraded, rather than ennobled, by the virtues of a monk and the learning of a sophist. Strong in the contempt of their sovereign and their own esteem, two generals at the head of the European and Asiatic legions, assumed the purple at Adrianople and Nice. Their revolt was in the same months; they bore the same name of Nicephorus; but the two candidates were distinguished by the surnames of Bryennius and Botaniates; the former in the maturity of wisdom and courage, the latter conspicuous only by the memory of his past exploits. While Botaniates advanced with cautious and dilatory steps, his active competitor stood in arms before the gates of Constantinople. The name of Bryennius was illustrious; his cause was popular; but his licentious troops could not be restrained from burning and pillaging a suburb; and the people, who would have hailed the rebel, rejected and repulsed the incendiary of his country. This change of the public opinion was favorable to Botaniates, who a length, with an army of Turks, approached the shores of Chalcedon. A formal invitation, in the name of the patriarch, the synod, and the senate, was circulated through the streets of Constantinople; and the general assembly, in the dome of St. Sophia, debated, with order and calmness, on the choice of their sovereign. The guards of Michael would have dispersed this unarmed multitude; but the feeble emperor, applauding his own moderation and clemency, resigned the ensigns of royalty, and was rewarded with the monastic habit, and the title of Archbishop of Ephesus. He left a son, a Constantine, born and educated in the purple; and a daughter of the house of Ducas illustrated the blood and confirmed the succession, of the Comnenian dynasty.

John Comnenus, the brother of the emperor Isaac, survived in peace and dignity his generous refusal of the sceptre. By his wife Anna, a woman of masculine spirit and policy, he left eight children: the three daughters multiplied the Comnenian alliance with the noblest of the Greeks: of the five sons, Manuel was stopped by a premature death; Isaac and Alexius restored the Imperial greatness of their house, which was enjoyed without toil or danger by the two younger brethren, Adrian and Nicephorus. Alexius, the third and most illustrious of the brothers, was endowed by nature with the choicest gifts both of mind and body: they were cultivated by a liberal education, and exercised in the school of obedience and adversity. The youth was dismissed from the perils of the Turkish war, by the paternal care of the emperor Romanus: but the mother of the Comneni, with her as-

piring race, was accused of treason, and banished, by the sons of
Ducas, to an island in the Propontis.   The two brothers soon
emerged into favor and action, fought by each other's side against
the rebels and barbarians, and adhered to the emperor Michael,
till he was deserted by the world and by himself.   In his first
interview with Botaniates, "Prince," said Alexius, with a noble
frankness, "my duty rendered me your enemy ; the decrees of
God and of the people have made me your subject.   Judge of my
future loyalty by my past opposition."   The successor of Michael
entertained him with esteem and confidence : his valor was employed against three rebels, who disturbed the peace of the empire, or at least of the emperors.   Ursel, Bryennius, and Basila-
cius, were formidable by their numerous forces and military fame :
they were successively vanquished in the field, and led in chains
to the foot of the throne ; and whatever treatment they might receive from a timid and cruel court, they applauded the clemency,
as well as the courage, of their conqueror.   But the loyalty of the
Comneni was soon tainted by fear and suspicion ; nor is it easy to
settle between a subject and a despot, the debt of gratitude
which the former is tempted to claim by a revolt, and the latter
to discharge by an executioner.   The refusal of Alexius to march
against a fourth rebel, the husband of his sister, destroyed the
merit or memory of his past services : the favorites of Botaniates
provoked the ambition which they apprehended and accused ;
and the retreat of the two brothers might be justified by the defence of their life and liberty.   The women of the family were
deposited in a sanctuary, respected by tyrants : the men, mounted
on horseback, sallied from the city, and erected the standard of
civil war.   The soldiers who had been gradually assembled in the
capital and the neighborhood, were devoted to the cause of a victorious and injured leader : the ties of common interest and domestic alliance secured the attachment of the house of Ducas ; and
the generous dispute of the Comneni was terminated by the decisive resolution of Isaac, who was the first to invest his younger
brother with the name and ensigns of royalty.   They returned to
Constantinople, to threaten rather than besiege that impregnable fortress ; but the fidelity of the guards was corrupted ; a gate
was surprised, and a fleet was occupied by the active courage of
George Palæologus, who fought against his father, without foreseeing that he labored for his posterity.   Alexius ascended the
throne ; and his aged competitor disappeared in a monastery.   An
army of various nations was gratified with the pillage of the city ;
but the public disorders were expiated by the tears and fasts of

the Comneni, who submitted to every penance compatible with the possession of the empire.

The life of the emperor Alexius has been delineated by a favorite daughter, who was inspired by a tender regard for his person and a laudable zeal to perpetuate his virtues. Conscious of the just suspicions of her readers, the princess Anna Comnena repeatedly protests, that, besides her personal knowledge, she had searched the discourse and writings of the most respectable veterans: and after an interval of thirty years, forgotten by, and forgetful of, the world, her mournful solitude was inaccessible to hope and fear; and that truth, the naked perfect truth, was more dear and sacred than the memory of her parent. Yet, instead of the simplicity of style and narrative which wins our belief, an elaborate affectation of rhetoric and science betrays in every page the vanity of a female author. The genuine character of Alexius is lost in a vague constellation of virtues; and the perpetual strain of panegyric and apology awakens our jealousy, to question the veracity of the historian and the merit of the hero. We cannot, however, refuse her judicious and important remark, that the disorders of the times were the misfortune and the glory of Alexius; and that every calamity which can afflict a declining empire was accumulated on his reign by the justice of Heaven and the vices of his predecessors. In the East, the victorious Turks had spread, from Persia to the Hellespont, the reign of the Koran and the Crescent: the West was invaded by the adventurous valor of the Normans; and, in the moments of peace, the Danube poured forth new swarms, who had gained, in the science of war, what they had lost in the ferociousness of manners. The sea was not less hostile than the land; and while the frontiers were assaulted by an open enemy, the palace was distracted with secret treason and conspiracy. On a sudden, the banner of the Cross was displayed by the Latins; Europe was precipitated on Asia; and Constantinople had almost been swept away by this impetuous deluge. In the tempest, Alexius steered the Imperial vessel with dexterity and courage. At the head of his armies, he was bold in action, skilful in stratagem, patient of fatigue, ready to improve his advantages, and rising from his defeats with inexhaustible vigor. The discipline of the camp was revived, and a new generation of men and soldiers was created by the example and precepts of their leader. In his intercourse with the Latins, Alexius was patient and artful: his discerning eye pervaded the new system of an unknown world; and I shall hereafter describe the superior policy with which he balanced the interests and passions of the champions of the first crusade. In a long reign of

thirty-seven years he subdued and pardoned the envy of his
equals : the laws of public and private order were restored : the
arts of wealth and science were cultivated : the limits of the empire were enlarged in Europe and Asia ; and the Comnenian
sceptre was transmitted to his children of the third and fourth
generation. Yet the difficulties of the times betrayed some defects
in his character ; and have exposed his memory to some just or
ungenerous reproach. The reader may possibly smile at the lavish
praise which his daughter so often bestows on a flying hero : the
weakness or prudence of his situation might be mistaken for a
want of personal courage ; and his political arts are branded by
the Latins with the names of deceit and dissimulation. The
increase of the male and female branches of his family adorned the
throne, and secured the succession ; but their princely luxury and
pride offended the patricians, exhausted the revenue, and insulted
the misery of the people. Anna is a faithful witness that his
happiness was destroyed, and his health was broken, by the cares
of a public life : the patience of Constantinople was fatigued by
the length and severity of his reign ; and before Alexius expired,
he had lost the love and reverence of his subjects. The clergy could
not forgive his application of the sacred riches to the defence of
the state ; but they applauded his theological learning and ardent
zeal for the orthodox faith, which he defended with his tongue,
his pen, and his sword. His character was degraded by the superstition of the Greeks ; and the same inconsistent principle of
human nature enjoined the emperor to found a hospital for the
poor and infirm, and to direct the execution of a heretic, who
was burnt alive in the square of St. Sophia. Even the sincerity of
his moral and religious virtues was suspected by the persons who
had passed their lives in his familiar confidence. In his last
hours, when he was pressed by his wife Irene to alter the succession, he raised his head, and breathed a pious ejaculation on the
vanity of this world. The indignant reply of the empress may be
inscribed as an epitaph on his tomb, " You die, as you have
lived—A HYPOCRITE !''

It was the wish of Irene to supplant the eldest of her surviving
sons, in favor of her daughter the princess Anna, whose philosophy
would not have refused the weight of a diadem. But the order
of male succession was asserted by the friends of their country ;
the lawful heir drew the royal signet from the finger of his insensible or conscious father ; and the empire obeyed the master of the
palace. Anna Comnena was stimulated by ambition and revenge
to conspire against the life of her brother, and when the design
was prevented by the fears or scruples of her husband, she pas-

sionately exclaimed, that nature had mistaken the two sexes, and had endowed Bryennius with the soul of a woman. The two sons of Alexius, John and Isaac, maintained the fraternal concord, the hereditary virtue of their race, and the younger brother was content with the title of *Sebastocrator*, which approached the dignity, without sharing the power, of the emperor. In the same person, the claims of primogeniture and merit were fortunately united ; his swarthy complexion, harsh features, and diminutive stature, had suggested the ironical surname of Calo-Johannes, or John the Handsome, which his grateful subjects more seriously applied to the beauties of his mind. After the discovery of her treason, the life and fortune of Anna were justly forfeited to the laws. Her life was spared by the clemency of the emperor ; but he visited the pomp and treasures of her palace, and bestowed the rich confiscation on the most deserving of his friends. That respectable friend, Axuch, a slave of Turkish extraction, presumed to decline the gift, and to intercede for the criminal : his generous master applauded and imitated the virtue of his favorite, and the reproach or complaint of an injured brother was the only chastisement of the guilty princess. After this example of clemency, the remainder of his reign was never disturbed by conspiracy or rebellion : feared by his nobles, beloved by his people, John was never reduced to the painful necessity of punishing, or even of pardoning, his personal enemies. During his government of twenty-five years, the penalty of death was abolished in the Roman empire, a law of mercy most delightful to the humane theorist, but of which the practice, in a large and vicious community, is seldom consistent with the public safety. Severe to himself, indulgent to others, chaste, frugal, abstemious, the philosophic Marcus would not have disdained the artless virtues of his successor, derived from his heart, and not borrowed from the schools. He despised and moderated the stately magnificence of the Byzantine court, so oppressive to the people, so contemptible to the eye of reason. Under such a prince, innocence had nothing to fear, and merit had every thing to hope ; and, without assuming the tyrannic office of a censor, he introduced a gradual though visible reformation in the public and private manners of Constantinople. The only defect of this accomplished character was the frailty of noble minds, the love of arms and military glory. Yet the frequent expeditions of John the Handsome may be justified, at least in their principle, by the necessity of repelling the Turks from the Hellespont and the Bosphorus. The sultan of Iconium was confined to his capital, the barbarians were driven to the mountains, and the maritime provinces of Asia enjoyed the transient blessings of their deliverance. From Constantinople to Antioch and Aleppo, he repeatedly marched at the head of a victorious army, and in the sieges and battles of this holy war, his Latin allies were astonished by the superior spirit and prowess of a Greek. As he began to indulge the ambitious hope of restoring the ancient limits of the empire, as he revolved in his mind, the Euphrates and Tigris, the dominion of Syria, and the conquest of Jerusalem, the thread of his life and of the public felicity was broken by a singular accident. He hunted the wild boar in the valley of Anazarbus, and had fixed his javelin in the body of the furious animal ; but in the struggle a poisoned arrow dropped from his quiver, and a slight wound in his hand, which produced a mortification, was fatal to the best and greatest of the Comnenian princes.

A premature death had swept away the two eldest sons of John the Handsome ; of the two survivors, Isaac and Manuel, his judgment or affection preferred the younger ; and the choice of their dying prince was ratified by the soldiers, who had applauded the valor of his favorite in the Turkish war. The faithful Axuch hastened to the capital, secured the person of Isaac in honorable confinement, and purchased, with a gift of two hundred pounds of silver, the leading ecclesiastics of St. Sophia, who possessed a decisive voice in the consecration of an emperor. With his veteran and affectionate troops, Manuel soon visited Constantinople ; his brother acquiesced in the title of Sebastocrator ; his subjects admired the lofty stature and martial graces of their new sovereign, and listened with credulity to the flattering promise, that he blended the wisdom of age with the activity and vigor of youth. By the experience of his government, they were taught, that he emulated the spirit, and shared the talents, of his father, whose social virtues were buried in the grave. A reign of thirty-seven years is filled by a perpetual though various warfare against the Turks, the Christians, and the hordes of the wilderness beyond the Danube. The arms of Manuel were exercised on Mount Taurus, in the plains of Hungary, on the coast of Italy and Egypt, and on the seas of Sicily and Greece : the influence of his negotiations extended from Jerusalem to Rome and Russia ; and the Byzantine monarchy, for a while, became an object of respect or terror to the powers of Asia and Europe. Educated in the silk and purple of the East, Manuel possessed the iron temper of a soldier, which cannot easily be paralleled, except in the lives of Richard the First of England, and of Charles the Twelfth of Sweden. Such was his strength and exercise in arms, that Raymond, surnamed the Hercules of Antioch, was incapable of wielding the lance and buckler of the Greek emperor. In a famous tournament he entered the lists on a fiery courser, and overturned in his first career two of the stoutest of the Italian knights. The first in the charge, the last in the retreat, his friends and his enemies alike trembled, the former for *his* safety, and the latter for their own. After posting an ambuscade in a wood, he rode forwards in search of some perilous adventure, accompanied only by his brother and the faithful Axuch, who refused to desert their sovereign. Eighteen horsemen, after a short combat, fled before them : but the numbers of the enemy increased ; the march of the re-enforcement was tardy and fearful, and Manuel, without receiving a wound, cut his way through a squadron of five hundred Turks. In a battle against the Hungarians, impatient of the slowness of his troops, he snatched a standard from the head of the column, and was the first, almost alone, who passed a bridge that separated him from the enemy. In the same country, after transporting his army beyond the Save, he sent back the boats, with an order, under pain of death, to their commander, that he should leave him to conquer or die on that hostile land. In the siege of Corfu, towing after him a captive galley, the emperor stood aloft on the poop, opposing against the volleys of darts and stones, a large buckler and a flowing sail ; nor could he have escaped inevitable death, had not the Sicilian admiral enjoined his archers to respect the person of a hero. In one day he is said to have slain above forty of the barbarians with his own hand ; he returned to the camp, dragging along four Turkish prisoners, whom he had tied to the rings of his saddle ; he was ever the foremost to provoke or to accept a single combat ; and the *gigantic* champions, who encountered his arm, were transpierced by the lance, or cut asunder by the sword, of the invincible Manuel. The story of his exploits, which appear as a model or a copy of the romances of chivalry, may induce a reasonable suspicion of the veracity of the Greeks : I will not, to vindicate their credit, endanger my own : yet I may observe, that, in the long series of their annals, Manuel is the only prince who has been the subject of similar exaggeration. With the valor of a soldier, he did not unite the skill or prudence of a general ; his victories were not productive of any permanent or useful conquest ; and his Turkish laurels were blasted in his last unfortunate campaign, in which he lost his army in the mountains of Pisidia, and owed his deliverance to the generosity of the sultan. But the most singular feature in the character of Manuel is the contrast and vicissitude of labor and sloth, of hardiness and effeminacy. In war he seemed ignorant of peace, in peace he appeared incapable of war. In the

field he slept in the sun or in the snow, tired in the longest
marches the strength of his men and horses, and shared with a smile
the abstinence or diet of the camp.   No sooner did he return to
Constantinople than he resigned himself to the arts and pleasures
of a life of luxury : the expense of his dress, his table, and his
palace, surpassed the measure of his predecessors, and whole summer days were idly wasted in the delicious isles of the Propontis,
in the incestuous love of his niece Theodora.   The double cost of
a warlike and dissolute prince exhausted the revenue, and multiplied the taxes ; and Manuel, in the distress of his last Turkish
campaign, endured a bitter reproach from the mouth of a desperate
soldier.   As he quenched his thirst, he complained that the water
of a fountain was mingled with Christian blood.   " It is not the
first time," exclaimed a voice from the crowd, " that you have
drank, O emperor, the blood of your Christian subjects."   Manuel
Comnenus was twice married, to the virtuous Bertha or Irene of
Germany, and to the beauteous Maria, a French or Latin princess
of Antioch.   The only daughter of his first wife was destined for
Bela, a Hungarian prince, who was educated at Constantinople
under the name of Alexius ; and the consummation of their nuptials
might have transferred the Roman sceptre to a race of free and
warlike barbarians.   But as soon as Maria of Antioch had given
a son and heir to the empire, the presumptive rights of Bela were
abolished, and he was deprived of his promised bride ; but the
Hungarian prince resumed his name and the kingdom of his
fathers, and displayed such virtues as might excite the regret and
envy of the Greeks.   The son of Maria was named Alexius ; and
at the age of ten years he ascended the Byzantine throne, after
his father's decease had closed the glories of the Comnenian line.

The fraternal concord of the two sons of the great Alexius had
been sometimes clouded by an opposition of interest and passion.
By ambition, Isaac the Sebastocrator was excited to flight and
rebellion, from whence he was reclaimed by the firmness and
clemency of John the Handsome.   The errors of Isaac, the father
of the emperors of Trebizond, were short and venial ; but John,
the elder of his sons, renounced forever his religion.   Provoked
by a real or imaginary insult of his uncle, he escaped from the
Roman to the Turkish camp : his apostasy was rewarded with
the sultan's daughter, the title of Chelebi, or noble, and the
inheritance of a princely estate ; and in the fifteenth century,
Mahomet the Second boasted of his Imperial descent from the
Comnenian family.   Andronicus, the younger brother of John,
son of Isaac, and grandson of Alexius Comnenus, is one of the
most conspicuous characters of the age ; and his genuine adven-

tures might form the subject of a very singular romance. To justify the choice of three ladies of royal birth, it is incumbent on me to observe, that their fortunate lover was cast in the best proportions of strength and beauty ; and that the want of the softer graces was supplied by a manly countenance, a lofty stature, athletic muscles, and the air and deportment of a soldier. The preservation, in his old age, of health and vigor, was the reward of temperance and exercise. A piece of bread and a draught of water was often his sole and evening repast ; and if he tasted of a wild boar or a stag, which he had roasted with his own hands, it was the well-earned fruit of a laborious chase. Dexterous in arms, he was ignorant of fear : his persuasive eloquence could bend to every situation and character of life : his style, though not his practice, was fashioned by the example of St. Paul ; and, in every deed of mischief, he had a heart to resolve, a head to contrive, and a hand to execute. In his youth, after the death of the emperor John, he followed the retreat of the Roman army ; but, in the march through Asia Minor, design or accident tempted him to wander in the mountains : the hunter was encompassed by the Turkish huntsmen, and he remained some time a reluctant or willing captive in the power of the sultan. His virtues and vices recommended him to the favor of his cousin : he shared the perils and the pleasures of Manuel ; and while the emperor lived in public incest with his niece Theodora, the affections of her sister Eudocia were seduced and enjoyed by Andronicus. Above the decencies of her sex and rank, she gloried in the name of his concubine ; and both the palace and the camp could witness that she slept, or watched, in the arms of her lover. She accompanied him to his military command of Cilicia, the first scene of his valor and imprudence. He pressed, with active ardor, the siege of Mopsuestia : the day was employed in the boldest attacks ; but the night was wasted in song and dance ; and a band of Greek comedians formed the choicest part of his retinue. Andronicus was surprised by the sally of a vigilant foe ; but, while his troops fled in disorder, his invincible lance transpierced the thickest ranks of the Armenians. On his return to the Imperial camp in Macedonia, he was received by Manuel with public smiles and a private reproof ; but the duchies of Naissus, Braniseba, and Castoria, were the reward or consolation of the unsuccessful general. Eudocia still attended her motions : at midnight their tent was suddenly attacked by her angry brothers, impatient to expiate her infamy in his blood : his daring spirit refused her advice, and the disguise of a female habit ; and, boldly starting from his couch, he drew his sword, and cut his way through the numerous assassins. It was here that he first betrayed his ingratitude and treachery: he engaged in a treasonable correspondence with the king of Hungary and the German emperor; approached the royal tent at a suspicious hour with a drawn sword, and, under the mask of a Latin soldier, avowed an intention of revenge against a mortal foe; and imprudently praised the fleetness of his horse as an instrument of flight and safety. The monarch dissembled his suspicions; but, after the close of the campaign, Andronicus was arrested and strictly confined in a tower of the palace of Constantinople.

In this prison he was left about twelve years; a most painful restraint, from which the thirst of action and pleasure perpetually urged him to escape. Alone and pensive, he perceived some broken bricks in a corner of the chamber, and gradually widened the passage, till he had explored a dark and forgotten recess. Into this hole he conveyed himself, and the remains of his provisions, replacing the bricks in their former position, and erasing with care the footsteps of his retreat. At the hour of the customary visit, his guards were amazed by the silence and solitude of the prison, and reported, with shame and fear, his incomprehensible flight. The gates of the palace and city were instantly shut: the strictest orders were despatched into the provinces, for the recovery of the fugitive; and his wife, on the suspicion of a pious act, was basely imprisoned in the same tower. At the dead of the night she beheld a spectre: she recognized her husband: they shared their provisions; and a son was the fruit of these stolen interviews, which alleviated the tediousness of their confinement. In the custody of a woman, the vigilance of the keepers was insensibly relaxed; and the captive had accomplished his real escape, when he was discovered, brought back to Constantinople, and loaded with a double chain. At length he found the moment, and the means, of his deliverance. A boy, his domestic servant, intoxicated the guards, and obtained in wax the impression of the keys. By the diligence of his friends, a similar key, with a bundle of ropes, was introduced into the prison, in the bottom of a hogshead. Andronicus employed, with industry and courage, the instruments of his safety, unlocked the doors, descended from the tower, concealed himself all day among the bushes, and scaled in the night the garden-wall of the palace. A boat was stationed for his reception: he visited his own house, embraced his children, cast away his chain, mounted a fleet horse, and directed his rapid course towards the banks of the Danube. At Anchialus in Thrace, an intrepid friend supplied him with horses and money: he passed the river, traversed with speed the desert of Moldavia and the Carpathian hills, and had almost reached the town of Halicz, in the Polish Russia, when he was intercepted by a party of Walachians, who resolved to convey their important captive to Constantinople. His presence of mind again extricated him from this danger. Under the pretence of sickness, he dismounted in the night, and was allowed to step aside from the troop : he planted in the ground his long staff, clothed it with his cap and upper garment ; and, stealing into the wood, left a phantom to amuse, for some time, the eyes of the Walachians. From Halicz he was honorably conducted to Kiow, the residence of the great duke : the subtle Greek soon obtained the esteem and confidence of Ieroslaus ; his character could assume the manners of every climate ; and the barbarians applauded his strength and courage in the chase of the elks and bears of the forest. In this northern region he deserved the forgiveness of Manuel, who solicited the Russian prince to join his arms in the invasion of Hungary. The influence of Andronicus achieved this important service : his private treaty was signed with a promise of fidelity on one side, and of oblivion on the other ; and he marched, at the head of the Russian cavalry, from the Borysthenes to the Danube. In his resentment Manuel had ever sympathized with the martial and dissolute character of his cousin ; and his free pardon was sealed in the assault of Zemlin, in which he was second, and second only, to the valor of the emperor.

No sooner was the exile restored to freedom and his country, than his ambition revived, at first to his own, and at length to the public, misfortune. A daughter of Manuel was a feeble bar to the succession of the more deserving males of the Comnenian blood : her future marriage with the prince of Hungary was repugnant to the hopes or prejudices of the princes and nobles. But when an oath of allegiance was required to the presumptive heir, Andronicus alone asserted the honor of the Roman name, declined the unlawful engagement, and boldly protested against the adoption of a stranger. His patriotism was offensive to the emperor, but he spoke the sentiments of the people, and was removed from the royal presence by an honorable banishment, a second command of the Cilician frontier, with the absolute disposal of the revenues of Cyprus. In this station the Armenians again exercised his courage and exposed his negligence ; and the same rebel, who baffled all his operations, was unhorsed, and almost slain by the vigor of his lance. But Andronicus soon discovered a more easy and pleasing conquest, the beautiful Philippa, sister of the empress Maria, and daughter of Raymond of Poitou, the Latin prince of Antioch. For her sake he deserted his station, and wasted the summer in balls and tournaments : to his love she sacrificed her innocence, her reputation, and the offer of an advantageous marriage. But the resentment of Manuel for this domestic affront interrupted his pleasures : Andronicus left the indiscreet princess to weep and to repent ; and, with a band of desperate adventurers, undertook the pilgrimage of Jerusalem. His birth, his martial renown, and professions of zeal, announced him as the champion of the Cross : he soon captivated both the clergy and the king ; and the Greek prince was invested with the lordship of Berytus, on the coast of Phœnicia. In his neighborhood resided a young and handsome queen, of his own nation and family, great-granddaughter of the emperor Alexis, and widow of Baldwin the Third, king of Jerusalem. She visited and loved her kinsman. Theodora was the third victim of his amorous seduction ; and her shame was more public and scandalous than that of her predecessors. The emperor still thirsted for revenge ; and his subjects and allies of the Syrian frontier were repeatedly pressed to seize the person, and put out the eyes, of the fugitive. In Palestine he was no longer safe ; but the tender Theodora revealed his danger and accompanied his flight. The queen of Jerusalem was exposed to the East, his obsequious concubine ; and two illegitimate children were the living monuments of her weakness. Damascus was his first refuge ; and, in the characters of the great Noureddin and his servant Saladin, the superstitious Greek might learn to revere the virtues of the Mussulmans. As the friend of Noureddin he visited, most probably, Bagdad, and the courts of Persia ; and, after a long circuit round the Caspian Sea and the mountains of Georgia, he finally settled among the Turks of Asia Minor, the hereditary enemies of his country. The sultan of Colonia afforded a hospitable retreat to Andronicus, his mistress and his band of outlaws : the debt of gratitude was paid by frequent inroads in the Roman province of Trebizond ; and he seldom returned without an ample harvest of spoil and of Christian captives. In the story of his adventures, he was fond of comparing himself to David, who escaped, by a long exile, the snares of the wicked. But the royal prophet (he presumed to add) was content to lurk on the borders of Judæa, to slay an Amalekite, and to threaten, in his miserable state, the life of the avaricious Nabal. The excursions of the Comnenian prince had a wider range ; and he had spread over the Eastern world the glory of his name and religion. By a sentence of the Greek church, the licentious rover had been separated from the faithful ; but even this excommunication may prove that he never abjured the profession of Christianity. His vigilance had eluded or repelled the open and secret persecution of the emperor; but he was at length insnared by the captivity of his female companion. The governor of Trebizond succeeded in his attempt to surprise the person of Theodora: the queen of Jerusalem and her two children were sent to Constantinople, and their loss imbittered the tedious solitude of banishment. The fugitive implored and obtained a final pardon, with leave to throw himself at the feet of his sovereign, who was satisfied with the submission of this haughty spirit. Prostrate on the ground, he deplored with tears and groans the guilt of his past rebellion; nor would he presume to arise, unless some faithful subject would drag him to the foot of the throne, by an iron chain with which he had secretly encircled his neck. This extraordinary penance excited the wonder and pity of the assembly; his sins were forgiven by the church and state; but the just suspicion of Manuel fixed his residence at a distance from the court, at Oenoe, a town of Pontus, surrounded with rich vineyards, and situate on the coast of the Euxine. The death of Manuel, and the disorders of the minority, soon opened the fairest field to his ambition. The emperor was a boy of twelve or fourteen years of age, without vigor, or wisdom, or experience: his mother, the empress Mary, abandoned her person and government to a favorite of the Comnenian name; and his sister, another Mary, whose husband, an Italian, was decorated with the title of Cæsar, excited a conspiracy, and at length an insurrection, against her odious step-mother. The provinces were forgotten, the capital was in flames, and a century of peace and order was overthrown in the vice and weakness of a few months. A civil war was kindled in Constantinople; the two factions fought a bloody battle in the square of the palace, and the rebels sustained a regular siege in the cathedral of St. Sophia. The patriarch labored with honest zeal to heal the wounds of the republic, the most respectable patriots called aloud for a guardian and avenger, and every tongue repeated the praise of the talents and even the virtues of Andronicus. In his retirement, he affected to revolve the solemn duties of his oath: "If the safety or honor of the Imperial family be threatened, I will reveal and oppose the mischief to the utmost of my power." His correspondence with the patriarch and patricians was seasoned with apt quotations from the Psalms of David and the epistles of St. Paul; and he patiently waited till he was called to her deliverance by the voice of his country. In his march from Oenoe to Constantinople, his slender train insensibly swelled to a crowd and an army: his professions of religion and loyalty were mistaken for the language of his heart; and the simplicity of a foreign dress, which showed to advantage his majestic stature, displayed a lively image of his poverty and exile. All opposition sunk before him ; he reached the straits of the Thracian Bosphorus ; the Byzantine navy sailed from the harbor to receive and transport the savior of the empire ; the torrent was loud and irresistible, and the insects who had basked in the sunshine of royal favor disappeared at the blast of the storm. It was the first care of Andronicus to occupy the palace, to salute the emperor, to confine his mother, to punish her minister, and to restore the public order and tranquillity. He then visited the sepulchre of Manuel : the spectators were ordered to stand aloof, but as he bowed in the attitude of prayer, they heard, or thought they heard, a murmur of triumph or revenge : "I no longer fear thee, my old enemy, who hast driven me a vagabond to every climate of the earth. Thou art safely deposited under a sevenfold dome, from whence thou canst never arise till the signal of the last trumpet. It is now my turn, and speedily will I trample on thy ashes and thy posterity." From his subsequent tyranny we may impute such feelings to the man and the moment ; but it is not extremely probable that he gave an articulate sound to his secret thoughts. In the first months of his administration, his designs were veiled by a fair semblance of hypocrisy, which could delude only the eyes of the multitude : the coronation of Alexius was performed with due solemnity, and his perfidious guardian, holding in his hands the body and blood of Christ, most fervently declared that he lived, and was ready to die, for the service of his beloved pupil. But his numerous adherents were instructed to maintain, that the sinking empire must perish in the hands of a child, that the Romans could only be saved by a veteran prince, bold in arms, skilful in policy, and taught to reign by the long experience of fortune and mankind ; and that it was the duty of every citizen to force the reluctant modesty of Andronicus to undertake the burden of the public care. The young emperor was himself constrained to join his voice to the general acclamation, and to solicit the association of a colleague, who instantly degraded him from the supreme rank, secluded his person, and verified the rash declaration of the patriarch, that Alexius might be considered as dead, so soon as he was committed to the custody of his guardian. But his death was preceded by the imprisonment and execution of his mother. After blackening her reputation, and inflaming against her the passions of the multitude, the tyrant accused and tried the empress for a treasonable correspondence with the king of Hungary. His own son, a youth of honor and humanity, avowed his abhorrence of this flagitious act, and three of the judges had the merit of preferring their conscience to their safety : but the obsequious tribunal, without requiring any re-proof, or hearing any defence, condemned the widow of Manuel ; and her unfortunate son subscribed the sentence of her death. Maria was strangled, her corpse was buried in the sea, and her memory was wounded by the insult most offensive to female vanity, a false and ugly representation of her beauteous form. The fate of her son was not long deferred ; he was strangled with a bowstring ; and the tyrant, insensible to pity or remorse, after surveying the body of the innocent youth, struck it rudely with his foot : "Thy father," he cried, "was a *knave*, thy mother a *whore*, and thyself a *fool!*"

The Roman sceptre, the reward of his crimes, was held by Andronicus about three years and a half as the guardian or sover-eign of the empire. His government exhibited a singular contrast of vice and virtue. When he listened to his passions, he was the scourge ; when he consulted his reason, the father, of his people. In the exercise of private justice, he was equitable and rigorous : a shameful and pernicious venality was abolished, and the offices were filled with the most deserving candidates, by a prince who had sense to choose, and severity to punish. He prohibited the in-human practice of pillaging the goods and persons of shipwrecked mariners ; the provinces, so long the objects of oppression or neglect, revived in prosperity and plenty ; and millions applauded the distant blessings of his reign, while he was cursed by the witnesses of his daily cruelties. The ancient proverb, That blood-thirsty is the man who returns from banishment to power, had been applied, with too much truth, to Marius and Tiberius ; and was now verified for the third time in the life of Andronicus. His memory was stored with a black list of the enemies and rivals, who had traduced his merit, opposed his greatness, or insulted his misfortunes ; and the only comfort of his exile was the sacred hope and promise of revenge. The necessary extinction of the young emperor and his mother imposed the fatal obligation of extirpating the friends, who hated, and might punish, the assassin; and the repetition of murder rendered him less willing, and less able, to forgive.* A horrid narrative of the victims whom he sac-

---

* Fallmerayer (Geschichte des Kaiserthums von Trapezunt, p. 29, 33) has highly drawn the character of Andronicus. In his view, the extermination of the Byzan-tine factions and dissolute nobility was part of a deep-laid and splendid plan for the regeneration of the empire. It was necessary for the wise and benevolent schemes of the father of his people to lop off those limbs which were infected with irremediable pestilence—

"and with necessity,
The tyrant's plea, excused his devilish deeds !"—

Still the fall of Andronicus was a fatal blow to the Byzantine empire.—M.

rificed by poison or the sword, by the sea or the flames, would be
less expressive of his cruelty than the appellation of the halcyon
days, which was applied to a rare and bloodless week of repose :
the tyrant strove to transfer, on the laws and the judges, some
portion of his guilt ; but the mask was fallen, and his subjects
could no longer mistake the true author of their calamities. The
noblest of the Greeks, more especially those who, by descent or
alliance, might dispute the Comnenian inheritance, escaped from
the monster's den : Nice and Prusa, Sicily or Cyprus, were their
places of refuge ; and as their flight was already criminal, they
aggravated their offence by an open revolt, and the Imperial title.
Yet Andronicus resisted the daggers and swords of his most formidable enemies : Nice and Prusa were reduced and chastised :
the Sicilians were content with the sack of Thessalonica ; and the
distance of Cyprus was not more propitious to the rebel than to
the tyrant. His throne was subverted by a rival without merit,
and a people without arms. Isaac Angelus, a descendant in the
female line from the great Alexius, was marked as a victim by the
prudence or superstition of the emperor.* In a moment of despair,
Angelus defended his life and liberty, slew the executioner, and
fled to the church of St. Sophia. The sanctuary was insensibly
filled with a curious and mournful crowd, who, in his fate, prog-
nosticated their own. But their lamentations were soon turned
to curses, and their curses to threats : they dared to ask, "Why
do we fear ? why do we obey ? We are many, and he is one : our
patience is the only bond of our slavery." With the dawn of day
the city burst into a general sedition, the prisons were thrown
open, the coldest and most servile were roused to the defence of
their country, and Isaac, the second of the name, was raised from
the sanctuary to the throne. Unconscious of his danger, the tyrant
was absent ; withdrawn from the toils of state, in the delicious
islands of the Propontis. He had contracted an indecent marriage
with Alice, or Agnes, daughter of Lewis the Seventh, of France,
and relict of the unfortunate Alexius ; and his society, more
suitable to his temper than to his age, was composed of a young
wife and a favorite concubine. On the first alarm, he rushed to
Constantinople, impatient for the blood of the guilty ; but he was
astonished by the silence of the palace, the tumult of the city,
and the general desertion of mankind. Andronicus proclaimed a
free pardon to his subjects ; they neither desired, nor would grant,
forgiveness ; he offered to resign the crown to his son Manuel ; but

---

* According to Nicetas (p. 444), Andronicus despised the imbecile Isaac too much
to fear him ; he was arrested by the officious zeal of Stephen, the instrument of
the emperor's cruelties.—M.

the virtues of the son could not expiate his father's crimes. The sea was still open for his retreat ; but the news of the revolution had flown along the coast ; when fear had ceased, obedience was no more : the Imperial galley was pursued and taken by an armed brigantine ; and the tyrant was dragged to the presence of Isaac Angelus, loaded with fetters, and a long chain round his neck. His eloquence, and the tears of his female companions, pleaded in vain for his life ; but, instead of the decencies of a legal execution, the new monarch abandoned the criminal to the numerous sufferers, whom he had deprived of a father, a husband or a friend. His teeth and hair, an eye and a hand, were torn from him, as a poor compensation for their loss ; and a short respite was allowed, that he might feel the bitterness of death. Astride on a camel, without any danger of rescue, he was carried through the city, and the basest of the populace rejoiced to trample on the fallen majesty of their prince. After a thousand blows and outrages, Andronicus was hung by the feet, between two pillars, that supported the statues of a wolf and a sow ; and every hand that could reach the public enemy, inflicted on his body some mark of ingenious or brutal cruelty, till two friendly or furious Italians, plunging their swords into his body, released him from all human punishment. In this long and painful agony, " Lord have mercy upon me !" and " Why will you bruise a broken reed ?" were the only words that escaped from his mouth. Our hatred for the tyrant is lost in pity for the man ; nor can we blame his pusillanimous resignation, since a Greek Christian was no longer master of his life.

I have been tempted to expatiate on the extraordinary character and adventures of Andronicus ; but I shall here terminate the series of the Greek emperors since the time of Heraclius. The branches that sprang from the Comnenian trunk had insensibly withered ; and the male line was continued only in the posterity of Andronicus himself, who, in the public confusion, usurped the sovereignty of Trebizond, so obscure in history, and so famous in romance. A private citizen of Philadelphia, Constantine Angelus, had emerged to wealth and honors, by his marriage with a daughter of the emperor Alexius. His son Andronicus is conspicuous only by his cowardice. His grandson Isaac punished and succeeded the tyrant : but he was dethroned by his own vices, and the ambition of his brother ; and their discord introduced the Latins to the conquest of Constantinople, the first great period in the fall of the Eastern empire.

If we compute the number and duration of the reigns, it will be found that a period of six hundred years is filled by sixty emperors, including in the Augustan list some female sovereigns ;

and deducting some usurpers who were never acknowledged in the capital, and some princes who did not live to possess their inheritance. The average proportion will allow ten years for each emperor, far below the chronological rule of Sir Isaac Newton, who, from the experience of more recent and regular monarchies, has defined about eighteen or twenty years as the term of an ordinary reign. The Byzantine empire was most tranquil and prosperous when it could acquiesce in hereditary succession : five dynasties, the Heraclian, Isaurian, Amorian, Basilian, and Comnenian families, enjoyed and transmitted the royal patrimony during their respective series of five, four, three, six, and four generations ; several princes number the years of their reign with those of their infancy ; and Constantine the Seventh and his two grandsons occupy the space of an entire century. But in the intervals of the Byzantine dynasties, the succession is rapid and broken, and the name of a successful candidate is speedily erased by a more fortunate competitor. Many were the paths that led to the summit of royalty : the fabric of rebellion was overthrown by the stroke of conspiracy, or undermined by the silent arts of intrigue : the favorites of the soldiers or people, of the senate or clergy, of the women and eunuchs, were alternately clothed with the purple : the means of their elevation were base, and their end was often contemptible or tragic. A being of the nature of men endowed with the same faculties, but with a longer measure of existence, would cast down a smile of pity and contempt on the crimes and follies of human ambition, so eager, in a narrow span, to grasp at a precarious and short-lived enjoyment. It is thus that the experience of history exalts and enlarges the horizon of our intellectual view. In a composition of some days, in a perusal of some hours, six hundred years have rolled away, and the duration of a life or reign is contracted to a fleeting moment ; the grave is ever beside the throne : the success of a criminal is almost instantly followed by the loss of his prize ; and our immortal reason survives and disdains the sixty phantoms of kings who have passed before our eyes, and faintly dwell on our remembrance. The observation that, in every age and climate, ambition has prevailed with the same commanding energy, may abate the surprise of a philosopher. But while he condemns the vanity, he may search the motive, of this universal desire to obtain and hold the sceptre of dominion. To the greater part of the Byzantine series we cannot reasonably ascribe the love of fame and of mankind. The virtue alone of John Comnenus was beneficent and pure : the most illustrious of the princes, who precede or follow that respectable name, have trod with some dexterity and vigor the crooked and bloody paths of a selfish policy : in scrutinizing the imperfect characters of Leo the Isaurian, Basil the First, and Alexius Comnenus, of Theophilus, the second Basil, and Manuel Comnenus, our esteem and censure are almost equally balanced ; and the remainder of the Imperial crowd could only desire and expect to be forgotten by posterity. Was personal happiness the aim and object of their ambition ? I shall not descant on the vulgar topics of the misery of kings ; but I may surely observe, that their condition, of all others, is the most pregnant with fear, and the least susceptible of hope. For these opposite passions, a larger scope was allowed in the revolutions of antiquity than in the smooth and solid temper of the modern world, which cannot easily repeat either the triumph of Alexander or the fall of Darius. But the peculiar infelicity of the Byzantine princes exposed them to domestic perils, without affording any lively promise of foreign conquest. From the pinnacle of greatness, Andronicus was precipitated by a death more cruel and shameful than that of the vilest malefactor ; but the most glorious of his predecessors had much more to dread from their subjects than to hope from their enemies. The army was licentious without spirit, the nation turbulent without freedom : the barbarians of the East and West pressed on the monarchy, and the loss of the provinces was terminated by the final servitude of the capital.

The entire series of Roman Emperors, from the first of the Cæsars to the last of the Constantines, extends above fifteen hundred years ; and the term of dominion, unbroken by foreign conquest, surpasses the measure of the ancient monarchies ; the Assyrians or Medes, the successors of Cyrus, or those of Alexander.

CHAPTER XLIX.

INTRODUCTION, WORSHIP, AND PERSECUTION OF IMAGES.— REVOLT OF ITALY AND ROME.—TEMPORAL DOMINION OF THE POPES.— CONQUEST OF ITALY BY THE FRANKS.—ESTABLISHMENT OF IMAGES.—CHARACTER AND CORONATION OF CHARLEMAGNE.—RESTORATION AND DECAY OF THE ROMAN EMPIRE IN THE WEST.— INDEPENDENCE OF ITALY.—CONSTITUTION OF THE GERMANIC BODY.

In the connection of the church and state, I have considered the former as subservient only, and relative, to the latter ; a salutary maxim, if in fact, as well as in narrative, it had ever been held sacred. The Oriental philosophy of the Gnostics, the dark abyss of predestination and grace, and the strange transformation of the Eucharist from the sign to the substance of Christ's body,[1] I have purposely abandoned to the curiosity of speculative divines. But I have reviewed, with diligence and pleasure, the objects of ecclesiastical history, by which the decline and fall of the Roman empire were materially affected, the propagation of Christianity, the constitution of the Catholic church, the ruin of Paganism, and the sects that arose from the mysterious controversies concerning the Trinity and incarnation. At the head of this class we may justly rank the worship of images, so fiercely disputed in the eighth and ninth centuries ; since a question of popular superstition produced the revolt of Italy, the temporal power of the popes, and the restoration of the Roman empire in the West.

The primitive Christians were possessed with an unconquerable repugnance to the use and abuse of images ; and this aversion may be ascribed to their descent from the Jews, and their enmity to the Greeks. The Mosaic law had severely proscribed all representations of the Deity ; and that precept was firmly established in the principles and practice of the chosen people. The wit of the Christian apologists was pointed against the foolish idolaters, who bowed before the workmanship of their own hands ; the images of brass and marble, which, had *they* been endowed with sense and motion, should have started rather from the pedestal to adore the creative powers of the artist.[2] Perhaps some recent and imperfect converts of the Gnostic tribe might crown the statues of Christ and St. Paul with the profane honors which they paid to those of Aristotle and Pythagoras ;[3] but the public religion of the Catholics was uniformly simple and spiritual ; and the first notice of the use of pictures is in the censure of the council of Illiberis, three hundred years after the Christian æra. Under the successors of Constantine, in the peace and luxury of the triumphant church, the more prudent bishops condescended to indulge a visible superstition, for the benefit of the multitude, and, after the ruin of Paganism, they were no longer restrained by the apprehension of an odious parallel. The first introduction of a symbolic worship was in the veneration of the cross and of relics. The saints and martyrs, whose intercession was implored, were seated on the right hand of God ; but the gracious and often supernatural favors which, in the popular belief, were showered round their tomb, conveyed an unquestionable sanction of the devout pilgrims, who visited, and touched, and kissed these lifeless remains, the memorials of their merits and sufferings.[4] But a memorial more interesting than the skull or the sandals of a departed worthy is the faithful copy of his person and features, delineated by the arts of painting or sculpture. In every age, such copies, so congenial to human feelings, have been cherished by the zeal of private friendship, or public esteem : the images of the Roman emperors were adored with civil, and almost religious honors ; a reverence less ostentatious, but more sincere, was applied to the statues of sages and patriots ; and these profane virtues, these splendid sins, disappeared in the presence of the holy men, who had died for their celestial and everlasting country. At first the experiment was made with caution and scruple ; and the venerable pictures were discreetly allowed to instruct the ignorant, to awaken the cold, and to gratify the prejudices of the heathen proselytes. By a slow though inevitable progression, the honors of the original were transferred to the copy : the devout Christian prayed before the image of a saint ; and the Pagan rites of genuflection, luminaries, and incense, again stole into the Catholic church. The scruples of reason, or piety, were silenced by the strong evidence of visions and miracles ; and the pictures which speak, and move, and bleed, must be endowed with a divine energy, and may be considered as the proper objects of religious adoration. The most audacious pencil might tremble in the rash attempt of defining, by forms and colors, the infinite Spirit, the eternal Father, who pervades and sustains the universe.[5] But the superstitious mind was more easily reconciled to paint and to worship the angels, and above all, the Son of God, under the human shape, which on earth they have condescended to assume. The second person of the Trinity had been clothed with a real and mortal body ; but that body had ascended into heaven : and had not some similitude been presented to the eyes of his disciples, the spiritual worship of Christ might have been obliterated by the visible relics and representations of the saints. A similar indulgence was requisite and propitious for the Virgin Mary : the place of her burial was unknown ; and the assumption of her soul and body into heaven was adopted by the credulity of the Greeks and Latins. The use, and even the worship, of images was firmly established before the end of the sixth century : they were fondly cherished by the warm imagination of the Greeks and Asiatics : the Pantheon and Vatican were adorned with the emblems of a new superstition ; but this semblance of idolatry was more coldly entertained by the rude barbarians and the Arian clergy of the West. The bolder forms of sculpture, in brass or marble, which peopled the temples of antiquity, were offensive to the fancy or conscience of the Christian Greeks : and a smooth surface of colors has ever been esteemed a more decent and harm-less mode of imitation.[6]

The merit and effect of a copy depends on its resemblance with the original ; but the primitive Christians were ignorant of the genuine features of the Son of God, his mother, and his apostles : the statue of Christ at Paneas in Palestine[7] was more probably that of some temporal savior ; the Gnostics and their profane monuments were reprobated ; and the fancy of the Christian ar-tists could only be guided by the clandestine imitation of some heathen model.   In this distress, a bold and dexterous invention assured at once the likeness of the image and the innocence of the worship.   A new superstructure of fable was raised on the popular basis of a Syrian legend, on the correspondence of Christ and Ab-garus, so famous in the days of Eusebius, so reluctantly deserted by our modern advocates. The bishop of Cæsarea[8] records the epistle,[9] but he most strangely forgets the picture of Christ ; [10] the perfect impression of his face on a linen, with which he gratified the faith of the royal stranger who had invoked his healing power, and offered the strong city of Edessa to protect him against the malice of the Jews.   The ignorance of the primitive church is explained by the long imprisonment of the image in a niche of the wall, from whence, after an oblivion of five hundred years, it was re-leased by some prudent bishop, and seasonably presented to the devotion of the times.   Its first and most glorious exploit was the deliverance of the city from the arms of Chosroes Nushirvan ; and it was soon revered as a pledge of the divine promise, that Edessa should never be taken by a foreign enemy.   It is true, in-deed, that the text of Procopius ascribes the double deliverance of Edessa to the wealth and valor of her citizens, who purchased the absence and repelled the assaults of the Persian monarch. He was ignorant, the profane historian, of the testimony which he is compelled to deliver in the ecclesiastical page of Evagius, that the Palladium was exposed on the rampart, and that the water which had been sprinkled on the holy face, instead of quenching, added new fuel to the flames of the besieged.   After this important service, the image of Edessa was preserved with respect and gratitude ; and if the Armenians rejected the legend, the more credulous Greeks adored the similitude, which was not the work of any mortal pencil, but the immediate creation of the divine original.   The style and sentiments of a Byzantine hymn will declare how far their worship was removed from the grossest idolatry.   " How can we with mortal eyes contemplate this image, whose celestial splendor the host of heaven presumes not to be-hold ?   HE who dwells in heaven, condescends this day to visit us by his venerable image : HE who is seated on the cherubim, visits us this day by a picture, which the Father has delineated with his immaculate hand, which he has formed in an ineffable manner, and which we sanctify by adoring it with fear and love." Before the end of the sixth century, these images, *made without hands* (in Greek it is a single word[11]), were propagated in the camps and cities of the Eastern empire :[12] they were the objects of worship, and the instruments of miracles ; and in the hour of danger or tumult their venerable presence could revive the hope, rekindle the courage, or repress the fury, of the Roman legions. Of these pictures, the far greater part, the transcripts of a human pencil could only pretend to a secondary likeness and improper title : but there were some of higher descent, who derived their resemblance from an immediate contact with the original, endowed, for that purpose, with a miraculous and prolific virtue. The most ambitious aspired from a filial to a fraternal relation with the image of Edessa ; and such is the *veronica* of Rome, or Spain, or Jerusalem, which Christ in his agony and bloody sweat applied to his face, and delivered to a holy matron. The fruitful precedent was speedily transferred to the Virgin Mary, and the saints and martyrs. In the church of Diospolis, in Palestine, the features of the Mother of God[13] were deeply inscribed in a marble column ; the East and West have been decorated by the pencil of St. Luke ; and the Evangelist, who was perhaps a physician, has been forced to exercise the occupation of a painter, so profane and odious in the eyes of the primitive Christians. The Olympian Jove, created by the muse of Homer and the chisel of Phidias, might inspire a philosophic mind with momentary devotion ; but these Catholic images were faintly and flatly delineated by monkish artists in the last degeneracy of taste and genius.[14]

The worship of images had stolen into the church by insensible degrees, and each petty step was pleasing to the superstitious mind as productive of comfort, and innocent of sin. But in the beginning of the eighth century, in the full magnitude of the abuse, the more timorous Greeks were awakened by an apprehension, that under the mask of Christianity, they had restored the religion of their fathers : they heard, with grief and impatience, the name of idolaters ; the incessant charge of the Jews and Mahometans,[15] who derived from the Law and the Koran an immortal hatred to graven images and all relative worship. The servitude of the Jews might curb their zeal, and depreciate their authority ; but the triumphant Mussulmans, who reigned at Damascus, and threatened Constantinople, cast into the scale of reproach the accumulated weight of truth and victory. The cities of Syria, Palestine, and Egypt had been fortified with the images of Christ, his mother, and his saints ; and each city presumed on the hope or promise of miraculous defence. In a rapid conquest of ten years, the Arabs subdued those cities and these images ; and, in their opinion, the Lord of Hosts pronounced a decisive judgment between the adoration and contempt of these mute and inanimate idols.* For a while Edessa had braved the Persian assaults ; but the chosen city, the spouse of Christ, was involved in the common ruin ; and his divine resemblance became the slave and trophy of the infidels. After a servitude of three hundred years, the Palladium was yielded to the devotion of Constantinople, for a ransom of twelve thousand pounds of silver, the redemption of two hundred Mussulmans, and a perpetual truce for the territory of Edessa.[16] In this season of distress and dismay, the eloquence of the monks was exercised in the defence of images ; and they attempted to prove that the sin and schism of the greatest part of the Orientals had forfeited the favor, and annihilated the virtue of these precious symbols. But they were now opposed by the murmurs of many simple or rational Christians, who appealed to the evidence of texts, of facts, and of the primitive times, and secretly desired the reformation of the church. As the worship of images had never been established by any general or positive law, its progress in the Eastern empire had been retarded, or accelerated, by the differences of men and manners, the local degrees of refinement, and the personal characters of the bishops. The splendid devotion was fondly cherished by the levity of the capital, and the inventive genius of the Byzantine clergy ; while the rude and remote districts of Asia were strangers to this innovation of sacred luxury. Many large congregations of Gnostics and Arians maintained, after their conversion, the simple worship which had preceded their separation ; and the Armenians, the most warlike subjects of Rome, were not reconciled, in the twelfth century, to the sight of images.[17] These various denominations of men afforded a fund of prejudice and aversion, of small account in the villages of Anatolia or Thrace, but which, in the fortune of a soldier, a prelate, or a eunuch, might be often connected with the powers of the church and state.

Of such adventurers, the most fortunate was the emperor Leo

---

* Yezid, ninth caliph of the race of the Ommiadæ, caused all the images in Syria to be destroyed about the year 719 ; hence the orthodox reproached the sectarians with following the example of the Saracens and the Jews. Fragm. Mon. Johan. Jerosylym. Script. Byzant. vol. xvi. p. 235. Hist. des Repub. Ital. par M. Sismondi, vol. i p. 126.—G.

the Third,[18] who, from the mountains of Isauria, ascended the throne of the East. He was ignorant of sacred and profane letters; but his education, his reason, perhaps his intercourse with the Jews and Arabs, had inspired the martial peasant with a hatred of images; and it was held to be the duty of a prince to impose on his subjects the dictates of his own conscience. But in the outset of an unsettled reign, during ten years of toil and danger, Leo submitted to the meanness of hypocrisy, bowed before the idols which he despised, and satisfied the Roman pontiff with the annual professions of his orthodoxy and zeal. In the reformation of religion, his first steps were moderate and cautious: he assembled a great council of senators and bishops, and enacted, with their consent, that all the images should be removed from the sanctuary and altar to a proper height in the churches, where they might be visible to the eyes, and inaccessible to the superstition, of the people. But it was impossible on either side to check the rapid though adverse impulse of veneration and abhorrence; in their lofty position, the sacred images still edified their votaries, and reproached the tyrant. He was himself provoked by resistance and invective; and his own party accused him of an imperfect discharge of his duty, and urged for his imitation the example of the Jewish king who had broken without scruple the brazen serpent of the temple. By a second edict, he proscribed the existence as well as the use of religious pictures; the churches of Constantinople and the provinces were cleansed from idolatry; the images of Christ, the Virgin, and the saints, were demolished, or a smooth surface of plaster was spread over the walls of the edifice. The sect of the Iconoclasts was supported by the zeal and despotism of six emperors, and the East and West were involved in a noisy conflict of one hundred and twenty years. It was the design of Leo the Isaurian to pronounce the condemnation of images as an article of faith, and by the authority of a general council: but the convocation of such an assembly was reserved for his son Constantine;[19] and though it is stigmatized by triumphant bigotry as a meeting of fools and atheists, their own partial and mutilated acts betray many symptoms of reason and piety. The debates and decrees of many provincial synods introduced the summons of the general council which met in the suburbs of Constantinople, and was composed of the respectable number of three hundred and thirty-eight bishops of Europe and Anatolia; for the patriarchs of Antioch and Alexandria were the slaves of the caliph, and the Roman pontiff had withdrawn the churches of Italy and the West from the communion of the Greeks. This Byzantine synod assumed the rank and powers of the seventh general council ; yet even this title was a recognition of the six preceding assemblies, which had laboriously built the structure of the Catholic faith. After a serious deliberation of six months, the three hundred and thirty-eight bishops pronounced and subscribed a unanimous decree, that all visible symbols of Christ, except in the Eucharist, were either blasphemous or heretical ; that image-worship was a corruption of Christianity and a renewal of Paganism ; that all such monuments of idolatry should be broken or erased ; and that those who should refuse to deliver the objects of their private superstition, were guilty of disobedience to the authority of the church and of the emperor. In their loud and loyal acclamations, they celebrated the merits of their temporal redeemer ; and to his zeal and justice they intrusted the execution of their spiritual censures. At Constantinople, as in the former councils, the will of the prince was the rule of episcopal faith ; but on this occasion I am inclined to suspect that a large majority of the prelates sacrificed their secret conscience to the temptations of hope and fear. In the long night of superstition the Christians had wandered far away from the simplicity of the Gospel: nor was it easy for them to discern the clew, and tread back the mazes of the labyrinth. The worship of images was inseparably blended, at least to a pious fancy, with the Cross, the Virgin, the Saints and their relics ; the holy ground was involved in a cloud of miracles and visions ; and the nerves of the mind, curiosity and scepticism, were benumbed by the habits of obedience and belief. Constantine himself is accused of indulging a royal license to doubt, or deny, or deride the mysteries of the Catholics,[20] but they were deeply inscribed in the public and private creed of his bishops ; and the boldest Iconoclast might assault with a secret horror the monuments of popular devotion, which were consecrated to the honor of his celestial patrons. In the reformation of the sixteenth century, freedom and knowledge had expanded all the faculties of man : the thirst of innovation superseded the reverence of antiquity ; and the vigor of Europe could disdain those phantoms which terrified the sickly and servile weakness of the Greeks.

The scandal of an abstract heresy can be only proclaimed to the people by the blast of the ecclesiastical trumpet ; but the most ignorant can perceive, the most torpid must feel, the profanation and downfall of their visible deities. The first hostilities of Leo were directed against a lofty Christ on the vestibule, and above the gate, of the palace. A ladder had been planted for the assault, but it was furiously shaken by a crowd of zealots and women : they beheld, with pious transport, the ministers of sacrilege tumbling from on high and dashed against the pavement; and the honors of the ancient martyrs were prostituted to these criminals, who justly suffered for murder and rebellion.[21] The execution of the Imperial edicts was resisted by frequent tumults in Constantinople and the provinces: the person of Leo was endangered, his officers were massacred, and the popular enthusiasm was quelled by the strongest efforts of the civil and military power. Of the Archipelago, or Holy Sea, the numerous islands were filled with images and monks: their votaries abjured, without scruple, the enemy of Christ, his mother, and the saints; they armed a fleet of boats and galleys, displayed their consecrated banners, and boldly steered for the harbor of Constantinople, to place on the throne a new favorite of God and the people. They depended on the succor of a miracle: but their miracles were inefficient against the *Greek fire;* and, after the defeat and conflagration of their fleet, the naked islands were abandoned to the clemency or justice of the conqueror. The son of Leo, in the first year of his reign, had undertaken an expedition against the Saracens: during his absence, the capital, the palace, and the purple were occupied by his kinsman Artavasdes, the ambitious champion of the orthodox faith. The worship of images was triumphantly restored: the patriarch renounced his dissimulation, or dissembled his sentiments, and the righteous claim of the usurper was acknowledged, both in the new, and in ancient Rome. Constantine flew for refuge to his paternal mountains; but he descended at the head of the bold and affectionate Isaurians; and his final victory confounded the arms and predictions of the fanatics. His long reign was distracted with clamor, sedition, conspiracy, and mutual hatred, and sanguinary revenge; the persecution of images was the motive, or pretence, of his adversaries; and, if they missed a temporal diadem, they were rewarded by the Greeks with the crown of martyrdom. In every act of open and clandestine treason, the emperor felt the unforgiving enmity of the monks, the faithful slaves of the superstition to which they owed their riches and influence. They prayed, they preached, they absolved, they inflamed, they conspired; the solitude of Palestine poured forth a torrent of invective; and the pen of St. John Damascenus,[22] the last of the Greek fathers, devoted the tyrant's head, both in this world and the next.[23] * I am not at leisure to examine how far the monks provoked, nor how much

---

* The patriarch Anastasius, an Iconoclast under Leo, an image worshipper under Artavasdes, was scourged, led through the streets on an ass, with his face to the tail; and, reinvested in his dignity, became again the obsequious minister of Constantine in his Iconoclastic persecutions. See Schlosser, p. 211.—M.

they have exaggerated, their real and pretended sufferings, nor how many lost their lives or limbs, their eyes or their beards, by the cruelty of the emperor.* From the chastisement of individuals, he proceeded to the abolition of the order ; and, as it was wealthy and useless, his resentment might be stimulated by avarice, and justified by patriotism. The formidable name and mission of the *Dragon*,[24] his visitor-general, excited the terror and abhorrence of the *black* nation : the religious communities were dissolved, the buildings were converted into magazines, or barracks ; the lands, movables, and cattle were confiscated ; and our modern precedents will support the charge, that much wanton or malicious havoc was exercised against the relics, and even the books, of the monasteries. With the habit and profession of monks, the public and private worship of images was rigorously proscribed ; and it should seem that a solemn abjuration of idolatry was exacted from the subjects, or at least from the clergy, of the Eastern empire.[25]

The patient East abjured, with reluctance, her sacred images ; they were fondly cherished, and vigorously defended, by the independent zeal of the Italians. In ecclesiastical rank and jurisdiction, the patriarch of Constantinople and the pope of Rome were nearly equal. But the Greek prelate was a domestic slave under the eye of his master, at whose nod he alternately passed from the convent to the throne, and from the throne to the convent. A distant and dangerous station, amidst the barbarians of the West, excited the spirit and freedom of the Latin bishops. Their popular election endeared them to the Romans : the public and private indigence was relieved by their ample revenue ; and the weakness or neglect of the emperors compelled them to consult, both in peace and war, the temporal safety of the city. In the school of adversity the priest insensibly imbibed the virtues and the ambition of a prince ; the same character was assumed, the same policy was adopted, by the Italian, the Greek, or the Syrian, who ascended the chair of St. Peter ; and, after the loss of her legions and provinces, the genius and fortune of the popes again restored the supremacy of Rome. It is agreed, that in the eighth century their dominion was founded on rebellion, and that the rebellion was produced, and justified, by the heresy of the Iconoclasts ; but the conduct of the second and third Gregory, in this memorable contest, is variously interpreted by the wishes of their friends and enemies. The Byzantine writers unanimously declare that, after a fruitless admonition, they pronounced the

---

* Compare Schlosser, p. 228-234.—M.

separation of the East and West, and deprived the sacrilegious tyrant of the revenue and sovereignty of Italy. Their excommunication is still more clearly expressed by the Greeks, who beheld the accomplishment of the papal triumphs ; and as they are more strongly attached to their religion than to their country, they praise, instead of blaming, the zeal and orthodoxy of these apostolical men.[26] The modern champions of Rome are eager to accept the praise and the precedent : this great and glorious example of the deposition of royal heretics is celebrated by the cardinals Baronius and Bellarmine ;[27] and if they are asked, why the same thunders were not hurled against the Neros and Julians of antiquity, they reply, that the weakness of the primitive church was the sole cause of her patient loyalty.[28] On this occasion, the effects of love and hatred are the same ; and the zealous Protestants, who seek to kindle the indignation, and to alarm the fears, of princes and magistrates, expatiate on the insolence and treason of the two Gregories against their lawful sovereign.[29] They are defended only by the moderate Catholics, for the most part, of the Gallican church,[30] who respect the saint, without approving the sin. These common advocates of the crown and the mitre circumscribe the truth of facts by the rule of equity, Scripture, and tradition, and appeal to the evidence of the Latins,[31] and the lives[32] and epistles of the popes themselves.

Two original epistles, from Gregory the Second to the emperor Leo, are still extant ;[33] and if they cannot be praised as the most perfect models of eloquence and logic, they exhibit the portrait, or at least the mask, of the founder of the papal monarchy. " During ten pure and fortunate years," says Gregory to the emperor, " we have tasted the annual comfort of your royal letters, subscribed in purple ink, with your own hand, the sacred pledges of your attachment to the orthodox creed of our fathers. How deplorable is the change ! how tremendous the scandal ! You now accuse the Catholics of idolatry ; and, by the accusation, you betray your own impiety and ignorance. To this ignorance we are compelled to adapt the grossness of our style and arguments : the first elements of holy letters are sufficient for your confusion ; and were you to enter a grammar-school, and avow yourself the enemy of our worship, the simple and pious children would be provoked to cast their horn-books at your head." After this decent salutation, the pope attempts the usual distinction between the idols of antiquity and the Christian images. The former were the fanciful representations of phantoms or dæmons, at a time when the true God had not manifested his person in any visible likeness. The latter are the genuine forms of Christ, his mother, and his saints, who had approved, by a crowd of miracles, the innocence and merit of this relative worship. He must indeed have trusted to the ignorance of Leo, since he could assert the perpetual use of images, from the apostolic age, and their venerable presence in the six synods of the Catholic church. A more specious argument is drawn from present possession and recent practice ; the harmony of the Christian world supersedes the demand of a general council ; and Gregory frankly confesses, that such assemblies can only be useful under the reign of an orthodox prince. To the impudent and inhuman Leo, more guilty than a heretic, he recommends peace, silence, and implicit obedience to his spiritual guides of Constantinople and Rome. The limits of civil and ecclesiastical powers are defined by the pontiff. To the former he appropriates the body ; to the latter, the soul : the sword of justice is in the hands of the magistrate : the more formidable weapon of excommunication is intrusted to the clergy ; and in the exercise of their divine commission a zealous son will not spare his offending father : the successor of St. Peter may lawfully chastise the kings of the earth. " You assault us, O tyrant ! with a carnal and military hand : unarmed and naked we can only implore the Christ, the prince of the heavenly host, that he will send unto you a devil, for the destruction of your body and the salvation of your soul. You declare, with foolish arrogance, I will despatch my orders to Rome : I will break in pieces the image of St. Peter ; and Gregory, like his predecessor Martin, shall be transported in chains, and in exile, to the foot of the Imperial throne. Would to God that I might be permitted to tread in the footsteps of the holy Martin ! but may the fate of Constans serve as a warning to the persecutors of the church ! After his just condemnation by the bishops of Sicily, the tyrant was cut off, in the fulness of his sins, by a domestic servant : the saint is still adored by the nations of Scythia, among whom he ended his banishment and his life. But it is our duty to live for the edification and support of the faithful people ; nor are we reduced to risk our safety on the event of a combat. Incapable as you are of defending your Roman subjects, the maritime situation of the city may perhaps expose it to your depredation ; but we can remove to the distance of four-and-twenty stadia,[34] to the first fortress of the Lombards, and then——you may pursue the winds. Are you ignorant that the popes are the bond of union, the mediators of peace, between the East and West ? The eyes of the nations are fixed on our humility ; and they revere, as a God upon earth, the apostle St. Peter, whose image you threaten to destroy.[35] The remote and interior kingdoms of the West present their homage to Christ and his vicegerent ; and we now prepare to visit one of their most powerful monarchs, who desires to receive from our hands the sacrament of baptism.[36] The barbarians have submitted to the yoke of the Gospel, while you alone are deaf to the voice of the Shepherd. These pious barbarians are kindled into rage : they thirst to avenge the persecution of the East. Abandon your rash and fatal enterprise ; reflect, tremble, and repent. If you persist, we are innocent of the blood that will be spilt in the contest ; may it fall on your own head !''

The first assault of Leo against the images of Constantinople had been witnessed by a crowd of strangers from Italy and the West, who related with grief and indignation the sacrilege of the emperor. But on the reception of his proscriptive edict, they trembled for their domestic deities : the images of Christ and the Virgin, of the angels, martyrs, and saints, were abolished in all the churches of Italy ; and a strong alternative was proposed to the Roman pontiff, the royal favor as the price of his compliance, degradation and exile as the penalty of his disobedience. Neither zeal nor policy allowed him to hesitate ; and the haughty strain in which Gregory addressed the emperor displays his confidence in the truth of his doctrine or the powers of resistance. Without depending on prayers or miracles, he boldly armed against the public enemy, and his pastoral letters admonished the Italians of their danger and their duty.[37] At this signal, Ravenna, Venice, and the cities of the Exarchate and Pentapolis, adhered to the cause of religion ; their military force by sea and land consisted, for the most part, of the natives ; and the spirit of patriotism and zeal was transfused into the mercenary strangers. The Italians swore to live and die in the defence of the pope and the holy images ; the Roman people was devoted to their father, and even the Lombards were ambitious to share the merit and advantage of this holy war. The most treasonable act, but the most obvious revenge, was the destruction of the statues of Leo himself : the most effectual and pleasing measure of rebellion was the withholding the tribute of Italy, and depriving him of a power which he had recently abused by the imposition of a new capitation.[38] A form of administration was preserved by the election of magistrates and governors ; and so high was the public indignation, that the Italians were prepared to create an orthodox emperor, and to conduct him with a fleet and army to the palace of Constantinople. In that palace, the Roman bishops, the second and third Gregory, were condemned as the authors of the revolt, and every attempt was made, either by fraud or force, to seize their persons, and to strike at their lives. The city was repeatedly visited or assaulted by captains of the guards, and dukes and exarchs of high dignity or secret trust ; they landed with foreign troops, they obtained some domestic aid, and the superstition of Naples may blush that her fathers were attached to the cause of heresy. But these clandestine or open attacks were repelled by the courage and vigilance of the Romans ; the Greeks were overthrown and massacred, their leaders suffered an ignominious death, and the popes, however inclined to mercy, refused to intercede for these guilty victims. At Ravenna,[39] the several quarters of the city had long exercised a bloody and hereditary feud ; in religious controversy they found a new aliment of faction ; but the votaries of images were superior in numbers or spirit, and the exarch, who attempted to stem the torrent, lost his life in a popular sedition. To punish this flagitious deed, and restore his dominion in Italy, the emperor sent a fleet and army into the Adriatic Gulf. After suffering from the winds and waves much loss and delay, the Greeks made their descent in the neighborhood of Ravenna : they threatened to depopulate the guilty capital, and to imitate, perhaps to surpass, the example of Justinian the Second, who had chastised a former rebellion by the choice and execution of fifty of the principal inhabitants. The women and clergy, in sackcloth and ashes, lay prostrate in prayer ; the men were in arms for the defence of their country ; the common danger had united the factions, and the event of a battle was preferred to the slow miseries of a siege. In a hard-fought day, as the two armies alternately yielded and advanced, a phantom was seen, a voice was heard, and Ravenna was victorious by the assurance of victory. The strangers retreated to their ships, but the populous sea-coast poured forth a multitude of boats ; the waters of the Po were so deeply infected with blood that during six years the public prejudice abstained from the fish of the river ; and the institution, of an annual feast perpetuated the worship of images, and the abhorrence of the Greek tyrant. Amidst the triumph of the Catholic arms, the Roman pontiff convened a synod of ninety-three bishops against the heresy of the Iconoclasts. With their consent, he pronounced a general excommunication against all who by word or deed should attack the tradition of the fathers and the images of the saints : in this sentence the emperor was tacitly involved,[40] but the vote of a last and hopeless remonstrance may seem to imply that the anathema was yet suspended over his guilty head. No sooner had they confirmed their own safety, the worship of images, and the freedom of Rome and Italy, than the popes appear to have relaxed of their severity, and to have spared the relics of the Byzantine dominion. Their moderate councils delayed and prevented the election of a new emperor, and they exhorted the Italians not to separate from the body of the Roman monarchy. The exarch was permitted to reside within the walls of Ravenna, a captive rather than a master ; and till the Imperial coronation of Charlemagne, the government of Rome and Italy was exercised in the name of the successors of Constantine.[41]

The liberty of Rome, which had been oppressed by the arms and arts of Augustus, was rescued, after seven hundred and fifty years of servitude, from the persecution of Leo the Isaurian. By the Cæsars, the triumphs of the consuls had been annihilated : in the decline and fall of the empire, the god Terminus, the sacred boundary, had insensibly receded from the ocean, the Rhine, the Danube, and the Euphrates ; and Rome was reduced to her ancient territory from Viterbo to Terracina, and from Narni to the mouth of the Tyber.[42] When the kings were banished, the republic reposed on the firm basis which had been founded by their wisdom and virtue. Their perpetual jurisdiction was divided between two annual magistrates : the senate continued to exercise the powers of administration and counsel ; and the legislative authority was distributed in the assemblies of the people by a well-proportioned scale of property and service. Ignorant of the arts of luxury, the primitive Romans had improved the science of government and war : the will of the community was absolute : the rights of individuals were sacred : one hundred and thirty thousand citizens were armed for defence or conquest ; and a band of robbers and outlaws was moulded into a nation deserving of freedom and ambitious of glory.[43] When the sovereignty of the Greek emperors was extinguished, the ruins of Rome presented the sad image of depopulation and decay : her slavery was a habit, her liberty an accident ; the effect of superstition, and the object of her own amazement and terror. The last vestige of the substance, or even the forms, of the constitution, was obliterated from the practice and memory of the Romans ; and they were devoid of knowledge, or virtue, again to build the fabric of a commonwealth. Their scanty remnant, the offspring of slaves and strangers, was despicable in the eyes of the victorious barbarians. As often as the Franks or Lombards expressed their most bitter contempt of a foe, they called him a Roman ; " and in this name," says the bishop Liutprand, " we include whatever is base, whatever is cowardly, whatever is perfidious, the extremes of avarice and luxury, and every vice that can prostitute the dignity of human nature." [44] * By the necessity of their situation, the inhabitants of Rome were cast into the rough model of a republican government : they were compelled to elect some judges in peace, and some leaders in war ; the nobles assembled to deliberate, and their resolves could not be executed without the union and consent of the multitude. The style of the Roman senate and people was revived, [45] but the spirit was fled ; and their new independence was disgraced by the tumultuous conflict of licentiousness and oppression. The want of laws could only be supplied by the influence of religion, and their foreign and domestic counsels were moderated by the authority of the bishop. His alms, his sermons, his correspondence with the kings and prelates of the West, his recent services, their gratitude, and oath, accustomed the Romans to consider him as the first magistrate or prince of the city. The Christian humility of the popes was not offended by the name of *Dominus*, or Lord ; and their face and inscription are still apparent on the most ancient coins. [46] Their temporal dominion is now confirmed by the reverence of a thousand years ; and their noblest title is the free choice of a people whom they had redeemed from slavery.

In the quarrels of ancient Greece, the holy people of Elis enjoyed a perpetual peace, under the protection of Jupiter, and in the exercise of the Olympic games. [47] Happy would it have been for the Romans, if a similar privilege had guarded the patrimony of St. Peter from the calamities of war ; if the Christians, who visited the holy threshold, would have sheathed their swords in the presence of the apostle and his successor. But this mystic circle could have been traced only by the wand of a legislator and a sage : this pacific system was incompatible with the zeal and ambition of the popes : the Romans were not addicted, like the inhabitants of Elis, to the innocent and placid labors of agriculture ; and the barbarians of Italy, though softened by the climate, were far below the Grecian states in the institutions of public and private life. A memorable example of repentance and piety was exhibited by Liutprand, king of the Lombards. In arms, at the gate of the Vatican, the conqueror listened to the voice of Gregory the Second, [48] withdrew his troops, resigned his conquests, respectfully visited the church of St. Peter, and after performing his devotions, offered his sword and dagger, his cuirass and mantle, his silver cross, and his crown of gold, on the tomb of the apostle. But this religious fervor was the illusion, perhaps the artifice, of the moment ; the

* Yet this contumelious sentence, quoted by Robertson (Charles V., note 2), as well as Gibbon, was applied by the angry bishop to the *Byzantine* Romans, whom, indeed, he admits to be the genuine descendants of Romulus.—M.

sense of interest is strong and lasting ; the love of arms and rapine was congenial to the Lombards ; and both the prince and people were irresistibly tempted by the disorders of Italy, the nakedness of Rome, and the unwarlike profession of her new chief. On the first edicts of the emperor, they declared themselves the champions of the holy images : Liutprand invaded the province of Romagna, which had already assumed that distinctive appellation ; the Catholics of the Exarchate yielded without reluctance to his civil and military power ; and a foreign enemy was introduced for the first time into the impregnable fortress of Ravenna. That city and fortress were speedily recovered by the active diligence and maritime forces of the Venetians ; and those faithful subjects obeyed the exhortation of Gregory himself, in separating the personal guilt of Leo from the general cause of the Roman empire.[49] The Greeks were less mindful of the service than the Lombards of the injury: the two nations, hostile in their faith, were reconciled in a dangerous and unnatural alliance : the king and the exarch marched to the conquest of Spoleto and Rome : the storm evaporated without effect, but the policy of Liutprand alarmed Italy with a vexatious alternative of hostility and truce. His successor Astolphus declared himself the equal enemy of the emperor and the pope : Ravenna was subdued by force or treachery,[50] and this final conquest extinguished the series of the exarchs, who had reigned with a subordinate power since the time of Justinian and the ruin of the Gothic kingdom. Rome was summoned to acknowledge the victorious Lombard as her lawful sovereign ; the annual tribute of a piece of gold was fixed as the ransom of each citizen, and the sword of destruction was unsheathed to exact the penalty of her disobedience. The Romans hesitated ; they entreated ; they complained ; and the threatening barbarians were checked by arms and negotiations, till the popes had engaged the friendship of an ally and avenger beyond the Alps.[51]

In his distress, the first * Gregory had implored the aid of a hero of the age, of Charles Martel, who governed the French monarchy with the humble title of mayor or duke ; and who, by his signal victory over the Saracens, had saved his country and perhaps Europe, from the Mahometan yoke. The ambassadors of the pope were received by Charles with decent reverence ; but the greatness of his occupations, and the shortness of his life, prevented his interference in the affairs of Italy, except by a friendly and ineffectual mediation. His son Pepin, the heir of his power and virtues, assumed the office of champion of the Roman church ;

* Gregory I. had been dead above a century ; read Gregory III.—M.

and the zeal of the French prince appears to have been prompted by the love of glory and religion. But the danger was on the banks of the Tyber, the succor on those of the Seine ; and our sympathy is cold to the relation of distant misery. Amidst the tears of the city, Stephen the Third embraced the generous resolution of visiting in person the courts of Lombardy and France, to deprecate the injustice of his enemy, or to excite the pity and indignation of his friend. After soothing the public despair by litanies and orations, he undertook this laborious journey with the ambassadors of the French monarch and the Greek emperor. The king of the Lombards was inexorable ; but his threats could not silence the complaints, nor retard the speed, of the Roman pontiff, who traversed the Pennine Alps, reposed in the abbey of St. Maurice, and hastened to grasp the right hand of his protector ; a hand which was never lifted in vain, either in war or friendship. Stephen was entertained as the visible successor of the apostle ; at the next assembly, the field of March or of May, his injuries were exposed to a devout and warlike nation, and he repassed the Alps, not as a suppliant, but as a conqueror, at the head of a French army, which was led by the king in person. The Lombards, after a weak resistance, obtained an ignominious peace, and swore to restore the possessions, and to respect the sanctity, of the Roman church. But no sooner was Astolphus delivered from the presence of the French arms, than he forgot his promise, and resented his disgrace. Rome was again encompassed by his arms ; and Stephen, apprehensive of fatiguing the zeal of his Transalpine allies, enforced his complaint and request by an eloquent letter in the name and person of St. Peter himself.[52] The apostle assures his adopted sons, the king, the clergy, and the nobles of France, that, dead in the flesh, he is still alive in the spirit ; that they now hear and must obey the voice of the founder and guardian of the Roman church ; that the Virgin, the angels, the saints, and the martyrs, and all the host of heaven, unanimously urge the request, and will confess the obligation ; that riches, victory, and paradise, will crown their pious enterprise, and that eternal damnation will be the penalty of their neglect, if they suffer his tomb, his temple, and his people, to fall into the hands of the perfidious Lombards. The second expedition of Pepin was not less rapid and fortunate than the first : St. Peter was satisfied, Rome was again saved, and Astolphus was taught the lessons of justice and sincerity by the scourge of a foreign master. After this double chastisement the Lombards languished about twenty years in a state of languor and decay. But their minds were not yet humbled to their condition ; and instead of affecting the pacific virtues of the feeble, they peevishly harassed the Romans with a repetition of claims, evasions, and inroads, which they undertook without reflection, and terminated without glory. On either side their expiring monarchy was pressed by the zeal and prudence of Pope Adrian the First, the genius, the fortune, and greatness of Charlemagne, the son of Pepin ; these heroes of the church and state were united in public and domestic friendship, and while they trampled on the prostrate they varnished their proceedings with the fairest colors of equity and moderation.[53] The passes of the Alps, and the walls of Pavia, were the only defence of the Lombards ; the former were surprised, the latter were invested, by the son of Pepin ; and after a blockade of two years,* Desiderius, the last of their native princes, surrendered his sceptre and his capital. Under the dominion of a foreign king, but in the possession of their national laws, the Lombards became the brethren, rather than the subjects, of the Franks ; who derived their blood, and manners, and language, from the same Germanic origin.[54]

The mutual obligations of the popes and the Carlovingian family form the important link of ancient and modern, of civil and ecclesiastical, history. In the conquest of Italy, the champions of the Roman church obtained a favorable occasion, a specious title, the wishes of the people, the prayers and intrigues of the clergy. But the most essential gifts of the popes to the Carlovingian race were the dignities of king of France,[55] and of patrician of Rome. I. Under the sacerdotal monarchy of St. Peter, the nations began to resume the practice of seeking, on the banks of the Tyber, their kings, their laws, and the oracles of their faith. The Franks were perplexed between the name and substance of their government. All the powers of royalty were exercised by Pepin, mayor of the palace ; and nothing, except the regal title, was wanting to his ambition. His enemies were crushed by his valor ; his friends were multiplied by his liberality ; his father had been the savior of Christendom ; and the claims of personal merit were repeated and ennobled in a descent of four generations. The name and image of royalty was still preserved in the last descendant of Clovis, the feeble Childeric ; but his obsolete right could only be used as an instrument of sedition : the nation was desirous of restoring the simplicity of the constitution ; and Pepin, a subject and a prince, was ambitious to ascertain his own rank and the fortune of his family. The mayor and the nobles were bound, by an oath of fidelity, to the royal

---

* Of fifteen months. James, Life of Charlemagne, p. 187.—M.

phantom : the blood of Clovis was pure and sacred in their eyes ; and their common ambassadors addressed the Roman pontiff, to dispel their scruples, or to absolve their promise. The interest of Pope Zachary, the successor of the two Gregories, prompted him to decide, and to decide in their favor : he pronounced that the nation might lawfully unite in the same person the title and authority of king ; and that the unfortunate Childeric, a victim of the public safety, should be degraded, shaved, and confined in a monastery for the remainder of his days. An answer so agreeable to their wishes was accepted by the Franks as the opinion of a casuist, the sentence of a judge, or the oracle of a prophet : the Merovingian race disappeared from the earth ; and Pepin was exalted on a buckler by the suffrage of a free people, accustomed to obey his laws, and to march under his standard. His coronation was twice performed, with the sanction of the popes, by their most faithful servant St. Boniface, the apostle of Germany, and by the grateful hands of Stephen the Third, who, in the monastery of St. Denys, placed the diadem on the head of his benefactor. The royal unction of the kings of Israel was dexterously applied : [56] the successor of St. Peter assumed the character of a divine ambassador : a German chieftain was transformed into the Lord's anointed ; and this Jewish rite has been diffused and maintained by the superstition and vanity of modern Europe. The Franks were absolved from their ancient oath ; but a dire anathema was thundered against them and their posterity, if they should dare to renew the same freedom of choice, or to elect a king except in the holy and meritorious race of the Carlovingian princes. Without apprehending the future danger, these princes gloried in their present security : the secretary of Charlemagne affirms, that the French sceptre was transferred by the authority of the popes ; [57] and, in their boldest enterprises, they insist, with confidence, on this signal and successful act of temporal jurisdiction.

II. In the change of manners and language, the patricians of Rome [58] were far removed from the senate of Romulus, or the palace of Constantine, from the free nobles of the republic, or the fictitious parents of the emperor. After the recovery of Italy and Africa by the arms of Justinian, the importance and danger of those remote provinces required the presence of a supreme magistrate ; he was indifferently styled the exarch or the patrician ; and these governors of Ravenna, who fill their place in the chronology of princes, extended their jurisdiction over the Roman city. Since the revolt of Italy and the loss of the Exarchate, the distress of the Romans had exacted some sacrifice of their independence. Yet, even in this act, they exercised the right of disposing of themselves ; and the decrees of the senate and people successively invested Charles Martel and his posterity with the honors of patrician of Rome. The leaders of a powerful nation would have disdained a servile title and subordinate office ; but the reign of the Greek emperors was suspended ; and, in the vacancy of the empire, they derived a more glorious commission from the pope and the republic. The Roman ambassadors presented these patricians with the keys of the shrine of St. Peter, as a pledge and symbol of sovereignty ; with a holy banner which it was their right and duty to unfurl in the defence of the church and city.[59] In the time of Charles Martel and of Pepin, the interposition of the Lombard kingdom covered the freedom, while it threatened the safety, of Rome ; and the *patriciate* represented only the title, the service, the alliance, of these distant protectors. The power and policy of Charlemagne annihilated an enemy, and imposed a master. In his first visit to the capital, he was received with all the honors which had formerly been paid to the exarch, the representative of the emperor ; and these honors obtained some new decorations from the joy and gratitude of Pope Adrian the First.[60] No sooner was he informed of the sudden approach of the monarch, than he despatched the magistrates and nobles of Rome to meet him, with the banner, about thirty miles from the city. At the distance of one mile, the Flaminian way was lined with the *schools*, or national communities, of Greeks, Lombards, Saxons, etc.: the Roman youth were under arms ; and the children of a more tender age, with palms and olive branches in their hands, chanted the praises of their great deliverer. At the aspect of the holy crosses, and ensigns of the saints, he dismounted from his horse, led the procession of his nobles to the Vatican, and, as he ascended the stairs, devoutly kissed each step of the threshold of the apostles. In the portico, Adrian expected him at the head of his clergy : they embraced as friends and equals ; but in their march to the altar, the king or patrician assumed the right hand of the pope. Nor was the Frank content with these vain and empty demonstrations of respect. In the twenty-six years that elapsed between the conquest of Lombardy and his Imperial coronation, Rome, which had been delivered by the sword, was subject, as his own, to the sceptre of Charlemagne. The people swore allegiance to his person and family : in his name money was coined, and justice was administered ; and the election of the popes was examined and confirmed by his authority. Except an original and self-inherent claim of sovereignty, there was not any prerogative remaining, which the title of emperor could add to the patrician of Rome.[61]

The gratitude of the Carlovingians was adequate to these obligations, and their names are consecrated as the saviors and benefactors of the Roman church. Her ancient patrimony of farms and houses was transformed by their bounty into the temporal dominion of cities and provinces ; and the donation of the Exarchate was the first-fruits of the conquests of Pepin.[62] Astolphus with a sigh relinquished his prey ; the keys and the hostages of the principal cities were delivered to the French ambassador ; and, in his master's name, he presented them before the tomb of St. Peter. The ample measure of the Exarchate[63] might comprise all the provinces of Italy which had obeyed the emperor and his vicegerent ; but its strict and proper limits were included in the territories of Ravenna, Bologna, and Ferrara : its inseparable dependency was the Pentapolis, which stretched along the Adriatic from Rimini to Ancona, and advanced into the midland country as far as the ridges of the Apennine. In this transaction, the ambition and avarice of the popes have been severely condemned. Perhaps the humility of a Christian priest should have rejected an earthly kingdom, which it was not easy for him to govern without renouncing the virtues of his profession. Perhaps a faithful subject, or even a generous enemy, would have been less impatient to divide the spoils of the barbarian ; and if the emperor had intrusted Stephen to solicit in his name the restitution of the Exarchate, I will not absolve the pope from the reproach of treachery and falsehood. But in the rigid interpretation of the laws, every one may accept, without injury, whatever his benefactor can bestow without injustice. The Greek emperor had abdicated, or forfeited, his right to the Exarchate ; and the sword of Astolphus was broken by the stronger sword of the Carlovingian. It was not in the cause of the Iconoclast that Pepin had exposed his person and army in a double expedition beyond the Alps ; he possessed, and might lawfully alienate, his conquests : and to the importunities of the Greeks he piously replied that no human consideration should tempt him to resume the gift which he had conferred on the Roman Pontiff for the remission of his sins, and the salvation of his soul. The splendid donation was granted in supreme and absolute dominion, and the world beheld for the first time a Christian bishop invested with the prerogatives of a temporal prince ; the choice of magistrates, the exercise of justice, the imposition of taxes, and the wealth of the palace of Ravenna. In the dissolution of the Lombard kingdom, the inhabitants of the duchy of Spoleto[64] sought a refuge from the storm, shaved their heads after the Roman fashion, declared themselves the servants and subjects of St. Peter, and completed, by this voluntary surrender, the present circle of the ecclesiastical state. That mysterious circle was enlarged to an indefinite extent, by the verbal or written donation of Charlemagne,[65] who, in the first transports of his victory, despoiled himself and the Greek emperor of the cities and islands which had formerly been annexed to the Exarchate. But, in the cooler moments of absence and reflection, he viewed, with an eye of jealousy and envy, the recent greatness of his ecclesiastical ally. The execution of his own and his father's promises was respectfully eluded: the king of the Franks and Lombards asserted the inalienable rights of the empire; and in his life and death, Ravenna,[66] as well as Rome, was numbered in the list of his metropolitan cities. The sovereignty of the Exarchate melted away in the hands of the popes; they found in the archbishops of Ravenna a dangerous and domestic rival:[67] the nobles and people disdained the yoke of a priest; and in the disorders of the times, they could only retain the memory of an ancient claim, which, in a more prosperous age, they have revived and realized.

Fraud is the resource of weakness and cunning; and the strong, though ignorant, barbarian was often entangled in the net of sacerdotal policy. The Vatican and Lateran were an arsenal and manufacture, which, according to the occasion, have produced or concealed a various collection of false or genuine, of corrupt or suspicious, acts, as they tended to promote the interest of the Roman church. Before the end of the eighth century, some apostolical scribe, perhaps the notorious Isidore, composed the decretals and the donation of Constantine, the two magic pillars of the spiritual and temporal monarchy of the popes. This memorable donation was introduced to the world by an epistle of Adrian the First, who exhorts Charlemagne to imitate the liberality, and revive the name, of the great Constantine.[68] According to the legend, the first of the Christian emperors was healed of the leprosy, and purified in the waters of baptism, by St. Silvester, the Roman bishop; and never was physician more gloriously recompensed. His royal proselyte withdrew from the seat and patrimony of St. Peter; declared his resolution of founding a new capital in the East; and resigned to the popes the free and perpetual sovereignty of Rome, Italy, and the provinces of the West.[69] This fiction was productive of the most beneficial effects. The Greek princes were convicted of the guilt of usurpation; and the revolt of Gregory was the claim of his lawful inheritance. The popes were delivered from their debt of gratitude; and the nominal gifts of the Carlovingians were no more than the just and irrevocable restitution of a scanty portion of the ecclesiastical state. The sovereignty of Rome no longer depended on the choice of a fickle people ; and the successors of St. Peter and Constantine were invested with the purple and prerogatives of the Cæsars. So deep was the ignorance and credulity of the times, that the most absurd of fables was received, with equal reverence, in Greece and in France, and is still enrolled among the decrees of the canon law.[70] The emperors, and the Romans, were incapable of discerning a forgery, that subverted their rights and freedom ; and the only opposition proceeded from a Sabine monastery, which, in the beginning of the twelfth century, disputed the truth and validity of the donation of Constantine.[71] In the revival of letters, this fictitious deed was transpierced by the pen of Laurentius Valla, the pen of an eloquent critic and a Roman patriot.[72] His contemporaries of the fifteenth century were astonished at his sacrilegious boldness ; yet such is the silent and irresistible progress of reason, that, before the end of the next age, the fable was rejected by the contempt of historians[73] and poets,[74] and the tacit or modest censure of the advocates of the Roman church.[75] The popes themselves have indulged a smile at the credulity of the vulgar ;[76] but a false and obsolete title still sanctifies their reign ; and, by the same fortune which has attended the decretals and the Sibylline oracles, the edifice has subsisted after the foundations have been undermined.

While the popes established in Italy their freedom and dominion, the images, the first cause of their revolt, were restored in the Eastern empire.[77] Under the reign of Constantine the Fifth, the union of civil and ecclesiastical power had overthrown the tree, without extirpating the root, of superstition. The idols (for such they were now held) were secretly cherished by the order and the sex most prone to devotion ; and the fond alliance of the monks and females obtained a final victory over the reason and authority of man. Leo the Fourth maintained with less rigor the religion of his father and grandfather ; but his wife, the fair and ambitious Irene, had imbibed the zeal of the Athenians, the heirs of the idolatry, rather than the philosophy, of their ancestors. During the life of her husband, these sentiments were inflamed by danger and dissimulation, and she could only labor to protect and promote some favorite monks whom she drew from their caverns, and seated on the metropolitan thrones of the East. But as soon as she reigned in her own name and that of her son, Irene more seriously undertook the ruin of Iconoclasts ; and the first step of her future persecution was a general edict for liberty of conscience. In the restoration of the monks, a thousand images were exposed to the public veneration ; a thousand legends were invented of their sufferings and miracles. By the opportunities of death or removal, the episcopal seats were judiciously filled ; the most eager competitors for earthly or celestial favor anticipated and flattered the judgment of their sovereign ; and the promotion of her secretary Tarasius gave Irene the patriarch of Constantinople, and the command of the Oriental church. But the decrees of a general council could only be repealed by a similar assembly :[78] the Iconoclasts whom she convened were bold in possession, and averse to debate ; and the feeble voice of the bishops was re-echoed by the more formidable clamor of the soldiers and people of Constantinople. The delay and intrigues of a year, the separation of the disaffected troops, and the choice of Nice for a second orthodox synod, removed these obstacles ; and the episcopal conscience was again, after the Greek fashion, in the hands of the prince. No more than eighteen days were allowed for the consummation of this important work : the Iconoclasts appeared, not as judges, but as criminals or penitents : the scene was decorated by the legates of Pope Adrian and the Eastern patriarchs,[79] the decrees were framed by the president Taracius, and ratified by the acclamations and subscriptions of three hundred and fifty bishops. They unanimously pronounced, that the worship of images is agreeable to Scripture and reason, to the fathers and councils of the church : but they hesitate whether that worship be relative or direct ; whether the Godhead, and the figure of Christ, be entitled to the same mode of adoration. Of this second Nicene council the acts are still extant ; a curious monument of superstition and ignorance, of falsehood and folly. I shall only notice the judgment of the bishops on the comparative merit of image-worship and morality. A monk had concluded a truce with the dæmon of fornication, on condition of interrupting his daily prayers to a picture that hung in his cell. His scruples prompted him to consult the abbot. "Rather than abstain from adoring Christ and his Mother in their holy images, it would be better for you," replied the casuist, "to enter every brothel, and visit every prostitute in the city."[80] For the honor of orthodoxy, at least the orthodoxy of the Roman church, it is somewhat unfortunate that the two princes who convened the two councils of Nice are both stained with the blood of their sons. The second of these assemblies was approved and rigorously executed by the despotism of Irene, and she refused her adversaries the toleration which at first she had granted to her friends. During the five succeeding reigns, a period of thirty-eight years, the contest was main-

tained, with unabated rage and various success, between the worshippers and the breakers of the images; but I am not inclined
to pursue with minute diligence the repetition of the same events.
Nicephorus allowed a general liberty of speech and practice;
and the only virtue of his reign is accused by the monks as the
cause of his temporal and eternal perdition.   Superstition and
weakness formed the character of Michael the First, but the saints
and images were incapable of supporting their votary on the
throne.   In the purple, Leo the Fifth asserted the name and religion of an Armenian; and the idols, with their seditious adherents, were condemned to a second exile.   Their applause
would have sanctified the murder of an impious tyrant, but his
assassin and successor, the second Michael, was tainted from his
birth with the Phrygian heresies: he attempted to mediate between the contending parties; and the intractable spirit of the
Catholics insensibly cast him into the opposite scale.   His moderation was guarded by timidity; but his son Theophilus, alike
ignorant of fear and pity, was the last and most cruel of the
Iconoclasts.   The enthusiasm of the times ran strongly against
them; and the emperors who stemmed the torrent were exasperated and punished by the public hatred.   After the death of Theophilus, the final victory of the images was achieved by a second
female, his widow Theodora, whom he left the guardian of the
empire.   Her measures were bold and decisive.   The fiction of a
tardy repentance absolved the fame and the soul of her deceased
husband; the sentence of the Iconoclast patriarch was commuted
from the loss of his eyes to a whipping of two hundred lashes:
the bishops trembled, the monks shouted, and the festival of
orthodoxy preserves the annual memory of the triumph of the
images.   A single question yet remained, whether they are endowed with any proper and inherent sanctity; it was agitated by
the Greeks of the eleventh century; [81] and as this opinion has the
strongest recommendation of absurdity, I am surprised that it was
not more explicitly decided in the affirmative.   In the West,
Pope Adrian the First accepted and announced the decrees of the
Nicene assembly, which is now revered by the Catholics as the
seventh in rank of the general councils.   Rome and Italy were
docile to the voice of their father; but the greatest part of the
Latin Christians were far behind in the race of superstition.   The
churches of France, Germany, England, and Spain steered a
middle course between the adoration and the destruction of
images, which they admitted into their temples, not as objects of
worship, but as lively and useful memorials of faith and history.
An angry book of controversy was composed and published in

the name of Charlemagne : [62] under his authority a synod of three hundred bishops was assembled at Frankfort : [63] they blamed the fury of the Iconoclasts, but they pronounced a more severe censure against the superstition of the Greeks, and the decrees of their pretended council, which was long despised by the barbarians of the West. [64] Among them the worship of images advanced with a silent and insensible progress ; but a large atonement is made for their hesitation and delay, by the gross idolatry of the ages which precede the reformation, and of the countries, both in Europe and America, which are still immersed in the gloom of super-stition.

It was after the Nicene synod, and under the reign of the pious Irene, that the popes consummated the separation of Rome and Italy, by the translation of the empire to the less orthodox Charlemagne. They were compelled to choose between the rival nations : religion was not the sole motive of their choice ; and while they dissembled the failings of their friends, they beheld, with reluctance and suspicion, the Catholic virtues of their foes. The difference of language and manners had perpetuated the enmity of the two capitals ; and they were alienated from each other by the hostile opposition of seventy years. In that schism the Romans had tasted of freedom, and the popes of sovereignty : their submission would have exposed them to the revenge of a jealous tyrant ; and the revolution of Italy had betrayed the impotence, as well as the tyranny, of the Byzantine court. The Greek emperors had restored the images, but they had not restored the Calabrian estates [85] and the Illyrian diocese, [86] which the Iconoclasts had torn away from the successors of St. Peter ; and Pope Adrian threatens them with a sentence of excommunication unless they speedily abjure this practical heresy. [87] The Greeks were now orthodox ; but their religion might be tainted by the breath of the reigning monarch : the Franks were now contumacious ; but a discerning eye might discern their approaching conversion, from the use, to the adoration, of images. The name of Charlemagne was stained by the polemic acrimony of his scribes ; but the conqueror himself conformed, with the temper of a statesman, to the various practice of France and Italy. In his four pilgrimages or visits to the Vatican, he embraced the popes in the communion of friendship and piety ; knelt before the tomb, and consequently before the image, of the apostle ; and joined, without scruple, in all the prayers and processions of the Roman liturgy. Would prudence or gratitude allow the pontiffs to renounce their benefactor ? Had they a right to alienate his gift of the Exarchate ? Had they power to abolish his government of Rome ?

The title of patrician was below the merit and greatness of Charlemagne ; and it was only by reviving the Western empire that they could pay their obligations or secure their establishment. By this decisive measure they would finally eradicate the claims of the Greeks ; from the debasement of a provincial town, the majesty of Rome would be restored : the Latin Christians would be united under a supreme head, in their ancient metropolis ; and the conquerors of the West would receive their crown from the successors of St. Peter. The Roman church would acquire a zealous and respectable advocate ; and, under the shadow of the Carlovingian power, the bishop might exercise, with honor and safety, the government of the city.[88]

Before the ruin of Paganism in Rome, the competition for a wealthy bishopric had often been productive of tumult and bloodshed. The people was less numerous, but the times were more savage; the prize more important, and the chair of St. Peter was fiercely disputed by the leading ecclesiastics who aspired to the rank of sovereign. The reign of Adrian the First[89] surpasses the measure of past or succeeding ages ;[90] the walls of Rome, the sacred patrimony, the ruin of the Lombards, and the friendship of Charlemagne, were the trophies of his fame : he secretly edified the throne of his successors, and displayed in a narrow space the virtues of a great prince. His memory was revered ; but in the next election, a priest of the Lateran, Leo the Third, was preferred to the nephew and the favorite of Adrian, whom he had promoted to the first dignities of the church. Their acquiescence or repentance disguised, above four years, the blackest intention of revenge, till the day of a procession, when a furious band of conspirators dispersed the unarmed multitude, and assaulted with blows and wounds the sacred person of the pope. But their enterprise on his life or liberty was disappointed, perhaps by their own confusion and remorse. Leo was left for dead on the ground : on his revival from the swoon, the effect of his loss of blood, he recovered his speech and sight ; and this natural event was impoved to the miraculous restoration of his eyes and tongue, of which he had been deprived, twice deprived, by the knife of the assassins.[91] From his prison he escaped to the Vatican : the duke of Spoleto hastened to his rescue, Charlemagne sympathized in his injury, and in his camp of Paderborn in Westphalia, accepted, or solicited, a visit from the Roman pontiff. Leo repassed the Alps with a commission of counts and bishops, the guards of his safety, and the judges of his innocence ; and it was not without reluctance that the conqueror of the Saxons delayed till the ensuing year the personal discharge of this pious office. In his fourth and last pilgrimage, he was received at Rome with the due honors of king and patrician : Leo was permitted to purge himself by oath of the crimes imputed to his charge : his enemies were silenced, and the sacrilegious attempt against his life was punished by the mild and insufficient penalty of exile. On the festival of Christmas, the last year of the eighth century, Charlemagne appeared in the church of St. Peter ; and, to gratify the vanity of Rome, he had exchanged the simple dress of his country for the habit of a patrician.[92] After the celebration of the holy mysteries, Leo suddenly placed a precious crown on his head,[93] and the dome resounded with the acclamations of the people, "Long life and victory to Charles, the most pious Augustus, crowned by God, the great and pacific emperor of the Romans!" The head and body of Charlemagne were consecrated by the royal unction : after the example of the Cæsars, he was saluted or adored by the pontiff : his coronation oath represents a promise to maintain the faith and privileges of the church ; and the first-fruits were paid in his rich offerings to the shrine of the apostle. In his familiar conversation, the emperor protested his ignorance of the intentions of Leo, which he would have disappointed by his absence on that memorable day. But the preparations of the ceremony must have disclosed the secret ; and the journey of Charlemagne reveals his knowledge and expectation : he had acknowledged that the Imperial title was the object of his ambition, and a Roman synod had pronounced, that it was the only adequate reward of his merit and services.[94]

The appellation of *great* has been often bestowed, and sometimes deserved ; but CHARLEMAGNE is the only prince in whose favor the title has been indissolubly blended with the name. That name, with the addition of *saint*, is inserted in the Roman calendar ; and the saint, by a rare felicity, is crowned with the praises of the historians and philosophers of an enlightened age.[95] His *real* merit is doubtless enhanced by the barbarism of the nation and the times from which he emerged : but the *apparent* magnitude of an object is likewise enlarged by an unequal comparison ; and the ruins of Palmyra derive a casual splendor from the nakedness of the surrounding desert. Without injustice to his fame, I may discern some blemishes in the sanctity and greatness of the restorer of the Western empire. Of his moral virtues, chastity is not the most conspicuous :[96] but the public happiness could not be materially injured by his nine wives or concubines, the various indulgence of meaner or more transient amours, the multitude of his bastards whom he bestowed on the church, and the long celibacy and licentious manners of his daughters,[97] whom the father was suspected of loving with too fond a passion.* I shall be scarcely permitted to accuse the ambition of a conqueror ; but in a day of equal retribution, the sons of his brother Carloman, the Merovingian princes of Aquitain, and the four thousand five hundred Saxons who were beheaded on the same spot, would have something to allege against the justice and humanity of Charlemagne. His treatment of the vanquished Saxons [93] was an abuse of the right of conquest ; his laws were not less sanguinary than his arms, and in the discussion of his motives, whatever is subtracted from bigotry must be imputed to temper. The sedentary reader is amazed by his incessant activity of mind and body ; and his subjects and enemies were not less astonished at his sudden presence, at the moment when they believed him at the most distant extremity of the empire ; neither peace nor war, nor summer nor winter, were a season of repose ; and our fancy cannot easily reconcile the annals of his reign with the geography of his expeditions.† But this activity was a national, rather than a personal, virtue ; the vagrant life of a Frank was spent in the chase, in pilgrimage, in military adventures ; and the journeys of Charlemagne were distinguished only by a more numerous train and a more important purpose. His military renown must be tried by the scrutiny of his troops, his enemies, and his actions. Alexander conquered with the arms of Philip, but the *two* heroes who preceded Charlemagne bequeathed him their name, their examples, and the companions of their victories. At the head of his veteran and superior armies, he oppressed the savage or degenerate nations, who were incapable of confederating for their common safety : nor did he ever encounter an equal antagonist in numbers, in discipline, or in arms. The science of war has been lost and revived with the arts of peace ;

---

* This charge of incest, as Mr. Hallam justly observes, "seems to have originated in a misinterpreted passage of Eginhard." Hallam's Middle Ages, vol. i. p. 16.—M.

† M. Guizot (Cours d'Histoire Moderne, p. 270, 273) has compiled the following statement of Charlemagne's military campaigns :

1	Against	the Aquitanians.
18	"	the Saxons.
5	"	the Lombards.
7	"	the Arabs in Spain.
1	"	the Thuringians.
4	"	the Avars.
2	"	the Bretons.
1	"	the Bavarians.
4	"	the Slaves beyond the Elbe.
5	"	the Saracens in Italy.
3	"	the Danes.
2	"	the Greeks.

53 total.—M.

but his campaigns are not illustrated by any siege or battle of singular difficulty and success ; and he might behold, with envy, the Saracen trophies of his grandfather. After the Spanish expedition, his rear-guard was defeated in the Pyrenæan mountains ; and the soldiers, whose situation was irretrievable, and whose valor was useless, might accuse, with their last breath, the want of skill or caution of their general.[99] I touch with reverence the laws of Charlemagne, so highly applauded by a respectable judge. They compose not a system, but a series, of occasional and minute edicts, for the correction of abuses, the reformation of manners, the economy of his farms, the care of his poultry, and even the sale of his eggs. He wished to improve the laws and the character of the Franks ; and his attempts, however feeble and imperfect, are deserving of praise : the inveterate evils of the times were suspended or mollified by his government :[100] but in his institutions I can seldom discover the general views and the immortal spirit of a legislator, who survives himself for the benefit of posterity. The union and stability of his empire depended on the life of a single man : he imitated the dangerous practice of dividing his kingdoms among his sons ; and after his numerous diets, the whole constitution was left to fluctuate between the disorders of anarchy and despotism. His esteem for the piety and knowledge of the clergy tempted him to intrust their aspiring order with temporal dominion and civil jurisdiction ; and his son Lewis, when he was stripped and degraded by the bishops, might accuse, in some measure, the imprudence of his father. His laws enforced the imposition of tithes, because the dæmons had proclaimed in the air that the default of payment had been the cause of the last scarcity.[101] The literary merits of Charlemagne are attested by the foundation of schools, the introduction of arts, the works which were published in his name, and his familiar connection with the subjects and strangers whom he invited to his court to educate both the prince and people. His own studies were tardy, laborious, and imperfect ; if he spoke Latin and understood Greek, he derived the rudiments of knowledge from conversation rather than from books : and in his mature age, the emperor strove to acquire the practice of writing, which every peasant now learns in his infancy.[102] The grammar and logic, the music and astronomy, of the times, were only cultivated as the handmaids of superstition ; but the curiosity of the human mind must ultimately tend to its improvement, and the encouragement of learning reflects the purest and most pleasing lustre on the character of Charlemagne.[103] The dignity of his person,[104] the length of his reign, the prosperity of his arms, the vigor of his government, and the reverence of distant nations, distinguish him from the royal crowd ; and Europe dates a new æra from his restoration of the Western empire.

That empire was not unworthy of its title ; [105] and some of the fairest kingdoms of Europe were the patrimony or conquest of a prince, who reigned at the same time in France, Spain, Italy, Germany, and Hungary. [106] I. The Roman province of Gaul had been transformed into the name and monarchy of FRANCE ; but, in the decay of the Merovingian line, its limits were contracted by the independence of the *Britons* and the revolt of *Aquitain.* Charlemagne pursued, and confined, the Britons on the shores of the ocean ; and that ferocious tribe, whose origin and language are so different from the French, was chastised by the imposition of tribute, hostages, and peace. After a long and evasive contest, the rebellion of the dukes of Aquitain was punished by the forfeiture of their province, their liberty, and their lives. Harsh and rigorous would have been such treatment of ambitious governors, who had too faithfully copied the mayors of the palace. But a recent discovery [107] has proved that these unhappy princes were the last and lawful heirs of the blood and sceptre of Clovis, a younger branch, from the brother of Dagobert, of the Merovingian house. Their ancient kingdom was reduced to the duchy of Gascogne, to the counties of Fesenzac and Armagnac, at the foot of the Pyrenees : their race was propagated till the beginning of the sixteenth century ; and after surviving their Carlovingian tyrants, they were reserved to feel the injustice, or the favors, of a third dynasty. By the reunion of Aquitain, France was enlarged to its present boundaries, with the additions of the Netherlands and Spain as far as the Rhine. II. The Saracens had been expelled from France by the grandfather and father of Charlemagne ; but they still possessed the greatest part of SPAIN, from the rock of Gibraltar to the Pyrenees. Amidst their civil divisions, an Arabian emir of Saragossa implored his protection in the diet of Paderborn. Charlemagne undertook the expedition, restored the emir, and, without distinction of faith, impartially crushed the resistance of the Christians, and rewarded the obedience and service of the Mahometans. In his absence he instituted the *Spanish march,* [108] which extended form the Pyrenees to the River Ebro : Barcelona was the residence of the French governor : he possessed the counties of *Rousillon* and *Catalonia ;* and the infant kingdoms of *Navarre* and *Arragon* were subject to his jurisdiction. III. As king of the Lombards, and patrician of Rome, he reigned over the greatest part of ITALY, [109] a tract of a thousand miles from the Alps to the borders of Calabria. The duchy of *Beneventum*, a Lombard fief, had spread, at the expense of the Greeks, over the modern kingdom of Naples. But Arrechis, the reigning duke, refused to be included in the slavery of his country ; assumed the independent title of prince ; and opposed his sword to the Carlovingian monarchy. His defence was firm, his submission was not inglorious, and the emperor was content with an easy tribute, the demolition of his fortresses, and the acknowledgment, on his coins, of a supreme lord. The artful flattery of his son Grimoald added the appellation of father, but he asserted his dignity with prudence, and Beneventum insensibly escaped from the French yoke.[119] IV. Charlemagne was the first who united GERMANY under the same sceptre. The name of *Oriental France* is preserved in the circle of *Franconia;* and the people of *Hesse* and *Thuringia* were recently incorporated with the victors, by the conformity of religion and government. The *Alemanni*, so formidable to the Romans, were the faithful vassals and confederates of the Franks ; and their country was inscribed within the modern limits of *Alsace, Swabia,* and *Switzerland.* The *Bavarians*, with a similar indulgence of their laws and manners, were less patient of a master : the repeated treasons of Tasillo justified the abolition of their hereditary dukes ; and their power was shared among the counts, who judged and guarded that important frontier. But the north of Germany, from the Rhine and beyond the Elbe, was still hostile and Pagan ; nor was it till after a war of thirty-three years that the Saxons bowed under the yoke of Christ and of Charlemagne. The idols and their votaries were extirpated : the foundation of eight bishoprics, of Munster, Osnaburgh, Paderborn, and Minden, of Bremen, Verden, Hildesheim, and Halberstadt, define, on either side of the Weser, the bounds of ancient Saxony ; these episcopal seats were the first schools and cities of that savage land ; and the religion and humanity of the children atoned, in some degree, for the massacre of the parents. Beyond the Elbe, the *Slavi*, or Sclavonians, of similar manners and various denominations, overspread the modern dominions of Prussia, Poland, and Bohemia, and some transient marks of obedience have tempted the French historian to extend the empire to the Baltic and the Vistula. The conquest or conversion of those countries is of a more recent age ; but the first union of *Bohemia* with the Germanic body may be justly ascribed to the arms of Charlemagne. V. He retaliated on the Avars, or Huns of Pannonia, the same calamities which they had inflicted on the nations. Their rings, the wooden fortifications which encircled their districts and villages, were broken down by the triple effort of a

French army, that was poured into their country by land and water, through the Carpathian mountains, and along the plain of the Danube. After a bloody conflict of eight years, the loss of some French generals was avenged by the slaughter of the most noble Huns: the relics of the nation submitted; the royal residence of the chagan was left desolate and unknown; and the treasures, the rapine of two hundred and fifty years, enriched the victorious troops, or decorated the churches of Italy and Gaul.[111] After the reduction of Pannonia, the empire of Charlemagne was bounded only by the conflux of the Danube with the Teyss and the Save: the provinces of Istria, Liburnia, and Dalmatia, were an easy though unprofitable accession; and it was an effect of his moderation that he left the maritime cities under the real or nominal sovereignty of the Greeks. But these distant possessions added more to the reputation than to the power of the Latin emperor; nor did he risk any ecclesiastical foundations to reclaim the barbarians from their vagrant life and idolatrous worship. Some canals of communication between the rivers, the Saône, and the Meuse, the Rhine and the Danube, were faintly attempted.[112] Their execution would have vivified the empire; and more cost and labor were often wasted in the structure of a cathedral.*

If we retrace the outlines of this geographical picture, it will be seen that the empire of the Franks extended, between east and west, from the Ebro to the Elbe or Vistula; between the north and south, from the duchy of Beneventum to the River Eyder, the perpetual boundary of Germany and Denmark. The personal and political importance of Charlemagne was magnified by the distress and division of the rest of Europe. The islands of Great Britain and Ireland were disputed by a crowd of princes of Saxon or Scottish origin: and, after the loss of Spain, the Christian and Gothic kingdom of Alphonso the Chaste was confined to the narrow range of the Asturian mountains. These petty sovereigns revered the power or virtue of the Carlovingian monarch, implored the honor and support of his alliance, and styled him their common parent, the sole and supreme emperor of the west.[113] He maintained a more equal intercourse with the caliph Harun al Rashid,[114] whose dominion stretched from Africa to India, and accepted from his ambassadors a tent, a water-clock, an elephant, and the keys of the Holy Sepulchre. It is not easy to conceive the private friendship of a Frank and an Arab, who were

---

*I should doubt this in the time of Charlemagne, even if the term "expended" were substituted for "wasted."—M.

strangers to each other's person and language and religion : but their public correspondence was founded on vanity, and their remote situation left no room for a competition of interest. Two thirds of the Western empire of Rome were subject to Charlemagne, and the deficiency was amply supplied by his command of the inaccessible or invincible nations of Germany. But in the choice of his enemies,* we may be reasonably surprised that he so often preferred the poverty of the north to the riches of the south. The three-and-thirty campaigns laboriously consumed in the woods and morasses of Germany would have sufficed to assert the amplitude of his title by the expulsion of the Greeks from Italy and the Saracens from Spain. The weakness of the Greeks would have insured an easy victory ; and the holy crusade against the Saracens would have been prompted by glory and revenge, and loudly justified by religion and policy. Perhaps, in his expeditions beyond the Rhine and the Elbe, he aspired to save his monarchy from the fate of the Roman empire, to disarm the enemies of civilized society, and to eradicate the seed of future emigrations. But it has been wisely observed that, in a light of precaution, all conquest must be ineffectual, unless it could be universal, since the increasing circle must be involved in a larger sphere of hostility.[115] The subjugation of Germany withdrew the veil which had so long concealed the continent or islands of Scandinavia from the knowledge of Europe, and awakened the torpid courage of their barbarous natives. The fiercest of the Saxon idolaters escaped from the Christian tyrant to their brethren of the North ; the Ocean and Mediterranean were covered with their piratical fleets ; and Charlemagne beheld with a sigh the destructive progress of the Normans, who, in less than seventy years, precipitated the fall of his race and monarchy.

Had the pope and the Romans revived the primitive constitution, the titles of emperor and Augustus were conferred on Charlemagne for the term of his life ; and his successors, on each vacancy, must have ascended the throne by a formal or tacit election. But the association of his son Lewis the Pious asserts the independent right of monarchy and conquest, and the emperor seems on this occasion to have foreseen and prevented the latent

---

* Had he the choice? M. Guizot has eloquently described the position of Charlemagne towards the Saxons. Il y fit face par le conquête ; la guerre défensive prit la forme offensive : il transporta la lutte sur le territoire des peuples qui voulaient envahir le sien ; il travailla à asservir les races étrangères, et extirper les croyances ennemies. De là son mode de gouvernement et la fondation de son empire: la guerre offensive et la conquête voulaient cette vaste et redoutable unité. Compare observations in the Quarterly Review, vol. xlviii., and James's Life of Charlemagne. —M.

claims of the clergy. The royal youth was commanded to take the crown from the altar, and with his own hands to place it on his head, as a gift which he held from God, his father, and the nation.[116] The same ceremony was repeated, though with less energy, in the subsequent associations of Lothaire and Lewis the Second ; the Carlovingian sceptre was transmitted from father to son in a lineal descent of four generations ; and the ambition of the popes was reduced to the empty honor of crowning and anointing these hereditary princes, who were already invested with their power and dominions. The pious Lewis survived his brothers, and embraced the whole empire of Charlemagne ; but the nations, and the nobles, his bishops, and his children, quickly discerned that this mighty mass was no longer inspired by the same soul ; and the foundations were undermined to the centre, while the external surface was yet fair and entire. After a war, or battle, which consumed one hundred thousand Franks, the empire was divided by treaty between his three sons, who had violated every filial and fraternal duty. The kingdoms of Germany and France were forever separated ; the provinces of Gaul, between the Rhone and the Alps, the Meuse and the Rhine, were assigned, with Italy, to the Imperial dignity of Lothaire. In the partition of his share, Lorraine and Arles, two recent and transitory kingdoms, were bestowed on the younger children ; and Lewis the Second, his eldest son, was content with the realm of Italy, the proper and sufficient patrimony of a Roman emperor. On his death, without any male issue, the vacant throne was disputed by his uncles and cousins, and the popes most dexterously seized the occasion of judging the claims and merits of the candidates, and of bestowing on the most obsequious, or most liberal, the Imperial office of advocate of the Roman church. The dregs of the Carlovingian race no longer exhibited any symptoms of virtue or power, and the ridiculous epithets of the *bard*, the *stammerer*, the *fat*, and the *simple*, distinguished the tame and uniform features of a crowd of kings alike deserving of oblivion. By the failure of the collateral branches, the whole inheritance devolved to Charles the Fat, the last emperor of his family : his insanity authorized the desertion of Germany, Italy, and France : he was deposed in a diet, and solicited his daily bread from the rebels by whose contempt his life and liberty had been spared. According to the measure of their force, the governors, the bishops, and the lords, usurped the fragments of the falling empire ; and some preference was shown to the female or illegitimate blood of Charlemagne. Of the greater part the title and possession were alike doubtful, and the merit was adequate to the contracted scale of their dominions. Those who could appear with an army at the gates of Rome were crowned emperors in the Vatican ; but their modesty was more frequently satisfied with the appellation of kings of Italy : and the whole term of seventy-four years may be deemed a vacancy, from the abdication of Charles the Fat to the establishment of Otho the First.

Otho [117] was of the noble race of the dukes of Saxony ; and if he truly descended from Witikind, the adversary and proselyte of Charlemagne, the posterity of a vanquished people was exalted to reign over their conquerors. His father, Henry the Fowler, was elected, by the suffrage of the nation, to save and institute the kingdom of Germany. Its limits [118] were enlarged on every side by his son, the first and greatest of the Othos. A portion of Gaul, to the west of the Rhine, along the banks of the Meuse and the Moselle, was assigned to the Germans, by whose blood and language it has been tinged since the time of Cæsar and Tacitus. Between the Rhine, the Rhone, and the Alps, the successors of Otho acquired a vain supremacy over the broken kingdoms of Burgundy and Arles. In the North, Christianity was propagated by the sword of Otho, the conqueror and apostle of the Slavic nations of the Elbe and Oder : the marches of Brandenburgh and Sleswick were fortified with German colonies ; and the king of Denmark, the dukes of Poland and Bohemia, confessed themselves his tributary vassals. At the head of a victorious army, he passed the Alps, subdued the kingdom of Italy, delivered the pope, and forever fixed the Imperial crown in the name and nation of Germany. From that memorable æra, two maxims of public jurisprudence were introduced by force and ratified by time. I. *That* the prince, who was elected in the German diet, acquired, from that instant, the subject kingdoms of Italy and Rome. II. But that he might not legally assume the titles of emperor and Augustus, till he had received the crown from the hands of the Roman pontiff. [119]

The Imperial dignity of Charlemagne was announced to the East by the alteration of his style ; and instead of saluting his fathers, the Greek emperors, he presumed to adopt the more equal and familiar appellation of brother. [120] Perhaps in his connection with Irene he aspired to the name of husband : his embassy to Constantinople spoke the language of peace and friendship, and might conceal a treaty of marriage with that ambitious princess, who had renounced the most sacred duties of a mother. The nature, the duration, the probable consequences of such a union between two distant and dissonant empires, it is impossible to conjecture ; but the unanimous silence of the Latins may teach us to suspect, that the report was invented by the enemies of Irene, to charge her with the guilt of betraying the church and state to the strangers of the West.[121]   The French ambassadors were the spectators, and had nearly been the victims, of the conspiracy of Nicephorus, and the national hatred.   Constantinople was exasperated by the treason and sacrilege of ancient Rome : a proverb, "That the Franks were good friends and bad neighbors," was in every one's mouth ; but it was dangerous to provoke a neighbor who might be tempted to reiterate, in the church of St. Sophia, the ceremony of his Imperial coronation.   After a tedious journey of circuit and delay, the ambassadors of Nicephorus found him in his camp, on the banks of the River Sala ; and Charlemagne affected to confound their vanity by displaying, in a Franconian village, the pomp, or at least the pride, of the Byzantine palace.[122]   The Greeks were successively led through four halls of audience : in the first they were ready to fall prostrate before a splendid personage in a chair of state, till he informed them that he was only a servant, the constable, or master of the house, of the emperor.   The same mistake, and the same answer, were repeated in the apartments of the count palatine, the steward, and the chamberlain ; and their impatience was gradually heightened, till the doors of the presence-chamber were thrown open, and they beheld the genuine monarch, on his throne, enriched with the foreign luxury which he despised, and encircled with the love and reverence of his victorious chiefs.   A treaty of peace and alliance was concluded between the two empires, and the limits of the East and West were defined by the right of present possession.   But the Greeks [123] soon forgot this humiliating equality, or remembered it only to hate the barbarians by whom it was extorted.   During the short union of virtue and power, they respectfully saluted the *august* Charlemagne, with the acclamations of *basileus*, and emperor of the Romans.   As soon as these qualities were separated in the person of his pious son, the Byzantine letters were inscribed, "To the king, or, as he styles himself, the emperor of the Franks and Lombards."   When both power and virtue were extinct, they despoiled Lewis the Second of his hereditary title, and with the barbarous appellation of rex or *rega*, degraded him among the crowd of Latin princes.   His reply [124] is expressive of his weakness : he proves, with some learning, that, both in sacred and profane history, the name of king is synonymous with the Greek word *basileus :* if, at Constantinople, it were assumed in a more exclusive and imperial sense, he claims from his ancestors, and from the pope, a just participation of the honors of the Roman purple.   The same controversy was revived in the reign of the Othos ; and their ambassador describes, in lively colors, the insolence of the Byzantine court.[125] The Greeks affected to despise the poverty and ignorance of the Franks and Saxons ; and in their last decline refused to prostitute to the kings of Germany the title of Roman emperors.

These emperors, in the election of the popes, continued to exercise the powers which had been assumed by the Gothic and Grecian princes ; and the importance of this prerogative increased with the temporal estate and spiritual jurisdiction of the Roman church. In the Christian aristocracy, the principal members of the clergy still formed a senate to assist the administration, and to supply the vacancy, of the bishop. Rome was divided into twenty-eight parishes, and each parish was governed by a cardinal priest, or presbyter, a title which, however common and modest in its origin, has aspired to emulate the purple of kings. Their number was enlarged by the association of the seven deacons of the most considerable hospitals, the seven palatine judges of the Lateran, and some dignitaries of the church. This ecclesiastical senate was directed by the seven cardinal-bishops of the Roman province, who were less occupied in the suburb dioceses of Ostia, Porto, Velitræ, Tusculum, Præneste, Tibur, and the Sabines, than by their weekly service in the Lateran, and their superior share in the honors and authority of the apostolic see. On the death of the pope, these bishops recommended a successor to the suffrage of the college of cardinals,[126] and their choice was ratified or rejected by the applause or clamor of the Roman people. But the election was imperfect ; nor could the pontiff be legally consecrated till the emperor, the advocate of the church, had graciously signified his approbation and consent. The royal commissioner examined, on the spot, the form and freedom of the proceedings ; nor was it till after a previous scrutiny into the qualifications of the candidates that he accepted an oath of fidelity, and confirmed the donations which had successively enriched the patrimony of St. Peter. In the frequent schisms, the rival claims were submitted to the sentence of the emperor ; and in a synod of bishops he presumed to judge, to condemn, and to punish, the crimes of a guilty pontiff. Otho the First imposed a treaty on the senate and people, who engaged to prefer the candidate most acceptable to his majesty : [127] his successors anticipated or prevented their choice : they bestowed the Roman benefice, like the bishoprics of Cologne or Bamberg, on their chancellors or preceptors ; and whatever might be the merit of a Frank or Saxon, his name sufficiently attests the interposition of foreign power. These acts of prerogative were most speciously excused

by the vices of a popular election. The competitor who had been
excluded by the cardinals appealed to the passions or avarice of
the multitude ; the Vatican and the Lateran were stained with
blood ; and the most powerful senators, the marquises of Tuscany
and the counts of Tusculum, held the apostolic see in a long and
disgraceful servitude. The Roman pontiffs, of the ninth and tenth
centuries, were insulted, imprisoned, and murdered, by their
tyrants ; and such was their indigence, after the loss and usurpation of the ecclesiastical patrimonies, that they could neither support the state of a prince, nor exercise the charity of a priest.[128]
The influence of two sister prostitutes, Marozia and Theodora, was
founded on their wealth and beauty, their political and amorous
intrigues : the most strenuous of their lovers were rewarded with
the Roman mitre, and their reign [129] may have suggested to the
darker ages [130] the fable [131] of a female pope.[132] The bastard son,
the grandson, and the great-grandson of Marozia, a rare genealogy, were seated in the chair of St. Peter, and it was at the
age of nineteen years that the second of these became the head of
the Latin church.* His youth and manhood were of a suitable
complexion ; and the nations of pilgrims could bear testimony to
the charges that were urged against him in a Roman synod, and
in the presence of Otho the Great. As John XII. had renounced
the dress and decencies of his profession, the *soldier* may not perhaps be dishonored by the wine which he drank, the blood that
he spilt, the flames that he kindled, or the licentious pursuits of
gaming and hunting. His open simony might be the consequence
of distress ; and his blasphemous invocation of Jupiter and Venus,
if it be true, could not possibly be serious. But we read, with
some surprise, that the worthy grandson of Marozia lived in public adultery with the matrons of Rome ; that the Lateran palace
was turned into a school for prostitution, and that his rapes of
virgins and widows had deterred the female pilgrims from visiting the tomb of St. Peter, lest, in the devout act, they should be
violated by his successor.[133] The Protestants have dwelt with
malicious pleasure on these characters of Antichrist ; but to a
philosophic eye, the vices of the clergy are far less dangerous than
their virtues. After a long series of scandal, the apostolic see was
reformed and exalted by the austerity and zeal of Gregory VII.
That ambitious monk devoted his life to the execution of two pro-

---

* John XI. was the son of her husband Alberic, not of her lover, Pope Sergius III.,
as Muratori has distinctly proved, Ann. ad. ann. 911, tom. v. p. 268. Her grandson,
Octavian, otherwise called John XII., was pope ; but a great-grandson cannot be
discovered in any of the succeeding popes ; nor does our historian himself, in his
subsequen narration seem to know of one. Hobhouse, Illustrations of Childe
Harold, p. 309.—M.

jects. I. To fix in the college of cardinals the freedom and independence of election, and forever to abolish the right or usurpation of the emperors and the Roman people. II. To bestow and resume the Western empire as a fief or benefice [134] of the church, and to extend his temporal dominion over the kings and kingdoms of the earth. After a contest of fifty years, the first of these designs was accomplished by the firm support of the ecclesiastical order, whose liberty was connected with that of their chief. But the second attempt, though it was crowned with some partial and apparent success, has been vigorously resisted by the secular power, and finally extinguished by the improvement of human reason.

In the revival of the empire of Rome, neither the bishop nor the people could bestow on Charlemagne or Otho the provinces which were lost, as they had been won, by the chance of arms. But the Romans were free to choose a master for themselves; and the powers which had been delegated to the patrician, were irrevocably granted to the French and Saxon emperors of the West. The broken records of the times [135] preserve some remembrance of their palace, their mint, their tribunal, their edicts, and the sword of justice, which, as late as the thirteenth century, was derived from Cæsar to the præfect of the city. [136] Between the arts of the popes and the violence of the people, this supremacy was crushed and annihilated. Content with the titles of emperor and Augustus, the successors of Charlemagne neglected to assert this local jurisdiction. In the hour of prosperity, their ambition was diverted by more alluring objects; and in the decay and division of the empire, they were oppressed by the defence of their hereditary provinces. Amidst the ruins of Italy, the famous Marozia invited one of the usurpers to assume the character of her third husband; and Hugh, king of Burgundy, was introduced by her faction into the mole of Hadrian or castle of St. Angelo, which commands the principal bridge and entrance of Rome. Her son by the first marriage, Alberic, was compelled to attend at the nuptial banquet; but his reluctant and ungraceful service was chastised with a blow by his new father. The blow was productive of a revolution. "Romans," exclaimed the youth, "once you were the masters of the world, and these Burgundians the most abject of your slaves. They now reign, these voracious and brutal savages, and my injury is the commencement of your servitude." [137] The alarum bell rang to arms in every quarter of the city: the Burgundians retreated with haste and shame; Marozia was imprisoned by her victorious son, and his brother, Pope John XI., was reduced to the exercise of his spiritual functions. With the title of prince, Alberic possessed above twenty years the government of Rome ; and he is said to have gratified the popular prejudice, by restoring the office, or at least the title, of consuls and tribunes. His son and heir Octavian assumed, with the pontificate, the name of John XII. : like his predecessor, he was provoked by the Lombard princes to seek a deliverer for the church and republic ; and the services of Otho were rewarded with the Imperial dignity. But the Saxon was imperious, the Romans were impatient, the festival of the coronation was disturbed by the secret conflict of prerogative and freedom, and Otho commanded his sword-bearer not to stir from his person, lest he should be assaulted and murdered at the foot of the altar.[138] Before he repassed the Alps, the emperor chastised the revolt of the people and the ingratitude of John XII. The pope was degraded in a synod ; the præfect was mounted on an ass, whipped through the city, and cast into a dungeon ; thirteen of the most guilty were hanged, others were mutilated or banished ; and this severe process was justified by the ancient laws of Theodosius and Justinian. The voice of fame has accused the second Otho of a perfidious and bloody act, the massacre of the senators, whom he had invited to his table under the fair semblance of hospitality and friendship.[139] In the minority of his son Otho the Third, Rome made a bold attempt to shake off the Saxon yoke, and the consul Crescentius was the Brutus of the republic. From the condition of a subject and an exile, he twice rose to the command of the city, oppressed, expelled, and created the popes, and formed a conspiracy for restoring the authority of the Greek emperors.* In the fortress of St. Angelo he maintained an obstinate siege, till the unfortunate consul was betrayed by a promise of safety : his body was suspended on a gibbet, and his head was exposed on the battlements of the castle. By a reverse of fortune, Otho, after separating his troops, was besieged three days, without food, in his palace ; and a disgraceful escape saved him from the justice or fury of the Romans. The senator Ptolemy was the leader of the people, and the widow of Crescentius enjoyed the pleasure or the fame of revenging her husband, by a poison which she administered to her Imperial lover. It was the design of Otho the Third to abandon the ruder countries of the North, to erect his throne in Italy, and to revive the institutions of the Roman monarchy. But his successors only once in their lives appeared on the banks of the Tyber, to receive their crown in the Vatican.[140]

---

* The Marquis Maffei's gallery contained a medal with Imp. Cæs. August. P. P. Crescentius. Hence Hobhouse infers that he affected the empire. Hobhouse, Illustrations of Childe Harold, p. 252.—M.

Their absence was contemptible, their presence odious and formidable. They descended from the Alps, at the head of their barbarians, who were strangers and enemies to the country ; and their transient visit was a scene of tumult and bloodshed.[141] A faint remembrance of their ancestors still tormented the Romans ; and they beheld with pious indignation the succession of Saxons, Franks, Swabians, and Bohemians, who usurped the purple and prerogatives of the Cæsars.

There is nothing perhaps more adverse to nature and reason than to hold in obedience remote countries and foreign nations, in opposition to their inclination and interest. A torrent of barbarians may pass over the earth, but an extensive empire must be supported by a refined system of policy and oppression ; in the centre, an absolute power, prompt in action and rich in resources ; a swift and easy communication with the extreme parts ; fortifications to check the first effort of rebellion ; a regular administration to protect and punish ; and a well-disciplined army to inspire fear, without provoking discontent and despair. Far different was the situation of the German Cæsars, who were ambitious to enslave the kingdom of Italy. Their patrimonial estates were stretched along the Rhine, or scattered in the provinces ; but this ample domain was alienated by the imprudence or distress of successive princes ; and their revenue, from minute and vexatious prerogative, was scarcely sufficient for the maintenance of their household. Their troops were formed by the legal or voluntary service of their feudal vassals, who passed the Alps with reluctance, assumed the license of rapine and disorder, and capriciously deserted before the end of the campaign. Whole armies were swept away by the pestilential influence of the climate : the survivors brought back the bones of their princes and nobles,[142] and the effects of their own intemperance were often imputed to the treachery and malice of the Italians, who rejoiced at least in the calamities of the barbarians. This irregular tyranny might contend on equal terms with the petty tyrants of Italy ; nor can the people, or the reader, be much interested in the event of the quarrel. But in the eleventh and twelfth centuries, the Lombards rekindled the flame of industry and freedom ; and the generous example was at length imitated by the republics of Tuscany.* In the Italian cities a municipal government had never been totally abolished ; and their first privileges were granted by the favor and policy of the emperors, who were desirous of erecting a

---

* Compare Sismondi, Histoire des Républiques Italiennes. Hallam's Middle Ages. Raumer, Geschichte der Hohenstauffen. Savigny, Geschichte des Römischen Rechts, vol. iii. p. 19, with the authors quoted.—M.

plebeian barrier against the independence of the nobles. But their rapid progress, the daily extension of their power and pretensions, were founded on the numbers and spirit of these rising communities.[143] Each city filled the measure of her diocese or district : the jurisdiction of the counts and bishops, of the marquises and counts, was banished from the land ; and the proudest nobles were persuaded or compelled to desert their solitary castles, and to embrace the more honorable character of freemen and magistrates. The legislative authority was inherent in the general assembly ; but the executive powers were intrusted to three consuls, annually chosen from the three orders of *captains, valvassors*,[144] and commons, into which the republic was divided. Under the protection of equal law, the labors of agriculture and commerce were gradually revived ; but the martial spirit of the Lombards was nourished by the presence of danger ; and as often as the bell was rung, or the standard[145] erected, the gates of the city poured forth a numerous and intrepid band, whose zeal in their own cause was soon guided by the use and discipline of arms. At the foot of these popular ramparts, the pride of the Cæsars was overthrown ; and the invincible genius of liberty prevailed over the two Frederics, the greatest princes of the middle age ; the first, superior perhaps in military prowess ; the second, who undoubtedly excelled in the softer accomplishments of peace and learning.

Ambitious of restoring the splendor of the purple, Frederic the First invaded the republics of Lombardy, with the arts of a statesman, the valor of a soldier, and the cruelty of a tyrant. The recent discovery of the Pandects had renewed a science most favorable to despotism ; and his venal advocates proclaimed the emperor the absolute master of the lives and properties of his subjects. His royal prerogatives, in a less odious sense, were acknowledged in the diet of Roncaglia ; and the revenue of Italy was fixed at thirty thousand pounds of silver,[146] which were multiplied to an indefinite demand, by the rapine of the fiscal officers. The obstinate cities were reduced by the terror or the force of his arms : his captives were delivered to the executioner, or shot from his military engines ; and, after the siege and surrender of Milan, the buildings of that stately capital were razed to the ground, three hundred hostages were sent into Germany, and the inhabitants were dispersed in four villages, under the yoke of the inflexible conqueror.[147] But Milan soon rose from her ashes ; and the league of Lombardy was cemented by distress : their cause was espoused by Venice, Pope Alexander the Third, and the Greek emperor : the fabric of oppression was overturned in a day ; and in the treaty of Constance, Frederic subscribed, with some reservations, the freedom of four-and-twenty cities. His grandson contended with their vigor and maturity ; but Frederic the Second [148] was endowed with some personal and peculiar advantages. His birth and education recommended him to the Italians ; and in the implacable discord of the two factions, the Ghibelins were attached to the emperor, while the Guelfs displayed the banner of liberty and the church. The court of Rome had slumbered, when his father Henry the Sixth was permitted to unite with the empire the kingdoms of Naples and Sicily ; and from these hereditary realms the son derived an ample and ready supply of troops and treasure. Yet Frederic the Second was finally oppressed by the arms of the Lombards and the thunders of the Vatican : his kingdom was given to a stranger, and the last of his family was beheaded at Naples on a public scaffold. During sixty years, no emperor appeared in Italy, and the name was remembered only by the ignominious sale of the last relics of sovereignty.

The barbarian conquerors of the West were pleased to decorate their chief with the title of emperor ; but it was not their design to invest him with the despotism of Constantine and Justinian. The persons of the Germans were free, their conquests were their own, and their national character was animated by a spirit which scorned the servile jurisprudence of the new or the ancient Rome. It would have been a vain and dangerous attempt to impose a monarch on the armed freemen, who were impatient of a magistrate ; on the bold, who refused to obey ; on the powerful, who aspired to command. The empire of Charlemagne and Otho was distributed among the dukes of the nations or provinces, the counts of the smaller districts, and the margraves of the marches or frontiers, who all united the civil and military authority as it had been delegated to the lieutenants of the first Cæsars. The Roman governors, who, for the most part, were soldiers of fortune, seduced their mercenary legions, assumed the Imperial purple, and either failed or succeeded in their revolt without wounding the power and unity of government. If the dukes, margraves, and counts of Germany, were less audacious in their claims, the consequences of their success were more lasting and pernicious to the state. Instead of aiming at the supreme rank, they silently labored to establish and appropriate their provincial independence. Their ambition was seconded by the weight of their estates and vassals, their mutual example and support, the common interest of the subordinate nobility, the change of princes and families, the minorities of Otho the Third and Henry the Fourth, the ambition of the popes, and the vain pursuit of the fugitive crowns of Italy and Rome. All the attributes of regal and territorial jurisdiction were gradually usurped by the commanders of the provinces : the right of peace and war, of life and death, of coinage and taxation, of foreign alliance and domestic economy. Whatever had been seized by violence was ratified by favor or distress, was granted as the price of a doubtful vote or a voluntary service ; whatever had been granted to one, could not, without injury, be denied to his successor or equal ; and every act of local or temporary possession was insensibly moulded into the constitution of the Germanic kingdom. In every province the visible presence of the duke or count was interposed between the throne and the nobles ; the subjects of the law became the vassals of a private chief ; and the standard which *he* received from his sovereign was often raised against him in the field. The temporal power of the clergy was cherished and exalted by the superstition or policy of the Carlovingian and Saxon dynasties, who blindly depended on their moderation and fidelity ; and the bishoprics of Germany were made equal in extent and privilege, superior in wealth and population, to the most ample states of the military order. As long as the emperors retained the prerogative of bestowing on every vacancy these ecclesiastic and secular benefices, their cause was maintained by the gratitude or ambition of their friends and favorites. But in the quarrel of the investitures, they were deprived of their influence over the episcopal chapters ; the freedom of election was restored, and the sovereign was reduced, by a solemn mockery, to his *first prayers*, the recommendation, once in his reign, to a single prebend in each church. The secular governors, instead of being recalled at the will of a superior, could be degraded only by the sentence of their peers. In the first age of the monarchy, the appointment of the son to the duchy or county of his father was solicited as a favor ; it was gradually obtained as a custom, and extorted as a right : the lineal succession was often extended to the collateral or female branches ; the states of the empire (their popular, and at length their legal, appellation) were divided and alienated by testament and sale ; and all idea of a public trust was lost in that of a private and perpetual inheritance. The emperor could not even be enriched by the casualties of forfeiture and extinction : within the term of a year he was obliged to dispose of the vacant fief ; and, in the choice of the candidate, it was his duty to consult either the general or the provincial diet.

After the death of Frederic the Second, Germany was left a monster with a hundred heads. A crowd of princes and prelates disputed the ruins of the empire : the lords of innumerable castles were less prone to obey, than to imitate, their superiors ; and, according to the measure of their strength, their incessant hostilities received the names of conquest or robbery. Such anarchy was the inevitable consequence of the laws and manners of Europe ; and the kingdoms of France and Italy were shivered into fragments by the violence of the same tempest. But the Italian cities and the French vassals were divided and destroyed, while the union of the Germans has produced, under the name of an empire, a great system of a federative republic. In the frequent and at last the perpetual institution of diets, a national spirit was kept alive, and the powers of a common lgislature are still exercised by the three branches or colleges of the electors, the princes, and the free and Imperial cities of Germany. I. Seven of the most powerful feudataries were permitted to assume, with a distinguished name and rank, the exclusive privilege of choosing the Roman emperor ; and these electors were the king of Bohemia, the duke of Saxony, the margrave of Brandenburgh, the count palatine of the Rhine, and the three archbishops of Mentz, of Treves, and of Cologne. II. The college of princes and prelates purged themselves of a promiscuous multitude : they reduced to four representative votes the long series of independent counts, and excluded the nobles or equestrian order, sixty thousand of whom, as in the Polish diets, had appeared on horseback in the field of election. III. The pride of birth and dominion, of the sword and the mitre, wisely adopted the commons as the third branch of the legislature, and, in the progress of society, they were introduced about the same æra into the national assemblies of France, England, and Germany. The Hanseatic League commanded the trade and navigation of the north : the confederates of the Rhine secured the peace and intercourse of the inland country ; the influence of the cities has been adequate to their wealth and policy, and their negative still invalidates the acts of the two superior colleges of electors and princes.[149]

It is in the fourteenth century that we may view in the strongest light the state and contrast of the Roman empire of Germany, which no longer held, except on the borders of the Rhine and Danube, a single province of Trajan or Constantine. Their unworthy successors were the counts of Hapsburgh, of Nassau, of Luxemburgh, and Schwartzenburgh : the emperor Henry the Seventh procured for his son the crown of Bohemia, and his grandson Charles the Fourth was born among a people strange and barbarous in the estimation of the Germans themselves.[150] After the excommunication of Lewis of Bavaria, he received the gift or promise of the vacant empire from the Roman pontiffs, who, in the exile and captivity of Avignon, affected the dominion of the earth. The death of his competitors united the electoral college, and Charles was unanimously saluted king of the Romans, and future emperor ; a title which, in the same age, was prostituted to the Cæsars of Germany and Greece. The German emperor was no more than the elective and impotent magistrate of an aristocracy of princes, who had not left him a village that he might call his own. His best prerogative was the right of presiding and proposing in the national senate, which was convened at his summons ; and his native kingdom of Bohemia, less opulent than the adjacent city of Nuremberg, was the firmest seat of his power and the richest source of his revenue. The army with which he passed the Alps consisted of three hundred horse. In the cathedral of St. Ambrose, Charles was crowned with the *iron* crown, which tradition ascribed to the Lombard monarchy ; but he was admitted only with a peaceful train ; the gates of the city were shut upon him ; and the king of Italy was held a captive by the arms of the Visconti, whom he confirmed in the sovereignty of Milan. In the Vatican he was again crowned with the *golden* crown of the empire ; but, in obedience to a secret treaty, the Roman emperor immediately withdrew without reposing a single night within the walls of Rome. The eloquent Petrarch,[151] whose fancy revived the visionary glories of the Capitol, deplores and upbraids the ignominious flight of the Bohemian ; and even his contemporaries could observe, that the sole exercise of his authority was in the lucrative sale of privileges and titles. The gold of Italy secured the election of his son ; but such was the shameful poverty of the Roman emperor, that his person was arrested by a butcher in the streets of Worms, and was detained in the public inn, as a pledge or hostage for the payment of his expenses.

From this humiliating scene let us turn to the apparent majesty of the same Charles in the diets of the empire. The golden bull, which fixes the Germanic constitution, is promulgated in the style of a sovereign and legislator. A hundred princes bowed before his throne, and exalted their own dignity by the voluntary honors which they yielded to their chief or minister. At the royal banquet, the hereditary great officers, the seven electors, who in rank and title were equal to kings, performed their solemn and domestic service of the palace. The seals of the triple kingdom were borne in state by the archbishops of Mentz, Cologne, and Treves, the perpetual arch-chancellors of Germany, Italy, and Arles. The great marshal, on horseback, exercised his function with a silver measure of oats, which he emptied on the ground, and immediately dismounted to regulate the order of the guests. The great steward, the count palatine of the Rhine, placed the dishes on the table. The great chamberlain, the margrave of Brandenburgh, presented, after the repast, the golden ewer and basin, to wash. The king of Bohemia, as great cup-bearer, was represented by the emperor's brother, the duke of Luxemburgh and Brabant; and the procession was closed by the great huntsmen, who introduced a boar and a stag, with a loud chorus of horns and hounds.[152] Nor was the supremacy of the emperor confined to Germany alone: the hereditary monarchs of Europe confessed the pre-eminence of his rank and dignity: he was the first of the Christian princes, the temporal head of the great republic of the West:[153] to his person the title of majesty was long appropriated; and he disputed with the pope the sublime prerogative of creating kings and assembling councils. The oracle of the civil law, the learned Bartolus, was a pensioner of Charles the Fourth; and his school resounded with the doctrine, that the Roman emperor was the rightful sovereign of the earth, from the rising to the setting sun. The contrary opinion was condemned, not as an error, but as a heresy, since even the Gospel had pronounced, "And there went forth a decree from Cæsar Augustus, that *all the world* should be taxed."[154]

If we annihilate the interval of time and space between Augustus and Charles, strong and striking will be the contrast between the two Cæsars; the Bohemian, who concealed his weakness under the mask of ostentation, and the Roman, who disguised his strength under the semblance of modesty. At the head of his victorious legions, in his reign over the sea and land, from the Nile and Euphrates to the Atlantic Ocean, Augustus professed himself the servant of the state and the equal of his fellow-citizens. The conqueror of Rome and her provinces assumed the popular and legal form of a censor, a consul, and a tribune. His will was the law of mankind, but in the declaration of his laws he borrowed the voice of the senate and people; and from their decrees their master accepted and renewed his temporary commission to administer the republic. In his dress, his domestics,[155] his titles, in all the offices of social life, Augustus maintained the character of a private Roman; and his most artful flatterers respected the secret of his absolute and perpetual monarchy.

CHAPTER L.

DESCRIPTION OF ARABIA AND ITS INHABITANTS.—BIRTH, CHAR-
ACTER, AND DOCTRINE OF MAHOMET.—HE PREACHES AT MECCA.
—FLIES TO MEDINA.—PROPAGATES HIS RELIGION BY THE
SWORD.—VOLUNTARY OR RELUCTANT SUBMISSION OF THE
ARABS.—HIS DEATH AND SUCCESSORS.—THE CLAIMS AND FOR-
TUNES OF ALI AND HIS DESCENDANTS.

AFTER pursuing above six hundred years the fleeting Cæsars of
Constantinople and Germany, I now descend, in the reign of
Heraclius, on the eastern borders of the Greek monarchy. While
the state was exhausted by the Persian war, and the church was
distracted by the Nestorian and Monophysite sects, Mahomet,
with the sword in one hand and the Koran in the other, erected
his throne on the ruins of Christianity and of Rome. The genius
of the Arabian prophet, the manners of his nation, and the spirit
of his religion, involve the causes of the decline and fall of the
Eastern empire ; and our eyes are curiously intent on one of the
most memorable revolutions, which have impressed a new and
lasting character on the nations of the globe.[1]

In the vacant space between Persia, Syria, Egypt, and Æthiopia, that Arabian peninsula[2] may be conceived as a triangle of
spacious but irregular dimensions. From the northern point of
Beles[3] on the Euphrates, a line of fifteen hundred miles is terminated by the Straits of Babelmandel and the land of frankincense. About half this length may be allowed for the middle
breadth, from east to west, from Bassora to Suez, from the Persian Gulf to the Red Sea.[4] The sides of the triangle are gradually
enlarged, and the southern basis presents a front of a thousand
miles to the Indian Ocean. The entire surface of the peninsula
exceeds in a fourfold proportion that of Germany or France ; but
the far greater part has been justly stigmatized with the epithets
of the *stony* and the *sandy*. Even the wilds of Tartary are decked
by the hand of nature, with lofty trees and luxuriant herbage ;
and the lonesome traveller derives a sort of comfort and society
from the presence of vegetable life. But in the dreary waste of
Arabia, a boundless level of sand is intersected by sharp and
naked mountains ; and the face of the desert, without shade or
shelter, is scorched by the direct and intense rays of a tropical
sun. Instead of refreshing breezes, the winds, particularly from
the south-west, diffuse a noxious and even deadly vapor ; the hil-

locks of sand which they alternately raise and scatter, are compared to the billows of the ocean, and whole caravans, whole armies, have been lost and buried in the whirlwind. The common benefits of water are an object of desire and contest ; and such is the scarcity of wood, that some art is requisite to preserve and propagate the element of fire. Arabia is destitute of navigable rivers, which fertilize the soil, and convey its produce to the adjacent regions : the torrents that fall from the hills are imbibed by the thirsty earth : the rare and hardy plants, the tamarind or the acacia, that strike their roots into the clefts of the rocks, are nourished by the dews of the night : a scanty supply of rain is collected in cisterns and aqueducts : the wells and springs are the secret treasure of the desert ; and the pilgrim of Mecca,⁵ after many a dry and sultry march, is disgusted by the taste of the waters which have rolled over a bed of sulphur or salt. Such is the general and genuine picture of the climate of Arabia. The experience of evil enhances the value of any local or partial enjoyments. A shady grove, a green pasture, a stream of fresh water, are sufficient to attract a colony of sedentary Arabs to the fortunate spots which can afford food and refreshment to themselves and their cattle, and which encourage their industry in the cultivation of the palm-tree and the vine. The high lands that border on the Indian Ocean are distinguished by their superior plenty of wood and water ; the air is more temperate, the fruits are more delicious, the animals and the human race more numerous : the fertility of the soil invites and rewards the toil of the husbandman ; and the peculiar gifts of frankincense ⁶ and coffee have attracted in different ages the merchants of the world. If it be compared with the rest of the peninsula, this sequestered region may truly deserve the appellation of the *happy ;* and the splendid coloring of fancy and fiction has been suggested by contrast, and countenanced by distance. It was for this earthly paradise that Nature had reserved her choicest favors and her most curious workmanship : the incompatible blessings of luxury and innocence were ascribed to the natives : the soil was impregnated with gold ⁷ and gems, and both the land and sea was taught to exhale the odors of aromatic sweets. This division of the *sandy,* the *stony,* and the *happy,* so familiar to the Greeks and Latins, is unknown to the Arabians themselves ; and it is singular enough that a country, whose language and inhabitants have ever been the same, should scarcely retain a vestige of its ancient geography. The maritime districts of *Bahrein* and *Oman* are opposite to the realm of Persia. The kingdom of *Yemen* displays the limits, or at least the situation, of Arabia Felix : the name of *Neged* is extended over the inland space ; and the birth of Mahomet has illustrated the province of *Hejaz* along the coast of the Red Sea.[8]

The measure of population is regulated by the means of subsistence ; and the inhabitants of this vast peninsula might be outnumbered by the subjects of a fertile and industrious province. Along the shores of the Persian Gulf, of the ocean, and even of the Red Sea, the *Icthyophagi*,[9] or fish-eaters, continued to wander in quest of their precarious food. In this primitive and abject state, which ill deserves the name of society, the human brute, without arts or laws, almost without sense or language, is poorly distinguished from the rest of the animal creation. Generations and ages might roll away in silent oblivion, and the helpless savage was restrained from multiplying his race by the wants and pursuits which confined his existence to the narrow margin of the sea-coast. But in an early period of antiquity the great body of the Arabs had emerged from this scene of misery ; and as the naked wilderness could not maintain a people of hunters, they rose at once to the more secure and plentiful condition of the pastoral life. The same life is uniformly pursued by the roving tribes of the desert ; and in the portrait of the modern *Bedoweens* we may trace the features of their ancestors,[10] who, in the age of Moses or Mahomet, dwelt under similar tents, and conducted their horses and camels and sheep to the same springs and the same pastures. Our toil is lessened, and our wealth is increased, by our dominion over the useful animals ; and the Arabian shepherd had acquired the absolute possession of a faithful friend and a laborious slave.[11] Arabia, in the opinion of the naturalist, is the genuine and original country of the *horse ;* the climate most propitious, not indeed to the size, but to the spirit and swiftness, of that generous animal. The merit of the Barb, the Spanish, and the English breed, is derived from a mixture of Arabian blood :[12] the Bedoweens preserve, with superstitious care, the honors and the memory of the purest race : the males are sold at a high price, but the females are seldom alienated ; and the birth of a noble foal was esteemed, among the tribes, as a subject of joy and mutual congratulation. These horses are educated in the tents, among the children of the Arabs, with a tender familiarity, which trains them in the habits of gentleness and attachment. They are accustomed only to walk and to gallop : their sensations are not blunted by the incessant abuse of the spur and the whip : their powers are reserved for the moments of flight and pursuit : but no sooner do they feel the touch of the hand or the stirrup than they dart away with the swiftness of the wind ; and if their friend be dismounted in the rapid career, they instantly stop till he has recovered his seat. In the sands of Africa and Arabia the *camel* is a sacred and precious gift. That strong and patient beast of burden can perform, without eating or drinking, a journey of several days ; and a reservoir of fresh water is preserved in a large bag, a fifth stomach of the animal, whose body is imprinted with the marks of servitude : the larger breed is capable of transporting a weight of a thousand pounds ; and the dromedary, of a lighter and more active frame, outstrips the fleetest courser in the race. Alive or dead, almost every part of the camel is serviceable to man : her milk is plentiful and nutritious : the young and tender flesh has the taste of veal : [13] a valuable salt is extrated from the urine : the dung supplies the deficiency of fuel ; and the long hair, which falls each year and is renewed, is coarsely manufactured into the garments, the furniture, and the tents of the Bedoweens. In the rainy seasons they consume the rare and insufficient herbage of the desert : during the heats of summer and the scarcity of winter they remove their encampments to the sea-coast, the hills of Yemen, or the neighborhood of the Euphrates, and have often extorted the dangerous license of visiting the banks of the Nile, and the villages of Syria and Palestine. The life of a wandering Arab is a life of danger and distress ; and though sometimes, by rapine or exchange, he may appropriate the fruits of industry, a private citizen in Europe is in the possession of more solid and pleasing luxury than the proudest emir, who marches in the field at the head of ten thousand horse.

Yet an essential difference may be found between the hordes of Scythia and the Arabian tribes ; since many of the latter were collected into towns, and employed in the labors of trade and agriculture. A part of their time and industry was still devoted to the management of their cattle : they mingled, in peace and war, with their brethren of the desert ; and the Bedoweens derived from their useful intercourse some supply of their wants, and some rudiments of art and knowledge. Among the forty-two cities of Arabia, [14] enumerated by Abulfeda, the most ancient and populous were situate in the *happy* Yemen : the towers of Saana, [15] and the marvellous reservoir of Merab, [16] were constructed by the kings of the Homerites ; but their profane lustre was eclipsed by the prophetic glories of MEDINA [17] and MECCA, [18] near the Red Sea, and at the distance from each other of two hundred and seventy miles. The last of these holy places was known to the Greeks under the name of Macoraba ; and the termination of the word is expressive of its greatness, which has not, indeed, in the most flourishing period, exceeded the size and populousness of Mar-

seilles. Some latent motive, perhaps of superstition, must have
impelled the founders, in the choice of a most unpromising situation. They erected their habitations of mud or stone, in a plain
about two miles long and one mile broad, at the foot of three
barren mountains ; the soil is a rock ; the water even of the holy
well of Zemzem is bitter or brackish ; the pastures are remote
from the city ; and grapes are transported above seventy miles
from the gardens of Tayef. The fame and spirit of the Koreishites, who reigned in Mecca, were conspicuous among the Arabian
tribes ; but their ungrateful soil refused the labors of agriculture,
and their position was favorable to the enterprises of trade. By
the seaport of Gedda, at the distance only of forty miles, they
maintained an easy correspondence with Abyssinia ; and that
Christian kingdom afforded the first refuge to the disciples of
Mahomet. The treasures of Africa were conveyed over the Peninsula to Gerrha or Katif, in the province of Bahrein, a city built,
as it is said, of rock-salt, by the Chaldæan exiles ; [19] and from
thence, with the native pearls of the Persian Gulf, they were
floated on rafts to the mouth of the Euphrates. Mecca is placed
almost at an equal distance, a month's journey, between Yemen
on the right, and Syria on the left hand. The former was the
winter, the latter the summer, station of her caravans ; and their
seasonable arrival relieved the ships of India from the tedious and
troublesome navigation of the Red Sea. In the markets of Saana
and Merab, in the harbors of Oman and Aden, the camels of the
Koreishites were laden with a precious cargo of aromatics ; a supply of corn and manufactures was purchased in the fairs of Bostra
and Damascus ; the lucrative exchange diffused plenty and riches
in the streets of Mecca ; and the noblest of her sons united the
love of arms with the profession of merchandise. [20]

The perpetual independence of the Arabs has been the theme of
praise among strangers and natives ; and the arts of controversy
transform this singular event into a prophecy and a miracle, in
favor of the posterity of Ismael. [21] Some exceptions, that can
neither be dismissed nor eluded, render this mode of reasoning as
indiscreet as it is superfluous ; the kingdom of Yemen has been
successively subdued by the Abyssinians, the Persians, the sultans
of Egypt, [22] and the Turks ; [23] the holy cities of Mecca and Medina have repeatedly bowed under a Scythian tyrant ; and the
Roman province of Arabia [24] embraced the peculiar wilderness in
which Ismael and his sons must have pitched their tents in the
face of their brethren. Yet these exceptions are temporary or
local ; the body of the nation has escaped the yoke of the most
powerful monarchies ; the arms of Sesostris and Cyrus, of Pompey

and Trajan, could never achieve the conquest of Arabia ; the present sovereign of the Turks [25] may exercise a shadow of jurisdiction, but his pride is reduced to solicit the friendship of a people, whom it is dangerous to provoke, and fruitless to attack. The obvious causes of their freedom are inscribed on the character and country of the Arabs. Many ages before Mahomet, [26] their intrepid valor had been severely felt by their neighbors in offensive and defensive war. The patient and active virtues of a soldier are insensibly nursed in the habits and discipline of a pastoral life. The care of the sheep and camels is abandoned to the women of the tribe ; but the martial youth, under the banner of the emir, is ever on horseback, and in the field, to practise the exercise of the bow, the javelin, and the cimeter. The long memory of their independence is the firmest pledge of its perpetuity, and succeeding generations are animated to prove their descent, and to maintain their inheritance. Their domestic feuds are suspended on the approach of a common enemy ; and in their last hostilities against the Turks, the caravan of Mecca was attacked and pillaged by fourscore thousands of the confederates. When they advance to battle, the hope of victory is in the front ; in the rear, the assurance of a retreat. Their horses and camels, who, in eight or ten days, can perform a march of four or five hundred miles, disappear before the conqueror ; the secret waters of the desert elude his search ; and his victorious troops are consumed with thirst, hunger, and fatigue, in the pursuit of an invisible foe, who scorns his efforts, and safely reposes in the heart of the burning solitude. The arms and deserts of the Bedoweens are not only the safeguards of their own freedom, but the barriers also of the happy Arabia, whose inhabitants, remote from war, are enervated by the luxury of the soil and climate. The legions of Augustus melted away in disease and lassitude ; [27] and it is only by a naval power that the reduction of Yemen has been successfully attempted. When Mahomet erected his holy standard, [28] that kingdom was a province of the Persian empire ; yet seven princes of the Homerites still reigned in the mountains ; and the vicegerent of Chosroes was tempted to forget his distant country and his unfortunate master. The historians of the age of Justinian represent the state of the independent Arabs, who were divided by interest or affection in the long quarrel of the East : the tribe of *Gassan* was allowed to encamp on the Syrian territory ; the princes of *Hira* were permitted to form a city about forty miles to the southward of the ruins of Babylon. Their service in the field was speedy and vigorous ; but their friendship was venal, their faith inconstant, their enmity capricious : it was an easier task to excite them to disarm these roving barbarians; and, in the familiar intercourse of war, they learned to see, and to despise, the splendid weakness both of Rome and of Persia. From Mecca to the Euphrates, the Arabian tribes [29] were confounded by the Greeks and Latins, under the general appellation of SARACENS, [30] a name which every Christian mouth has been taught to pronounce with terror and abhorrence.

The slaves of domestic tyranny may vainly exult in their national independence : but the Arab is personally free ; and he enjoys, in some degree, the benefits of society, without forfeiting the prerogatives of nature. In every tribe, superstition, or gratitude, or fortune, has exalted a particular family above the heads of their equals. The dignities of sheik and emir invariably descend in this chosen race ; but the order of succession is loose and precarious ; and the most worthy or aged of the noble kinsmen are preferred to the simple, though important, office of composing disputes by their advice, and guiding valor by their example. Even a female of sense and spirit has been permitted to command the countrymen of Zenobia. [31] The momentary junction of several tribes produces an army : their more lasting union constitutes a nation ; and the supreme chief, the emir of emirs, whose banner is displayed at their head, may deserve, in the eyes of strangers, the honors of the kingly name. If the Arabian princes abuse their power, they are quickly punished by the desertion of their subjects, who had been accustomed to a mild and parental jurisdiction. Their spirit is free, their steps are unconfined, the desert is open, and the tribes and families are held together by a mutual and voluntary compact. The softer natives of Yemen supported the pomp and majesty of a monarch ; but if he could not leave his palace without endangering his life [32] the active powers of government must have been devolved on his nobles and magistrates. The cities of Mecca and Medina present, in the heart of Asia, the form, or rather the substance, of a commonwealth. The grandfather of Mahomet, and his lineal ancestors, appear in foreign and domestic transactions as the princes of their country ; but they reigned, like Pericles at Athens, or the Medici at Florence, by the opinion of their wisdom and integrity ; their influence was divided with their patrimony ; and the sceptre was transferred from the uncles of the prophet to a younger branch of the tribe of Koreish. On solemn occasions they convened the assembly of the people ; and, since mankind must be either compelled or persuaded to obey, the use and reputation of oratory among the ancient Arabs is the clearest evidence of public freedom. [33] But their simple freedom was of a very different cast from the nice and artificial machinery of the Greek and Roman republics, in which each member possessed an undivided share of the civil and political rights of the community. In the more simple state of the Arabs, the nation is free, because each of her sons disdains a base submission to the will of a master. His breast is fortified by the austere virtues of courage, patience, and sobriety ; the love of independence prompts him to exercise the habits of self-command ; and the fear of dishonor guards him from the meaner apprehension of pain, of danger, and of death. The gravity and firmness of the mind is conspicuous in his outward demeanor ; his speech is low, weighty, and concise ; he is seldom provoked to laughter ; his only gesture is that of stroking his beard, the venerable symbol of manhood ; and the sense of his own importance teaches him to accost his equals without levity, and his superiors without awe.[34] The liberty of the Saracens survived their conquests : the first caliphs indulged the bold and familiar language of their subjects ; they ascended the pulpit to persuade and edify the congregation ; nor was it before the seat of empire was removed to the Tigris that the Abbasides adopted the proud and pompous ceremonial of the Persian and Byzantine courts.

In the study of nations and men we may observe the causes that render them hostile or friendly to each other, that tend to narrow or enlarge, to mollify or exasperate, the social character. The separation of the Arabs from the rest of mankind has accustomed them to confound the ideas of stranger and enemy ; and the poverty of the land has introduced a maxim of jurisprudence, which they believe and practise to the present hour. They pretend that, in the division of the earth, the rich and fertile climates were assigned to the other branches of the human family ; and that the posterity of the outlaw Ismael might recover, by fraud or force, the portion of inheritance of which he had been unjustly deprived. According to the remark of Pliny, the Arabian tribes are equally addicted to theft and merchandise ; the caravans that traverse the desert are ransomed or pillaged ; and their neighbors, since the remote times of Job and Sesostris,[35] have been the victims of their rapacious spirit. If a Bedoween discovers from afar a solitary traveller, he rides furiously against him, crying, with a loud voice, " Undress thyself, thy aunt (*my wife*) is without a garment." A ready submission entitles him to mercy ; resistance will provoke the aggressor, and his own blood must expiate the blood which he presumes to shed in legitimate defence. A single robber, or a few associates, are branded with their genuine name ; but the exploits of a numerous band assume the character of lawful and honorable war. The temper of a people thus armed against mankind was doubly inflamed by the domestic license of rapine, murder, and revenge. In the constitution of Europe, the right of peace and war is now confined to a small, and the actual exercise to a much smaller, list of respectable potentates ; but each Arab, with impunity and renown, might point his javelin against the life of his countryman. The union of the nation consisted only in a vague resemblance of language and manners ; and in each community the jurisdiction of the magistrate was mute and impotent. Of the time of ignorance which preceded Mahomet, seventeen hundred battles[36] are recorded by tradition : hostility was imbittered with the rancor of civil faction ; and the recital, in prose or verse, of an obsolete feud, was sufficient to rekindle the same passions among the descendants of the hostile tribes. In private life every man, at least every family, was the judge and avenger of his own cause. The nice sensibility of honor, which weighs the insult rather than the injury, sheds its deadly venom on the quarrels of the Arabs : the honor of their women, and of their *beards*, is most easily wounded ; an indecent action, a contemptuous word, can be expiated only by the blood of the offender ; and such is their patient inveteracy, that they expect whole months and years the opportunity of revenge. A fine or compensation for murder is familiar to the barbarians of every age : but in Arabia the kinsmen of the dead are at liberty to accept the atonement, or to exercise with their own hands the law of retaliation. The refined malice of the Arabs refuses even the head of the murderer, substitutes an innocent for the guilty person, and transfers the penalty to the best and most considerable of the race by whom they have been injured. If he falls by their hands, they are exposed, in their turn, to the danger of reprisals, the interest and principal of the bloody debt are accumulated : the individuals of either family lead a life of malice and suspicion, and fifty years may sometimes elapse before the account of vengeance be finally settled.[37] This sanguinary spirit, ignorant of pity or forgiveness, has been moderated, however, by the maxims of honor, which require in every private encounter some decent equality of age and strength, of numbers and weapons. An annual festival of two, perhaps of four, months, was observed by the Arabs before the time of Mahomet, during which their swords were religiously sheathed both in foreign and domestic hostility ; and this partial truce is more strongly expressive of the habits of anarchy and warfare.[38]

But the spirit of rapine and revenge was attempered by the milder influence of trade and literature. The solitary peninsula is encompassed by the most civilized nations of the ancient world ; the merchant is the friend of mankind ; and the annual caravans imported the first seeds of knowledge and politeness into the cities, and even the camps of the desert. Whatever may be the pedigree of the Arabs, their language is derived from the same original stock with the Hebrew, the Syriac, and the Chaldæan tongues : the independence of the tribes was marked by their peculiar dialects ; [39] but each, after their own, allowed a just preference to the pure and perspicuous idiom of Mecca. In Arabia, as well as in Greece, the perfection of language outstripped the refinement of manners ; and her speech could diversify the fourscore names of honey, the two hundred of a serpent, the five hundred of a lion, the thousand of a sword, at a time when this copious dictionary was intrusted to the memory of an illiterate people. The monuments of the Homerites were inscribed with an obsolete and mysterious character ; but the Cufic letters, the groundwork of the present alphabet, were invented on the banks of the Euphrates ; and the recent invention was taught at Mecca by a stranger who settled in that city after the birth of Mahomet. The arts of grammar, of metre, and of rhetoric, were unknown to the freeborn eloquence of the Arabians ; but their penetration was sharp, their fancy luxuriant, their wit strong and sententious, [40] and their more elaborate compositions were addressed with energy and effect to the minds of their hearers. The genius and merit of a rising poet was celebrated by the applause of his own and the kindred tribes. A solemn banquet was prepared, and a chorus of women, striking their tymbals, and displaying the pomp of their nuptials, sung in the presence of their sons and husbands the felicity of their native tribe ; that a champion had now appeared to vindicate their rights ; that a herald had raised his voice to immortalize their renown. The distant or hostile tribes resorted to an annual fair, which was abolished by the fanaticism of the first Moslems ; a national assembly that must have contributed to refine and harmonize the barbarians. Thirty days were employed in the exchange, not only of corn and wine, but of eloquence and poetry. The prize was disputed by the generous emulation of the bards ; the victorious performance was deposited in the archives of princes and emirs ; and we may read in our own language the seven original poems which were inscribed in letters of gold, and suspended in the temple of Mecca. [41] The Arabian poets were the historians and moralists of the age ; and if they sympathized with the prejudices, they inspired and crowned the virtues, of their countrymen. The indissoluble union of generosity and valor was the darling theme of their song ; and when they pointed their keenest satire against a despicable race, they affirmed, in the bitterness of reproach, that the men knew not how to give, nor the women to deny.[42] The same hospitality, which was practised by Abraham, and celebrated by Homer, is still renewed in the camps of the Arabs. The ferocious Bedoweens, the terror of the desert, embrace, without inquiry or hesitation, the stranger who dares to confide in their honor and to enter their tent. His treatment is kind and respectful : he shares the wealth, or the poverty, of his host ; and, after a needful repose, he is dismissed on his way, with thanks, with blessings, and perhaps with gifts. The heart and hand are more largely expanded by the wants of a brother or a friend ; but the heroic acts that could deserve the public applause must have surpassed the narrow measure of discretion and experience. A dispute had arisen who, among the citizens of Mecca, was entitled to the prize of generosity ; and a successive application was made to the three who were deemed most worthy of the trial. Abdallah, the son of Abbas, had undertaken a distant journey, and his foot was in the stirrup when he heard the voice of a suppliant, " O son of the uncle of the apostle of God, I am a traveller, and in distress !" He instantly dismounted to present the pilgrim with his camel, her rich caparison, and a purse of four thousand pieces of gold, excepting only the sword, either for its intrinsic value, or as the gift of an honored kinsman. The servant of Kais informed the second suppliant that his master was asleep : but he immediately added, "Here is a purse of seven thousand pieces of gold (it is all we have in the house), and here is an order that will entitle you to a camel and a slave ;" the master, as soon as he awoke, praised and enfranchised his faithful steward, with a gentle reproof, that by respecting his slumbers he had stinted his bounty. The third of these heroes, the blind Arabah, at the hour of prayer, was supporting his steps on the shoulders of two slaves. "Alas !" he replied, " my coffers are empty ! but these you may sell ; if you refuse, I renounce them." At these words, pushing away the youths, he groped along the wall with his staff. The character of Hatem is the perfect model of Arabian virtue ; [43] he was brave and liberal, an eloquent poet, and a successful robber ; forty camels were roasted at his hospitable feast ; and at the prayer of a suppliant enemy he restored both the captives and the spoil. The freedom of his countrymen disdained the laws of justice ; they proudly indulged the spontaneous impulse of pity and benevolence.

The religion of the Arabs,[44] as well as of the Indians, consisted in the worship of the sun, the moon, and the fixed stars ; a primitive and specious mode of superstition. The bright luminaries of the sky display the visible image of a Deity : their number and distance convey to a philosophic, or even a vulgar, eye, the idea of boundless space : the character of eternity is marked on these solid globes, that seem incapable of corruption or decay : the regularity of their motions may be ascribed to a principle of reason or instinct ; and their real, or imaginary, influence encourages the vain belief that the earth and its inhabitants are the object of their peculiar care. The science of astronomy was cultivated at Babylon ; but the school of the Arabs was a clear firmament and a naked plain. In their nocturnal marches they steered by the guidance of the stars : their names, and order, and daily station, were familiar to the curiosity and devotion of the Bedoween ; and he was taught by experience to divide, in twenty-eight parts, the zodiac of the moon, and to bless the constellations who refreshed, with salutary rains, the thirst of the desert. The reign of the heavenly orbs could not be extended beyond the visible sphere ; and some metaphysical powers were necessary to sustain the transmigration of souls and the resurrection of bodies : a camel was left to perish on the grave, that he might serve his master in another life ; and the invocation of departed spirits implies that they were still endowed with consciousness and power. I am ignorant, and I am careless, of the blind mythology of the barbarians ; of the local deities, of the stars, the air, and the earth, of their sex or titles, their attributes or subordination. Each tribe, each family, each independent warrior, created and changed the rites and the object of his fantastic worship ; but the nation, in every age, has bowed to the religion, as well as to the language, of Mecca. The genuine antiquity of the CAABA ascends beyond the Christian æra ; in describing the coast of the Red Sea, the Greek historian Diodorus [45] has remarked, between the Thamudites and the Sabæans, a famous temple, whose superior sanctity was revered by *all* the Arabians ; the linen or silken veil, which is annually renewed by the Turkish emperor, was first offered by a pious king of the Homerites, who reigned seven hundred years before the time of Mahomet. [46] A tent, or a cavern, might suffice for the worship of the savages, but an edifice of stone and clay has been erected in its place ; and the art and power of the monarchs of the East have been confined to the simplicity of the original model. [47] A spacious portico encloses the quadrangle of the Caaba ; a square chapel, twenty-four cubits long, twenty-three broad, and twenty-seven high : a door and a window admit the light ; the double roof is supported by three pillars of wood ; a spout (now of gold) discharges the rain-water, and the well Zemzem is protected by a dome from accidental pollution. The tribe of Koreish, by fraud and force, had acquired the custody of the Caaba; the sacerdotal office devolved through four lineal descents to the grandfather of Mahomet; and the family of the Hashemites, from whence he sprung, was the most respectable and sacred in the eyes of their country.[48] The precincts of Mecca enjoyed the rights of sanctuary; and, in the last month of each year, the city and the temple were crowded with a long train of pilgrims, who presented their vows and offerings in the house of God. The same rites which are now accomplished by the faithful Mussulman were invented and practised by the superstition of the idolaters. At an awful distance they cast away their garments: seven times, with hasty steps, they encircled the Caaba, and kissed the black stone: seven times they visited and adored the adjacent mountains: seven times they threw stones into the valley of Mina; and the pilgrimage was achieved, as at the present hour, by a sacrifice of sheep and camels, and the burial of their hair and nails in the consecrated ground. Each tribe either found or introduced in the Caaba their domestic worship: the temple was adorned, or defiled, with three hundred and sixty idols of men, eagles, lions, and antelopes; and most conspicuous was the statue of Hebal, of red agate, holding in his hand seven arrows, without heads or feathers, the instruments and symbols of profane divination. But this statue was a monument of Syrian arts: the devotion of the ruder ages was content with a pillar or a tablet; and the rocks of the desert were hewn into gods or altars, in imitation of the black stone[49] of Mecca, which is deeply tainted with the reproach of an idolatrous origin. From Japan to Peru, the use of sacrifice has universally prevailed; and the votary has expressed his gratitude, or fear, by destroying or consuming, in honor of the gods, the dearest and most precious of their gifts. The life of a man[50] is the most precious oblation to deprecate a public calamity: the altars of Phœnicia and Egypt, of Rome and Carthage, have been polluted with human gore: the cruel practice was long preserved among the Arabs; in the third century, a boy was annually sacrificed by the tribe of the Dumatians;[51] and a royal captive was piously slaughtered by the prince of the Saracens, the ally and soldier of the emperor Justinian.[52] A parent who drags his son to the altar exhibits the most painful and sublime effort of fanaticism: the deed, or the intention, was sanctified by the example of saints and heroes; and the father of Mahomet himself was devoted by a rash vow, and hardly ransomed for the equivalent of a hundred camels. In the time of ignorance, the Arabs, like the Jews and Egyptians, abstained from the taste of swine's flesh ; [53] they circumcised [54] their children at the age of puberty : the same customs, without the censure or the precept of the Koran, have been silently transmitted to their posterity and proselytes. It has been sagaciously conjectured that the artful legislator indulged the stubborn prejudices of his countrymen. It is more simple to believe that he adhered to the habits and opinions of his youth without foreseeing that a practice congenial to the climate of Mecca might become useless or inconvenient on the banks of the Danube or the Volga.

Arabia was free : the adjacent kingdoms were shaken by the storms of conquest and tyranny, and the persecuted sects fled to the happy land where they might profess what they thought, and practise what they professed. The religions of the Sabians and Magians, of the Jews and Christians, were disseminated from the Persian Gulf to the Red Sea. In a remote period of antiquity, Sabianism was diffused over Asia by the science of the Chaldæans [55] and the arms of the Assyrians. From the observations of two thousand years, the priests and astronomers of Babylon [56] deduced the eternal laws of nature and providence. They adored the seven gods, or angels, who directed the course of the seven planets, and shed their irresistible influence on the earth. The attributes of the seven planets, with the twelve signs of the zodiac, and the twenty-four constellations of the northern and southern hemisphere, were represented by images and talismans ; the seven days of the week were dedicated to their respective deities ; the Sabians prayed thrice each day ; and the temple of the moon at Haran was the term of their pilgrimage. [57] But the flexible genius of their faith was always ready either to teach or to learn : in the tradition of the creation, the deluge, and the patriarchs, they held a singular agreement with their Jewish captives ; they appealed to the secret books of Adam, Seth, and Enoch ; and a slight infusion of the Gospel has transformed the last remnant of the Polytheists into the Christians of St. John, in the territory of Bassora. [58] The altars of Babylon were overturned by the Magians ; but the injuries of the Sabians were revenged by the sword of Alexander ; Persia groaned above five hundred years under a foreign yoke ; and the purest disciples of Zoroaster escaped from the contagion of idolatry, and breathed with their adversaries the freedom of the desert. [59] Seven hundred years before the death of Mahomet, the Jews were settled in Arabia ; and a far greater multitude was expelled from the Holy Land in the wars of Titus and Hadrian. The industrious exiles aspired to liberty and power : they erected synagogues in the cities, and castles in the wilderness, and their Gentile converts were confounded with the children of Israel, whom they resembled in the outward mark of circumcision. The Christian missionaries were still more active and successful : the Catholics asserted their universal reign ; the sects whom they oppressed, successively retired beyond the limits of the Roman empire ; the Marcionites and Manichæans dispersed their *fantastic* opinions and apocryphal gospels ; the churches of Yemen, and the princes of Hira and Gassan, were instructed in a purer creed by the Jacobite and Nestorian bishops.[60] The liberty of choice was presented to the tribes : each Arab was free to elect or to compose his private religion : and the rude superstition of his house was mingled with the sublime theology of saints and philosophers. A fundamental article of faith was inculcated by the consent of the learned strangers ; the existence of one supreme God, who is exalted above the powers of heaven and earth, but who has often revealed himself to mankind by the ministry of his angels and prophets, and whose grace or justice has interrupted, by seasonable miracles, the order of nature. The most rational of the Arabs acknowledged his power, though they neglected his worship ;[61] and it was habit rather than conviction that still attached them to the relics of idolatry. The Jews and Christians were the people of the *Book ;* the Bible was already translated into the Arabic language,[62] and the volume of the Old Testament was accepted by the concord of these implacable enemies. In the story of the Hebrew patriarchs, the Arabs were pleased to discover the fathers of their nation. They applauded the birth and promises of Ismael ; revered the faith and virtue of Abraham ; traced his pedigree and their own to the creation of the first man, and imbibed, with equal credulity, the prodigies of the holy text, and the dreams and traditions of the Jewish rabbis.

The base and plebeian origin of Mahomet is an unskilful calumny of the Christians,[63] who exalt instead of degrading the merit of their adversary. His descent from Ismael was a national privilege or fable ; but if the first steps of the pedigree[64] are dark and doubtful, he could produce many generations of pure and genuine nobility : he sprung from the tribe of Koreish and the family of Hashem, the most illustrious of the Arabs, the princes of Mecca, and the hereditary guardians of the Caaba. The grandfather of Mahomet was Abdol Motalleb, the son of Hashem, a wealthy and generous citizen, who relieved the distress of famine with the supplies of commerce. Mecca, which had been fed by the liberality of the father, was saved by the courage of the son. The kingdom of Yemen was subject to the Christian princes of Abyssinia ; their vassal Abrahah was provoked by an insult to avenge the honor of the cross ; and the holy city was invested by a train of elephants and an army of Africans. A treaty was proposed ; and, in the first audience, the grandfather of Mahomet demanded the restitution of his cattle. "And why," said Abrahah, "do you not rather implore my clemency in favor of your temple, which I have threatened to destroy ?" "Because," replied the intrepid chief, "the cattle is my own ; the Caaba belongs to the gods, and *they* will defend their house from injury and sacrilege." The want of provisions, or the valor of the Koreish, compelled the Abyssinians to a disgraceful retreat ; their discomfiture has been adorned with a miraculous flight of birds, who showered down stones on the heads of the infidels ; and the deliverance was long commemorated by the æra of the elephant.[65] The glory of Abdol Motalleb was crowned with domestic happiness ; his life was prolonged to the age of one hundred and ten years ; and he became the father of six daughters and thirteen sons. His best beloved Abdallah was the most beautiful and modest of the Arabian youth ; and in the first night, when he consummated his marriage with Amina,* of the noble race of the Zahrites, two hundred virgins are said to have expired of jealousy and despair. Mahomet, or more properly Mohammed, the only son of Abdallah and Amina, was born at Mecca, four years after the death of Justinian, and two months after the defeat of the Abyssinians,[66] whose victory would have introduced into the Caaba the religion of the Christians. In his early infancy, he was deprived of his father, his mother, and his grandfather ; his uncles were strong and numerous ; and, in the division of the inheritance, the orphan's share was reduced to five camels and an Æthiopian maid-servant. At home and abroad, in peace and war, Abu Taleb, the most respectable of his uncles, was the guide and guardian of his youth ; in his twenty-fifth year, he entered into the service of Cadijah, a rich and noble widow of Mecca, who soon rewarded his fidelity with the gift of her hand and fortune. The marriage contract, in the simple style of antiquity, recites the mutual love of Mahomet and Cadijah ; describes him as the most accomplished of the tribe of Koreish ; and stipulates a dowry of twelve ounces of gold and twenty camels, which was supplied by the liberality of his uncle.[67] By this alliance, the son of Abdallah was restored to the station of his ancestors ; and the judicious matron was content with his domestic virtues, till, in the fortieth

---

* Amina, or Emina, was of Jewish birth. V. Hammer, Geschichte der Assass. p. 10.—M.

year of his age,[68] he assumed the title of a prophet, and proclaimed the religion of the Koran.

According to the tradition of his companions, Mahomet[69] was distinguished by the beauty of his person, an outward gift which is seldom despised, except by those to whom it has been refused. Before he spoke, the orator engaged on his side the affections of a public or private audience. They applauded his commanding presence, his majestic aspect, his piercing eye, his gracious smile, his flowing beard, his countenance that painted every sensation of the soul, and his gestures that enforced each expression of the tongue. In the familiar offices of life he scrupulously adhered to the grave and ceremonious politeness of his country : his respectful attention to the rich and powerful was dignified by his condescension and affability to the poorest citizens of Mecca : the frankness of his manner concealed the artifice of his views ; and the habits of courtesy were imputed to personal friendship or universal benevolence. His memory was capacious and retentive ; his wit easy and social ; his imagination sublime ; his judgment clear, rapid, and decisive. He possessed the courage both of thought and action ; and, although his designs might gradually expand with his success, the first idea which he entertained of his divine mission bears the stamp of an original and superior genius. The son of Abdallah was educated in the bosom of the noblest race, in the use of the purest dialect of Arabia ; and the fluency of his speech was corrected and enhanced by the practice of discreet and seasonable silence. With these powers of eloquence, Mahomet was an illiterate barbarian : his youth had never been instructed in the arts of reading and writing ;[70] the common ignorance exempted him from shame or reproach, but he was reduced to a narrow circle of existence, and deprived of those faithful mirrors, which reflect to our mind the minds of sages and heroes. Yet the book of nature and of man was open to his view ; and some fancy has been indulged in the political and philosophical observations which are ascribed to the Arabian *traveller.*[71] He compares the nations and the religions of the earth ; discovers the weakness of the Persian and Roman monarchies ; beholds, with pity and indignation, the degeneracy of the times ; and resolves to unite under one God and one king the invincible spirit and primitive virtues of the Arabs. Our more accurate inquiry will suggest, that, instead of visiting the courts, the camps, the temples, of the East, the two journeys of Mahomet into Syria were confined to the fairs of Bostra and Damascus ; that he was only thirteen years of age when he accompanied the caravan of his uncle ; and that his duty compelled him to return as soon as he had disposed of the merchandise of Cadijah. In these hasty and superficial excursions, the eye of genius might discern some objects invisible to his grosser companions ; some seeds of knowledge might be cast upon a fruitful soil ; but his ignorance of the Syriac language must have checked his curiosity ; and I cannot perceive, in the life or writings of Mahomet, that his prospect was far extended beyond the limits of the Arabian world. From every region of that solitary world, the pilgrims of Mecca were annually assembled, by the calls of devotion and commerce : in the free concourse of multitudes a simple citizen, in his native tongue, might study the political state and character of the tribes, the theory and practice of the Jews and Christians. Some useful strangers may be tempted, or forced, to implore the rights of hospitality ; and the enemies of Mahomet have named the Jew, the Persian, and the Syrian monk, whom they accuse of lending their secret aid to the composition of the Koran.[72] Conversation enriches the understanding, but solitude is the school of genius ; and the uniformity of a work denotes the hand of a single artist. From his earliest youth Mahomet was addicted to religious contemplation ; each year during the month of Ramadan, he withdrew from the world, and from the arms of Cadijah : in the cave of Hera, three miles from Mecca,[73] he consulted the spirit of fraud or enthusiasm, whose abode is not in the heavens, but in the mind of the prophet. The faith which, under the name of *Islam*, he preached to his family and nation, is compounded of an eternal truth, and a necessary fiction, THAT THERE IS ONLY ONE GOD, AND THAT MAHOMET IS THE APOSTLE OF GOD.

It is the boast of the Jewish apologists, that while the learned nations of antiquity were deluded by the fables of polytheism, their simple ancestors of Palestine preserved the knowledge and worship of the true God. The moral attributes of Jehovah may not easily be reconciled with the standard of *human* virtue : his metaphysical qualities are darkly expressed ; but each page of the Pentateuch and the Prophets is an evidence of his power : the unity of his name is inscribed on the first table of the law ; and his sanctuary was never defiled by any visible image of the invisible essence. After the ruin of the temple, the faith of the Hebrew exiles was purified, fixed, and enlightened, by the spiritual devotion of the synagogue ; and the authority of Mahomet will not justify his perpetual reproach, that the Jews of Mecca or Medina adored Ezra as the son of God.[74] But the children of Israel had ceased to be a people ; and the religions of the world were guilty, at least in the eyes of the prophet, of giving sons, or daughters, or companions to the supreme God. In the rude idolatry of the Arabs, the crime is manifest and audacious : the Sabians are poorly excused by the pre-eminence of the first planet, or intelligence, in their celestial hierarchy ; and in the Magian system the conflict of the two principles betrays the imperfection of the conqueror. The Christians of the seventh century had insensibly relapsed into a semblance of Paganism : their public and private vows were addressed to the relics and images that disgraced the temples of the East : the throne of the Almighty was darkened by a cloud of martyrs, and saints, and angels, the objects of popular veneration ; and the Collyridian heretics, who flourished in the fruitful soil of Arabia, invested the Virgin Mary with the name and honors of a goddess.[75] The mysteries of the Trinity and Incarnation *appear* to contradict the principle of the divine unity. In their obvious sense, they introduce three equal deities, and transform the man Jesus into the substance of the Son of God :[76] an orthodox commentary will satisfy only a believing mind : intemperate curiosity and zeal had torn the veil of the sanctuary ; and each of the Oriental sects was eager to confess that all, except themselves, deserved the reproach of idolatry and polytheism. The creed of Mahomet is free from suspicion or ambiguity ; and the Koran is a glorious testimony to the unity of God. The prophet of Mecca rejected the worship of idols and men, of stars and planets, on the rational principle that whatever rises must set, that whatever is born must die, that whatever is corruptible must decay and perish.[77] In the Author of the universe, his rational enthusiasm confessed and adored an infinite and eternal being, without form or place, without issue or similitude, present to our most secret thoughts, existing by the necessity of his own nature, and deriving from himself all moral and intellectual perfection. These sublime truths, thus announced in the language of the prophet,[78] are firmly held by his disciples, and defined with metaphysical precision by the interpreters of the Koran. A philosophic theist might subscribe the popular creed of the Mahometans ;[79] a creed too sublime, perhaps, for our present faculties. What object remains for the fancy, or even the understanding, when we have abstracted from the unknown substance all ideas of time and space, of motion and matter, of sensation and reflection ? The first principle of reason and revelation was confirmed by the voice of Mahomet : his proselytes, from India to Morocco, are distinguished by the name of *Unitarians ;* and the danger of idolatry has been prevented by the interdiction of images. The doctrine of eternal decrees and absolute predestination is strictly embraced by the Mahometans ; and they struggle, with the common difficulties, *how* to reconcile the prescience of God with the freedom and responsibility of man ; *how* to explain the permission of evil under the reign of infinite power and infinite goodness.

The God of nature has written his existence on all his works, and his law in the heart of man. To restore the knowledge of the one, and the practice of the other, has been the real or pretended aim of the prophets of every age : the liberality of Mahomet allowed to his predecessors the same credit which he claimed for himself ; and the chain of inspiration was prolonged from the fall of Adam to the promulgation of the Koran.[80] During that period, some rays of prophetic light had been imparted to one hundred and twenty-four thousand of the elect, discriminated by their respective measure of virtue and grace ; three hundred and thirteen apostles were sent with a special commission to recall their country from idolatry and vice ; one hundred and four volumes have been dictated by the Holy Spirit ; and six legislators of transcendent brightness have announced to mankind the six successive revelations of various rites, but of one immutable religion. The authority and station of Adam, Noah, Abraham, Moses, Christ, and Mahomet, rise in just gradation above each other ; but whosoever hates or rejects any one of the prophets is numbered with the infidels. The writings of the patriarchs were extant only in the apocryphal copies of the Greeks and Syrians :[81] the conduct of Adam had not entitled him to the gratitude or respect of his children ; the seven precepts of Noah were observed by an inferior and imperfect class of the proselytes of the synagogue ;[82] and the memory of Abraham was obscurely revered by the Sabians in his native land of Chaldæa : of the myriads of prophets, Moses and Christ alone lived and reigned ; and the remnant of the inspired writings was comprised in the books of the Old and the New Testament. The miraculous story of Moses is consecrated and embellished in the Koran ;[83] and the captive Jews enjoy the secret revenge of imposing their own belief on the nations whose recent creeds they deride. For the author of Christianity, the Mahometans are taught by the prophet to entertain a high and mysterious reverence.[84] " Verily, Christ Jesus, the son of Mary, is the apostle of God, and his word, which he conveyed unto Mary, and a Spirit proceeding from him ; honorable in this world, and in the world to come ; and one of those who approach near to the presence of God."[85] The wonders of the genuine and apocryphal gospels[86] are profusely heaped on his head ; and the Latin church has not disdained to borrow from the Koran the immaculate conception[87] of his virgin mother. Yet Jesus was a mere mortal ; and, at the day of judgment, his testimony will serve to condemn both the Jews, who reject him as a prophet, and the Christians, who adore him as the Son of God. The malice of his enemies aspersed his reputation, and conspired against his life ; but their intention only was guilty ; a phantom or a criminal was substituted on the cross ; and the innocent saint was translated to the seventh heaven.[88] During six hundred years the gospel was the way of truth and salvation ; but the Christians insensibly forgot both the laws and example of their founder ; and Mahomet was instructed by the Gnostics to accuse the church, as well as the synagogue, of corrupting the integrity of the sacred text.[89] The piety of Moses and of Christ rejoiced in the assurance of a future prophet, more illustrious than themselves : the evangelic promise of the *Paraclete*, or Holy Ghost, was prefigured in the name, and accomplished in the person, of Mahomet,[90] the greatest and the last of the apostles of God.

The communication of ideas requires a similitude of thought and language : the discourse of a philosopher would vibrate without effect on the ear of a peasant ; yet how minute is the distance of *their* understandings, if it be compared with the contact of an infinite and a finite mind, with the word of God expressed by the tongue or the pen of a mortal ! The inspiration of the Hebrew prophets, of the apostles and evangelists of Christ, might not be incompatible with the exercise of their reason and memory ; and the diversity of their genius is strongly marked in the style and composition of the books of the Old and New Testament. But Mahomet was content with a character, more humble, yet more sublime, of a simple editor ; the substance of the Koran,[91] according to himself or his disciples, is uncreated and eternal ; subsisting in the essence of the Deity, and inscribed with a pen of light on the table of his everlasting decrees. A paper copy, in a volume of silk and gems, was brought down to the lowest heaven by the angel Gabriel, who, under the Jewish economy, had indeed been despatched on the most important errands ; and this trusty messenger successively revealed the chapters and verses to the Arabian prophet. Instead of a perpetual and perfect measure of the divine will, the fragments of the Koran were produced at the discretion of Mahomet ; each revelation is suited to the emergencies of his policy or passion ; and all contradiction is removed by the saving maxim, that any text of Scripture is abrogated or modified by any subsequent passage. The word of God, and of the apostle, was diligently recorded by his disciples on palm-leaves and the shoulder-bones of mutton ; and the pages, without order or connection, were cast into a domestic chest, in the custody of one of his wives. Two years after the death of Mahomet, the sacred volume was collected and published by his friend and successor Abubeker : the work was revised by the caliph Othman, in the thirtieth year of the Hegira ; and the various editions of the Koran assert the same miraculous privilege of a uniform and incorruptible text. In the spirit of enthusiasm or vanity, the prophet rests the truth of his mission on the merit of his book ; audaciously challenges both men and angels to imitate the beauties of a single page ; and presumes to assert that God alone could dictate this incomparable performance.[92] This argument is most powerfully addressed to a devout Arabian, whose mind is attuned to faith and rapture ; whose ear is delighted by the music of sounds ; and whose ignorance is incapable of comparing the productions of human genius.[93] The harmony and copiousness of style will not reach, in a version, the European infidel : he will peruse with impatience the endless incoherent rhapsody of fable, and precept, and declamation, which seldom excites a sentiment or an idea, which sometimes crawls in the dust, and is sometimes lost in the clouds. The divine attributes exalt the fancy of the Arabian missionary ; but his loftiest strains must yield to the sublime simplicity of the book of Job, composed in a remote age, in the same country, and in the same language.[94] If the composition of the Koran exceed the faculties of a man, to what superior intelligence should we ascribe the Iliad of Homer, or the Philippics of Demosthenes ? In all religions, the life of the founder supplies the silence of his written revelation : the sayings of Mahomet were so many lessons of truth ; his actions so many examples of virtue ; and the public and private memorials were preserved by his wives and companions. At the end of two hundred years, the *Sonna*, or oral law, was fixed and consecrated by the labors of Al Bochari, who discriminated seven thousand two hundred and seventy-five genuine traditions, from a mass of three hundred thousand reports, of a more doubtful or spurious character. Each day the pious author prayed in the temple of Mecca, and performed his ablutions with the water of Zemzem : the pages were successively deposited on the pulpit and the sepulchre of the apostle ; and the work has been approved by the four orthodox sects of the Sonnites.[95]

The mission of the ancient prophets, of Moses and of Jesus, had been confirmed by many splendid prodigies ; and Mahomet was repeatedly urged, by the inhabitants of Mecca and Medina, to produce a similar evidence of his divine legation ; to call down from heaven the angel or the volume of his revelation, to create a garden in the desert, or to kindle a conflagration in the unbelieving city. As often as he is pressed by the demands of the Kore-

ish, he involves himself in the obscure boast of vision and prophecy, appeals to the internal proofs of his doctrine, and shields
himself behind the providence of God, who refuses those signs
and wonders that would depreciate the merit of faith, and aggravate the guilt of infidelity.   But the modest or angry tone of his
apologies betrays his weakness and vexation ; and these passages
of scandal established, beyond suspicion, the integrity of the
Koran.[96] The votaries of Mahomet are more assured than himself of his miraculous gifts ; and their confidence and credulity
increase as they are farther removed from the time and place of
his spiritual exploits.   They believe or affirm that trees went
forth to meet him ; that he was saluted by stones ; that water
gushed from his fingers ; that he fed the hungry, cured the sick,
and raised the dead ; that a beam groaned to him ; that a camel
complained to him ; that a shoulder of mutton informed him of
its being poisoned ; and that both animate and inanimate nature
were equally subject to the apostle of God.[97] His dream of a
nocturnal journey is seriously described as a real and corporeal
transaction.   A mysterious animal, the Borak, conveyed him from
the temple of Mecca to that of Jerusalem : with his companion
Gabriel he successively ascended the seven heavens, and received
and repaid the salutations of the patriarchs, the prophets, and
the angels, in their respective mansions. Beyond the seventh
heaven, Mahomet alone was permitted to proceed ; he passed the
veil of unity, approached within two bow-shots of the throne, and
felt a cold that pierced him to the heart, when his shoulder was
touched by the hand of God.   After this familiar, though important conversation, he again descended to Jerusalem, remounted
the Borak, returned to Mecca, and performed in the tenth part of
a night the journey of many thousand years.[98] According to another legend, the apostle confounded in a national assembly the
malicious challenge of the Koreish. His resistless word split asunder the orb of the moon ; the obedient planet stooped from her
station in the sky, accomplished the seven revolutions round the
Caaba, saluted Mahomet in the Arabian tongue, and, suddenly
contracting her dimensions, entered at the collar, and issued forth
through the sleeve, of his shirt.[99] The vulgar are amused with
these marvellous tales ; but the gravest of the Mussulman doctors
imitate the modesty of their master, and indulge a latitude of
faith or interpretation.[100] They might speciously allege, that in
preaching the religion it was needless to violate the harmony of
nature ; that a creed unclouded with mystery may be excused
from miracles ; and that the sword of Mahomet was not less
potent than the rod of Moses.

The polytheist is oppressed and distracted by the variety of superstition : a thousand rites of Egyptian origin were interwoven with the essence of the Mosaic law ; and the spirit of the gospel had evaporated in the pageantry of the church. The prophet of Mecca was tempted by prejudice, or policy, or patriotism, to sanctify the rites of the Arabians, and the custom of visiting the holy stone of the Caaba. But the precepts of Mahomet himself inculcate a more simple and rational piety : prayer, fasting, and alms, are the religious duties of a Mussulman ; and he is encouraged to hope, that prayer will carry him half way to God, fasting will bring him to the door of his palace, and alms will gain him admittance.[101] I. According to the tradition of the nocturnal journey, the apostle, in his personal conference with the Deity, was commanded to impose on his disciples the daily obligation of fifty prayers. By the advice of Moses, he applied for an alleviation of this intolerable burden ; the number was gradually reduced to five ; without any dispensation of business or pleasure, or time or place : the devotion of the faithful is repeated at daybreak, at noon, in the afternoon, in the evening, and at the first watch of the night ; and in the present decay of religious fervor, our travellers are edified by the profound humility and attention of the Turks and Persians. Cleanliness is the key of prayer : the frequent lustration of the hands, the face, and the body, which was practised of old by the Arabs, is solemnly enjoined by the Koran ; and a permission is formally granted to supply with sand the scarcity of water. The words and attitudes of supplication, as it is performed either sitting, or standing, or prostrate on the ground, are prescribed by custom or authority ; but the prayer is poured forth in short and fervent ejaculations ; the measure of zeal is not exhausted by a tedious liturgy ; and each Mussulman for his own person is invested with the character of a priest. Among the theists, who reject the use of images, it has been found necessary to restrain the wanderings of the fancy, by directing the eye and the thought towards a *kebla*, or visible point of the horizon. The prophet was at first inclined to gratify the Jews by the choice of Jerusalem ; but he soon returned to a more natural partiality ; and five times every day the eyes of the nations at Astracan, at Fez, at Delhi, are devoutly turned to the holy temple of Mecca. Yet every spot for the service of God is equally pure : the Mahometans indifferently pray in their chamber or in the street. As a distinction from the Jews and Christians, the Friday in each week is set apart for the useful institution of public worship : the people is assembled in the mosch ; and the imam, some respectable elder, ascends the pulpit, to begin the prayer and pronounce the sermon. But the Mahometan religion is destitute of priesthood or sacrifice ; and the independent spirit of fanaticism looks down with contempt on the ministers and the slaves of superstition.* II. The voluntary [102] penance of the ascetics, the torment and glory of their lives, was odious to a prophet who censured in his companions a rash vow of abstaining from flesh, and women, and sleep ; and firmly declared, that he would suffer no monks in his religion.[103] Yet he instituted, in each year, a fast of thirty days ; and strenuously recommended the observance as a discipline which purifies the soul and subdues the body, as a salutary exercise of obedience to the will of God and his apostle. During the month of Ramadan, from the rising to the setting of the sun, the Mussulman abstains from eating, and drinking, and women, and baths, and perfumes ; from all nourishment that can restore his strength, from all pleasure that can gratify his senses. In the revolution of the lunar year, the Ramadan coincides, by turns, with the winter cold and the summer heat ; and the patient martyr, without assuaging his thirst with a drop of water, must expect the close of a tedious and sultry day. The interdiction of wine, peculiar to some orders of priests or hermits, is converted by Mahomet alone into a positive and general law ; [104] and a considerable portion of the globe has abjured, at his command, the use of that salutary, though dangerous, liquor. These painful restraints are, doubtless, infringed by the libertine, and eluded by the hypocrite ; but the legislator, by whom they are enacted, cannot surely be accused of alluring his prosleytes by the indulgence of their sensual appetites. III. The charity of the Mahometans descends to the animal creation ; and the Koran repeatedly inculcates, not as a merit, but as a strict and indispensable duty, the relief of the indigent and unfortunate. Mahomet, perhaps, is the only lawgiver who has defined the precise measure of charity : the standard may vary with the degree and nature of property, as it consists either in money, in corn or cattle, in fruits or merchandise ; but the Mussulman does not accomplish the law, unless he bestows a *tenth* of his revenue ; and if his conscience

---

* Such is Mahometanism beyond the precincts of the Holy City. But Mahomet retained, and the Koran sanctions (Sale's Koran, c. 5, in init. c. 22, vol. ii. p. 171, 172), the sacrifice of sheep and camels (probably according to the old Arabian rites) at Mecca ; and the pilgrims complete their ceremonial with sacrifices, sometimes as numerous and costly as those of King Solomon. Compare note, vol. iv. c. xxiii. p. 96, and Forster's Mahometanism Unveiled, vol. i. p. 420. This author quotes the questionable authority of Benjamin of Tudela, for the sacrifice of a camel by the caliph at Bosra ; but sacrifice undoubtedly forms no part of the ordinary Mahometan ritual ; nor will the sanctity of the caliph, as the earthly representative of the prophet, bear any close analogy to the priesthood of the Mosaic or Gentile religions. —M.

accuses him of fraud or extortion, the tenth, under the idea of restitution, is enlarged to a *fifth*.[105] Benevolence is the foundation of justice, since we are forbid to injure those whom we are bound to assist. A prophet may reveal the secrets of heaven and of futurity ; but in his moral precepts he can only repeat the lessons of our own hearts.

The two articles of belief, and the four practical duties, of Islam, are guarded by rewards and punishments ; and the faith of the Mussulman is devoutly fixed on the event of the judgment and the last day. The prophet has not presumed to determine the moment of that awful catastrophe, though he darkly announces the signs, both in heaven and earth, which will precede the universal dissolution, when life shall be destroyed, and the order of creation shall be confounded in the primitive chaos. At the blast of the trumpet, new worlds will start into being : angels, genii, and men will arise from the dead, and the human soul will again be united to the body. The doctrine of the resurrection was first entertained by the Egyptians ; [106] and their mummies were embalmed, their pyramids were constructed, to preserve the ancient mansion of the soul, during a period of three thousand years. But the attempt is partial and unavailing ; and it is with a more philosophic spirit that Mahomet relies on the omnipotence of the Creator, whose word can reanimate the breathless clay, and collect the innumerable atoms, that no longer retain their form or substance.[107] The intermediate state of the soul it is hard to decide ; and those who most firmly believe her immaterial nature, are at a loss to understand how she can think or act without the agency of the organs of sense.

The reunion of the soul and body will be followed by the final judgment of mankind ; and in his copy of the Magian picture, the prophet has too faithfully represented the forms of proceeding, and even the slow and successive operations, of an earthly tribunal. By his intolerant adversaries he is upbraided for extending, even to themselves, the hope of salvation, for asserting the blackest heresy, that every man who believes in God, and accomplishes good works, may expect in the last day a favorable sentence. Such rational indifference is ill adapted to the character of a fanatic ; nor is it probable that a messenger from heaven should depreciate the value and necessity of his own revelation. In the idiom of the Koran [108] the belief of God is inseparable from that of Mahomet : the good works are those which he has enjoined, and the two qualifications imply the profession of Islam, to which all nations and all sects are equally invited. Their spiritual blindness, though excused by ignorance and crowned with virtue, will be scourged with everlasting torments ; and the tears which Mahomet shed over the tomb of his mother, for whom he was forbidden to pray, display a striking contrast of humanity and enthusiasm.[109] The doom of the infidels is common : the measure of their guilt and punishment is determined by the degree of evidence which they have rejected, by the magnitude of the errors which they have entertained : the eternal mansions of the Christians, the Jews, the Sabians, the Magians, and idolaters, are sunk below each other in the abyss ; and the lowest hell is reserved for the faithless hypocrites who have assumed the mask of religion. After the greater part of mankind has been condemned for their opinions, the true believers only will be judged by their actions. The good and evil of each Mussulman will be accurately weighed in a real or allegorical balance ; and a singular mode of compensation will be allowed for the payment of injuries : the aggressor will refund an equivalent of his own good actions, for the benefit of the person whom he has wronged ; and if he should be destitute of any moral property, the weight of his sins will be loaded with an adequate share of the demerits of the sufferer. According as the shares of guilt or virtue shall preponderate, the sentence will be pronounced, and all, without distinction, will pass over the sharp and perilous bridge of the abyss ; but the innocent, treading in the footsteps of Mahomet, will gloriously enter the gates of paradise, while the guilty will fall into the first and mildest of the seven hells. The term of expiation will vary from nine hundred to seven thousand years ; but the prophet has judiciously promised, that *all* his disciples, whatever may be their sins, shall be saved, by their own faith and his intercession, from eternal damnation. It is not surprising that superstition should act most powerfully on the fears of her votaries, since the human fancy can paint with more energy the misery than the bliss of a future life. With the two simple elements of darkness and fire, we create a sensation of pain, which may be aggravated to an infinite degree by the idea of endless duration. But the same idea operates with an opposite effect on the continuity of pleasure ; and too much of our present enjoyments is obtained from the relief, or the comparison, of evil. It is natural enough that an Arabian prophet should dwell with rapture on the groves, the fountains, and the rivers of paradise ; but instead of inspiring the blessed inhabitants with a liberal taste for harmony and science, conversation and friendship, he idly celebrates the pearls and diamonds, the robes of silk, palaces of marble, dishes of gold, rich wines, artificial dainties, numerous attendants, and the whole train of sensual and costly luxury, which becomes insipid to the owner, even in the short period of this mortal life. Seventy-two *Houris*, or black-eyed girls, of resplendent beauty, blooming youth, virgin purity, and exquisite sensibility, will be created for the use of the meanest believer ; a moment of pleasure will be prolonged to a thousand years, and his faculties will be increased a hundredfold, to render him worthy of his felicity. Notwithstanding a vulgar prejudice, the gates of heaven will be open to both sexes ; but Mahomet has not specified the male companions of the female elect, lest he should either alarm the jealousy of their former husbands, or disturb their felicity, by the suspicion of an everlasting marriage. This image of a carnal paradise has provoked the indignation, perhaps the envy, of the monks : they declaim against the impure religion of Mahomet ; and his modest apologists are driven to the poor excuse of figures and allegories. But the sounder and more consistent party adhere, without shame, to the literal interpretation of the Koran : useless would be the resurrection of the body, unless it were restored to the possession and exercise of its worthiest faculties ; and the union of sensual and intellectual enjoyment is requisite to complete the happiness of the double animal, the perfect man. Yet the joys of the Mahometan paradise will not be confined to the indulgence of luxury and appetite ; and the prophet has expressly declared that all meaner happiness will be forgotten and despised by the saints and martyrs, who shall be admitted to the beatitude of the divine vision.[110]

The first and most arduous conquests of Mahomet [111] were those of his wife, his servant, his pupil, and his friend ; [112] since he presented himself as a prophet to those who were most conversant with his infirmities as a man. Yet Cadijah believed the words, and cherished the glory, of her husband ; the obsequious and affectionate Zeid was tempted by the prospect of freedom ; the illustrious Ali, the son of Abu Taleb, embraced the sentiments of his cousin with the spirit of a youthful hero ; and the wealth, the moderation, the veracity of Abubeker confirmed the religion of the prophet whom he was destined to succeed. By his persuasion, ten of the most respectable citizens of Mecca were introduced to the private lessons of Islam ; they yielded to the voice of reason and enthusiasm ; they repeated the fundamental creed, "There is but one god, and Mahomet is the apostle of God ;" and their faith, even in this life, was rewarded with riches and honors, with the command of armies and the government of kingdoms. Three years were silently employed in the conversion of fourteen proselytes, the first-fruits of his mission ; but in the fourth year he assumed the prophetic office, and resolving to impart to his family the light of divine truth, he prepared a banquet, a lamb, as it is said, and a bowl of milk, for the entertainment of forty guests of the race of Hashem. "Friends and kinsmen," said Mahomet to the assembly, "I offer you, and I alone can offer, the most precious of gifts, the treasures of this world and of the world to come. God has commanded me to call you to his service. Who among you will support my burden? Who among you will be my companion and my vizier?"[113] No answer was returned, till the silence of astonishment, and doubt, and contempt, was at length broken by the impatient courage of Ali, a youth in the fourteenth year of his age. "O prophet, I am the man: whosoever rises against thee I will dash out his teeth, tear out his eyes, break his legs, rip up his belly. O prophet, I will be thy vizier over them." Mahomet accepted his offer with transport, and Abu Taleb was ironically exhorted to respect the superior dignity of his son. In a more serious tone, the father of Ali advised his nephew to relinquish his impracticable design. "Spare your remonstrances," replied the intrepid fanatic to his uncle and benefactor; "if they should place the sun on my right hand, and the moon on my left, they should not divert me from my course." He persevered ten years in the exercise of his mission; and the religion which has overspread the East and the West advanced with a slow and painful progress within the walls of Mecca. Yet Mahomet enjoyed the satisfaction of beholding the increase of his infant congregation of Unitarians, who revered him as a prophet, and to whom he seasonably dispensed the spiritual nourishment of the Koran. The number of proselytes may be esteemed by the absence of eighty-three men and eighteen women, who retired to Æthiopia in the seventh year of his mission; and his party was fortified by the timely conversion of his uncle Hamza, and of the fierce and inflexible Omar, who signalized in the cause of Islam the same zeal which he had exerted for its destruction. Nor was the charity of Mahomet confined to the tribe of Koreish, or the precincts of Mecca: on solemn festivals, in the days of pilgrimage, he frequented the Caaba, accosted the strangers of every tribe, and urged, both in private converse and public discourse, the belief and worship of a sole Deity. Conscious of his reason and of his weakness, he asserted the liberty of conscience, and disclaimed the use of religious violence:[114] but he called the Arabs to repentance, and conjured them to remember the ancient idolaters of Ad and Thamud, whom the divine justice had swept away from the face of the earth.[115]

The people of Mecca were hardened in their unbelief by superstition and envy. The elders of the city, the uncles of the prophet, affected to despise the presumption of an orphan, the reformer of his country : the pious orations of Mahomet in the Caaba were answered by the clamors of Abu Taleb. "Citizens and pilgrims, listen not to the tempter, hearken not to his impious novelties. Stand fast in the worship of Al Lâta and Al Uzzah." Yet the son of Abdallah was ever dear to the aged chief : and he protected the fame and person of his nephew against the assaults of the Koreishites, who had long been jealous of the pre-eminence of the family of Hashem. Their malice was colored with the pretence of religion : in the age of Job, the crime of impiety was punished by the Arabian magistrate ; [16] and Mahomet was guilty of deserting and denying the national deities. But so loose was the policy of Mecca, that the leaders of the Koreish, instead of accusing a criminal, were compelled to employ the measures of persuasion or violence. They repeatedly addressed Abu Taleb in the style of reproach and menace. "Thy nephew reviles our religion ; he accuses our wise forefathers of ignorance and folly ; silence him quickly, lest he kindle tumult and discord in the city. If he persevere, we shall draw our swords against him and his adherents, and thou wilt be responsible for the blood of thy fellow-citizens." The weight and moderation of Abu Taleb eluded the violence of religious faction ; the most helpless or timid of the disciples retired to Æthiopia, and the prophet withdrew himself to various places of strength in the town and country. As he was still supported by his family, the rest of the tribe of Koreish engaged themselves to renounce all intercourse with the children of Hashem, neither to buy nor sell, neither to marry nor to give in marriage, but to pursue them with implacable enmity, till they should deliver the person of Mahomet to the justice of the gods. The decree was suspended in the Caaba before the eyes of the nation ; the messengers of the Koreish pursued the Mussulman exiles in the heart of Africa : they besieged the prophet and his most faithful followers, intercepted their water, and inflamed their mutual animosity by the retaliation of injuries and insults. A doubtful truce restored the appearances of concord till the death of Abu Taleb abandoned Mahomet to the power of his enemies, at the moment when he was deprived of his domestic comforts by the loss of his faithful and generous Cadijah. Abu Sophian, the chief of the branch of Ommiyah, succeeded to the principality of the republic of Mecca. A zealous votary of the idols, a mortal foe of the line of Hashem, he convened an assembly of the Koreishites and their allies, to decide the fate of the apostle. His imprisonment might provoke the despair of his enthusiasm ; and the exile of an eloquent and popular fanatic would diffuse the mischief through the provinces

of Arabia. His death was resolved ; and they agreed that a
sword from each tribe should be buried in his heart, to divide the
guilt of his blood, and baffle the vengeance of the Hashemites.
An angel or a spy revealed their conspiracy ; and flight was the
only resource of Mahomet.[117]   At the dead of night, accompanied
by his friend Abubeker, he silently escaped from his house : the
assassins watched at the door, but they were deceived by the figure of Ali, who reposed on the bed, and was covered with the
green vestment of the apostle. The Koreish respected the piety
of the heroic youth ; but some verses of Ali, which are still extant, exhibit an interesting picture of his anxiety, his tenderness,
and his religious confidence. Three days Mahomet and his companion were concealed in the cave of Thor, at the distance of a
league from Mecca ; and in the close of each evening, they received from the son and daughter of Abubeker a secret supply of
intelligence and food. The diligence of the Koreish explored
every haunt in the neighborhood of the city : they arrived at the
entrance of the cavern ; but the providential deceit of a spider's
web and a pigeon's nest is supposed to convince them that the
place was solitary and inviolate. " We are only two," said the
trembling Abubeker. " There is a third," replied the prophet ;
" it is God himself." No sooner was the pursuit abated than the
two fugitives issued from the rock, and mounted their camels : on
the road to Medina, they were overtaken by the emissaries of the
Koreish ; they redeemed themselves with prayers and promises
from their hands. In this eventful moment, the lance of an Arab
might have changed the history of the world. The flight of the
prophet from Mecca to Medina has fixed the memorable æra of the
Hegira,[118] which, at the end of twelve centuries, still discriminates
the lunar years of the Mahometan nations.[119]

The religion of the Koran might have perished in its cradle, had
not Medina embraced with faith and reverence the holy outcasts
of Mecca. Medina, or the *city*, known under the name of Yathreb, before it was sanctified by the throne of the prophet, was
divided between the tribes of the Charegites and the Awsites,
whose hereditary feud was rekindled by the slightest provocations : two colonies of Jews, who boasted a sacerdotal race, were
their humble allies, and without converting the Arabs, they introduced the taste of science and religion, which distinguished Medina as the city of the Book. Some of her noblest citizens, in a
pilgrimage to the Caaba, were converted by the preaching of Mahomet ; on their return, they diffused the belief of God and his
prophet, and the new alliance was ratified by their deputies in
two secret and nocturnal interviews on a hill in the suburbs of

Mecca. In the first, ten Charegites and two Awsites united in faith and love, protested, in the name of their wives, their children, and their absent brethren, that they would forever profess the creed, and observe the precepts, of the Koran. The second was a political association, the first vital spark of the empire of the Saracens.[120] Seventy-three men and two women of Medina held a solemn conference with Mahomet, his kinsman, and his disciples ; and pledged themselves to each other by a mutual oath of fidelity. They promised, in the name of the city, that if he should be banished, they would receive him as a confederate, obey him as a leader, and defend him to the last extremity, like their wives and children. "But if you are recalled by your country," they asked with a flattering anxiety, "will you not abandon your new allies ?" "All things," replied Mahomet with a smile, "are now common between us ; your blood is as my blood, your ruin as my ruin. We are bound to each other by the ties of honor and interest. I am your friend, and the enemy of your foes." "But if we are killed in your service, what," exclaimed the deputies of Medina, "will be our reward ?" "PARADISE," replied the prophet. "Stretch forth thy hand." He stretched it forth, and they reiterated the oath of allegiance and fidelity. Their treaty was ratified by the people, who unanimously embraced the profession of Islam ; they rejoiced in the exile of the apostle, but they trembled for his safety, and impatiently expected his arrival. After a perilous and rapid journey along the sea-coast, he halted at Koba, two miles from the city, and made his public entry into Medina, sixteen days after his flight from Mecca. Five hundred of the citizens advanced to meet him ; he was hailed with acclamations of loyalty and devotion ; Mahomet was mounted on a she-camel, an umbrella shaded his head, and a turban was unfurled before him to supply the deficiency of a standard. His bravest disciples, who had been scattered by the storm, assembled round his person ; and the equal, though various, merit of the Moslems was distinguished by the names of *Mohagerians* and *Ansars*, the fugitives of Mecca, and the auxiliaries of Medina. To eradicate the seeds of jealousy, Mahomet judiciously coupled his principal followers with the rights and obligations of brethren ; and when Ali found himself without a peer, the prophet tenderly declared, that *he* would be the companion and brother of the noble youth. The expedient was crowned with success ; the holy fraternity was respected in peace and war, and the two parties vied with each other in a generous emulation of courage and fidelity. Once only the concord was slightly ruffled by an accidental quarrel : a patriot of Medina arraigned the insolence of the strangers, but the hint of their expulsion was heard with abhorrence ; and his own son most eagerly offered to lay at the apostle's feet the head of his father.

From his establishment at Medina, Mahomet assumed the exercise of the regal and sacerdotal office ; and it was impious to appeal from a judge whose decrees were inspired by the divine wisdom. A small portion of ground, the patrimony of two orphans, was acquired by gift or purchase ; [121] on that chosen spot he built a house and a mosch, more venerable in their rude simplicity than the palaces and temples of the Assyrian caliphs. His seal of gold, or silver, was inscribed with the apostolic title ; when he prayed and preached in the weekly assembly, he leaned against the trunk of a palm-tree ; and it was long before he indulged himself in the use of a chair or pulpit of rough timber. [122] After a reign of six years, fifteen hundred Moslems, in arms and in the field, renewed their oath of allegiance ; and their chief repeated the assurance of protection till the death of the last member, or the final dissolution of the party. It was in the same camp that the deputy of Mecca was astonished by the attention of the faithful to the words and looks of the prophet, by the eagerness with which they collected his spittle, a hair that dropped on the ground, the refuse water of his lustrations, as if they participated in some degree of the prophetic virtue. " I have seen," said he, " the Chosroes of Persia and the Cæsar of Rome, but never did I behold a king among his subjects like Mahomet among his companions." The devout fervor of enthusiasm acts with more energy and truth than the cold and formal servility of courts.

In the state of nature, every man has a right to defend, by force of arms, his person and his possessions, to repel, or even to prevent, the violence of his enemies, and to extend his hostilities to a reasonable measure of satisfaction and retaliation. In the free society of the Arabs, the duties of subject and citizen imposed a feeble restraint ; and Mahomet, in the exercise of a peaceful and benevolent mission, had been despoiled and banished by the injustice of his countrymen. The choice of an independent people had exalted the fugitive of Mecca to the rank of a sovereign ; and he was invested with the just prerogative of forming alliances, and of waging offensive or defensive war. The imperfection of human rights was supplied and armed by the plenitude of divine power : the prophet of Medina assumed, in his new revelations, a fiercer and more sanguinary tone, which proves that his former moderation was the effect of weakness : [123] the means of persuasion had been tried, the season of forbearance was elapsed, and he was now commanded to propagate his religion by the sword, to destroy the monuments of idolatry, and, without regarding the sanctity of days or months, to pursue the unbelieving nations of the earth. The same bloody precepts, so repeatedly inculcated in the Koran, are ascribed by the author to the Pentateuch and the Gospel. But the mild tenor of the evangelic style may explain an ambiguous text, that Jesus did not bring peace on the earth, but a sword : his patient and humble virtues should not be confounded with the intolerant zeal of princes and bishops, who have disgraced the name of his disciples. In the prosecution of religious war, Mahomet might appeal with more propriety to the example of Moses, of the Judges, and the kings of Israel. The military laws of the Hebrews are still more rigid than those of the Arabian legislator. [124] The Lord of hosts marched in person before the Jews : if a city resisted their summons, the males, without distinction, were put to the sword : the seven nations of Canaan were devoted to destruction ; and neither repentance nor conversion could shield them from the inevitable doom, that no creature within their precincts should be left alive.* The fair option of friendship, or submission, or battle, was proposed to the enemies of Mahomet. If they professed the creed of Islam, they were admitted to all the temporal and spiritual benefits of his primitive disciples, and marched under the same banner to extend the religion which they had embraced. The clemency of the prophet was decided by his interest : yet he seldom trampled on a prostrate enemy ; and he seems to promise that, on the payment of a tribute, the least guilty of his unbelieving subjects might be indulged in their worship, or at least in their imperfect faith. In the first months of his reign he practised the lessons of holy warfare, and displayed his white banner before the gates of Medina : the martial apostle fought in person at nine battles or sieges ; [125] and fifty enterprises of war were achieved in ten years by himself or his lieutenants. The Arab continued to unite the professions of a merchant and a robber ; and his petty excursions for the defence or the attack of a caravan insensibly prepared his troops for the conquest of Arabia. The distribution of the spoil was regulated by a divine law : [126] the whole was faithfully collected in one common mass : a fifth of the gold and silver, the prisoners and cattle, the movables and immovables, was reserved by the prophet for pious and charitable uses ; the remainder was shared in adequate portions by the soldiers who had obtained the victory or guarded the camp : the rewards of the slain devolved to their

---

* The editor's opinions on this subject may be read in the History of the Jews, vol. i. p. 137.—M.

widows and orphans ; and the increase of cavalry was encouraged by the allotment of a double share to the horse and to the man. From all sides the roving Arabs were allured to the standard of religion and plunder : the apostle sanctified the license of embracing the female captives as their wives or concubines, and the enjoyment of wealth and beauty was a feeble type of the joys of paradise prepared for the valiant martyrs of the faith. "The sword," says Mahomet, "is the key of heaven and of hell ; a drop of blood shed in the cause of God, a night spent in arms, is of more avail than two months of fasting or prayer : whosoever falls in battle, his sins are forgiven : at the day of judgment his wounds shall be resplendent as vermilion, and odoriferous as musk ; and the loss of his limbs shall be supplied by the wings of angels and cherubim." The intrepid souls of the Arabs were fired with enthusiasm : the picture of the invisible world was strongly painted on their imagination ; and the death which they had always despised became an object of hope and desire. The Koran inculcates, in the most absolute sense, the tenets of fate and predestination, which would extinguish both industry and virtue, if the actions of man were governed by his speculative belief. Yet their influence in every age has exalted the courage of the Saracens and Turks. The first companions of Mahomet advanced to battle with a fearless confidence : there is no danger where there is no chance : they were ordained to perish in their beds ; or they were safe and invulnerable amidst the darts of the enemy.[127]

Perhaps the Koreish would have been content with the flight of Mahomet, had they not been provoked and alarmed by the vengeance of an enemy, who could intercept their Syrian trade as it passed and repassed through the territory of Medina. Abu Sophian himself, with only thirty or forty followers, conducted a wealthy caravan of a thousand camels ; the fortune or dexterity of his march escaped the vigilance of Mahomet ; but the chief of the Koreish was informed that the holy robbers were placed in ambush to await his return. He despatched a messenger to his brethren of Mecca, and they were roused, by the fear of losing their merchandise and their provisions, unless they hastened to his relief with the military force of the city. The sacred band of Mahomet was formed of three hundred and thirteen Moslems, of whom seventy-seven were fugitives, and the rest auxiliaries ; they mounted by turns a train of seventy camels (the camels of Yathreb were formidable in war); but such was the poverty of his first disciples that only two could appear on horseback in the field.[128] In the fertile and famous vale of Peder,[129] three stations from Medina, he was informed by his scouts of the caravan that approached on one side ; of the Koreish, one hundred horse, eight hundred and fifty foot, who advanced on the other. After a short debate, he sacrificed the prospect of wealth to the pursuit of glory and revenge ; and a slight intrenchment was formed, to cover his troops, and a stream of fresh water, that glided through the valley. "O God," he exclaimed, as the numbers of the Koreish descended from the hills, "O God, if these are destroyed, by whom wilt thou be worshipped on the earth ?—Courage, my children ; close your ranks ; discharge your arrows, and the day is your own." At these words he placed himself, with Abubeker, on a throne or pulpit,[130] and instantly demanded the succor of Gabriel and three thousand angels. His eye was fixed on the field of battle : the Mussulmans fainted and were pressed : in that decisive moment the prophet started from his throne, mounted his horse, and cast a handful of sand into the air : "Let their faces be covered with confusion." Both armies heard the thunder of his voice : their fancy beheld the angelic warriors :[131] the Koreish trembled and fled : seventy of the bravest were slain ; and seventy captives adorned the first victory of the faithful. The dead bodies of the Koreish were despoiled and insulted : two of the most obnoxious prisoners were punished with death ; and the ransom of the others, four thousand drams of silver compensated in some degree the escape of the caravan. But it was in vain that the camels of Abu Sophian explored a new road through the desert and along the Euphrates : they were overtaken by the diligence of the Mussulmans ; and wealthy must have been the prize, if twenty thousand drams could be set apart for the fifth of the apostle. The resentment of the public and private loss stimulated Abu Sophian to collect a body of three thousand men, seven hundred of whom were armed with cuirasses, and two hundred were mounted on horseback ; three thousand camels attended his march ; and his wife Henda, with fifteen matrons of Mecca, incessantly sounded their timbrels to animate the troops, and to magnify the greatness of Hobal, the most popular deity of the Caaba. The standard of God and Mahomet was upheld by nine hundred and fifty believers : the disproportion of numbers was not more alarming than in the field of Beder ; and their presumption of victory prevailed against the divine and human sense of the apostle. The second battle was fought on Mount Ohud, six miles to the north of Medina :[132] the Koreish advanced in the form of a crescent ; and the right wing of cavalry was led by Caled, the fiercest and most successful of the Arabian warriors. The troops of Mahomet were skilfully posted on the declivity of the hill ; and their rear was guarded by a detachment of fifty archers. The weight of their charge impelled and broke the centre of the idolaters : but in the pursuit they lost the advantage of their ground : the archers deserted their station : the Mussulmans were tempted by the spoil, disobeyed their general, and disordered their ranks. The intrepid Caled, wheeling his cavalry on their flank and rear, exclaimed, with a loud voice, that Mahomet was slain. He was indeed wounded in the face with a javelin : two of his teeth were shattered with a stone ; yet, in the midst of tumult and dismay, he reproached the infidels with the murder of a prophet ; and blessed the friendly hand that stanched his blood, and conveyed him to a place of safety. Seventy martyrs died for the sins of the people : they fell, said the apostle, in pairs, each brother embracing his lifeless companion ; [133] their bodies were mangled by the inhuman females of Mecca ; and the wife of Abu Sophian tasted the entrails of Hamza, the uncle of Mahomet. They might applaud their superstition, and satiate their fury ; but the Mussulmans soon rallied in the field, and the Koreish wanted strength or courage to undertake the siege of Medina. It was attacked the ensuing year by an army of ten thousand enemies ; and this third expedition is variously named from the *nations*, which marched under the banner of Abu Sophian, from the *ditch* which was drawn before the city, and a camp of three thousand Mussulmans. The prudence of Mahomet declined a general engagement : the valor of Ali was signalized in single combat ; and the war was protracted twenty days, till the final separation of the confederates. A tempest of wind, rain, and hail overturned their tents : their private quarrels were fomented by an insidious adversary ; and the Koreish, deserted by their allies, no longer hoped to subvert the throne, or to check the conquests, of their invincible exile. [134]

The choice of Jerusalem for the first kebla of prayer discovers the early propensity of Mahomet in favor of the Jews ; and happy would it have been for their temporal interest had they recognized, in the Arabian prophet, the hope of Israel and the promised Messiah. Their obstinacy converted his friendship into implacable hatred, with which he pursued that unfortunate people to the last moment of his life ; and, in the double character of an apostle and a conqueror, his persecution was extended to both worlds. [135] The Kainoka dwelt at Medina under the protection of the city ; he seized the occasion of an accidental tumult, and summoned them to embrace his religion, or contend with him in battle. "Alas !" replied the trembling Jews, "we are ignorant of the use of arms, but we persevere in the faith and worship of our fathers ; why wilt thou reduce us to the necessity of a just defence ?'' The unequal conflict was terminated in fifteen days ; and it was with extreme reluctance that Mahomet yielded to the importunity of his allies, and consented to spare the lives of the captives. But their riches were confiscated, their arms became more effectual in the hands of the Mussulmans ; and a wretched colony of seven hundred exiles was driven, with their wives and children, to implore a refuge on the confines of Syria. The Nad-hirites were more guilty, since they conspired, in a friendly inter-view, to assassinate the prophet. He besieged their castle, three miles from Medina ; but their resolute defence obtained an honor-able capitulation ; and the garrison, sounding their trumpets and beating their drums, was permitted to depart with the honors of war. The Jews had excited and joined the war of the Koreish : no sooner had the *nations* retired from the *ditch* than Mahomet, without laying aside his armor, marched on the same day to ex-tirpate the hostile race of the children of Koraidha. After a resistance of twenty-five days, they surrendered at discretion. They trusted to the intercession of their old allies of Medina ; they could not be ignorant that fanaticism obliterates the feelings of humanity. A venerable elder, to whose judgment they ap-pealed, pronounced the sentence of their death : seven hundred Jews were dragged in chains to the market-place of the city ; they descended alive into the grave prepared for their execution and burial ; and the apostle beheld with an inflexible eye the slaughter of his helpless enemies. Their sheep and camels were inherited by the Mussulmans : three hundred cuirasses, five hun-dred pikes, a thousand lances, composed the most useful portion of the spoil. Six days' journey to the north-east of Medina, the ancient and wealthy town of Chaibar, was the seat of the Jewish power in Arabia : the territory, a fertile spot in the desert, was covered with plantations and cattle, and protected by eight cas-tles, some of which were esteemed of impregnable strength. The forces of Mahomet consisted of two hundred horse and fourteen hundred foot : in the succession of eight regular and painful sieges they were exposed to danger and fatigue and hunger ; and the most undaunted chiefs despaired of the event. The apostle revived their faith and courage by the example of Ali, on whom he bestowed the surname of the Lion of God : perhaps we may believe that a Hebrew champion of gigantic stature was cloven to the chest by his irresistible cimeter ; but we cannot praise the modesty of romance, which represents him as tearing from its hinges the gate of a fortress and wielding the ponderous buckler in his left hand.[136] After the reduction of the castles, the town of Chaibar submitted to the yoke. The chief of the tribe was tortured, in the presence of Mahomet, to force a confession of his hidden treasure : the industry of the shepherds and husbandmen was rewarded with a precarious toleration ; they were permitted, so long as it should please the conqueror, to improve their patrimony, in equal shares, for *his* emolument and their own. Under the reign of Omar, the Jews of Chaibar were transplanted to Syria ; and the caliph alleged the injunction of his dying master, that one and the true religion should be professed in his native land of Arabia.[137]

Five times each day the eyes of Mahomet were turned towards Mecca,[138] and he was urged by the most sacred and powerful motives to revisit, as a conqueror, the city and the temple from whence he had been driven as an exile. The Caaba was present to his waking and sleeping fancy : an idle dream was translated into vision and prophecy ; he unfurled the holy banner ; and a rash promise of success too hastily dropped from the lips of the apostle. His march from Medina to Mecca displayed the peaceful and solemn pomp of a pilgrimage : seventy camels, chosen and bedecked for sacrifice, preceded the van ; the sacred territory was respected ; and the captives were dismissed without ransom to proclaim his clemency and devotion. But no sooner did Mahomet descend into the plain, within a day's journey of the city, than he exclaimed, "They have clothed themselves with the skins of tigers." The numbers and resolution of the Koreish opposed his progress ; and the roving Arabs of the desert might desert or betray a leader whom they had followed for the hopes of spoil. The intrepid fanatic sunk into a cool and cautious politician : he waived in the treaty his title of apostle of God ; concluded with the Koreish and their allies a truce of ten years ; engaged to restore the fugitives of Mecca who should embrace his religion ; and stipulated only, for the ensuing year, the humble privilege of entering the city as a friend, and of remaining three days to accomplish the rites of the pilgrimage. A cloud of shame and sorrow hung on the retreat of the Mussulmans, and their disappointment might justly accuse the failure of a prophet who had so often appealed to the evidence of success. The faith and hope of the pilgrims were rekindled by the prospect of Mecca : their swords were sheathed ; * seven times in the footsteps of the apostle they encompassed the Caaba : the Koreish had retired to the hills, and Mahomet, after the customary sacrifice, evacuated the

---

* This peaceful entrance into Mecca took place, according to the treaty, the following year. Weil, p. 202.—M. 1845.

city on the fourth day. The people was edified by his devotion ;
the hostile chiefs were awed, or divided, or seduced ; and both
Kaled and Amrou, the future conquerors of Syria and Egypt,
most seasonably deserted the sinking cause of idolatry. The
power of Mahomet was increased by the submission of the Arabian tribes ; ten thousand soldiers were assembled for the conquest of Mecca ; and the idolaters, the weaker party, were easily
convicted of violating the truce. Enthusiasm and discipline impelled the march, and preserved the secret till the blaze of ten
thousand fires proclaimed to the astonished Koreish the design,
the approach, and the irresistible force of the enemy. The
haughty Abu Sophian presented the keys of the city, admired the
variety of arms and ensigns that passed before him in review ; observed that the son of Abdallah had acquired a mighty kingdom,
and confessed, under the cimeter of Omar, that he was the apostle of the true God. The return of Marius and Scylla was stained
with the blood of the Romans : the revenge of Mahomet was stimulated by religious zeal, and his injured followers were eager to
execute or to prevent the order of a massacre. Instead of indulging their passions and his own,[139] the victorious exile forgave the
guilt, and united the factions of Mecca. His troops, in three
divisions, marched into the city : eight-and-twenty of the inhabitants were slain by the sword of Caled ; eleven men and six
women were proscribed by the sentence of Mahomet ; but he
blamed the cruelty of his lieutenant ; and several of the most obnoxious victims were indebted for their lives to his clemency or
contempt. The chiefs of the Koreish were prostrate at his feet.
"What mercy can you expect from the man whom you have
wronged ?" "We confide in the generosity of our kinsman." "And
you shall not confide in vain : begone ! you are safe, you are free."
The people of Mecca deserved their pardon by the profession of
Islam ; and after an exile of seven years, the fugitive missionary
was enthroned as the prince and prophet of his native country.[140]
But the three hundred and sixty idols of the Caaba were ignominiously broken : the house of God was purified and adorned : as an
example to future times, the apostle again fulfilled the duties of a
pilgrim ; and a perpetual law was enacted that no unbeliever
should dare to set his foot on the territory of the holy city.[141]

The conquest of Mecca determined the faith and obedience of
the Arabian tribes ;[142] who, according to the vicissitudes of fortune, had obeyed, or disregarded, the eloquence or the arms of
the prophet. Indifference for rites and opinions still marks the
character of the Bedoweens ; and they might accept, as loosely as
they hold, the doctrine of the Koran. Yet an obstinate remnant

still adhered to the religion and liberty of their ancestors, and the war of Honain derived a proper appellation from the *idols* whom Mahomet had vowed to destroy, and whom the confederates of Tayef had sworn to defend.[143] Four thousand Pagans advanced with secrecy and speed to surprise the conqueror : they pitied and despised the supine negligence of the Koreish, but they depended on the wishes, and perhaps the aid, of a people who had so lately renounced their gods, and bowed beneath the yoke of their enemy. The banners of Medina and Mecca were displayed by the prophet ; a crowd of Bedoweens increased the strength or numbers of the army, and twelve thousand Mussulmans entertained a rash and sinful presumption of their invincible strength. They descended without precaution into the valley of Honain : the heights had been occupied by the archers and slingers of the confederates ; their numbers were oppressed, their discipline was confounded, their courage was appalled, and the Koreish smiled at their impending destruction. The prophet, on his white mule, was encompassed by the enemies : he attempted to rush against their spears in search of a glorious death : ten of his faithful companions interposed their weapons and their breasts ; three of these fell dead at his feet : " O my brethren," he repeatedly cried, with sorrow and indignation, " I am the son of Abdallah, I am the apostle of truth ! O man, stand fast in the faith ! O God, send down thy succor !" His uncle Abbas, who, like the heroes of Homer, excelled in the loudness of his voice, made the valley resound with the recital of the gifts and promises of God : the flying Moslems returned from all sides to the holy standard ; and Mahomet observed with pleasure that the furnace was again rekindled : his conduct and example restored the battle, and he animated his victorious troops to inflict a merciless revenge on the authors of their shame. From the field of Honain, he marched without delay to the siege of Tayef, sixty miles to the south-east of Mecca, a fortress of strength, whose fertile lands produce the fruits of Syria in the midst of the Arabian desert. A friendly tribe, instructed (I know not how) in the art of sieges, supplied him with a train of battering-rams and military engines, with a body of five hundred artificers. But it was in vain that he offered freedom to the slaves of Tayef ; that he violated his own laws by the extirpation of the fruit-trees ; that the ground was opened by the miners ; that the breach was assaulted by the troops. After a siege of twenty days, the prophet sounded a retreat ; but he retreated with a song of devout triumph, and affected to pray for the repentance and safety of the unbelieving city. The spoil of this fortunate expedition amounted to six thousand captives, twenty-four thousand camels, forty thousand sheep, and four thousand ounces of silver : a tribe who had fought at Honain redeemed their prisoners by the sacrifice of their idols ; but Mahomet compensated the loss, by resigning to the soldiers his fifth of the plunder, and wished, for their sake, that he possessed as many head of cattle as there were trees in the province of Tehama. Instead of chastising the disaffection of the Koreish, he endeavored to cut out their tongues (his own expression), and to secure their attachment by a superior measure of liberality : Abu Sophian alone was presented with three hundred camels and twenty ounces of silver ; and Mecca was sincerely converted to the profitable religion of the Koran.

The *fugitives* and *auxiliaries* complained that they who had borne the burden were neglected in the season of victory. " Alas !" replied their artful leader, " suffer me to conciliate these recent enemies, these doubtful proselytes, by the gift of some perishable goods. To your guard I intrust my life and fortunes. You are the companions of my exile, of my kingdom, of my paradise." He was followed by the deputies of Tayef, who dreaded the repetition of a siege. " Grant us, O apostle of God ! a truce of three years, with the toleration of our ancient worship." " Not a month, not an hour." " Excuse us at least from the obligation of prayer." " Without prayer religion is of no avail." They submitted in silence : their temples were demolished, and the same sentence of destruction was executed on all the idols of Arabia. His lieutenants, on the shores of the Red Sea, the Ocean, and the Gulf of Persia, were saluted by the acclamations of a faithful people ; and the ambassadors, who knelt before the throne of Medina, were as numerous (says the Arabian proverb) as the dates that fall from the maturity of a palm-tree. The nation submitted to the God and the sceptre of Mahomet : the opprobrious name of tribute was abolished : the spontaneous or reluctant oblations of arms and tithes were applied to the service of religion ; and one hundred and fourteen thousand Moslems accompanied the last pilgrimage of the apostle.[144]

When Heraclius returned in triumph from the Persian war, he entertained, at Emesa, one of the ambassadors of Mahomet, who invited the princes and nations of the earth to the profession of Islam. On this foundation the zeal of the Arabians has supposed the secret conversion of the Christian emperor : the vanity of the Greeks has feigned a personal visit of the prince of Medina, who accepted from the royal bounty a rich domain, and a secure retreat, in the province of Syria.[145] But the friendship of Heraclius and Mahomet was of short continuance : the new religion had inflamed rather than assuaged the rapacious spirit of the Saracens; and the murder of an envoy afforded a decent pretence for invading, with three thousand soldiers, the territory of Palestine, that extends to the eastward of the Jordan. The holy banner was intrusted to Zeid; and such was the discipline or enthusiasm of the rising sect that the noblest chiefs served without reluctance under the slave of the prophet. On the event of his decease, Jaafar and Abdallah were successively substituted to the command; and if the three should perish in the war, the troops were authorized to elect their general. The three leaders were slain in the battle of Muta,[146] the first military action, which tried the valor of the Moslems against a foreign enemy. Zeid fell, like a soldier, in the foremost ranks: the death of Jaafar was heroic and memorable: he lost his right hand: he shifted the standard to his left: the left was severed from his body: he embraced the standard with his bleeding stumps, till he was transfixed to the ground with fifty honorable wounds.* "Advance," cried Abdallah, who stepped into the vacant place, "advance with confidence: either victory or paradise is our own." The lance of a Roman decided the alternative; but the falling standard was rescued by Caled, the proselyte of Mecca: nine swords were broken in his hand; and his valor withstood and repulsed the superior numbers of the Christians. In the nocturnal council of the camp he was chosen to command: his skilful evolutions of the ensuing day secured either the victory or the retreat of the Saracens; and Caled is renowned among his brethren and his enemies by the glorious appellation of the *Sword of God*. In the pulpit Mahomet described, with prophetic rapture, the crowns of the blessed martyrs; but in private he betrayed the feelings of human nature: he was surprised as he wept over the daughter of Zeid: "What do I see?" said the astonished votary. "You see," replied the apostle, "a friend who is deploring the loss of his most faithful friend." After the conquest of Mecca, the sovereign of Arabia affected to prevent the hostile preparations of Heraclius; and solemnly proclaimed war against the Romans, without attempting to disguise the hardships and dangers of the enterprise.[147] The Moslems were discouraged: they alleged the want of money, or horses, or provisions; the season of harvest, and the intolerable

---

* To console the afflicted relatives of his kinsman Jauffer, he (Mahomet) represented that, in Paradise, in exchange for the arms which he had lost, he had been furnished with a pair of wings, resplendent with the blushing glories of the ruby, and with which he was become the inseparable companion of the archangel Gabriel, in his volitations through the regions of eternal bliss. Hence, in the catalogue of the martyrs, he has been denominated Jauffer teyaur, the winged Jauffer. Price, Chronological Retrospect of Mohammedan History, vol. i. p. 5.—M.

heat of the summer : "Hell is much hotter," said the indignant prophet. He disdained to compel their service : but on his return he admonished the most guilty, by an excommunication of fifty days. Their desertion enhanced the merit of Abubeker, Othman, and the faithful companions who devoted their lives and fortunes ; and Mahomet displayed his banner at the head of ten thousand horse and twenty thousand foot. Painful indeed was the distress of the march : lassitude and thirst were aggravated by the scorching and pestilential winds of the desert : ten men rode by turns on the same camel ; and they were reduced to the shameful necessity of drinking the water from the belly of that useful animal. In the mid-way, ten days' journey from Medina and Damascus, they reposed near the grove and fountain of Tabuc. Beyond that place Mahomet declined the prosecution of the war : he declared himself satisfied with the peaceful intentions, he was more probably daunted by the martial array, of the emperor of the East. But the active and intrepid Caled spread around the terror of his name ; and the prophet received the submission of the tribes and cities, from the Euphrates to Ailah, at the head of the Red Sea. To his Christian subjects, Mahomet readily granted the security of their persons, the freedom of their trade, the property of their goods, and the toleration of their worship.[148] The weakness of their Arabian brethren had restrained them from opposing his ambition ; the disciples of Jesus were endeared to the enemy of the Jews ; and it was the interest of a conqueror to propose a fair capitulation to the most powerful religion of the earth.

Till the age of sixty-three years the strength of Mahomet was equal to the temporal and spiritual fatigues of his mission. His epileptic fits, an absurd calumny of the Greeks, would be an object of pity rather than abhorrence ;[149] but he seriously believed that he was poisoned at Chaibar by the revenge of a Jewish female.[150] During four years the health of the prophet declined ; his infirmities increased ; but his mortal disease was a fever of fourteen days, which deprived him by intervals of the use of reason. As soon as he was conscious of his danger he edified his brethren by the humility of his virtue or penitence. "If there be any man," said the apostle from the pulpit, "whom I have unjustly scourged, I submit my own back to the lash of retaliation. Have I aspersed the reputation of a Mussulman ? let him proclaim *my* thoughts in the face of the congregation. Has any one been despoiled of his goods ? the little that I possess shall compensate the principal and the interest of the debt." "Yes," replied a voice from the crowd, "I am entitled to three drams of silver."

Mahomet heard the complaint, satisfied the demand, and thanked his creditor for accusing him in this world rather than at the day of judgment. He beheld with temperate firmness the approach of death: enfranchised his slaves (seventeen men, as they are named, and eleven women); minutely directed the order of his funeral, and moderated the lamentations of his weeping friends, on whom he bestowed the benediction of peace. Till the third day before his death, he regularly performed the function of public prayer: the choice of Abubeker to supply his place appeared to mark that ancient and faithful friend as his successor in the sacerdotal and regal office; but he prudently declined the risk and envy of a more explicit nomination. At a moment when his faculties were visibly impaired, he called for pen and ink to write, or, more properly, to dictate, a divine book, the sum and accomplishment of all his revelations: a dispute arose in the chamber, whether he should be allowed to supersede the authority of the Koran; and the prophet was forced to reprove the indecent vehemence of his disciples. If the slightest credit may be afforded to the traditions of his wives and companions, he maintained, in the bosom of his family, and to the last moments of his life, the dignity * of an apostle, and the faith of an enthusiast; described the visits of Gabriel, who bade an everlasting farewell to the earth, and expressed his lively confidence, not only of the mercy, but of the favor, of the Supreme Being. In a familiar discourse he had mentioned his special prerogative, that the angel of death was not allowed to take his soul till he had respectfully asked the permission of the prophet. The request was granted; and Mahomet immediately fell into the agony of his dissolution: his head was reclined on the lap of Ayesha, the best beloved of all his wives; he fainted with the violence of pain; recovering his spirits, he raised his eyes towards the roof of the house, and, with a steady look, though a faltering voice, uttered the last broken, though articulate, words: "O God! . . . . pardon my sins. . . . Yes, . . . I come, . . . among my fellow-citizens on

* Major Price, who writes with the authority of one widely conversant with the original sources of Eastern knowledge, and in a very candid tone, takes a very different view of the prophet's death. "In tracing the circumstances of Mahommed's illness, we look in vain for any proofs of that meek and heroic firmness which might be expected to dignify and embellish the last moments of the apostle of God. On some occasions he betrayed such want of fortitude, such marks of childish impatience, as are in general to be found in men only of the most ordinary stamp; and such as extorted from his wife Ayesha, in particular, the sarcastic remark that in herself, or any of her family, a similar demeanor would long since have incurred his severe displeasure. . . . He said that the acuteness and violence of his sufferings were necessarily in the proportion of those honors with which it had ever pleased the hand of Omnipotence to distinguish its peculiar favorites." Price, vol. i. p. 13.—M.

high ;'' and thus peaceably expired on a carpet spread upon the floor. An expedition for the conquest of Syria was stopped by this mournful event : the army halted at the gates of Medina ; the chiefs were assembled round their dying master. The city, more especially the house, of the prophet, was a scene of clamorous sorrow or silent despair : fanaticism alone could suggest a ray of hope and consolation. " How can he be dead, our witness, our intercessor, our mediator, with God ? By God he is not dead : like Moses and Jesus, he is wrapped in a holy trance, and speedily will he return to his faithful people.'' The evidence of sense was disregarded ; and Omar, unsheathing his cimeter, threatened to strike off the heads of the infidels who should dare to affirm that the prophet was no more. The tumult was appeased by the weight and moderation of Abubeker. " Is it Mahomet,'' said he to Omar and the multitude, " or the God of Mahomet, whom you worship ? The God of Mahomet liveth forever ; but the apostle was a mortal like ourselves, and, according to his own prediction, he has experienced the common fate of mortality.'' He was piously interred by the hands of his nearest kinsman, on the same spot on which he expired :[151] Medina has been sanctified by the death and burial of Mahomet ; and the innumerable pilgrims of Mecca often turn aside from the way, to bow, in voluntary devotion,[152] before the simple tomb of the prophet.[153]

At the conclusion of the life of Mahomet, it may perhaps be expected that I should balance his faults and virtues ; that I should decide whether the title of enthusiast or impostor more properly belongs to that extraordinary man. Had I been intimately conversant with the son of Abdallah, the task would still be difficult, and the success uncertain : at the distance of twelve centuries, I darkly contemplate his shade through a cloud of religious incense ; and could I truly delineate the portrait of an hour, the fleeting resemblance would not equally apply to the solitary of Mount Hera, to the preacher of Mecca, and to the conqueror of Arabia. The author of a mighty revolution appears to have been endowed with a pious and contemplative disposition : so soon as marriage had raised him above the pressure of want, he avoided the paths of ambition and avarice ; and till the age of forty he lived with innocence, and would have died without a name. The unity of God is an idea most congenial to nature and reason ; and a slight conversation with the Jews and Christians would teach him to despise and detest the idolatry of Mecca. It was the duty of a man and a citizen to impart the doctrine of salvation, to rescue his country from the dominion of sin and error. The energy of a mind incessantly bent on the same object would convert a general obligation into a particular call ; the warm suggestions of the understanding or the fancy would be felt as the inspirations of Heaven ; the labor of thought would expire in rapture and vision ; and the inward sensation, the invisible monitor, would be described with the form and attributes of an angel of God.[154]   From enthusiasm to imposture, the step is perilous and slippery : the dæmon of Socrates [155] affords a memorable instance, how a wise man may deceive himself, how a good man may deceive others, how the conscience may slumber in a mixed and middle state between self-illusion and voluntary fraud.   Charity may believe that the original motives of Mahomet were those of pure and genuine benevolence ; but a human missionary is incapable of cherishing the obstinate unbelievers who reject his claims, despise his arguments, and persecute his life ; he might forgive his personal adversaries, he may lawfully hate the enemies of God ; the stern passions of pride and revenge were kindled in the bosom of Mahomet, and he sighed, like the prophet of Nineveh, for the destruction of the rebels whom he had condemned.   The injustice of Mecca and the choice of Medina transformed the citizen into a prince, the humble preacher into the leader of armies ; but his sword was consecrated by the example of the saints ; and the same God who afflicts a sinful world with pestilence and earthquakes, might inspire for their conversion or chastisement the valor of his servants.   In the exercise of political government, he was compelled to abate of the stern rigor of fanaticism, to comply in some measure with the prejudices and passions of his followers, and to employ even the vices of mankind as the instruments of their salvation.   The use of fraud and perfidy, of cruelty and injustice, were often subservient to the propagation of the faith ; and Mahomet commanded or approved the assassination of the Jews and idolaters who had escaped from the field of battle. By the repetition of such acts, the character of Mahomet must have been gradually stained ; and the influence of such pernicious habits would be poorly compensated by the practise of the personal and social virtues which are necessary to maintain the reputation of a prophet among his sectaries and friends.   Of his last years, ambition was the ruling passion ; and a politician will suspect that he secretly smiled (the victorious impostor !) at the enthusiasm of his youth, and the credulity of his proselytes.[156]   A philosopher will observe that *their* credulity and *his* success would tend more strongly to fortify the assurance of his divine mission, that his interest and religion were inseparably connected, and that his conscience would be soothed by the persuasion, that he alone was absolved by the Deity from the obligation of positive ard moral laws. If he retained any vestige of his native innocence, the sins of Mahomet may be allowed as an evidence of his sincerity. In the support of truth, the arts of fraud and fiction may be deemed less criminal; and he would have started at the foulness of the means had he not been satisfied of the importance and justice of the end. Even in a conqueror or a priest, I can surprise a word or action of unaffected humanity; and the decree of Mahomet, that, in the sale of captives, the mothers should never be separated from their children, may suspend, or moderate, the censure of the historian.[157]

The good sense of Mahomet [158] despised the pomp of royalty: the apostle of God submitted to the menial offices of the family: he kindled the fire, swept the floor, milked the ewes, and mended with his own hands his shoes and his woollen garment. Disdaining the penance and merit of a hermit, he observed, without effort or vanity, the abstemious diet of an Arab and a soldier. On solemn occasions he feasted his companions with rustic and hospitable plenty; but in his domestic life many weeks would elapse without a fire being kindled on the hearth of the prophet. The interdiction of wine was confirmed by his example; his hunger was appeased with a sparing allowance of barley-bread: he delighted in the taste of milk and honey; but his ordinary food consisted of dates and water. Perfumes and women were the two sensual enjoyments which his nature required, and his religion did not forbid; and Mahomet affirmed that the fervor of his devotion was increased by these innocent pleasures. The heat of the climate inflames the blood of the Arabs; and their libidinous complexion has been noticed by the writers of antiquity.[159] Their incontinence was regulated by the civil and religious laws of the Koran: their incestuous alliances were blamed; the boundless license of polygamy was reduced to four legitimate wives or concubines; their rights both of bed and of dowry were equitably determined; the freedom of divorce was discouraged, adultery was condemned as a capital offence; and fornication, in either sex, was punished with a hundred stripes.[160] Such were the calm and rational precepts of the legislator: but in his private conduct, Mahomet indulged the appetites of a man, and abused the claims of a prophet. A special revelation dispensed him from the laws which he had imposed on his nation: the female sex, without reserve, was abandoned to his desires; and this singular prerogative excited the envy, rather than the scandal, the veneration, rather than the envy, of the devout Mussulmans. If we remember the seven hundred wives and three hundred concubines of the wise Solomon, we shall applaud the modesty of the Arabian, who espoused no more than seventeen or fifteen wives; eleven are enumerated who occupied at Medina their separate apartments round the house of the apostle, and enjoyed in their turns the favor of his conjugal society. What is singular enough, they were all widows, excepting only Ayesha, the daughter of Abubeker. *She* was doubtless a virgin, since Mahomet consummated his nuptials (such is the premature ripeness of the climate) when she was only nine years of age. The youth, the beauty, the spirit of Ayesha, gave her a superior ascendant: she was beloved and trusted by the prophet; and, after his death, the daughter of Abubeker was long revered as the mother of the faithful. Her behavior had been ambiguous and indiscreet: in a nocturnal march she was accidentally left behind; and in the morning Ayesha returned to the camp with a man. The temper of Mahomet was inclined to jealousy; but a divine revelation assured him of her innocence: he chastised her accusers, and published a law of domestic peace, that no woman should be condemned unless four male witnesses had seen her in the act of adultery.[161] In his adventures with Zeineb, the wife of Zeid, and with Mary, an Egyptian captive, the amorous prophet forgot the interest of his reputation. At the house of Zeid, his freedman and adopted son, he beheld, in a loose undress, the beauty of Zeineb, and burst forth into an ejaculation of devotion and desire. The servile, or grateful, freedman understood the hint, and yielded without hesitation to the love of his benefactor. But as the filial relation had excited some doubt and scandal, the angel Gabriel descended from heaven to ratify the deed, to annul the adoption, and gently to reprove the apostle for distrusting the indulgence of his God. One of his wives, Hafna, the daughter of Omar, surprised him on her own bed, in the embraces of his Egyptian captive: she promised secrecy and forgiveness; he swore that he would renounce the possession of Mary. Both parties forgot their engagements; and Gabriel again descended with a chapter of the Koran, to absolve him from his oath, and to exhort him freely to enjoy his captives and concubines, without listening to the clamors of his wives. In a solitary retreat of thirty days, he labored, alone with Mary, to fulfil the commands of the angel. When his love and revenge were satiated, he summoned to his presence his eleven wives, reproached their disobedience and indiscretion, and threatened them with a sentence of divorce, both in this world and in the next; a dreadful sentence, since those who had ascended the bed of the prophet were forever excluded from the hope of a second marriage. Perhaps the incontinence of Mahomet may be palliated by the tradition of his natural or preternatural gifts;[162] he united the manly virtue of thirty of the children of Adam : and the apostle might rival the thirteenth labor [163] of the Grecian Hercules. [164] A more serious and decent excuse may be drawn from his fidelity to Cadijah. During the twenty-four years of their marriage her youthful husband abstained from the right of polygamy, and the pride or tenderness of the venerable matron was never insulted by the society of a rival. After her death, he placed her in the rank of the four perfect women, with the sister of Moses, the mother of Jesus, and Fatima, the best beloved of his daughters. "Was she not old ?" said Ayesha, with the insolence of a blooming beauty ; "has not God given you a better in her place ?" "No, by God," said Mahomet, with an effusion of honest gratitude, "there never can be a better ! She believed in me when men despised me ; she relieved my wants when I was poor and persecuted by the world." [165]

In the largest indulgence of polygamy, the founder of a religion and empire might aspire to multiply the chances of a numerous posterity and a lineal succession. The hopes of Mahomet were fatally disappointed. The virgin Ayesha, and his ten widows of mature age and approved fertility, were barren in his potent embraces. The four sons of Cadijah died in their infancy. Mary, his Egyptian concubine, was endeared to him by the birth of Ibrahim. At the end of fifteen months the prophet wept over his grave ; but he sustained with firmness the raillery of his enemies, and checked the adulation or credulity of the Moslems, by the assurance that an eclipse of the sun was *not* occasioned by the death of the infant. Cadijah had likewise given him four daughters, who were married to the most faithful of his disciples : the three eldest died before their father ; but Fatima, who possessed his confidence and love, became the wife of her cousin Ali, and the mother of an illustrious progeny. The merit and misfortunes of Ali and his descendants will lead me to anticipate, in this place, the series of the Saracen caliphs, a title which describes the commanders of the faithful as the vicars and successors of the apostle of God. [166]

The birth, the alliance, the character of Ali, which exalted him above the rest of his countrymen, might justify his claim to the vacant throne of Arabia. The son of Abu Taleb was, in his own right, the chief of the family of Hashem, and the hereditary prince or guardian of the city and temple of Mecca. The light of prophecy was extinct ; but the husband of Fatima might expect the inheritance and blessing of her father : the Arabs had sometimes been patient of a female reign ; and the two grandsons of the prophet had often been fondled in his lap, and shown in his pulpit, as the hope of his age, and the chief of the youth of paradise. The first of the true believers might aspire to march before them in this world and in the next ; and if some were of a graver and more rigid cast, the zeal and virtue of Ali were never outstripped by any recent proselyte. He united the qualifications of a poet, a soldier, and a saint : his wisdom still breathes in a collection of moral and religious sayings ; [167] and every antagonist, in the combats of the tongue or of the sword, was subdued by his eloquence and valor. From the first hour of his mission to the last rites of his funeral the apostle was never forsaken by a generous friend, whom he delighted to name his brother, his vicegerent, and the faithful Aaron of a second Moses. The son of Abu Taleb was afterwards reproached for neglecting to secure his interest by a solemn declaration of his right, which would have silenced all competition, and sealed his succession by the decrees of Heaven. But the unsuspecting hero confided in himself : the jealousy of empire, and perhaps the fear of opposition, might suspend the resolutions of Mahomet ; and the bed of sickness was besieged by the artful Ayesha, the daughter of Abubeker, and the enemy of Ali.*

The silence and death of the prophet restored the liberty of the people ; and his companions convened an assembly to deliberate on the choice of his successor. The hereditary claim and lofty spirit of Ali were offensive to an aristocracy of elders, desirous of bestowing and resuming the sceptre by a free and frequent election : the Koreish could never be reconciled to the proud pre-eminence of the line of Hashem ; the ancient discord of the tribes was rekindled, the *fugitives* of Mecca and the *auxiliaries* of Medina asserted their respective merits ; and the rash proposal of choosing two independent caliphs would have crushed in their infancy the religion and empire of the Saracens. The tumult was appeased

---

* Gibbon wrote chiefly from the Arabic or Sunnite account of these transactions, the only sources accessible at the time when he composed his History. Major Price, writing from Persian authorities, affords us the advantage of comparing throughout what may be fairly considered the Shiite Version. The glory of Ali is the constant burden of their strain. He was destined, and, according to some accounts, designated, for the caliphate by the prophet ; but while the others were fiercely pushing their own interests, Ali was watching the remains of Mahomet with pious fidelity. His disinterested magnanimity, on each separate occasion, declined the sceptre, and gave the noble example of obedience to the appointed caliph. He is described, in retirement, on the throne, and in the field of battle, as transcendently pious, magnanimous, valiant, and humane. He lost his empire through his excess of virtue and love for the faithful ; his life through his confidence in God, and submission to the decrees of fate.

Compare the curious account of this apathy in Price, chap. ii. It is to be regretted, I must add, that Major Price has contented himself with quoting the names of the Persian works which he follows, without any account of their character, age, and authority.—M.

by the disinterested resolution of Omar, who, suddenly renouncing his own pretensions, stretched forth his hand, and declared himself the first subject of the mild and venerable Abubeker.* The urgency of the moment, and the acquiescence of the people, might excuse this illegal and precipitate measure ; but Omar himself confessed from the pulpit that if any Mussulman should hereafter presume to anticipate the suffrage of his brethren, both the elector and the elected would be worthy of death.[168] After the simple inauguration of Abubeker, he was obeyed in Medina, Mecca, and the provinces of Arabia : the Hashemites alone declined the oath of fidelity ; and their chief, in his own house, maintained, above six months, a sullen and independent reserve, without listening to the threats of Omar, who attempted to consume with fire the habitation of the daughter of the apostle. The death of Fatima, and the decline of his party, subdued the indignant spirit of Ali : he condescended to salute the commander of the faithful, accepted his excuse of the necessity of preventing their common enemies, and wisely rejected his courteous offer of abdicating the government of the Arabians. After a reign of two years, the aged caliph was summoned by the angel of death. In his testament, with the tacit approbation of his companions, he bequeathed the sceptre to the firm and intrepid virtue of Omar. "I have no occasion," said the modest candidate, "for the place." "But the place has occasion for you," replied Abubeker, who expired with a fervent prayer, that the God of Mahomet would ratify his choice, and direct the Mussulmans in the way of concord and obedience. The prayer was not ineffectual, since Ali himself, in a life of privacy and prayer, professed to revere the superior worth and dignity of his rival, who comforted him for the loss of empire by the most flattering marks of confidence and esteem. In the twelfth year of his reign Omar received a mortal wound from the hand of an assassin : he rejected with equal impartiality the names of his son and of Ali, refused to load his conscience with the sins of his successor, and devolved on six of the most respectable companions the arduous task of electing a commander of the faithful. On this occasion Ali was again blamed by his friends[169] for submitting his right to the judgment of men, for recognizing their jurisdiction by accepting a place among the six electors. He might have obtained their suffrage had he deigned to promise a strict and servile conformity, not only to the Koran and tradition, but likewise to the determinations of two *seniors*.[170] With these limitations, Othman, the secretary of Mahomet, accepted the govern-

---

* Abubeker, the father of the virgin Ayesha. St. Martin, vol. xi. p. 188.—M.

ment ; nor was it till after the third caliph, twenty-four years after
the death of the prophet, that Ali was invested, by the popular
choice, with the regal and sacerdotal office.   The manners of the
Arabians retained their primitive simplicity, and the son of Abu
Taleb despised the pomp and vanity of this world.   At the hour
of prayer he repaired to the mosch of Medina clothed in a thin
cotton gown, a coarse turban on his head, his slippers in one hand,
and his bow in the other, instead of a walking-staff.   The companions of the prophet, and the chiefs of the tribes, saluted their
new sovereign, and gave him their right hands as a sign of fealty
and allegiance.

The mischiefs that flow from the contests of ambition are
usually confined to the times and countries in which they have
been agitated.   But the religious discord of the friends and
enemies of Ali has been renewed in every age of the Hegira, and
is still maintained in the immortal hatred of the Persians and
Turks.[171] The former, who are branded with the appellation of
Shiites or sectaries, have enriched the Mahometan creed with a
new article of faith ; and if Mahomet be the apostle, his companion
Ali is the vicar, of God.   In their private converse, in their public
worship, they bitterly execrate the three usurpers who intercepted
his indefeasible right to the dignity of Imam and Caliph ; and the
name of Omar expresses in their tongue the perfect accomplishment of wickedness and impiety.[172]   The *Sonnites,* who are
supported by the general consent and orthodox tradition of the
Mussulmans, entertain a more impartial, or at least a more decent,
opinion.   They respect the memory of Abubeker, Omar, Othman,
and Ali, the holy and legitimate successors of the prophet.   But
they assign the last and most humble place to the husband of Fatima, in the persuasion that the order of succession was determined
by the degrees of sanctity.[173]   An historian who balances the four
caliphs with a hand unshaken by superstition, will calmly pronounce that their manners were alike pure and exemplary ; that
their zeal was fervent, and probably sincere ; and that, in the
midst of riches and power, their lives were devoted to the practise
of moral and religious duties.   But the public virtues of Abubeker
and Omar, the prudence of the first, the severity of the second,
maintained the peace and prosperity of their reigns.   The feeble
temper and declining age of Othman were incapable of sustaining
the weight of conquest and empire.   He chose, and he was deceived ; he trusted, and he was betrayed : the most deserving of
the faithful became useless or hostile to his government, and his
lavish bounty was productive only of ingratitude and discontent.
The spirit of discord went forth in the provinces : their deputies

assembled at Medina ; and the Charegites, the desperate fanatics who disclaimed the yoke of subordination and reason, were confounded among the free-born Arabs, who demanded the redress of their wrongs and the punishment of their oppressors. From Cufa, from Bassora, from Egypt, from the tribes of the desert, they rose in arms, encamped about a league from Medina, and despatched a haughty mandate to their sovereign, requiring him to execute justice, or to descend from the throne. His repentance began to disarm and disperse the insurgents ; but their fury was rekindled by the arts of his enemies ; and the forgery of a perfidious secretary was contrived to blast his reputation and precipitate his fall. The caliph had lost the only guard of his predecessors, the esteem and confidence of the Moslems : during a siege of six weeks his water and provisions were intercepted, and the feeble gates of the palace were protected only by the scruples of the more timorous rebels. Forsaken by those who had abused his simplicity, the hopeless and venerable caliph expected the approach of death : the brother of Ayesha marched at the head of the assassins ; and Othman, with the Koran in his lap, was pierced with a multitude of wounds.* A tumultuous anarchy of five days was appeased by the inauguration of Ali : his refusal would have provoked a general massacre. In this painful situation he supported the becoming pride of the chief of the Hashemites ; declared that he had rather serve than reign ; rebuked the presumption of the strangers ; and required the formal, if not the voluntary, assent of the chiefs of the nation. He has never been accused of prompting the assassin of Omar ; though Persia indiscreetly celebrates the festival of that holy martyr. The quarrel between Othman and his subjects was assuaged by the early mediation of Ali ; and Hassan, the eldest of his sons, was insulted and wounded in the defence of the caliph. Yet it is doubtful whether the father of Hassan was strenuous and sincere in his opposition to the rebels ; and it is certain that he enjoyed the benefit of their crime. The temptation was indeed of such magnitude as might stagger and corrupt the most obdurate virtue. The ambitious candidate no longer aspired to the barren sceptre of Arabia ; the Saracens had been victorious in the East and West ; and the wealthy kingdoms of Persia, Syria, and Egypt were the patrimony of the commander of the faithful.

A life of prayer and contemplation had not chilled the martial activity of Ali ; but in a mature age, after a long experience of mankind, he still betrayed in his conduct the rashness and indis-

---

* Compare Price, p. 180.—M.

cretion of youth.* In the first days of his reign, he neglected to
secure, either by gifts or fetters, the doubtful allegiance of Telha
and Zobeir, two of the most powerful of the Arabian chiefs. They
escaped from Medina to Mecca, and from thence to Bassora;
erected the standard of revolt; and usurped the government of
Irak, or Assyria, which they had vainly solicited as the reward of
their services. The mask of patriotism is allowed to cover the
most glaring inconsistencies; and the enemies, perhaps the
assassins, of Othman now demanded vengeance for his blood.
They were accompanied in their flight by Ayesha, the widow of the
prophet, who cherished, to the last hour of her life, an implacable hatred against the husband and the posterity of Fatima. The
most reasonable Moslems were scandalized, that the mother of the
faithful should expose in a camp her person and character;† but
the superstitious crowd was confident that her presence would
sanctify the justice, and assure the success, of their cause. At
the head of twenty thousand of his loyal Arabs and nine thousand
valiant auxiliaries of Cufa, the caliph encountered and defeated
the superior numbers of the rebels under the walls of Bassora.‡
Their leaders, Telha and Zobeir,§ were slain in the first battle
that stained with civil blood the arms of the Moslems.‖ After
passing through the ranks to animate the troops, Ayesha had
chosen her post amidst the dangers of the field. In the heat of
the action, seventy men, who held the bridle of her camel, were
successively killed or wounded; and the cage or litter, in which
she sat, was stuck with javelins and darts like the quills of a
porcupine. The venerable captive sustained with firmness the
reproaches of the conqueror, and was speedily dismissed to her
proper station at the tomb of Mahomet, with the respect and tenderness that was still due to the widow of the apostle.¶ After
this victory, which was styled the Day of the Camel, Ali marched

---

* Ali had determined to supersede all the lieutenants in the different provinces.
Price, p. 191. Compare, on the conduct of Telha and Zobeir, p. 193.—M.
† See the very curious circumstances which took place before and during her
flight. Price, p. 196.—M.
‡ The reluctance of Ali to shed the blood of true believers is strikingly described
by Major Price's Persian historians. Price, p. 222.—M.
§ See (in Price) the singular adventures of Zobeir. He was murdered after having abandoned the army of the insurgents. Telha was about to do the same, when
his leg was pierced with an arrow by one of his own party. The wound was mortal. Price, p. 222.—M.
‖ According to Price, two hundred and eighty of the Benni Beiangiai alone lost a
right hand in this service (p. 225).—M.
¶ She was escorted by a guard of females disguised as soldiers. When she discovered this, Ayesha was as much gratified by the delicacy of the arrangement, as
she had been offended by the familiar approach of so many men. Price, p. 229.
—M.

against a more formidable adversary ; against Moawiyah, the son of Abu Sophian, who had assumed the title of caliph, and whose claim was supported by the forces of Syria and the interest of the house of Ommiyah. From the passage of Thapsacus, the plain of Siffin [174] extends along the western bank of the Euphrates. On this spacious and level theatre, the two competitors waged a desultory war of one hundred and ten days. In the course of ninety actions or skirmishes, the loss of Ali was estimated at twenty-five, that of Moawiyah at forty-five, thousand soldiers ; and the list of the slain was dignified with the names of five-and-twenty veterans who had fought at Beder under the standard of Mahomet. In this sanguinary contest the lawful caliph displayed a superior character of valor and humanity.* His troops were strictly enjoined to await the first onset of the enemy, to spare their flying brethren, and to respect the bodies of the dead, and the chastity of the female captives. He generously proposed to save the blood of the Moslems by a single combat ; but his trembling rival declined the challenge as a sentence of inevitable death. The ranks of the Syrians were broken by the charge of a hero who was mounted on a piebald horse, and wielded with irresistible force his ponderous and two-edged sword. As often as he smote a rebel, he shouted the Allah Acbar, "God is victorious !" and in the tumult of a nocturnal battle, he was heard to repeat four hundred times that tremendous exclamation. The prince of Damascus already meditated his flight ; but the certain victory was snatched from the grasp of Ali by the disobedience and enthusiasm of his troops. Their conscience was awed by the solemn appeal to the books of the Koran which Moawiyah exposed on the foremost lances ; and Ali was compelled to yield to a disgraceful truce and an insidious compromise. He retreated with sorrow and indignation to Cufa ; his party was discouraged ; the distant provinces of Persia, of Yemen, and of Egypt, were subdued or seduced by his crafty rival ; and the stroke of fanaticism, which was aimed against the three chiefs of the nation, was fatal only to

---

* The Shiite authors have preserved a noble instance of Ali's magnanimity. The superior generalship of Moawiyah had cut off the army of Ali from the Euphrates ; his soldiers were perishing from want of water. Ali sent a message to his rival to request free access to the river, declaring that under the same circumstances he would not allow any of the faithful, though his adversaries, to perish from thirst. After some debate, Moawiyah determined to avail himself of the advantage of his situation, and to reject the demand of Ali. The soldiers of Ali became desperate ; forced their way through that part of the hostile army which commanded the river ; and in their turn entirely cut off the troops of Moawiyah from the water. Moawiyah was reduced to make the same supplication to Ali. The generous caliph instantly complied ; and both armies, with their cattle, enjoyed free and unmolested access to the river. Price, vol. i. p. 268, 272.—M.

the cousin of Mahomet. In the temple of Mecca, three Charegites or enthusiasts discoursed of the disorders of the church and state: they soon agreed that the deaths of Ali, of Moawiyah, and of his friend Amrou, the viceroy of Egypt, would restore the peace and unity of religion. Each of the assassins chose his victim, poisoned his dagger, devoted his life, and secretly repaired to the scene of action. Their resolution was equally desperate: but the first mistook the person of Amrou, and stabbed the deputy who occupied his seat; the prince of Damascus was dangerously hurt by the second; the lawful caliph, in the mosch of Cufa, received a mortal wound from the hand of the third. He expired in the sixty-third year of his age, and mercifully recommended to his children, that they would despatch the murderer by a single stroke.* The sepulchre of Ali [175] was concealed from the tyrants of the house of Ommiyah; [176] but in the fourth age of the Hegira, a tomb, a temple, a city, arose near the ruins of Cufa. [177] Many thousands of the Shiites repose in holy ground at the feet of the vicar of God; and the desert is vivified by the numerous and annual visits of the Persians, who esteem their devotion not less meritorious than the pilgrimage of Mecca.

The persecutors of Mahomet usurped the inheritance of his children; and the champions of idolatry became the supreme heads of his religion and empire. The opposition of Abu Sophian had been fierce and obstinate; his conversion was tardy and reluctant; his new faith was fortified by necessity and interest; he served, he fought, perhaps he believed; and the sins of the time of ignorance were expiated by the recent merits of the family of Ommiyah. Moawiyah, the son of Abu Sophian, and of the cruel Henda, was dignified, in his early youth, with the office or title of secretary of the prophet: the judgment of Omar intrusted him with the government of Syria; and he administered that important province above forty years, either in a subordinate or supreme rank. Without renouncing the fame of valor and liberality, he affected the reputation of humanity and moderation: a grateful people was attached to their benefactor; and the victorious Moslems were enriched with the spoils of Cyprus and Rhodes. The sacred duty of pursuing the assassins of Othman was the engine and pretence of his ambition. The bloody shirt of the martyr was exposed in the mosch of Damascus: the emir deplored the fate of his injured kinsman; and sixty thousand Syrians were engaged in his service by an oath of fidelity and revenge. Amrou,

* His son Hassan was recognized as caliph in Arabia and Irak; but voluntarily abdicated the throne, after six or seven months, in favor of Moawiyah. St. Martin, vol. xi. p. 375.—M.

the conqueror of Egypt, himself an army, was the first who saluted the new monarch, and divulged the dangerous secret, that the Arabian caliphs might be created elsewhere than in the city of the prophet.[178] The policy of Moawiyah eluded the valor of his rival ; and, after the death of Ali, he negotiated the abdication of his son Hassan, whose mind was either above or below the government of the world, and who retired without a sigh from the palace of Cufa to an humble cell near the tomb of his grandfather. The aspiring wishes of the caliph were finally crowned by the important change of an elective to an hereditary kingdom. Some murmurs of freedom or fanaticism attested the reluctance of the Arabs, and four citizens of Medina refused the oath of fidelity ; but the designs of Moawiyah were conducted with vigor and address ; and his son Yezid, a feeble and dissolute youth, was proclaimed as the commander of the faithful and the successor of the apostle of God.

A familiar story is related of the benevolence of one of the sons of Ali. In serving at table, a slave had inadvertently dropped a dish of scalding broth on his master : the heedless wretch fell prostrate, to deprecate his punishment, and repeated a verse of the Koran : " Paradise is for those who command their anger :"—" I am not angry :"—" and for those who pardon offences :"—" I pardon your offence :"—" and for those who return good for evil :"—" I give you your liberty, and four hundred pieces of silver." With an equal measure of piety, Hosein, the younger brother of Hassan, inherited a remnant of his father's spirit, and served with honor against the Christians in the siege of Constantinople. The primogeniture of the line of Hashem, and the holy character of grandson of the apostle, had centred in his person, and he was at liberty to prosecute his claim against Yezid, the tyrant of Damascus, whose vices he despised, and whose title he had never deigned to acknowledge. A list was secretly transmitted from Cufa to Medina, of one hundred and forty thousand Moslems, who professed their attachment to his cause, and who were eager to draw their swords so soon as he should appear on the banks of the Euphrates. Against the advice of his wisest friends, he resolved to trust his person and family in the hands of a perfidious people. He traversed the desert of Arabia with a timorous retinue of women and children ; but as he approached the confines of Irak he was alarmed by the solitary or hostile face of the country, and suspected either the defection or ruin of his party. His fears were just : Obeidollah, the governor of Cufa, had extinguished the first sparks of an insurrection ; and Hosein, in the plain of Kerbela, was encompassed by a body of five thousand horse, who intercepted his communication with the city and the river. He might still have escaped to a fortress in the desert, that had defied the power of Cæsar and Chosroes, and confided in the fidelity of the tribe of Tai, which would have armed ten thousand warriors in his defence. In a conference with the chief of the enemy, he proposed the option of three honorable conditions : that he should be allowed to return to Medina, or be stationed in a frontier garrison against the Turks, or safely conducted to the presence of Yezid. But the commands of the caliph, or his lieutenant, were stern and absolute ; and Hosein was informed that he must either submit as a captive and a criminal to the commander of the faithful, or expect the consequences of his rebellion. " Do you think," replied he, " to terrify me with death ?" And, during the short respite of a night,* he prepared with calm and solemn resignation to encounter his fate. He checked the lamentations of his sister Fatima, who deplored the impending ruin of his house. " Our trust," said Hosein, " is in God alone. All things, both in heaven and earth, must perish and return to their Creator. My brother, my father, my mother, were better than me, and every Mussulman has an example in the prophet." He pressed his friends to consult their safety by a timely flight : they unanimously refused to desert or survive their beloved master ; and their courage was fortified by a fervent prayer and the assurance of paradise. On the morning of the fatal day he mounted on horseback, with his sword in one hand and the Koran in the other : his generous band of martyrs consisted only of thirty-two horse and forty foot ; but their flanks and rear were secured by the tent-ropes, and by a deep trench which they had filled with lighted fagots, according to the practice of the Arabs. The enemy advanced with reluctance, and one of their chiefs deserted, with thirty followers, to claim the partnership of inevitable death. In every close onset or single combat, the despair of the Fatimites was invincible ; but the surrounding multitudes galled them from a distance with a cloud of arrows, and the horses and men were successively slain : a truce was allowed on both sides for the hour of prayer ; and the battle at length expired by the death of the last companions of Hosein. Alone, weary, and wounded, he seated himself at the door of his tent. As he tasted a drop of water, he was pierced in the mouth with a dart ; and his son and nephew, two beautiful youths, were killed in his arms.

---

* According to Major Price's authorities, a much longer time elapsed (p. 400, etc.)—M.

He lifted his hands to heaven ; they were full of blood ; and he uttered a funeral prayer for the living and the dead. In a transport of despair, his sister issued from the tent, and adjured the general of the Cufians, that he would not suffer Hosein to be murdered before his eyes : a tear trickled down his venerable beard ; and the boldest of his soldiers fell back on every side as the dying hero threw himself among them. The remorseless Shamer, a name detested by the faithful, reproached their cowardice ; and the grandson of Mahomet was slain with three-and-thirty strokes of lances and swords. After they had trampled on his body, they carried his head to the castle of Cufa, and the inhuman Obeidollah struck him on the mouth with a cane : " Alas !" exclaimed an aged Mussulman, " on these lips have I seen the lips of the apostle of God !" In a distant age and climate, the tragic scene of the death of Hosein will awaken the sympathy of the coldest reader.[179] * On the annual festival of his martyrdom, in the devout pilgrimage to his sepulchre, his Persian votaries abandon their souls to the religious frenzy of sorrow and indignation.[180]

When the sisters and children of Ali were brought in chains to the throne of Damascus, the caliph was advised to extirpate the enmity of a popular and hostile race, whom he had injured beyond the hope of reconciliation. But Yezid preferred the counsels of mercy ; and the mourning family was honorably dismissed to mingle their tears with their kindred at Medina. The glory of martyrdom superseded the right of primogeniture ; and the twelve IMAMS, [181] or pontiffs, of the Persian creed, are Ali, Hassan, Hosein, and the lineal descendants of Hosein to the ninth generation. Without arms, or treasures, or subjects, they successively

---

* The account of Hosein's death, in the Persian Tarikh Tebry, is much longer ; in some circumstances, more pathetic than that of Ockley, followed by Gibbon. His family, after his defenders were all slain, perished in succession before his eyes. They had been cut off from the water, and suffered all the agonies of thirst. His eldest son, Ally Akbar, after ten different assaults on the enemy, in each of which he slew two or three, complained bitterly of his sufferings from heat and thirst. "His father arose, and introducing his own tongue within the parched lips of his favorite child, thus endeavored to alleviate his sufferings by the only means of which his enemies had not yet been able to deprive him." Ally was slain and cut to pieces in his sight : this wrung from him his first and only cry ; then it was that his sister Zeyneb rushed from the tent. The rest, including his nephew, fell in succession. Hosein's horse was wounded—he fell to the ground. The hour of prayer, between noon and sunset, had arrived ; the Imaum began the religious duties :—as Hosein prayed he heard the cries of his infant child Abdallah, only twelve months old. The child was, at his desire, placed on his bosom : as he wept over it, it was transfixed by an arrow. Hosein dragged himself to the Euphrates : as he slaked his burning thirst, his mouth was pierced by an arrow : he drank his own blood. Wounded in four-and-thirty places, he still gallantly resisted. A soldier named Zeraiah gave the fatal wound : his head was cut off by Zilrousheng. Price, p. 402, 410.— M.

enjoyed the veneration of the people, and provoked the jealousy
of the reigning caliphs : their tombs at Mecca or Medina, on the
banks of the Euphrates, or in the province of Chorosan, are still
visited by the devotees of their sect.   Their names were often the
pretence of sedition and civil war ; but these royal saints despised
the pomp of the world : submitted to the will of God and the injustice of man ; and devoted their innocent lives to the study and
practice of religion.   The twelfth and last of the Imams, conspicuous by the title of *Mahadi*, or the Guide, surpassed the solitude and sanctity of his predecessors.   He concealed himself in
a cavern near Bagdad : the time and place of his death are unknown ; and his votaries pretend that he still lives, and will appear before the day of judgment to overthrow the tyranny of De-
jal, or the Antichrist.[182]   In the lapse of two or three centuries,
the posterity of Abbas, the uncle of Mahomet, had multiplied to
the number of thirty-three thousand :[183] the race of Ali might be
equally prolific : the meanest individual was above the first and
greatest of princes ; and the most eminent were supposed to
excel the perfection of angels.   But their adverse fortune, and
the wide extent of the Mussulman empire, allowed an ample scope
for every bold and artful impostor, who claimed affinity with the
holy seed : the sceptre of the Almohades, in Spain and Africa ; of
the Fatimites, in Egypt and Syria ;[184] of the Sultans of Yemen ;
and of the Sophis of Persia ;[185] has been consecrated by this vague
and ambiguous title.   Under their reigns it might be dangerous
to dispute the legitimacy of their birth ; and one of the Fatimite
caliphs silenced an indiscreet question by drawing his cimeter :
" This," said Moez, " is my pedigree ; and these," casting a
handful of gold to his soldiers—" and these are my kindred and
my children."   In the various conditions of princes, or doctors,
or nobles, or merchants, or beggars, a swarm of the genuine or
fictitious descendants of Mahomet and Ali is honored with the
appellation of sheiks, or sherifs, or emirs.   In the Ottoman empire, they are distinguished by a green turban ; receive a stipend
from the treasury ; are judged only by their chief ; and, however
debased by fortune or character, still assert the proud pre-eminence
of their birth.   A family of three hundred persons, the pure and
orthodox branch of the caliph Hassan, is preserved without taint
or suspicion in the holy cities of Mecca and Medina, and still retains, after the revolutions of twelve centuries, the custody of the
temple and the sovereignty of their native land.   The fame and
merit of Mahomet would ennoble a plebeian race, and the ancient
blood of the Koreish transcends the recent majesty of the kings
of the earth.[186]

The talents of Mahomet are entitled to our applause ; but his success has, perhaps, too strongly attracted our admiration. Are we surprised that a multitude of proselytes should embrace the doctrine and the passions of an eloquent fanatic ? In the heresies of the church, the same seduction has been tried and repeated from the time of the apostles to that of the reformers. Does it seem incredible that a private citizen should grasp the sword and the sceptre, subdue his native country, and erect a monarchy by his victorious arms ? In the moving picture of the dynasties of the East, a hundred fortunate usurpers have arisen from a baser origin, surmounted more formidable obstacles, and filled a larger scope of empire and conquest. Mahomet was alike instructed to preach and to fight ; and the union of these opposite qualities, while it enhanced his merit, contributed to his success : the operation of force and persuasion, of enthusiasm and fear, continually acted on each other, till every barrier yielded to their irresistible power. His voice invited the Arabs to freedom and victory, to arms and rapine, to the indulgence of their darling passions in this world and the other : the restraints which he imposed were requisite to establish the credit of the prophet, and to exercise the obedience of the people ; and the only objection to his success was his rational creed of the unity and perfections of God. It is not the propagation, but the permanency of his religion, that deserves our wonder : the same pure and perfect impression which he engraved at Mecca and Medina, is preserved, after the revolutions of twelve centuries, by the Indian, the African, and the Turkish proselytes of the Koran. If the Christian apostles, St. Peter or St. Paul, could return to the Vatican, they might possibly inquire the name of the Deity who is worshipped with such mysterious rites in that magnificent temple : at Oxford or Geneva they would experience less surprise ; but it might still be incumbent on them to peruse the catechism of the church, and to study the orthodox commentators on their own writings and the words of their Master. But the Turkish dome of St. Sophia, with an increase of splendor and size, represents the humble tabernacle erected at Medina by the hands of Mahomet. The Mahometans have uniformly withstood the temptation of reducing the object of their faith and devotion to a level with the senses and imagination of man. " I believe in one God, and Mahomet the apostle of God," is the simple and invariable profession of Islam. The intellectual image of the Deity has never been degraded by any visible idol ; the honors of the prophet have never transgressed the measure of human virtue ; and his living precepts have restrained the gratitude of his disciples within the bounds of

reason and religion. The votaries of Ali have, indeed, consecrated
the memory of their hero, his wife, and his children ; and some
of the Persian doctors pretend that the divine essence was incarnate in the person of the Imams ; but their superstition is universally condemned by the Sonnites ; and their impiety has afforded
a seasonable warning against the worship of saints and martyrs.
The metaphysical questions on the attributes of God, and the liberty of man, have been agitated in the schools of the Mahometans,
as well as in those of the Christians ; but among the former they
have never engaged the passions of the people, or disturbed the
tranquillity of the state. The cause of this important difference
may be found in the separation of union of the regal and sacerdotal characters. It was the interest of the caliphs, the successors
of the prophet and commanders of the faithful, to repress and dis-
courage all religious innovations : the order, the discipline, the
temporal and spiritual ambition of the clergy, are unknown to the
Moslems ; and the sages of the law are the guides of their conscience and the oracles of their faith. From the Atlantic to the
Ganges, the Koran is acknowledged as the fundamental code, not
only of theology, but of civil and criminal jurisprudence ; and
the laws which regulate the actions and the property of mankind
are guarded by the infallible and immutable sanction of the will of
God. This religious servitude is attended with some practical
disadvantage ; the illiterate legislator had been often misled by
his own prejudices and those of his country ; and the institutions
of the Arabian desert may be ill adapted to the wealth and numbers of Ispahan and Constantinople. On these occasions the
Cadhi respectfully places on his head the holy volume, and substitutes a dexterous interpretation more apposite to the principles
of equity, and the manners and policy of the times.

His beneficial or pernicious influence on the public happiness is
the last consideration in the character of Mahomet. The most
bitter or most bigoted of his Christian or Jewish foes will surely
allow that he assumed a false commission to inculcate a salutary
doctrine, less perfect only than their own. He piously supposed,
as the basis of his religion, the truth and sanctity of *their* prior
revelations, the virtues and miracles of their founders. The idols
of Arabia were broken before the throne of God ; the blood of
human victims was expiated by prayer, and fasting, and alms, the
laudable or innocent arts of devotion ; and his rewards and punishments of a future life were painted by the images most congenial
to an ignorant and carnal generation. Mahomet was, perhaps,
incapable of dictating a moral and political system for the use of
his countrymen : but he breathed among the faithful a spirit of

charity and friendship ; recommended the practice of the social virtues ; and checked, by his laws and precepts, the thirst of revenge, and the oppression of widows and orphans. The hostile tribes were united in faith and obedience, and the valor, which had been idly spent in domestic quarrels, was vigorously directed against a foreign enemy. Had the impulse been less powerful, Arabia, free at home and formidable abroad, might have flourished under a succession of her native monarchs. Her sovereignty was lost by the extent and rapidity of conquest. The colonies of the nation were scattered over the East and West, and their blood was mingled with the blood of their converts and captives. After the reign of three caliphs, the throne was transported from Medina to the valley of Damascus and the banks of the Tigris ; the holy cities were violated by impious war ; Arabia was ruled by the rod of a subject, perhaps of a stranger ; and the Bedoweens of the desert, awakening from their dream of dominion, resumed their old and solitary independence.[187]

CHAPTER LI.

THE CONQUEST OF PERSIA, SYRIA, EGYPT, AFRICA, AND SPAIN, BY THE ARABS OR SARACENS.—EMPIRE OF THE CALIPHS OR SUCCESSORS OF MAHOMET.—STATE OF THE CHRISTIANS, ETC., UNDER THEIR GOVERNMENT.

THE revolution of Arabia had not changed the character of the Arabs : the death of Mahomet was the signal of independence ; and the hasty structure of his power and religion tottered to its foundations. A small and faithful band of his primitive disciples had listened to his eloquence and shared his distress ; had fled with the apostle from the persecution of Mecca, or had received the fugitive in the walls of Medina. The increasing myriads, who acknowledged Mahomet as their king and prophet, had been compelled by his arms or allured by his prosperity. The polytheists were confounded by the simple idea of a solitary and invisible God ; the pride of the Christians and Jews disdained the yoke of a mortal and contemporary legislator. Their habits of faith and obedience were not sufficiently confirmed ; and many of the new converts regretted the venerable antiquity of the law of Moses ; or the rites and mysteries of the Catholic church ; or the idols, the sacrifices, the joyous festivals, of their Pagan ancestors. The jarring interests and hereditary feuds of the Arabian tribes had not yet coalesced in a system of union and subordination; and the barbarians were impatient of the mildest and most salutary laws that curbed their passions, or violated their customs. They submitted with reluctance to the religious precepts of the Koran, the abstinence from wine, the fast of the Ramadan, and the daily repetition of five prayers; and the arms and tithes, which were collected for the treasury of Medina, could be distinguished only by a name from the payment of a perpetual and ignominious tribute. The example of Mahomet had excited a spirit of fanaticism or imposture, and several of his rivals presumed to imitate the conduct, and defy the authority, of the living prophet. At the head of the *fugitives* and *auxiliaries*, the first caliph was reduced to the cities of Mecca, Medina, and Tayef; and perhaps the Koreish would have restored the idols of the Caaba, if their levity had not been checked by a seasonable reproof. "Ye men of Mecca, will ye be the last to embrace, and the first to abandon, the religion of Islam?" After exhorting the Moslems to confide in the aid of God and his apostle, Abubeker resolved, by a vigorous attack, to prevent the junction of the rebels. The women and children were safely lodged in the cavities of the mountains: the warriors, marching under eleven banners, diffused the terror of their arms; and the appearance of a military force revived and confirmed the loyalty of the faithful. The inconstant tribes accepted, with humble repentance, the duties of prayer, and fasting, and alms; and, after some examples of success and severity, the most daring apostates fell prostrate before the sword of the Lord and of Caled. In the fertile province of Yemanah,[1] between the Red Sea and the Gulf of Persia, in a city not inferior to Medina itself, a powerful chief (his name was Moseilama) had assumed the character of a prophet, and the tribe of Hanifa listened to his voice. A female prophetess * was attracted by his reputation; the decencies of words and actions were spurned by these favorites of Heaven;[2] and they employed several days in mystic and amorous converse. An obscure sentence of his Koran, or book, is yet extant;[3] and in the pride of his mission, Moseilama condescended to offer a partition of the earth. The proposal

---

* This extraordinary woman was a Christian; she was at the head of a numerous and flourishing sect; Moseilama professed to recognize her inspiration. In a personal interview he proposed their marriage and the union of their sects. The handsome person, the impassioned eloquence, and the arts of Moseilama, triumphed over the virtue of the prophetess, who was rejected with scorn by her lover, and by her notorious unchastity lost her influence with her own followers. Gibbon, with that propensity too common, especially in his later volumes, has selected only the grosser part of this singular adventure.—M.

was answered by Mahomet with contempt; but the rapid progress of the impostor awakened the fears of his successor: forty thousand Moslems were assembled under the standard of Caled; and the existence of their faith was resigned to the event of a decisive battle.* In the first action they were repulsed with the loss of twelve hundred men; but the skill and perseverance of their general prevailed: their defeat was avenged by the slaughter of ten thousand infidels; and Moseilama himself was pierced by an Æthiopian slave with the same javelin which had mortally wounded the uncle of Mahomet. The various rebels of Arabia, without a chief or a cause, were speedily suppressed by the power and discipline of the rising monarchy; and the whole nation again professed, and more steadfastly held, the religion of the Koran. The ambition of the caliphs provided an immediate exercise for the restless spirit of the Saracens: their valor was united in the prosecution of a holy war; and their enthusiasm was equally confirmed by opposition and victory.

From the rapid conquests of the Saracens a presumption will naturally arise, that the caliphs † commanded in person the armies of the faithful, and sought the crown of martyrdom in the foremost ranks of the battle. The courage of Abubeker,[4] Omar,[5] and Othman,[6] had indeed been tried in the persecution and wars of the prophet; and the personal assurance of paradise must have taught them to despise the pleasures and dangers of the present world. But they ascended the throne in a venerable or mature age; and esteemed the domestic cares of religion and justice the most important duties of a sovereign. Except the presence of Omar at the siege of Jerusalem, their longest expeditions were the frequent pilgrimage from Medina to Mecca; and they calmly received the tidings of victory as they prayed or preached before the sepulchre of the prophet. The austere and frugal measure of their lives was the effect of virtue or habit, and the pride of their simplicity insulted the vain magnificence of the kings of the earth. When Abubeker assumed the office of caliph, he enjoined his daughter Ayesha to take a strict account of his private patrimony, that it might be evident whether he were enriched or impoverished by the service of the state. He thought himself entitled to a stipend of three pieces of gold, with the sufficient maintenance of a single camel and a black slave; but on the Friday of each week he distributed the residue of his own and the public money, first to the most worthy, and then to the most indigent,

---

* Compare a long account of this battle in Price, p. 42.—M.

† In Arabic, "successors." V. Hammer, Geschichte der Assas. p. 16.—M.

of the Moslems. The remains of his wealth, a coarse garment, and five pieces of gold, were delivered to his successor, who lamented with a modest sigh his own inability to equal such an admirable model. Yet the abstinence and humility of Omar were not inferior to the virtues of Abubeker : his food consisted of barley bread or dates ; his drink was water ; he preached in a gown that was torn or tattered in twelve places ; and a Persian satrap, who paid his homage to the conqueror, found him asleep among the beggars on the steps of the mosch of Medina. Economy is the source of liberality, and the increase of the revenue enabled Omar to establish a just and perpetual reward for the past and present services of the faithful. Careless of his own emolument, he assigned to Abbas, the uncle of the prophet, the first and most ample allowance of twenty-five thousand drachms or pieces of silver. Five thousand were allotted to each of the aged warriors, the relics of the field of Beder ; and the last and meanest of the companions of Mahomet was distinguished by the annual reward of three thousand pieces. One thousand was the stipend of the veterans who had fought in the first battles against the Greeks and Persians ; and the decreasing pay, as low as fifty pieces of silver, was adapted to the respective merit and seniority of the soldiers of Omar. Under his reign, and that of his predecessor, the conquerors of the East were the trusty servants of God and the people ; the mass of the public treasure was consecrated to the expenses of peace and war ; a prudent mixture of justice and bounty maintained the discipline of the Saracens, and they united, by a rare felicity, the despatch and execution of despotism with the equal and frugal maxims of a republican government. The heroic courage of Ali,[7] the consummate prudence of Moawiyah,[8] excited the emulation of their subjects ; and the talents which had been exercised in the school of civil discord were more usefully applied to propagate the faith and dominion of the prophet. In the sloth and vanity of the palace of Damascus, the succeeding princes of the house of Ommiyah were alike destitute of the qualifications of statesmen and of saints.[9] Yet the spoils of unknown nations were continually laid at the foot of their throne, and the uniform ascent of the Arabian greatness must be ascribed to the spirit of the nation rather than the abilities of their chiefs. A large deduction must be allowed for the weakness of their enemies. The birth of Mahomet was fortunately placed in the most degenerate and disorderly period of the Persians, the Romans, and the barbarians of Europe : the empires of Trajan or even of Constantine or Charlemagne, would have repelled the assault of the naked Saracens, and the torrent of fanaticism might have been obscurely lost in the sands of Arabia.

In the victorious days of the Roman republic, it had been the aim of the senate to confine their councils and legions to a single war, and completely to suppress a first enemy before they provoked the hostilities of a second. These timid maxims of policy were disdained by the magnanimity or enthusiasm of the Arabian caliphs. With the same vigor and success they invaded the successors of Augustus and those of Artaxerxes; and the rival monarchies at the same instant became the prey of an enemy whom they had been so long accustomed to despise. In the ten years of the administration of Omar, the Saracens reduced to his obedience thirty-six thousand cities or castles, destroyed four thousand churches or temples of the unbelievers, and edified fourteen hundred moschs for the exercise of the religion of Mahomet. One hundred years after his flight from Mecca, the arms and the reign of his successors extended from India to the Atlantic Ocean, over the various and distant provinces, which may be comprised under the names of, I. Persia; II. Syria; III. Egypt; IV. Africa; and V. Spain. Under this general division, I shall proceed to unfold these memorable transactions; despatching with brevity the remote and less interesting conquests of the East, and reserving a fuller narrative for those domestic countries which had been included within the pale of the Roman empire. Yet I must excuse my own defects by a just complaint of the blindness and insufficiency of my guides. The Greeks, so loquacious in controversy, have not been anxious to celebrate the triumphs of their enemies.[10] After a century of ignorance, the first annals of the Mussulmans were collected in a great measure from the voice of tradition.[11] Among the numerous productions of Arabic and Persian literature,[12] our interpreters have selected the imperfect sketches of a more recent age.[13] The art and genius of history have ever been unknown to the Asiatics;[14] they are ignorant of the laws of criticism; and our monkish chronicles of the same period may be compared to their most popular works, which are never vivified by the spirit of philosophy and freedom. The *Oriental library* of a Frenchman[15] would instruct the most learned mufti of the East; and perhaps the Arabs might not find in a single historian so clear and comprehensive a narrative of their own exploits as that which will be deduced in the ensuing sheets.

I. In the first year of the first caliph, his lieutenant Caled, the Sword of God, and the scourge of the infidels, advanced to the banks of the Euphrates, and reduced the cities of Anbar and Hira. Westward of the ruins of Babylon, a tribe of sedentary Arabs had

fixed themselves on the verge of the desert ; and Hira was the
seat of a race of kings who had embraced the Christian religion,
and reigned above six hundred years under the shadow of the
throne of Persia.[16] The last of the Mondars * was defeated and
slain by Caled ; his son was sent a captive to Medina ; his nobles
bowed before the successor of the prophet ; the people was
tempted by the example and success of their countrymen ; and
the caliph accepted as the first-fruits of foreign conquest an annual
tribute of seventy thousand pieces of gold. The conquerors, and
even their historians, were astonished by the dawn of their future
greatness : "In the same year," says Elmacin, "Caled fought
many signal battles : an immense multitude of the infidels was
slaughtered ; and spoils infinite and innumerable were acquired
by the victorious Moslems."[17] But the invincible Caled was soon
transferred to the Syrian war : the invasion of the Persian frontier
was conducted by less active or less prudent commanders : the
Saracens were repulsed with loss in the passage of the Euphrates ;
and, though they chastised the insolent pursuit of the Magians,
their remaining forces still hovered in the desert of Babylon.†

The indignation and fears of the Persians suspended for a moment their intestine divisions. By the unanimous sentence of the
priests and nobles, their queen Arzema was deposed ; the sixth of
the transient usurpers, who had arisen and vanished in three or
four years since the death of Chosroes, and the retreat of Heraclius. Her tiara was placed on the head of Yezdegerd, the grandson of Chosroes ; and the same æra, which coincides with an
astronomical period,[18] has recorded the fall of the Sassanian dynasty and the religion of Zoroaster.[19] The youth and inexperience of the prince (he was only fifteen years of age) declined a
perilous encounter : the royal standard was delivered into the
hands of his general Rustam ; and a remnant of thirty thousand
regular troops was swelled in truth, or in opinion, to one hundred
and twenty thousand subjects, or allies, of the great king. The
Moslems, whose numbers were re-enforced from twelve to thirty
thousand, had pitched their camp in the plains of Cadesia :[20] and
their line, though it consisted of fewer *men*, could produce more
soldiers, than the unwieldy host of the infidels. I shall here observe, what I must often repeat, that the charge of the Arabs was
not, like that of the Greeks and Romans, the effort of a firm and
compact infantry : their military force was chiefly formed of cavalry and archers ; and the engagement, which was often inter-

* Eichhorn and Silvestre de Sacy have written on the obscure history of the
Mondars.—M.
† Compare throughout, Malcolm, vol. ii. p. 136.—M.

rupted and often renewed by single combats and flying skirmishes, might be protracted without any decisive event to the continuance of several days. The periods of the battle of Cadesia were distinguished by their peculiar appellations. The first, from the well-timed appearance of six thousand of the Syrian brethren, was denominated the day of *succor*. The day of *concussion* might express the disorder of one, or perhaps of both, of the contending armies. The third, a nocturnal tumult, received the whimsical name of the night of *barking*, from the discordant clamors, which were compared to the inarticulate sounds of the fiercest animals. The morning of the succeeding day * determined the fate of Persia ; and a seasonable whirlwind drove a cloud of dust against the faces of the unbelievers. The clangor of arms was re-echoed to the tent of Rustam, who, far unlike the ancient hero of his name, was gently reclining in a cool and tranquil shade, amidst the baggage of his camp, and the train of mules that were laden with gold and silver. On the sound of danger, he started from his couch ; but his flight was overtaken by a valiant Arab, who caught him by the foot, struck off his head, hoisted it on a lance, and instantly returning to the field of battle, carried slaughter and dismay among the thickest ranks of the Persians. The Saracens confess a loss of seven thousand five hundred men ; † and the battle of Cadesia is justly described by the epithets of obstinate and atrocious.[21] The standard of the monarchy was overthrown and captured in the field—a leathern apron of a blacksmith, who, in ancient times, had arisen the deliverer of Persia ; but this badge of heroic poverty was disguised, and almost concealed, by a profusion of precious gems.[22] After this victory, the wealthy province of Irak, or Assyria, submitted to the caliph, and his conquests were firmly established by the speedy foundation of Bassora,[23] a place which ever commands the trade and navigation of the Persians. At the distance of fourscore miles from the Gulf, the Euphrates and Tigris unite in a broad and direct current, which is aptly styled the river of the Arabs. In the midway, between the junction and the mouth of these famous streams, the new settlement was planted on the western bank : the first colony was composed of eight hundred Moslems ; but the influence of the situation soon reared a flourishing and populous capital. The air, though excessively hot, is pure and healthy : the meadows are

---

* The day of cormorants, or according to another reading, the day of re-enforcements. It was the night which was called the night of snarling. Price, p. 114.—M.

† According to Malcolm's authorities, only three thousand ; but he adds, "This is the report of Mahomedan historians, who have a great disposition to the wonderful in relating the first actions of the faithful." Vol. i p. 139.—M.

filled with palm-trees and cattle ; and one of the adjacent valleys has been celebrated among the four paradises or gardens of Asia. Under the first caliphs the jurisdiction of this Arabian colony extended over the southern provinces of Persia : the city has been sanctified by the tombs of the companions and martyrs ; and the vessels of Europe still frequent the port of Bassora, as a convenient station and passage of the Indian trade.

After the defeat of Cadesia, a country intersected by rivers and canals might have opposed an insuperable barrier to the victorious cavalry ; and the walls of Ctesiphon or Madayn, which had resisted the battering-rams of the Romans, would not have yielded to the darts of the Saracens. But the flying Persians were overcome by the belief, that the last day of their religion and empire was at hand ; the strongest posts were abandoned by treachery or cowardice ; and the king, with a part of his family and treasures, escaped to Holwan, at the foot of the Median hills. In the third month after the battle, Said, the lieutenant of Omar, passed the Tigris without opposition ; the capital was taken by assault, and the disorderly resistance of the people gave a keener edge to the sabres of the Moslems, who shouted with religious transport, "This is the white palace of Chosroes ; this is the promise of the apostle of God !" The naked robbers of the desert were suddenly enriched beyond the measure of their hope or knowledge. Each chamber revealed a new treasure secreted with art, or ostentatiously displayed ; the gold and silver, the various wardrobes and precious furniture surpassed (says Abulfeda) the estimate of fancy or numbers ; and another historian defines the untold and almost infinite mass, by the fabulous computation of three thousands of thousands of thousands of pieces of gold.[24] Some minute though curious facts represent the contrast of riches and ignorance. From the remote islands of the Indian Ocean a large provision of camphire[25] had been imported, which is employed with a mixture of wax to illuminate the palaces of the East. Strangers to the name and properties of that odoriferous gum, the Saracens, mistaking it for salt, mingled the camphire in their bread, and were astonished at the bitterness of the taste. One of the apartments of the palace was decorated with a carpet of silk, sixty cubits in length, and as many in breadth : a paradise or garden was depictured on the ground : the flowers, fruits, and shrubs, were imitated by the figures of the gold embroidery, and the colors of the precious stones ; and the ample square was encircled by a variegated and verdant border.*

---

* Compare Price, p. 122.—M.

The Arabian general persuaded his soldiers to relinquish their claim, in the reasonable hope that the eyes of the caliph would be delighted with the spendid workmanship of nature and industry. Regardless of the merit of art, and the pomp of royalty, the rigid Omar divided the prize among his brethren of Medina : the picture was destroyed ; but such was the intrinsic value of the materials, that the share of Ali alone was sold for twenty thousand drachms. A mule that carried away the tiara and cuirass, the belt and bracelets of Chosroes, was overtaken by the pursuers ; the gorgeous trophy was presented to the commander of the faithful ; and the gravest of the companions condescended to smile when they beheld the white beard, the hairy arms, and uncouth figure of the veteran, who was invested with the spoils of the Great King.[26] The sack of Ctesiphon was followed by its desertion and gradual decay. The Saracens disliked the air and situation of the place, and Omar was advised by his general to remove the seat of government to the western side of the Euphrates. In every age, the foundation and ruin of the Assyrian cities has been easy and rapid : the country is destitute of stone and timber ; and the most solid structures [27] are composed of bricks baked in the sun, and joined by a cement of the native bitumen. The name of *Cufa* [28] describes a habitation of reeds and earth ; but the importance of the new capital was supported by the numbers, wealth, and spirit, of a colony of veterans ; and their licentiousness was indulged by the wisest caliphs, who were apprehensive of provoking the revolt of a hundred thousand swords : " Ye men of Cufa," said Ali, who solicited their aid, " you have been always conspicuous by your valor. You conquered the Persian king and scattered his forces, till you had taken possession of his inheritance." This mighty conquest was achieved by the battles of Jalula and Nehavend. After the loss of the former, Yezdegerd fled from Holwan, and concealed his shame and despair in the mountains of Farsistan, from whence Cyrus had descended with his equal and valiant companions. The courage of the nation survived that of the monarch : among the hills to the south of Ecbatana or Hamadan, one hundred and fifty thousand Persians made a third and final stand for their religion and country ; and the decisive battle of Nehavend was styled by the Arabs the victory of victories. If it be true that the flying general of the Persians was stopped and overtaken in a crowd of mules and camels laden with honey, the incident, however slight or singular, will denote the luxurious impediments of an Oriental army.[29]

The geography of Persia is darkly delineated by the Greeks and Latins ; but the most illustrious of her cities appear to be more ancient than the invasion of the Arabs. By the reduction of Hamadan and Ispahan, of Caswin, Tauris, and Rei, they gradually approached the shores of the Caspian Sea ; and the orators of Mecca might applaud the success and spirit of the faithful, who had already lost sight of the northern bear, and had almost transcended the bounds of the habitable world.[30] Again turning towards the West and the Roman empire, they repassed the Tigris over the bridge of Mosul, and, in the captive provinces of Armenia and Mesopotamia, embraced their victorious brethren of the Syrian army. From the palace of Madayn their Eastern progress was not less rapid or extensive. They advanced along the Tigris and the Gulf ; penetrated through the passes of the mountains into the valley of Estachar or Persepolis, and profaned the last sanctuary of the Magian empire. The grandson of Chosroes was nearly surprised among the falling columns and mutilated figures ; a sad emblem of the past and present fortune of Persia :[31] he fled with accelerated haste over the desert of Kirman, implored the aid of the warlike Segestans, and sought an humble refuge on the verge of the Turkish and Chinese power. But a victorious army is insensible of fatigue : the Arabs divided their forces in the pursuit of a timorous enemy ; and the caliph Othman promised the government of Chorasan to the first general who should enter that large and populous country, the kingdom of the ancient Bactrians. The condition was accepted ; the prize was deserved ; the standard of Mahomet was planted on the walls of Herat, Merou, and Balch ; and the successful leader neither halted nor reposed till his foaming cavalry had tasted the waters of the Oxus. In the public anarchy, the independent governors of the cities and castles obtained their separate capitulations : the terms were granted or imposed by the esteem, the prudence, or the compassion, of the victors ; and a simple profession of faith established the distinction between a brother and a slave. After a noble defence, Harmozan, the prince or satrap of Ahwaz and Susa, was compelled to surrender his person and his state to the discretion of the caliph ; and their interview exhibits a portrait of the Arabian manners. In the presence, and by the command, of Omar, the gay barbarian was despoiled of his silken robes embroidered with gold, and of his tiara bedecked with rubies and emeralds : " Are you now sensible," said the conqueror to his naked captive ; " are you now sensible of the judgment of God, and of the different rewards of infidelity and obedience ?" " Alas !" replied Harmozan, " I feel them too deeply. In the days of our common ignorance, we fought with the weapons of the flesh, and my nation was superior. God was then neuter :

since he has espoused your quarrel, you have subverted our king-dom and religion." Oppressed by this painful dialogue, the Per-sian complained of intolerable thirst, but discovered some appre-hension lest he should be killed whilst he was drinking a cup of water. "Be of good courage," said the caliph; "your life is safe till you have drunk this water:" the crafty satrap accepted the assurance, and instantly dashed the vase against the ground. Omar would have avenged the deceit, but his companions repre-sented the sanctity of an oath; and the speedy conversion of Harmozan entitled him not only to a free pardon, but even to a stipend of two thousand pieces of gold. The administration of Persia was regulated by an actual survey of the people, the cat-tle, and the fruits of the earth;[32] and this monument, which at-tests the vigilance of the caliphs, might have instructed the phi-losophers of every age.[33]

The flight of Yezdegerd had carried him beyond the Oxus, and as far as the Jaxartes, two rivers[34] of ancient and modern renown, which descend from the mountains of India towards the Caspian Sea. He was hospitably entertained by Tarkhan, prince of Far-gana,[35] a fertile province on the Jaxartes: the king of Samar-cand, with the Turkish tribes of Sogdiana and Scythia, were moved by the lamentations and promises of the fallen monarch; and he solicited, by a suppliant embassy, the more solid and pow-erful friendship of the emperor of China.[36] The virtuous Tait-song,[37] the first of the dynasty of the Tang, may be justly com-pared with the Antonines of Rome: his people enjoyed the bless-ings of prosperity and peace; and his dominion was acknowl-edged by forty-four hordes of the barbarians of Tartary. His last garrisons of Cashgar and Khoten maintained a frequent inter-course with their neighbors of the Jaxartes and Oxus; a recent colony of Persians had introduced into China the astronomy of the Magi; and Taitsong might be alarmed by the rapid progress and dangerous vicinity of the Arabs. The influence, and perhaps the supplies, of China revived the hopes of Yezdegerd and the zeal of the worshippers of fire; and he returned with an army of Turks to conquer the inheritance of his fathers. The fortunate Moslems, without unsheathing their swords, were the spectators of his ruin and death. The grandson of Chosroes was betrayed by his servant, insulted by the seditious inhabitants of Merou, and oppressed, defeated, and pursued by his barbarian allies. He reached the banks of a river, and offered his rings and bracelets for an instant passage in a miller's boat. Ignorant or insensible of royal distress, the rustic replied, that four drachms of silver were the daily profit of his mill, and that he would not suspend his work unless the loss were repaid. In this moment of hesitation and delay, the last of the Sassanian kings was overtaken and slaughtered by the Turkish cavalry, in the nineteenth year of his unhappy reign.[38] * His son Firuz, an humble client of the Chinese emperor, accepted the station of captain of his guards ; and the Magian worship was long preserved by a colony of loyal exiles in the province of Bucharia.† His grandson inherited the regal name ; but after a faint and fruitless enterprise, he returned to China, and ended his days in the palace of Sigan. The male line of the Sassanides was extinct ; but the female captives, the daughters of Persia, were given to the conquerors in servitude, or marriage ; and the race of the caliphs and imams was ennobled by the blood of their royal mothers.[39]

After the fall of the Persian kingdom, the River Oxus divided the territories of the Saracens and of the Turks. This narrow boundary was soon overleaped by the spirit of the Arabs ; the governors of Chorasan extended their successive inroads ; and one of their triumphs was adorned with the buskin of a Turkish queen, which she dropped in her precipitate flight beyond the hills of Bochara.[40] But the final conquest of Transoxiana,[41] as well as of Spain, was reserved for the glorious reign of the inactive Walid ; and the name of Catibah, the camel-driver, declares the origin and merit of his successful lieutenant. While one of his colleagues displayed the first Mahometan banner on the banks of the Indus, the spacious regions between the Oxus, the Jaxartes, and the Caspian Sea, were reduced by the arms of Catibah to the obedience of the prophet and of the caliph.[42] A tribute of two millions of pieces of gold was imposed on the infidels ; their idols were burnt or broken ; the Mussulman chief pronounced a sermon in the new mosch of Carizme ; after several battles, the Turkish hordes were driven back to the desert ; and the emperors of China solicited the friendship of the victorious Arabs. To their industry, the prosperity of the province, the Sogdiana of the ancients, may in a great measure be ascribed ; but the advantages of the soil and climate had been understood and cultivated since the reign of the Macedonian kings. Before the invasion of the Saracens, Carizme, Bochara, and Samarcand were rich and populous

---

* The account of Yezdegerd's death in the Habeib 'usseyr and Rouzut uzzuffa (Price, p. 162) is much more probable. On the demand of the few dhirems, he offered to the miller his sword, and royal girdle, of inestimable value. This awoke the cupidity of the miller, who murdered him, and threw the body into the stream.—M.

† Firouz died leaving a son called Ni-ni-cha by the Chinese, probably Narses. Yezdegerd had two sons, Firouz and Bahram. St. Martin, vol. xi. p. 318.—M.

under the yoke of the shepherds of the north.* These cities were surrounded with a double wall ; and the exterior fortification, of a larger circumference, enclosed the fields and gardens of the adjacent district. The mutual wants of India and Europe were supplied by the diligence of the Sogdian merchants ; and the inestimable art of transforming linen into paper has been diffused from the manufacture of Samarcand over the western world.[43]

II. No sooner had Abubeker restored the unity of faith and government, than he despatched a circular letter to the Arabian tribes. "In the name of the most merciful God, to the rest of the true believers. Health and happiness, and the mercy and blessing of God, be upon you. I praise the most high God, and I pray for his prophet Mahomet. This is to acquaint you, that I intend to send the true believers into Syria[44] to take it out of the hands of the infidels. And I would have you know, that the fighting for religion is an act of obedience to God." His messengers returned with the tidings of pious and martial ardor which they had kindled in every province ; and the camp of Medina was successively filled with the intrepid bands of the Saracens, who panted for action, complained of the heat of the season and the scarcity of provisions, and accused with impatient murmurs the delays of the caliph. As soon as their numbers were complete, Abubeker ascended the hill, reviewed the men, the horses, and the arms, and poured forth a fervent prayer for the success of their undertaking. In person, and on foot, he accompanied the first day's march ; and when the blushing leaders attempted to dismount, the caliph removed their scruples by a declaration, that those who rode, and those who walked, in the service of religion, were equally meritorious. His instructions[45] to the chiefs of the Syrian army were inspired by the warlike fanaticism which advances to seize, and affects to despise, the objects of earthly ambition. "Remember," said the successor of the prophet, "that you are always in the presence of God, on the verge of death, in the assurance of judgment, and the hope of paradise. Avoid injustice and oppression, consult with your brethren, and study to preserve the love and confidence of your troops. When you fight the battles of the Lord, acquit yourselves like men, without turning your backs ; but let not your victory be stained with the blood of women or children. Destroy no palm-trees, nor burn any fields of corn. Cut down no fruit-trees, nor do any mischief

---

* The manuscript Arabian and Persian writers in the royal library contain very circumstantial details on the contest between the Persians and Arabians. M. St. Martin declined this addition to the work of Le Beau, as extending to too great length. St. Martin, vol. xi. p. 320.—M.

to cattle, only such as you kill to eat. When you make any covenant or article, stand to it, and be as good as your word. As you go on, you will find some religious persons who live retired in monasteries, and propose to themselves to serve God that way : let them alone, and neither kill them nor destroy their monasteries : [46] And you will find another sort of people, that belong to the synagogue of Satan, who have shaven crowns ; [47] be sure you cleave their skulls, and give them no quarter till they either turn Mahometans or pay tribute." All profane or frivolous conversation, all dangerous recollection of ancient quarrels, was severely prohibited among the Arabs : in the tumult of a camp, the exercises of religion were assiduously practised ; and the intervals of action were employed in prayer, meditation, and the study of the Koran. The abuse, or even the use, of wine was chastised by fourscore strokes on the soles of the feet, and in the fervor of their primitive zeal, many secret sinners revealed their fault, and solicited their punishment. After some hesitation, the command of the Syrian army was delegated to Abu Obeidah, one of the fugitives of Mecca, and companions of Mahomet ; whose zeal and devotion were assuaged, without being abated, by the singular mildness and benevolence of his temper. But in all the emergencies of war, the soldiers demanded the superior genius of Caled ; and whoever might be the choice of the prince, the *Sword of God* was both in fact and fame the foremost leader of the Saracens. He obeyed without reluctance ; [*] he was consulted without jealousy ; and such was the spirit of the man, or rather of the times, that Caled professed his readiness to serve under the banner of the faith, though it were in the hands of a child or an enemy. Glory, and riches, and dominion, were indeed promised to the victorious Mussulman ; but he was carefully instructed, that if the goods of this life were his only incitement, *they* likewise would be his only reward.

One of the fifteen provinces of Syria, the cultivated lands to the eastward of the Jordan, had been decorated by Roman vanity with the name of *Arabia ;* [48] and the first arms of the Saracens were justified by the semblance of a national right. The country was enriched by the various benefits of trade ; by the vigilance of the emperors it was covered with a line of forts ; and the populous cities of Gerasa, Philadelphia, and Bosra, [49] were secure, at least from a surprise, by the solid structure of their walls. The last of these cities was the eighteenth station from Medina : the road was familiar to the caravans of Hejaz and Irak, who annu-

---

* Compare Price, p. 60.—M.

ally visited this plenteous market of the province and the desert : the perpetual jealousy of the Arabs had trained the inhabitants to arms ; and twelve thousand horse could sally from the gates of Bosra, an appellation which signifies, in the Syriac language, a strong tower of defence. Encouraged by their first success against the open towns and flying parties of the borders, a detachment of four thousand Moslems presumed to summon and attack the fortress of Bosra. They were oppressed by the numbers of the Syrians ; they were saved by the presence of Caled, with fifteen hundred horse : he blamed the enterprise, restored the battle, and rescued his friend, the venerable Serjabil, who had vainly invoked the unity of God and the promises of the apostle. After a short repose, the Moslems performed their ablutions with sand instead of water ;[50] and the morning prayer was recited by Caled before they mounted on horseback. Confident in their strength, the people of Bosra threw open their gates, drew their forces into the plain, and swore to die in the defence of their religion. But a religion of peace was incapable of withstanding the fanatic cry of " Fight, fight ! Paradise, paradise !" that reechoed in the ranks of the Saracens ; and the uproar of the town, the ringing of bells,[51] and the exclamations of the priests and monks increased the dismay and disorder of the Christians. With the loss of two hundred and thirty men, the Arabs remained masters of the field; and the ramparts of Bosra, in expectation of human or divine aid, were crowded with holy crosses and consecrated banners. The governor Romanus had recommended an early submission : despised by the people, and degraded from his office, he still retained the desire and opportunity of revenge. In a nocturnal interview, he informed the enemy of a subterraneous passage from his house under the wall of the city ; the son of the caliph, with a hundred volunteers, were committed to the faith of this new ally, and their successful intrepidity gave an easy entrance to their companions. After Caled had imposed the terms of servitude and tribute, the apostate or convert avowed in the assembly of the people his meritorious treason : " I renounce your society," said Romanus, " both in this world and the world to come. And I deny him that was crucified, and whosoever worships him. And I choose God for my Lord, Islam for my faith, Mecca for my temple, the Moslems for my brethren, and Mahomet for my prophet ; who was sent to lead us into the right way, and to exalt the true religion in spite of those who join partners with God."

The conquest of Bosra, four days' journey from Damascus,[52] encouraged the Arabs to besiege the ancient capital of Syria.[53]

At some distance from the walls, they encamped among the groves and fountains of that, delicious territory,[54] and the usual option of the Mahometan faith, of tribute or of war, was proposed to the resolute citizens, who had been lately strengthened by a re-enforcement of five thousand Greeks. In the decline, as in the infancy, of the military art, a hostile defiance was frequently offered and accepted by the generals themselves :[55] many a lance was shivered in the plain of Damascus, and the personal prowess of Caled was signalized in the first sally of the besieged. After an obstinate combat, he had overthrown and made prisoner one of the Christian leaders, a stout and worthy antagonist. He instantly mounted a fresh horse, the gift of the governor of Palmyra, and pushed forwards to the front of the battle. "Repose yourself for a moment," said his friend Derar, "and permit me to supply your place : you are fatigued with fighting with this dog." "O Derar!" replied the indefatigable Saracen, "we shall rest in the world to come. He that labors to-day shall rest to-morrow." With the same unabated ardor, Caled answered, encountered, and vanquished a second champion ; and the heads of his two captives, who refused to abandon their religion, were indignantly hurled into the midst of the city. The event of some general and partial actions reduced the Damascenes to a closer defence : but a messenger, whom they dropped from the walls, returned with the promise of speedy and powerful succor, and their tumultuous joy conveyed the intelligence to the camp of the Arabs. After some debate, it was resolved by the generals to raise, or rather to suspend, the siege of Damascus, till they had given battle to the forces of the emperor. In the retreat, Caled would have chosen the more perilous station of the rear-guard ; he modestly yielded to the wishes of Abu Obeidah. But in the hour of danger he flew to the rescue of his companion, who was rudely pressed by a sally of six thousand horse and ten thousand foot, and few among the Christians could relate at Damascus the circumstances of their defeat. The importance of the contest required the junction of the Saracens, who were dispersed on the frontiers of Syria and Palestine ; and I shall transcribe one of the circular mandates which was addressed to Amrou, the future conqueror of Egypt. "In the name of the most merciful God : from Caled to Amrou, health and happiness. Know that thy brethren the Moslems design to march to Aiznadin, where there is an army of seventy thousand Greeks, who purpose to come against us, *that they may extinguish the light of God with their mouths ; but God preserveth his light in spite of the infidels.*[56] As soon therefore as this letter of mine shall be delivered to thy hands, come with those that are with thee to Aiznadin, where thou shalt find us, if it please the most high God." The summons was cheerfully obeyed, and the forty-five thousand Moslems who met on the same day, on the same spot, ascribed to the blessing of Providence the effects of their activity and zeal.

About four years after the triumphs of the Persian war, the repose of Heraclius and the empire was again disturbed by a new enemy, the power of whose religion was more strongly felt, than it was clearly understood, by the Christians of the East. In his palace of Constantinople or Antioch, he was awakened by the invasion of Syria, the loss of Bosra, and the danger of Damascus.* An army of seventy thousand veterans, or new levies, was assembled at Hems or Emesa, under the command of his general Werdan : [57] and these troops, consisting chiefly of cavalry, might be indifferently styled either Syrians, or Greeks, or Romans : *Syrians*, from the place of their birth or warfare ; *Greeks*, from the religion and language of their sovereign ; and *Romans*, from the proud appellation which was still profaned by the successors of Constantine. On the plain of Aiznadin, as Werdan rode on a white mule decorated with gold chains, and surrounded with ensigns and standards, he was surprised by the near approach of a fierce and naked warrior, who had undertaken to view the state of the enemy. The adventurous valor of·Derar was inspired, and has perhaps been adorned, by the enthusiasm of his age and country. The hatred of the Christians, the love of spoil, and the contempt of danger, were the ruling passions of the audacious Saracen ; and the prospect of instant death could never shake his religious confidence, or ruffle the calmness of his resolution, or even suspend the frank and martial pleasantry of his humor. In the most hopeless enterprises, he was bold, and prudent, and fortunate : after innumerable hazards, after being thrice a prisoner in the hands of the infidels, he still survived to relate the achievements, and to enjoy the rewards, of the Syrian conquest. On this occasion, his single lance maintained a flying fight against thirty Romans, who were detached by Werdan ; and, after killing or unhorsing seventeen of their number, Derar returned in safety to his applauding. brethren. When his rashness was mildly censured by the general, he excused himself with the simplicity of a soldier. " Nay," said Derar, " I did not begin first : but they came out to take me, and I was afraid that God should see me turn my back : and indeed I fought in good earnest, and without doubt God assisted

---

* It is difficult here to reconcile the Persian authorities of Major Price with the Arabian writers consulted by Gibbon.

me against them ; and had I not been apprehensive of disobeying your orders, I should not have come away as I did ; and I perceive already that they will fall into our hands.'' In the presence of both armies, a venerable Greek advanced from the ranks with a liberal offer of peace ; and the departure of the Saracens would have been purchased by a gift to each soldier, of a turban, a robe, and a piece of gold ; ten robes and a hundred pieces to their leader ; one hundred robes and a thousand pieces to the caliph. A smile of indignation expressed the refusal of Caled. '' Ye Christian dogs, you know your option ; the Koran, the tribute, or the sword. We are a people whose delight is in war, rather than in peace : and we despise your pitiful alms, since we shall be speedily masters of your wealth, your families, and your persons.'' Notwithstanding this apparent disdain, he was deeply conscious of the public danger : those who had been in Persia, and had seen the armies of Chosroes, confessed that they never beheld a more formidable array. From the superiority of the enemy, the artful Saracen derived a fresh incentive of courage : '' You see before you,'' said he, '' the united force of the Romans ; you cannot hope to escape, but you may conquer Syria in a single day. The event depends on your discipline and patience. Reserve yourselves till the evening. It was in the evening that the Prophet was accustomed to vanquish.'' During two successive engagements, his temperate firmness sustained the darts of the enemy, and the murmurs of his troops. At length, when the spirits and quivers of the adverse line were almost exhausted, Caled gave the signal of onset and victory. The remains of the Imperial army fled to Antioch, or Cæsarea, or Damascus ; and the death of four hundred and seventy Moslems was compensated by the opinion that they had sent to hell above fifty thousand of the infidels. The spoil was inestimable ; many banners and crosses of gold and silver, precious stones, silver and gold chains, and innumerable suits of the richest armor and apparel. The general distribution was postponed till Damascus should be taken ; but the seasonable supply of arms became the instrument of new victories. The glorious intelligence was transmitted to the throne of the caliph ; and the Arabian tribes, the coldest or most hostile to the prophet's mission, were eager and importunate to share the harvest of Syria.

The sad tidings were carried to Damascus by the speed of grief and terror ; and the inhabitants beheld from their walls the return of the heroes of Aiznadin. Amrou led the van at the head of nine thousand horse : the bands of the Saracens succeeded each other in formidable review ; and the rear was closed by Caled in person, with the standard of the black eagle. To the activity of Derar he intrusted the commission of patrolling round the city with two thousand horse, of scouring the plain, and of intercepting all succor or intelligence. The rest of the Arabian chiefs were fixed in their respective stations before the seven gates of Damascus ; and the siege was renewed with fresh vigor and confidence. The art, the labor, the military engines, of the Greeks and Romans are seldom to be found in the simple, though successful, operations of the Saracens : it was sufficient for them to invest a city with arms, rather than with trenches ; to repel the sallies of the besieged ; to attempt a stratagem or an assault ; or to expect the progress of famine and discontent. Damascus would have acquiesced in the trial of Aiznadin, as a final and peremptory sentence between the emperor and the caliph : her courage was rekindled by the example and authority of Thomas, a noble Greek, illustrious in a private condition by the alliance of Heraclius.[58] The tumult and illumination of the night proclaimed the design of the morning sally ; and the Christian hero, who affected to despise the enthusiasm of the Arabs, employed the resource of a similar superstition. At the principal gate, in the sight of both armies, a lofty crucifix was erected ; the bishop, with his clergy, accompanied the march, and laid the volume of the New Testament before the image of Jesus ; and the contending parties were scandalized or edified by a prayer that the Son of God would defend his servants and vindicate his truth. The battle raged with incessant fury ; and the dexterity of Thomas,[59] an incomparable archer, was fatal to the boldest Saracens, till their death was revenged by a female heroine. The wife of Aban, who had followed him to the holy war, embraced her expiring husband. "Happy," said she, "happy art thou, my dear : thou art gone to thy Lord, who first joined us together, and then parted us asunder. I will revenge thy death, and endeavor to the utmost of my power to come to the place where thou art, because I love thee. Henceforth shall no man ever touch me more, for I have dedicated myself to the service of God." Without a groan, without a tear, she washed the corpse of her husband, and buried him with the usual rites. Then grasping the manly weapons, which in her native land she was accustomed to wield, the intrepid widow of Aban sought the place where his murderer fought in the thickest of the battle. Her first arrow pierced the hand of his standard-bearer ; her second wounded Thomas in the eye ; and the fainting Christians no longer beheld their ensign or their leader. Yet the generous champion of Damascus refused to withdraw to his palace : his wound was dressed on the rampart ; the fight was continued till the evening ; and the Syrians rested on their arms. In the silence of the night, the signal was given by a stroke on the great bell ; the gates were thrown open, and each gate discharged an impetuous column on the sleeping camp of the Saracens. Caled was the first in arms : at the head of four hundred horse he flew to the post of danger, and the tears trickled down his iron cheeks, as he uttered a fervent ejaculation : " O God, who never sleepest, look upon thy servants, and do not deliver them into the hands of their enemies." The valor and victory of Thomas were arrested by the presence of the *Sword of God;* with the knowledge of the peril, the Moslems recovered their ranks, and charged the assailants in the flank and rear. After the loss of thousands, the Christian general retreated with a sigh of despair, and the pursuit of the Saracens was checked by the military engines of the rampart.

After a siege of seventy days,[60] the patience, and perhaps the provisions, of the Damascenes were exhausted ; and the bravest of their chiefs submitted to the hard dictates of necessity. In the occurrences of peace and war, they had been taught to dread the fierceness of Caled, and to revere the mild virtues of Abu Obeidah. At the hour of midnight, one hundred chosen deputies of the clergy and people were introduced to the tent of that venerable commander. He received and dismissed them with courtesy. They returned with a written agreement, on the faith of a companion of Mahomet, that all hostilities should cease ; that the voluntary emigrants might depart in safety, with as much as they could carry away of their effects ; and that the tributary subjects of the caliph should enjoy their lands and houses, with the use and possession of seven churches. On these terms, the most respectable hostages, and the gate nearest to his camp, were delivered into his hands : his soldiers imitated the moderation of their chief ; and he enjoyed the submissive gratitude of a people whom he had rescued from destruction. But the success of the treaty had relaxed their vigilance, and in the same moment the opposite quarter of the city was betrayed and taken by assault. A party of a hundred Arabs had opened the eastern gate to a more inexorable foe. " No quarter," cried the rapacious and sanguinary Caled, " no quarter to the enemies of the Lord :" his trumpets sounded, and a torrent of Christian blood was poured down the streets of Damascus. When he reached the church of St. Mary, he was astonished and provoked by the peaceful aspect of his companions ; their swords were in the scabbard, and they were surrounded by a multitude of priests and monks. Abu Obeidah saluted the general : " God," said he, " has delivered the city into my hands by way of surrender, and has saved the believers the trouble of fighting." "And am *I* not," replied the indignant Caled, " am *I* not the lieutenant of the commander of the faithful ? Have I not taken the city by storm ? The unbelievers shall perish by the sword. Fall on." The hungry and cruel Arabs would have obeyed the welcome command ; and Damascus was lost, if the benevolence of Abu Obeidah had not been supported by a decent and dignified firmness. Throwing himself between the trembling citizens and the most eager of the barbarians, he adjured them, by the holy name of God, to respect his promise, to suspend their fury, and to wait the determination of their chiefs. The chiefs retired into the church of St. Mary ; and after a vehement debate, Caled submitted in some measure to the reason and authority of his colleague ; who urged the sanctity of a covenant, the advantage as well as the honor which the Moslems would derive from the punctual performance of their word, and the obstinate resistance which they must encounter from the distrust and despair of the rest of the Syrian cities. It was agreed that the sword should be sheathed, that the part of Damascus which had surrendered to Abu Obeidah, should be immediately entitled to the benefit of his capitulation, and that the final decision should be referred to the justice and wisdom of the caliph.[61] A large majority of the people accepted the terms of toleration and tribute ; and Damascus is still peopled by twenty thousand Christians. But the valiant Thomas, and the free-born patriots who had fought under his banner, embraced the alternative of poverty and exile. In the adjacent meadow, a numerous encampment was formed of priests and laymen, of soldiers and citizens, of women and children : they collected, with haste and terror, their most precious movables ; and abandoned, with loud lamentations, or silent anguish, their native homes, and the pleasant banks of the Pharpar. The inflexible soul of Caled was not touched by the spectacle of their distress : he disputed with the Damascenes the property of a magazine of corn ; endeavored to exclude the garrison from the benefit of the treaty ; consented, with reluctance, that each of the fugitives should arm himself with a sword, or a lance, or a bow ; and sternly declared, that, after a respite of three days, they might be pursued and treated as the enemies of the Moslems.

The passion of a Syrian youth completed the ruin of the exiles of Damascus. A nobleman of the city, of the name of Jonas,[62] was betrothed to a wealthy maiden ; but her parents delayed the consummation of his nuptials, and their daughter was persuaded to escape with the man whom she had chosen. They corrupted the nightly watchmen of the gate Keisan ; the lover, who led the way, was encompassed by a squadron of Arabs ; but his exclamation in the Greek tongue, " The bird is taken," admonished his mistress to hasten her return. In the presence of Caled, and of death, the unfortunate Jonas professed his belief in one God and his apostle Mahomet ; and continued, till the season of his martyrdom, to discharge the duties of a brave and sincere Mussulman. When the city was taken, he flew to the monastery, where Eudocia had taken refuge ; but the lover was forgotten ; the apostate was scorned ; she preferred her religion to her country ; and the justice of Caled, though deaf to mercy, refused to detain by force a male or female inhabitant of Damascus. Four days was the general confined to the city by the obligation of the treaty, and the urgent cares of his new conquest. His appetite for blood and rapine would have been extinguished by the hopeless computation of time and distance ; but he listened to the importunities of Jonas, who assured him, that the weary fugitives might yet be overtaken. At the head of four thousand horse, in the disguise of Christian Arabs, Caled undertook the pursuit. They halted only for the moments of prayer ; and their guide had a perfect knowledge of the country. For a long way the footsteps of the Damascenes were plain and conspicuous : they vanished on a sudden ; but the Saracens were comforted by the assurance that the caravan had turned aside into the mountains, and must speedily fall into their hands. In traversing the ridges of the Libanus, they endured intolerable hardships, and the sinking spirits of the veteran fanatics were supported and cheered by the unconquerable ardor of a lover. From a peasant of the country, they were informed that the emperor had sent orders to the colony of exiles to pursue without delay the road of the sea-coast, and of Constantinople, apprehensive, perhaps, that the soldiers and people of Antioch might be discouraged by the sight and the story of their sufferings. The Saracens were conducted through the territories of Gabala [63] and Laodicea, at a cautious distance from the walls of the cities ; the rain was incessant, the night was dark, a single mountain separated them from the Roman army ; and Caled, ever anxious for the safety of his brethren, whispered an ominous dream in the ear of his companion. With the dawn of day, the prospect again cleared, and they saw before them, in a pleasant valley, the tents of Damascus. After a short interval of repose and prayer, Caled divided his cavalry into four squadrons, committing the first to his faithful Derar, and reserving the last for himself. They successively rushed on the promiscuous multitude, insufficiently provided with arms, and already vanquished by sorrow and fatigue. Except a captive, who was pardoned and dismissed, the Arabs enjoyed the satisfaction of believing that not a Christian of either sex escaped the edge of their cimeters. The gold and silver of Damascus was scattered over the camp, and a royal wardrobe of three hundred loads of silk might clothe an army of naked barbarians. In the tumult of the battle, Jonas sought and found the object of his pursuit: but her resentment was inflamed by the last act of his perfidy; and as Eudocia struggled in his hateful embraces, she struck a dagger to her heart. Another female, the widow of Thomas, and the real or supposed daughter of Heraclius, was spared and released without a ransom; but the generosity of Caled was the effect of his contempt; and the haughty Saracen insulted, by a message of defiance, the throne of the Cæsars. Caled had penetrated above a hundred and fifty miles into the heart of the Roman province: he returned to Damascus with the same secrecy and speed. On the accession of Omar, the *Sword of God* was removed from the command; but the caliph, who blamed the rashness, was compelled to applaud the vigor and conduct, of the enterprise.

Another expedition of the conquerors of Damascus will equally display their avidity and their contempt for the riches of the present world. They were informed that the produce and manufactures of the country were annually collected in the fair of Abyla,[64] about thirty miles from the city; that the cell of a devout hermit was visited at the same time by a multitude of pilgrims; and that the festival of trade and superstition would be ennobled by the nuptials of the daughter of the governor of Tripoli. Abdallah, the son of Jaafar, a glorious and holy martyr, undertook, with a banner of five hundred horse, the pious and profitable commission of despoiling the infidels. As he approached the fair of Abyla, he was astonished by the report of the mighty concourse of Jews and Christians, Greeks and Armenians, of natives of Syria and of strangers of Egypt, to the number of ten thousand, besides a guard of five thousand horse that attended the person of the bride. The Saracens paused: "For my own part," said Abdallah, "I *dare not* go back: our foes are many, our danger is great, but our reward is splendid and secure, either in this life or in the life to come. Let every man, according to his inclination, advance or retire." Not a Mussulman deserted his standard. "Lead the way," said Abdallah to his Christian guide, "and you shall see what the companions of the prophet can perform." They charged in five squadrons; but after the first advantage of the surprise, they were encompassed and almost overwhelmed by the multitude of their enemies; and their valiant band is fancifully

compared to a white spot in the skin of a black camel.[65]   About
the hour of sunset, when their weapons dropped from their hands,
when they panted on the verge of eternity, they discovered an
approaching cloud of dust, they heard the welcome sound of the
tecbir,[66] and they soon perceived the standard of Caled, who flew
to their relief with the utmost speed of his cavalry.   The Christians were broken by his attack, and slaughtered in their flight,
as far as the river of Tripoli.   They left behind them the various
riches of the fair ; the merchandises that were exposed for sale,
the money that was brought for purchase, the gay decorations of
the nuptials, and the governor's daughter, with forty of her
female attendants.   The fruits, provisions, and furniture, the
money, plate, and jewels, were diligently laden on the backs of
horses, asses, and mules ; and the holy robbers returned in triumph to Damascus.   The hermit, after a short and angry controversy with Caled, declined the crown of martyrdom, and was left
alive in the solitary scene of blood and devastation.

Syria,[67] one of the countries that have been improved by the
most early cultivation, is not unworthy of the preference.[68]   The
heat of the climate is tempered by the vicinity of the sea and
mountains, by the plenty of wood and water ; and the produce of
a fertile soil affords the subsistence, and encourages the propagation, of men and animals.   From the age of David to that of Heraclius, the country was overspread with ancient and flourishing
cities : the inhabitants were numerous and wealthy ; and, after
the slow ravage of despotism and superstition, after the recent
calamities of the Persian war, Syria could still attract and reward
the rapacious tribes of the desert.   A plain of ten days' journey,
from Damascus to Aleppo and Antioch, is watered, on the western side, by the winding course of the Orontes.   The hills of Libanus and Anti-Libanus are planted from north to south, between the Orontes and the Mediterranean ; and the epithet of
hollow (Cœlesyria) was applied to a long and fruitful valley,
which is confined in the same direction by the two ridges of
snowy mountains.[69]   Among the cities, which are enumerated by
Greek and Oriental names in the geography and conquest of Syria,
we may distinguish Emesa or Hems, Heliopolis or Baalbec, the
former as the metropolis of the plain, the latter as the capital of
the valley.   Under the last of the Cæsars, they were strong and
populous ; the turrets glittered from afar : an ample space was
covered with public and private buildings ; and the citizens were
illustrious by their spirit, or at least by their pride ; by their
riches, or at least by their luxury.   In the days of Paganism, both
Emesa and Heliopolis were addicted to the worship of Baal, or

the sun ; but the decline of their superstition and splendor has been marked by a singular variety of fortune. Not a vestige remains of the temple of Emesa, which was equalled in poetic style to the summits of Mount Libanus,[70] while the ruins of Baalbec, invisible to the writers of antiquity, excite the curiosity and wonder of the European traveller.[71] The measure of the temple is two hundred feet in length, and one hundred in breadth : the front is adorned with a double portico of eight columns ; fourteen may be counted on either side ; and each column, forty-five feet in height, is composed of three massy blocks of stone or marble. The proportions and ornaments of the Corinthian order express the architecture of the Greeks : but as Baalbec has never been the seat of a monarch, we are at a loss to conceive how the expense of these magnificent structures could be supplied by private or municipal liberality.[72] From the conquest of Damascus the Saracens proceeded to Heliopolis and Emesa ; but I shall decline the repetition of the sallies and combats which have been already shown on a larger scale. In the prosecution of the war, their policy was not less effectual than their sword. By short and separate truces they dissolved the union of the enemy ; accustomed the Syrians to compare their friendship with their enmity ; familiarized the idea of their language, religion, and manners ; and exhausted, by clandestine purchase, the magazines and arsenals of the cities which they returned to besiege. They aggravated the ransom of the more wealthy, or the more obstinate ; and Chalcis alone was taxed at five thousand ounces of gold, five thousand ounces of silver, two thousand robes of silk, and as many figs and olives as would load five thousand asses. But the terms of truce or capitulation were faithfully observed ; and the lieutenant of the caliph, who had promised not to enter the walls of the captive Baalbec, remained tranquil and immovable in his tent till the jarring factions solicited the interposition of a foreign master. The conquest of the plain and valley of Syria was achieved in less than two years. Yet the commander of the faithful reproved the slowness of their progress ; and the Saracens, bewailing their fault with tears of rage and repentance, called aloud on their chiefs to lead them forth to fight the battles of the Lord. In a recent action, under the walls of Emesa, an Arabian youth, the cousin of Caled, was heard aloud to exclaim, " Methinks I see the black-eyed girls looking upon me ; one of whom, should she appear in this world, all mankind would die for love of her. And I see in the hand of one of them a handkerchief of green silk, and a cap of precious stones, and she beckons me, and calls out, Come hither quickly, for I love thee." With these words, charging the Christians, he made havoc wherever he went, till, observed at length by the governor of Hems, he was struck through with a javelin.

It was incumbent on the Saracens to exert the full powers of their valor and enthusiasm against the forces of the emperor, who was taught, by repeated losses, that the rovers of the desert had undertaken, and would speedily achieve, a regular and permanent conquest. From the provinces of Europe and Asia, fourscore thousand soldiers were transported by sea and land to Antioch and Cæsarea: the light troops of the army consisted of sixty thousand Christian Arabs of the tribe of Gassan. Under the banner of Jabalah, the last of their princes, they marched in the van; and it was a maxim of the Greeks, that for the purpose of cutting diamond, a diamond was the most effectual. Heraclius withheld his person from the dangers of the field; but his presumption, or perhaps his despondency, suggested a peremptory order, that the fate of the province and the war should be decided by a single battle. The Syrians were attached to the standard of Rome and of the cross; but the noble, the citizen, the peasant, were exasperated by the injustice and cruelty of a licentious host, who oppressed them as subjects, and despised them as strangers and aliens.[73] A report of these mighty preparations was conveyed to the Saracens in their camp of Emesa; and the chiefs, though resolved to fight, assembled a council: the faith of Abu Obeidah would have expected on the same spot the glory of martyrdom; the wisdom of Caled advised an honorable retreat to the skirts of Palestine and Arabia, where they might await the succors of their friends, and the attack of the unbelievers. A speedy messenger soon returned from the throne of Medina, with the blessings of Omar and Ali, the prayers of the widows of the prophet, and a re-enforcement of eight thousand Moslems. In their way they overturned a detachment of Greeks, and when they joined at Yermuk the camp of their brethren, they found the pleasing intelligence, that Caled had already defeated and scattered the Christian Arabs of the tribe of Gassan. In the neighborhood of Bosra, the springs of Mount Hermon descend in a torrent to the plain of Decapolis, or ten cities; and the Hieromax, a name which has been corrupted to Yermuk, is lost, after a short course, in the Lake of Tiberias.[74] The banks of this obscure stream were illustrated by a long and bloody encounter.* On this momentous occasion, the public voice, and the modesty of

---

* Compare Price, p. 79. The army of the Romans is swollen to 400,000 men, of which 70,000 perished.—M.

Abu Obeidah, restored the command to the most deserving of the Moslems. Caled assumed his station in the front, his colleague was posted in the rear, that the disorder of the fugitives might be checked by his venerable aspect, and the sight of the yellow banner which Mahomet had displayed before the walls of Chaibar. The last line was occupied by the sister of Derar, with the Arabian women who had enlisted in this holy war, who were accustomed to wield the bow and the lance, and who in a moment of captivity had defended, against the uncircumcised ravishers, their chastity and religion.[75] The exhortation of the generals was brief and forcible : "Paradise is before you, the devil and hell-fire in your rear." Yet such was the weight of the Roman cavalry, that the right wing of the Arabs was broken and separated from the main body. Thrice did they retreat in disorder, and thrice were they driven back to the charge by the reproaches and blows of the women. In the intervals of action, Abu Obeidah visited the tents of his brethren, prolonged their repose by repeating at once the prayers of two different hours, bound up their wounds with his own hands, and administered the comfortable reflection, that the infidels partook of their sufferings without partaking of their reward. Four thousand and thirty of the Moslems were buried in the field of battle ; and the skill of the Armenian archers enabled seven hundred to boast that they had lost an eye in that meritorious service. The veterans of the Syrian war acknowledged that it was the hardest and most doubtful of the days which they had seen. But it was likewise the most decisive : many thousands of the Greeks and Syrians fell by the swords of the Arabs ; many were slaughtered, after the defeat, in the woods and mountains ; many, by mistaking the ford, were drowned in the waters of the Yermuk ; and however the loss may be magnified,[76] the Christian writers confess and bewail the bloody punishment of their sins.[77] Manuel, the Roman general, was either killed at Damascus, or took refuge in the monastery of Mount Sinai. An exile in the Byzantine court, Jabalah lamented the manners of Arabia, and his unlucky preference of the Christian cause.[78] He had once inclined to the profession of Islam ; but in the pilgrimage of Mecca, Jabalah was provoked to strike one of his brethren, and fled with amazement from the stern and equal justice of the caliph. These victorious Saracens enjoyed at Damascus a month of pleasure and repose : the spoil was divided by the discretion of Abu Obeidah : an equal share was allotted to a soldier and to his horse, and a double portion was reserved for the noble coursers of the Arabian breed.

After the battle of Yermuk, the Roman army no longer appeared in the field ; and the Saracens might securely choose, among the fortified towns of Syria, the first object of their attack. They consulted the caliph whether they should march to Cæsarea or Jerusalem ; and the advice of Ali determined the immediate siege of the latter. To a profane eye, Jerusalem was the first or second capital of Palestine ; but after Mecca and Medina, it was revered and visited by the devout Moslems, as the temple of the Holy Land which had been sanctified by the revelation of Moses, of Jesus, and of Mahomet himself. The son of Abu Sophian was sent with five thousand Arabs to try the first experiment of surprise or treaty ; but on the eleventh day the town was invested by the whole force of Abu Obeidah. He addressed the customary summons to the chief commanders and people of *Ælia.* " Health and happiness to every one that follows the right way ! We require of you to testify that there is but one God, and that Mahomet is his apostle. If you refuse this, consent to pay tribute, and be under us forthwith. Otherwise I shall bring men against you who love death better than you do the drinking of wine or eating hog's flesh. Nor will I ever stir from you, if it please God, till I have destroyed those that fight for you, and made slaves of your children." But the city was defended on every side by deep valleys and steep ascents ; since the invasion of Syria, the walls and towers had been anxiously restored ; the bravest of the fugitives of Yermuk had stopped in the nearest place of refuge ; and in the defence of the sepulchre of Christ, the natives and strangers might feel some sparks of the enthusiasm which so fiercely glowed in the bosoms of the Saracens. The siege of Jerusalem lasted four months ; not a day was lost without some action of sally or assault ; the military engines incessantly played from the ramparts ; and the inclemency of the winter was still more painful and destructive to the Arabs. The Christians yielded at length to the perseverance of the besiegers. The patriarch Sophronius appeared on the walls, and by the voice of an interpreter demanded a conference.* After a vain attempt to dissuade the lieutenant of the caliph from his impious enterprise, he proposed, in the name of the people, a fair capitulation, with this extraordinary clause, that the articles of security should be ratified by the authority and presence of Omar himself. The question was debated in the council of Medina ; the sanctity of the place, and the advice of Ali, persuaded the caliph to gratify the wishes of his soldiers and enemies ; and the simplicity of his

* See the explanation of this in Price, with the prophecy which was thereby fulfilled, p. 85.—M.

journey is more illustrious than the royal pageants of vanity and oppression. The conqueror of Persia and Syria was mounted on a red camel, which carried, besides his person, a bag of corn, a bag of dates, a wooden dish, and a leathern bottle of water. Wherever he halted, the company, without distinction, was invited to partake of his homely fare, and the repast was consecrated by the prayer and exhortation of the commander of the faithful.[80] But in this expedition, or pilgrimage, his power was exercised in the administration of justice : he reformed the licentious polygamy of the Arabs, relieved the tributaries from extortion and cruelty, and chastised the luxury of the Saracens, by despoiling them of their rich silks, and dragging them on their faces in the dirt. When he came within sight of Jerusalem, the caliph cried, with a loud voice, "God is victorious. O Lord, give us an easy conquest!" and, pitching his tent of coarse hair, calmly seated himself on the ground. After signing the capitulation, he entered the city without fear or precaution ; and courteously discoursed with the patriarch concerning its religious antiquities.[81] Sophronius bowed before his new master, and secretly muttered, in the words of Daniel, "The abomination of desolation is in the holy place."[82] At the hour of prayer they stood together in the church of the resurrection ; but the caliph refused to perform his devotions, and contented himself with praying on the steps of the church of Constantine. To the patriarch he disclosed his prudent and honorable motive. "Had I yielded," said Omar, "to your request, the Moslems of a future age would have infringed the treaty under color of imitating my example." By his command the ground of the temple of Solomon was prepared for the foundation of a mosch ;[83] and, during a residence of ten days, he regulated the present and future state of his Syrian conquests. Medina might be jealous, lest the caliph should be detained by the sanctity of Jerusalem or the beauty of Damascus ; her apprehensions were dispelled by his prompt and voluntary return to the tomb of the apostle.[84]

To achieve what yet remained of the Syrian war, the caliph had formed two separate armies ; a chosen detachment, under Amrou and Yezid, was left in the camp of Palestine ; while the larger division, under the standard of Abu Obeidah and Caled, marched away to the north against Antioch and Aleppo. The latter of these, the Berœa of the Greeks, was not yet illustrious as the capital of a province or a kingdom ; and the inhabitants, by anticipating their submission and pleading their poverty, obtained a moderate composition for their lives and religion. But the castle of Aleppo,[85] distinct from the city, stood erect on a lofty arti-

ficial mound : the sides were sharpened to a precipice, and faced
with freestone ; and the breadth of the ditch might be filled with
water from the neighboring springs. After the loss of three
thousand men, the garrison was still equal to the defence ; and
Youkinna, their valiant and hereditary chief, had murdered his
brother, a holy monk, for daring to pronounce the name of peace.
In a siege of four or five months, the hardest of the Syrian war,
great numbers of the Saracens were killed and wounded : their
removal to the distance of a mile could not seduce the vigilance of
Youkinna ; nor could the Christians be terrified by the execution
of three hundred captives whom they beheaded before the castle
wall. The silence, and at length the complaints, of Abu Obeidah
informed the caliph that their hope and patience were consumed
at the foot of this impregnable fortress. "I am variously affected," replied Omar, "by the difference of your success ; but I
charge you by no means to raise the siege of the castle. Your retreat would diminish the reputation of our arms, and encourage
the infidels to fall upon you on all sides. Remain before Aleppo
till God shall determine the event, and forage with your horse
round the adjacent country." The exhortation of the commander
of the faithful was fortified by a supply of volunteers from all the
tribes of Arabia, who arrived in the camp on horses or camels.
Among these was Dames, of a servile birth, but of gigantic size and
intrepid resolution. The forty-seventh day of his service he proposed, with only thirty men, to make an attempt on the castle.
The experience and testimony of Caled recommended his offer ;
and Abu Obeidah admonished his brethren not to despise the
baser origin of Dames, since he himself, could he relinquish the
public care, would cheerfully serve under the banner of the slave.
His design was covered by the appearance of a retreat ; and the
camp of the Saracens was pitched about a league from Aleppo.
The thirty adventurers lay in ambush at the foot of the hill ; and
Dames at length succeeded in his inquiries, though he was provoked by the ignorance of his Greek captives. "God curse these
dogs," said the illiterate Arab ; "what a strange barbarous language they speak !" At the darkest hour of the night he scaled
the most accessible height, which he had diligently surveyed, a
place where the stones were less entire, or the slope less perpendicular, or the guard less vigilant. Seven of the stoutest Saracens mounted on each other's shoulders, and the weight of the
column was sustained on the broad and sinewy back of the gigantic slave. The foremost in this painful ascent could grasp and
climb the lowest part of the battlements ; they silently stabbed
and cast down the sentinels ; and the thirty brethren, repeating a

pious ejaculation, " O apostle of God, help and deliver us !" were successively drawn up by the long folds of their turbans. With bold and cautious footsteps, Dames explored the palace of the governor, who celebrated, in riotous merriment, the festival of his deliverance. From thence, returning to his companions, he assaulted on the inside the entrance of the castle. They overpowered the guard, unbolted the gate, let down the drawbridge, and defended the narrow pass, till the arrival of Caled, with the dawn of day, relieved their danger and assured their conquest. Youkinna, a formidable foe, became an active and useful proselyte ; and the general of the Saracens expressed his regard for the most humble merit, by detaining the army at Aleppo till Dames was cured of his honorable wounds. The capital of Syria was still covered by the castle of Aazaz and the iron bridge of the Orontes. After the loss of those important posts, and the defeat of the last of the Roman armies, the luxury of Antioch[86] trembled and obeyed. Her safety was ransomed with three hundred thousand pieces of gold ; but the throne of the successors of Alexander, the seat of the Roman government in the East, which had been decorated by Cæsar with the titles of free and holy and inviolate, was degraded under the yoke of the caliphs to the secondary rank of a provincial town.[87]

In the life of Heraclius, the glories of the Persian war are clouded on either hand by the disgrace and weakness of his more early and his later days. When the successors of Mahomet unsheathed the sword of war and religion, he was astonished at the boundless prospect of toil and danger ; his nature was indolent, nor could the infirm and frigid age of the emperor be kindled to a second effort. The sense of shame, and the importunities of the Syrians, prevented his hasty departure from the scene of action ; but the hero was no more ; and the loss of Damascus and Jerusalem, the bloody fields of Aiznadin and Yermuk, may be imputed in some degree to the absence or misconduct of the sovereign. Instead of defending the sepulchre of Christ, he involved the church and state in a metaphysical controversy for the unity of his will ; and while Heraclius crowned the offspring of his second nuptials, he was tamely stripped of the most valuable part of their inheritance. In the cathedral of Antioch, in the presence of the bishops, at the foot of the crucifix, he bewailed the sins of the prince and people ; but his confession instructed the world, that it was vain, and perhaps impious, to resist the judgment of God. The Saracens were invincible in fact, since they were invincible in opinion ; and the desertion of Youkinna, his false repentance and repeated perfidy, might justify the suspicion of the emperor, that he was encompassed by traitors and apostates, who conspired to betray his person and their country to the enemies of Christ. In the hour of adversity, his superstition was agitated by the omens and dreams of a falling crown ; and after bidding an eternal farewell to Syria, he secretly embarked with a few attendants, and absolved the faith of his subjects.[88] Constantine, his eldest son, had been stationed with forty thousand men at Cæsarea, the civil metropolis of the three provinces of Palestine. But his private interest recalled him to the Byzantine court ; and, after the flight of his father, he felt himself an unequal champion to the united force of the caliph. His vanguard was boldly attacked by three hundred Arabs and a thousand black slaves, who, in the depth of winter, had climbed the snowy mountains of Libanus, and who were speedily followed by the victorious squadrons of Caled himself. From the north and south the troops of Antioch and Jerusalem advanced along the sea-shore till their banners were joined under the walls of the Phœnician cities : Tripoli and Tyre were betrayed ; and a fleet of fifty transports, which entered without distrust the captive harbors, brought a seasonable supply of arms and provisions to the camp of the Saracens. Their labors were terminated by the unexpected surrender of Cæsarea : the Roman prince had embarked in the night ;[89] and the defenceless citizens solicited their pardon with an offering of two hundred thousand pieces of gold. The remainder of the province, Ramlah, Ptolemais or Acre, Sichem or Neapolis, Gaza, Ascalon, Berytus, Sidon, Gabala, Laodicea, Apamea, Hierapolis, no longer presumed to dispute the will of the conqueror ; and Syria bowed under the sceptre of the caliphs seven hundred years after Pompey had despoiled the last of the Macedonian kings.[90]

The sieges and battles of six campaigns had consumed many thousands of the Moslems. They died with the reputation and the cheerfulness of martyrs ; and the simplicity of their faith may be expressed in the words of an Arabian youth, when he embraced, for the last time, his sister and mother : " It is not," said he, " the delicacies of Syria, or the fading delights of this world, that have prompted me to devote my life in the cause of religion. But I seek the favor of God and his apostle ; and I have heard, from one of the companions of the prophet, that the spirits of the martyrs will be lodged in the crops of green birds, who shall taste the fruits, and drink of the rivers, of paradise. Farewell, we shall meet again among the groves and fountains which God has provided for his elect." The faithful captives might exercise a passive and more arduous resolution ; and a cousin of Mahomet is celebrated for refusing, after an abstinence of three days, the wine and pork, the only nourishment that was allowed by the malice of the infidels. The frailty of some weaker brethren exasperated the implacable spirit of fanaticism ; and the father of Amer deplored, in pathetic strains, the apostasy and damnation of a son, who had renounced the promises of God, and the intercession of the prophet, to occupy, with the priests and deacons, the lowest mansions of hell. The more fortunate Arabs, who survived the war and persevered in the faith, were restrained by their abstemious leader from the abuse of prosperity. After a refreshment of three days, Abu Obeidah withdrew his troops from the pernicious contagion of the luxury of Antioch, and assured the caliph that their religion and virtue could only be preserved by the hard discipline of poverty and labor. But the virtue of Omar, however rigorous to himself, was kind and liberal to his brethren. After a just tribute of praise and thanksgiving, he dropped a tear of compassion ; and sitting down on the ground, wrote an answer, in which he mildly censured the severity of his lieutenant : " God," said the successor of the prophet, has not forbidden the use of the " good things of this world to faithful men, and such as have performed good works. Therefore you ought to have given them leave to rest themselves, and partake freely of those good things which the country affordeth. If any of the Saracens have no family in Arabia, they may marry in Syria ; and whosoever of them wants any female slaves, he may purchase as many as he hath occasion for." The conquerors prepared to use, or to abuse, this gracious permission ; but the year of their triumph was marked by a mortality of men and cattle ; and twenty-five thousand Saracens were snatched away from the possession of Syria. The death of Abu Obeidah might be lamented by the Christians ; but his brethren recollected that he was one of the ten elect whom the prophet had named as the heirs of paradise.[91] Caled survived his brethren about three years ; and the tomb of the Sword of God is shown in the neighborhood of Emesa. His valor, which founded in Arabia and Syria the empire of the caliphs, was fortified by the opinion of a special providence ; and as long as he wore a cap, which had been blessed by Mahomet, he deemed himself invulnerable amidst the darts of the infidels.[*]

The place of the first conquerors was supplied by a new generation of their children and countrymen : Syria became the seat and

---

[*] Khaled, according to the Rouzont Uzzuffa (Price, p. 90), after having been deprived of his ample share of the plunder of Syria by the jealousy of Omar, died, possessed only of his horse, his arms, and a single slave. Yet Omar was obliged to acknowledge to his lamenting parent that never mother had produced a son like Khaled.—M.

support of the house of Ommiyah ; and the revenue, the soldiers, the ships of that powerful kingdom, were consecrated to enlarge on every side the empire of the caliphs. But the Saracens despise a superfluity of fame ; and their historians scarcely condescend to mention the subordinate conquests which are lost in the splendor and rapidity of their victorious career. To the *north* of Syria they passed Mount Taurus, and reduced to their obedience the province of Cilicia, with its capital Tarsus, the ancient monument of the Assyrian kings. Beyond a second ridge of the same mountains they spread the flame of war, rather than the light of religion, as far as the shores of the Euxine and the neighborhood of Constantinople. To the *east* they advanced to the banks and sources of the Euphrates and Tigris : [92] the long-disputed barrier of Rome and Persia was forever confounded ; the walls of Edessa and Amida, of Dara and Nisibis, which had resisted the arms and engines of Sapor or Nushirvan, were levelled in the dust ; and the holy city of Abgarus might vainly produce the epistle or the image of Christ to an unbelieving conqueror. To the *west* the Syrian kingdom is bounded by the sea : and the ruin of Aradus, a small island or peninsula on the coast, was postponed during ten years. But the hills of Libanus abounded in timber ; the trade of Phœnicia was populous in mariners ; and a fleet of seventeen hundred barks was equipped and manned by the natives of the desert. The Imperial navy of the Romans fled before them from the Pamphylian rocks to the Hellespont ; but the spirit of the emperor, a grandson of Heraclius, had been subdued before the combat by a dream and a pun. [93] The Saracens rode masters of the sea ; and the islands of Cyprus, Rhodes, and the Cyclades, were successively exposed to their rapacious visits. Three hundred years before the Christian era, the memorable though fruitless siege of Rhodes [94] by Demetrius had furnished that maritime republic with the materials and the subject of a trophy. A gigantic statue of Apollo, or the sun, seventy cubits in height, was erected at the entrance of the harbor, a monument of the freedom and the arts of Greece. After standing fifty-six years, the colossus of Rhodes was overthrown by an earthquake ; but the massy trunk, and huge fragments, lay scattered eight centuries on the ground, and are often described as one of the wonders of the ancient world. They were collected by the diligence of the Saracens, and sold to a Jewish merchant of Edessa, who is said to have laden nine hundred camels with the weight of the brass metal ; an enormous weight, though we should include the hundred colossal figures, [95] and the three thousand statues, which adorned the prosperity of the city of the sun.

II. The conquest of Egypt may be explained by the character of the victorious Saracen, one of the first of his nation, in an age when the meanest of the brethren was exalted above his nature by the spirit of enthusiasm. The birth of Amrou was at once base and illustrious; his mother, a notorious prostitute, was unable to decide among five of the Koreish; but the proof of resemblance adjudged the child to Aasi, the oldest of her lovers.[96] The youth of Amrou was impelled by the passions and prejudices of his kindred: his poetic genius was exercised in satirical verses against the person and doctrine of Mahomet; his dexterity was employed by the reigning faction to pursue the religious exiles who had taken refuge in the court of the Æthiopian king.[97] Yet he returned from his embassy a secret proselyte; his reason or his interest determined him to renounce the worship of idols; he escaped from Mecca with his friend Caled; and the prophet of Medina enjoyed at the same moment the satisfaction of embracing the two firmest champions of his cause. The impatience of Amrou to lead the armies of the faithful was checked by the reproof of Omar, who advised him not to seek power and dominion, since he who is a subject to-day may be a prince to-morrow. Yet his merit was not overlooked by the two first successors of Mahomet; they were indebted to his arms for the conquest of Palestine; and in all the battles and sieges of Syria, he united with the temper of a chief the valor of an adventurous soldier. In a visit to Medina, the caliph expressed a wish to survey the sword which had cut down so many Christian warriors; the son of Aasi unsheathed a short and ordinary cimeter; and as he perceived the surprise of Omar, "Alas," said the modest Saracen, "the sword itself, without the arm of its master, is neither sharper nor more weighty than the sword of Pharezdak the poet."[98] After the conquest of Egypt, he was recalled by the jealousy of the caliph Othman; but in the subsequent troubles, the ambition of a soldier, a statesman, and an orator, emerged from a private station. His powerful support, both in council and in the field, established the throne of the Ommiades; the administration and revenue of Egypt were restored by the gratitude of Moawiyah to a faithful friend who had raised himself above the rank of a subject; and Amrou ended his days in the palace and city which he had founded on the banks of the Nile. His dying speech to his children is celebrated by the Arabians as a model of eloquence and wisdom: he deplored the errors of his youth; but if the penitent was still infected by the vanity of a poet, he might exaggerate the venom and mischief of his impious compositions.[99]

From his camp in Palestine, Amrou had surprised or anticipated

the caliph's leave for the invasion of Egypt.[100]   The magnanimous
Omar trusted in his God and his sword, which had shaken the
thrones of Chosroes and Cæsar : but when he compared the slender force of the Moslems with the greatness of the enterprise, he
condemned his own rashness, and listened to his timid companions. The pride and the greatness of Pharaoh were familiar to the
readers of the Koran ; and a tenfold repetition of prodigies had
been scarcely sufficient to effect, not the victory, but the flight, of
six hundred thousand of the children of Israel : the cities of
Egypt were many and populous ; their architecture was strong
and solid ; the Nile, with its numerous branches, was alone an insuperable barrier ; and the granary of the Imperial city would be
obstinately defended by the Roman powers. In this perplexity,
the commander of the faithful resigned himself to the decision of
chance, or, in his opinion, of Providence. At the head of only
four thousand Arabs, the intrepid Amrou had marched away from
his station of Gaza, when he was overtaken by the messenger of
Omar. "If you are still in Syria," said the ambiguous mandate,
"retreat without delay ; but if, at the receipt of this epistle, you
have already reached the frontiers of Egypt, advance with confidence, and depend on the succor of God and of your brethren."
The experience, perhaps the secret intelligence, of Amrou had
taught him to suspect the mutability of courts ; and he continued
his march till his tents were unquestionably pitched on Egyptian
ground. He there assembled his officers, broke the seal, perused
the epistle, gravely inquired the name and situation of the place,
and declared his ready obedience to the commands of the caliph.
After a siege of thirty days, he took possession of Furmah or
Pelusium ; and that key of Egypt, as it has been justly named,
unlocked the entrance of the country as far as the ruins of
Heliopolis and the neighborhood of the modern Cairo.

On the western side of the Nile, at a small distance to the east
of the Pyramids, at a small distance to the south of the Delta,
Memphis, one hundred and fifty furlongs in circumference, displayed the magnificence of ancient kings. Under the reign of the
Ptolemies and Cæsars, the seat of government was removed to the
sea-coast ; the ancient capital was eclipsed by the arts and opulence of Alexandria ; the palaces, and at length the temples, were
reduced to a desolate and ruinous condition : yet, in the age of
Augustus, and even in that of Constantine, Memphis was still
numbered among the greatest and most populous of the provincial
cities.[101] The banks of the Nile, in this place of the breadth of
three thousand feet, were united by two bridges of sixty and of
thirty boats, connected in the middle stream by the small island

of Rouda, which was covered with gardens and habitations.[102] The eastern extremity of the bridge was terminated by the town of Babylon and the camp of a Roman legion, which protected the passage of the river and the second capital of Egypt. This important fortress, which might fairly be described as a part of Memphis or *Misrah*, was invested by the arms of the lieutenant of Omar : a re-enforcement of four thousand Saracens soon arrived in his camp ; and the military engines, which battered the walls, may be imputed to the art and labor of his Syrian allies. Yet the siege was protracted to seven months ; and the rash invaders were encompassed and threatened by the inundation of the Nile.[103] Their last assault was bold and successful : they passed the ditch, which had been fortified with iron spikes, applied their scaling ladders, entered the fortress with the shout of " God is victorious !" and drove the remnant of the Greeks to their boats and the Isle of Rouda. The spot was afterwards recommended to the conqueror by the easy communication with the gulf and the peninsula of Arabia ; the remains of Memphis were deserted ; the tents of the Arabs were converted into permanent habitations ; and the first mosch was blessed by the presence of fourscore companions of Mahomet.[104] A new city arose in their camp, on the eastward bank of the Nile ; and the contiguous quarters of Babylon and Fostat are confounded in their present decay by the appellation of old Misrah, or Cairo, of which they form an extensive suburb. But the name of Cairo, the town of victory, more strictly belongs to the modern capital, which was founded in the tenth century by the Fatimite caliphs.[105] It has gradually receded from the river ; but the continuity of buildings may be traced by an attentive eye from the monuments of Sesostris to those of Saladin.[106]

Yet the Arabs, after a glorious and profitable enterprise, must have retreated to the desert had they not found a powerful alliance in the heart of the country. The rapid conquest of Alexander was assisted by the superstition and revolt of the natives : they abhorred their Persian oppressors, the disciples of the Magi, who had burnt the temples of Egypt, and feasted with sacrilegious appetite on the flesh of the god Apis.[107] After a period of ten centuries, the same revolution was renewed by a similar cause ; and in the support of an incomprehensible creed, the zeal of the Coptic Christians was equally ardent. I have already explained the origin and progress of the Monophysite controversy, and the persecution of the emperors, which converted a sect into a nation, and alienated Egypt from their religion and government. The Saracens were received as the deliverers of the Jacobite church ; and a secret and effectual treaty was opened during the siege of Memphis between a victorious army and a people of slaves. A rich and noble Egyptian, of the name of Mokawkas, had dissembled his faith to obtain the administration of his province : in the disorders of the Persian war he aspired to independence : the embassy of Mahomet ranked him among princes ; but he declined, with rich gifts and ambiguous compliments, the proposal of a new religion.[108] The abuse of his trust exposed him to the resentment of Heraclius : his submission was delayed by arrogance and fear ; and his conscience was prompted by interest to throw himself on the favor of the nation and the support of the Saracens. In his first conference with Amrou, he heard without indignation the usual option of the Koran, the tribute, or the sword. "The Greeks," replied Mokawkas, "are determined to abide the determination of the sword : but with the Greeks I desire no communion, either in this world or in the next, and I abjure forever the Byzantine tyrant, his synod of Chalcedon, and his Melchite slaves. For myself and my brethren, we are resolved to live and die in the profession of the Gospel and unity of Christ. It is impossible for us to embrace the revelations of your prophet ; but we are desirous of peace, and cheerfully submit to pay tribute and obedience to his temporal successors." The tribute was ascertained at two pieces of gold for the head of every Christian ; but old men, monks, women, and children, of both sexes, under sixteen years of age, were exempted from this personal assessment : the Copts above and below Memphis swore allegiance to the caliph, and promised a hospitable entertainment of three days to every Mussulman who should travel through their country. By this charter of security, the ecclesiastical and civil tyranny of the Melchites was destroyed :[109] the anathemas of St. Cyril were thundered from every pulpit ; and the sacred edifices, with the patrimony of the church, were restored to the national communion of the Jacobites, who enjoyed without moderation the moment of triumph and revenge. At the pressing summons of Amrou, their patriarch Benjamin emerged from his desert ; and after the first interview, the courteous Arab affected to declare that he had never conversed with a Christian priest of more innocent manners and a more venerable aspect.[110] In the march from Memphis to Alexandria, the lieutenant of Omar intrusted his safety to the zeal and gratitude of the Egyptians : the roads and bridges were diligently repaired ; and in every step of his progress, he could depend on a constant supply of provisions and intelligence. The Greeks of Egypt, whose numbers could scarcely equal a tenth of the natives, were overwhelmed by the universal defection : they had ever been hated, they were no longer feared :

the magistrate fled from his tribunal, the bishop from his altar ; and the distant garrisons were surprised or starved by the surrounding multitudes. Had not the Nile afforded a safe and ready conveyance to the sea, not an individual could have escaped who, by birth, or language, or office, or religion, was connected with their odious name.

By the retreat of the Greeks from the provinces of Upper Egypt, a considerable force was collected in the Island of Delta ; the natural and artificial channels of the Nile afforded a succession of strong and defensible posts ; and the road to Alexandria was laboriously cleared by the victory of the Saracens in two-and-twenty days of general or partial combat. In their annals of conquest, the siege of Alexandria [111] is perhaps the most arduous and important enterprise. The first trading city in the world was abundantly replenished with the means of subsistence and defence. Her numerous inhabitants fought for the dearest of human rights, religion, and property ; and the enmity of the natives seemed to exclude them from the common benefit of peace and toleration. The sea was continually open ; and if Heraclius had been awake to the public distress, fresh armies of Romans and barbarians might have been poured into the harbor to save the second capital of the empire. A circumference of ten miles would have scattered the forces of the Greeks, and favored the stratagems of an active enemy ; but the two sides of an oblong square were covered by the sea and the Lake Mareotis, and each of the narrow ends exposed a front of no more than ten furlongs. The efforts of the Arabs were not inadequate to the difficulty of the attempt and the value of the prize. From the throne of Medina, the eyes of Omar were fixed on the camp and city : his voice excited to arms the Arabian tribes and the veterans of Syria ; and the merit of a holy war was recommended by the peculiar fame and fertility of Egypt. Anxious for the ruin or expulsion of their tyrants, the faithful natives devoted their labors to the service of Amrou : some sparks of martial spirit were perhaps rekindled by the example of their allies ; and the sanguine hopes of Mokawkas had fixed his sepulchre in the church of St. John of Alexandria. Eutychius the patriarch observes that the Saracens fought with the courage of lions : they repulsed the frequent and almost daily sallies of the besieged, and soon assaulted in their turn the walls and towers of the city. In every attack, the sword, the banner of Amrou, glittered in the van of the Moslems. On a memorable day he was betrayed by his imprudent valor : his followers who had entered the citadel were driven back ; and the general, with a friend and a slave, remained a

prisoner in the hands of the Christians. When Amrou was conducted before the præfect, he remembered his dignity, and forgot
his situation : a lofty demeanor, and resolute language, revealed
the lieutenant of the caliph, and the battle-axe of a soldier was
already raised to strike off the head of the audacious captive.
His life was saved by the readiness of his slave, who instantly
gave his master a blow on the face, and commanded him, with an
angry tone, to be silent in the presence of his superiors. The
credulous Greek was deceived : he listened to the offer of a treaty,
and his prisoners were dismissed in the hope of a more respectable
embassy, till the joyful acclamations of the camp announced the
return of their general, and insulted the folly of the infidels. At
length, after a siege of fourteen months, [112] and the loss of three-
and-twenty thousand men, the Saracens prevailed : the Greeks
embarked their dispirited and diminished numbers, and the standard of Mahomet was planted on the walls of the capital of
Egypt. "I have taken," said Amrou to the caliph, "the great
city of the West. It is impossible for me to enumerate the variety of its riches and beauty ; and I shall content myself with observing that it contains four thousand palaces, four thousand
baths, four hundred theatres or places of amusement, twelve thousand shops for the sale of vegetable food, and forty thousand tributary Jews. The town has been subdued by force of arms, without treaty or capitulation, and the Moslems are impatient to seize
the fruits of their victory." [113]   The commander of the faithful
rejected with firmness the idea of pillage, and directed his lieutenant to reserve the wealth and revenue of Alexandria for the
public service and the propagation of the faith : the inhabitants
were numbered ; a tribute was imposed ; the zeal and resentment
of the Jacobites were curbed, and the Melchites who submitted to
the Arabian yoke were indulged in the obscure but tranquil exercise of their worship. The intelligence of this disgraceful and
calamitous event afflicted the declining health of the emperor ;
and Heraclius died of a dropsy about seven weeks after the loss of
Alexandria. [114]   Under the minority of his grandson, the clamors
of a people, deprived of their daily sustenance, compelled the
Byzantine court to undertake the recovery of the capital of Egypt.
In the space of four years the harbor and fortifications of Alexandria were twice occupied by a fleet and army of Romans. They
were twice expelled by the valor of Amrou, who was recalled by
the domestic peril from the distant wars of Tripoli and Nubia.
But the facility of the attempt, the repetition of the insult, and
the obstinacy of the resistance, provoked him to swear that if a
third time he drove the infidels into the sea, he would render

Alexandria as accessible on all sides as the house of a prostitute. Faithful to his promise, he dismantled several parts of the walls and towers ; but the people was spared in the chastisement of the city, and the mosch of *Mercy* was erected on the spot where the victorious general had stopped the fury of his troops.

I should deceive the expectation of the reader if I passed in silence the fate of the Alexandrian library, as it is described by the learned Abulpharagius. The spirit of Amrou was more curious and liberal than that of his brethren, and in his leisure hours the Arabian chief was pleased with the conversation of John, the last disciple of Ammonius, and who derived the surname of *Philoponus* from his laborious studies of grammar and philosophy.[115] Emboldened by this familiar intercourse, Philoponus presumed to solicit a gift, inestimable in *his* opinion, contemptible in that of the barbarians—the royal library, which alone, among the spoils of Alexandria, had not been appropriated by the visit and the seal of the conqueror. Amrou was inclined to gratify the wish of the grammarian, but his rigid integrity refused to alienate the minutest object without the consent of the caliph ; and the well-known answer of Omar was inspired by the ignorance of a fanatic. "If these writings of the Greeks agree with the book of God, they are useless, and need not be preserved ; if they disagree, they are pernicious, and ought to be destroyed." The sentence was executed with blind obedience ; the volumes of paper or parchment were distributed to the four thousand baths of the city ; and such was their incredible multitude that six months were barely sufficient for the consumption of this precious fuel. Since the Dynasties of Abulpharagius[115] have been given to the world in a Latin version, the tale has been repeatedly transcribed ; and every scholar, with pious indignation, has deplored the irreparable shipwreck of the learning, the arts, and the genius, of antiquity. For my own part, I am strongly tempted to deny both the fact and the consequences.* The fact

---

* Since this period several new Mahometan authorities have been adduced to support the authority of Abulpharagius. That of I. Abdollatiph, by Professor White ; II. Of Makrizi ; I have seen a MS. extract from this writer; III. Of Ibn Chaledun ; and after them Hadschi Chalfa. See Von Hammer, Geschichte der Assassinen, p. 17. Reinhard, in a German Dissertation, printed at Göttingen, 1792, and St. Croix (Magasin Encyclop. tom. iv. p. 433), have examined the question. Among Oriental scholars, Professor White, M. St. Martin, Von Hammer, and Silv. de Sacy, consider the fact of the burning the library, by the command of Omar, beyond question. Compare St. Martin's note, vol. xi. p. 296. A Mahometan writer brings a similar charge against the Crusaders. The library of Tripoli is said to have contained the incredible number of three millions of volumes. On the capture of the city, Count Bertram of St. Giles, entering the first room, which contained nothing but the Koran, ordered the whole to be burnt, as the works of the false prophet of Arabia. See Wilken, Gesch. der Kreuzzüge, vol. ii. p. 211.—M.

is indeed marvellous. "Read and wonder!" says the historian himself: and the solitary report of a stranger who wrote at the end of six hundred years on the confines of Media is overbalanced by the silence of two annalists of a more early date, both Christians, both natives of Egypt, and the most ancient of whom, the patriarch Eutychius, has amply described the conquest of Alexandria.[117] The rigid sentence of Omar is repugnant to the sound and orthodox precept of the Mahometan casuists: they expressly declare that the religious books of the Jews and Christians, which are acquired by the right of war, should never be committed to the flames; and that the works of profane science, historians or poets, physicians or philosophers, may be lawfully applied to the use of the faithful.[118] A more destructive zeal may perhaps be attributed to the first successors of Mahomet; yet in this instance, the conflagration would have speedily expired in the deficiency of materials. I shall not recapitulate the disasters of the Alexandrian library, the involuntary flame that was kindled by Cæsar in his own defence,[119] or the mischievous bigotry of the Christians, who studied to destroy the monuments of idolatry.[120] But if we gradually descend from the age of the Antonines to that of Theodosius, we shall learn from a chain of contemporary witnesses that the royal palace and the temple of Serapis no longer contained the four, or the seven, hundred thousand volumes, which had been assembled by the curiosity and magnificence of the Ptolemies.[121] Perhaps the church and seat of the patriarchs might be enriched with a repository of books; but if the ponderous mass of Arian and Monophysite controversy were indeed consumed in the public baths,[122] a philosopher may allow, with a smile, that it was ultimately devoted to the benefit of mankind. I sincerely regret the more valuable libraries which have been involved in the ruin of the Roman empire; but when I seriously compute the lapse of ages, the waste of ignorance, and the calamities of war, our treasures, rather than our losses, are the object of my surprise. Many curious and interesting facts are buried in oblivion: the three great historians of Rome have been transmitted to our hands in a mutilated state, and we are deprived of many pleasing compositions of the lyric, iambic, and dramatic poetry of the Greeks. Yet we should gratefully remember that the mischances of time and accident have spared the classic works to which the suffrage of antiquity[123] had adjudged the first place of genius and glory: the teachers of ancient knowledge, who are still extant, had perused and compared the writings of their predecessors;[124] nor can it fairly be presumed that any important truth, any useful discovery in art or nature, has been snatched away from the curiosity of modern ages.

In the administration of Egypt,[125] Amrou balanced the demands of justice and policy ; the interest of the people of the law, who were defended by God ; and of the people of the alliance, who were protected by man. In the recent tumult of conquest and deliverance, the tongue of the Copts and the sword of the Arabs were most adverse to the tranquillity of the province. To the former Amrou declared that faction and falsehood would be doubly chastised ; by the punishment of the accusers, whom he should detest as his personal enemies, and by the promotion of their innocent brethren, whom their envy had labored to injure and supplant. He excited the latter by the motives of religion and honor to sustain the dignity of their character, to endear themselves by a modest and temperate conduct to God and the caliph, to spare and protect a people who had trusted to their faith, and to content themselves with the legitimate and splendid rewards of their victory. In the management of the revenue, he disapproved the simple but oppressive mode of a capitation, and preferred with reason a proportion of taxes deducted on every branch from the clear profits of agriculture and commerce. A third part of the tribute was appropriated to the annual repairs of the dikes and canals, so essential to the public welfare. Under his administration the fertility of Egypt supplied the dearth of Arabia ; and a string of camels, laden with corn and provisions, covered almost without an interval the long road from Memphis to Medina.[126] But the genius of Amrou soon renewed the maritime communication which had been attempted or achieved by the Pharaohs, the Ptolemies, or the Cæsars ; and a canal, at least eighty miles in length, was opened from the Nile to the Red Sea.* This inland navigation, which would have joined the Mediterranean and the Indian Ocean, was soon discontinued as useless and dangerous : the throne was removed from Medina to Damascus, and the Grecian fleets might have explored a passage to the holy cities of Arabia.[127]

---

* Many learned men have doubted the existence of a communication by water between the Red Sea and the Mediterranean by the Nile. Yet the fact is positively asserted by the ancients. Diodorus Siculus (l. i. p. 33) speaks of it in the most distinct manner as existing in his time. So, also, Strabo (l. xvii. p. 805). Pliny (vol. vi. p. 29) says that the canal which united the two seas was navigable (alveus navigabilis). The indications furnished by Ptolemy and by the Arabic historian, Makrisi, show that works were executed under the reign of Hadrian to repair the canal and extend the navigation ; it then received the name of the River of Trajan. Lucian (in his Pseudomantis, p. 44) says that he went by water from Alexandria to Clysma, on the Red Sea. Testimonies of the sixth and of the eighth century show that the communication was not interrupted at that time. See the French translation of Strabo, vol. v. p. 382. St. Martin, vol. xi. p. 299.—M,

Of his new conquest, the caliph Omar had an imperfect knowledge from the voice of fame and the legends of the Koran. He requested that his lieutenant would place before his eyes the realm of Pharaoh and the Amalekites ; and the answer of Amrou exhibits a lively and not unfaithful picture of that singular country.[128] "O commander of the faithful, Egypt is a compound of black earth and green plants between a pulverized mountain and a red sand. The distance from Syene to the sea is a month's journey for a horseman. Along the valley descends a river, on which the blessing of the Most High reposes both in the evening and morning, and which rises and falls with the revolutions of the sun and moon. When the annual dispensation of Providence unlocks the springs and fountains that nourish the earth, the Nile rolls his swelling and sounding waters through the realm of Egypt : the fields are overspread by the salutary flood ; and the villages communicate with each other in their painted barks. The retreat of the inundation deposits a fertilizing mud for the reception of the various seeds : the crowds of husbandmen who blacken the land may be compared to a swarm of industrious ants ; and their native indolence is quickened by the lash of the task-master, and the promise of the flowers and fruits of a plentiful increase. Their hope is seldom deceived ; but the riches which they extract from the wheat, the barley, and the rice, the legumes, the fruit-trees, and the cattle, are unequally shared between those who labor and those who possess. According to the vicissitudes of the seasons, the face of the country is adorned with a *silver* wave, a verdant *emerald*, and the deep yellow of a *golden* harvest."[129] Yet this beneficial order is sometimes interrupted ; and the long delay and sudden swell of the river in the first year of the conquest might afford some color to an edifying fable. It is said that the annual sacrifice of a virgin[130] had been interdicted by the piety of Omar ; and that the Nile lay sullen and inactive in his shallow bed till the mandate of the caliph was cast into the obedient stream, which rose in a single night to the height of sixteen cubits. The admiration of the Arabs for their new conquest encouraged the license of their romantic spirit. We may read, in the gravest authors, that Egypt was crowded with twenty thousand cities or villages :[131] *that,* exclusive of the Greeks and Arabs, the Copts alone were found, on the assessment, six millions of tributary subjects,[132] or twenty millions of either sex, and of every age : *that* three hundred millions of gold or silver were annually paid to the treasury of the caliphs.[133] Our reason must be startled by these extravagant assertions ; and they will become more palpable if we assume the compass and measure the extent of habitable ground ; a valley from the tropic to Memphis seldom broader than twelve miles, and the triangle of the Delta, a flat surface of two thousand one hundred square leagues, compose a twelfth part of the magnitude of France.[134] A more accurate research will justify a more reasonable estimate. The three hundred millions, created by the error of a scribe, are reduced to the decent revenue of four millions three hundred thousand pieces of gold, of which nine hundred thousand were consumed by the pay of the soldiers.[135] Two authentic lists, of the present and of the twelfth century, are circumscribed within the respectable number of two thousand seven hundred villages and towns.[136] After a long residence at Cairo, a French consul has ventured to assign about four millions of Mahometans, Christians, and Jews, for the ample, though not incredible, scope of the population of Egypt.[137]

IV. The conquest of Africa, from the Nile to the Atlantic Ocean,[138] was first attempted by the arms of the caliph Othman. The pious design was approved by the companions of Mahomet and the chiefs of the tribes ; and twenty thousand Arabs marched from Medina, with the gifts and the blessing of the commander of the faithful. They were joined in the camp of Memphis by twenty thousand of their countrymen ; and the conduct of the war was intrusted to Abdallah,[139] the son of Said and the foster-brother of the caliph, who had lately supplanted the conqueror and lieutenant of Egypt. Yet the favor of the prince, and the merit of his favorite, could not obliterate the guilt of his apostasy. The early conversion of Abdallah, and his skilful pen, had recommended him to the important office of transcribing the sheets of the Koran : he betrayed his trust, corrupted the text, derided the errors which he had made, and fled to Mecca to escape the justice, and expose the ignorance, of the apostle. After the conquest of Mecca, he fell prostrate at the feet of Mahomet ; his tears, and the entreaties of Othman, extorted a reluctant pardon ; but the prophet declared that he had so long hesitated to allow time for some zealous disciple to avenge his injury in the blood of the apostate. With apparent fidelity and effective merit, he served the religion which it was no longer his interest to desert : his birth and talents gave him an honorable rank among the Koreish ; and, in a nation of cavalry, Abdallah was renowned as the boldest and most dexterous horseman of Arabia. At the head of forty thousand Moslems, he advanced from Egypt into the unknown countries of the West. The sands of Barca might be impervious to a Roman legion ; but the Arabs were attended by their faithful camels ; and the natives of the desert beheld without terror the familiar aspect of the soil and climate. After a painful march, they pitched their tents before the walls of Tripoli,[140] a maritime city in which the *name*, the wealth, and the inhabitants of the province had gradually centred, and which now maintains the third rank among the states of barbary. A re-enforcement of Greeks was surprised and cut in pieces on the sea-shore ; but the fortifications of Tripoli resisted the first assaults ; and the Saracens were tempted by the approach of the præfect Gregory [141] to relinquish the labors of the siege for the perils and the hopes of a decisive action. If his standard was followed by one hundred and twenty thousand men, the regular bands of the empire must have been lost in the naked and disorderly crowd of Africans and Moors, who formed the strength, or rather the numbers, of his host. He rejected with indignation the option of the Koran or the tribute ; and during several days the two armies were fiercely engaged from the dawn of light to the hour of noon, when their fatigue and the excessive heat compelled them to seek shelter and refreshment in their respective camps. The daughter of Gregory, a maid of incomparable beauty and spirit, is said to have fought by his side : from her earliest youth she was trained to mount on horseback, to draw the bow, and to wield the cimeter ; and the richness of her arms and apparel were conspicuous in the foremost ranks of the battle. Her hand, with a hundred thousand pieces of gold, was offered for the head of the Arabian general, and the youths of Africa were excited by the prospect of the glorious prize. At the pressing solicitation of his brethren, Abdallah withdrew his person from the field ; but the Saracens were discouraged by the retreat of their leader, and the repetition of these equal or unsuccessful conflicts.

A noble Arabian, who afterwards became the adversary of Ali, and the father of a caliph, had signalized his valor in Egypt, and Zobeir [142] was the first who planted the scaling ladder against the walls of Babylon. In the African war he was detached from the standard of Abdallah. On the news of the battle, Zobeir, with twelve companions, cut his way through the camp of the Greeks, and pressed forwards, without tasting either food or repose, to partake of the dangers of his brethren. He cast his eyes round the field : " Where," said he, " is our general ?" " In his tent." " Is the tent a station for the general of the Moslems ?" Abdallah represented with a blush the importance of his own life, and the temptation that was held forth by the Roman præfect. " Retort," said Zobeir, " on the infidels their ungenerous attempt. Proclaim through the ranks that the head of Gregory shall be repaid with his captive daughter, and the equal sum of one hundred thousand pieces of gold." To the courage and discretion of

Zobeir the lieutenant of the caliph intrusted the execution of his own stratagem, which inclined the long-disputed balance in favor of the Saracens. Supplying by activity and artifice the deficiency of numbers, a part of their forces lay concealed in their tents, while the remainder prolonged an irregular skirmish with the enemy till the sun was high in the heavens. On both sides they retired with fainting steps : their horses were unbridled, their armor was laid aside, and the hostile nations prepared, or seemed to prepare, for the refreshment of the evening, and the encounter of the ensuing day. On a sudden the charge was sounded ; the Arabian camp poured forth a swarm of fresh and intrepid warriors ; and the long line of the Greeks and Africans was surprised, assaulted, overturned, by new squadrons of the faithful, who, to the eye of fanaticism, might appear as a band of angels descending from the sky. The præfect himself was slain by the hand of Zobeir : his daughter, who sought revenge and death, was surrounded and made prisoner ; and the fugitives involved in their disaster the town of Sufetula, to which they escaped from the sabres and lances of the Arabs. Sufetula was built one hundred and fifty miles to the south of Carthage : a gentle declivity is watered by a running stream, and shaded by a grove of juniper-trees ; and, in the ruins of a triumphal arch, a portico, and three temples of the Corinthian order, curiosity may yet admire the magnificence of the Romans.[143] After the fall of this opulent city, the provincials and barbarians implored on all sides the mercy of the conqueror. His vanity or his zeal might be flattered by offers of tribute or professions of faith : but his losses, his fatigues, and the progress of an epidemical disease, prevented a solid establishment ; and the Saracens, after a campaign of fifteen months, retreated to the confines of Egypt, with the captives and the wealth of their African expedition. The caliph's fifth was granted to a favorite, on the nominal payment of five hundred thousand pieces of gold ;[144] but the state was doubly injured by this fallacious transaction, if each foot-soldier had shared one thousand, and each horseman three thousand, pieces, in the real division of the plunder. The author of the death of Gregory was expected to have claimed the most precious reward of the victory : from his silence it might be presumed that he had fallen in the battle, till the tears and exclamations of the præfect's daughter at the sight of Zobeir revealed the valor and modesty of that gallant soldier. The unfortunate virgin was offered, and almost rejected, as a slave, by her father's murderer, who coolly declared that his sword was consecrated to the service of religion ; and that he labored for a recompense far above the charms of mortal beauty, or the riches of this transitory life. A reward congenial to his temper was the honorable commission of announcing to the caliph Othman the success of his arms. The companions, the chiefs, and the people, were assembled in the mosch of Medina, to hear the interesting narrative of Zobeir - and as the orator forgot nothing except the merit of his own counsels and actions, the name of Abdallah was joined by the Arabians with the heroic names of Caled and Amrou.[145]

The Western conquests of the Saracens were suspended near twenty years, till their dissensions were composed by the establishment of the house of Ommiyah ; and the caliph Moawiyah was invited by the cries of the Africans themselves. The successors of Heraclius had been informed of the tribute which they had been compelled to stipulate with the Arabs ; but instead of being moved to pity and relieve their distress, they imposed, as an equivalent or a fine, a second tribute of a similar amount. The ears of the Byzantine ministers were shut against the complaints of their poverty and ruin : their despair was reduced to prefer the dominion of a single master ; and the extortions of the patriarch of Carthage, who was invested with civil and military power, provoked the sectaries, and even the Catholics of the Roman province, to abjure the religion as well as the authority of their tyrants. The first lieutenant of Moawiyah acquired a just renown, subdued an important city, defeated an army of thirty thousand Greeks, swept away fourscore thousand captives, and enriched with their spoils the bold adventures of Syria and Egypt.[146] But the title of conqueror of Africa is more justly due to his successor Akbah. He marched from Damascus at the head of ten thousand of the bravest Arabs ; and the genuine force of the Moslems was enlarged by the doubtful aid and conversion of many thousand barbarians. It would be difficult, nor is it necessary, to trace the accurate line of the progress of Akbah. The interior regions have been peopled by the Orientals with fictitious armies and imaginary citadels. In the warlike province of Zab, or Numidia, fourscore thousand of the natives might assemble in arms ; but the number of three hundred and sixty towns is incompatible with the ignorance or decay of husbandry ;[147] and a circumference of three leagues will not be justified by the ruins of Erbe or Lambesa, the ancient metropolis of that inland country. As we approach the sea-coast, the well-known cities of Bugia[148] and Tangier[149] define the more certain limits of the Saracen victories. A remnant of trade still adheres to the commodious harbor of Bugia, which, in a more prosperous age, is said to have contained about twenty thousand houses ; and the plenty of iron which is dug from the adjacent mountains might have supplied a braver people with the instruments of defence. The remote position and venerable antiquity of Tingi, or Tangier, have been decorated by the Greek and Arabian fables ; but the figurative expressions of the latter, that the walls were constructed of brass, and that the roofs were covered with gold and silver, may be interpreted as the emblems of strength and opulence. The province of Mauritania Tingitana, [150] which assumed the name of the capital, had been imperfectly discovered and settled by the Romans ; the five colonies were confined to a narrow pale, and the more southern parts were seldom explored except by the agents of luxury, who searched the forests for ivory and the citron-wood, [151] and the shores of the ocean for the purple shell-fish. The fearless Akbah plunged into the heart of the country, traversed the wilderness in which his successors erected the splendid capitals of Fez and Morocco, [152] and at length penetrated to the verge of the Atlantic and the great desert. The river Sus descends from the western sides of Mount Atlas, fertilizes, like the Nile, the adjacent soil, and falls into the sea at a moderate distance from the Canary, or Fortunate, Islands. Its banks were inhabited by the last of the Moors, a race of savages, without laws, or discipline, or religion ; they were astonished by the strange and irresistible terrors of the Oriental arms ; and as they possessed neither gold nor silver, the richest spoil was the beauty of the female captives, some of whom were afterwards sold for a thousand pieces of gold. The career, though not the zeal, of Akbah was checked by the prospect of a boundless ocean. He spurred his horse into the waves, and raising his eyes to heaven, exclaimed with a tone of a fanatic, " Great God ! if my course were not stopped by this sea, I would still go on, to the unknown kingdoms of the West, preaching the unity of thy holy name, and putting to the sword the rebellious nations who worship any other Gods than thee." [153] Yet this Mahometan Alexander, who sighed for new worlds, was unable to preserve his recent conquests. By the universal defection of the Greeks and Africans, he was recalled from the shores of the Atlantic, and the surrounding multitudes left him only the resource of an honorable death. The last scene was dignified by an example of national virtue. An ambitious chief, who had disputed the command and failed in the attempt, was led about as a prisoner in the camp of the Arabian general. The insurgents had trusted to his discontent and revenge ; he disdained their offers, and revealed their designs. In the hour of danger, the grateful Akbah unlocked his fetters and advised him to retire ; he chose to die under the banner of his rival. Embracing as friends and martyrs, they unsheathed their cimeters, broke their scabbards, and maintained an obstinate combat, till they fell by each other's side on the last of their slaughtered countrymen. The third general or governor of Africa, Zuheir, avenged and encountered the fate of his predecessor. He vanquished the natives in many battles; he was overthrown by a powerful army, which Constantinople had sent to the relief of Carthage.

It had been the frequent practice of the Moorish tribes to join the invaders, to share the plunder, to profess the faith, and to revolt to their savage state of independence and idolatry, on the first retreat or misfortune of the Moslems. The prudence of Akbah had proposed to found an Arabian colony in the heart of Africa; a citadel that might curb the levity of the barbarians, a place of refuge to secure, against the accidents of war, the wealth and the families of the Saracens. With this view, and under the modest title of the station of a caravan, he planted this colony in the fiftieth year of the Hegira. In the present decay, Cairoan [154] still holds the second rank in the kingdom of Tunis, from which it is distant about fifty miles to the south: [155] its inland situation, twelve miles westward of the sea, has protected the city from the Greek and Sicilian fleets. When the wild beasts and serpents were extirpated, when the forest, or rather wilderness, was cleared, the vestiges of a Roman town were discovered in a sandy plain: the vegetable food of Cairoan is brought from afar; and the scarcity of springs constrains the inhabitants to collect in cisterns and reservoirs a precarious supply of rain-water. These obstacles were subdued by the industry of Akbah; he traced a circumference of three thousand and six hundred paces, which he encompassed with a brick wall; in the space of five years, the governor's palace was surrounded with a sufficient number of private habitations; a spacious mosch was supported by five hundred columns of granite, porphyry, and Numidian marble; and Cairoan became the seat of learning as well as of empire. But these were the glories of a later age; the new colony was shaken by the successive defeats of Akbah and Zuheir, and the western expeditions were again interrupted by the civil discord of the Arabian monarchy. The son of the valiant Zobeir maintained a war of twelve years, a siege of seven months against the house of Ommiyah. Abdallah was said to unite the fierceness of the lion with the subtlety of the fox, but if he inherited the courage, he was devoid of the generosity of his father. [156]

The return of domestic peace allowed the caliph Abdalmalek to resume the conquest of Africa; the standard was delivered to Hassan, governor of Egypt, and the revenue of that

kingdom, with an army of forty thousand men, was consecrated
to the important service. In the vicissitudes of war, the interior
provinces had been alternately won and lost by the Saracens.
But the sea-coast still remained in the hands of the Greeks ; the
predecessors of Hassan had respected the name and fortifications
of Carthage ; and the number of its defenders was recruited
by the fugitives of Cabes and Tripoli. The arms of Hassan were
bolder and more fortunate : he reduced and pillaged the metropolis of Africa ; and the mention of scaling-ladders may justify
the suspicion that he anticipated, by a sudden assault, the more
tedious operations of a regular siege. But the joy of the conquerors was soon disturbed by the appearance of the Christian
succors. The præfect and patrician John, a general of experience and renown, embarked at Constantinople the forces of the
Eastern empire ;[157] they were joined by the ships and soldiers of
Sicily, and a powerful re-enforcement of Goths[158] was obtained
from the fears and religion of the Spanish monarch. The weight
of the confederate navy broke the chain that guarded the entrance of the harbor ; the Arabs retired to Cairoan, or Tripoli ;
the Christians landed ; the citizens hailed the ensign of the cross,
and the winter was idly wasted in the dream of victory or deliverance. But Africa was irrecoverably lost ; the zeal and resentment of the commander of the faithful[159] prepared in the ensuing spring a more numerous armament by sea and land ; and the
patrician in his turn was compelled to evacuate the post and
fortifications of Carthage. A second battle was fought in the
neighborhood of Utica : the Greeks and Goths were again defeated ; and their timely embarkation saved them from the sword
of Hassan, who had invested the slight and insufficient rampart of
their camp. Whatever yet remained of Carthage was delivered
to the flames, and the colony of Dido[160] and Cæsar lay desolate
above two hundred years, till a part, perhaps a twentieth, of the
old circumference, was repeopled by the first of the Fatimite caliphs. In the beginning of the sixteenth century, the second
capital of the West was represented by a mosch, a college without students, twenty-five or thirty shops, and the huts of five
hundred peasants, who, in their abject poverty, displayed the
arrogance of the Punic senators. Even that paltry village was
swept away by the Spaniards whom Charles the Fifth had stationed in the fortress of the Goletta. The ruins of Carthage have
perished ; and the place might be unknown if some broken
arches of an aqueduct did not guide the footsteps of the inquisitive traveller.[161]

The Greeks were expelled, but the Arabians were not yet masters of the country. In the interior provinces the Moors or *Ber-bers*,[162] so feeble under the first Cæsars, so formidable to the Byzantine princes, maintained a disorderly resistance to the religion and power of the successors of Mahomet. Under the standard of their queen Cahina, the independent tribes acquired some degree of union and discipline ; and as the Moors respected in their females the character of a prophetess, they attacked the invaders with an enthusiasm similar to their own. The veteran bands of Hassan were inadequate to the defence of Africa : the conquests of an age were lost in a single day ; and the Arabian chief, overwhelmed by the torrent, retired to the confines of Egypt, and expected, five years, the promised succors of the caliph. After the retreat of the Saracens, the victorious prophetess assembled the Moorish chiefs, and recommended a measure of strange and savage policy. "Our cities," said she, "and the gold and silver which they contain, perpetually attract the arms of the Arabs. These vile metals are not the objects of *our* ambition ; we content ourselves with the simple productions of the earth. Let us destroy these cities ; let us bury in their ruins those pernicious treasures ; and when the avarice of our foes shall be destitute of temptation, perhaps they will cease to disturb the tranquillity of a warlike people." The proposal was accepted with unanimous applause. From Tangier to Tripoli, the buildings, or at least the fortifications, were demolished, the fruit-trees were cut down, the means of subsistence were extirpated, a fertile and populous garden was changed into a desert, and the historians of a more recent period could discern the frequent traces of the prosperity and devastation of their ancestors. Such is the tale of the modern Arabians. Yet I strongly suspect that their ignorance of antiquity, the love of the marvellous, and the fashion of extolling the philosophy of barbarians, has induced them to describe, a one voluntary act, the calamities of three hundred years since the first fury of the Donatists and Vandals. In the progress of the revolt, Cahina had most probably contributed her share of destruction ; and the alarm of universal ruin might terrify and alienate the cities that had reluctantly yielded to her unworthy yoke. They no longer hoped, perhaps they no longer wished, the return of their Byzantine sovereigns : their present servitude was not alleviated by the benefits of order and justice ; and the most zealous Catholic must prefer the imperfect truths of the Koran to the blind and rude idolatry of the Moors. The general of the Saracens was again received as the savior of the province : the friends of civil society conspired against the savages of the land ; and the royal prophetess was slain in the first battle, which overturned the baseless fabric of her superstition and empire. The same spirit revived under the successor of Hassan : it was finally quelled by the activity of Musa and his two sons ; but the number of the rebels may be presumed from that of three hundred thousand captives ; sixty thousand of whom, the caliph's fifth, were sold for the profit of the public treasury. Thirty thousand of the barbarian youth were enlisted in the troops ; and the pious labors of Musa, to inculcate the knowledge and practice of the Koran, accustomed the Africans to obey the apostle of God and the commander of the faithful. In their climate and government, their diet and habitation, the wandering Moors resembled the Bedoweens of the desert. With the religion they were proud to adopt the language, name, and origin of Arabs : the blood of the strangers and natives was insensibly mingled ; and from the Euphrates to the Atlantic, the same nation might seem to be diffused over the sandy plains of Asia and Africa. Yet I will not deny that fifty thousand tents of pure Arabians might be transported over the Nile, and scattered through the Libyan desert ; and I am not ignorant that five of the Moorish tribes still retain their *barbarous* idiom, with the appellation and character of *white* Africans.[163]

V. In the progress of conquest from the north and south, the Goths and the Saracens encountered each other on the confines of Europe and Africa. In the opinion of the latter, the difference of religion is a reasonable ground of enmity and warfare.[164]

As early as the time of Othman,[165] their piratical squadrons had ravaged the coast of Andalusia ;[166] nor had they forgotten the relief of Carthage by the Gothic succors. In that age, as well as in the present, the kings of Spain were possessed of the fortress of Ceuta ; one of the columns of Hercules, which is divided by a narrow strait from the opposite pillar or point of Europe. A small portion of Mauritania was still wanting to the African conquest ; but Musa, in the pride of victory, was repulsed from the walls of Ceuta by the vigilance and courage of Count Julian, the general of the Goths. From his disappointment and perplexity, Musa was relieved by an unexpected message of the Christian chief, who offered his place, his person, and his sword, to the successors of Mahomet, and solicited the disgraceful honor of introducing their arms into the heart of Spain.[167] If we inquire into the cause of his treachery, the Spaniards will repeat the popular story of his daughter Cava ;[168]* of a virgin, who was

---

* But, says M. Condé, the name of La Cava, that of Alifa assigned to her attendant, and all the circumstances with which the tale is embellished, distinctly prove that this anecdote is nothing more than an Arabian fiction, founded on some of the

seduced, or ravished, by her sovereign ; of a father who sacrificed his religion and country to the thirst of revenge.   The passions of princes have often been licentious and destructive ; but this well-known tale, romantic in itself, is indifferently supported by external evidence ; and the history of Spain will suggest some motives of interest and policy more congenial to the breast of a veteran statesman.[169]   After the decease or deposition of Witiza, his two sons were supplanted by the ambition of Roderic, a noble Goth, whose father, the duke or governor of a province, had fallen a victim to the preceding tyranny.   The monarchy was still elective ; but the sons of Witiza, educated on the steps of the throne, were impatient of a private station.   Their resentment was the more dangerous, as it was varnished with the dissimulation of courts : their followers were excited by the remembrance of favors and the promise of a revolution ; and their uncle Oppas, archbishop of Toledo and Seville, was the first person in the church, and the second in the state.   It is probable that Julian was involved in the disgrace of the unsuccessful faction ; that he had little to hope and much to fear from the new reign ; and that the imprudent king could not forget or forgive the injuries which Roderic and his family had sustained.   The merit and influence of the count rendered him a useful or formidable subject : his estates were ample, his followers bold and numerous ; and it was too fatally shown, that, by his Andalusian and Mauritanian commands, he held in his hand the keys of the Spanish monarchy. Too feeble, however, to meet his sovereign in arms, he sought the aid of a foreign power ; and his rash invitation of the Moors and Arabs produced the calamities of eight hundred years.   In his epistles, or in a personal interview, he revealed the wealth and nakedness of his country ; the weakness of an unpopular prince ; the degeneracy of an effeminate people.   The Goths were no longer the victorious barbarians, who had humbled the pride of Rome, despoiled the queen of nations, and penetrated from the Danube to the Atlantic Ocean.   Secluded from the world by the Pyrenæan mountains, the successors of Alaric had slumbered in a long peace : the walls of the cities were mouldered into dust : the youth had abandoned the exercise of arms ; and the presumption of their ancient renown would expose them in a field of battle to the first assault of the invaders.   The ambitious Saracen was fired by the ease and importance of the attempt ; but the execution was delayed till he had consulted the commander of the faithful ; and his messenger returned with the permission of Walid to annex

popular poetic romances of the country. De Marles (the abbreviator of Condé), Hist. des Arabes en Espagne, vol. i. p. 63.—M.

the unknown kingdoms of the West to the religion and throne of the caliphs. In his residence of Tangier, Musa, with secrecy and caution, continued his correspondence and hastened his preparations. But the remorse of the conspirators was soothed by the fallacious assurance that he should content himself with the glory and spoil, without aspiring to establish the Moslems beyond the sea that separates Africa from Europe.[170]

Before Musa would trust an army of the faithful to the traitors and infidels of a foreign land, he made a less dangerous trial of their strength and veracity. One hundred Arabs, and four hundred Africans, passed over, in four vessels, from Tangier or Ceuta: the place of their descent on the opposite shore of the strait is marked by the name of Tarif their chief; and the date of this memorable event[171] is fixed to the month of Ramadan, of the ninety-first year of the Hegira, to the month of July, seven hundred and forty-eight years from the Spanish æra of Cæsar,[172] seven hundred and ten after the birth of Christ. From their first station they marched eighteen miles through a hilly country to the castle and town of Julian:[173] on which (it is still called Algezire) they bestowed the name of the Green Island, from a verdant cape that advances into the sea. Their hospitable entertainment, the Christians who joined their standard, their inroad into a fertile and unguarded province, the richness of their spoil, and the safety of their return, announced to their brethren the most favorable omens of victory. In the ensuing spring five thousand veterans and volunteers were embarked under the command of Tarik, a dauntless and skilful soldier, who surpassed the expectation of his chief; and the necessary transports were provided by the industry of their too faithful ally. The Saracens landed[174] at the pillar or point of Europe; the corrupt and familiar appellation of Gibraltar (*Gebel al Tarik*) describes the mountain of Tarik; and the intrenchments of his camp were the first outline of those fortifications, which, in the hands of our countrymen, have resisted the art and power of the house of Bourbon. The adjacent governors informed the court of Toledo of the descent and progress of the Arabs; and the defeat of his lieutenant Edeco, who had been commanded to seize and bind the presumptuous strangers, admonished Roderic of the magnitude of the danger. At the royal summons, the dukes and counts, the bishops and nobles of the Gothic monarchy, assembled at the head of their followers; and the title of King of the Romans, which is employed by an Arabic historian, may be excused by the close affinity of language, religion, and manners, between the nations of Spain. His army consisted of ninety or a hundred thousand men ; a formidable power, if their fidelity and discipline had been adequate to their numbers. The troops of Tarik had been augmented to twelve thousand Saracens ; but the Christian malecontents were attracted by the influence of Julian, and a crowd of Africans most greedily tasted the temporal blessings of the Koran. In the neighborhood of Cadiz, the town of Xeres [175] has been illustrated by the encounter which determined the fate of the kingdom ; the stream of the Guadalete, which falls into the bay, divided the two camps, and marked the advancing and retreating skirmishes of three successive and bloody days. On the fourth day, the two armies joined a more serious and decisive issue ; but Alaric would have blushed at the sight of his unworthy successor, sustaining on his head a diadem of pearls, encumbered with a flowing robe of gold and silken embroidery, and reclining on a litter or car of ivory drawn by two white mules. Notwithstanding the valor of the Saracens, they fainted under the weight of multitudes, and the plain of Xeres was overspread with sixteen thousand of their dead bodies. "My brethren," said Tarik to his surviving companions, "the enemy is before you, the sea is behind ; whither would ye fly ? Follow your general : I am resolved either to lose my life, or to trample on the prostrate king of the Romans." Besides the resource of despair, he confided in the secret correspondence and nocturnal interviews of Count Julian with the sons and the brother of Witiza. The two princes and the archbishop of Toledo occupied the most important posts : their well-timed defection broke the ranks of the Christians ; each warrior was prompted by fear or suspicion to consult his personal safety ; and the remains of the Gothic army were scattered or destroyed in the flight and pursuit of the three following days. Amidst the general disorder, Roderic started from his car, and mounted Orelia, the fleetest of his horses ; but he escaped from a soldier's death to perish more ignobly in the waters of the Bœtis or Guadalquivir. His diadem, his robes, and his courser, were found on the bank ; but as the body of the Gothic prince was lost in the waves, the pride and ignorance of the caliph must have been gratified with some meaner head, which was exposed in triumph before the palace of Damascus. "And such," continues a valiant historian of the Arabs, "is the fate of those kings who withdraw themselves from a field of battle." [176]

Count Julian had plunged so deep into guilt and infamy that his only hope was in the ruin of his country. After the battle of Xeres, he recommended the most effectual measures to the victorious Saracens. "The king of the Goths is slain ; their princes have fled before you, the army is routed, the nation is astonished.

Secure with sufficient detachments the cities of Bœtica, but in person, and without delay, march to the royal city of Toledo, and allow not the distracted Christians either time or tranquillity for the election of a new monarch." Tarik listened to his advice. A Roman captive and proselyte, who had been enfranchised by the caliph himself, assaulted Cordova with seven hundred horse: he swam the river, surprised the town, and drove the Christians into the great church, where they defended themselves above three months. Another attachment reduced the sea-coast of Bœtica, which in the last period of the Moorish power has comprised in a narrow space the populous kingdom of Grenada. The march of Tarik from the Bœtis to the Tagus [177] was directed through the Sierra Morena, that separates Andalusia and Castille, till he appeared in arms under the walls of Toledo. [178] The most zealous of the Catholics had escaped with the relics of their saints; and if the gates were shut, it was only till the victor had subscribed a fair and reasonable capitulation. The voluntary exiles were allowed to depart with their effects; seven churches were appropriated to the Christian worship; the archbishop and his clergy were at liberty to exercise their functions, the monks to practise or neglect their penance; and the Goths and Romans were left in all civil and criminal cases to the subordinate jurisdiction of their own laws and magistrates. But if the justice of Tarik protected the Christians, his gratitude and policy rewarded the Jews, to whose secret or open aid he was indebted for his most important acquisitions. Persecuted by the kings and synods of Spain, who had often pressed the alternative of banishment or baptism, that outcast nation embraced the moment of revenge: the comparison of their past and present state was the pledge of their fidelity; and the alliance between the disciples of Moses and of Mahomet was maintained till the final æra of their common expulsion. From the royal seat of Toledo, the Arabian leader spread his conquests to the north, over the modern realms of Castille and Leon; but it is needless to enumerate the cities that yielded on his approach, or again to describe the table of emerald, [179] transported from the East by the Romans, acquired by the Goths among the spoils of Rome, and presented by the Arabs to the throne of Damascus. Beyond the Asturian mountains, the maritime town of Gijon was the term [180] of the lieutenant of Musa, who had performed, with the speed of a traveller, his victorious march of seven hundred miles, from the Rock of Gibraltar to the Bay of Biscay. The failure of land compelled him to retreat; and he was recalled to Toledo to excuse his presumption of subduing a kingdom in the absence of his general. Spain, which in a more savage and disorderly state had resisted, two hundred years, the arms of the Romans, was overrun in a few months by those of the Saracens; and such was the eagerness of submission and treaty, that the governor of Cordova is recorded as the only chief who fell, without conditions, a prisoner into their hands. The cause of the Goths had been irrevocably judged in the field of Xeres; and, in the national dismay, each part of the monarchy declined a contest with the antagonist who had vanquished the united strength of the whole.[181] That strength had been wasted by two successive seasons of famine and pestilence; and the governors, who were impatient to surrender, might exaggerate the difficulty of collecting the provisions of a siege. To disarm the Christians, superstition likewise contributed her terrors: and the subtle Arab encouraged the report of dreams, omens, and prophecies, and of the portraits of the destined conquerors of Spain, that were discovered on breaking open an apartment of the royal palace. Yet a spark of the vital flame was still alive: some invincible fugitives preferred a life of poverty and freedom in the Asturian valleys; the hardy mountaineers repulsed the slaves of the caliph; and the sword of Pelagius has been transformed into the sceptre of the Catholic kings.[182]

On the intelligence of this rapid success, the applause of Musa degenerated into envy; and he began, not to complain, but to fear, that Tarik would leave him nothing to subdue. At the head of ten thousand Arabs and eight thousand Africans, he passed over in person from Mauritania to Spain: the first of his companions were the noblest of the Koreish; his eldest son was left in the command of Africa; the three younger brethren were of an age and spirit to second the boldest enterprises of their father. At his landing in Algezire, he was respectfully entertained by Count Julian, who stifled his inward remorse, and testified, both in words and actions, that the victory of the Arabs had not impaired his attachment to their cause. Some enemies yet remained for the sword of Musa. The tardy repentance of the Goths had compared their own numbers and those of the invaders; the cities from which the march of Tarik had declined considered themselves as impregnable; and the bravest patriots defended the fortifications of Seville and Merida. They were successively besieged and reduced by the labor of Musa, who transported his camp from the Bœtis to the Anas, from the Guadalquivir to the Guadiana. When he beheld the works of Roman magnificence, the bridge, the aqueducts, the triumphal arches, and the theatre of the ancient metropolis of Lusitania, "I should imagine," said he to his four companions, "that the human race must have united their art and power in the foundation of this city : happy is the man who shall become its master !'' He aspired to that happiness, but the *Emeritans* sustained on this occasion the honor of their descent from the veteran legionaries of Augustus.[183] Disdaining the confinement of their walls, they gave battle to the Arabs on the plain ; but an ambuscade, rising from the shelter of a quarry, or a ruin, chastised their indiscretion, and intercepted their return. The wooden turrets of assault were rolled forwards to the foot of the rampart ; but the defence of Merida was obstinate and long ; and the *castle of the martyrs* was a perpetual testimony of the losses of the Moslems. The constancy of the besieged was at length subdued by famine and despair ; and the prudent victor disguised his impatience under the names of clemency and esteem. The alternative of exile or tribute was allowed ; the churches were divided between the two religions ; and the wealth of those who had fallen in the siege, or retired to Gallicia, was confiscated as the reward of the faithful. In the midway between Merida and Toledo, the lieutenant of Musa saluted the vicegerent of the caliph, and conducted him to the palace of the Gothic kings. Their first interview was cold and formal : a rigid account was exacted of the treasures of Spain : the character of Tarik was exposed to suspicion and obloquy ; and the hero was imprisoned, reviled, and ignominiously scourged by the hand, or the command, of Musa. Yet so strict was the discipline, so pure the zeal, or so tame the spirit, of the primitive Moslems, that, after this public indignity, Tarik could serve and be trusted in the reduction of the Tarragonest province. A mosch was erected at Saragossa, by the liberality of the Koreish : the port of Barcelona was opened to the vessels of Syria ; and the Goths were pursued beyond the Pyrenæan mountains into their Gallic province of Septimania or Languedoc.[184] In the church of St. Mary at Carcassone, Musa found, but it is improbable that he left, seven equestrian statues of massy silver ; and from his *term* or column of Narbonne, he returned on his footsteps to the Gallician and Lusitanian shores of the ocean. During the absence of the father, his son Abdelaziz chastised the insurgents of Seville, and reduced, from Malaga to Valentia, the seacoast of the Mediterranean : his original treaty with the discreet and valiant Theodemir[185] will represent the manners and policy of the terms. '' *The conditions of peace agreed and sworn between Abdelaziz, the son of Musa, the son of Nassir, and Theodemir prince of the Goths.* In the name of the most merciful God, Abdelaziz makes peace on these conditions : *that* Theodemir shall not be disturbed in his principality ; nor any injury be offered to the life or property, the wives and children, the religion and temples, of the Christians : *that* Theodemir shall freely deliver his seven* cities, Orihuela, Valentola, Alicant, Mola, Vacasora, Bigerra, (now Bejar), Ora (or Opta), and Lorca : *that* he shall not assist or entertain the enemies of the caliph, but shall faithfully communicate his knowledge of their hostile designs : *that* himself, and each of the Gothic nobles, shall annually pay one piece of gold, four measures of wheat, as many of barley, with a certain proportion of honey, oil, and vinegar ; and that each of their vassals shall be taxed at one moiety of the said imposition. Given the fourth of Regeb, in the year of the Hegira ninety-four, and subscribed with the names of four Mussulman witnesses." [186] Theodemir and his subjects were treated with uncommon lenity ; but the rate of tribute appears to have fluctuated from a tenth to a fifth, according to the submission or obstinacy of the Christians. [187] In this revolution many partial calamities were inflicted by the carnal or religious passions of the enthusiasts : some churches were profaned by the new worship : some relics or images were confounded with idols : the rebels were put to the sword ; and one town (an obscure place between Cordova and Seville) was razed to its foundations. Yet if we compare the invasion of Spain by the Goths, or its recovery by the kings of Castille and Arragon, we must applaud the moderation and discipline of the Arabian conquerors.

The exploits of Musa were performed in the evening of life, though he affected to disguise his age by coloring with a red powder the whiteness of his beard. But in the love of action and glory, his breast was still fired with the ardor of youth ; and the possession of Spain was considered only as the first step to the monarchy of Europe. With a powerful armament by sea and land, he was preparing to repass the Pyrenees, to extinguish in Gaul and Italy the declining kingdoms of the Franks and Lombards, and to preach the unity of God on the altar of the Vatican. From thence, subduing the barbarians of Germany, he proposed to follow the course of the Danube from its source to the Euxine Sea, to overthrow the Greek or Roman empire of Constantinople, and returning from Europe to Asia, to unite his new acquisitions with Antioch and the provinces of Syria. [188] But his vast enterprise, perhaps of easy execution, must have seemed extravagant to vulgar minds ; and the visionary conqueror was soon reminded of his dependence and servitude. The friends of Tarik had effectually stated his services and wrongs : at the court of Damascus,

---

* Gibbon has made eight cities ; in Condé's translation Bigerra does not appear.—M.

the proceedings of Musa were blamed, his intentions were suspected, and his delay in complying with the first invitation was chastised by a harsher and more peremptory summons. An intrepid messenger of the caliph entered his camp at Lugo in Gallicia, and in the presence of the Saracens and Christians arrested the bridle of his horse. His own loyalty, or that of his troops, inculcated the duty of obedience : and his disgrace was alleviated by the recall of his rival and the permission of investing with his two governments his two sons, Abdallah and Abdelaziz. His long triumph from Ceuta to Damascus displayed the spoils of Africa and the treasures of Spain : four hundred Gothic nobles, with gold coronets and girdles, were distinguished in his train ; and the number of male and female captives, selected for their birth or beauty, was computed at eighteen, or even at thirty, thousand persons. As soon as he reached Tiberias in Palestine, he was apprised of the sickness and danger of the caliph, by a private message from Soliman, his brother and presumptive heir ; who wished to reserve for his own reign the spectacle of victory. Had Walid recovered, the delay of Musa would have been criminal : he pursued his march, and found an enemy on the throne. In his trial before a partial judge against a popular antagonist, he was convicted of vanity and falsehood ; and a fine of two hundred thousand pieces of gold either exhausted his poverty or proved his rapaciousness. The unworthy treatment of Tarik was revenged by a similar indignity ; and the veteran commander, after a public whipping, stood a whole day in the sun before the palace gate, till he obtained a decent exile, under the pious name of a pilgrimage to Mecca. The resentment of the caliph might have been satiated with the ruin of Musa ; but his fears demanded the extirpation of a potent and injured family. A sentence of death was intimated with secrecy and speed to the trusty servants of the throne both in Africa and Spain ; and the forms, if not the substance, of justice were superseded in this bloody execution. In the mosch or palace of Cordova, Abdelaziz was slain by the swords of the conspirators ; they accused their governor of claiming the honors of royalty ; and his scandalous marriage with Egilona, the widow of Roderic, offended the prejudices both of the Christians and Moslems. By a refinement of cruelty, the head of the son was presented to the father, with an insulting question whether he acknowledged the features of the rebel ? "I know his features," he exclaimed with indignation : "I assert his innocence ; and I imprecate the same, a juster fate, against the authors of his death." The age and despair of Musa raised him above the power of kings, and he expired at Mecca of the anguish of a broken heart. His rival was more favorably treated : his services were forgiven ; and Tarik was permitted to mingle with the crowd of slaves.[189] I am ignorant whether Count Julian was rewarded with the death which he deserved indeed, though not from the hands of the Saracens ; but the tale of their ingratitude to the sons of Witiza is disproved by the most unquestionable evidence. The two royal youths were reinstated in the private patrimony of their father ; but on the decease of Eba, the elder, his daughter was unjustly despoiled of her portion by the violence of her uncle Sigebut. The Gothic maid pleaded her cause before the caliph Hashem, and obtained the restitution of her inheritance ; but she was given in marriage to a noble Arabian, and their two sons, Isaac and Ibrahim, were received in Spain with the consideration that was due to their origin and riches.

A province is assimilated to the victorious state by the introduction of strangers and the imitative spirit of the natives ; and Spain, which had been successively tinctured with Punic, and Roman, and Gothic blood, imbibed, in a few generations, the name and manners of the Arabs. The first conquerors, and the twenty successive lieutenants of the caliphs, were attended by a numerous train of civil and military followers, who preferred a distant fortune to a narrow home : the private and public interest was promoted by the establishment of faithful colonies ; and the cities of Spain were proud to commemorate the tribe or country of their Eastern progenitors. The victorious though motley bands of Tarik and Musa asserted, by the name of *Spaniards*, their original claim of conquest ; yet they allowed their brethren of Egypt to share their establishments of Murcia and Lisbon. The royal legion of Damascus was planted at Cordova ; that of Emesa at Seville ; that of Kinnisrin or Chalcis at Jaen ; that of Palestine at Algezire and Medina Sidonia. The natives of Yemen and Persia were scattered round Toledo and the inland country, and the fertile seats of Grenada were bestowed on ten thousand horsemen of Syria and Irak, the children of the purest and most noble of the Arabian tribes.[190] A spirit of emulation, sometimes beneficial, more frequently dangerous, was nourished by these hereditary factions. Ten years after the conquest, a map of the province was presented to the caliph ; the seas, the rivers, and the harbors, the inhabitants and cities, the climate, the soil, and the mineral productions of the earth.[191] In the space of two centuries, the gifts of nature were improved by the agriculture,[192] the manufactures, and the commerce, of an industrious people ; and the effects of their diligence have been magnified by the idleness of their fancy. The first of the Ommiades who reigned in Spain solicited the support of the Christians ; and in his edict of peace and protection, he contents himself with a modest imposition of ten thousand ounces of gold, ten thousand pounds of silver, ten thousand horses, as many mules, one thousand cuirasses, with an equal number of helmets and lances.[193] The most powerful of his successors derived from the same kingdom the annual tribute of twelve millions and forty-five thousand dinars or pieces of gold, about six millions of sterling money ;[194] a sum which, in the tenth century, most probably surpassed the united revenues of the Christian monarchs. His royal seat of Cordova contained six hundred moschs, nine hundred baths, and two hundred thousand houses ; he gave laws to eighty cities of the first, to three hundred of the second and third order ; and the fertile banks of the Guadalquivir were adorned with twelve thousand villages and hamlets. The Arabs might exaggerate the truth, but they created and they described the most prosperous æra of the riches, the cultivation, and the populousness of Spain.[195]

The wars of the Moslems were sanctified by the prophet ; but among the various precepts and examples of his life, the caliphs selected the lessons of toleration that might tend to disarm the resistance of the unbelievers. Arabia was the temple and patrimony of the God of Mahomet ; but he beheld with less jealousy and affection the nations of the earth. The polytheists and idolaters, who were ignorant of his name, might be lawfully extirpated by his votaries;[196] but a wise policy supplied the obligation of justice ; and after some acts of intolerant zeal, the Mahometan conquerors of Hindostan have spared the pagods of that devout and populous country. The disciples of Abraham, of Moses, and of Jesus, were solemnly invited to accept the more *perfect* revelation of Mahomet ; but if they preferred the payment of a moderate tribute, they were entitled to the freedom of conscience and religious worship.[197] In a field of battle the forfeit lives of the prisoners were redeemed by the profession of *Islam;* the females were bound to embrace the religion of their masters, and a race of sincere proselytes was gradually multiplied by the education of the infant captives. But the millions of African and Asiatic converts, who swelled the native band of the faithful Arabs, must have been allured, rather than constrained, to declare their belief in one God and the apostle of God. By the repetition of a sentence and the loss of a foreskin, the subject or the slave, the captive or the criminal, arose in a moment the free and equal companion of the victorious Moslems. Every sin was expiated, every engagement was dissolved : the vow of celibacy was superseded by the indulgence of nature ; the active spirits who slept in the cloister were awakened by the trumpet of the Saracens ; and in the convulsion of the world, every member of a new society ascended to the natural level of his capacity and courage. The minds of the multitude were tempted by the invisible as well as temporal blessings of the Arabian prophet ; and charity will hope that many of his proselytes entertained a serious conviction of the truth and sanctity of his revelation. In the eyes of an inquisitive polytheist, it must appear worthy of the human and the divine nature. More pure than the system of Zoroaster, more liberal than the law of Moses, the religion of Mahomet might seem less inconsistent with reason than the creed of mystery and superstition, which, in the seventh century, disgraced the simplicity of the gospel.

In the extensive provinces of Persia and Africa, the national religion has been eradicated by the Mahometan faith. The ambiguous theology of the Magi stood alone among the sects of the East : but the profane writings of Zoroaster [198] might under the reverend name of Abraham, be dexterously connected with the chain of divine revelation. Their evil principle, the dæmon Ahriman, might be represented as the rival, or as the creature, of the God of light. The temples of Persia were devoid of images ; but the worship of the sun and of fire might be stigmatized as a gross and criminal idolatry. [199] The milder sentiment was consecrated by the practice of Mahomet [200] and the prudence of the caliphs ; the Magians or Ghebers were ranked with the Jews and Christians among the people of the written law ; [201] and as late as the third century of the Hegira, the city of Herat will afford a lively contrast of private zeal and public toleration. [202] Under the payment of an annual tribute, the Mahometan law secured to the Ghebers of Herat their civil and religious liberties : but the recent and humble mosch was overshadowed by the antique splendor of the adjoining temple of fire. A fanatic Iman deplored, in his sermons, the scandalous neighborhood, and accused the weakness or indifference of the faithful. Excited by his voice, the people assembled in tumult ; the two houses of prayer were consumed by the flames, but the vacant ground was immediately occupied by the foundations of a new mosch. The injured Magi appealed to the sovereign of Chorasan ; he promised justice and relief ; when, behold ! four thousand citizens of Herat, of a grave character and mature age, unanimously swore that the idolatrous fane had *never* existed ; the inquisition was silenced, and their conscience was satisfied (says the historian Mirchond [203]) with this holy and meritorious perjury. [204] But the greatest part of the temples of Persia were ruined by the insensible and general desertion of their votaries. It was *insensible*, since it is not accompanied with any memorial of time or place, of persecution or resistance. It was *general*, since the whole realm, from Shiraz to Samarcand, imbibed the faith of the Koran; and the preservation of the native tongue reveals the descent of the Mahometans of Persia.[205] In the mountains and deserts, an obstinate race of unbelievers adhered to the superstition of their fathers; and a faint tradition of the Magian theology is kept alive in the province of Kirman, along the banks of the Indus, among the exiles of Surat, and in the colony which, in the last century, was planted by Shaw Abbas at the gates of Ispahan. The chief pontiff has retired to Mount Elbourz, eighteen leagues from the city of Yezd: the perpetual fire (if it continue to burn) is inaccessible to the profane; but his residence is the school, the oracle, and the pilgrimag eof the Ghebers, whose hard and uniform features attest the unmingled purity of their blood. Under the jurisdiction of their elders, eighty thousand families maintain an innocent and industrious life: their subsistence is derived from some curious manufactures and mechanic trades; and they cultivate the earth with the fervor of a religious duty. Their ignorance withstood the despotism of Shaw Abbas, who demanded with threats and tortures the prophetic books of Zoroaster; and this obscure remnant of the Magians is spared by the moderation or contempt of their present sovereigns.[206]

The Northern coast of Africa is the only land in which the light of the gospel, after a long and perfect establishment, has been totally extinguished. The arts, which had been taught by Carthage and Rome, were involved in a cloud of ignorance; the doctrine of Cyprian and Augustin was no longer studied. Five hundred episcopal churches were overturned by the hostile fury of the Donatists, the Vandals, and the Moors. The zeal and numbers of the clergy declined; and the people, without discipline, or knowledge, or hope, submissively sunk under the yoke of the Arabian prophet. Within fifty years after the expulsion of the Greeks, a lieutenant of Africa informed the caliph that the tribute of the infidels was abolished by their conversion;[207] and, though he sought to disguise his fraud and rebellion, his specious pretence was drawn from the rapid and extensive progress of the Mahometan faith. In the next age, an extraordinary mission of five bishops was detached from Alexandria to Cairoan. They were ordained by the Jacobite patriarch to cherish and revive the dying embers of Christianity:[208] but the interposition of a foreign prelate, a stranger to the Latins, an enemy to the Catholics, supposes the decay and dissolution of the African hierarchy. It was no longer the time when the successor of St. Cyprian, at the head of a numerous synod, could maintain an equal contest with the ambition of the Roman pontiff. In the eleventh century, the unfortunate priest who was seated on the ruins of Carthage implored the arms and the protection of the Vatican ; and he bitterly complains that his naked body had been scourged by the Saracens, and that his authority was disputed by the four suffragans, the tottering pillars of his throne. Two epistles of Gregory the Seventh [209] are destined to soothe the distress of the Catholics and the pride of a Moorish prince. The pope assures the sultan that they both worship the same God, and may hope to meet in the bosom of Abraham ; but the complaint that three bishops could no longer be found to consecrate a brother, announces the speedy and inevitable ruin of the episcopal order. The Christians of Africa and Spain had long since submitted to the practice of circumcision and the legal abstinence from wine and pork ; and the name of *Mozarabes* [210] (adoptive Arabs) was applied to their civil or religious conformity. [211] About the middle of the twelfth century, the worship of Christ and the succession of pastors were abolished along the coast of Barbary, and in the kingdoms of Cordova and Seville, of Valencia and Grenada. [212] The throne of the Almohades, or Unitarians, was founded on the blindest fanaticism, and their extraordinary rigor might be provoked or justified by the recent victories and intolerant zeal of the princes of Sicily and Castille, of Arragon and Portugal. The faith of the Mozarabes was occasionally revived by the papal missionaries ; and, on the landing of Charles the Fifth, some families of Latin Christians were encouraged to rear their heads at Tunis and Algiers. But the seed of the gospel was quickly eradicated, and the long province from Tripoli to the Atlantic has lost all memory of the language and religion of Rome. [213]

After the revolution of eleven centuries, the Jews and Christians of the Turkish empire enjoy the liberty of conscience which was granted by the Arabian caliphs. During the first age of the conquest, they suspected the loyalty of the Catholics, whose name of Melchites betrayed their secret attachment to the Greek emperor, while the Nestorians and Jacobites, his inveterate enemies, approved themselves the sincere and voluntary friends of the Mahometan government. [214] Yet this partial jealousy was healed by time and submission ; the churches of Egypt were shared with the Catholics ; [215] and all the Oriental sects were included in the common benefits of toleration. The rank, the immunities, the domestic jurisdiction of the patriarchs, the bishops, and the clergy, were protected by the civil magistrate : the learning of individuals recommended them to the employments of secretaries and physicians : they were enriched by the lucrative collection of the revenue ; and their merit was sometimes raised to the command of cities and provinces. A caliph of the house of Abbas was heard to declare that the Christians were most worthy of trust in the administration of Persia. " The Moslems," said he, " will abuse their present fortune ; the Magians regret their fallen greatness ; and the Jews are impatient for their approaching deliverance."[216] But the slaves of despotism are exposed to the alternatives of favor and disgrace. The captive churches of the East have been afflicted in every age by the avarice or bigotry of their rulers ; and the ordinary and legal restraints must be offensive to the pride, or the zeal, of the Christians.[217] About two hundred years after Mahomet, they were separated from their fellow-subjects by a turban or girdle of a less honorable color ; instead of horses or mules, they were condemned to ride on asses, in the attitude of women. Their public and private buildings were measured by a diminutive standard ; in the streets or the baths it is their duty to give way or bow down before the meanest of the people ; and their testimony is rejected, if it may tend to the prejudice of a true believer. The pomp of processions, the sound of bells or of psalmody, is interdicted in their worship ; a decent reverence for the national faith is imposed on their sermons and conversations ; and the sacrilegious attempt to enter a mosch, or to seduce a Mussulman, will not be suffered to escape with impunity. In a time, however, of tranquillity and justice, the Christians have never been compelled to renounce the Gospel, or to embrace the Koran ; but the punishment of death is inflicted upon the apostates who have professed and deserted the law of Mahomet. The martyrs of Cordova provoked the sentence of the cadhi, by the public confession of their inconstancy, or their passionate invectives against the person and religion of the prophet.[218]

At the end of the first century of the Hegira, the caliphs were the most potent and absolute monarchs of the globe. Their prerogative was not circumscribed, either in right or in fact, by the power of the nobles, the freedom of the commons, the privileges of the church, the votes of a senate, or the memory of a free constitution. The authority of the companions of Mahomet expired with their lives ; and the chiefs or emirs of the Arabian tribes left behind, in the desert, the spirit of equality and independence. The regal and sacerdotal characters were united in the successors of Mahomet ; and if the Koran was the rule of their actions, they were the supreme judges and interpreters of that divine book. They reigned by the right of conquest over the nations of the East, to whom the name of liberty was unknown, and who were accustomed to applaud in their tyrants the acts of violence and

severity that were exercised at their own expense.   Under the last
of the Ommiades, the Arabian empire extended two hundred days'
journey from east to west, from the confines of Tartary and India
to the shores of the Atlantic Ocean.   And if we retrench the sleeve
of the robe, as it is styled by their writers, the long and narrow
province of Africa, the solid and compact dominion from Fargana
to Aden, from Tarsus to Surat, will spread on every side to the
measure of four or five months of the march of a caravan.[219]   We
should vainly seek the indissoluble union and easy obedience that
pervaded the government of Augustus and the Antonines; but
the progress of the Mahometan religion diffused over this ample
space a general resemblance of manners and opinions.   The language and laws of the Koran were studied with equal devotion at
Samarcand and Seville : the Moor and the Indian embraced as
countrymen and brothers in the pilgrimage of Mecca ; and the
Arabian language was adopted as the popular idiom in all the
provinces to the westward of the Tigris.[220]

END OF VOLUME III.